The History
of the Ship

D1076527

Praise for *The History of the Ship*

'One of the most comprehensive books ever written
about seafaring'
Sea Breezes

'Woodman writes with a buoyant love for his subject girded by
vast scholarship... Naval and history buffs will be riveted.'
Publishers Weekly

'A handsome, readable volume, often thought-provoking, and an
excellent introduction to "one of the human
race's greatest ventures".'
The Mermaid

'One of the most important books of the decade.'
International Association of Institutes of Navigation

'This book is a treasure for the way in which it reminds the
world of the importance of the sea, of ships and of seafarers.'
NUMAST Telegraph

The History of the Ship

The comprehensive story of seafaring from the earliest times to the present day

RICHARD WOODMAN

CONWAY MARITIME PRESS

This book is dedicated to Ronald Hope

© Richard Woodman, 1997
Epilogue © Richard Woodman, 2005

First published in Great Britain in 1997

This edition published in Great Britain in 2005 by
Conway Maritime Press

An imprint of **Chrysalis** Books Group plc

The Chrysalis Building
Bramley Road
London W10 6SP
www.conwaymaritime.com

ISBN 1 84486 004 3

A CIP catalogue record for this book is available from the British
Library

All images: Chrysalis Image Library

Typeset by SX Composing DTP, Rayleigh, Essex
Printed and bound in Great Britain

Contents

Acknowledgements

A work of this complexity cannot be undertaken without help and encouragement, and I would like to thank Rob Gardiner and Julian Mannering for so ably laying the keel. My gratitude also goes to Alison Moss for her good-natured forbearance in editing the typescript and, in particular, Antony Preston for his invaluable help and advice about warships and weapons technology. As always, I have received much support from my agent Barbara Levy.

Despite being a member of that dwindling breed of seamen who spent their working lives under the red ensign, I would be foolish to claim that this book is exhaustive. A concise history of something so generic as 'the ship' is almost a contradiction in terms. To further complicate matters, for a working sailor such as myself, the opportunity of writing such a book inevitably invites a partisan approach to a vast subject. Yet to avoid such an approach would geld the text of the enthusiasm I first felt for ships when, as a small boy, I was taken on a tour of the then thriving London docks. The opinions in this book are therefore my own.

Richard Woodman

*'Take it all in all, a ship is the most honourable thing
a man has ever produced.'*

John Ruskin

Introduction

Ships are among the most powerful artefacts produced by the hand of man. They have transcended mere practical use and become instruments of great influence, furthering causes for good or evil by acting as manifestations of political power, military might, or commercial exploitation.

The inventiveness of the human race in overcoming the challenges of the natural environment is a recurring theme in history, and is one in which the ship plays a significant role. For the history of the ship belongs to the era of our struggle to dominate the world about us, and has become, for better or worse, a tool with which we have shaped our civilisation. J.B. Priestley, writing in the mid twentieth century, said that the ship was the greatest construction of the age, likening it to the cathedral of the middle ages. Today, like the medieval cathedral, the ship has slipped to the margins of public perception. The wonders of our own age are smaller, more complex and electronic.

Nevertheless, during our great era of conquest, we explored by ship; we have destroyed alien civilisations by means of ships, shifted whole populations by ships, supplied great war-hosts, fought battles and dominated continents by ships. At a more mundane but more important level, we continue to supply our daily needs by ships, transporting huge quantities of the world's natural resources and our own manufactured goods around the globe. At a more sinister level, we have unintentionally permitted disease to migrate and pollution to spread by ship.

Much of this activity centres round what we call Western Civilisation, though, as we shall see, the very repudiation of the ship by China, the world's oldest culture, exposed it first to a tentative nibbling at its borders, and then the inroads of an aggressive, amoral Western commerce, backed by sea-power. This is an irony, since it was the Chinese who produced the world's first most efficient and seaworthy sailing ship in the misnamed junk. But the Ming emperors abandoned all thought of exploration after a major effort in the fourteenth century failed to penetrate the western hemisphere. Not long afterwards the Portuguese, rounding the southern tip of Africa from the opposite direction, established themselves in Macao, and were soon followed by the British and other Europeans.

Although dominated by the nations of the West, the history of the ship does not belong exclusively to the white race, particularly in the twentieth century. Nevertheless, it was the proactive nature of Western societies which encouraged Europeans, in particular, to seek political freedom and ascendancy by way of the sea.

Whatever its origins, the history of the ship was to become dominated by successive 'powers', of which the most influential was Great Britain. This is a matter of fact, and while Britain was ultimately impoverished by war and lost her maritime preeminence to the United States of America, much of what follows relates to British developments. This is, however, not an essay in either jingoism or naval history. The purpose of this book is to present the informed reader who has an interest, perhaps even a love of ships, with an account of the development of this most fascinating, important and influential invention.

To abstract so complex an evolution within a single volume is to set a course perilous with danger and contention. It falls to all attempting the distillation of a vast topic, to make subjective decisions in selecting material. In so doing they run the risk of stirring up controversy, of adopting partisan approaches, of ignoring one and elevating another when claiming this person or that was the father of some significant development. In accordance with my brief, this book in general follows the arguments propounded in the widely acclaimed Conway's History of the Ship. This is not to say that this book is a mere condensation of the data contained in the twelve volumes in the series, merely to state that for my primary source material, it is to this magnificent collection of essays to which I have referred. In fact my own lifelong involvement with ships has provided the mainspring for this book. I would like to think I have communicated the excitement and enthusiasm that ships in general, and some ships in particular, provoke in me. The same might also be said for the people associated with them. I have always had a partiality for the maverick or the forgotten hero; some of these characters may be found in the following pages. Nor, I hope, have I entirely neglected those who manned ships. Countless hundreds of thousands of them are quite unknown, but from time to time a name demands a mention, for without their commanders and companies to breathe life into them, ships are inert.

Whatever uses have been made of them, and some of these are indefensible, the ship, venturing out upon the huge and hostile ocean, still does so at its peril. Long before I was born, the 'unsinkable' *Titanic* met her end in the icy calm of a North Atlantic night; but in my own lifetime the huge LASH ship *München* and the bulker *Derbyshire* have foundered mysteriously, presumably overwhelmed by the indifferent sea. Moreover, in my everyday working life, it has been my business to attend several wrecks, for the sea remains an implacably hostile environment, notwithstanding all the manifold advances of technology.

The future will undoubtedly have a place for the ship, but its influence can never exceed what it has already accomplished. What we review in these pages is not the so-called romance of the sea, something few sailors believe in, but the sheer dogged achievement of successive generations in producing a machine which combined the utility and efficiency of harsh, uncompromising pragmatic requirements, with the adaptability to adjust to constant innovation and development. That this machine was often also beautiful has inspired a fascination close to love, an emotion very different from romance!

Richard Woodman
Harwich, 1997

CHAPTER ONE

Towards the Middle Sea

The first English word relating to ships on record is 'keel' (found in a Latin history of 545 AD), from which one may infer the ship in its primitive form was an object useful to man from earliest times. To ascribe its origins precisely is, of course, impossible; but although 'keel' appears in early Anglo-Saxon chronicles, mention of human exploits upon the sea predates this. A Phoenician named Sanchoniathon improbably attributes the 'invention' of a primitive boat to one Onous, who allegedly cut the branches from a tree, sat astride the log and paddled through water.

In addition to ancient writings, representations of water-borne craft appear in carved reliefs and frescoes, in the tombs of kings and on such lesser objects as seals and vases. Such images, however, are usually of significant craft, not the mundane; much conjecture must therefore be employed in trying to unravel the past. Occasional archaeological digs provide evidence of a more tangible and accurate nature, but primitive boats and ships were made of organic materials that have since rotted, leaving only tantalising hints, and raising more questions for academic speculation and debate. Such argument never produces certainty, only informed conjecture.

What we do see in the development of the ship is that phenomenon of simultaneous progress which may be observed in all human activities; this is to say that despite a diversity of raw materials, different climates and the demands of the user, the development of the earliest craft around the world is remarkably similar.

What might be termed 'primitive buoyancy aids' for the individual, such as inflated animal bladders or rafts, both of which rely upon the natural flotation of their constituents, are not boats. The true boat derives its buoyancy from its ability to displace water equal to its own weight and that of its cargo and crew without submerging. It follows that even if such a craft is made out of lightweight materials, like a coracle, it is the quality of being hollow and having a freeboard that marks the boat as a significant advance on the raft.

But this is not a history of the boat; the diversity of boats beggars description and could not be attempted in a single volume, so it is necessary to define the ship as a natural development of the boat which itself went on to live and prosper alongside its larger offspring. Indeed the matter is complicated, for the two words are used synonymously. Submariners refer to their modern mammoth warships as 'boats', following a tradition established when the first submersibles were regarded as maverick craft manned by youthful madmen. Similarly seamen will refer to having been 'in the such-and-such boats', as a term of familiarity, but take exception if a landlubber refers to the same craft as 'boats'.

Such complicated usage, rooted in the deep prejudices of a now arcane argot, are not really intended to confuse; in fact they are intended merely to establish those rites of passage peculiar to humankind. Such a familiar abuse of a jealously guarded technical term establishes one as a member of a confraternity. Nevertheless, a study of 'the ship,' if we can establish that particular noun as our generic norm, needs some definition.

By the beginning of the nineteenth century, the different types of sailing ship were specifically referred to by rig. The common noun then in use was 'vessel' or 'bottom', both of which had displaced the earlier 'keel'. Thus a vessel could be known as a 'brig', 'barque', 'schooner' or 'snow', the word 'ship' referring exclusively to one form of rig. This was a three-masted vessel having three, square-rigged masts. She might have triangular fore and aft jibs and staysails, even a lateen or gaff-spanker, but the presence of yards on fore, main and mizen masts, marked her as a proper ship, and such a vessel was said to be 'ship-rigged'. Nelson's flagship HMS *Victory* was therefore a true ship, but so was the tea clipper *Cutty Sark* and as modern visitors to Portsmouth and Greenwich can verify, in appearance and purpose, they are two very different things.

In the chapters where this distinction is critical, I have avoided using the noun 'ship' indiscriminately, but the term is too well rooted in our subconscious to warrant this pedantry taken to extremes. Elsewhere, I have followed modern practice.

As for the distinction between a ship and a boat, it is, of course, largely a matter of scale. Ships tend to carry boats and boats, whether built for commerce or pleasure, remain comparatively small. By contrast ships are not only larger, it sometimes seems there is no limit to their size!

None of this helps us determine the origin of the ship herself, but since ships have their origins in boats, it is necessary to trace the earliest waterborne craft to the point at which the boat reached a state capable of sustaining her crew for a voyage across a sea, out of sight and refuge of land. Application of what might be termed the 'pelagic principle' thus determines the nascent moment of the ship herself.

Of course it is quite impossible to determine when or where this happened, for the first intrepid mariners would have pushed their river craft into an estuary, then into the open sea beyond, to venture tentatively along a coast. It is probable that in differing parts of the world, people were doing this at roughly the same time. It seems that survival, trade or war could create the conditions likely to prompt such an expedition and it is these primal motives of human behaviour that, for better or worse, have been the dynamic engines of historical progress. From these three causes have descended the merchant ship and the warship.

But there is another motive that prompted and continues to send humans to sea: the quest for food itself. Among the world's fishing vessels may be found some of the most efficient, ingenious and beautiful craft ever created. To distinguish between a fishing boat and a ship intended for fishing, is sometimes difficult, but application of the pelagic principle resolves the matter (see Chapter Eighteen). Moreover, in our own time, mere survival has produced a number of craft which are indisputably ships, that is those relatively small vessels which prospect for, establish and support the offshore gas and oil industries.

Our ancestors must first have encountered water as an obstacle that thwarted their intentions. They must then have attempted the crossing of rivers in pursuit of game or an enemy, or perhaps as a means of escape from attack. The sight of decaying trees floating upon the surface of the water must have attracted attention and prompted an inventive brain. We can be fairly certain that at some stage, a log rolled and threw this inventor off, illustrating the first lesson in seamanship: that a craft has to be stable to be serviceable. Shortly thereafter the discovery was probably made that this fate could be avoided by the simple expedient of having two trees secured alongside one another.

Primitive humans must also have realised that they could eat fish and that a boat enabled them to catch species which could not be snared or speared in the shallows. It cannot have been long before they devised the dug-out, and stabilised it with an out-rigger, enabling them to put a small cargo aboard, a catch perhaps, or game caught on the far side of a lake or river.

That an animal corpse, its hide expanding under the gases of corruption, floated persistently and offensively, must, in its turn, have led an adventurous predecessor of ours, to clean and inflate the hide of a butchered animal. With this he could support his own weight to cross a river. This, however, would have proved difficult, not to say uncomfortable, and he would have discovered that if he contrived to secure four or perhaps six such leather bags together and build a platform of sticks over them, he could transport not merely himself, but two or three fellows, armed and dry-shod. Sealed pots or even gourds might be substituted for these bladders, depending upon local circumstances.

Elsewhere, bundles of reeds might make a raft, but the adaptation of a woven reed basket covered with hide could provide a coracle. The waterproof membrane need not be of leather; instead bitumen might be used on bark. The method formed a displacement craft, one of the primitive antecedents of the ship.

Curiously, many of these types of boat still exist in parts of the world today, or have only recently been superseded. Others were recorded by the first Western explorers penetrating what they believed to be alien cultures. In the sixteenth century, for instance, Spanish adventurers reported the indigenous Chileans using boats made of sewn planks, the seams of which were caulked with crushed bark held in place with splines of cane. It would seem that larch and beech were split with wedges and the adjacent plank lands bored and threaded with fibre rope. This craft, the *dalca*, was used and modified by the Spaniards themselves to penetrate the country, proving usefully portable, a feature which may have been exploited by the Chilean

Amerindians. Further north, in southern California, a tribe known as the Chumash were observed by the Spaniard Cabrillo in 1542 to use a sewn, planked boat called the *tomolo*. Cabrillo's report was successively corroborated by others, including George Vancouver in 1793. The *tomolo* was sealed with bitumen, deposits of which occur naturally in the locality of modern Los Angeles. Both the *dalca* and the *tomolo* craft achieved sizes of some 30 feet (10 metres).

Today, in remote Tibet, nomads still carry animal skins to inflate when their path is barred by unfordable mountain torrents. The modern forms of primitive boats found in places as widely divergent as Lake Chad in Africa, Lake Titicaca in South America, the rivers of mid Wales or the seas of the cold Arctic Ocean give us not only a positive notion of what may have existed in a locality for thousands of years, satisfactorily serving its purpose, but a clue to the methodology used elsewhere in ancient times. Yet while the coracle of Wales corresponds closely to the round 'bull boat' of the Sioux indians, the best known bark boat, the birch-bark canoe used by the indians of the Six Nations on the River St Lawrence and first observed by the French explorer Jacques Cartier in 1535, is very different from that of the Alacalufs and Yahgans of Patagonian Chile, reported by the Spanish in 1553. In the case of the coracle and the bull boat, the materials to hand were similar: light, pliable timber and hide; in the case of the bark canoes, the characteristics of the barks appear quite different and thus the boats derived from them are dissimilar.

The *zaima* of the Marsh Arabs of southern Iraq is a bitumen-proofed reed-boat with a light, internal frame which probably has not much altered in manufacture since ancient times. The same principle applies to the *kayak* and *umiak* of the Arctic innuit. These simple craft demonstrate the resource of human beings, and their ability to take the materials to hand and to produce an object which is close to ideal for its purpose and its environment. For while the *zaima* is propelled among the placid reed-beds of the Tigris and Euphrates, the *kayak* is capable of proceeding offshore. It is this adaptability and problem-solving skill that drives development. In the evolution of the ship perhaps more than any other 'invention' until the late twentieth century, this process is remorseless.

Most of the primitive craft encountered by Western explorers were relatively small, up to some 10 metres or so. Most were propelled by paddles. Some, like the log-boats seen by Columbus in 1492 were larger, up to 90 feet, some 30 metres, and bore simple sails spread by poles. Rowing with oars, or 'pulling' as it is properly called by seamen, is a more powerful way of using the strength of the human body and appears to originate in Europe. Poling, or quanting a boat, can only be done in shallow, level-bottomed waters and contributes little to the history of the ship.

As for form, the experience of early humans with logs and rafts must soon have persuaded them to make the front of their craft pointed, and thus reduce water resistance. Beam, on the other hand, conferred stability. Similarly, early encounters with waves must have made them realise the advantage of freeboard, and almost immediately they would have found a conflict between the need for paddlers to reach down to the water, and the boat to have sides high enough to keep the crests of waves out. So they learnt the lesson that no boat is perfect, and that to function it becomes a set of compromises. In the more recent history of the ship these have become complex and delicate, but to the first mariners, the first compromise was to reconcile their desire to go afloat with the raw materials to hand.

But at what period did we first attempt to put to sea?

Modern studies suggest *Homo erectus* was probably capable of transporting himself across water before 200,000 BC and that Neanderthal man was doing likewise on a raft. Around 30,000 BC, *Homo sapiens sapiens* of the Upper Palaeolithic period was venturing across what is now the Bering Strait from Asia to North America and southwards to Australia. Of course sea levels were lower and the Bering Strait may have been little more than a narrow passage. So, while we say with certainty that *Homo sapiens* was unlikely to venture far across water, we can speculate with a fair degree of certainty that if our direct ancestors had determined to migrate, provided the farther shore was visible and the sea-surface conditions encouraging, they possessed the will and the skill to make the attempt.

The coincidental discovery of pelagic fish bones and possible hollowed log boats found in both Scotland and The Netherlands, and dating from the Mesolithic period when the last European ice age ended, suggest the hunting instinct may have made fishermen out of our forebears between 7000 and 6000 BC. From this date onwards, with the increasing certainty conferred by carbon-dating and pollen analysis, archaeologists have concluded humans had become fishermen and users of water-transport. By the succeeding Neolithic era (7000 – 2000 BC), rafts had been adopted, and skin boats made their appearance in Western Europe. By the Bronze Age that followed, reed boats, bark boats, log boats and boats made of sewn planks were being produced.

Birch-bark, balsa wood, ambatche, papyrus and ox hide, all provided the local materials for such early craft. But these remained boats, to be used on rivers and lakes. Though they were the progenitors of the ship, they were not ships in any sense of the word.

However, before men considered venturing on the open sea, the demands of war and commerce, both of which required larger craft with some form of hold capable of bearing a payload, were required on the rivers along whose margins the first progressive societies were established. Most notable of these was the Nile. Models of boats estimated to be 11,000 years old have been excavated from its banks. Representations of reed-hulled river craft appear on pottery of the so-called pre-dynastic period of Egyptian history – that is before about 3400 BC when Menes became the first pharaoh. By the accession of Menes, the Egyptians had fitted such reed-boats with a sail and steering oars on either quarter. Wooden hull construction followed, though precisely when is uncertain. Sycamore or acacia was used to produce blocks rather than planks, which were pegged and also held in place by ropes girding the hull. Additional help was at hand by the agency of the compression of water pressure. Such boats, built of short timber lengths, bent, or hogged at their extremities, were thus further supported, not by a keel running under the hull, but by a great rope stretched <u>over</u> it, in the form of a truss. This was tensioned by inserting a stout piece of wood between the strands and twisting them in the form of what was later called by seamen, a 'Spanish windlass'.

However, it was known that cedar, in addition to being light, could be cut into long planks and about 2900 BC, the Pharoah

Sneferu, or Snofru, sent a fleet of some two score ships to make the sea crossing to Byblos in the Lebanon and bring back cargoes of cedar. These early ships were fitted with oars as well as compound steering sweeps, but when the wind was fair a bipod mast was raised and a square sail hoisted. Sneferu's craft were embellished with the eye of Horus, still to be found decorating the bows of Mediterranean boats.

It was not long before more aggressive use was made of such craft and about 2700 BC the Pharoah Sahure despatched a squadron of eight armed ships to ravage the coast of Syria. Thus the ship emerges on the stage of history as an expression of royal puissance, usually, though not always malicious. A benevolent example occurred in about 1500 BC when Queen Hatshepsut, sister and consort of the Pharaoh Thotmes II, sent a trading embassy to acquire monkeys, ivory and ebony from the land of Punt, supposedly modern Somalia. The temple reliefs depicting these ships show the ends of deck beams as conspicuous features of the side elevation. It is supposed that longitudinal rigidity was supplied by the solid block construction of at least the lower hull, but the rope truss overall prevented sag. Bow and stern curved upwards, forward in a beak-head, aft into a decorated fan-shaped lotus flower. A single pole-mast spread a wide sail between an upper and lower yard; otherwise propulsion was obtained by oars, with twin steering sweeps over either quarter.

The same reliefs also show a huge barge used for the transportation of commemorative obelisks. The actual size of these is disputed, for the Egyptians did not use perspective and the illustrations may be merely representational. Certainly it was realised that a vessel was capable of bearing and transporting a weight which on land, would prove exceptionally difficult. Again the block method seems to have been used, stiffened by several longitudinal trusses and rows of athwartships beams. Four steering sweeps were provided, but the barges were towed by smaller, oared boats, and the trip was one-way only: down-stream. Thus Queen Hatshepsut's obelisk barges illustrate one of the problems of historiography: they represent the exceptional, not the ordinary. Nevertheless, they might with some justice be seen as distant forbears of the very large crude-oil tanker in their purpose, namely the transportation of a huge mass of material.

*

To make their ships the Egyptians used tools edged with obsidian. This volcanic material originated from Crete and may have been presented to them by the Minoans who seem to have been the first regular sea traders, carrying this cargo as early as 3000 BC. The cradle of this marine culture probably lay among the islands of the Aegean. Early representations of such craft dated around 2800 BC show a dugout hull with a raised and decorated stern, its freeboard augmented by a bulwark or washboard.

Somewhere about 1400 to 1200 BC Minoan merchantmen were sailing between Sicily, Crete and the Nile delta, exporting wine, olive oil, pottery and metal artefacts. Little is known about these ships, but representations of them show multi-masted vessels. What scholars have concluded, however, is that to make commercially successful voyages, space had to be devoted to cargo, not a large crew of oarsmen. Thus it would appear that these Cretan merchantmen were seagoing sailing ships. Their builders also had access to more superior forms of timber than the Egyptians and in order to produce hulls capable of carrying a load of cargo and having even rudimentary sailing characteristics, they were building vessels with keels and ribs.

Whether the wealth thus accrued attracted the jealousy of their neighbours or not, the prosperous Minoan civilisation was doomed. The population was driven out of Crete by its Greek neighbours from the north in about 1400 BC. Seeking a new land, they in turn attempted the invasion of Egypt where they were known as 'the people from the sea.'

The defeat of this invasion was achieved by Rameses III, and his tomb at Medinet Habu depicts the first recorded naval battle. Although our knowledge of this action is limited, it is clear that there is little distinction between the vessels of the opposing fleets, and that this similarity marks a transition away from the traditional Nile design and an adoption on the part of Rameses of methods also used by the Minoans. Precise hull details are not known, but the absence of the fore and aft truss-rope suggests stiffening of the hull by more advanced means, perhaps even ribbed construction, for a bulwark protecting the oarsmen is clearly shown and the sails are brailed up to the yards. There are also fighting tops, or baskets, at the mastheads for lookouts or archers when battle was joined.

Such war-vessels would have been built under royal sanction. As late as 400 BC the historian Herodotus described Egyptian merchantmen as being built of brick-like blocks of acacia, caulked with papyrus and held together with pegs.

Rameses III's victory marked the peak of Egyptian power. The 'people from the sea' might have been defeated, but the Egyptians failed to follow up their victory and establish themselves as a sea-power. Their society then fell into a long decline.

It was the Sidonian Phoenicians who founded the first trading empire. Having their origins on the shores of the Persian Gulf, they like the Minoans were immigrants and established themselves in the coastal cities of Tyre and Sidon at the eastern end of the Mediterranean.

This was not to suffice them, for they were a restless people. Manufacturing glassware, bronze artefacts, dyes and so forth, they worked westwards, making trading voyages along the littoral, seeking imports of linen, oil, honey, ivory and founding colonies on the Mediterranean coasts of France and Spain and landing at Carthage, Corsica and Sardinia. Eventually they passed the Pillars of Hercules and ventured north, up the Atlantic coast of the Iberian peninsula to eventually enter the rias of southern Cornwall to trade for tin with the Brythonic Celts of that ancient kingdom. There are also unsubstantiated suggestions that the Phoenicians circumnavigated Africa but, even if true, these argue only for an extended coasting voyage, daring and prolonged though it might have been.

Phoenician success lay chiefly in the Mediterranean which conferred a beneficial local climate upon these early seafarers not found in many other places on the globe. As its name suggests, the Mediterranean is surrounded by land and therefore its weather, and in particular its winds, are dominated by the land-masses of North Africa and Southern Europe. The seasonal passage of the sun generates stable pressure systems over land which in turn produce winds of steady strength and direction. These change with a degree of predictability which would have enabled the Phoenicians to make planned voyages both in the Mediterranean and in the Red Sea.

Phoenician vessels fell into two types, a coasting craft known as a *gaulus*, and a seagoing ship called a *hippo*, able to make the fearful voyage into the strange, tidal Hyperborean seas. The *hippo* was fully decked and pierced with hatches. She boasted stem and stern posts which bore decorations such as horses' heads. According to the Old Testament, Ezekiel reports one such ship to have 'ship boards of fir trees of Senhir' and 'cedars of Lebanon to make masts... Of the oaks of Bashan have they made their oars.' What is perhaps significant is that these ships made no mere random voyages, but those requiring organisational effort, skill and knowledge. One can assume with a fair degree of certainty that hitherto, primitive ships were manned and commanded by men whose knowledge of their trade was that of boatmen. As such, the Phoenicians can be seen as the first true seafarers, founding the art of pilotage, cabotage and navigation, documenting the process and jealously guarding their trade routes with tales of the improbable denizens of the outer deeps. Equally, the *hippo*, for all its ungainly connotations to our modern sensibilities, would appear to be the first true ship, built of planks, capable of carrying a deadweight cargo and being sailed and steered, thus possessing an endurance beyond the mere physical strength of her company and proving the pelagic principle.

But Phoenician domination of the Mediterranean was to come to an end with the explosion of the power of the Greeks whose gathering momentum had brought them into direct competition with first the Minoans and then, by about 800 BC, with the Phoenicians. The beginnings of this lay in the arrival of the Dorians, a savage tribe who settled on the shores of the Aegean from the north about the same time as the pre-dynastic period came to an end in Egypt. Fantastic conclusions have been drawn as to their vessels, largely based on false assumptions made without applying practical theories of seamanship. Whatever the details, the Dorians possessed war canoes, probably dugouts, a form of construction that conferred the gift of a ram almost automatically to the form of the hull.

The Greeks sought to found colonies in Calabria, Sardinia and North Africa. Much as their rivals had done, these colonies were founded as trading posts, where imports of home-produced commodities were bartered for indigenous products. The Greeks also ventured into the Black Sea in search of grain. Although the ship-type employed is obscure, there was probably little difference in essence to the early merchantmen of the Phoenicians.

While the civilised Phoenicians may have protected their trade, and were known to scuttle their boats rather than have them taken by an enemy, their aggression was not manifest, unlike their warring Greek successors. To what extent the Phoenicians went to war is uncertain, but theorists believe them to have possessed oared warships, with the oars configured in the double-banked system known as a bireme, and representations of such vessels, armed with rams at the bow, are shown on Assyrian reliefs from the Sargon and Sennacherib palaces, dated 700 BC.

Harnessing a favourable wind made voyaging simpler, but even in the Mediterranean, it was still hampered by submission to the vagaries of the breeze. Drilled oarsmen, although limited in endurance, could provide the speed and manoeuvrability necessary to lay early warships board-to-board, or close an enemy and attack with archers. The slave cultures of the ancient world provided a ready supply of brawn and muscle, either by chaining criminals or prisoners of war. Such vessels were engaged by both sides when Rameses III defeated the 'people from the sea'.

The greatest early exponents of the war galley were the Greeks, who developed the oared galley into a powerful warship, which could not only provide a useful weapons' platform, but could attack with a reinforced ram and sink the opposition. This simple, primitive man-of-war was ultimately to dominate the Mediterranean for well over two thousand years.

Like the Phoenician merchant ship, the Greek war galley marks a turning point in maritime history. Under the impetus of war, the galley underwent a dramatic transformation from a simple dugout to a relatively sophisticated vessel. Theories as to early construction abound and interpretations of iconographic evidence are as fanciful as they are speculative, but it seems probable that a dugout hull, with a pointed bow and supported on each side by an out-rigger, the *parexeiresia* which supported the fulcrum of the oar loom, was the original form. The later adoption of the planked hull removed the limitation on size and the ingenuity of man soon ensured that more than one bank of oars was deployed on each side.

The fifty-oared galley formed the *pentecontor* of Homer's *Iliad* and *Oddysey*, the smaller thirty-oared galley formed the *triacontor*, but Homer's literary work is scarcely a reliable source for such claims. Nor are the Greek historians much help; Thucydides, who was born only nine years after the battle of Salamis in 480 BC, states the Corinthians were the first in Greece to build a trireme.

The Royal Hellenic Navy's modern reconstruction of a trireme, the *Olympias*, proves beyond doubt, however, that the descending rows of *thranite*, *zygite* and *thalamite*, could indeed have plied their oars and manoeuvred a long vessel for prolonged periods, removing all doubts as to the overall practicalities of galley operation. And although many questions of detail are left unanswered, this demonstration shifts the deeds of mythical heroes into the realms of the possible.

Some authorities claim that the Phoenician biremes were developed because early planked construction was incapable of producing a hull long enough to support more than about twenty-five oars a side, hence the *pentecontor*. Perhaps it was from these seventh-century BC craft that the Corinthians imported the idea, immediately augmenting the power of their galleys by going one better, and adding another row of oars to produce the trireme. Whether or not further banks were added seems unlikely, although multi-manned oars may answer this knotty problem.

The Greek city-states that mustered navies for the Peloponnesian and Persian wars eschewed the use of slaves as oarsmen. They relied upon poor citizens to ply the fir oars, and these men sat upon benches. That the oarsmen sat at different levels is amusingly confirmed by the playwright Aristophanes who indicated that the higher oarsmen 'made wind into the face of the *thalamite*.'

It was Athens that emerged as the primary naval power in Greece. Suffering the rapacity of pirates, the Athenians quickly became alerted to the effectiveness of ships of war. In 492 BC the Persian King Xerxes attempted to invade Greece, but lost his ship-borne supplies by bad weather. (He had the surface of the sea whipped for its impertinence!) A second invasion followed, but was repulsed at the battle of Marathon in 490 BC and almost alone among the Greeks, the voice of Themistocles maintained that the defeat would only aggravate the situation and that the

Athenians must build a fleet in anticipation of a third invasion. Elected the leader of the Athenian state for the statutory year as *archon*, Themistocles fortified the natural harbours of the Piraeus, but failed to raise the money for a fleet to replace two score of ageing *pentecontors* then in commission.

Then, in 483 BC, in a *deus ex machina* intervention of providence in the finest traditions of Greek drama, a rich lode of silver was discovered in the state mines. It yielded wealth enough to pay the expenses of the Athenian state, give its citizens a tax rebate *and* build a fleet. Themistocles lost no time, denuding Attica of trees to provide the Athenian navy with 200 triremes.

The galleys' hulls were made of pine, payed with pitch below the waterline and decorated brightly on their topsides. They bore sails for running before a favourable wind, but this top-hamper could be lowered and stowed along the centreline, for the trireme went into action under her triple banks of oars.

Preparations were barely completed when in 480 BC an enormous Persian army crossed the Bosphorus supported by an equally large fleet, and pushed down the coast of Macedonia. There, at the defensive battle at Thermopylae, the advance of the Persians was delayed by the Spartans under Leonidas, giving the Greek confederation the precious time they needed to organise. In Athens the citizens reluctantly agreed to Themistocles's plan to leave the city and take refuge on the island of Salamis. The hope of defending the Acropolis was abandoned and the helpless Athenians and their allies watched the mighty Persian fleet round the southern capes of Attica and anchor off Phalerum. Salamis sealed the Bay of Eleusis with an east and west channel and King Xerxes sent an Egyptian squadron to blockade the western, concentrating his main force against the eastern channel. Corinthian galleys prevented the Egyptians taking the main force in the rear and the rest of the Greek fleet mustered in the eastern narrows to oppose the larger Persian squadrons that contained both Phoenician and Ionian Greek vessels, the latter having been conquered by Xerxes and changed sides. Anticipating victory, Xerxes had his throne set up on a promontory overlooking the strait and the island of Salamis.

The diurnal predictability of the Mediterranean winds persuaded Themistocles to await its freshening before committing his ships to battle. Meanwhile the Persians under

Ariabignes, Xerxes' brother, pulled on, already tiring from a night of forming up, and bore down towards the strait where the Greek fleet waited in three lines. As the Persian fleet advanced, led by Phoenicians, the Greek centre fell back just as the wind rose, raising a sea and swell from the open water beyond the Persian rear. At this point the drummers and flautists whose music controlled the ardour of the Greek oarsmen, burst into action and the wings of the Greek fleet closed on the centre of the Persian column.

The Phoenician galleys were becoming difficult to handle as the wind caught their high sterns. While they attempted to drive off theirtormentors with arrows and javelins, the low Greek triremes tore into their flanks with their bronze-tipped rams. After this ferocious assault they back-watered clear and let the Persian galleys fill and roll over. As the poet Aeschylus, who fought in the action, afterwards wrote, the Greek 'hoplites and archers did wonders and soon threw the enemy into confusion'. Xerxes witnessed the humiliating defeat and ordered survivors who swam ashore from his own fleet to be killed for their failure. Those who fell victim to the Greeks on the opposite shore were slaughtered in their turn 'as men gaff tunny fish'.

Themistocles did not follow up his victory immediately – the sea running outside the strait was wreaking its own havoc on the fleeing Persians – but when the wind was light the following morning, the Greek fleet pulled into Phalerum Bay to find it deserted. Deprived of his seaborne communications, Xerxes was compelled to retreat for lack of supplies and thus the Greek fleet demonstrated the effect sea power could have upon a land campaign by depriving the Persians of their support. The remnants of the Persian fleet were utterly destroyed at Mycale in Asia Minor the following year.

The description of Salamis is, after all the academic speculation about the galley, perhaps the best evidence of how the trireme was used, and it is in a ship's use, rather than its construction that her chief interest lies. On the same day another battle was fought at Himera on the north coast of Sicily which has its own part in this history.

The Phoenician colony at Carthage, in modern Tunisia, was in active alliance with Persia and sent a fleet to attack Greek colonies in Sicily, suffering coincidental defeat at Himera. This disaster persuaded the increasingly autonomous Carthaginian authorities to build up their own shipping and it seems likely that this enjoyed a brief flowering, for Punic coins have been found as far west as the Azores. But Greek sea-power was to dominate the Mediterranean for several centuries, even while the country was in decline, for the star of Rome had begun to rise and the Romans employed their Greek allies in ageing triremes as a bulwark against the Carthaginians during the First Punic War (264 BC).

The Greeks were, however, now to be outclassed by a new form of galley, the quadrereme and quinquereme of Carthage, whose raids ruined Roman trade in the western Mediterranean and harried the very beaches of the Italian peninsula. Essentially these more effective galleys relied not upon a huge multiplicity of banks of oars, but a more sophisticated method of manning them with a greater number of oarsmen. These unfortunates, especially those at the inboard ends of the oar looms, must have had to run back and forth with frantic energy, encouraged no doubt by the whip. But when a quinquereme was wrecked on the Sicilian coast, the Roman Senate ordered Greek shipwrights who had settled in Roman territory to supervise the building of 100 copies and a fleet was constructed and placed under the command of a consul, Caius Duilius, who engaged a Carthaginian fleet, securing his galleys alongside by means of grappling, and by this method carried boarding parties of Roman infantry directly to the enemy vessels.

Thereafter Roman power dominated the Mediterranean. Annual grain convoys sailed from the fertile Nile to bring much needed food to the growing conurbation of Rome itself. For this and trade elsewhere, the Romans developed a handsome merchant vessel which may have derived from the ships of the Phoenicians. There are a number of depictions of these ships over a fairly wide period and they are remarkably similar. A sturdy, broad-beamed, capacious wooden keel-based hull, planked and decked, and clearly capable of lifting a reasonable deadweight, seems therefore to have been rather commonplace. The vessel had a high stern with its stern-post being fashioned into a decorative finial, usually a swan's neck and head. The hull was double ended, but the deck was carried out over the stern, into a rudimentary poop with a deck cabin and on either quarter protrusions of the deck enabled the twin steering oars to be fitted and handled. These vessels also bore a single mast supported by shrouds and a forestay, tensioning being achieved by deadeyes and lanyards. On the mast a square sail was hoisted on a yard by a halliard (or 'haul-yard') and which was clewed by brails. The sail and yard could then be lowered to the deck. The yard was braced and the clews of the sail sheeted. Above the yard a triangular rafee could be set. From the heavy stem-post a bowsprit, or artemon, bore a small yard and sprit-sail and this would have made the vessel much more manoeuvrable than earlier, simpler craft.

There is a recognisable form to these merchantmen; they are not so different from early medieval ships and were entirely wind dependent. Less glamorous were their holds, those capacious spaces by which every merchant ship in history has earned her keep. According to a description of a Roman grain ship seen in the Piraeus by the satirist Lucian around AD 250, these vessels were about 180 feet (55 metres) long, over 40 feet (12 metres) in the beam and with a similar depth from deck to keelson. Such a vessel, conceived and built with a purpose, able, as the old phrase had it, 'to keep the sea' and to fulfil her function, was a true ship.

As for her heavy galleys, Rome increased their power by the addition of catapults. Rocks or lead shot were said to be hurled several hundred yards, as were iron-shod poles, while 'Greek fire', an inextinguishable mixture of burning naphtha, sulphur and pitch delivered either in bombs thrown by catapult or blown through long pipes, was a terrible weapon. The Romans developed not only war galleys, but transports capable of sea-borne invasion which were built near the locality in which they were required to serve. By this means Julius Caesar made his reconnaissance in force into southern Britain in 55 BC, to be followed by full scale invasion and annexation under the Emperor Claudius a century later.

Galleys engaged in the Battle of Actium in 31 BC during the civil war that followed the assassination of Caesar. In this action damage seems to have been deliberately inflicted on the oars of Mark Anthony's ships, although accounts of the battle are not clear and are confused by the enigmatic action of Cleopatra's galleys, which ran off under sail. After this incident, the galley was to continue to dominate naval warfare in the Mediterranean for a millennium.

To a degree the conventions of war meant that fleets would not engage unless conditions werereasonably stable; so, while merchant ships had come to rely entirely upon sail by about AD 1200, war fleets could still decide the fates of nations under oars. By this time the trireme had been superseded by the *dromon* and the *selander* and these vessels had adopted the Chinese innovation of the stern-hung rudder and the Arab lateen sail, which are discussed in Chapter Three. The ram became a remnant, giving a long, threatening bow to the war galleys of the fourteenth, fifteenth and sixteenth centuries AD, but by then they had been outdated by the gun. Galleys, by virtue of their beam and open bows, could carry a small battery of cannon set athwartships and were able to fire directly ahead, an advantage not possessed by any warship until the invention of the barbette. Moreover such an approach presented the narrowest aspect, if one excepts those banks of vulnerable oars.

There were smaller denominations of galley which underwent slow transformations and mutations. The *panfilo* was a tenth-century development of the dromon which then developed into a merchant ship with a single tier of oars, each pulled by two men. The *bergantina* was a fast, open vessel common in the fourteenth century, which outgrew the Mediterranean to become the forbear of the brigantine. Another small, very light, narrow and fast form of the galley was the *posticco*, and another galley, the *saettia*, was named for the arrow which, with its long oars to give it speed, it was said to resemble. Finally a three-masted, seventy-oared merchant version of the *galleass* (see below) was called a *baleniero*, or whaler, and seems to have been developed by the Venetians, Genoese and Catalans from a Basque form. This pedigree suggests an able sea-keeper, imported to the Middle Sea from the Atlantic and capable of serving as trader, transport or warship.

Almost continuously from the beginnings of recorded history and up until the very end of the eighteenth century, galleys formed the main constituents of the war fleets of all the Mediterranean maritime powers: Spain and France, the knights of Malta and most significantly the city-state of Venice. The Venetians, whose trading interests were vast, also carried the galley to its final sophistication, the *galleass*, a sort of oared frigate which was a high freeboard vessel with a gundeck above the oarsmen and three masts bearing fore-and-aft lateen sails.

Such a vessel was quickly copied by other nations, most particularly the Spanish. Even the English had a form of galleass in their fleet of 1545, though the type was not widely adopted outside the Mediterranean.

One of the most extraordinary feats of arms, and one of the least known, concerns galleys and began in the middle of winter, in January 1439, when a state of war existed between the Italian city-states of Venice and Milan. The contest centred on Lake Garda where the Duke of Milan had a naval squadron and whose forces lay in seige of Brescia. Deprived of a direct river-route by way of the Po and Mincio, the Venetian Senate seemed on the verge of losing Brescia when a Greek seaman who had long been in the service of the republic, suggested transporting a fleet overland. Sorbolo Candioto was eventually given command of a small fleet of a pair of galleys and some smaller ships and boats. Moving up the Adige to Verona with an army of mariners, soldiers, workmen and carpenters together with a vast herd of oxen, the craft were hauled ashore and dragged on rollers. With the workmen clearing a path and using streams and tracks to haul their burden through a pass over 1000 feet above sea level, the galleys and boats were then lowered some 800 feet to Torbole, only to be mauled by the more numerous Milanese. Large quantities of timber were brought over the mountains and a new fleet was built at Torbole to fight the Milanese who were eventually defeated, and Venetian supremacy was re-established on Lake Garda and Brescia. After the victory the fleet was laid up and later, in the face of a more powerful combination against Venice, the ships were scuttled in the lake, weighed down with stones. One of these was rediscovered in the mid 1960s and proved to have been over 100 feet long, planked and framed, and complete with a mast-step and three anchors.

The Venetians appreciated the increased endurance and manoeuvrability of the galley and they formed a small proportion of that state's contribution to the combined fleet of the Holy Alliance which met the Ottoman Turks under Ali Pasha at Lepanto in October 1571.

This was the greatest naval engagement in which the galley featured, and was fought off the Gulf of Corinth. The Christian fleet was an allied product of papal diplomacy and commanded by Don Juan of Austria, a bastard of the Holy Roman Emperor Charles V. It comprised vessels from Spain, Venice, the Papal States, Naples, Sicily, Genoa and Malta. In all 208 galleys, 6 galleasses, a dozen *nefs* and some 50 other vessels, of which Venice alone contributed 116, were manned by some 75,000 soldiers and mariners. Ali Pasha's fleet, fresh from its successful raid on the Venetian possession of Cyprus, was of roughly equal man-power and slightly larger size – 210 galleys and three score of smaller vessels. Relying upon archers the Turks were out-manoeuvred and out-gunned, permanently damaging Ottoman power in the Mediterranean.

The galley continued to thrive, though it was no longer manned by free men and after the accession of Louis XIV in 1643, it was France which became the dominant power in the Mediterranean basin and continued to maintain a fleet of galleys and galleasses. Such vessels had undergone only minor changes. In the galleass, the long ram had been replaced by a more conventional beak-head, bowsprit and spritsail, and the weight of metal thrown by the broadside guns had increased. The flagship of the French commander was called *La Réale*. This name was also generic, applying to the largest size of war-galley in the French Mediterranean squadrons. Seven to a thwart, some 462 men manned each of these elaborate craft which were supported by galleys of two lesser classes, the 'ordinaries' and 'extra-ordinaries'. The wretched men who ran about in chains beneath the overseer's lash were of course, condemned convicts, and although they were relieved in favourable winds by the two lateen sails, they had perforce, not merely to pull the galley forward, but to manoeuvre it to bring her fixed guns to bear. The overseeing staff moved up and down a centre gang-way which also provided access fore-and-aft for the soldiers. Fighting platforms were fitted over the gundeck forward and as a command post aft. But the day of the galley was effectively over. In 1651 the small French frigate *Lion Couronné* held off an attack by eleven galleys for many hours and in 1684 *Le Bon* defeated thirty-five galleys by the power of her broadside guns.

Nevertheless in 1717, off Cape Matapan, a combined squadron of fifty-seven Papal, Spanish, Venetian and Portuguese warships, among which were several galleys, beat off an attack by a Turkish force. Furthermore the celebrated Swedish naval architect Fredrik Henrik af Chapman designed a type of galleass specifically for service among the islands off the Finnish coast. Although poor at manoeuvring, the support of their guns was decisive when the Swedish 'Archipelago Fleet' defeated the Russians at Svenskund in 1790. Some of these oared warships served in a later action at Ratan on 20 August 1809, in the Second Russo-Swedish War, an offshoot of the greater Napoleonic conflict.

The Baltic is a long way from the Mediterranean, but it shares the characteristic of being an inland sea, its weather dominated by its surrounding land masses. It is full of narrow, sheltered straits lying in the lee of many islands, so it is not surprising that until steam replaced sail, oars should have remained a practicable way of manoeuvring a man-of-war. The significance of the galley is that it co-existed in modified form and with modified application, alongside the true, manoeuvrable sailing vessel for as long as it was capable of performing a role. In addition it was powered by human brawn, howsoever brutal the regime which obtained such energy. The galley, the most durable warship form in history, was largely eclipsed by the romantic associations attached to the sailing man-of-war, for although this too was provided for by human energy, much of which was acquired by the press gang, the sailing warship harnessed the wind. Brute force was partly replaced by a touch of science.

CHAPTER TWO

The Long Ship

Whatever the claims that the Phoenicians pioneered mercantile voyaging, no seafarer could dispute the achievements of the Vikings, who ventured far from their coasts and set their keels at the distant horizon. Yet this was no sudden and impulsive movement and much about the Norsemen has been misunderstood, or misrepresented. What we know as fact about Norse maritime culture is sparse, but the legacy of their contribution to the history of the ship is enduring and may be found in many wooden hulled clinker-built yachts and fishing vessels that exist today.

At the end of the last Ice Age, humans seem to have followed the retreating ice northwards, and the presence of fishbones, especially on islands, indicates that primitive settlements not only existed close to open water but sustained themselves from the fruits of the sea. Modern scholarship suggests the inhabitants of Scandinavia developed their extraordinarily attractive long ships from early skin boats in which animal hides were sewn together and stretched over a light timber frame. The overlap necessary to stitch leather inspired, it is theorised, the overlapping planks that we call clinker or lapstrake. The latter name means 'over-lapping planks' and is perhaps more apposite than clinker, which is a corruption of 'clencher' and refers to the clenching of nails, a means of securing the overlapping planks.

A lapstrake hull is built by first constructing the shell of overlapping planks and then inserting the frames to stiffen the structure afterwards, a method more akin to reinforcing reed or log boats. Whatever its origins, archaeological and iconographical evidence exists of planked boats being in use about 350 – 300 BC. Indeed right across Scandinavia there are rock scratchings and carvings that represent such boats and span the epoch 2000 BC to around the 250 BC. Debate as to the precise nature of these can, of course, offer only conjectural solutions to the questions they provoke, but given the nature of the probable use to which such craft were put and the materials to hand, the hide boat with its wooden formers, seems the most likely explanation for them.

In short, the representations are of early fishing boats, capable of being drawn up on a strand.

We know the hide-boat was well-established in the cold waters of northwestern Europe, and that it was used by the Celts who were a sea-faring people before the Vikings. Indeed, Julius Caesar left the provocative, but wholly unhelpful comment that 'their ships were built and rigged in a different manner from ours'. Whether this refers to wooden or hide boats we have no idea, but we can conjecture that the early wooden boats, being sewn, copy the method used to link the fairly obvious resource of hides which were readily available. Moreover the lingering presence of skin boats in remote, but culturally Celtic regions, does more than merely suggest the Celts used such boats. That which most closely approaches an early ship capable of the putative voyages claimed by such navigators as Prince Madoc, St Patrick and St Brendan, was the curragh. Caesar does record that in 49 BC his legionaries made skin boats when on campaign in Spain 'of the kind that his knowledge of Britain a few years earlier had taught him. First, the keels and ribs were made of light timber, then the rest of the hull of the boats was wrought in wickerwork and covered with hides.' The Roman historian Pliny, writing in the first century, refers to boats 'made in [sic] the British Ocean of wickerwork covered with hides', and Solinus records in the third century that 'the sea which separates Hibernia (Ireland) from Britain, is rough and stormy throughout the year [and] ... they voyage in small boats formed of pliant twigs, covered with skins of oxen'. Solinus also adds the pertinent remark that during the trip 'the voyagers abstain from food'. Irish scholars point to the Mesolithic invasion of Ireland around 8000 BC as being by sea and in hide boats. Modern curraghs, or more properly 'currachs', are capable of carrying two cows and a score of sheep, which gives some idea of the size and stability which could have been built into such a craft. Iconographical evidence of a curragh of the seventh or eighth centuries shows a hide boat with a steering oar and four oars a side, secured to the stiffened gunwale by thole pins. For the benefit of the diarist and nautical enthusiast Samuel Pepys in 1685, a Captain Phillips illustrated a sailing curragh 'ordinarily used by the Wild Irish'.

*

While it is quite possible to see how the hide boat developed in Scandinavian waters as much as Ireland, the leap from hide to clinker planking needs some further explanation and this is likely to have grown out of a marriage of disparate forms. The other early primitive boat-form is the dugout. But the dugout is limited to tree size which, in terms of girth, is not great among the pines and firs of the northern forests, or indeed of the deciduous woodlands, prolific in oaks, which stood upon the Baltic shores. The narrow dugout is almost as unstable as the bare log and the outrigger seems never to have been used in Northern Europe. Why should it have been? Northern waters are cold and when one wants a large boat it is usually because one wants to put bulky objects in it such as livestock or a cargo. The Norsemen used the dugout from the Stone Age and numerous examples have been found in bogs, marshes and lakes across the region. They show development taking another tack: the augmentation of the dugout hull first increasing stability by lashing side stringers outside the hull, then by lashing two dugouts side by side. This innovation would have conferred immediate advantages in terms of capacity, but for the inconvenience of a double ridge running the length of the hull where the inboard gunwales of the two hulls met. As the facility and sophistication of tools improved, particularly the use of the adze as a derivative of the axe, the boat was made from two side pieces separated by a central widening timber, a sort of primitive flat keel. The weatherliness of such a hull could then be increased dramatically by the longitudinal extension of this central keel, and the addition of side planks, set on edge, and increasing freeboard by as much as their width.

It takes no great leap of the imagination to see the embryonic hull form of the traditional north European boat emerging once man had mastered the art of cutting or splitting a tree trunk into planks. The degree to which woodworking skills had advanced by about 350 BC is indicated by the remains of a boat found in 1921 in a bog at Hjortspring on the island of Als in southern Denmark. Wide lime planking was sewn together to produce a hull over 50 feet long with a central flat keel, either side of which a garboard strake is found to have been secured and topped off by a plank on each side. The keel is tapered and projects beyond the point at which the planks sweep up at either end to meet vertical posts. The hull is stiffened by light hazel frames which are lashed to the planks which have been cleverly fashioned with 'cleats' to accept these lashings. Ten thwarts and a quantity of weapons suggest this light narrow hull was used for warlike activities, but which could as easily been a fishing craft and perhaps served both roles, propelled by paddles.

Later discoveries suggest vestigial remains of rowlocks, indicating the adoption of oars, but there is little evidence of this until about AD 350, the date of the Nydam ship which was discovered in 1863 in a peat bog in southern Denmark. Built of oak, the 82-feet long planks of which the hull is constructed are a triumph of long-lost ingenuity, for only fifteen pieces were used in the construction. Simple in concept, the strakes are secured by iron nails driven through overlaps and clenched over iron roves. The hull was stiffened internally by oak branches and once again these were tied to cleats in the planks by bass-lashings. Rowlocks against which the oar looms were pulled, were lashed to the gunwale. A vessel of this type could have made a long voyage such as would have enabled the Angles and Saxons to reach Britain, particularly as the narrow form and sharp rise of floor suggests the Nydam ship was never equipped to sail, but relied entirely upon oars. With relief oarsmen, surprising distances could have been covered. Notwithstanding the lack of mast and sail, a quantity of rocks were found in the bottom, suggesting the need for ballast, while a steering oar was located near one end of the excavated hull.

The Sutton Hoo find in England in 1939 proved to be a rich burial ship, built during the sixth century, but thought to have been old when she was buried under a tumulus beside the River Deben in Suffolk laden with a quite marvellous treasure. The real significance of the Sutton Hoo burial ship was that it had a more complex hull, with narrower, more cunningly fashioned planks. The ship was almost 90 feet long, with a depth of hull of 4.5 feet and a forward beak which rose nearly 13 feet above the keel. The planks, nine a side and one inch thick, were not continuous lengths, but were overlapped longitudinally, scarphed and clenched. The keel was about 3 inches deep and the stem and sternposts were bolted to it. Strengthening of the starboard quarter suggested the original presence of a steering oar, but it was clear that the elderly hull had been stripped out prior to use for the burial. Nevertheless, this positioning of the steering oar has been enshrined in the *lingua franca* of the seaman, for 'starboard' derives directly from 'steerboard' and its original opposite, 'larboard' originates from 'lading board', or the favoured side for loading over so as to avoid damaging the steering gear.

Whether or not these early long ships ever used sail is disputed due to lack of clear evidence. That they were rowed is not in doubt, and efficient galleys they must have made, but it seems that their commanders and crews cannot have been unaware of the potential of a sail even if they did not arrive with one, for the galleys of the Romano-British Comes Britanniorum, the 'Count of the Saxon Shore' whose task was to maintain a navy to prevent the Saxon predators landing, were probably fitted with them. The likely explanation seems to be that they were not so rigged initially, but later a demountable rig was adopted, as was the case in the Mediterranean galley, permitting the long ship to load cargo or booty, or providing a war-galley clear of encumbrances. Such versatility would have been consonant with what we understand of the Norse way of life.

Such a long hull would hog and sag, a flexing that would discourage the permanent establishment of a mast with its associated rigging stresses. At Kvalsund, in western Norway, two hulls were found in 1920, the larger of which was 60 feet in length with a longitudinal bracing piece at right angles to the flat keel plank, thus stiffening the hull at about the station of a mast. Another feature of this ship, which dates from around AD 700, is the lashed frames which are made of pine, whilst the planks of the hull are of oak. Extra athwartships stiffening is provided forward, on the shoulders of the hull, and aft, on the quarters, in way of the steering oar fastening. Here heavy frames, which almost amount to bulkheads are notched to take the planking which is nailed, rather than lashed. Corroborative evidence of this general state of progress is found in relics throughout Scandinavia. The larger Kvalsund ship is an advance on the Nydam hull, possessing a much flatter 'U' shaped midships section. This, with the more rigid keel form, would have provided greater athwartships stability, quite sufficient to step a mast and support rigging, though there is no hard evidence to suggest this was done.

The Long Ship

The precise date of the adoption of sail in the long ships is uncertain. When we consider the lightness of the hulls and the fact that the greater part of Norse voyages were either coastal, inland or up the great rivers into Russia and beyond, the oar seems to be a perfectly satisfactory means of propulsion. Moreover the low freeboard, which was exactly correct for long sessions at the oars, was quite unsuitable for sailing when a moderate angle of heel would have had water pouring inboard over the lee gunwale. Nor is the North Sea a tolerant or kindly nursery and we must assume that losses among early seafarers were at least of similar magnitude to those of the Victorians for whom the sailing cargo ship and fishing vessel operating in coastal waters was still an essential part of the fabric of society. But when external pressures compelled the Norsemen to look westward, they cannot have contemplated voyaging far into the west without sails.

Exactly what these pressures were is difficult to say, though increasing population is the most acceptable. Modern scholarship is persuaded to challenge, if not to deny the rapacity of the so-called Vikings. Even their fearsome name seems to be of rather a dubious origin. It is probable that 'raids' were opportunist foraging, more in search of victuals than plunder, for when met by armed resistance, it was usually the defenders who held the field and the fearsome 'Vikings' who retreated to their long ships. Whatever the truth of the matter, one thing is certain, that in these voyages they gained experience and skill, and thereafter perfected an ocean-going hull some time in the second half of the eighth century.

From about AD 800 onwards, the long ships sailed to the westward, making landings on the coasts of England, Ireland, Scotland, Wales, Iceland and eventually across to Greenland and North America. Simultaneously they were venturing out of the Baltic and along the coasts of Flanders, France, Spain and into the Mediterranean to found Norse settlements in what later became Normandy, and the Vandal Kingdoms of the central Mediterranean.

This date was a watershed in the development of the ship, for iconographical evidence indicates a sturdy merchant hull which was sail-propelled offshore and which possessed a deep cutwater necessary to give good course holding characteristics together with an upward curving stem and stern. This seems to have been the 'identical ends' of the ships of the Northmen identified by the Roman historian Tacitus writing of the ships of the Sviones as early as the first century.

The significant and certain fact that emerges from the archaeological finds at Hjortspring, Nydam and Kvalsund, as well as others at North Ferriby on the banks of the River Humber, at Björke in Sweden, or on the island of Bornholm, is that the Scandinavian hull was built by overlapping planks. This 'northern tradition' of building the skin and later reinforcing it with ribs, was at variance with the 'southern' or Mediterranean practice of building a framework and cladding it. Ultimately, of course, the rivetting of frames to over-lapping planks, provided a hull of enormous strength, and the Scandinavians were fortunate in this business of clenching, for, by drawing the planks up together between the frames or ribs, the natural expansion of the waterlogged fibres of the wood made the hull watertight without driving in caulking.

Such a boat could, by about AD 800, make an annual voyage to the westwards and about AD 860, one such had sighted Iceland, although it was to be 874 before colonists, escaping the tyranny of the ruler of Norway, landed to settle the island. There are suggestions that they discovered evidence of earlier visitors from Britain or Ireland who must have come thither in the hide curragh in which St Brendan is said to have traversed the Atlantic some four centuries earlier. In about 982 Thorwald and his son Eric the Red, being guilty of murder, then left Iceland and sailed further west, discovering Greenland and landing there. A later Norse navigator, Bjorn, attempting to reach his father in Greenland, was driven far to the south west by bad weather and made a landing in a well-provided, temperate country. Getting back to Greenland he afterwards related his adventures to Leif Ericsson, heir to the Redhead. Equipping a ship, Leif and Bjorn set out and landed in North America. According to Sir John Barrow's *Chronological History of Voyages into the Arctic Regions*, a German sailor in Leif's crew discovered grapes such as were made into wine in his native land, so the place upon which they had landed was named Vinland.

Whatever the fate of any early colonists in either Vinland or Greenland, these passages are not disputed. Moreover, sufficient accurate evidence has been gathered by voyages in replicas of

Norse ships, even of curraghs, to suggest that the northern route is not only feasible, but in the right summer weather conditions, not unpleasant.

These voyages, made at the end of the first millennium, were carried out in what we recognise as 'typical' Viking ships – that is long, elegant, double-ended clinker-built vessels, propelled by oars or a single sail. Fortunately, examples of these attractive Norwegian vessels have survived at Oseberg, Tune and Gokstad. All are burial ships which owe their survival to the blue clay sub-soil of the area surrounding Oslo Fiord. Both wood and iron are preserved in remarkably fine condition, though at Tune and Gokstad a loose earth tumulus had allowed air to rot the ships' upperworks.

The earliest example of the type is that found at Oseberg farm, near Tønsberg in 1904, and is said to date from the ninth century burial of a high-born female member of the ruling clan of Vestfold, a family which later bore future kings of Norway. The ship was found beneath a mound protected by turves, which preserved her well. She is highly decorated and of a low free-board, suggesting her use was exclusively for royal pleasure in placid waters. A number of artefacts found in the ship confirm the assertion of the Norse sagas that when on passage, only cold food was eaten, but that landings were made to cook and camp, though leather sleeping bags provided overnight comfort when at sea.

Overall the hull is some 70 feet long and 17 feet in the beam. Twelve planks rise either side of a substantial keel. The ribs lie loose across the keel and are bound to the planks with bass lashings in the old way, being rivetted to the ninth and tenth planks, the latter of which is angle-sectioned to give added beam and strength. This strong plank or 'meginhufr' is both plank and stringer, marks the vessel's waterline, and provides the lodgement for the athwartships beams, each coincident with a rib. The oak planks are clenched together and rise sharply at both ends into tall, highly decorated beaks. The inside of the hull contained a planked deck laid on cross beams which were fitted at the tenth plank level. The sheer-strake is pierced for oars.

The Oseberg ship, whose hull shape is said by the marine historian and artist Bjorn Landstrom to conform to the small coastal vessel known as a *karv*, although steered by a sophisticated steering board bound against a block by a withe, lashed and moved by a short tiller, was not a seagoing ship. It is, however, the earliest extant Norse hull which was definitely fitted for sailing, having a heavy fore and aft timber as a step, set across two floors which are rebated to take it. Further support is provided by mast partners which lie on the deck planking and they open aft to allow the mast to be raised when required. Interestingly, the stepping of the mast bears evidence of repair. A remarkably fine anchor was found with the ship, together with some odds and ends of chandlery, including blocks, toggles, cleats and fragments of rope.

The subsequent archaeological discoveries, dating from some fifty to one hundred years later show the remarkable advances that attest to the greater endurance of Norse ships and confirms the expansion recorded in the sagas. The Tune ship is a shallow draught, low freeboard vessel, but the extreme width and outward rake of its top strakes, suggest a more seaworthy hull than that of the Oseberg ship. It has, moreover, a much more substantial mast stepping arrangement wherein the load is spread over a greater area of the lower hull and which is better braced and rebated, suggesting at the very least a change in building practice as mast and sail became more commonly used. This arrangement also appears in the Gokstad ship which was discovered in 1880 on a farm near Sandejord.

Only a few feet longer than the Oseberg vessel and of almost identical beam, the Gokstad ship is also of oak, with sixteen planks between keel and gunwale. The hull is decked and pierced for sixteen oars on each side. The positioning of these oar-holes, or 'rowlocks' is such that the ship could be rowed with ease, but the planking rises a further two strakes, raising the freeboard for sea-sailing and the rowlocks could be made watertight by inserting wooden discs. There are no thwarts and it is conjectured that the oarsmen sat on benches or chests containing their belongings. Such chests were found in the Oseberg ship.

The hull at Gokstad was decked and the mast stepping arrangement, though larger and heavier, follows the same form as that in the Tune hull. A vertical timber, known as a 'beitass' was set up to straighten the weather leech of the sail, clear evidence that such a ship was capable of sailing to windward. Among the debris surrounding the wreck was the stock of an anchor and some 'blocks'. Although their location is impossible to guess, they clearly indicated familiarity with the concept of mechanical advantage for, although devoid of revolving sheaves, their comb-like shape, shows how ropes could be rove over them to make a purchase.

The fact that these well preserved relics were burial ships begs the question of how typical were they? Other archaeological finds in Norway suggest local differences, particularly in respect of the method of fastening. The northernmost finds favoured lashing with minimal clench nailing or trenailing. Nevertheless, the stiffened keel was widespread, requiring the nailing of the garboards to it, and providing the backbone of a hull now using sail whenever circumstances demanded or made possible.

The preservation of a long tradition of boat-building skills, passed from master-craftsman to apprentice by example for over a thousand years, suggests the typical form changed little. A graceful hull like that of the Gokstad ship could scarcely be bettered, reminding one of the old empirical boat-building principal that 'if it looks right, it is right'. Moreover, to prove the feasibility of a Gokstad-type ship having been similar to that of Bjorn and Leif Ericsson, and capable of the epic voyages claimed by the sagas, a replica was built in 1893 and crossed the Atlantic in twenty-eight days. This and subsequent experiments with other replicas also proved the windward capability of the Norse longship.

Analysis of iconographical finds has led to the conclusion that Norse sails were made of homespun, rather a weak sail-cloth, but which was reinforced by leather doublings criss-crossed diagonally to provide strong clews and a head to the sail. Clearly such a sail was stretched along a yard which was hoisted aloft. Whether or not a lower boom was fitted seems to be a matter of conjecture. Indeed the personal choice of the chieftain concerned was probably decisive.

Whatever the details of the Norse ship, it was no more than part of a continuum. What history has come to regard as the Viking longship with its dragon's head prow, its square, striped sail, its oarsmen crowding behind their painted shield-wall ready to drop the oar loom and rush ashore wielding a battle axe, led by demented berserkers, is probably as inaccurate as the legend of winged helmets – not a single example of which has been found. Our sophisticated historical taste has become too used to such inventions and thus the ordinarily beautiful has been overlooked.

Nevertheless, the 'Viking' legacy is that their ships were of a double-ended hull form which could run in a heavy sea and which was both flexible and yet resiliently strong. The clinker hull became the hall-mark of the northern ship as the age of the single masted sailing ship dawned, and the northern ship was to be in the vanguard of early medieval expansion.

This type of hull produced derivatives other than those that have passed into a somewhat specious legend. The *karv* and the *knorr*, or *knarr*, were both variants used for the carriage of cargoes and by inference from the sagas, we know the latter was high-sided, as would have been necessary if it was to pay its way. We can only speculate as to what constituted a ninth or tenth century cargo, but it may well have included cattle which would have required a sturdy, stable hull with a good beam. Such a stolid merchant ship was found in 1956 among the five ships which appear to have been scuttled in the Peberrenden channel leading to Roskilde, near the village of Skuldelev on the Danish island of Sjæland. About 54 feet long and 15 feet wide, with a deep stem, the hull is pine planked, but the keel and much of the lower ribs are heavy oak, the remainder of the framing being of lime. Such a stout hull convinced the archaeologists that the little ship had been built for the North Atlantic trade, from Norway to Iceland and beyond, almost certainly to Greenland and perhaps to Vinland itself. Sunk around 1050 when Norwegians raided the substantial Danish town of Roskilde, the *knarr*'s building is thus dated around 1000. This ship, and a smaller merchantman are key elements in the archaeology of the period and they provide the additional intelligence that their upper strakes were only pierced for a few oars forward and aft, just sufficient to move the ship inshore, and leaving her full midships section clear for cargo. Her main propulsion was therefore a sail.

As is usual, few merchant vessels are available to us and we are left largely with descriptions of the contemporary man-of-war as the exemplar of the northern ship at the close of the first millennium. Almost all our evidence comes from the sagas which, like most propaganda, are prone to exaggeration, but there seems little doubt that Norse chiefs like Olav Tryggvason and Jarl

Håkon possessed war vessels of considerable size, long ships of seventy or eighty oars. These great warships, or *drakkars*, were the very fabric of legend, their size attesting to the prowess of their commanders. Olav's is known to us by name, *Ormen Lange*, though its length may have been much enlarged by poetic licence, while the *drakkar* of Knut, the Danish king of England, was allegedly larger, though this probably reflects the greater prestige attaching to Knut's name.

The diaspora of the Norsemen was widespread by this time. The rapprochement between Charles the Simple, King of the Franks, and the Norse chieftain Rollo in 912, established them in what was to be known as Normandy and from where, a century and a half later, William the Bastard was to invade southern England. William's invasion was in long ships which are depicted in the Bayeux tapestry and they show the fearsome dragon's head stem of legend. The tapestry is useful in that it shows the invasion fleet being constructed. By this time other roughly contemporaneous representations show still the homespun sail crisscrossed with reinforcing strips, but also bowlines along the sides, or leeches of the square sail which have replaced the beitass and enable the leading edge of the sail which was pointed to windward, to be kept taught and allow a clean flow of air over the aerofoil of the sharply braced sail when the *drakkar* was close hauled on a wind. This arrangement was to continue until the nineteenth century, when the double topsail and topgallant split the deep square sail into more manageable areas. Such sophisticated sailing techniques are suggested in the chronicles by the presence of gilt windvanes at the mast-trucks, which 'shone like fire in the sun'.

Ships of this period carried iron anchors little different from those borne by ships a thousand years later, wooden stocked, with a shank, flukes and forged palms. In an excavation of 1935 at Ladby on the Danish island of Fyn, one such anchor was found complete with a ring in its crown for breaking it out of the sea-bed, and more than 30 feet (10 metres) of chain to which was secured the remnant of a rope hawser. Although the form of an efficient anchor was known to the Romans and, judging from a native British example dredged up off Dorset, anchors with chains were used from early times, this anchor with its chain ganger and crown ring, argues in favour of a comprehensive understanding of seamanship, for in a sailing vessel a good anchor and ground tackle are essential. An anchor was found at Oseberg and the stock of one lay with the buried ship at Gokstad, but such an anchor as was found at Ladby is clear evidence of a vessel either too large or too laden to haul up on a beach, as might have been done with an earlier craft. This confirms the period of the ninth to the tenth centuries as marking the departure of the Norsemen from large oared coastal vessels to sailing ships capable of real sea-keeping.

In 1922, the discovery of a buried ship at Ellingaa, near Frederikshavn in Jutland, Denmark, provides another clue as to the progress of cargo-ship development. Excavation did not take place until 1968, by which time archaeologists not only possessed the expertise to preserve the wreck, but to date it as coming from the twelfth century, and thus it was later than the Skuldelev merchantman. The remains of the 50-feet hull show a closing up of frame spacing, essential if the hull is to be strong enough to lift a substantial deadweight, together with remains of cross beams, showing the existence of a half deck and what amounts to an early hold space.

Although the Bayeux tapestry shows Duke William's long ships carried anchors, they were driven upon the strand of Pevensey Bay to enable the Normans to land their fearsome horses. Their Norse forbears, it is said, fought at sea, with great rafts of their ships lashed together and driven at the opposition. Such a battle took place off the Scanian coast of southern Sweden around 755. The oared ships of the period were decked, as we have remarked, and these decks were raised at bow and stern into a slightly higher platform as the gunwales swept upwards into the curved extremities of the hull. These platforms were called the 'lyfting' and upon them the most reputable warriors, known as the 'stem-dwellers' or *stafnbui*, fought hand-to-hand while flights of arrows flew overhead. Such fighting must have been awkward in the extreme and probably had more taunting and posturing in it than the infliction of grievous bodily harm, but the platforms were to become significant features of the medieval ship as it was to emerge from the longship.

Popular myth aside, modern scholarship advocates the view that the sea-faring Vikings were mostly emigrants looking for a place to settle. Evidence of their swift occlusion by local culture in such diverse places as Normandy (where Rollo and his descendants became titular fief-holders of the Frankish kings), to Sicily where absorption was almost complete, is adduced in support of this theory. Perhaps the truth lies midway between this apologist school of thought and the depredations of Sweyn Forkbeard, Harald Hardrada and their kin. If they left little ashore beyond their reputation, it is their legacy that has become permanent.

But it is necessary to look at how developments in shipbuilding elsewhere may have inspired the Norsemen in the final flowering of their own technique. In 897 Alfred, King of the West Saxons in England, built a fleet of ships which were twice as long as the raiding vessels of the Northmen. Some of these vessels had upwards of sixty oars, which suggests they were roughly the same size as the Viking long ships of a hundred years later. 'They were both swifter and steadier and also higher ... shaped neither like the Frisian nor the Danish ...' the Anglo-Saxon Chronicle records. The Frisian Islands and the waters lying behind them provided a network along which cargoes could be shipped in relative safety. Shallow draught was a requisite here, and a form of curved construction seems to have been the hull form favoured. In 1930 a hull 57 feet long was found near Utrecht in the old bed of the Rhine which, up to 866, had flowed into Lake Flevo. This was later breached by the sea to become part of the Zuider Zee, while the river was sealed off to wander seawards further south.

The Utrecht ship consists of wide planks which draw together at bow and stern. The centre plank is thus tapered, but amidships is 6.5 feet (2 metres) wide. Of oak, this plank supports a mast step situated well forward, in a position which elsewhere enabled it to be towed, and this seems to have been the case, for similar craft are found on coins and in ecclesiastical locations from the Carolingian period (AD 690–987) onwards. Carbon dating puts the Utrecht vessel at around 800, and the significance of the find is not the inland employment of the vessel, but the fact that it provides evidence of an alternative form of hull construction which, by the curious coincidence of appearing upon a town seal at Hulksmouth, now New Shoreham, has become known as a 'hulk'. The name hulk did not originally connote a broken-down ship, but derives from the Greek for a towed cargo hull. Moreover, the hulk was not confined to inland waters, but matured into a seagoing cargo ship, probably from the Frisian Islands which established and maintained a coastal trade throughout the extensive Rhine delta and via the Wadden Zee to the estuaries of the Jade, Weser and Elbe, and along the Danish coast to the Limfiord and the Baltic beyond.

But here too another 60-feet cargo hull emerges from the mud, this time that of Kolding Fiord. Although the bottom was flat and made of planks laid edge to edge, suitable for shallow water navigation, there was a sharp angle at the turn of the bilge and the topsides were clinker built. The ends were no curved rise of the keel, but an equally acute-angled stem and sternpost. Most remarkably, the latter bore rusting evidence of rudder hangings which, among other things, dated the wreck to around the end of the twelfth century at the earliest. This hull form was known as a 'cog', famous for being the trading vessel associated with the Hanseatic League.

Trading is known to have taken place between the Frisians and Scania, and the Scanian port of Birka, part of which disappeared around 1000, and which was known as Kugghamn, or cog-haven. The inevitable conclusion is that the wide waters of the Rhine estuary and the Frisian archipelago, produced a flat bottomed, hard-chine cog which was unequivocally a merchant vessel. The trade these cogs were engaged in seems to have been destroyed, or at least interrupted by Norse expansion, but later both the cog and the hulk reappear.

CHAPTER THREE

Medieval Merchantmen

Europe was to emerge from the 'Dark Ages' (the late fifth century AD to about AD 1000) as a collection of loosely 'united' kingdoms under the titular authority of the pope and the remit of the Roman Catholic church. Insofar as this went, it conferred a degree of stability which thus encouraged trade, but it also fomented and spawned wars of religion to add to those generated by the lust for land and for power.

These twin influences were to have momentous effects upon the history of the ship. The Papal See was to precipitate the Crusades and thus create a need for the sea transport of armies, while flourishing trade was to increasingly concentrate wealth in the hands of merchants, thereby stimulating the development of shipping to support trade.

Evidence of this promotion of the ship as a means to both mercantile and military ends is reflected in the common use of the image of ships on town seals, and these images are clearly derivatives of the long ship. Despite the distortions necessary to fit them on circular grounds, together with the interpretation of any representations made before the understanding of perspective, it is possible to mark the steady refinement of the long ship as a military vessel. Gone are the platforms for the *stafnbui*, replaced by the raised and castellated emplacements for archers known as fore and after castles. Occasionally these appear at the mastheads as topcastles, but the clinker hull form remains substantially as in the knarr and while provision might be made to manoeuvre these vessels with sweeps, they are essentially sailing vessels, for there is evidence of reef points to decrease the sail area in strengthening winds, and forward bumkins are fitted to take the bowlines used to stiffen the leading edge of the mainsail as the ship worked to windward. This replaced the *beitass* and was later adapted into the bowsprit.

Mercantile requirements called for the enlargement of the hull to accommodate bigger cargoes. Increased depth of hull led to greater draught and, as we shall see, this facilitated the introduction of the stern-hung rudder, for the old side-mounted steerboard possessed weaknesses and was inefficient in a deeper hull. The steerboard lingered longer in the Mediterranean, where the prototype was the Roman round ship. Carvel construction continued to be favoured with beams carried through the planking to be fastened outboard with pegs. There was a significant difference in the rig, the lateen sail being favoured, giving improved windward performance.

There were thus broadly two traditions, the 'northern' and the 'southern' and the differences, small at first, nevertheless possessed a potential for further development. In due course, the southern carvel tradition called for a frame to be erected, upon which a skin of planking was secured. This method ultimately enabled larger hulls to be built than could be achieved using the clinker, or 'northern' method, which required the shell to be framed up afterwards.

As a result of increased commerce, coupled with the upheavals caused by the Crusades, these two traditions came into contact and methods migrated. It is this merging of ideas and practices that drives the development of the ship during the medieval period towards what subsequently became the dominant type – 'the full-rigged ship' – which was to emerge by about 1550 and thereafter remained substantially unchanged for three centuries when it gave way to the steam ship. It was this 'true ship' that was to enable the expansionist nation states of Europe to shape the modern world, and to enable political power to be wielded far beyond the wildest dreams of the greatest warriors of either the Norse sagas or classical mythology. However, such pre-eminence was a consequence of luck, not providential superiority, for unbeknown to the nations of Christendom, or their sophisticated Muslim rivals, far beyond the Holy City of Jerusalem, the distant court of Cathay, a great power in its own right, had its own interest in the sea and had developed a ship-form which was to reach such a state of sophistication that it changed little in two thousand years.

The existence of China and the wonders it contained had long been rumoured in Europe and was confirmed after the return of the Venetian Marco Polo in 1295. Not content with retirement after his long sojourn abroad, Polo fought for Venice and was captured and imprisoned by the Genoese. During his incarceration, he wrote his *Travels*, a book which gave substance to conjecture. The extent to which the ambition of the Ming emperors prompted exploration will be discussed in Chapter Four; it is the development of the ship-form we know as the 'junk' which demands attention at this point in time. Although there is considerable diversity in local variants, the big ocean-going junk embraces the general principles of Chinese ship-construction. There was no spinal keel; instead a flat bottom of planks was laid upon sandbags so that the gradually increasing weight of the junk adjusted its bed to suit its growing shape. Upon this foundation athwartships bulkheads were raised. These were made of close-grained laurel or camphor-wood and conferred an immense strength to the hull, as well as splitting it into separate integral units, a circumstance which not only gave a degree of tolerance to flooding, but allowed liquid cargoes to be carried. In the eighteenth century, western observers found the Chinese running 'tankers' capable of shipping about 50 tonnes of liquid cargo. Legend and tradition claim that the idea of sub-dividing a hull with water-tight bulkheads originated from the nodes in the shaft of the bamboo stalk.

Longitudinal strength was provided by five rows of split, half-logs, laid as massive stringers. Planking of quick growing *sha-mui* pine, either overlapping or butting together, was then secured using iron pins, after which the hull was caulked with a mixture of Tung oil and lime mixed with bamboo tow. Tung oil contains alpha-elaeostearic acid which polymerises rapidly and provides a drying agent and medium, sealing the hull very effectively. Rot, where it did occur, was overcome by doubling the timbers, so such a hull was virtually indestructible.

No less trouble was taken over the masts which were traditionally made from a single teak log strengthened by burial in damp ground from which it was disinterred after absorbing natural preservatives. The main mast was stepped to transfer weight forward and across a main beam forming part of a bulkhead. Long before European craft sported more than one mast, the junk bore several and these were supported by bamboo ropes, resistant to chafe, decay and stretch, and having a very high tensile strength. The junk's sails were made of small sections of cloth in such a way that the most beggarly patchwork, a large percentage of which might be rent in tatters, will hardly affect the aerodynamic perfection of the airflow produced. This woven sail was stiffened laterally by light bamboo battens, each of which led to sheets and euphroe blocks. These, like the other blocks and pulleys, were made of teak and camphor wood. The sails were mounted fore and aft, held to the mast by bamboo rods and woven ropes. So highly sophisticated in their ability to harness the wind were they, that today eccentric yachtsmen use modern adaptations of the junk to power ocean-going sailing craft.

Adoption of bulkheads and the fore and aft rig mark the junk, already old practice when Marco Polo returned to Venice in the last decade of the thirteenth century, as a highly technologically advanced sailing ship, incomparably finer than anything produced in Europe. That the junk bore a high stern and a bow platform, giving it a rather clumsy appearance to western eyes, belies the effectiveness of hull and rig to fulfil its function. But there was yet another quality which, when it finally appeared in European ship-design, was to have a revolutionary effect. And this additional feature was the stern-hung rudder.

The Chinese rudder differs in two significant ways from the rudder finally fitted to European hulls: it was proportionately much larger, and it lifted and lowered, doubling as an effective leeboard to counteract down-wind drift, or 'leeway'. Its greater size made it extremely effective, particularly when fitted to river craft required to be exceptionally handy under sail. But this large size, conferring advantages inherent in levers, also made it difficult to handle, and this was overcome by cutting relieving holes, usually lozenge-shaped, to allow water to pass through it without much affecting its efficiency when in use.

The development of the tall, narrow and fixed rudder in Europe, argues against the direct importation of the stern-hung rudder from China. Whether the concept of the rudder was the result of turning travellers' tales to advantage, the separate realisation of the idea in the west, or a simultaneous invention, will never be known. As with so much in this history, conjecture can be diverting, but rarely satisfying, unless employed solely as a vehicle for the imagination. Hard evidence comes to us from the thirteenth century in an excavation of 1934 at Kalmar in Sweden where, in the drained castle moat, eighteen sunken hulls were discovered, among which was a small sailing coasting vessel dating from the thirteenth century. It was to prove a remarkable find.

Vague and uncertain iconographical evidence, mainly from town seals, suggested the existence of stern hung rudders from about the last quarter of the twelfth century. This is guesswork, but the Kalmar boat proves a definite shift of gear in the development of the ship, yet she remains a direct descendant of the long ship. Oak planks secured clinker fashion, with knees and beams passing through the planking, gave the hull strength, as did the rivetted, or clenched fastenings. Small decked areas existed fore and aft, the latter incorporating a simple, handspike windlass which could be used for several applications such as hoisting the yard and sail, weighing the anchor and lowering or hoisting the mast, which was raised between two longitudinal partners. On the sternpost is hung a rudder.

The advantages of the stern-hung rudder over the side-mounted version must have been immediately appreciated by its users, and while a more complex means of hinging it was necessary, the positive handling characteristics would have seemed a joy. Yet it is not so much the rudder, as the straight sternpost upon which it hangs that is ultimately so important.

By fitting a straight sternpost, the curves and twists of the after strakes differ from those of the forward running planks, so the shape of the hull takes on a new sophistication, possessing an entry forward and a run aft. These differences would have had an effect on the characteristics of the hull's performance. The solution to the geometrical problem this produced would later facilitate the adaption of all-carvel construction, uniting the best elements of the northern and southern traditions.

The Kalmar ship, small and probably insignificant though she was in life, possesses in death a unique quality; that of the long ship in transition, the first example of a northern European hull with differing end forms. The importance of this is that the lines of the stern are finer than those of the rounder, 'fuller' bow. This also produces diverse waterlines and distribution of hull form which when heeled under sail, drives the hull away from the wind. To keep such a hull on course required the application of lee helm and to counteract this a small after, or mizen mast was fitted, to carry a fore and aft lateen sail which had to shove the bow back up to windward. Such a primitive ketch could work to windward with more certainty than the single masted vessel exemplified by the Kalmar boat. Such a vessel must have been commonplace and was known by the generic term 'nef'.

At about the same time as the Kalmar boat and her contemporary sisters were working the coast of southeast Sweden, the Hanseatic League had united a number of northern city states in a commercial and legal confederation of mutual benefit. While it would be foolish to claim the League possessed a single, typical ship, there seems little doubt that the common carrier employed upon its many trades was the simple, effective and capacious 'cog'. Fortunately remains of such a craft were discovered at Bremen on the River Weser in 1962, confirming the depictions on the seals of ports such as Elbing, the modern Elblag in Poland, Lübeck, Stralsund, Wismar and Damme in northern Germany and Harderwijk, once a coastal port on the Zuider Zee in The Netherlands. All of these ports were within the Hanseatic Pale, while contemporary representations outside, at Ipswich in England for instance, continue to show the unmistakable long ship derivative, though this has the stern-hung rudder of the nef.

The Bremen discovery was crucially important in defining this important merchantman, ancestor of Indiamen, clippers, tramps and container ships, a functional carrier of raw materials and manufactured goods, a workhorse of the maritime world and a primitive argosy. At the time of the discovery in 1962, the word 'cog' had fallen into disuse, being used for an old boat, almost as we might use the word 'hulk' today. But the cog featured in Hanseatic records from about AD 1200 onwards, and appeared to conform to images on seals, particularly that of the Pomeranian port of Stralsund, which was dated from 1329. Dendochronolgy established the oak used in the Bremen cog had been felled in 1378. Not only did the seal enable identification of the cog, but the discovery of the wreck, which sank on her starboard side and so preserved a considerable portion of her upper fabric on that side, offered explanations as to certain details of the seal which hitherto had been puzzling.

An energetic and thorough analysis resolved that the cog derived from the log boat and that several had been unknowingly disinterred, notably alongside the boat found at Kalmar in 1934, but at the time not considered so noteworthy. Moreover, like the long ship, the cog was to disappear quite suddenly, through derivatives of both were to survive as small craft, mainly in the form of fishing boats, into the present century.

The characteristics of the cog are however very different from the long ship. The cog has a flat, flush laid bottom which turns sharply at the bilge and rises in steep, widening sides of overlapping clinker planking, fastened with iron spikes. These were not clenched, as in the Norse tradition, but bent over at both ends and buried in the timber. The hull terminates in straight, raked stem and stern posts, but a curious deficiency exists in the decking, which might reasonably be expected to preserve the cargo in an enclosed hold. In fact the cog's deck planks were laid athwartships, and a gap was left to allow water to run below, rather than lie on deck, and from where it was pumped out by a rudimentary lift pump, remains of which have been discovered in the cog at Kalmar. Cargoes which were susceptible to taint, damp or mildew had to be carried in barrels, and prevented the cog's capacity being maximised. Nevertheless this method of carriage meant that a cog's yard might be pressed into use as a derrick to handle cargo. On the quayside of important ports such as Lübeck, masts and crossed yards, or *Wippes* made their appearance as early cranes. The word 'whip' passed into English as the name of a simple pulley and line arrangement, although the original meaning was 'see-saw' from the nodding motion of the spar as it hoisted cargo in and out of a vessel. Bulwarks guarded the working area of a cog's deck while a commanding after castle had protective shingles down to the line of the hull's rail enclosing the tiller and forming a 'steerage'. The cog also boasted a windlass, hatches and a forecastle. Her single masted rig hoisted the usual single square sail.

Perhaps it was not surprising that so little care was taken over the cargo when the creature comforts afforded to the crew were minimal. The 'steerage' under the after castle provided some shelter for the ship-master and any passengers, but for the rest, the leather sleeping bag, hide-side out, seems to have sufficed. Privy seats have been found, though to what extent hot food was prepared at sea remains a matter for conjecture.

The Hanseatic League was established to facilitate trade and protect those trades that were members, not only against pirates, but against extortionate tariffs and dues levied by foreign princes. The word 'hanse' itself means an association or fellowship, and the mutual advantages of the agreement reached between the merchant seafarers of Frisia and their land-bound colleagues in Westphalia which resulted in the inauguration of the Hanseatic League and the establishment of Lübeck in 1159, soon spread its influence far beyond the immediate environs of the new Baltic port to finally embrace some eighty-four cities. The Frisian traded his knowledge of the sea and distant ports with the Westphalians' knowledge of the demands of the inland markets. This mercantile activity 'across sand and sea' soon increased enormously, to the detriment of competitors. It was not long before the League virtually monopolised Baltic trade. The Hanseatic remit ran up the Rhine, and east to Reval. Overseas concessions were obtained and trading bases were established in places as diverse as Bruges, London, Bergen, Visby (Gotland) and Novgorod. As the power of the League increased, the cog assumed its role as the principal Baltic and North European carrier.

To service this widespread commercial empire, larger cogs were built. The example at Bremen, some 80 feet (24 metres) in length, had a capacity of about 80 tons, but there is mention of a cog of 1241 capable of carrying 240 tons. It is thought that these had a sweeter, rounder bilge, easier in a seaway than the sharp 'chine' in the Bremen example. Nevertheless, even this development did not alter the simpler construction method used in the cog when compared with the long ship derivative. Wider planks could be used, cutting down the number of seams, and sawing them rather than splitting was less wasteful of timber. The watertight integrity of the hull was increasingly important to the preservation of a cargo, despite the run-off from the deck. While Rhenish wines in barrels, a staple export, might resist bilge-water, English wool en route to the Flemish weavers was not so tolerant, and a spoilt cargo meant massive loss. The cargoes carried were many and various, providing evidence of a complex web of cross-trades: grain and grain products such as beer were exported from Germany, and Norwegian stockfish and Scanian herrings were imported to feed devout German Catholics on fast-days. These were often preserved in salt from Lüneberg, which also found ready markets abroad. Swedish iron and copper were carried, as were Russian timber, furs, potash and wax, with small valuable consignments of jewels and amber providing profitable dividends. Tar was widely used, especially in ship-building, as was turpentine, obtained from the coniferous forests which abounded on the shores of the Baltic, and these commodities were also transported by cog.

The commercial dominance and widespread influence of the Hanseatic League was to do more than elevate the simple cog to the status of primary carrier; it was to encourage the supporting 'science' of navigation. Much of the navigational skill of the master of a cog was cabotage, requiring a detailed and compre-hensive knowledge of conspicuous features, leads and transits, anchorages, shoals and deeps which lay along the proposed route. Such knowledge was often hard-won and jealously guarded. The swashways and gats, narrow 'gates' or 'gaps' through often long sandbanks, could shorten a passage, or allow a master to slip to leeward of a bank and shelter from a heavy sea. Indeed the verb 'to conn' a ship, meaning to give the helm orders and to watch and monitor her progress, also forms the root of the word 'cunning', originally meaning to possess a special knowledge.

Moreover, once a cog had ventured out of the almost tide-less Baltic, the tidal rivers and turbulent, tide-riven North Sea offered an altogether different kind of challenge: cabotage had of necessity to transform itself into something more nearly approaching modern navigation.

The magnetic compass appeared as a navigational instrument about 1400, and was indispensable when making passage off-shore. Courses were recorded on maps or 'cartes' and written sailing directions began to appear in which pilotage directions and compass courses were recorded for future use, one of the earliest of these being the *Niederdeutsche Seebuch* produced for the Hanseatic ships and containing directions for voyaging between Cadiz and Reval. These books, called 'rutters' or 'ruttiers' in English, became common outside the League after about 1500. An English version, *The Book of the Sea Carte*, gave directions for the 'whole Ile of Brytanye' and contained 'ye tydes, courses, [and] kennynges,' the old form of 'cunning' or knowledge, referred to earlier.

In addition to these resources on board, the regular trading patterns established by the League also encouraged the establishment of seamarks. The often flat and featureless coasts of the Baltic could often confuse, particularly in fogs and summer mists. Many large wooden beacons with distinctive topmarks were erected to identify a locality and assist navigation, a practice still maintained in northern Europe. Lighted beacons were established to mark the entrance to the River Maas about 1280 and at Nieuport some four years later. The approaches to the Zuider Zee boasted buoys from 1323, and the Maas from 1358. Trouble arose almost immediately in levying and sharing the *Tonnengeld*, or dues to pay for them. But it was the River Weser which is believed to have had the first buoyed channels as early as 1066, and a major lighthouse was established at Lübeck in about 1202. The thirteenth century saw more lighthouses established in the Baltic near Copenhagen, at Wismar and Travemünde. There are instances of channels being marked by buoys of different shapes, even bearing topmarks, besoms with their points uppermost marking one side of a channel, besoms with their points downwards, the other.

Ultimately, the Hanseatic League attracted a degree of jealousy both from the wealthy feudal barony, and the less fortunate who found piracy the only road to democracy. But just as feudal lords were turning increasingly to the employment of mercenaries rather than deplete their productive lands of peasants as the price for raising inexpert soldiers, so the League itself could employ professional military expertise and wage war when the protection of its interests were necessary. In 1234 and 1239 the merchants of Lübeck mobilised and armed their cogs against the King of Denmark who sought domination over their city.

Attempts to limit the League's power in Norway and to wrest some of its trade back into Norwegian bottoms led to piracy and sequestration of Hanseatic vessels in Norwegian waters. This culminated in the seizure of the cog carrying the League's delegation travelling to hold negotiations in Norway, and war was declared. With the exception of Bremen, all adjacent Hanseatic ports and towns united in manning a fleet of cogs which blockaded the Norwegian coast and enforced a trade embargo interdicting Norwegian exports and southern imports. The blockading force was organised into squadrons which actively raided the Norwegian coastal villages, but it was the embargo on grain imports that forced the King of Norway to seek an armistice in 1285. He was forced to accept humiliating conditions in which all prisoners and captured merchandise was returned, while the Hanseatic merchants in his kingdom were restored to all their privileges.

The Norwegian king had a treaty of alliance with Edward I of England, but the Hammer of the Scots was too busy cudgelling his northern neighbours, so that during the war the only thing that came out of England was the concept of fore and after castles, observed on English ships. These provided crossbowmen with firing platform and also, it was realised, a shelter underneath, created by shingling in the steerage. This feature was to develop into the poop.

The conquest of England by Duke William of Normandy was to divert English attention away from its connections with Northern Europe after 1066 and concentrate mercantile acumen in establishing a new trade. The Saxon home-produced staples of ale and mead were despised by the new gentry and a flourishing wine trade soon grew up with the French fiefdoms of succeeding Norman kings of England. The ship depicted on the seal of Ipswich, differing from the cog of northern Europe, seems to be typical of the merchant vessel engaged in shipping those large barrels then known as 'tuns', of some 252 gallons capacity, or 35 cubic feet and by which the burthen of a cargo ship was henceforward determined. It was this volumetric measure that constituted a 'space ton' in cargo liners used to the very end of break-bulk carriage of general cargoes. (The word also passed into German as that for a buoy, early buoys being coopered in the same way as barrels.)

English nefs like the one on the Ipswich seal, were clinker built, and it may be assumed that many were taken up from trade to convey the Crusaders across the Channel for the long march through France and re-embarkation at a Mediterranean port. Their main trade, however, was the wine trade from the Gironde where France's oldest lighthouse was established by Charlemagne on the island of Cordouan in a primitive form, a chapel equipped with a light. The record of 1409 attributing credit to Edward, the Black Prince, in founding the light around 1370 is more credible and probably refers to the first erection of a proper tower. Equally important were regulations governing the conduct of ships and forming the beginnings of international maritime jurisprudence. The Laws of Oléron, incorporated into English law around 1185 during the short reign of Richard I, derived from an island in the king's French possessions. They were chiefly intended to govern the lucrative and important wine trade. Among other things they permitted the master of a ship wrecked by the incompetence of a pilot, to summarily behead the offending man.

In England, from the thirteenth century, ships for royal service were provided for by the five 'cinque ports'. This number was later expanded to seven, all of which were located along the shoreline of the Strait of Dover. In return for certain financial privileges, the town authorities would contribute to the raising of a fleet for the monarch's service when so commanded. As a result lighthouses were established at one of these, Winchelsea, in 1261, and another on the Isle of Wight in 1314, and it may reasonably be inferred that the Roman pharos at Dover was revived upon occasion. From this period lights began to be established wherever shipping needed them.

Cogs appear in English records under English ownership and were not infrequently used by pirates. The cog *Johan* of Yarmouth seized 30 tuns of white wine out of a Flemish vessel in 1360. On the other hand, the *Great Cog of St Mary* of Great Yarmouth, the *Seintmaricog* of Colchester and the *Beate Marie* and *Coga* of Valencia, Ireland, were themselves raided by Flemings in 1308. Wars between kings stopped trade and it seemed to many frustrated merchants, to be a legitimate practice to employ your cog to raid the commerce of the enemy if he would not trade with you like a gentleman; thus the privateer-cum-pirate was born. During the protracted dynastic conflict between England and France known as The Hundred Years' War (1337–1453), which arose from the English King Edward III's claim to the French throne, the cog was widely used as a military transport. Sailing from the River Orwell in June 1340, King Edward led a fleet of some 200 vessels, including many cogs, towards the Flanders coast and, on the 24th, engaged a French fleet guarding the approaches to Bruges, off Sluys. The battle was an English victory largely attributable to the superiority of the English archery, but the subsequent seige of Tournai was a failure and ended in a truce in September.

More significantly, about 1400, armed cogs acted as escort to the wine trade from Bordeaux, establishing the significant concept of convoy, which was to have so profound an effect upon naval strategy in the future. It was this occasional use for military purposes which had resulted in the building of the fore and after castles being adopted in its design.

The greater and greater voyaging required of the cog eventually resulted in it being superseded by the hulk which possessed a rounder, more refined and seaworthy clinker hull with a far greater cargo capacity. The defects of the cog must have lain in the difficulty of preserving perishable cargoes, a degree of leeway which made navigation in tidal waters uncertain, and a hull which had poor sea-keeping qualities outside the comparatively sheltered waters of the Baltic where coastal passages were the norm and where anchorages and havens of refuge abounded.

The hulk had been developed out of the long ship by the English. As already noted, the 1295 town seal of New Shoreham, then known as Hulksmouth, indicates the existence of these ships, though no archaeological confirmation has yet been discovered. In about 1400 the hulk seems to have been adopted by the League, if the iconographical evidence of the seal of Danzig is to be accepted. The Danzig ship bore a single mast, with a top and fore and after castles, but these structures appear to have become integral parts of the ship, not mere appendages. The Shoreham seal indicates the existence of ratlines to facilitate entry into the top, which is of a slightly different design than seen hitherto. Like the cog, the hulk had a stern-hung rudder. It had eclipsed the cog about 1450, the latter disappearing entirely.

Interestingly, it was in Danzig that the next phase of development affecting the innovative League took place. Such a willingness to adapt and accept change, argues powerfully that the League accepted the principle of market forces, for in 1462 a merchant from the French Biscay port of La Rochelle abandoned his huge merchantman at Danzig. Why he did this is open to conjecture, but coercion is not impossible and since imitation is the sincerest form of flattery, we should not be surprised to learn that the Danzig shipwrights studied this monster from the stormy shores of the Western Ocean with more than a superficial degree of curiosity. Thus the *Peter de la Rochelle* became the *Peter von*

Danzig, suggesting a prize. She was a three masted, carvel built ship with lapping planks nailed onto a frame of keel, hog and ribs. Fitted out for the Hanseatic war against England of 1470, she proved her worth, actually being armed with nineteen small bore cannon. Although arming ships on their upper decks with heavy artillery was to threaten stability, the earliest record of mounting them lower, to reduce the height of the centre of gravity and fitting opening gunports, occurs on the seal of Maximilian, Prefect of Burgundy, dated 1493. This too depicts a three masted ship and while the Hanseatic League was late in adopting this arrangement, its final conformity marks the end for the descendants of the long ship and of the northern tradition. A multitude of small craft preserved the Norse techniques into the twentieth century, but it was the Mediterranean, or southern ship-type which was to subsume the northern tradition to provide the crucial stage in the development of the true, full-rigged sailing ship.

The maritime history of the Mediterranean in the second half of the first millennium, is something of a closed book. The idea that the collapse of the Roman Empire ushered in a dark age is a conceit of classicism, but it did transform the Mediterranean from a Roman *mare nostrum* to a frontier with all the activity associated with borders. In the west the boorish feudal states emerged under the titular leadership of a papal Rome, while in the east the imperial remnant of Byzantium kept the faith for a thousand years. But from the Levant in the east, to Granada in the west, stretched the dominions of 'the Moors', a refined, sophisticated and advanced civilisation, mathematically inclined and imbued with the zeal of a newer religion. And while the stinking crusaders embarked at Genoa and Marseilles to wrest Jerusalem from the scented infidel and establish the Frankish version of the Kingdom of God in the Holy Land, they did so in ships which owed much to the enemy.

Archaeological evidence with which to track the development of the ship in these southern waters is rare. Iconographical sources are more numerous, but with the distortions inherent in the pre-perspective age, not much more helpful. However, certain developments are beyond peradventure and seem to be confirmed by the existing traditional building methods found in fishing vessels at the turn of the century, elsewhere a good indication of earlier methods, if preserved in diminutive form.

As we have already noted in the first chapter, the galley remained the dominant war ship, but insofar as merchant vessels are concerned, the debt owed to the great Roman grain ships remained. Indeed, their size was probably never equalled and certainly not surpassed, though our knowledge of the medieval merchantman is limited. There have been three significant archaeological sites rendering clues for the period. Sadly two of these excavations have left us no hard evidence, only the results of contemporary scholarship. A pair of these are close together, on the Turkish coast at Yassi Ada and Serçe Liman near the island of Rhodes, where hulls of the seventh and eleventh centuries respectively were found. The third find, a vessel known as the Contarina Ship and dated around 1300, was found in 1898 in the Po Estuary at the head of the Adriatic. Other ancient wreck sites are known to exist, three off the coast of Languedoc, another at Mazara on the west coast of Sicily and one off the Greek island of Pelagos. None of these have yielded hulls.

The Yassi Ada ship was excavated between 1960 and 1964 and although it was not preserved, provided some facts about typical construction methods during the seventh century. These showed the continuing tradition of binding the hull with through-beams which became external projections. At the stern these were used to hold the twin steering oars, while amidships they became mast partners. Keel and endposts (the stem was never discovered) were made of cypress, the frames of elm and the planking of pine. Iron spikes and bolts held the ship's 20.5-metre hull together and she could carry some 61 metric tonnes which, at the time of her loss, consisted chiefly of about 900 amphorae of wine. In the stern a cabin and tiled galley contained several artifacts, including a steelyard with the name of her master, or naukleros, George the elder. Like many Mediterranean wrecks she was found with a large number of anchors, eleven in this case, which suggests their use perhaps for mooring offshore to work cargo, and possible frequent loss. But it is in the hull construction that the chief interest of the Yassi Ada ship lies. The keel and end posts were set up, the latter elegantly curved and rising quite high. Then a series of strakes were laid side by side alongside the keel and secured to each other by tenons morticed into each adjacent plank and pinned by trenails in the classical way. Once the bottom had been started, floors were laid across them and spiked to the planks and this procedure was repeated until the hull had been formed up to the waterline. Thereafter the frames were raised directly to the line of the gunwale and the sides planked up, being nailed directly onto the frames without the use of tenons or trenails. Thus the old technique provided the under-water body and a new, plank on frame method was used for the topsides.

In 1973, an American team located a ship not far away, at Serçe Liman. She was thought to have sunk in 1015 or 1024 from the dates on the coins found in the wreck. She had been carrying a cargo largely of glassware and from evidence of other cargo, is thought to have been trading between the Muslim Fatimid caliphate of Egypt and the Christian empire of Byzantium. She too carried numerous anchors, some struck into the hold and others at either bow, with one missing and found some distance away, the failure of which was probably the cause of her driving ashore and being wrecked.

Her keel comprised three scarphed pieces of elm, while pine was used for the rest of the hull and her construction method marks another stage in the process we know to have taken place in changing Mediterranean technique from skin to skeletal construction. Keel and end posts were laid down and then four frames, two short and two long, were laid out amidships, one of each on either side. The short frames were flat, while the longer pair took in the beam of the ship and the turn of the bilge. Thus the first two full floors extended each side from keel to the sharp angle of the bilge, though the station on the keel at which this was achieved was staggered. Futtocks were then scarphed to the long frames, while more futtocks were scarphed to the short frames, extending them up the side and completing two full frames. Eight additional floor frames were then added, forward and aft, with their first long, curving sections sweeping alternately round the bilge to port and starboard. This alternating of the scarphed joints meant there was no continuous line of joints to provide a weakness in the hull and this was further strengthened by the addition of the lower outer planking. The basic form of the hull was now configured, and the remaining ribs were set up between the primary frames. The planking was then continued up to the gunwale without mortices and tenons,

Iconographic evidence of a waterborne craft on a prehistoric Norwegian rock carving; two men in a boat, one with a bow and arrow, the other with snowshoes.

The wall relief from the palace of Sennacherib showing galleys evacuating Luli, King of Tyre and Sidon, from Tyre; Nineveh 702 BC.

One combination of oar and sail produced the more weatherly galleasse which appeared at Lepanto in 1571.

A Flemish representation of a kraek or carrack. Thirty large models of these were made for the nuptials of Charles the Bold, Duke of Burgundy, and Margaret of York in 1468. The carrack was the precursor of the three-masted, full-rigged ship.

A large Dutch galleon engraved by Barentsoen, dated 1594, has topgallant yards and a fourth, bonaventure mast.

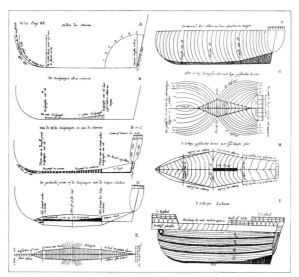

Early attempts to convey hull form by graphical representation appeared in the seventeenth century. These are diagrams by the Portuguese Fernando de Oliveira from his *Livra da fábrica das Naos* published by the Dutchman Witsen in his *Scheepsbouw* of 1671.

The expansion of Dutch trade and the nature of The Netherlands' coastline called for the development of numerous shoal draft coasters and a multitude of fishing vessels. Here a *boeijer* and a *galijoot* have been engraved by Reinier Nooms. Note the loose-footed gaff main sails, the fore and aft rig and the leeboards to aid windward performance.

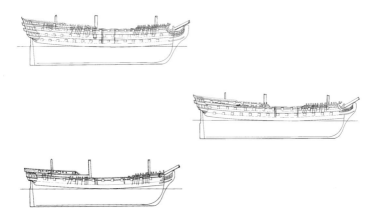

Top: The *Royal George* of 1788, successor to the ship lost in 1782 and one of the last 100-gun ships before they were superseded by 110s and 120s. Right: A standard 74-gun ship, typical of many built between 1757 and 1780, 168ft long on the gundeck. Many survived to fight in the wars of 1793 to 1815. Bottom: A 28-gun sixth rate of 1775. Some of this type survived to fight from 1793 to 1815, though no new ones were built.

A Dutch East Indiaman, her draught reduced by 'camels', is towed across the shallow waters of the Zuider Zee by *waterschepen* from the island of Marken.

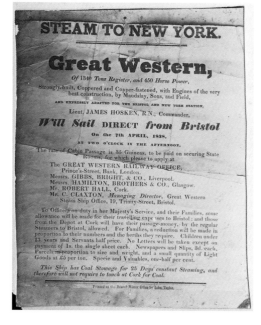

B runel's *Great Western* was conceived literally as a westwards extension of the Great Western Railway across the Atlantic, as this advertisement implies. Note that her master is a former naval officer, a fact of significance in lulling the fears of would-be passengers.

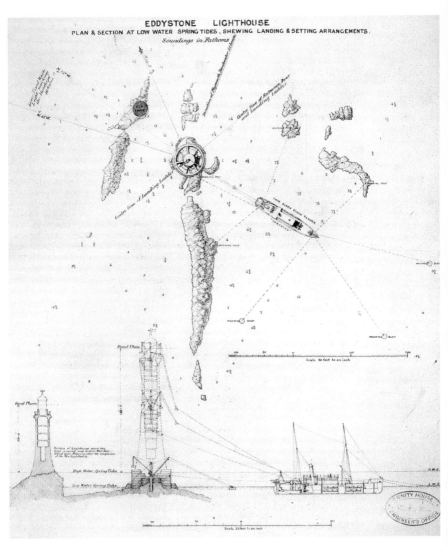

EDDYSTONE LIGHTHOUSE
PLAN & SECTION AT LOW WATER SPRING TIDES, SHEWING LANDING & SETTING ARRANGEMENTS.
Soundings in Fathoms

Steam and steamships greatly facilitated the building of the rock lighthouses, crucial to coastal navigation during the expansion of trade in the nineteenth century. Here the Trinity House steamer *Hercules*, specially built for the carriage and delivery of prepared masonry, assists in the building of Sir James Douglass' Eddystone Light of 1881.

The inventors of gunpowder are out-gunned by the inventors of steam engines. The primitive sailing war-junks of the Chinese are shot to pieces by the steamships of the Royal Navy in the ignoble Opium Wars.

The 1866 race between the *Taeping* and *Ariel* was the most famous of all the tea races, with both ships entering the Channel neck and neck after a passage of 13,000 miles, with *Serica* only minutes astern.

Dupuy de Lôme's 90-gun *Napoleon* was the first purpose-built screw line-of-battle ship. She was commissioned in 1852 and was followed by ten sister-ships.

HMS *Warrior* was built in response to France's *Gloire*, but far exceeded her in capability. As an iron, armoured version of the large wooden steam frigate *Mersey*, *Warrior* was a true cruiser, capable of extended operations.

but spiked to the frames. Finally, a keelson was laid and bolted through the keel and three stringers were run across the floor timbers from bow to stern on each side. To line this hull for cargo, a removable ceiling was fitted. Thus the basic, 16-metre hull shape was essentially formed by designed primary frames to which the planking was secured and it was not the curve of the strakes that decided the form of the hull, but the curve and station of the frames. However, this is only partially true. The insertion of secondary frames reflected a convenient reversion to the old methodology, while the ends of the ship were allowed to take up the shape the strakes conferred. Short timber lengths and a large number of scarphed joints suggests a Muslim builder, if only because of the dearth of long timber lengths, but whoever built her wanted a capacious, cargo bearing hull, and they achieved this by dictating the midships cross-section.

The Contarina ship of 1300, though lost to us, was excavated with the painstaking care in documenting everything which bespeaks the curiosity of the nineteenth century. With the exception of her larch stringers, the Contarina ship is oak-built and some 21 metres overall in length. Her keel is in two sections and was laid with both end posts raised upon it. Again the midships section was defined by setting up three frames attached to the floors which crossed the keel and were secured by a keelson through-rivetted to the keel. The central frames consisted of a floor, extended on each side by two further futtocks, each of which overlapped by some 75 centimetres. Thereafter an upper futtock was added to each side, in line with the floor, and extended to the gunwale. There were slight variations at each end to allow the lines of the hull to converge on the stem and sternposts and the lower to upper futtock joints were stiffened by an internal stringer and an external wale. Unlike either of the other two finds, the Contarina ship yields evidence of her masts, in the form of steps, one forward and one aft. Additionally, there is evidence of a single through beam near the stern, which probably bore the stern rudders. Thus, with this single anachronism, we have arrived at the basic construction method which essentially became the standard technique for ship construction until after the Napoleonic Wars, some eight centuries later.

What we remain ignorant of, is the rig of such ships.

*

Documentary evidence of the same period as the Contarina wreck is obtained from contracts made by King Louis IX of France (St Louis) with the merchants of Genoa, Venice and Marseilles for transport for his two crusades (1248–54). King Louis IX was canonised and thereby attracted a biographer, Jean de Joinville, a contemporary and servant of the King, who tells us that the King's ships had more than one deck, for when 'we entered into our ship, they opened the door of the ship and put therein all the horses we wanted to take oversea [sic]; and then they reclosed the door, and caulked it well … because, when the ship is on the high seas, all the said door is under water.'

Notwithstanding the limitations of size when compared to Roman merchant vessels, St Louis' transports were clearly ships of some substance. There appear to have been several three decked ships taken up from trade and chartered to the King for military transport. Others had two decks and some half-decks at either end, connected along the inner sides by *corridoria*, necessary for swift fore and aft access and forerunners of the later gangway and the open waist which let air and light into the deck below.

These ships were lateen rigged, with huge triangular sails spread by a long yard made from several tree trunks and raised upon an immensely strong, short mast by a prodigious halliard tackle. Despite this early fore and aft rig, the weight of the gear needed a large crew, about 10 men per 100 tonnes and again there were several anchors and every vessel bore several boats. Such transports ran up to 35 metres in length with displacements thought to have reached 800 tonnes. The largest could embark about a hundred horses or some one thousand people, including the crew of about eighty.

There is substantial evidence to suggest that for seagoing ships, the square sail remained the norm until about AD 500 and the gradual dissolution of the old Roman Empire. By the ninth century and until the thirteenth, the square sail entirely disappears from the Mediterranean and is replaced by the triangular, high-peaked lateen. A single, wide, square sail could be braced sharp up and cockbilled, a logical evolution as the wind hauled ahead of a vessel, producing a rough aerofoil approaching the lateen and improving windward performance. It would have taken no great mind to reconfigure the square sail to operate in this way, squaring the yard and slacking the forward corner when the wind hauled aft. This empiric approach was probably the origin of the primitive Egyptian lug rig such as survived on the Nile nuggar. It was used to work down the River Nile against the prevailing northerly wind. There seems little doubt therefore, that the lateen sail was effectively of 'Moorish' inception, but it was soon taken up by others.

To indicate his senior ships when sailing to engage Gellimer, King of the Vandals, the Byzantium Emperor Justinian's great commander Belisarius had the 'upper corner' of his sails painted red, suggesting the use of lateen sails in the third decade of the sixth century. Lateen sails are depicted on Byzantine dromons of the late fifth and sixth centuries in a manuscript of the Iliad, while a more unequivocal representation appears about AD 880 in a manuscript of the sermons of St Gregory of Nazianzus.

The lateen sail was cut to produce a baggier and therefore more aerodynamically satisfactory shape than a square sail. Wind trapped in its foot spiralled upwards to produce a fine aerofoil shape which created substantial lift to improve windward performance, hence the extreme length of these yards and the power of the gear necessary to get them at as sharp an angle as possible in the largest ships. The evolution of tacking a lateen sail was complicated, but could be achieved with a well-disciplined crew, even with very large sails, a method still practiced in Arab dhows.

The significance of the adoption of the lateen sail is not so much its windward capability, as the obviously increased necessity for a ship to be able to set her course, if not directly to windward, then in as many directions as possible, for in the post-Roman Mediterranean, all sea-roads did not lead to Rome. Trade had become extensive; ships now ran between many ports.

Following the capture of Jerusalem by the First Crusade in 1099, traffic the length of the Mediterranean increased, for not only did this event initiate a large movement of pilgrims, but the demands of an independent though essentially Frankish kingdom stimulated a vast trade. In 1102 an Anglo-Saxon pilgrim named Saewulf recorded thirty large ships in Jaffa harbour, and seventy years later another pilgrim named Theodorich, passing through Acre at Easter in 1172, counted eighty ships there. The mercantile republic of Venice had concluded a treaty with Basil II of

Byzantium in 991, and by the late eleventh century, Genoa and Amalfi had established links with Egypt. Pisa, Barcelona and Marseilles soon followed suit. Though the crusaders were destined to lose Jerusalem and the Kingdom was to be destroyed, the trade routes were to prove more enduring. Merchant fleets were established and merchants acted as middle-men and facilitators. The Italians, for instance, trafficked in Ukrainian and Caucasian slaves, selling them to Muslim dealers at Alexandria, while Genoese and Venetian outposts echoed the foreign bases of the Hanseatic League, founding enclaves in the Levant, while Muslim merchants established themselves, like the Jews, in many western ports and cities.

Rich though many became by this lucrative trade, it was not conducted without risk. The perils of the sea were not to be conquered by a mere triangular sail. Cunning though the Contarina ship and her sisters were, capable of working painstakingly to windward, they were still using a steering oar and their builders as yet possessed no clear understanding of hydrodynamics. While the lateen sail enabled a ship to point up reasonably well, her hull would sag away to leeward, frustrating her master and complicating navigation. It is not surprising to note that a Muslim pilgrim named Ibn Jubayr, returning to Messina in Sicily from Acre in 1183, passed Crete 'on Saturday the 10th of Sha'ban ... and made speed under a favourable north wind ... At midnight on Sunday the 11th, the wind changed to the west ... Strongly the wind blew ... Morning had scarcely come when to our misfortune we saw the coast of Crete again'. And the experiences of an Egyptian Jew coasting from Tyre to Jaffa were even less pleasant. A storm 'drove us out into the midst of the sea, where we remained for four days, giving up all hope for life. We were without sails ... likewise the sailyards were broken and the waves burst into the ship'. Passages were as slow as they might be uncertain. It took St Louis' ships twenty-four days to work from Aigues Mortes on the French coast to Cyprus in 1254 and in 1183 a passage from Almeria to Alexandria took thirty-one days. But the following year a Genoese ship took fifty-one days to travel from Acre to Messina against the prevailing wind and speeds made good in any direction rarely exceeded 2 knots.

Navigation was basically confined to cabotage, the successful masters being those most skilled in using the complex local winds of the Mediterranean. But the often featureless coasts could entrap an unwary navigator, especially that of the Nile Delta. The pharos in Alexandria, erected in ancient times, had endured in a reduced state to aid navigation, and lighthouses began to appear in other ports. Genoa possessed one by 1161 and in later years the keeper was one Antonio Columbus, reputedly the uncle of the Genoese-born Christopher. While these aids to navigation might make more certain a landfall, they scarcely ameliorated the miseries of contemporary voyaging.

The conditions endured by passengers and crews alike were uncomfortable and primitive, even by the standards of the time. Unsurprisingly the pilgrim trade stimulated some rudimentary regulations, such as the Statutes of Marseilles of 1253 which stipulated the space for each pilgrim or crusader who clearly demanded value for money. Sleeping was on the deck and victualling depended upon the status of the passenger. The most luxurious diet consisted of rusks, or double baked bread, with wine, salt meat or salt fish, cheese, beans and lentils, figs, garlic and onions, rice and almonds. Cooking was done over wood fires and the attendant risks must have been considerable. St Louis assigned to his afterwards biographer, Jean de Joinville, the important duty of supervising the dousing of all fires on board at nightfall, except the central hearth from which all others were rekindled next morning and which was constantly under guard.

But the world stood on the threshold of radical change, and that change was to affect the history of the ship. By the time of the Crusades, the cog had appeared in the Mediterranean and by the early fourteenth century, had become commonplace. In the cultural melting pot the Mediterranean had now become, there was to occur a fusion of the northern and southern traditions that was to produce the first true, full-rigged sailing ship, the carrack.

CHAPTER FOUR

Towards the Ocean Sea

In 1405, during the reign of Yongle, the second Ming Emperor of China, one of the emperor's trusted servants, the eunuch Sanbao (also known as Zheng He), began a remarkable series of exploratory voyages. As a young man, Zheng He had been captured and castrated when the Ming forces defeated the Yuan army in which he had been serving in his home province of Yunnan. At the time of his capture, Zheng He had acquired a reputation for courage and subsequently entered the household of the Ming prince who, after staging a coup, seized the Peacock Throne as the Emperor Yongle.

Zheng He was a Muslim whose father had made the *haj* (the pilgrimage to Mecca that every Muslim must make in their lifetime), a circumstance which may well have contributed to the young man's interest in the world beyond the borders of the Celestial Kingdom. Between 1405 and 1433, Zheng He made seven voyages to 'the Western Ocean', south to modern Surabaya in eastern Java, through the Malacca Strait to ports on the coast of the Bay of Bengal, across the Arabian Sea to Hormuz, then penetrating the Red Sea as far north as Jeddah. Zheng He also doubled the Horn of Africa and coasted southwards. This was no speculative voyage of discovery such as were being mooted by the Portuguese Prince Henry at Sagres. These were full blown expeditions and Zheng He commanded the largest fleet the world had yet seen – some 200 ships of varying sizes with over 27,000 people of all ranks and stations embarked. Chief among these was the *Treasured Ship*, whose 'sails, anchors and rudders ... cannot be moved without two or three hundred people', and which is reputed to have been about 152 metres in length, with a beam of 62 metres. So vast a ship, even allowing for a degree of inflating exaggeration, was a triumph of Chinese naval architecture. The *Treasured Ship* bore nine masts with a dozen sails and was supported by a host of smaller vessels which were deployed in a complex formation over which control was exerted by 'flags in the daytime, lanterns at night'. When the visibility closed in, drums, trumpets and gongs were used and these audible signals were used in clear weather to manoeuvre.

The fleet left China in the autumn and crossed the Indian Ocean westward during the northeast monsoon. The wilder, southwest monsoon was harnessed for the return voyage, and the fleet contained men who knew the arcana of weather lore through verses not dissimilar to those occasionally still taught to yachtsmen today.

During the passages, observations for future cabotage were made, and recent studies have concluded that errors in courses of not more than five degrees were made, using the magnetic compasses with which the whole fleet was equipped. It is clear that dead reckoning was the main method of navigation, and it may be assumed that the efficient sailing qualities of the junk, conferred a greater degree of accuracy on this than was possible with the European vessels then fitting out on the other side of the world. The fleet's navigators also used a primitive form of astro-navigation derived from the Arabic method known as Al Kemal. This depended upon observing the heights of known stars, measured with star plates made of persimmon wood and inscribed with linear graduations. In his sailing directions, Zheng He marked the altitudes of ten selected stars at certain locations to plot his course.

Arab influence, together with native Chinese development ensured that the Ming fleet was better equipped than any similar expedition by a western prince, both in terms of technological ability and methodology and in the superior quality of its ships, the junks, the advantages of which have been discussed in Chapter Two.

Zheng He died at Calicut, India, during his seventh voyage, unequivocally one of the world's greatest maritime explorers and the first true admiral. His body was borne honourably home and buried in Niusou Hill, Nanjing.

Modern scholarship suggests that in 1420, a Chinese ship sailed around the south of Africa. Whether this junk was a speculative offshoot of the main fleet or not, neither this nor Zheng He's enterprise seems to have stimulated a desire to capitalise on the discoveries made. China traded overland in the riches of Arabia and Moghul India; the coast of Africa appeared to offer nothing comparable, nor was it conducive to the sophisticated appetites of the emissaries of the Celestial Kingdom. China was to pay heavily for this disdain, if disdain it was. Subsequent emperors were to consider that everything desirable lay within the imperial pale, or was connected with it by the ancient silk-road. Theirs was the 'Middle Kingdom' subsisting supreme and all powerful, at the centre of the world.

Seventy years later the Portuguese doubled Africa to burst into the Indian Ocean and in succeeding decades a whole pack of 'foreign devils' followed in their wake.

The fusion of the northern and southern traditions of shipbuilding discussed in the last chapter was one contributing factor to the upsurge in the collective energies of the Europeans and which we know as the Renaissance. From it came the first 'orrible, greete and stoute' ship, generically known as the 'carrack'.

In her day, the extravagant carrack rivalled the great cathedrals in her claim on superlatives; Chaucer, for instance, used the image of a carrack's mainsail to describe the width of the devil's tail. Carracks were regarded as symbolic of temporal might, and thirty huge models of them were borne in the marriage ceremony of Charles the Bold, Duke of Burgundy, to Margaret of York in 1468. To our modern eye, the carrack is a somewhat impossible sort of ship, yet her form is recognisable: she has the three masts of the true ship, a pronounced sheer, a stern rudder and high fore and after castles.

By the last quarter of the thirteenth century, major Mediterranean ports such as Genoa, had produced some large, multi-decked ships. By adopting ideas from the cog, Genoese owners eschewed the traditional galley when despatching ships north to Flemish waters and began building *coche baonesche*, or 'Biscayan cogs,' a pragmatic hybrid that earned itself the English soubriquet of 'carrack'. The etymology of the word is confused and may owe something to Arabic, given the Moorish influence in the Iberian peninsula; it was most likely a handy, possibly slang name which stuck. As this type of ship proliferated in the Mediterranean, the name *coche* declined, replaced by the Italian *nave*, or Spanish *não*, literally translated into English as 'ship'.

An engraving of about 1470, and possibly connected with the Burgundian marriage of 1468, is that of a *kraeck*, the Flemish equivalent of carrack, and it is significant in that it shows a three-masted vessel with square-rigged fore and main masts and a lateen mizen. The hull is heavily carvel built, suggesting skeletal construction, with a massively imposing forecastle and lesser after castle. The degree to which the artist has distorted the image is debatable, but the presence of a loading port and the freeboard of the carrack indicates at least two decks. The transitional *coche* adopted the square-sailed main and added the lateen mizen for the reasons described in connection with the Kalmar boat in Chapter Three, and it is clear that an additional forward mast was later the means by which greater sail was added to the increasing size of hulls. For despite impressions to the contrary, the big lateen required a larger crew to handle it.

By 1353, a vessel described as having a bowsprit, a main mast and an *arbre de mig*, or mizen, sailed from Barcelona to Alexandria. In 1410 a former Genoese two masted carrack called the *Sancta Maria & Sancta Brigida* was bought into English crown service and renamed *Le Carake*. An inventory of this ship dated 1411 noted the presence of 'one great mast and one small mast.' In the renewal of the dynastic war with France by Henry V in 1416, the English captured eight more Genoese ships in the service of King Charles of France. They were comparatively large ships of up to 600 tons burthen and six had two masts. The smaller after mast was called the mesan, an Italian or Spanish word deriving from the sail it bore. By 1420, the term mizen mast was an accepted anglicization.

Importing Mediterranean shipwrights and caulkers to build frame-on-plank, the English began to construct a fleet, but neglect led to the loss of some of these ships which simply foundered. Nevertheless, the influence of carvel-built Portuguese caravels gradually overcame English difficulties with the new method. Determined to secure dominance over the sea around his kingdom, Henry is thought to have built four 'grete ships' between his accession in 1413 and 1420. They were the 540-ton *Trinity Royale*, the 760-ton *Holigost*, the *Jesus* of 1000 tons and the *Grace Dieu* of 1400 tons. The first two of these took part in the war capturing the Genoese carracks, a fact which suggests they were actually themselves large clinker-built versions of the carrack. Their precise rig is uncertain, but by the middle of the fifteenth century, the adoption of the mizen was closely followed by an additional sail above the main, the topsail. Then, well before the turn of the century, a second lateen-rigged mast, then called the bonaventure, was added abaft the mizen. By 1500 topsails were carried on all four masts, with a topgallant gracing the main and foremasts. Such a rapid proliferation of spars and sails is unsurprising when seen against the rapidity of change ashore in the innovative cultural, scientific and artistic fervour of the times.

This has led to difficulties in charting the precise nature of changes as they occurred, but construction of an English carrack is best exemplified by the *Mary Rose*, built in 1510, which sank at Spithead in 1545. A warship, the *Mary Rose* was one of the largest and most heavily armed of King Henry VIII's fleet which sailed from Portsmouth on 19 July 1545 to engage the French. Artillery had gone to sea some years earlier and had been adopted on the various decks, by piercing the hull with opening gunports. With guns run out and sails set, the *Mary Rose* heeled to a sudden gust of wind. Set too low, her open lee ports were quickly swamped and this swift down-flooding led to her capsize within a few minutes; fewer than forty of her five hundred-strong company survived. Her hull lay partially buried in the mud for four-and-a-quarter centuries, and may now be seen disinterred at Portsmouth. The armament of the *Mary Rose* consisted of a bewildering array of guns of different sizes and calibres. Essentially they were the same, smooth-bore barrels that were to serve navies world-wide until the nineteenth century, the heaviest carried as low as possible, to reduce the ship's centre of gravity. Guns were cast of both iron and bronze, and some curiously bored 'scatter-guns' were found around the wreck site, as were examples of that standard English weapon, the bow and arrow.

The keel of the *Mary Rose* was 105 feet (32 metres) in length and she had a beam of 37 feet (11.4 metres) on a draught thought to be about 14.8 feet (4.5 metres). Regarded as a huge ship in her day, she was some 20 feet shorter than the Swedish *Stora Kravfel* (great caravel) otherwise known as *Elefant*, whose forecastle rose 52 feet (16 metres) above the water. Another English carrack, the *Regent* of 1488 had a main mast only 8 feet shorter than the *Elefant's*, a 'tree' of 114 feet (35 metres) with a main yard made of two fished spars each of 31 feet (25 metres). The *Regent* carried at least four masts and the great tree amidships was over three metres in circumference.

It seems clear that the *Regent* was not pierced with gunports, for naval tactics were then confined to exchanging arrow shots, then grappling, boarding and fighting 'a land battle at sea'. A later ship , the *Mary Rose* was so fitted, tending to support the assertion that the hinged artillery port appeared at sea around 1510. On the other hand, the *Mary Rose* was extensively refitted in 1536, at which time these gunports may have been cut in the hull. It seems likely, however, that the ship was probably built with gunports, evidence reinforcing otherwise putative claims for a Brest shipwright named Descharges to have done so about 1501. Clearly, however, gunports were no real innovation, since openings had long facilitated the loading of cargo and were to do so in the hulls of merchantmen long after naval vessels had adopted a more efficient killing machine than the muzzle-loading cannon.

Although the hull of the *Mary Rose* was far from intact when she was lifted from the ooze of Spithead, modern analysis suggests she was not the towering, castellated carrack of the Flemish engravers of 1468. Doubtless a degree of exaggeration emphasised the prestige of a state ship, but there is sufficient iconographical evidence to suggest the castles were dominating features and that they could have been comparatively lightly scantled, and not the threat to stability that they so often seem.

The great size of the carrack tended to make her expensive to build and run, although she offered some economies in manning, requiring a crew member for every 5 to 8 tons of burthen, with English ships being more generously manned with one man for every 3 tons. To what degree this additional manpower was needed for serving her armament is now impossible to say, but crew costs were not then an overwhelming consideration in royal ships. While the cost of a royal 'grete ship' was about £1650, a captured carrack was sold to a Bristol owner in 1423 for just under £167. This price must have reflected her running costs of £647 over the seven years she had been in crown ownership, and a year later two Venetians purchased another for £133, her costs during the eight years since her capture amounting to almost £1000.

Whether fitted for war or trade (and a distinction was emerging), the carrack form was capable of both undertakings. She would have wallowed, and been unhandy; she would have been slow and ponderous, but if one did not cut gunports too low down in the hull, she would have, as they said, 'swum' well and provided a good gun platform. In such a 'orrible, grete and stoute' ship one might venture anywhere on the oceans of the world.

While Punic coins have been found as far west as the Azores, no seaman had ever ventured south along the Saharan coast past Cape Bojador, for beyond lay the edge of the world. The *drear littoral* gave less encouragement to the European than that of southeast Africa to the Chinese. The land was arid, occasional strong harmattan winds whirled off the desert, while unpredictable currents confused navigation and the dry, sandy cliffs of the coast itself had a disconcerting habit of collapsing into the sea which appeared to boil as this disintegration took place. To any observer used to northern shores, this inhospitable locality was a God-given warning of the utter darkness that lay beyond, and this seemed confirmed by a low, sandy cape beyond which a long, shallow reef ran 15 miles out to seaward. Moreover, beyond this cape, the winds swing round and freshen, combining with the North Equatorial Drift to sweep a ship to the westward and the feared, misunderstood 'glutinous' Sargasso Sea discovered by the Phoenicians. No sensible mariner stood past Cape Bojador.

Until, that is, Prince Henry of Portugal decided otherwise. The third surviving son of King John I of Portugal and Queen Philippa, daughter of John of Gaunt, this enigmatic man is known to history as 'The Navigator'. Part visionary, part mystic, part pragmatist, part opportunist, his obsession with the sea, and what lay beyond the horizon, was to provide a dynamic for the energies of Portuguese seamen and almost bankrupt a relatively poor country. Prince Henry established his *tercona naval*, a maritime think-tank, at Sagres on the Atlantic coast, and gathered around him a fantastic court. Balearic Jews known for their cartographical skills rubbed shoulders with astronomers and instrument-makers who understood the astrolabe and men who knew the secrets of the *Al Kemal*, the Arab device which, adapted by Zheng He, could determine the altitude of a star and lead men to foreign ports across the featureless ocean. Shipwrights from Lisbon and the distant Rhine argued the merits of hull form, while the prince cajoled and debated with a college of sea-captains, arguing in favour of the vast profits to be made from sailing south.

Under this royal patronage and pressure, Henry's captains went forth to voyage with God. While some deceived the prince and turned pirates, others rediscovered Madeira and the Azores, whereupon Henry took a step which was to alter the course of history and transform the world: he ordered the islands colonised. Wood, sugar and wine returned to Portugal and settlers named their offspring after Adam and Eve, for they found they lived in what seemed an Earthly Paradise. But between 1419 and 1433, no seaman was obedient enough, foolish enough, or bold enough to sail south and double Cape Bojador. Until that is, a young squire from Lagos named Gil Eannes came forward. Failing on his first voyage, for Eannes turned aside to the Canaries, he was persuaded to make a second by Henry, apparently a man of near infinite patience. Reaching the dreaded Cape, Gil Eannes ran parallel with the 'boiling' reef until he could work round its extremity, standing back inshore until he reached the coast, upon which he landed and picked flowers. Returning to Sagres, he reported to Prince Henry that beyond the cape the character of the landscape altered dramatically.

Having announced that Cape Bojador did not mark the edge of the world, Gil Eannes thereafter disappears into obscurity. Oddly his claim to fame rests not so much on doubling the fearful Cape, significant though that was, but in changing the perception of his generation: the horizon was no longer a limitation; it had become a challenge. In this, his achievement was far greater than that of Columbus.

Gil Eannes and his contemporary colleagues did not venture forth at Prince Henry's behest in carracks. Such large and unwieldy ships could only prove successful as merchantmen once a route had been opened up and roughly charted. Exploration such as Gil Eannes undertook, had to be in a far handier vessel, and such was the smooth-sided caravel.

It is uncertain in exactly what kind of ship Gil Eannes ventured south. The Portuguese *barinel*, the English *balinger* and the Galician, Catalan and Castilian *balener* were commonplace at the time. There were similar trading vessels working round from the Atlantic coasts into the Mediterranean in the first quarter of the fifteenth century where they were copied or bought, and these operated alongside the Portuguese *barca*, or *barque*. Both types bore stern rudders and possessed windward ability, although we cannot be sure of their precise design.

The caravel was to be the outstanding windward-working ship-type of the period. The name, which was to pass into English as the adjective 'carvel', describing a smooth hull planked butt-to-butt. This adoption of the word into popular useage to define a method very different to the more traditional clinker-built technique marks its impact upon English seafarers and shipbuilding. In Portuguese the word 'caravela' appears first in a Portuguese manuscript of 1255 and describes open fishing boats, but the name migrated, or perhaps kept pace with increasing size. The caravel had a beautiful hull with an elegantly curved stem post, hollow waterlines in her entrance and a fine sweeping sheer, rising in the stern to a long, low poop which carried out over the stern. The stern itself did not consist of planks converging on a stern post, but was transom built. The transom-hung rudder was acted upon by the water flowing aft along the run of the hull below the wide transom. Such a stern shape was extremely buoyant and gave the hull a good grip on the water. The caravel clearly owed much to Moorish influence and is kindred to the dhow, as much in its hull as in its early, lateen rig. The two- or three-masted *caravela latina*, was of less draught than the *barinel* and its cousins, and had a generally better performance. But the most successful ships are never vessels which excel at one particular aspect of seagoing. Such excellence is usually purchased at the cost of some other, but vital quality. The most successful ships are those that best answer their purpose, and they are always compromises. For deliberate voyages of exploration, good windward performance is handy, but not at the expense of requiring a huge crew with the additional logistic problems of supply. Nor is speed an essential if it sacrifices sea-kindliness; nor size at the expense of manoeuvrability. While the *caravela latina* was held to be a superior vessel, pragmatists recognised all its virtues were not essential, and some could prove dangerous. In a heavy sea, the great yard was a liability, and the Spaniard Juan

Escalante de Mendoza commented of the lateen, 'if you do not know me, do not touch me'. Columbus, fighting his way westward into wind and current along the south coast of Cuba in the summer of 1494 with the *Niña* and two lateen caravels, wrote 'nobody attempts to struggle close-hauled, for in one day they would lose what they gained in seven; nor do I except caravels, *even Portuguese lateeners*' (author's italics).

What is interesting in this comment is the fact that Columbus had altered the rig of his beloved *Niña* on his first voyage in 1492. She had left Palos with the *Santa Maria* and *Pinta* as a lateen-rigged caravel, while the *Pinta* was a *caravela redonda*, square-rigged on her main mast, her lateen mizen a small mast at the very stern, and a fore mast, also square rigged, and stayed to a bowsprit. This configuration was not only better suited to Columbus's requirements, it was remarkably similar to the rig then being adopted in the larger, clumsier carrack. The *caravela redonda* would not have pointed so sharply to windward, but clearly her all-round performance better answered her admiral's purpose.

We must recall that the mariner's only motive resource was the wind, and the most positive configuration of sails to harness it had to be found. Sailing ships only beat to windward when it was imperative, and the lateen sail was not very efficient when running downwind for days on end, such as a trade wind passage required.

In 1487, Bartolomeu Dias extended Prince Henry's original intent and doubled the Cape of Good Hope. His success confirmed the ability of the *caravela redonda* to sail long distances over the high seas and produced a refinement known as the *caravela da armada*. This bore a pair of square sails on a forward raking foremast, with a lateen-rigged main and mizen. Such a ship proved an able cargo carrier, a good sea-keeper and thus a stable gun platform, as well as being an effective windward performer.

Columbus, lionised by history for a lesser achievement than many of his contemporaries, nevertheless commanded a disparate squadron. While the *Niña* and *Pinta* were caravels, almost the only thing we know for certain about his flagship, the *Santa Maria*, is that she was not. Columbus refers to her as *La não*, 'the ship', and she was described by the priest Las Casas as 'somewhat larger' than the caravels. In October 1492, Columbus himself records that he 'let them set all the sails, the main course with two bonnets (extensions along the sail's foot), the fore course, the spritsail, the mizen, the [main] topsail and the boat's sail on the half deck', from which she may be broadly reconstructed. But she drew too much and was slow, and Columbus preferred the smaller, handier caravels comparable with the *Niña* at 60 *toneladas* (tuns). The *Santa Maria* was probably a small carrack, though no-one knows for certain. However, the mention of the spritsail is interesting, for, having set a bowsprit to which to lead the forestays, advantage is taken of this additional spar to set another sail. The spritsail is to be of more than passing interest as we trace the history of the sailing ship and this casual mention of it suggests it was already a feature of the *caravela redonda* and the carrack by 1492. It should not be confused with the quadrilateral fore and aft spritsail set on a mast in small craft.

But the caravel possessed an additional benefit; she could be converted back. As such, when the Portuguese navigator Vasco da Gama made his first voyage to India (1497–1503), his fleet sailed east under square rig, but reverted to lateen in the Indian Ocean. Thus the caravel became a prime instrument in Spanish and Portuguese exploration, often scouting ahead of the main fleet or acting as a despatch boat. The estuaries of the Amazon and the Plate were first penetrated by caravels and in 1511 a caravel was despatched from Malacca to reconnoitre a route further east to the Moluccas.

In 1519 Ferdinando Magellan set out on what was to be the first circumnavigation of the globe. Among his ships was the caravel *Santiago* which was lost on the coast of South America. By this time the extreme length of the exploratory voyages were rendering the small caravel less ideal. Longer voyages required larger ships and the proliferation of sails such as Columbus had described in the *Santa Maria* broke up a vessel's sail area and thus made her manageable by a smaller crew. With the use of bowlines and euphroes, a reasonable track could be made to windward, often enough to satisfy the demands of sixteenth-century navigators.

The caravel continued to answer specialist needs; having pioneered the Portuguese fishery on the Grand Banks off

Newfoundland, she would continue for centuries as a fishing craft. She was also handy as a swift cargo carrier, carrying fish to markets and salt to Ireland. She brought back spices, gold and pepper from West Africa, and also distributed the first Indian cargoes from Lisbon to other European ports. She was capable of acting as a military transport and a fast warship, suiting state navy, corsair or pirate. From 1453 the King of Castile maintained a protective squadron of a carrack and a number of caravels in the Bay of Biscay and fifty years later Dom João II, King of Portugal, mounted heavy cannon in caravels sent to protect trade passing the Strait of Gibraltar, while inward convoys were met by squadrons of caravels off the Azores and escorted home from 'the Brazils'.

It is no coincidence that the name *frigata* is that of the twentieth-century Portuguese wine boats of the Tagus, direct descendants of the caravel, nor that that name was later adopted by the British and French to define a new, distant water cruiser with qualities of sea-keeping, endurance and relative power, which could also act as the eyes of a fleet, a messenger or convoy escort.

The reputation of the caravel soon attracted imitators, among them the English and the Flemings, the Sicilians and Italians. Such small ships were used as slavers and coral fishers, trading with North Africa, and proved so successful that in 1478 Andrea Satler wrote on behalf of a German trading company from Bruges: 'The small ships have quite displaced the large ones'. Caravels rarely exceeded 100 tons and it was increasing familiarity with them that induced the English to adopt skeletal construction. Regular traders in English Channel ports were Breton caravels, which were then the most numerous in northern waters.

Despite all her advantages, the caravel would eventually founder in the hands of bureaucrats. It was the Spanish, not the Portuguese, who were to emerge as the dominant maritime nation in the Atlantic. Increasing greed for imports of American raw materials, loot and the insatiable thirst of governments for taxes, caused the Spanish authorities to ban vessels of less than 100 tons from the Carrera de Indias, the passage to the Indies, in 1552. By 1587, nothing less than a 300-ton ship was permitted to make the voyage.

In a sense the caravel was to 'southern' ship development what the long ship had been to 'northern', an adaptable, durable tool, exactly fitted to the hand of man at a given moment in history. Naval use of the caravel continued and smaller developments of coastal ships derived from it. The *saetta-polaccra*, or *polacre*, of the nineteenth century is reminiscent of the *caravela redonda*, and once again, like the Tagus *frigata*, demonstrated that a successful type will survive where the conditions remain right for it to prosper.

In a painting of Venice executed by Jacopo de Barbari in 1500, the artist has shown a large carrack. She has a bonaventure mizen, a spritsail and a main topsail, a sail plan complementing the advances we have already noted. In form she is reminiscent of the Flemish *kraeck*, but her more sophisticated rig requires ratlines, which differentiates her from the other ships in the Venetian scene. The curious awning of spars set up over her castles may have been to support defensive nets, for she is armed with some fifty-six cannon and would have had to run the gauntlet of Turkish corsairs when she proceeded to sea. But the carrack was deficient in speed and handiness and, even when fitted for war, could be outmanoeuvred in light airs by galleys. Because man will always spend treasure on warfare, another type of ship, faster, more manoeuvrable and a better gun and fighting platform than the carrack, was to appear before the second half of the sixteenth century. This was to become known as the *galleon*.

As usual, the origin of the noun is confused, but would seem to derive from galley, or more properly the Italian *gallioni*, perhaps a reference to a superior form of sailable galley out of which the galleon evolved. There exists a Venetian document of about 1550 which refers to '*un galion che voga a remi*', 'a galleon moved by oars'. Local variations are to be expected, but the type had common features wherever it was built and became a powerful tool of foreign policy during the period between about 1540 and 1650. She was the first 'capital ship' and the first man-of-war to be involved in what can reasonably be called fleet actions – that is sea battles which were not merely land battles fought at sea.

There is a paucity of evidence for the period, though an increasing number of artists painted seascapes, with detailed depictions of ships and shipping, so that iconographical evidence improves rapidly from the mid sixteenth century. Other sources consist of documents such as the Anthony Anthony Roll, showing drawings of the English navy of King Henry VIII executed about 1545. As an artillerist, Anthony's chief interest lay understandably in their cannon. Other documents showing contemporary ships are the *Carta Universal* of Diego Ribero, cosmographer to Charles I of Spain. This, held in the Vatican's Apostolic Library, dates from 1529 and predates by some sixty years the 'Fragments of Ancient English Shipwrightry' held in the Pepysian Library. This document was said to have been produced by one Matthew Baker, a master shipwright, and gives a more accurate insight into ship design than anything hitherto. It is of particular interest since it shows Elizabethan English men-of-war, the very ships which drubbed the mighty Spanish during the last quarter of the sixteenth century.

The acquisition of a great overseas empire by the Spanish after Columbus's epochal first voyage, made that country the richest in Europe and her kings the most powerful. Spanish sway extended over the Low Countries and Spanish military might predominated. Partly to protect the fabulous trade of 'The Indies' and partly as an expression of power, the Spanish led galleon design, adapting the basic carrack into a powerful form of warship.

In 1580 King Henry of Portugal died and Philip II of Spain seized the throne. A Catholic zealot, Philip also vigorously supressed the Protestant schismatics and the Spanish Netherlands erupted in open and bloody rebellion which eventually resulted in their independence as the United Provinces of the Netherlands. To fight their enemy, the Dutch acquired galleons to match those of their oppressor. Moreover, deprived of their traditional trade with Lisbon and Spain, they went further afield, to the East Indies.

Philip also attempted to suppress English piracy on Spanish trade and sought to invade the Protestant England of Elizabeth I. His great enterprise, the Armada of 1588, was harried by English galleons, attacked by fireships and finally dispersed, to be destroyed piecemeal by bad weather as the great ships attempted to return home by passing north around Scotland and so southwards to Spain.

The galleons of these three protagonists, as well as those of the Portuguese and Venetians varied greatly. From accounts of the defeat of the Spanish Armada, we know that the English fleet consisted of smaller, handier and better served ships than their enemy. These were capable of tactical manoeuvre and superior gunfire. Nevertheless, all galleons seem to have had certain qualities in common which distinguished them from their forebears, particularly carracks.

They were lower in profile, with the forecastles built into the forward hull rather than on it. A projection, reminiscent of the galley's ram, formed a beak head, providing a working platform running under the root of the bowsprit for handling the spritsail. Aft there was less of a castle and more of an extended raised upper, or quarterdeck and the hulls were pierced with gunports on two or more decks. The galleon's hull was slimmer than the carrack's; the proportion of length of hull (roughly stem to stern), to length of keel, to beam was 3:2:1 in the carrack, but 4:3:1 in the galleon. The shape of the hull is even more interesting, for Matthew Baker's drawings show a section through one hull together with a cross section. The former, stripped of its upperworks, has the flat, transom stern swelling out above the waterline, and the wonderfully elegant upwards sweep of the curved stem of a caravel. Such a stern enabled the aftercastle to be faired into the hull and, as a consequence, the stern was much narrower than before and often rose to considerable height.

The cross section of the hull in Baker's drawings is also reminiscent of the caravel, with a flattish bottom and wide outward curving sides which, at the point where the caravel's rail would be, they turn sharply inwards and taper upwards in the pronounced tumblehome that gave a low centre of gravity both for sailing and carrying artillery as high as possible.

Insofar as rig was concerned, this usually consisted of a four-masted rig with a towering main mast and a foremast set well forward. Both of these masts carried square sails. The courses, and in particular the main course, were still the dominant sails. Topsails and topgallants were now borne above the courses, but these were wide footed and narrow headed, not at all the useful sails they were later to become. From the raised deck or decks aft, the mizen and bonaventure mizen spread lateen sails.

Paintings of several galleons show lateen topsails set above these, but they may have been either artistic licence, or mere kites, used to impress, to be struck below as soon as the galleon proceeded to sea. Contemporary paintings, particularly of Pieter Breughel the Elder, show galleons with two continuous gundecks the length of the hull, with additional light cannon on the raised castles fore and aft.

The rivalry between Henry VIII of England and Francis I of France which predated the Anglo-Spanish wars produced a remarkable vessel in the Royal Navy of King Henry. Henry may be credited with the foundation of several British institutions, most notable of which were a national church and the Royal Navy. A man of extremes, he had built a great ship, named after himself, the *Henri Grâce à Dieu*. Constructed at enormous expense in 1514, she was a huge ship for her day and like many classes of line-of-battle ship that followed, was extensively rebuilt between 1536 and 1539. According to Anthony Anthony, she had the projecting forecastle of a carrack, but the high narrow and transom stern of a galleon. Given her date she might be regarded as a transitional hybrid, if such terminology did not imply some kind of rule applied to nomenclature. It did not; nor were such ships ever built to plans, or on scientific principles. Things developed slowly and empirically. Fast ships tended to be copied, extremes avoided because they often ended in disaster. What looked right, probably was right; small advantages were sought, not quantum and risky leaps in progress. Shipwrights kept the secrets of their trade, but they had no thorough knowledge of the science of hydrostatics or dynamics. Ships floated because they were made of wood.

The *Great Harry*, as she was colloquially known, was no exception; the purpose behind her was diplomatic, not scientific. She was built to impress, and when she conveyed Henry to France for his historic meeting with Francis, her sails are said to have been of gold, or at least painted yellow.

Anthony Anthony depicts her with a lateen topsail and topgallant, with great grappling irons on the arms of her lower yards and at the end of her tremendous bowsprit. Whether all these details are strictly accurate is doubtful. Nevertheless, after her refit we know she bore 21 heavy bronze guns, 130 iron guns of lesser weight of metal and 100 hand guns. Below her lowest continuous gundeck, she had an orlop.

In reality we know very little about the *Great Harry* beyond the fact that she was a truly magnificent ship. Baker's drawings are more practically likely, and are consonant with what we know were the characteristics of the English men-of-war which engaged the Spanish armada. The nimbler performance suggests not so much a lack of waterline length, but perhaps less superstructure, with lower castles and more efficient guns, for we know the Spanish regarded the gunnery of the English as superior to their own. This concession was the more likely if it could be attributed to efficiency, rather than inherent English ability.

While the defeat of the Spanish Armada was as much due to the flawed strategy of its master and the hostility of the weather, it was a true defeat in that it conceded the mastery of the English Channel to the English, a fact that was by no means certain when the great Spanish fleet entered it. The running battle fought in the late summer of 1588 was solely about mastery of the narrow seas, but the perspective of history shows it achieved much more. It was not fought to decide whether the remit of the Queen of England or the King of Spain was the dominant maritime feature thereafter, but its outcome was to shift the balance of power in favour of the adaptable, energetic and rapacious islanders whose heretic religion called forth the vengeance of God. After the events of that summer, Spain's power began a long decline and England, shortly to become Great Britain when Elizabeth died without issue, was to begin her climb to pre-eminence.

Though not specifically called 'galleons', the word tending to be reserved in English perception for the ships of the Armada, the English ships which, under Lord Howard of Effingham and his able vice-admiral, Sir Francis Drake, so bothered the Spanish, were as much galleons as those of their enemy.

The galleon was not a specified type, merely a generic, even a general and rather loose title. The Spanish Armada contained a score of vessels actually listed as galleons, with 29 naos among a total fleet of 130. However, while the battle decided the fate of England, the galleons which contested it were suited to major, trans-oceanic voyages. They were designed for service at sea, their hulls containing considerable cross-bracing and strengthening timbers, and while they incorporated national characteristics, these were as much to do with whether they carried cargo, as to whether they had high or low aftercastles. Moreover, a substantial part of the Spanish fleet consisted of galleasses, lateen rigged and propelled also by oars which gave them a very foreign look to the Englishmen who chased after them.

At about this time, however, there occurred a significant change in steering a ship which was a consequence of increasing the number of decks. The tiller had to be brought inboard at a relatively low level and, in order for the helmsman to steer from a higher deck, an extension in the form of a whipstaff was fitted. This was pivoted on the deck between the end of the tiller in the 'steerage' and the deck upon which the helmsman had his station and its somewhat unsatisfactory qualities are not hard to imagine, but it was to be some years yet before the introduction of a wheel.

Perhaps the contribution of the galleon to the history of the ship is more philosophical than practical, though many were used for the carriage of cargo. Indeed the Spanish *flota* which brought the annual riches of the Indies home to Spain always consisted of state-owned galleons. The galleon was essentially a gun platform and is the ancestor of the ship of the line. For it was by relatively small refinements and developments that ships were now to change as, in the wake of Zheng He's retreat, European shipping was to spread across the oceans of the world.

CHAPTER FIVE

Princes and Predators

By the end of the sixteenth century, the Portuguese, Spanish, Dutch and English had spent two centuries in their sea-questing. Portuguese exploitation of the Grand Banks fishery, the Dutch foray into the Arctic whaling grounds, the Spanish conquest of the Indies with cross and sword and the initially modest claims of Cabot in Newfoundland on behalf of King Henry VII, had only been possible by means of capable ships.

These events highlighted the importance of 'the ship' as an instrument of political and economic policy. With the dawn of the seventeenth century, a period of terrible religious division, war and emigration, Henry the Navigator's concept of colonisation found eager imitators. From small and uncertain beginnings, overseas settlements started to transform the world with the first European claims to imperial dominion. The first decade saw the founding and failure of the commercial English colony at Roanoke in Virginia, but in 1620, the *Mayflower* sailed to the New World. Like the *Santa Maria*, her name enters history as an icon, though the name of her master, Christopher Jones, is not as famous as that of Christopher Columbus. Jones was to be one of those seafarers who, in the words of Conrad, followed 'a useful calling' virtually unnoticed.

And it is at the beginning of the seventeenth century that the man-of-war and merchantman begin to take on those distinctions of purpose that ensured a distinction of appearance. When King Henry VIII of England ordered the *Henri Grâce à Dieu* to be built in 1514, he was not the first monarch to demand a 'great ship' as a reflection of his own puissance, but he was the first to invest a vast sum of money to create a vessel of totalitarian omnipotence. In this he established an enduring fashion among European governments, a fashion greatly to be lamented, as we shall see, both as an imposition on the populace and as a false strategic assumption. Wars are not won by large, single ships, no matter what their individual might. But political desire often overrode common sense, to produce the seductive notion that the intimidating presence of such a man-of-war would excite not envy, but compliance.

Despite squandering vast sums of money, Henry VIII may justly claim to have established an English 'Royal' navy to protect his own dominions. He also sought to regulate his subjects' trade and encourage the professionalism of seafarers by endowing the Trinity House of London with a royal charter in 1514, granting it statutory powers. The Trinity House was a guild 'of shipmen and mariners', one of whom, Sir Thomas Spert, was the sailing master of Henry's great ship. The charter empowered the brethren of Trinity House to license pilots and thus assist ships making the dangerous approach to London through the complex channels of the Thames Estuary. The guild was also encouraged to lay buoys, erect beacons and sanction lighthouses along the coasts of England and Wales.

Such royal recognition of trade in tandem with the acquisition of 'king's ships', marks the first real division between mercantile activity and the military profession, establishing embryonic bureaucracies seeking to govern both activities. The royal charter granted to Trinity House states in its preamble justifying the need for experienced pilots, that these should not be young men 'unwilling to take the labour and adventure of learning the shipmen's craft on the high seas', and emphasises the dangers of allowing foreigners, particularly 'Scots, Flemings and Frenchmen' to learn 'the secrets of the King's Streams [channels]'.

While distinctions between the designs of naval and merchant ships were to remain blurred for some time, they were increasingly important. For by arming and equipping a ship solely for war, different design parameters were set, just as they were for merchant shipping in the matter of cargo capacity. The treatise of Matthew Baker one hundred years later refers to an 'ancient English shipwrightry,' clearly implying a traditional element to his record. It was but one of a number of such documents which sought to detach shipbuilding from its slow, safe, hand-me-down development based upon the relationship between a master craftsman and his apprentice, and elevate it to a proto-science. The new thinking of the Renaissance demanded a more academic rigour, and so did the requirements of war.

Preservation of dimensional details of successful war galleys was governed by regulation in both Venice and Genoa during the fourteenth century and it was in Venice that an early treatise on shipbuilding was produced. The Venetian Arsenale had become a centre of excellence for the design and production of war galleys, largely due to the expertise of a Greek master shipwright named Theodoro Baxon, or Bassanus. Baxon seemed able to combine speed with strength so successfully that it persuaded the Senate to offer him lifetime employment at an inflated salary. To preserve his technical expertise, models were made of his best hulls and their dimensions were recorded so that this data was available after his death in 1407. It appears that Baxon's providence encouraged this maintaining of data, the compilation of records and probably espionage. In consonance with the 'rules' being established for painting and architecture in Italy at the time, Baxon's secrets seem to have been as much to do with immutable concepts of proportion as exact measurements. By dividing a hull into sections, which roughly equated to the entry, parallel body and run, a system of curves was built up using a semicircle, sometimes known as a *mezzaluna*, for different stations and by striking chords parallel to the diameter, taking the diminishing lengths of these chords to form the dimensions of various parts of the ship, such as the floors, or the breadth at deck level. By such ratios, a harmonious hull could be constructed for any set of extreme dimensions.

Works of the time by men such as Zorzi da Modon (the pen name for a man called Giorgio Timbotta) and Theodoro de Nicoló enabled Italian master craftsmen to work outside Italy, where others were anxious to hire them, because their treatises dealt with vessels other than galleys. The spread of such scholarship was inevitable and was soon taken up by the Spanish in particular, where on the shores of the tempestuous Atlantic, desire for perfection in ship design was driven by more robust imperatives. Thus interestingly, Diego Garcia de Palacio's *Instrucción náutica para navegar*, was published in 1587 in Mexico City and intended for use in the Spanish maritime empire of the Indies. It is more of a seamanship manual, for it contains chapters on navigation, meteorology, tides and astronomy as well as on sails and rigging, with hull details for a *nao* of 400 *toneladas*. Greater emphasis is placed on hull technology in other studies, many of which were unpublished in their day. In 1611 the *Arte para fabricar y aparejar naos* was published in Seville. It was written by Thomé Cano and agrees with Palacio's work on ocean-going ships, or *naos*, being in proportion to their beam as having a length of keel of twice the beam, and an overall hull length of three times the beam. Further details of *naos* and galleons are contained in the 1616 illustrated manuscript *Livro de Tracas de Carpintaria* by the Portuguese, Manuel Fernandes.

It seems that many of these works were conceived not for use by seafarers or even shipbuilders, but as reference books for the increasing number of bureaucrats and administrators who fastened onto the imperial corpus. Nevertheless the literature of the sea was copied elsewhere, many northern Europeans using Italian ideas and expertise. The German Joseph Furttenbach produced a lavishly baroque *Architectura Navalis* in Ulm in 1629, the Frenchman Georges Fournier published his *Hydrographie* in 1643, and Robert Dudley his *Arcana del Mare* in Florence in 1646. Other Englishmen, Henry Mainwaring and John Smith, compiled nautical glossaries, and Nathaniel Boteler wrote a dialogue between a sea-captain and an inexperienced admiral by way of an instructional device, athough it also serves as an interesting social comment. Fournier's book gives details of a specific ship, the *La Couronne*, of which more later.

Translations burgeoned, as did native works in, for instance, Dutch. These had by now advanced from Matthew Baker's 'Fragments of Ancient English Shipwrightry', where the craftsman's eye is paramount and Baker likens the underwater body of a ship to a fish. Not that there was much wrong with the concept; cod-headed and mackerel tailed was the watchword of many a wooden fishing boat builder well into the twentieth century and the bluff bow and finer run of European ships may be traced from the first ruddered boat found at Kalmar to the advent of the hollow entry six hundred years later. Howsoever sketchy and imperfect, the advent of quasi-scientific shipbuilding was established principally for the better perfection of warships. It was left for the growing class of bourgeois merchants to develop their own vessels.

The closure of Lisbon and Cadiz to their shipping in the sixteenth century as a consequence of their revolt against Spanish overlords sent the energetic Dutch further afield, not just to increase trade, but to finance their rebellion against the Spanish and secure an independent economic base. In a short time this would entirely eclipse the fabled wealth of the Spanish Indies and the silver mines of Potosi.

Just as the Hanseatic cog came to dominate earlier merchant shipping, the emerging Dutch were to assert their influence and produce the definitive cargo-carrier of the late sixteenth and early seventeenth centuries. The adoption of the framed, skeletal hull by northern shipwrights had not been without its troubles, for it required, if not the actual design of a hull, at least the conceptualising of it first. Gone were the days of allowing it to take on the shape that nature intended with the lapstrake method, although the Dutch, unlike the English, according to information laid before the French minister Colbert by a spy named Arnould, did lay the bottom planking first. This was undoubtedly due to the shallower draught and flatter hull required for navigation in Dutch waters.

What was required to conduct a reliable, safe and profitable trade was a cheap but efficient hull with a cheap and efficient rig. Such a vessel had to be capable of carrying large quantities of cargo, often in bulk, in a safe, dry manner, and if that vessel could, when economic factors altered, be switched with equal advantage to another trade, then so much the better. The result of this broad and basic specification was the '*fluit*' or 'flute'.

The Dutch had already developed an extensive range of small trading and fishing vessels. Among these were a number of innovations, not least of which was a northern competitor for windward work, the spritsail, a fore and aft sail set abaft the mast to which its leading edge, or luff, was hooped or laced. The sail was stretched from its lower forward corner to its upper after corner by a spar known as the 'sprit'. Unlike the cumbersome lateen, the spritsail could be tacked automatically and furled away by drawing it, curtain-like, towards the mast by brails, leaving the sprit standing. They also discovered that in the fore triangle produced between the mast and the stem, another sail could be set. Since a stay supported the mast forward, this was hoisted on the stay and called the 'staysail'. Moreover, by extending a 'bowsprit' beyond the stemhead, a second triangular sail called the 'jib' could be set, allowing an increase in the size of the sprit-rigged main which this balanced. Also adopted was a small mizen, usually lateen or sprit-rigged. Such a rig formed the antecedent of the ketch and yawl.

Although a plethora of configurations existed, these coasters and short-sea traders, which could also carry a topsail above the head of the sprit-rigged mainsail, were generally known as *boeijers*, or boyers. Short, demanding trips on the extensive waterways of the Low Countries doubtless assisted the quest for a generally more efficient rig and the expertise thus gained was to have an initially oblique effect upon the larger ocean carrier. Not least among the lessons learned by the hardy and industrious Dutch, was that it was perfectly possible to send quite a large ship to sea with a relatively small crew; the economic advantages of this were obvious.

Another important step in the development of the *fluit* (or fluyt) was the *buss*, a capaciously hulled fishing vessel which brought home barrels of salted fish from the North Sea grounds. Two of its three masts could be lowered, allowing the process of fishing to be carried out and to facilitate this, the *buss* was a very long ship in terms of beam to length ratio. Experience thus gained produced a hybrid, the *buyscarveel*, whose name suggests the marriage of skeletal construction with length, and the combination of square-rigged fore and main masts, with a lateen mizen.

'Invention' of the *fluit* is attributed to one Pieter Jansz Liorne from the town of Hoorn on the western side of the Zuider Zee (after which Schouten named the fearsome cape). In 1595 Liorne launched a ship whose beam was a quarter of its length, and this ratio was soon exceeded. The *fluit* was box-like, with sharp, inward curving planking; her forecastle was low and, because of the tumblehome necessary to its extreme length, the aftercastle was narrow. It is said that this looked like a slender wine glass, giving the *fluit* her name. Be that as it may, the term 'flute-sterned' was to describe this method of construction, with the rudder fastened to a huge sternpost above which the tiller went inboard, superimposed, often on a wing transom, by the narrowing poop. The poop ran forward, descending to the waist in half and quarter decks, to give a commanding view over the ship. The larger *fluits* had a through 'between' deck, and those fitted for the dangerous passage to the East Indies may have mounted a few guns on what became known as the 'tween deck'.

Sizes and burthen varied. Where the *boeijer* rarely seems to have exceeded 100 tons, the *fluit* varied from between 200 and 500 tons, the smaller being some 93 feet (28.5 metres) in length by 20 feet (6.2 metres) in the beam. According to Nicolaes Witsen a *fluit* of 400 tons was 115.2 feet by 22.3 feet (35.1 metres by 6.8 metres). Occasionally larger fluits of 800 tons are found, but it seems that profits were best earned by vessels in the medium range which could enter and leave most ports at will, without undue delays.

This, of course, had as much to do with the efficiency of the rig and the number of the crew, as with cargo capacity. It was claimed that the companies of Dutch ships were a third the size of English crews on vessels of comparative sizes. Seven men and a boy could handle a 150-ton *fluit* in the Norwegian trade and as early as 1603 Sir Walter Ralegh complained that where thirty English sailors were needed to sail a 100-ton ship, ten Dutchmen could do the same in a *fluit*.

The advantage lay in the *fluit*'s more efficient rig. Typically, she did not carry topgallants, but significantly for European sail plans in the years to come, the topsails had increased enormously in size, widening across the head, while the courses had diminished. There were a number of reasons for this. First, the course had become so large as to be verging on the uncontrollable; secondly, it was not only a large sail, but when set it was unhandy, particularly for manoeuvring; and, being low on the mast, was often blanketed by the buildings along a commercial waterfront. The higher, handier topsail gave a ship steerage way and was much more easily worked, leaving the master, his officers and a pilot if there was one, a much better view of their surroundings. This philosophy, incidentally, applied equally to warships manoeuvring for battle. The topsail moreover, was controlled at both clews, by yards, making it safer to handle in heavy weather than the heavy clews of a course with its sheet and tack gear. It could also be systematically reduced by reefing.

The mizen continued to sport the lateen yard, and the bowsprit carried its spritsail, a square sail set under the yard. Some larger *fluits* carried a square mizen topsail, and some a sprit topsail, hoisted on a small vertical mast raised at the end of the bowsprit. Echoes of these developments can be found in the sail plans of men-of-war, but in the *fluit* they meant the crew numbers could be minimised. The standard *fluit*, with spritsail, fore and main courses and topsails, and a lateen mizen, could be crewed more efficiently than any comparative ship.

A degree of standardisation seems to have governed *fluit* building and this would have helped to keep down costs. The cost of a *fluit* was about forty per cent of a comparable English ship. The extensive substitution of pine for oak meant a hull was lighter and could take more cargo for a given draught. Such ships may have been less durable in the long term, but were similar to modern ships with a life expectancy of twenty years.

Standardisation also enabled the completed *fluit* to be adaptable, either to trade to the Mediterranean or the Baltic, or act as a whaler venturing into the Arctic Ocean. As time passed and trade picked up, the *fluit* increased in size. One factor encouraging this was the alteration of the tonnage rules for vessels passing the Sound into the Baltic. Subject to a levy by the Danish customs at Helsingør, the narrow beam of a *fluit* gave it a huge advantage over its competitors, for until 1669 the dues were based on a beam-related formula. At this time over half the shipping thus levied was Dutch, and the total number of Dutch merchant ships at sea was estimated to have been about 10,000.

Construction on such a level in a relatively short timespan was possible because of the contained and familiar nature of *fluit* building. Much of this was done at Zaanstreek, on the River Ij on the outskirts of Amsterdam in an area called the Lastage. This became the world's first mass-production shipbuilding yard where pre-Industrial Revolution technology used windmill powered saws, efficient capstans and cranes, all of which eliminated waste and shaved costs.

After 1650, as the demand for larger ships increased, the *fluit* spawned derivative types. The northern versions, the *Noortsvaerder* and the *Oostervaeder*, traded to Norway and the Baltic. So successful were they that they could load Polish and Latvian grain in bulk, not in sacks, and they also bore cargoes of timber, potash and other wood products as well as coal and furs. The *Noortsvaerder* was especially modified for the Norwegian timber trade and in particular the carriage of very long tree trunks intended for masts, for which special ports were cut in the *fluit*'s hull. These were caulked securely before the ship made her passage, a method that stuck, many fine sailing ships in the late nineteenth and early twentieth centuries ending their days in timber trades, their fine hulls pierced by these entrances.

Other, smaller variants of the *fluit* existed. The *katschip* was a simpler version with a gaff mizen and no square topsails, while a similar, beamier version was called a *hekboot*. Most uneconomic of the larger fluit-types was the Mediterranean trader which had to pass the Strait of Gibraltar and was thus known as the *Straetsvaeder*. Heavier sparred and armed against Barbary corsairs, among others, it was quite different from its northern cousin with an extending beak-head and a much more complex rig. The guns were carried at the cost of cargo capacity and required greater manpower, for nothing was so labour intensive or demanding as a muzzle-loading cannon. These factors, combined with the greater complexities of the rig, which incorporated main and fore topgallants, a mizen topsail and a sprit topsail, increased the operating costs significantly. Nevertheless, these ships made severe inroads on the native trades, carrying fish and grain, stone and oil cheaper than the Italians, for instance. With the exception of the *Straetsvaeder*, the *fluit* was minimally armed, if at all. For this reason the expression 'to be armed *en flûte*', passed into the jargon of both the French and British navies to mean a warship reduced to minimum armament and used as a transport or troop ship.

Although the *fluit* was never taken up by the Dutch East India Company, it was a remarkably successful merchant ship, far more so than either the cog or the hulk. It was, moreover, the precursor of the standard ship, and offered all the predatory advantages that rewarded the vigorous commercialism of the Dutch of the seventeenth century, destroying the coastal and short-sea trade of their competitors, chief among whom were the British.

When protection was required, the admiralties, into which the marine administration of the United Provinces of the Netherlands was divided, provided pinnaces. These small, fast flat-sterned single decked warships escorted *fluits* and herring *busses* alike and were full-rigged ships. Often called *yachts*, both words existed in one form or another in English. The presentation of a beautiful yacht by the States-General to King Charles II ensured the word came to mean a pleasure-craft and eclipsed pinnace entirely. In fact the word *yacht* is a corruption of *jaght* which derives from *jaghen*, meaning 'to hunt'. The true definition is thus of a pursuit craft and a *jachtschip* is defined in a seventeenth-century dictionary (along with fifteen alternative spellings) as 'a ship for chasing, a light sailing vessel, a fast piratical ship'. Be that as it may, the pinnace (or *pinas*) and the *fluit* equate to the corvette and Liberty ship of three hundred years later in more ways than one. In the seventeenth century they were sharply distinct types, the former a man-of-war, the latter a merchantman.

While the industrious burghers of the Low Countries were laying the foundations of a great commercial empire, untroubled by heady notions of monarchical supremacy, the English were emerging from a bloody civil war. Driven from England, the Royalists continued to fight their lost cause at sea, where generals like Prince Rupert became admirals and their parliamentary pursuers like Robert Blake became Generals-at-Sea. Both, one presumes, required Nathaniel Boteler's dialogues as a means of learning their new profession!

One of the causes of the English civil war had been the insistence of King Charles I to raise a tax known as 'ship money' with which to refurbish his navy. The tax was unpopular from the start, particularly among the squirearchy from the shires who had little or no interest in matters maritime and who would have to bear the cost of the imposition. The act was reluctantly passed in 1634 and to be fair, a number of fine men-of-war were added to the Royal Navy by this legislation. On 26 June, however, King Charles visited the building yard at Woolwich where one such ship, the *Leopard*, was under construction. During his visit Charles, acting with typical tactlessness, is said to have instructed the master shipwright Phineas Pett to design the largest ship in the world. Word must have leaked out, for the brethren of Trinity House, by now well established as the repository of the nation's maritime technical expertise, formally complained that the projected vessel would prove ungovernable in English waters. They might also have added it would prove ruinously expensive, but they rested their case on their collective wisdom as shipmasters.

Experiment in warship design was not uncommon, a direct and significant contrast with *fluit*-building, and when experiments went wrong in men-of-war, it was usually in the imperfectly understood matter of stability. Little scientific analysis of this had yet taken place, but every seaman knew instinctively if his ship 'felt right'. We have already noted the case of the *Mary Rose* in Chapter Four, but a worse case of disastrous experimentation occurred a few years prior to Charles' request in Sweden, then the major maritime power in the Baltic. The Swedes had commissioned Dutch shipwrights to build a new galleon with two gundecks, but King Gustavus Vasa interferred and ordained the incorporation of certain features. The outcome of the King's modifications was a ship that had the length to beam ratio of a *fluit*, with so shallow a draught that she could not be ballasted to bear her sail plan without bringing her lower gunports dangerously close to the water.

The 800-ton *Vasa* was completed in 1628 and set sail from Stockholm in full view of the king, his court and an excited population. The wind gusted into her sails, she overset and foundered. It was the *Mary Rose* all over again and the *Vasa* lay on the bottom until raised from the seabed in a stunning salvage operation begun in the 1960s. She may now be seen in Stockholm, close to the scene of her nemesis, a monument to monarchical ambition, but a tribute also to the skills of craftsmen of a bygone era.

Ignoring all protests and precedent, however, King Charles I commanded and Mr Pett obeyed. The *Sovereign of the Seas* was Pett's masterpiece, a grandiloquent ship in every sense of the word. Huge by the standards of the times, 127 feet in the keel (some 90 odd metres), 48 feet (16 metres) in the beam, with a draught of 23.5 feet (7.5 metres), and with a tonnage of over 1500, she exceeded even the *Vasa* or other, earlier 'great ships' such as the three decker British *Prince Royal* of 1610 in the extravagance of her decorations. These lavish, but entirely useless embellish-ments are said to have been executed by the master carver Gerard Christmas, his sons and apprentices, from drawings by the court artist, Anthony Van Dyck. Her figurehead was King Edgar the Peaceful mounted on horseback and ironically riding down seven enemy kings; the beakhead was decorated with coursing hounds, the dragon of Cadwallader, the lion and the unicorn (representing the union of England and

Scotland formed by the accession of Charles's father James I of England who was also James VI of Scotland). As a residual echo of the English claim to the throne of France, the fleur-de-lis were included with the Irish harp, royal ciphers, cupid mounted upon a lion, satyrs, and goddesses representing counsel, care, industry, strength, valour and victory. Along the ship's sides were friezes of other mythological figures, musical instruments, weapons and armour, the signs of the zodiac and the portraits of Roman emperors. Her stern galleries consisted of cupolas and royal coats of arms and the towering aedifice bore representations of Victory, Neptune, Jason, Jupiter and Hercules together with an inscription invoking the protection of the God whom the winds and tides obeyed, in protecting this ship of the great Charles! There was scarcely an image from the whole pantheon of European mythology that the king did not cause to have hung about her.

A full-rigged ship with spritsail and sprit topsail, the *Sovereign of the Seas* carried royals above her topgallants on the fore and main masts, with a topsail and topgallant above her lateen mizen. Whereas the *Prince Royal* had carried 56 guns, the *Sovereign of the Seas* boasted 100. Launched in 1637 she was at least something of a success. With much of her costly decoration and upperworks removed to improve her stability and allow her lee guns to operate in a breeze, she was rendered stable and thereafter served successfully against the Dutch, who called her 'the golden devil'. But much of this service took place under the English Commonwealth, that period of republican rule with Cromwell as Lord Protector. The great ship finally returned to royal 'ownership' as the *Royal Sovereign* with the restoration of King Charles II in 1660. Ironically, she was destroyed by fire after an overset candle put paid to her in 1696. Despite her final service, it was her opulence as well as her expense which inflamed the Puritan souls of her enemies, for she seemed the very essence of all they were set against. With the average cost of a 40–50-gun ship at about £6–7,000, *Sovereign of the Seas* cost £65,587, a sum of unimaginable magnitude in the English political climate of 1637. The *Prince Royal* of 56 guns, built by Pett in 1610, had then been the most splendid ship in the world. Her carving, painting and gilding had cost the extravagant sum of £1,309, but it proved paltry against the *Sovereign*.

Although too heavy and therefore riding dangerously low at her building, the *Sovereign* was fundamentally sound when reduced and as a warship she was ahead of her time. Her extravagance caused a reactive diminution of decoration in subsequent British men-of-war and the wood carvers thus put out of business turned their attention to the decoration of parish churches, though even this was said to be idolatrous. Her instigator, the unfortunate and intransigent King Charles I, duly paid for his presumption and lost his head in 1649.

The *Sovereign of the Seas* may be seen in historical terms as the crown of an extravagant age. The turmoil of seventeenth-century Europe was little better than that of the preceding hundred years, for while civil war raged in England, the continent was deluged in the horrors of the Thirty Years War. Both conflicts were manifestations of deep religious divisions. France was transformed under Cardinal Richelieu, minister to King Louis XIII, who sought to make her the first power in Europe. Richelieu recognised the significance of a navy as a manifestation of that ambition. Within two years of coming to power in 1624, the French had acquired a major warship, the *Saint Louis,* a two-decked 60-gun ship built by Dutch master shipwrights and dedicated to fighting with her artillery. They also responded to the *Sovereign of the Seas* with *La Couronne* commissioned a year earlier than her English rival in 1636. Of almost identical dimensions, the French ship, grossing a staggering 2000 tons, had only two gundecks and mounted a mere 72 guns and therefore failed in the essential matter of overwhelming flamboyance compared to her rival. She was, however, the more effective man-of-war. In fact, *La Couronne* was the predecessor of the most successful wooden man-of-war, the 74-gun, two-decked ship of the line. She rode with greater freeboard than the *Sovereign* and, well served, might deliver as heavy a broadside in all but calm weather.

It is difficult at this remove to understand the importance attached to such ships. Prestige was a matter that preoccupied the courts of Europe. One manifestation of this was the abundance of decoration that these great capital ships bore, which served to reinforce the pre-eminence of a certain sovereign over a certain patch of water. The Danish king, for instance, claimed the Sound as his own and thus levied dues on all ships which passed Helsingør; English monarchs required ships navigating in the Channel to salute them by lowering their topsails when an English naval ship hove in sight and from this developed the traditional dipping of ensigns as a mark of respect or exchange of courtesies.

This matter of maritime precedence was of profound importance in the sixteenth and seventeenth centuries. Colbert, who became the Minister to the king of France nineteen years after Richelieu's death in 1642, wrote 'nothing is more impressive, *nor so befits the Majesty of the King* than that his ships bear the finest ornament on the high seas' (author's italics). By the time Colbert came to power, the navy built up by Richelieu had fallen into decay under his successor, Cardinal Mazarin. Colbert had to begin again.

Under Colbert, the French navy, initially falling behind the standards of the British and Dutch, was to develop a highly sophisticated dockyard system coupled with a more disciplined and scientific approach to the design and building of their ships of war. In 1663, for instance, Samuel Pepys, who was by then Secretary to the Navy and Master of Trinity House, recorded the fact that a French man-of-war of 70 guns carried her lower gundeck 4 feet above the waterline, compared to the Royal Navy's 3 feet. This was mainly due to a greater beam, a feature which made a more stable gun platform.

In the naval battles against the Dutch, English warships had generally proved superior because of their larger size, deeper draught and by the larger numbers of 'great guns' which they bore. English gunfire in the age of the muzzle-loading cannon was always formidable. The superiority of French ships began to dawn on the British when they were out-sailed. On a visit to Spithead in 1672, the French 74-gun *Superbe* attracted a great deal of interest, for she was noticeably higher out of the water than her British equivalents, and had a wider hull, prompting Pepys to write that English shipwrights did not appear to understand the advantages conferred by a beamy hull. As a consequence Sir Anthony Deane, author of *The Doctrine of Naval Architecture* was ordered to build a copy, HMS *Harwich*, which was followed by nine sister-ships.

After the Catholic King James II was overthrown in 1688, war with the France of Louis XIV brought these ships into conflict. When French men-of-war were captured, they were often copied, while English ships falling into French hands, usually had their establishment of guns reduced to lighten them and make them more manageable. The French were also constrained to moderate the extreme decoration of their First-Rate ships and introduce a slightly more rational standard. They also concentrated some thought on providing all-round cover with their guns, lowering the rails of the beakhead to enable forward firing guns to be mounted across the decks abaft the bowsprit, and fitting stern chasers. This defensive armament was to oppose the attacks of galleys in the sometimes windless Mediterranean.

One of the most significant factors emerging from the naval wars between the Dutch and the British, and the French and British in the second half of the seventeenth century, was the formalisation of the 'line of battle.' Whereas the medieval sea battle was a land battle fought at sea, the harrying of the Armada had proved the efficacy of gunfire alone. The English had demonstrated this on several occasions thereafter, the most spectacular of which had been the single-handed fight of the *Revenge* in the Azores. For fifteen hours, from three o'clock in the afternoon of 31 August 1591, until dawn the following morning, this single ship out-gunned a fleet of fifty-three Spanish warships, sinking two of them outright, a difficult enough feat in the days of wooden ships with large crews to man pumps. The English fought to the last grain of powder before striking their ensign, and although the *Revenge* was reduced to an absolute shambles and foundered later in bad weather, her defiance proved the ability of well-served guns to hold off any adversary from boarding.

However, until a century later, national 'fleets' remained largely composed of a mixture of 'king's ships' alongside merchantmen taken up from trade and adapted for war. These now proved inadequate and the 'line-of-battle ship', designed and trained to stand in a line, stem to stern, 'following the motions of the admiral', was proving an effective way of bringing the greatest number of guns to bear on an enemy without exposing one's own fleet to piecemeal destruction. Some of the battles of the Dutch wars were pell-mell affairs, running fights in strong winds, but others, like the decisive Battle of the Gabbard of June 1653, were fought between huge fleets, broadside to broadside. Similarly the Battle of Beachy Head of 1690 was fought between an Anglo-Dutch fleet of fifty-six ships, opposed to eighty-four French, much larger than those engaged at Trafalgar 115 years later.

Standardisation of tactics was made possible by the more scientific approach to ship design and marine artillery. Ships fit to stand in the line of battle were rated according to the number of their guns, and the guns themselves were cast and bored to more rational and standard calibres and thus weight of shot. While less attention was being lavished on the carvings on a ship of the line, a great deal was being paid to her armament and her ability to fight alongside her neighbours. These must all have similar sailing characteristics if the line of battle was not to prove ungovernable. Hence was born the concept of an organised fleet of classed or equivalent ships, an even more potent manifestation of temporal power than a single, gaudy galleon, no matter how large.

CHAPTER SIX

An Explosion of Enterprise

The 'great ship', of which King Charles I's *Sovereign of the Seas* was perhaps the ill-conceived apogee, left an indelible mark upon the history of the ship. Unwittingly, Stuart pride determined the direction the sailing warship was to take in the next two centuries, and the determination of this elevated the power of a fleet to a position where it could greatly augment the power of a state.

The prestigious 'great ship' transmuted itself by degrees into the ship of the line, a large floating battery mounting over 100 guns and capable of keeping the sea in any season, in any part of the world. But whilst they were called upon to do this from time to time it was usually only necessary for a country to maintain a 'fleet-in-being', with the *potential* to intervene and impose its will on an enemy, for its rival to be compelled to maintain a fleet of similar force, or to seek alliance with another state with whom it might combine its naval might.

Wars between European states were incessant between 1650 and 1815 and the ship was duly summoned to play her role. In fact the last battle in which the sailing warship took part was at Navarino in 1827 when a combined British, French and Russian fleet annihilated that of Turkey in a brief campaign. By the time the three allies had become enemies and were fighting the Crimean War of the mid nineteenth century, the auxiliary steam battleship was displacing the old sailing wooden wall. But by then, far more than the form of warships had altered; the American and French revolutions had taken place, accelerating the rates of intellectual and political change, and the Industrial Revolution, led by Great Britain, had forced the pace of technological and social development. Arising from these shifts, an influential intelligentsia whose curiosity about the world extended far beyond philosophical debate, had begun to systematise the natural sciences. Navigation, hydrography and what was then called 'atmosphereology' were receiving greater attention from savants and seamen alike.

*

An Explosion of Enterprise

The turmoil generated by European aspirations in the form of religious, political and commercial conflict was to generate this long series of wars. The successive dynastic conflicts of the Wars of the Spanish and Austrian Successions, conflicts of colonisation leading to the Seven Years War and its consequent aspiration of self-government which culminated in American independence, provided the dynamic for this explosion of enterprise. Having lost America, Great Britain went on to consolidate a world-wide empire and other European powers also acquired imperial ambitions and status, most notably France and Russia. Earlier maritime powers, such as Spain and Portugal, had gone into decline and as early as the 1820s the former had lost her overseas empire which had been transformed into the independent republics of South America.

To give form to these complex events, the ship played a fundamental role; both the merchantman and the man-of-war contributed to, responded to and influenced their course.

At the middle of the seventeenth century, the Anglo-Dutch Wars, which also embroiled the French though not to a significant maritime extent, developed the concept of the line of battle, in which extended columns of warships fought broadside to broadside until one fleet conceded the ground to the other by withdrawing, usually after a number of its ships had been overwhelmed and forced to surrender. Although large sailing warships did destroy each other upon occasion, it was not common. Once a ship's spars had been reduced to a shambles making her unmanoeuvrable, and once a respectable percentage of her company had been shot to ribbons, the honour of her flag was said to have been upheld and her captain was entitled to strike his ensign. But the concept of maintenance of the line was paramount, and woe betide any commander who did not do his utmost to support his admiral, or fell out of the line for any reason other than having been overwhelmed. Such conduct was held to be unthinkable. As the design of line-of-battle ships converged to give little advantage to the attacker, this led to the strangulation of initiative. Drawn and inconclusive battles were the result. Out of this stalemate developed the tactic of breaking the line, discovered almost accidentally by Rodney at The Saintes (1782), brought on by circumstances advantageous to Duncan at Camperdown (1797) and exploited by Nelson at Trafalgar (1805).

For Rodney a fortuitous gap opened up in the enemy line, whereas Duncan was eager to get to leeward of his enemy and prevent the Dutch from escaping into port. Nelson's approach at Trafalgar, on the other hand, was quite deliberate. On a previous occasion, when still a commodore, Nelson supported by his friend and colleague Collingwood, had daringly broken out of the formal line and pinned down the van of a Spanish fleet off Cape St Vincent (1797), thus allowing the British to cripple it. Nelson's action at St Vincent is all the more striking because he risked a court martial in the process. His admiral Sir John Jervis, however, perceived the advantage thus delivered to his command and was unstinting in his praise. At Trafalgar, Nelson, with Collingwood as his second-in-command, attacked quite deliberately in two columns, to fall upon and annihilate a portion of the Franco-Spanish fleet. Curiously, the enemy Commander-in-Chief, the French Admiral Villeneuve, had not only warned his captains a year before of this danger, but had actually drawn up plans for a division of his fleet to hold aloof from the main line, and thereby to mount a counter-attack. Unfortunately for Villeneuve, his fleet was hampered by lack of experience, poor co-ordination, light wind, the early wounding of the Spanish admiral commanding this division of ships and the sheer energy of Nelson and Collingwood's attack. Villeneuve's unsuccessful, though ingenious plan, has received little recognition, for no subsequent opportunity to exploit it ever arose. By the time the next major fleet action was fought at The Battle of Jutland a century later in the First World War, the post-mortem arguments as to the tactics of the contending admirals would focus on entirely different concerns, as will be discussed in Chapter Fourteen.

Despite the deficiency in the Franco-Spanish fleet in Trafalgar, it nevertheless contained some of the most advanced line-of-battle ships then in existence. While the *Sovereign of the Seas* had been a precursor of the First Rate of the late eighteenth century, her predecessor, the *Prince Royal* of 1610 may be more truthfully said to have been a proto-line-of-battle ship because she might be replicated and thus produce a class of warship unlike the *Sovereign* which was too expensive and thus stands alone. Both of these ships have been mentioned in the previous chapter, as have the French responses, the *Couronne* and the

Superbe. In these may be discerned the progenitors of the ships who in the succeeding century were to contest the mastery of the seas. We have already remarked upon the foolishness of cramming too many guns at too low a freeboard into too narrow a ship, and it was clear that while heavy guns threw an overwhelming weight of metal and were thus more destructive than many lighter weapons, the structure which supported them had to be seaworthy. Thus development of the ship of the line followed a very defined path: as armament size increased to a gun capable of firing a 42-pound shot, the largest a man may reasonably load on board a ship in action, hull form became increasingly concerned with providing a long, continuous and stable gundeck. Consequently decoration and high stern castles reduced dramatically and the demands of war impinged upon rig, to enable warships to keep the seas in any season. In the mid seventeenth century, the sea-fights of the Anglo-Dutch Wars had generally been waged in home waters during the summer months. By the late eighteenth century, Hughes and Suffren were battling it out in Indian waters and Rodney fell on the Spanish fleet off Cadiz on a moonlit night in January.

To accomplish a stable gundeck, the size of large men-of-war increased steadily throughout the period. A three-decked First Rate of 1650 displaced about 1500 tons and while it might have carried as many guns as its descendant in 1805, these were neither as large in calibre, nor as well served. The guns employed at Trafalgar were better placed within the gundecks, with more space and hence their crews could achieve a faster rate of fire. Thus the First Rate of 1805 displaced some 2500 tons, with a gundeck perhaps fifty or sixty feet longer than her predecessor.

This steady increase in size and tonnage dislocated one major maritime state: The Netherlands. In the first rank of naval powers in 1650, the constraints imposed on the size of men-of-war by her shallow ports and waterways made it virtually impossible for the Dutch to compete. Moreover, when part of their fleet was frozen in the icebound Texel during January 1795, a division of Revolutionary French cavalry and house artillery galloped across the ice and captured the Dutch squadron. Finally the remaining ships were out-gunned by Admirals Adam Duncan and Richard Onslow off Camperdown in October 1797, an ignominious end for a brave and hitherto successful naval power.

It was the tragedy of the Dutch to risk contention with navies able to develop world-class warships, but other countries suffered from similar geographical limitations. The Baltic powers, particularly Russia and Sweden, both built fleets to suit their own coasts, but these were designed to seize local initiatives, not argue the fates of empires. Despite this, national characteristics in warship design tended to reduce dramatically during this period, as refinement towards the ideal progressively limited the options. Much has been made of the British 'craft' tradition of empirical shipbuilding as opposed to the French 'scientific' approach, and this is based upon sound evidence. The British, although suffering occasional defeat and more frequent governmental indifference, nevertheless constantly maintained a more-or-less capable fleet. There were periods of neglect, incompetence and complacency, particularly in the Navy Board and in the Surveyor's department charged with the design and building programmes, but even a poorly conceived ship of the line formed a useful element in a fleet-in-being. For its part, the French navy also suffered a greater proportion of neglect, but there were periodic revivals which were politically inspired and, by virtue of the greater absolutism of their monarchy, better resourced. As a consequence, a higher degree of expertise was brought in to generate these revitalisations. Spain, still maintaining her overseas possessions, tended to follow a similar methodology to the British. The Spanish, having access to Honduran mahogany, built some very fine ships of the line, or *navios*, of which the greatest, perhaps the greatest wooden ship of the line of them all, must be the *Santissima Trinidad*, which stood in the Franco-Spanish line at Trafalgar.

The trade of the shipwright was highly valued in the eighteenth century. Tsar Peter the Great of Russia came to Deptford on the Thames in London to learn it, returning to his newly established capital of St Petersburg to build his first man-of-war, the frigate *Shtandart* (1703). Peter was no exception in his enthusiasm, merely the most august example. As we have already noted in the galley builders of Venice, shipbuilders were able to command high salaries, position and influence. The Swedes succeeded in persuading an Englishman named Sheldon to settle and found a dynasty of shipwrights in Stockholm, and Frederic af Chapman, the great Swedish designer who produced a portfolio of ship designs called the *Architectura Navalis Mercatoria*, was of English descent. *Inter alia*, af Chapman's work of analysis and development of design calculation contributed enormously to the nascent sciences of naval architecture and hydrostatics.

Not only did this 'brain drain' of talent exist, but reports bordering on espionage were not uncommonly submitted by 'observers' travelling through foreign countries. Developments in The Netherlands and England were reported to Paris by Arnoul in 1673, and in response to the need to rebuild the French Navy in the 1730s, Blaise Ollivier studied British methods. This was not condoned; while Tsar Peter's stay in Deptford might have diplomatic status, Frederic af Chapman's curiosity landed him briefly in an English gaol. On the other hand, Danish trainees were sent to Britain and France to learn design and building methods in the naval yards of those countries, and Spain drew on French and British talent, among the latter of whom was an Irishman, Matthew Mullan, who in 1769 built the great *Santissima Trinidad* at Havana, Cuba. Finally, revolution itself cast desperate emigrants upon foreign soil. Men like M. Barrallier, arriving destitute in England to escape the French guillotine, turned their hands against their fellow-countrymen and designed ships for the British.

While the three-decked *Sovereign of the Seas* might have been said to have set a bench-mark of artillery at 100 guns, the two-decked French *Superbe*, attracting attention on her visit to Spithead in 1673, was clearly a more generally useful ship. Indications of the superiority of weatherly two-decked ships of the line had been provided earlier by the Dutch flagship at the Four Days Battle in 1666. *De Zeven Provencien* bore 80 guns on a beam of 40 feet (12 metres) and a length of about 160 feet (50 metres). Unable to increase draught, her Dutch builders had compensated for this limitation and conferred great stability by increasing her beam. In boisterous weather it was observed that the older British ships (despite holding the so-called advantage of the weather gauge) could not operate their lower-deck guns, while *De Zeven Provencien* was able to fire both broadsides. In time, the general increase in size robbed the Dutch of this temporary advantage, more especially because the British came increasingly to consider the two-decked 'Third Rate' as the standard line-of-battle ship.

As time passed and Great Britain was obliged to maintain a large fleet, cost became an important consideration. The three-decked First and Second Rates were hugely expensive ships, not only in terms of capital investment, but in their running costs. They required a substantially larger crew than Third Rates, with immense amounts of stores, victuals, cordage and canvas, whereas a standard Third Rate of 74 guns was a much more viable proposition yet could stand in the line of battle and deliver a comparable weight of shot. She was, moreover, a much more handy and seaworthy ship. And while admirals might require ships of 90- or 100-gun size to support the added burden of their staffs and their diplomatic responsibilities, several complained about the unweatherliness of their lumbering flagships. Nelson's 100-gun *Victory*, built to the design of Sir Thomas Slade at Chatham was, in this respect, something of a rarity. When she joined the fleet in 1765 she rapidly became renowned for her superior sailing qualities, rivalling a two-decker in her performance.

During the reforms of the French navy carried out by Colbert in the 1730s, the system of rating was introduced and this was soon adopted in other European navies. In the Royal Navy, it was based upon the 'great guns', the ship's principal armament on the gundecks, together with her chase guns at bow and stern. It did not include anti-personnel weapons such as swivel guns or the heavy, short-range carronades introduced on quarterdecks and forecastles late in the eighteenth century. As the Napoleonic War progressed, therefore, the exact conformity of a ship's guns to the strictures of her rate became increasingly vague. Nevertheless, the system was too well rooted to be swept aside. In the 'Establishment of 1780', warships carrying 100 guns were said to be of the First Rate, with 42-pounders on the lower deck, 32-pounders on the middle deck and 12-pounders on the upper deck. Their complement was officially 850 men, whereas a Second Rate three-decker of 90 guns, bore 750 men. Her armament was 32-pounders, 18-pounders and 12-pounders. The Third Rate at this time mounted between 60 and 80 guns, though the classes bearing 74 became the most numerous and bore a complement of 650 men.

The '74' was a remarkably successful ship, a contrast with the three-decked '80' which was little short of a scandalous disaster. Her very seaworthy predecessor, the '70', had been unable to carry heavier guns than 24-pounders on her main deck, and these were no match for the 36-pounders of the French 70-gun ships of the first half of the eighteenth century. At the time the British naval establishment was complacent to a fault. Even the reforming Admiral Lord Anson, First Lord of the Admiralty, found it difficult to shift the hidebound functionaries who sat on the Navy Board charged with warship design. However, in 1755 Thomas Slade began a design programme which culminated in December 1757 with orders for three 74-gun line-of-battle ships, the *Dragon*, *Superb* and *Bellona*, with a gundeck length of 168 feet and a tonnage of 1615. Approximately forty similar sisters were thereafter constructed, Slade's designs being reverted to after his death following the failure of his successor to produce an improved version. It was only when Sir Robert Seppings took over as Surveyor to the Navy in 1811 that his innovative method of construction allowed gundeck lengths to increase in excess of 180 feet without prejudice to hull strength. Thereafter the 80-gun two-decker succeeded the faithful 74.

In the 74 the freeboard amidships between the lower sills of the gun-ports and the waterline was 5.3 feet, and this was achieved with a main armament on the main (lower) deck of twenty-eight 32-pounders. Twenty-eight 18-pounders were carried on the upper deck with the remaining eighteen guns being 9-pounders, four of which were 'long' and especially suitable for ranging and chasing shots. This, the basic armament of the class in 1761, was later augmented with carronades, 12-pounders in 1793 and 18 and 32-pounders around 1812.

For the first sixty years of the eighteenth century Fourth Rates of between 50 and 60 guns diminished in importance as line-of-battle ships, or indeed as a viable class of warship. (The last British Fourth Rate to fight in the line was HMS *Isis* at Camperdown in 1797.) Much the same could be said of the Fifth Rate of 40 to 50 guns. Despite this, many of these served useful lives as troop ships, armed *en flûte*, or, particularly in the case of the obsolescent 44-gun two-deckers, as hospital or prison ships.

By the Napoleonic War most ships of these classes were unfit for active service and had been displaced by the Sixth Rate, better known as the frigate. Classes of frigates had increased in size and importance, and below the Sixth Rates lay a plethora of sloops and lesser cruisers, more of which later.

The extreme longevity of wooden ships, albeit with rebuilds, made them much more economical investments than their steel successors. The *Sovereign of the Seas* underwent extensive reconstruction which finally rendered her useful as HMS *Royal Sovereign* during the reign of Charles II, and this became a common occurrence in a large ship's life. Nelson's *Victory*, laid down to Slade's design in 1759 and launched in 1765 as a 100-gun First Rate, had been rebuilt twice by the time she led Nelson's column into action at Trafalgar (Collingwood's flagship in the Battle was HMS *Royal Sovereign*, lineal descendant of the renamed *Sovereign of the Seas*). In common with contemporary 'modernisations' *Victory*'s open stern galleries were closed in and her chain-wales, or channels, the horizontal platforms by which her shrouds were spread and secured to the hull, were moved up level with her forecastle and quarterdeck. In 1808, she was reduced to a 98-gun Second Rate, later being restored to 100 guns. Her sailing qualities were exceptional for her size, which was a hull of 226 feet, on a keel of 150 feet with a gundeck of 186 feet (61 metres) and a beam of 52 feet (17 metres).

Although HMS *Victory* represented the largest class of ship in the British Royal Navy, she was by no means the largest ship to date. In Colbert's French navy a *premier rang extraordinaire* topped the rating list with ships of up to 120 guns, and the three-decked *Commerce de Marseille*, built at Toulon in 1788, bore 118 guns. But it was Spain who possessed the largest warship in the world, the *Santissima Trinidad*, mentioned on page 82. Although having a gundeck equal in length to *Victory*, she was six feet wider in the beam and was armed with 120 guns. In 1796, she was extensively rebuilt and given a fourth full-length gundeck which increased her armament to 136. Thus fitted, she appeared in the Franco-Spanish line at Trafalgar, bearing the divisional flag of Rear-Admiral Cisneros. Captured, she either foundered or was sent to the bottom in the bad weather which followed the battle, although there are accounts that Collingwood, who succeeded to command after the death of Nelson, ordered her destruction. 'Everything alive was taken out [of her]', a British officer wrote, 'including the ship's cat ... [which] ran out on the muzzle of one of the lower deck guns and by a plaintive mew, seemed to beg for assistance ...'

The opposing fleets which fought off Cape Trafalgar on 21 October 1805 had taken the egocentric vision of King Charles I of England to new heights. Charles's concept of his 'great ship' as an expression of monarchical splendour and omnipotence, a reflection of the glory of his kingdom and the dignity of his crown, had been transformed into floating gun-platforms, capable of a remarkable degree of control and manoeuvre, in which all endeavour was bent on overwhelming, annihilating and destroying the enemy. Nelson's most influential signal was not 'England expects that every man will do his duty': but the one found in the signal book as No 16 – 'Engage the enemy more closely'.

To facilitate communications along the formal line of battle, usually stationed well out on the unengaged flank, were the 'repeating frigates'. Having spied out an enemy squadron, these 'eyes of the fleet' fell back on their own main body and repeated the signals of flag-officers so that line-of-battle ships engulfed in the smoke of their own and their enemy's discharges, their line-of-sight to the admiral obscured, could see what was required of them. It was tacitly understood by all parties that frigates thus employed were left unattacked by line-of-battle ships whose business was to engage ships of equal force to their own. Thus, in addition to repeating signals, the frigates were free to lower boats to assist disabled men-of-war or pick up casualties, tow dismasted 'liners' out of action to help them avoid surrender and act as tenders in the aftermath.

In reality these formal duties were infrequently performed, for frigates were more often employed upon a multitude of other duties, most unconnected directly with fleet operations. The most common of these was cruising a given area to prey on the enemy's trade or protect friendly merchantmen, and acting as escorts to convoys of merchant ships. Nelson, as Commander-in-Chief of the Mediterranean in 1798, had only the brig-sloop *Mutine* for reconnaissance and consequently lost touch with the enemy before cornering a French fleet off the Nile delta, complaining bitterly of his 'want of ... these eyes of the fleet'.

Sixth Rate frigates and all the lesser men-of-war in the British Royal Navy, descended in order and prestige through the 20-gun, ship-rigged sloops-of-war, via brig-sloops, bomb-vessels, gun-brigs, armed schooners and cutters which were usually referred to under the widely used generic term 'cruiser'. Foreign navies had their own types of smaller craft. The Spanish, for instance, employed luggers and xebec-frigates as well as galleys. Prior to the revolution, galleys were also used by the Bourbon navy and the French *chasse marée* lugger was an exceptional challenge to the Royal Navy in its home waters. Heavily armed gunboats and shallow water craft were developed by the Scandinavian navies, but most of these small vessels were boats, not ships, and thus lie outside this history.

The term cruiser or 'cruizer' applied to any naval ship sent 'upon a cruise', usually meaning a general policing, reconnaissance or intercepting role, where the commander was allowed wide latitude in the interpretation of his orders, though the general tenor of these would be understood by all. While many such small cruisers operated against smugglers and, during the frequent wars with France, in the interception of spies, there were important factors governing the employment of all cruisers, irrespective of their size and function. These will be examined in Chapter Eight.

By 1805, both the ship of the line, irrespective of rate, the frigate, irrespective of the number of guns she bore, and the ship-sloop, all shared a common rig. This had come to be called the 'ship rig'. In fact anything less than the ship-rigged sloop of 20 guns was not considered a 'post-ship' in the British navy. Post-ships were commanded by post-captains, officers who had earned their rank by influence, ability or daring, but whose future was assured since, once they had 'been made post', they automatically rose through the seniority list to become in succession rear, vice and full admirals. Officers who commanded ships of lesser force were either entitled Master and Commander in the Royal Navy (Master Commandant in the United States Navy), or held lesser ranks such as lieutenant-in-command, from which the rank of lieutenant-commander eventually derived. Similar distinctions existed in the French, Russian and Spanish navies of the day.

The importance of the ship rig was partly due to this hierarchical distinction, and to it accrued all sorts of prerequisites connected with the establishment of the ship, the number of her officers and complement and hence the emoluments attaching to the salary of her commander. There were exceptions, of course; the British Royal Yachts, ship-sloops in size and tonnage, paid their court-favourite and privileged senior captains salaries equivalent to the post-captains of First Rates. In contrast bomb vessels were ranked as sloops because they were used as such most of the time, only being commissioned as 'bombs' when on special assignment.

The ship rig consisted of a three-masted configuration. By the late eighteenth century, the lateen mizen had given way to a loose-footed quadrilateral sail which, although laced by its head to a lateen yard, did not itself extend forward of the mizen mast, though the yard did. This counterbalance could be controlled by tackles at its lower, forward end, and provided a large, spare spar to replace losses. But, by the end of the century the lateen yard had given way to a proper gaff and the loose foot was extended beyond the taffrail by a boom.

Gone too was the square sprit topsail on its mast at the end of the bowsprit. Instead, this heavy spar was extended by a jib-boom upon which several triangular staysails and jibs were set. More staysails were set between the masts. However a sail was still carried on the bowsprit, extended by its yard below the spar and this was doubled in large ships. These apparent anachronisms were crucially important if a ship was shot to pieces in action, for although all the masts and sails might have been destroyed, the bowsprit rarely was, and the ability to set a single small sail under that sturdy spar could take a hard-pressed ship out of action and thus preserve her. It was always comparatively easy to re-rig a sailing warship, given time, means and material, and a damaged man-of-war that could avoid the ignominy of being boarded and captured thus lived to fight another day.

As mentioned, by the last quarter of the eighteenth century, the dominating sails were no longer the courses, but the deep topsails, crossed by three rows of reef-points and easier to manage than the loose-footed course. Above the topsail a single topgallant was spread, while the royal, appearing first on the main mast and later upon the fore and mizen, was found upon line-of-battle ships after about 1805, and somewhat earlier on frigates, a class of warship more open to individual experimentation by their commanders. The first royals were set flying, the whole spar and sail being sent aloft when required and struck down when the wind freshened. Warships, especially frigates, had the luxury of large crews, and even when nominally short of complement, inevitably had far more men than merchantmen of similar tonnage, so such adaptations were possible.

The development of the frigate is a complex one, since there was no standard type even within the British Royal Navy, let alone her enemies or allies. Generally accepted as Sixth-Rates, this classification for men-of-war other than those intended for the line of battle fell into disuse, and colloquial reference to frigates tended to refer to the number of guns and weight of metal they could 'throw'. Thus reference to 'a 12-pounder, thirty-two gun frigate' would, to a British naval officer of the 1780s, have indicated a ship of a medium size and weatherly type, generally dating from about 1760 to 1780 in build, whereas 'a 9-pounder, thirty-two' would indicate a smaller, older and less effective ship.

As the lesser rates of line-of-battle ships were replaced by the handier and more adaptable frigate, these in turn steadily increased in size. Sometimes these larger frigates actually derived from the Fourth and Fifth Rates they had replaced.

Captain Edward Pellew's *Indefatigable*, for instance, had been built as a 64-gun ship of the line in 1780, a sister to Nelson's favourite ship, HMS *Agamemnon*. Both were designed by Slade as part of the eight-strong *Ardent* class with gundecks 131 feet long and a main armament of twenty-six 24-pounders, twenty-six 18-pounders and a dozen 9-pounder chase guns. In 1795, two years after the outbreak of the 'Great War' with France, the *Indefatigable* was taken in hand and 'cut-down', reduced to a single main gundeck, and converted to a heavy frigate. This type of conversion was called a *'razée'*. As such her main armament consisted of thirty-eight 24-pounders with additional chase guns bringing her up to a strength and standard to have her reclassified as a 44-gun frigate. This initiative had been prompted as a response to the powerful French frigate *Pomone*, captured in 1794 and found to be armed with these heavy calibre, 24-pounder guns. A straight copy, HMS *Endymion*, was ordered, and

Indefatigable and two similar ships were converted to produce a trio of very successful frigates.

It was in fact French stimulus which had prompted the emergence of the true frigate in the first place. The criteria set for the type were that she should carry her main armament on a single gundeck, be supremely weatherly, a good, if not an excellent sailer, and possess an immense endurance. Almost self-sustaining, the frigate was expected to operate anywhere in the world and such ships frequently exerted an influence far outweighing their size. The reasons as to why the French pursued this concept will be dealt with in Chapter Eight.

'Esteemed as excellent cruizers', the frigate became 'a light, nimble ship, built for the purposes of sailing swiftly'. In fact the name had earlier referred both to a small, two-decked warship and to a class of merchant ship, which was said to be frigate-built and which we shall examine in the next chapter. Like many other common nouns in maritime use, the meaning of the word later crystallised around a particular type of vessel. After the demise of the wooden frigate, her grander, steam-powered iron and steel successors came to be called 'cruisers', defining a specific ship type. The name 'frigate' was revived in 1943 for an entirely different form of warship, but one which was destined to play an equally crucial role in a very different war.

In 1746, during the War of the Austrian Succession, the British captured the French frigate *Embuscade*. She carried twenty-eight 12-pounders on a single main deck, with ten 6-pounders on her quarterdeck and two upon her forecastle. The freeboard of her gundeck was thus high and her second deck could be virtually given over to accommodate her company in relative comfort. With a freeboard of about 8 feet, the gundeck could bear a reasonably heavy-calibre armament, while the ship offered good weatherly qualities with equally good stability. Such a compromise proved an 'excellent cruizer' and was copied by her captors with the building of the *Pallas* and *Brilliant* in 1757. Surprisingly the type was slow to catch on, the unarmed berth-deck continuing to be called a gundeck for a further fifty years, so conservative was British naval thinking. It was this tardy response to French innovation that caused the '24-pounder scare' after the capture of the *Pomone* and prompted Slade's response with his class of 44-gun frigates.

British tardiness was only partly a result of the conservative thinking of the Navy Board. In fact the Royal Navy was a victim of its own success in the dynastic wars of the first half of the eighteenth century and the astonishing triumph of the Seven Years War which ended in 1763. Thereafter the British suffered a series of rude shocks, the first of which occurred when the American colonists revolted in 1776. Soon the French, Spanish and Dutch navies were ranged against them and their attempts to defend their remaining empire relied heavily upon 'excellent cruizers', not a few of which fell short of this standard. Their hand was forced in 1779 when a combined Franco-Spanish fleet entered the Channel almost unopposed at a time when the depredations of French, American and even illegal Irish privateers were having such a devastating effect upon British trade. The economic impact was almost to bring Britain to her knees. To police the trade routes, to hunt down privateers and enemy frigates prowling on the lookout for merchant ships, to scout for the fleets of any enemies and to escort the convoys of their own merchantmen, the British built numerous cruisers, though not all were of a large enough size to qualify as frigates and too many of them were the useless and obsolescent Fourth and Fifth Rates.

At the height of the Napoleonic War there were sixty frigates of more-or-less similar classes, based upon HMS *Southampton* of 1756. The *Southampton*'s lower deck was 124.3 feet in length, her beam was 35 feet and her burthen 672 tons. With a crew of 210 men to man her artillery and sail her, she proved a good ship, though was not exceptionally fast. Fortunately her successors improved upon this. Built originally to carry twenty-six 12-pounders as her main armament with six 6-pounders on forecastle and quarterdeck, *Southampton* was later rearmed and, while retaining her main complement of 12-pounders, her light forecastle and quarterdeck guns were replaced by carronades, culminating in four 24-pounders on the quarterdeck and two on the forecastle. By an Admiralty order affecting all ships, she also carried a smaller carronade to fit into her heaviest boat.

The carronade, originally called the 'smasher', took its name from the foundry at Carron in Stirlingshire, Scotland, where the first of these short-barrelled guns was cast in 1778 after a series of foundry errors had debarred the Carron Company from supplying the Royal Navy with conventional long guns. Designed as short-range weapons with a more carefully reamed bore than ordinary guns, carronades lacked trunnions, but were fitted with a single lug and mounted upon slides. The better fitting of their shot into the bore allowed more of the explosive energy of the charge to propel a heavier ball, for they were lightly scantled and could operate on markedly less charges than conventional long guns. So short were they, that earlier models frequently set fire to surrounding rigging and they were later lengthened slightly. Their design owed much to the military howitzer and French attempts to copy the carronade resulted in the less successful *obusier*. Eventually all major navies adopted the carronade, the British even occasionally using it for the main armament of odd men-of-war such as the brig *Wolverene*, or the converted East Indiaman, HMS *Glatton*, which was commanded by Captain William Bligh at Copenhagen in 1801. The *Glatton*, armed as an experiment with 68-pounder carronades, proved a formidable close-range antagonist, but sailed poorly.

By far the worst shock the British received occurred in 1812, when war broke out with the United States of America. The new navy fielded some powerful frigates of 40 or more guns, which proved more than a match for the ageing, smaller British ships whose tasks brought them into contact with their brash new challengers. These super-frigates posed the greatest threat to British naval supremacy in terms of their technical superiority; we shall see how this was countered in Chapter Eight.

Below the frigates were a cluster of smaller 'cruisers,' of which the light ship- and brig-sloops were virtually small frigates. The chief advantage of these sloops was that they required a smaller crew. The brig-sloop should not be confused with the light, shallow draughted gun-brigs which tended to be employed in home and near-continental waters. Almost all these lesser classes were employed in trade protection, while schooners and cutters doubled as despatch vessels, or 'advice boats' as they were sometimes known.

Towards the end of the Napoleonic War and in the years following, the term 'sloop' began to fall from favour and underwent an even more complicated shift of meaning than frigate, though surfacing a century later for broadly similar reasons. In its place the imported French term 'corvette' was adopted. This was to prove slightly more enduring, surviving the transition to steam, then later joining the sloop and frigate as the main opposition to the submarine in the mid twentieth century.

Sloops and corvettes had originated as small support craft deriving from merchant vessels of the same name. Indeed the British Admiralty declined to build small warships, but hired merchantmen to serve as auxiliary warships. Faced with the need to patrol Scottish and Irish waters to protect his new throne from French-backed Jacobite interference and rebellion, William III resorted to this policy in the last decade of the seventeenth century. This precedent was followed in the succeeding dynastic wars of the Spanish and Austrian succession, to combat the increased war upon trade practised by the French. However, hiring proved less profitable than either the ships' owners or the Admiralty supposed, and eventually the decision was taken to use up quantities of redundant short timber lengths held in naval yards to construct minor men-of-war.

France too, built small warships, often to sail with the fleet. The most numerous class were corvettes and Tourville's fleet of 1693 contained thirteen corvettes in preference to four frigates, to support eighty-seven ships of the line. Other navies possessed a bewildering list of small warships whose duties included scouting, dispatch bearing, the protection of trade and the general patrolling then called cruising.

The decision by the British Admiralty to accept the advice of the Navy Board and build proper small men-of-war arose largely to 'guard the coasts from enemy privateers'. It was not so much the actual coasts, but more rather the busy coastal trade that, in 1709, was fundamental to the prosperity of the national economy and in particular the well-being of London. This alarm over the coastal trade arose from a significant switch in French naval policy, away from fleet confrontation to the more subtle and far more deadly *guerre de course*, the war upon trade, at which they were to prove awesomely adept. While British seamen prided themselves on their doggedness and the thunderous superiority of their gunnery, the French bedazzled with their audacity. From an economical point of view, the national debt was considerably relieved by the arming of private ships of war operating under 'letters of marque and reprisal'. These became 'privateers' which preyed upon merchant shipping, a form of warfare to which the British were highly vulnerable. Protection came in the form of a cheap and numerous class of small warship, the regular British sloop-of-war, not an over-grown boat, but a lightweight, cheap frigate, similar to the French corvette. Sloops of varying design were built in both naval and private yards. They were still pierced for sweeps, large oars for use in calms, but gradually the necessity to 'keep the sea' raised freeboard and while they had in general only one continuous gundeck, the quarterdeck and forecastle of the increasingly standard warship design was eventually adopted. In 1732 Stacey, the Master Shipwright at the Deptford Yard, laid down three sloops of the Cruiser class, and these seem to have been the first built to a common draught. They were snow-rigged, that is two-masted, but with a loose-footed gaff main, the luff of which laced to a spar set slightly aft of, but parallel to the main lower mast.

The renewal of war in 1739 prompted the British to accelerate their sloop-building, whereas neither the French nor Spanish felt this pressing necessity, relying upon privateers to strike the death-blow to their enemy's trade. This first 'war-emergency' building programme produced the *Swallow* class, with wheel-steering displacing the exposed tiller. The *Swallows* were initially armed with ten and later twelve 6-pounder cannon. Although of 270-tons burthen, their clinker hulls possessed a sharp sheer that still owed something to the lines of large cutters. Being short lived and constantly pitched against the fastest products of French private yards, both the demand for more sloops and the quest for speed dominated their design. There were thirty-four in the Royal Navy by 1753 and forty-two three years later at the outbreak of the Seven Years War. Various rigs were tried, and the accusation that some were over-canvassed was debunked by the Surveyor of the Navy. 'If they are designed to sail fast', Sir Jacob Acworth wisely pronounced with an oblique thrust at imprudence in the young officers commanding sloops, 'they must have a quantity of canvas to assist them, and in a gale of wind care must be taken to hand or shorten sail in time, and in my opinion such vessels...that do not sail fast, should not be employed but laid up as quite useless'.

In 1753 the *Cruizer* was modified to a ship-rig and a plethora of small, derivative classes proliferated, varying from 200 to 300 tons and based on originals as diverse as fast royal yachts, French privateers, a French frigate and even the scaled down lines of a fast French 74, the captured *Monarche*. But there were also original designs by the surveyors Thomas Slade and William Bately. In fact the period produced the first ship-rigged sloop class with the *Favourite*, built at Shoreham in 1757. She bore sixteen 6-pounders, measured just under 100 feet on the gundeck (29 metres), 27 feet beam (8.22 metres), and, with a depth of hold of 8.6 feet (2.59 metres), had a burthen of 309 tons. In addition to her 6-pounders and in common with all early sloops, she fairly bristled with small swivel guns.

Such a ship and her successors were diminutive frigates, having a single gundeck, wheel-steering and raised quarterdeck and forecastle connected by narrow gangways across the waist. Unfortunately for their companies they lacked the continuous lower berth deck which gave a degree of comfort to their crew. In common with all other warships, supplementary accommodation space was provided by fitting the holds out with platforms at different levels. Indeed such were the similarities that the 16-gun *Favourites* and another class of 14 guns were initially considered Sixth Rate frigates.

Although the French royal navy continued to build corvettes, a series of them being designed by Coulomb at the same time as Slade's *Favourites*, they were neither so numerous, nor so heavily armed as the British sloops and whenever they were captured by the British, their lighter cannon were replaced by the standard 6-pounder. Even France's opportunist intervention in Britain's civil war with her rebellious American subjects failed to prompt a real expansion of the corvette class. Instead they resorted to building the much cheaper cutter. This proved a mistake, for they were too big and their huge mainsails were difficult to handle, particularly in a strong wind. Several were later converted to brigs and several purpose-built brig classes then followed.

Due to the extreme pressure placed on the British Royal Navy during the war by the emerging United States of America and her extensive European allies, the need for small cruisers became desperate and the demand for both ship-sloops and brig-sloops increased. The existing 300-ton, 14-gun *Swallow* of 1767, for instance, became the prototype for twenty-six sisters by 1779. In 1778 a further six, 200-ton brig-sloops of the *Childers* class were built, armed initially with twelve, and later fourteen 4-pounders. Nomenclature of these 'brigs' is somewhat confusing, particularly as they often bore hallmarks of merchant practice in their rigging. The distinctions between a brig and snow lay principally in the nature of the quadrilateral, fore and aft mizen, whether the luff of this was laced to the main mast proper or a parallel spar, known as a horse, whether the foot was loose or extended by a boom, and whether or not this sail was the real 'mainsail' or merely set abaft a square main course. To confuse the issue, their plans call them brigantines, but this is a conundrum we shall attempt to unravel in the next chapter. HM Brig *Childers,* as the history books denote her, was engaged by the batteries at Pointe Ste Matthieu as she reconnoitred into the Roadstead of Brest on Saturday, 29 December 1792. For over a year France had been in the hands of the revolutionaries, a source of anxiety to the British. The exchange of shot with the little *Childers* was to open the 'Great War' which was to turn into the struggle with Napoleon and raise Great Britain from a country humiliated by the loss of her American empire in 1783, to the most dominating exponent of sea-power the world has ever seen.

Notwithstanding her defeat in 1783 when her troops finally left New York under the terms of the Treaty of Paris, Great Britain had shown resilience. Though generally uninspiringly led, her navy provided a school of hard-knocks for future admirals, many of whom had in these modest little sloops, taken their first commands. And the most numerous class of wooden warship ever produced were the sloops deriving from the 1795 brig-sloop *Cruizer* (not to be confused with the earlier *Cruizer* of 1732). Built at Ipswich on the charming River Orwell in Suffolk, she was of 335 tons burthen, 100 feet (30.5 metres) on the gundeck, with a beam of 30.5 feet (9.3 metres) and a depth of hold of 12.75 feet (3.9 metres), she was armed with eighteen 32-pounder carronades, making her and her sisters able to pack a punch much harder than their lightly armed predecessors.

The sea-power of Great Britain often derived from the presence of such small men-of-war, their influence being out of all proportion to their size. When, in final obedience to his commander-in-chief's signal to withdraw at Copenhagen in 1801, Nelson left before the city a line of bomb vessels, still capable of throwing their explosive shells into the Danish capital and wreaking disruptive and terrifying havoc. Similarly, in 1809, when a French fleet took shelter in the Basque and Aix Roads on the west coast of France, the British sent in against them a handful of explosion vessels and a single frigate, HMS *Imperieuse* commanded by Lord Cochrane. The approach of these flaming craft caused utter confusion and subsequent heavy losses among Contre-Amiral Willaumez's squadron in its attempts to escape.

Both these classes of warship were small in number, but are of great interest. Initially fireships and explosion vessels were small chartered merchantmen, but later hulls were specially constructed, to be used as sloops-of-war until required for their fell purpose. Fireships had been used by Tudor seamen against the Spanish, and the Dutch attacked the English with them, as did the French, whose fiery assault against Admiral Saunders's fleet before Quebec in 1759 was a failure. The British navy possessed three fireships in 1675, and twenty-six by 1688. Four years later these were used successfully against the remnants of a French fleet at Cherbourg and La Hogue after the Battle of Barfleur. A mere handful were maintained during the greater part of the eighteenth century, though in 1780, during the confrontation with most European navies, there was a sudden increase to eighteen. After Cochrane's attack, this declined to none. Small frigates were either built or converted by cutting additional downward opening ports, fitting grapnels to yard arms, removing planking from part of the decks, providing chocks for barrels of gunpowder, inflammable pitch, spirits and other combustibles. The only development worthy of the name, was Cochrane's insistence that instead of 'fire' ships, his little squadron should be explosive vessels, stuffed with powder tamped down with bricks so that the energy of the explosions should be vented outwards rather than just upwards.

Mention has been made earlier of the bomb vessel being employed as a sloop, usually on convoy duty where they proved slow sailers, and weakly armed escorts, for their defensive armament were only a few guns, most useful of which were their two stern-chasers. In 1682 the French engineer Bernard Renau d'Elicagary built a few very strong hulls based on the Dutch *galiot*. They were to be used for shore bombardment and required an open deck upon which to mount the mortars and hence the ketch rig was adopted, with square course, topsail and topgallant upon the main mast, crossjack and topsail on the mizen, along with a lateen sail. Staysails hoisted upon the forestays and a spritsail set under the bowsprit, but the essence of the ship was a clear foredeck and the forestay was of chain, to enable it to withstand the hot gases produced by the discharges of the mortars. Set low in the hull in a strong timber bed, the mortar, with a bore of 13 inches, lay surrounded by earth, intended to absorb the huge recoil.

In 1687 the English followed suit with HMS *Salamander*, similar in size to the French *Ardente* at around 70 feet (21 metres). The initial practice of anchoring before the target, and then training the rigidly mounted mortars by sheering the bomb vessel by the application of a spring upon the anchor cable was fine in table-top theory, but largely ineffective in practice. Wind and tide played upon the symmetry of this arrangement, destroying the accuracy that could be obtained from the same weapon on land. The shell, or 'carcase', was fitted with a fuse and it was the length of this fuse that determined the point at which it exploded. The shell was not therefore constrained within a long barrel, which would have caused it to explode prematurely, but thrown by the charge, the size of which depended upon the range required, for elevation was fixed at forty-five degrees. Thus direction, range and explosion at target-point were highly dependent upon getting these elements accurate. Clearly this was a matter for skilled artillerymen; it was also a matter for improvement, and the British took the French idea further, bedding their mortars on strong oak frames which traversed. Such an innovation allowed firing to take place across the ship, dispensing with the requirement to traverse by cable and spring. Instead the ship could be allowed to take up her natural position, even steadied by the backing of a sail or two, and then open a systematic and accurate fire, as several bomb vessels did before Copenhagen in 1801. In this case their mortars were manned by Royal Artillery officers placed on board for the purpose. Later the Royal Marine Artillery was formed to obviate the necessity of employing land soldiers on board ship.

By Copenhagen the British bomb vessel was no longer a ketch; the Royal Navy improved the massive hulls' otherwise unspectacular sailing qualities by rigging them as ships. This modification allowed the bombs to double as sloops and also permitted the fitting of two mortars between the masts, an 11-inch forward and a 13-inch aft. These bomb vessels were massively constructed to absorb the tremendous recoil of their main armament. In this their scantlings approximated to a First Rate's, with massive futtocks, and their hulls were incredibly strong, a circumstance that was to give them a new lease of life after the end of the Napoleonic War.

Consumption of timber by naval dockyards and merchant slipways was prodigious. It took about 5750 oak trees to construct a 100-gun line-of-battle ship. Miles of hemp cordage and numerous spruce and pine trees furnished masts and spars. Turpentine and natural resins, like gum arabic and gum copal formed the bases for paints and varnishes; flax and jute the canvas for sails and tarpaulins. Supplies of timber became crucial, especially to the British after they had decimated their native forests, and became an important consideration in their sensitivity to attacks on their trade.

Throughout the 165 years under review in this chapter, the enduring design faults of men-of-war remained: too little freeboard, lack of stability and too lofty a rig. Such deficiencies were why good designs were copied and development was cautious.

Ship-stability was more 'mysterie' than 'arte' until the publication of Bouguer's *Traité du Navire* in 1746. Bouguer expounded the concept of the 'metacentre', individual to every ship, and the establishment of which eventually enabled a post-building inclining experiment to determine the statical stability of a vessel. This was devised by Jean-Charles Borda, who was appointed France's Inspector of Naval Shipbuilding in 1784. Hitherto, complicated calculations had attempted to determine a ship's centre of gravity before she was built and these were demonstrably unsuccessful, as the infamous case of the French 74 *Scipio* testified in 1779. This ship was so crank, as instability was then known, that its cause defied understanding. It was this conundrum which inspired Borda, and led to the formal inclining experiment being universally carried out on new tonnage. The worst British naval disaster of the period must be the dramatic loss of Rear-Admiral Kempenfelt's flagship, HMS *Royal George*, which sank at her moorings in Spithead on 29 August 1782.

While loading stores she was also heeled over to repair a leak and her lower deck ports were thus brought close to the waterline. It was widely supposed that 'a land-breeze shook her shrouds', water entered through the low gunports and she capsized and sank with terrible loss of life. At the enquiry other testimony suggested a 'material part of her frame gave way'. The *Royal George* was known to have a proportion of rotten timber in her and was scheduled for a drydocking, though these facts were concealed from the public at the time. This was an ignominious end to a famous ship, for she had led Hawke's fleet in a raging gale in hot pursuit of De Conflans' ships onto a lee shore at Quiberon Bay in November 1759 during the Seven Years' War. Whatever the cause, and it was likely to be a combination of several contributory flaws, her own officers' lack of under-standing of stability must be numbered among them.

But disaster could result from reasons other than faulty methodology. Bad practice, corruption and neglect were just as dangerous. 'Devil bolts', bolts fitted with inadequate shanks during repairs were widely suspected for the loss of several ships, not least Troubridge's flagship, HMS *Blenheim* in 1807. And while *Victory*'s longevity is ascribed to the long weathering of her oak frames while building, this exposure was not always so enthusiastically greeted and at least one British ship of the line was scrapped while still in frame, since these had become too rotten to proceed with her construction. One wonders how many were commissioned with the process at least partially under way.

Irrespective of their rating, wooden ships were organic. Built of hundreds of pieces of natural material, they contained the seeds of their own destruction. They were often fastened with unsuitable iron nails which turned the surrounding oak 'sick', becoming soft and rotten. When made of cheaper and perhaps more available timber, such as pine and fir, they decayed faster and splintered lethally in action. Teak was used in the Parsee shipyards of Bombay which built first Indiamen and later warships for the British Admiralty. But splinter wounds received from teak were greatly feared, usually turning septic.

Moreover, wooden ships were not rigid constructions; they 'worked' in a seaway, leaked and needed constant attention. This was rarely disastrous and with a sufficient crew they could be kept afloat by dint of effort for astonishing periods. Lieutenant Edward Riou's old 44-gun, two-decked Fifth Rate *Guardian*, had become a transport armed *en flûte* by 1789. She was transporting convicts, mail and stores to Botany Bay, when she hit an iceberg while running her easting down to Australia. Although so damaged that part of her crew deemed it better to take their chance by boat, Riou and his remaining men brought her back to Table Bay, pumping constantly in an astounding epic of fortitude and endurance.

Constantly wet, poorly ventilated, infested by a large population of rats, full of rust, fungus, animal droppings, the chemical conditions for corruption of a more corporeal sort than that which infested the dockyards (and naval authorities), highlights the reality of the British achievement of keeping a mighty navy at sea, a subject we shall look at further in Chapter Eight. To these internal threats must be added the malice of the sea, exemplified by the iceberg with which the *Guardian* collided in the dark. And there were others, though less dramatic.

Barnacles and weed were also things to be avoided, since they retarded a ship's speed. Poor Captain Keats's *Superb* had been so long out of dock, that she could not keep up with Nelson's squadron as it chased Villeneuve across the Atlantic in the summer of 1805. These twin inhibitors had long been combatted by 'paying', that is spreading a mixture of train-oil and rosin or sulphur over the underwater hull. This so-called 'white-stuff' was much favoured as an anti-fouling agent in the late seventeenth century and was sometimes topped with a smearing of tallow, thought to give a ship the lubricity necessary for her to go faster. A common cheaper alternative, much used on coasters and fishing craft well into the twentieth century, was 'black-stuff', a mixture of pitch and tar, and by adding sulphur a further composition was made, unsurprisingly called 'brown-stuff'.

But there was a yet more insidious menace, encountered in northern waters, but proliferating in the placid seas of the tropics. The ship-worm is commonly known as 'the gribble' in temperate waters, but its tropical cousin the *teredo navalis* is a vigorous consumer of timber. Invasion of a ship's timbers by the *teredo* was not easy to discover, since the worm entered by a small hole and then ate longitudinally, so that the outer surface of a worm-eaten plank appeared sound. Voyages to India or the Caribbean could prove disastrous if a vessel was attacked, and many were. Early attempts to combat the *teredo* were to pay the vessel with a foul layer of animal hair and tar over which light planking was nailed. This sheathing with its noxious barrier of hirsute gunge was supposed to appease the hungry worm, but failed to do so effectively.

As early as the 1670s British warships had been sheathed with lead, at first thought to be an excellent anti-fouling, for neither weed nor worm liked it much and it served as outboard ballast. Alas, ignorance of stability was only exceeded by ignorance of electrolysis and action between the lead and iron fastenings around such essential fittings as the rudder pintles and gudgeons, helpfully facilitated by the omnipresent sea-water, caused these to erode. Consequently rudders fell off and the experiment was hastily abandoned. In 1708 copper sheathing was suggested, but rejected on the grounds of expense. Partial experimentation began again in the late 1750s and in 1761, HM Frigate *Alarm* was fully coppered with thin sheets, but electrolytic action occurred again with a wasting of the iron bolts underneath. A reversion to lead was tried on the 74s *Marlborough* and *Egmont*, but this wore away and was abandoned in turn as the answer was found by using copper bolts underwater. This was predicted to be ruinously expensive and a compromise solution was found in 1769 by making rudder fittings of cuprous alloy. This still represented a considerable expense and it needed the prompting of war, in the form of the American rebellion to initiate a coppering programme for small sloops in defiance of the effects of electrolysis.

By 1779, with the escalation of the war drawing in most maritime European states on the side of the Americans, coppering became general for all warships. Any deleterious effects were combatted by laying tar and brown paper over the hulls before the copper was nailed on. After the peace in 1783 it was decided to refasten the whole fleet as the ships came into dock, a practice copied by the Bourbon navy of France. The most valuable achievement of Lord Sandwich's tenure of office as First Lord of the Admiralty during the otherwise undistinguished years of the American War of Independence was this wholesale coppering of the fleet. In retrospect it seems a mundane if expensive decision in itself, but for the British it was vital. Whatever the effects of electrolysis, coppering was to preserve a powerful fleet-in-being for the future.

This great fleet, and those of its rivals, existed for the purpose of bringing its weight to bear upon an enemy, driven by an efficient ship-rig and contained in a hull which, whatever its drawbacks and vulnerability, was still relatively long-lived and capable of bearing its burden of 'great guns' to almost every corner of the known world.

These wooden men-of-war operated by harnessing the wind, yet even this could not be done without one essential component. Nor could a cask be stowed, nor an anchor weighed, nor a topsail hoisted without the brawn and skill of a ship's company. Her officers might direct, but it was her 'people', the 'mariners' of Drake's famous phrase and without whom the 'gentlemen' were largely powerless, who turned political ambition into strategy and tactical intent into victory. They served the guns in action and they worked the sails; they weighed anchors and stowed stores. And they ate, slept, fought and died largely between decks, alongside their brute cannon, in conditions of abject deprivation. Only in a frigate was there a sufficiency of space for them not to live in close proximity to the cold and sweating cannon on which condensation formed, to run off eventually into the bilges.

Others enjoyed a degree of privilege. The marines and midshipmen lived in some rudimentary corporate privacy, a rough common berth in the orlop, which turned into the ship's operating theatre in action. The officers, both commissioned and warrant, lived in small cabins, which in 1780 might consist of no more than a canvas partition, though a generation later would be formed by folding bulkheads. The warrant officers were either the essential tradesmen, such as the carpenter and boatswain, who lived on the orlop, or specialists like the surgeon or the sailing master, who was the ship's professional navigator and who lived on one of the gundecks. The specialists usually messed with the officers, but it was 1805 before masters, many of whom had served as officers in the merchant service, were accorded the social standing of young commissioned officers whose only claim to status was their birth.

An Explosion of Enterprise

Preparing for action, the wood or canvas bulkheads were removed, as were those which gave the captain or commander his privacy, revealing the continuous length of the gundecks and turning the ship into the killing machine she was designed to be.

There was only a single fire allowed on board, in the brick-lined galley, usually just abaft the foremast. The multitudinous stores were carried in the hold, along with the ship's cables, her ammunition and powder. The latter was contained in lined magazines, lit by special lanterns shining through glass from outside the magazine itself. By the end of the Napoleonic War the British navy carried fresh water in iron tanks and had adopted tinned food, though not without inflicting lead-poisoning upon those who ate it over a long period. Up to this time salting and casking was the only way of preserving meat, while flour, dried peas, cheese and raisins supplemented the diet. Daily rations of spirits were doled out to make up for dietary deficiencies.

Small beer kept better than water and on foreign stations where this or wine was not available, expedient concoctions like spruce beer were adopted. Though a seaman might be allowed 8 pints of beer a day, he could be flogged for drunkenness, and since he might have been snatched from his home by the press-gang, it is scarcely to be wondered at that he might attempt to inebriate himself. He was unlikely to return home if sent on a foreign commission, and if he did he would probably have been ruptured at the very least. Trusses were widely used in the Georgian navy where, despite the long wars, only about seven per cent of deaths at sea were caused by action. Ship fever, also known as gaol fever or typhus, was an epidemic killer, spread by the human louse usually brought aboard by pressed gaol-birds. And if he did return home he might not be paid. The elegant screen wall set before the old British Admiralty building in Whitehall, London, was built to keep unpaid seamen from importuning their Lordships too vigorously. During the Napoleonic Wars HMS *Centurion* was in the East Indies for eleven years and HMS *Rattlesnake* was on a foreign station for fourteen, so that when she finally paid off only one man remained from her original crew. As for HMS *Fox*, a frigate on foreign service in the Red Sea and Indian waters, her commission lasted for fifteen years. During this time not one penny was paid to her people. Yet, despite these paradoxes and injustices, supported by draconian laws which alone among the British king's subjects removed even a pretence of civil liberty from seamen, the Royal Navy kept the sea and exercised sea-power to the greater glory and dignity of the nation to an extent unimaginable even to the inflated self-esteem of Charles Stuart.

But the expense of a fleet was considerable, even to an absolutist monarchy like France, which enjoyed a brief moment of sea-power in 1782. Within six years of the French naval victory off the Virginia Capes which turned the irresolute British fleet from succouring Lord Cornwallis's army at Yorktown and delivered independence to the Americans, the French monarchy lay wrecked, bankrupted by its own extravagances and the huge injustices heaped upon its subjects. Among its expenses was that of its fleet. Only trade could sustain such vast expenditure. The Spanish had derived their wealth from the silver mines of Potosi, the Portuguese from the less glamorous but more enduring cod-fishery of the Newfoundland Grand Banks. For the Dutch and British, the sugar and spices of the East and West Indies underpinned growing commercial empires, for the energy and ambition which had driven the development of the man-of-war was as nothing when compared with the enterprise of merchant-men and their masters.

CHAPTER SEVEN

Exploitation and Exploration

Behind the grandeur of the great sailing navies of the seventeenth and eighteenth centuries, lay the day-to-day shipping of commerce. Arising from a conversation in a coffee house in February 1664, Samuel Pepys noted in his diary that there was insufficient trade to support both England and the Netherlands. A Captain Cocke had told him one must give way to the other, and at the time the position of the United Provinces of the Netherlands seemed unassailable. Not only had the Dutch fought the Royal Navy, they had entered the Thames and Medway and humiliated the English by capturing and burning ships, including HMS *Royal Charles*. Dutch maritime energies seemed invulnerable, dominating European trade and expanding rapidly into the void left by Spain and Portugal.

Mention has already been made in Chapters Four and Five of the acceleration of Dutch navigation to the Far East after the closure of Iberian ports during their rebellion against their Spanish overlord, King Philip II. The struggle lasted intermittently from 1568 to 1648. The key both to the survival of a viable Dutch economy during this period, and to subsequent expansion, was the successful policy of the Dutch authorities, in keeping the maritime provinces of Zeeland, Holland, Friesland and Groningen almost completely free from the effects of war. Set amidst upheaval and turbulence both within the Netherlands and outside (the devastating Thirty Years War preoccupied central Europe and ended, like the English Civil War, in about 1650), this comparative stability provided the dynamo for rapid mercantile expansion, but this expansion was aided by the fortunate occurrence of other, more random factors.

There also occurred a curious migration of the herring shoals from the Baltic to the North Sea, encouraging a rapid growth of the fisheries; there was a failure of crops in Italy to which the Dutch responded, entering the Mediterranean trade, and a steady growth of the traditional 'mother-trade' long enjoyed between the Netherlands and the Baltic states. All thesecontributed to the rise of Dutch maritime fortune.

Equally important, the fall of Antwerp to Parma's Spanish forces in 1585 caused a migration of Protestant merchants to Amsterdam. Parma's military victory was neither the first nor the last to be an economic defeat, but it was perhaps one of the most spectacular in history. The rebellious and defiant Dutch Lowlanders took with their religion, their acumen, contacts, money and businesses, stood on the threshold of unimaginable riches. In the wake of this, Amsterdam flourished. In addition to supporting the shipping houses, shipbuilding yards, wharves and docks associated with the management of so great a multitude of shipping, Amsterdam became a great entrepôt. The city provided expert knowledge of market conditions, facilities for brokering and insurance, surveying and loss adjusting, general merchandising, and banks offering credit and exchange. The Amsterdam Bourse and Exchange Bank (the *Wisselbank*) were institutions of great power and influence, held in universal respect. More prosaically, commodity-dealing ensured the growth of storage and warehousing which has left its indelible impression on the city.

The ships of the Dutch West Indies Company, the multitude of fluits and other vessels operating on behalf of private trading houses coasting the Baltic, and hundreds of vessels in the herring and whale fisheries, were now augmented by the magnificent 'Indiamen' of the Dutch East Indies Company. Altogether these ships made up the largest mercantile fleet the world had yet seen, making the Dutch supreme masters of all the maritime skills.

The first foraging by the Dutch into the East Indies took place in 1595 when four ships left Amsterdam on a voyage to Asia. Three quarters of their companies died and one ship was lost, but although this 'First Voyage' was essentially a failure, it did stimulate interest and competition. This prompted further voyages, which began to attract increased interest from investors so that by 1602, sixty-five ships had ventured eastward, sent out by merchants from Zeeland and Holland. The result of their endeavours was to depreciate the prices of East Indian spices, much sought after by the rich burghers of Amsterdam and other cities. This economic crisis was addressed in 1604 by the quaintly named 'Old Pensionary', Johan van Oldenbarnevelt, whose high government rank enabled him to call together all the interested parties and to form the world's first joint-stock company, the *Vereenigde Oostindische Compagnie* (VOC), or Dutch East Indies Company. The VOC became the role model for other nations, and in a generation had established a commercial empire in the east. The VOC was granted a twenty-one year trade monopoly east of the Cape of Good Hope, and west through the Strait of Magellan (Cape Horn not yet having been discovered). The VOC's charter also empowered it to build forts and factories, appoint governors and raise troops, and enabled it to make treaties with local rulers.

Within ten years the VOC's *Bewindhebbers*, or directors, had flouted one clause of the charter which stated that investors could withdraw their investment after ten years. Sheltering behind the unexpired years of the charter, they effectively generated a permanent capital stock by forcing sale of VOC shares only through the stock market. It was clear the directors had very long-term vision.

Their pro-consular exponent of Dutch vision in the orient was Governor-General Jan Pieterszoon Coen. In 1605, the Dutch had dislodged the Portuguese from their Moluccan fortress-factory on Amboina and by 1609 possessed seven fortresses and a small number of factories in the East Indies. In 1619, Coen founded Batavia on the Javanese *kampong* of Jakarta and the place became the centre of Dutch colonial rule.

Also in 1609, the VOC established a toehold in Japan, first at Hirado, then in 1641 moving to the island of De-jima at Nagasaki. Unlike Jakarta and Amboina, this was no colonial transplant; the move to 'Decima' was on the orders of the *shogun*, for Japan was extremely hostile to foreign interference. Decima became a highly restricted and controlled trading post, the only one allowed by the Japanese to any Western nation until the mid nineteenth century.

In 1617 an Indian settlement was established at Surat and in 1621 Coen ordered the population of the Banda Islands slaughtered and the islands resettled, to ensure acceptably priced supplies of the humble nutmeg. For thirty years the VOC maintained a settlement off the coast of Taiwan before being driven out by the disaffected Chinese. To offset this, the important post of Malacca on the Malay peninsula was taken from the Portuguese in 1641 and by 1658 the Portuguese had also lost the fortress of Galle in Ceylon (Sri Lanka). Thereafter other Portuguese settlements on the coast of India fell to the Dutch and the VOC's troops conquered the Celebes (Sulawesi) to stop what they claimed was an 'illicit' trade in spices through Macassar (modern Uyung Pandan). Treaties were concluded with Javanese and Sumatran sultans allowing either garrisons to be established on their territory, or making them vassal-rulers under Dutch 'protection'.

Thus, in less than a century the Dutch acquired a commercial and political empire in the east which sent back home, furs, crops, minerals and spices. To service ships and men making their way to and from these possessions, 'an inn for travellers' was founded at Cape Town, but in Amsterdam the directors were unhappy with territorial responsibilities: they were expensive, especially the troops who contributed little to the generation of wealth. Their 'servants' in the Far East felt differently; bourgeois democracy had reached its high-water mark and 'the merchant had become king'. There were fortunes to be made, not least in the 'country trade' – local voyaging within the eastern sphere of influence. Profits from this were crucial to the VOC's viability, for they funded much of the VOC's trade since European exports found no markets in the east. Notwithstanding these drawbacks, the income received directly by the VOC and the cash flow passing into the home economy made The Netherlands the richest country on earth in terms of *per capita* income.

However this state of affairs was not to last. Further restricted by the Japanese *shogun*, profits fell in the country trade which was also subject to inroads by the vigorously competitive English whose Honourable East India Company of London was, in some ways a mirror image of the VOC, although it concentrated its endeavours in India, where ousting the French had become a priority. Until about 1720 the VOC's income exceeded its expenditure, but dividends were too large and a decline began. The company was finally wound up during the Napoleonic War, by which time The Netherlands had effectively become a vassal state of the French Empire. At this time its liabilities were fourteen times the value of its assets and its place had been taken by the British.

The East Indiamen of the VOC were large, ornate vessels and while many proceeded across the shallow Zuider Zee to berth near Amsterdam's Damrak, it was necessary for their draught to be reduced by means of 'camels'. These acted like a floating dock and consisted of a pair of pontoons, the inner surfaces of which approximated the underwater body of an Indiaman. Filled with water, they were warped underneath the expectant ship and pumped empty, to raise her perhaps as much as three metres and allow her to be towed and thus to negotiate the shoals at Enkhuizen or the notorious Pampus in the mouth of the Ij. Towage was accomplished by a line of *waterschepen* from Marken, an island in the Zuider Zee (now in the Markermeer), along with help from the Indiaman's own sails. The alternative to this long towage was discharge and trans-shipment at an outer port such as Den Helder and the cargoes were held in intermediary storage in such warehouses as may still be seen at Enkhuizen, a process which was slow, expensive and gave opportunities for pilferage.

The British had no such problem. Like the design of their warships, there were no limiting constraints upon the build of their Indiamen and these had the superficial appearance of large frigates. Whereas the VOC had been essentially a large ship-owning concern (and the Honourable East India Company (HEIC) was founded on the same model), the British institution soon relinquished the actual ownership of its vessels, building only small teak frigates and dispatch vessels in India for the Bombay and Bengal Marines, the private auxiliary navies used to police its Indian possessions. Instead, the Company hired ships, retaining its yards at Blackwall and Deptford which built for syndicates of private speculators and then chartered the vessels thus produced. The long independent existence of the HEIC should nail that old Victorian lie that trade followed the flag. It was unquestionably the other way round: acquisition of an empire by the British was a direct consequence of the vigour of its merchants and its merchant seamen.

Marine staff employed on Indiamen were said to be in the Company's service, although they in turn were allowed space on board according to rank, to carry out a private trade. To command an Indiaman was popularly believed to guarantee a fortune, although this was not actually true. It did, however, confer a social status and was uniquely considered to be markedly superior to service in the Royal Navy. There was however, no guarantee to success, and notification of a shortage of a commodity, such as that of glassware in Madras in 1768, ensured that a glut arrived the following season, all outward commanders having invested heavily in the stuff. The losses said to have ensued were in the region of sixty per cent. One commander who lost a fortune was John Wordsworth, brother of the poet, who also lost his life when the Indiaman *Earl of Abergavenny* sank on the Shambles off Portland Bill. Nevertheless, profits were possible: 'the gains to a prudent commander averaged from four to five thousand pounds a voyage, sometimes falling as low as two, but at others rising to ten or twelve,' commented a Captain Eastwick, who commanded country ships in the closing years of the eighteenth century. 'Three or four voyages assured any man a very handsome fortune.'

The frigate-like appearance of these ships was such that in 1804, Commodore Nathaniel Dance, senior officer of a large group of Indiamen and country ships in the Strait of Malacca, was able to outwit the French Admiral Linois. Linois refused battle with what he took to be a squadron of British frigates as Dance manoeuvred his Indiamen with the apparent aggression of convoying men-of-war. This was perhaps Dance's greatest moment, for like Captain Wordsworth he lost money on all his voyages, 'never finding himself richer, but on the contrary poorer at the end of a voyage', according to the society gossip William Hickey.

Speed was of little interest to the Indiamen of both the British and the Dutch companies which made their sedate voyages by harnessing the prevailing seasonal monsoon winds in the Indian Ocean (and to a lesser extent the South China Sea). The favourable wind for the outward passage was the southwest monsoon, between May and October, and for the homeward passage the northeast monsoon between November and April. Using these winds, commanders of East Indiamen sought to avoid the early autumn cyclones of the Bay of Bengal and the typhoons of the South China Sea.

It is outside the scope of this history to describe the acquisition of an empire by the British, but much of the wealth with which the British oligarchy lined their own pockets and, it has to be said, subsidised the nations of Europe in their fight against Napoleon, came from India, an India run not as a national colony, but as a private one, virtually owned and certainly administered by the Honourable East India Company. The Company, or 'John Company' as it was familiarly known became even more powerful, rich and enduring than its exemplar, the VOC. It made treaties, appointed governors and raised troops. Moreover, it drove the French out of India.

The other great focus for European trade during the seventeenth and eighteenth centuries, was the sugar islands of the West Indies. Here again the Dutch seized the initiative. In 1591 Willem Usselinckx had migrated from Antwerp to Middelburg, the capital of Zeeland. A Calvinist zealot, Usselinckx waged war on Iberian interests in the Americas and West Indies by proposing a chartered company which would control shipping and colonial interests in this area to the detriment of the Spanish enemy. The *West-Indische Compagnie* (WIC) was founded in 1621 and its trade monopoly covered Africa south of the Tropic of Cancer, America and the Atlantic islands between the meridians of the Cape of Good Hope and New Guinea. In 1638 Dutch privateers seized the Spanish *flota*, or treasure fleet, and in 1630 the Portuguese settlements at Olinda and Recife were taken. Seven years later John-Maurice of Nassau-Siegen, the Governor of Dutch Brazil, took the African slaving station of Elmina. Known for his successfully temporising policies towards the Portuguese colonists, the governor was less kind to the negroes, sending an expedition to Loanda and Sao Tomé in Angola, to secure a source of slaves and sugar. However a revolt in Portugal against Spanish rule and Dutch political changes in attitude towards the Portuguese, culminated in the loss of these overseas possessions by 1654. The WIC was saved from ruin by reorganisation, centred chiefly on its retained possessions on the African coast, most important of which was the Gold Coast station of Elmina. In the West Indies the islands of Aruba, Bonaire, Curaçao, Saba and St Eustatius were retained, and remain Dutch to this day. Part of St Martin is also Dutch and these colonies became important for sugar, salt and slaves. The WIC also acquired plantation colonies at Essequibo, Demerara, Berbice and Surinam (exchanged with England for New York in 1667). These formed dolorous markets for African slaves.

The predominating position enjoyed by The Netherlands declined steadily during the eighteenth century. It was given its death-blow after the States-General concluded a commercial treaty with the emerging United States, from whose independence they mistakenly anticipated a large increase in trade. As a consequence of these negotiations, the British and Dutch again went to war and the widespread British navy swept up numerous Dutch merchantmen, including seven laden and homeward bound Indiamen and five on the outward passage. The crisis threatened both the VOC and the *Wisselbank* which annually advanced the VOC credit to finance its outward voyages. In the ensuing treaty, The Netherlands lost possessions in India and the monopoly of its Indonesian trade. Ten years later, during the Napoleonic upheaval, the VOC disappeared with no compensation being paid to its shareholders. Thereafter, despite a number of expedient solutions to maintain trade, the Continental System of Napoleon, the blockade of the British navy, Dutch republicanism and French intervention all combined to ruin The Netherlands. Dutch overseas possessions and their trade fell almost wholesale to the British. To these inexorable forces can be added the adoption by larger neighbours of the mercantilist practices pioneered and established by the Dutch themselves. The native Dutch internal market was unable to sustain such pressure, while such subtleties as a change in dietary habit impacted severely upon the traditional herring fishery.

By the time independence was restored to the country in 1813, The Netherlands had finally been outstripped by Great Britain as a maritime power, despite efforts to promote an organised colonial system which required the restored colony of Java to produce commodities such as coffee and sugar on demand from The Netherlands. Although the shipping of these was highly orchestrated, the ships which brought these cash crops home for sale fell from the vanguard of technical development.

This reversal of Anglo-Dutch fortunes was staggering, for in the seventeenth century the British, in direct competition with the Dutch, had had to protect their trade by the Navigation Acts because the latter were more efficient with their cheaper and effective *fluits*, cheaper freight rates and cheaper seamen. The Navigation Acts compelled all British and colonial trade to be carried in British or colonially owned vessels, the crews of which had to be three-quarters British. If certain goods such as tobacco and sugar were intended for a European market, they had first to be shipped to Britain from where they were re-exported after payment of custom house dues. This close protection of shipping as a national asset was a major contributor to Britain's rise to maritime supremacy, not least because it provided a supply of seamen for the navy. The fisheries, the coastal trade and the slave trade were all held to be 'nurseries' for British seamen. However, this perception of the merchant marine as a pool of manpower for the navy is only partly correct. In fact the British nation was dependent upon its merchant shipping, which was far more than a mere naval reserve. Masters and mates of merchant ships had a tough time getting commissions in warships. When the ageing Admiral Lord Howe asked his Master of the Fleet James Bowen – a former merchant officer who held senior warrant rank from which he could advance no further – what he could do for him to express his gratitude for Bowen's services in manoeuvring the fleet during the Battle of the Glorious First of June (1794), the sardonic Bowen replied he wanted nothing so much as a junior lieutenant's commission. The request was granted and Bowen eventually rose to flag-rank.

As an instrument of power, the Royal Navy existed in its own right, but it also existed to protect the nation's trade, a lesson it learned during the struggle against America and her active maritime allies.

Sadly, the fragmented nature of private shipbuilding and ship-operation has resulted in poor documentation of British merchant shipping during the eighteenth century. With the exception of the lordly Indiamen, merchant ships were ordinary, engaged in trade and therefore not noteworthy. Yet East Indiamen, West Indiamen, Guinea slavers, barque, brigs and bilanders, even merchantmen named 'frigates', fell into convoy in time of war and were guarded jealously by the frigates and sloops-of-war assigned to their protection.

Lasting evidence of this mercantile ascendancy is to be found in London. Cheated of its inheritance as much by the Continental System of Napoleon and the opposing British blockade, as by the shallow waters of the Zuider Zee, Amersterdam relinquished its maritime importance to London. Difficult of approach, through tortuous shoals, the Estuary of the Thames, though wide and forbidding, possessed channels deep enough to accommodate the largest ships of the day. Thus Cobbett's 'Great Wen' became Conrad's great port, the hub of a vast commercial empire as much as the capital of a political one.

In the pre-scientific age the world had yet to become obsessed with classification and the common nouns associated with various types of ships were flimsy and vague. Merchant ships were described both by their rig and their build in a bewildering mixture of terminology.

Take for instance the 'sloop'. The term describes a small warship below the rating of a frigate. When ship-rigged and of 20 guns or more, a sloop was a junior post-captain's command, when brig-rigged or of lesser power, a commander's. But a sloop might also describe a smaller warship, looking very much like a cutter, with one mast, a large fore and aft gaff mainsail, a staysail and jib. Under such a rig she might also be a small merchantman, a privateer in time of war, or a small passenger 'packet'. This is somewhat at variance with the modern sloop-rigged yacht which is differentiated from a cutter by having a single headsail to the cutter's two. In the eighteenth century, the distinction was that the merchant sloop's bowsprit was a standing spar and could not be shortened, or reefed, as it could in a cutter. This spar on a private cutter usually meant she was intended for speed and therefore smuggling, and this reefing spar was often referred to at the time as an 'illegal' bowsprit, indicating it should properly only be carried on revenue or naval cutters.

The complexities of rig confuse further when alluding to two-masted vessels. An early eighteenth-century form of full-bodied, two-masted merchantman was the bilander, which bore a fore course and fore topsail, a quadrilateral lateen mainsail with a square course above it and a spritsail set on a yard beneath her bowsprit. The schooner, snow, brig and brigantine all had the superior main mast abaft a foremast, but in the schooner the main and fore sails were quadrilateral and set on gaffs, though a fore square fore course might be carried and both masts usually carried square topsails. As the eighteenth century gave way to the nineteenth the square sails were gradually dropped, though two were often retained on the foremast, to produce the topsail schooner, a contraction for the 'square topsail' schooner, for most carried triangular topsails above their gaff sails. Later, of course, the schooner enjoyed a multiplicity of masts up to seven in number, as we shall see in Chapter Eight.

The brig and snow have been discussed in the previous chapter, but the brigantine and its relative, the 'hermaphrodite' brig, are uneasy companions, the latter actually describing a two-masted vessel upon the foremast of which are square yards, the main supporting only fore and aft sails, a gaff main above which was carried a gaff topsail. The so-called 'true' brigantine was similar to a brig except that it did not carry a square main course *and* a gaff spanker, the 'main' sail being the gaff-rigged spanker.

The ketch, originally a two-masted square-rigged vessel with the main forward and thus only a mizen aft, metamorphosed into a handsome fore and aft rig, although even some of these carried a square topsail right up to the last days of coastal sail. Odd rigs were introduced with auxiliary steam power and were usually known as 'jackass barques'. Today such subtleties have become matters of arcana.

Similar bewilderment is caused to the modern mind by the names of hull forms, although the seaman of the eighteenth century would have understood the nuances which, betwixt hull, purpose and rig, differentiated one 'type' of vessel from another. F. H. Chapman, in his *Architectura Navalis Mercatoria*, attempts to classify merchantmen common in 1768, noting that the chief differences lie in the construction of the stern. The 'pink' was a development of the fluit, a round-sterned hull, tapering upwards; the 'hagboat's' stern planking terminated in a beam just beneath the taffrail, while to be 'frigate-built', a merchant ship was flat sterned with her planking ending at the counter, just beneath the decorated stern which was common to all three of these types. They also all had a carved beak-head just like a man-of-war. To be frigate-built did not therefore mean that a merchant ship necessarily had any warlike pretensions, nor did her rig have to be that of a ship.

A bark, on the other hand, was plain stem headed, the most famous being the collier *Endeavour*, used by James Cook on his first voyage (1768–71).

The fluit, flûte or flyboat, as the English called it, enjoyed a long and useful life but, although merchant ship development was to be a gradual evolution, sudden changes were unavoidable as the shifts of supply and demand influenced trade and hence shipbuilding. An increase in the timber trade, for example, produced what the Dutch called the 'bootship', the English the 'cat': a wider sterned, stem-headed vessel. Nevertheless, old forms persisted, and such was the quality of Blackwall-built Indiamen that after the HEIC lost its shipping monopoly, passenger ships built at Blackwall were known as 'Blackwall-frigates', a hangover of this eighteenth-century habit of classifying a ship by her hull form. This was rapidly to be replaced in the nineteenth, by the neater system of denoting a vessel by her rig, a method that made the use of the word 'ship' highly specific.

In general, however, the 'frigate-built' merchant vessel was 'ship' rigged during the eighteenth century, so too were some others, such as Cook's bark, *Endeavour*. Merchantmen increasingly carried topgallants above topsails, though the royal was generally reserved for the lordly East Indiaman towards the end of the century.

British ports other than London rose to prominence during the second half of the eighteenth century, often due to a particular trade or commodity. For example, whereas jute contributed to the prosperity of Dundee, it was the slave trade that made Liverpool rich, so rich that soon it had become an alternative centre of imperial trade to London and demanded so much manpower to service its infrastructure that there was a huge influx of Irish immigrants to fulfil this need. Epidemics proliferated in the insanitary housing thrown up to accommodate them, and as a result, Liverpool became the first city in the world to appoint public health officers.

Slaves, however, were rarely to be seen in the city itself, for Liverpool ship-owners conducted their profitable commerce by means of what was called 'the triangular trade'. 'Trade-goods' consisting of trinkets and small arms were taken outwards to the East African or Guinea coast where they were bartered for the slaves stockaded by native chiefs and Arab traders on the banks of malarial river estuaries. These were embarked and conveyed across the Atlantic on the notorious 'middle-passage' to work the plantations of the West Indies or the southern provinces of the American Colonies (later to become the United States). The highly valued sugar crops resulting from their enforced labour was then shipped back to Liverpool for distribution.

Prior to the prohibition of this trade, initiated by William Wilberforce's Act and passed by the British Parliament in 1807, a wide variety of ships were used in this cruel traffic. An open 'tween deck was essential for the primitive care afforded the human cargo during the infamous middle-passage. Little humanity attended this consideration beyond preservation of 'the cargo', for it was extremely lucrative. In 1766, the slaver *Vine*, under a Captain Simmons, loaded 400 slaves at Bonny on the Guinea coast, and sold them in Dominica, returning to Liverpool after seven-and-a-half months. The market value of her human cargo was about £13,000. In September 1764 the ship *African* embarked her 268 slaves at Malemba and landed them at Kingston in Jamaica for a net profit of £8131. In fact in the decade between 1783 and 1793 eight-hundred-and-seventy-eight voyages transhipping 303,737 slaves yielded a value of £15,186,850, giving an average value of £50 per human shipped successfully. The logs of these 'Guineamen' are, however, studded with entries such as 'buried a man slave of flux and fever'; 'died one man boy slave [sic] of the fever after a sickness of 6 days'.

Wilberforce's Abolition Act prohibited any slaver clearing a British port after 1 May 1807 and outlawed the landing of any slave in any British possession after March 1808. The traffic nevertheless continued, with lucrative pickings for the unscrupulous, since the plantations of the southern American states and the sugar islands of the West Indies still wanted this kind of labour, as did the silver mines and sugar groves of the newly independent republics of South America. Small 'cruisers' of the British Royal Navy pursued a vigorous anti-slavery policy in the years following the Napoleonic War, but it was 1888 before slavery was finally abolished in Brazil. The illegality of this trade and the challenge to the right assumed by the British to police the world's oceans, revolutionised hull design as the serious search for speed began.

Slavers had always been renowned for moving at a fine 'clip', if only to preserve the negroes in their 'tween decks and, in time of war, they made able privateers. In addition to a turn of speed they were usually armed and their crews well drilled, though this discipline did not necessarily extend to the care of their miserable cargo. Liverpool produced some notable privateers as did other British ports, but it was the French and Americans who excelled at this method of warfare and for whom the merchantmen of the British Empire provided a ready prey, a subject we shall return to in the next chapter.

During the French Revolutionary and Napoleonic Wars the British built up their domination of world-wide trade. The beginning of the Peninsular campaign in 1808 saw a British army operating with the Portuguese against the French in Portugal and Spain. It was British policy not to live off the country, as the French did, and either to pay for what the Allied army consumed, or supply it from home. This created a huge demand for chartered shipping, as well as placing a strain on the ability of the British to provide sufficient manpower for its naval and mercantile fleets. Such was the demand that it was not uncommon to find many foreign nationals serving even in ships of the Royal Navy. The Honourable East India Company had for some time adopted the expedient of crewing their ships with a proportion of men from the Indian sub-continent and China.

Although a physician named Lind had determined the cause of scurvy by the middle of the eighteenth century, the significance of his discovery, a vitamin C deficiency, was not recognised for some time, nor, even among intelligent and reforming commanders like Cook were the best and most efficacious remedies employed to combat it. Less interest was probably paid by merchant masters. Scurvy thus continued to take its toll, as did other diseases, so that the merchant seaman's life was almost as precarious as his naval cousin, although his pay was generally better and, more to the point, actually given to him. Perhaps the greatest risk run by the common merchant able seaman of the eighteenth century was that of involuntary impressment into King George III's navy. Certainly fear of this would have preoccupied him more than the traditional dangers, which he would have accepted with a degree of fatalism and which were gradually being recognised and combatted.

William Hutchinson, harbour master in Liverpool during the 1770s and who produced a manual of seamanship, introduced tide-tables for the Mersey and a buoyage system which became the precursor of the modern American method. Pilotage was becoming better regulated and an increasing number of light-houses were being built throughout the world. John Smeeton's Eddystone, although not the first lighthouse upon the notorious reef off Plymouth, was the first to employ the technique of interlocking and keying the courses of stones which was to become the standard practice for the building of lighthouses on remote rocks and reefs in the succeeding 150 years.

As for deep-sea navigation, for many generations mariners had employed parallel sailing as a means of finding a destination; that is placing themselves upon the latitude of a port and then running east or west towards it. Determining latitude was not difficult and successive instruments had improved the accuracy of so doing. The astrolabe, cross-staff and backstaff had been succeeded by the quadrant, developed by the London instrument maker John Hadley in the 1750s. In 1757 a Captain Campbell and the instrument maker John Bird took matters a stage further, extending the instrument's arc to sixty degrees and thereby producing the sextant. By a vernier mechanism, the sextant could measure angles of up to 120 degrees to an accuracy of one sixtieth of a degree and was to prove indispensable not only in astro-navigation, but in surveying.

By this time the issue of solving the longitude problem was regarded as acute, so much so that the British authorities offered the then immense prize of £20,000 to anyone capable of determining it. There was already in existence a complex method using sights of the moon, but this was considered too difficult and prolonged for practical use as sea. Nevertheless, when the British produced their first official nautical almanac under the aegis of the fifth Astronomer Royal, Nevil Maskelyne, tables for determining the longitude by lunar observations were included. The 'longitude problem' revolved around the provision of an accurate timepiece capable of operating for long periods on a ship where the traditional pendulum mechanism was quite useless. Although Christian Huyghens had invented the spiral balance-spring in 1675, a pocket watch could only keep time to within a minute, over a six hour period; much greater accuracy was necessary to determine longitude at sea.

Time-keeping at sea had, for hundreds of years, been done with the sand-glass. This was turned every half-hour, whereupon a bell was rung, resulting in the complex system of single and double bell-rings marking the passage of the ship's working day. The lunar method of computing longitude used the predictable movements of the moon as the 'hands' of a celestial clock, with the sun, planets and stars as indicators. It still needed a watch that could measure small differences of time, for which the standard pocket-watch of the day was adequate. The calculations required to resolve longitude by this means are best described as formidable, and while the first solo-yachtsman to circumnavigate the globe, the American ship-master Joshua Slocum used it as late as 1895 (employing an old tin alarm clock for the short, intermediate times between sights), it never found favour among the generality of navigators, for an error of one minute of arc in a lunar distance, threw a lunar-obtained longitude out by as much as half a degree. Such a margin of error was justifiably unacceptable.

It was another Briton, John Harrison, a Yorkshire carpenter by trade, who worked on the chronological problem. He built three chrono-meters of sufficient accuracy, but these remained unsuitable for use at sea. However, in 1762, he improved the accuracy of the pocket-watch to produce his 'fourth chronometer'. James Cook took one of Harrison's watches with him on his second voyage in 1772 and at its end in 1775 pronounced his complete satisfaction with it.

The means were now at hand to navigate safely, given the two other variables of clear skies and a sharp horizon. Later refinements were developed by navigators and the compilers of navigational tables who capitalised upon such 'patent' methods. Most notable of these were those of Sumner and St Hilaire. Thomas Sumner was an American ship-master who, uncertain of his position off the Welsh coast on 18 December 1837, discovered the position line, long called the Sumner Line in his honour. Being doubtful of his dead-reckoning position, Sumner used several different estimated locations to determine his local time from a single observation of the sun. He then compared these with his time by chronometer, discovering that all the positions he calculated lay on a straight line. His findings linked latitude with longitude and made possible the simultaneous determination of both, it hitherto having only been possible to find them out by separate observations and calculations. Finally in a series of papers written between 1875 and 1878, the French naval captain, Marcq St Hilaire, extended this principal to show that calculations can be made from any assumed position to produce 'intercepts' which, if there is more than one, can, like a series of bearings, denote a ship's position. Thereafter, generations of ships' navigators were brought up on these methods and the patent extensions developed by navigational publishers. The names of Norie, Imray and Burdwood became familiar to British apprentices and midshipmen, and that of Nathaniel Bowditch to their American cousins.

The subject of astro-navigation is dealt with further in Chapter Sixteen, for these methods were to be common practice until the electronic age in the twentieth century. But at the time, neither the British Admiralty, nor the average merchant ship-owner, expected to supply a commander or master with these necessities. Many of these men were in turn too mean to consider them important enough to purchase their own. This was not entirely unreasonable, for until 1834 the British Nautical Almanac remained dedicated to supplying data for the lunar method, and without accurate charts mere knowledge of latitude and longitude did not guarantee a vessel's safety. Nevertheless, an increasing interest was being shown in hydrography, or marine surveying, a new science that had arisen from the exploration which in turn had developed from the desire of Europeans to seize colonies from the more primitive peoples of the world.

Mention has already been made of the falsity of the claim that 'trade follows the flag'. The prospecting voyages of the Portuguese, Dutch, Spanish and English were commercial, not political, though imperial claims soon followed. By the beginning of the eighteenth century, however, a quasi-alliance between an increasingly vociferous scientific lobby and the state were under-writing voyages of discovery which conformed more to our modern notion of 'expeditions'.

These later voyages of exploration may with some justice be touched upon in a history of the ship, because they contributed, not simply to the increase of human knowledge, but to that of navigation and the conduct of ships upon the oceans of the globe. It is also of some passing interest that the vessels in which these explorers undertook their voyages were standard merchantmen. In October 1698, the 'pink' *Paramore*, under the command of the newly and irregularly appointed commander Edmond Halley (better known for his comet), who had hitherto occupied the office of secretary to the Royal Society, proceeded on a voyage to the South Atlantic 'to observe ... the variations of the Compasse [sic]...'. The *Paramore* was tiny, only 52 feet on her deck, but, despite difficulties with his first lieutenant, Halley succeeded in producing a chart showing the variation of the compass, a critical factor, since a magnetic compass is influenced by the highly variable nature of the earth's constantly moving magnetic field without which a ship's commander is unable to set an accurate course. Until the advent of the gyrocompass in the late nineteenth century (which is discussed in Chapter Eighteen), charts derived from Halley's prototype were constantly used. Ignorance of the variation could spring surprises upon even experienced navigators and when Halley's contemporary, William Dampier, bound himself upon a voyage of exploration, found his ship, HMS *Roebuck*, close to the French coast soon after leaving The Downs, Dampier reassured his sailing master Hughes that it was not to be wondered at because it arose from 'not allowing for the change in the Variations since the making of the Charts, which Captain Hally [sic] has observed to be very considerable'.

William Dampier has secured himself an enigmatic reputation of 'hydrographer and pirate'. That he served on privateers is indisputable, but it is an unjustified calumny, arising from an animadversion that Dampier, like Halley, was not a regular naval officer and received his commission to command because of his personal ability. Both commanders had trouble with their first lieutenants. Certainly Dampier's career was irregular, but during its vicissitudes he became a first-class navigator for his day and a talented surveyor. His contributions to English literature are but by-blows of his maverick talent, though they indicate the popular image of the ship in the cultural life of his day. Having marooned Alexander Selkirk at Selkirk's own request, and thus inspired Defoe's *Robinson Crusoe*, Dampier's own life is said to have prompted Defoe to conceive a less well-known novel, *Captain Singleton*. Dampier is also thought to have influenced Jonathan Swift in formulating the plot for *Gulliver's Travels*. Alternatively disgraced and lauded, Dampier nevertheless made major contributions in the understanding of the trade winds and in the early mapping of the East Indies and New Holland (Australia) in 1699.

Exploitation and Exploration

Dampier was not the first European to venture into the South Seas. Magellan, De Retes and Drake had preceded him in the sixteenth century and in the seventeenth, Schouten and Le Maire, Tasman, Torres, Hartog, Jansz and Castenz had all made their mark on the growing map of the world as known to Europeans. Some had left their names upon their charts, others, like Schouten, named features after their sponsors or birthplaces.

These voyages contributed knowledge bit by bit to the accuracy of a seaman's charts. Magellan had died in the Philippines, leaving Sebastian del Cano to bring the remnants of his expedition home to Spain in 1522. De Saavedra touched the coast at New Guinea in 1528, but died at sea and the succeeding Spanish trans-Pacific expeditions of Grijalva (1537) and Villalobos (1542) were disasters. Under Philip II, Spanish efforts increased, feeding on speculation about the mysterious Terra Australis, a vast southern land alluded to in the Bible as Tarshish and Ophir visited by the seamen of King Solomon's day. Mendaña de Neira and Sarmiento y Gamboa failed to find it, but in 1568 the latter named an archipelago after Solomon in the southwest Pacific. Such was the state of navigation at the time that he failed to find the Solomon Islands again when permitted to return and colonise them twenty-seven years later. Instead he discovered the Marquesas and the Santa Cruz Islands. His colleague, the Portuguese navigator Fernandes de Queiros, accompanying Luis Vaez de Torres, found Tuamotu and the New Hebrides while Torres independently found the strait that bears his name and proved New Guinea not to be part of Terra Australis, but a separate island. So bad were the surveying methods used by these men, that the positions of these places remained uncertain and subsequently were repeatedly and confusingly 'rediscovered'. It was the incursions of the Dutch that improved the general knowledge of the positions and potential of these distant 'Indies'. Jansz named Australia, New Holland on his voyage of 1605–6. A decade later Jakob Le Maire and Willem Schouten reconnôitred the tip of South America south of Magellan's Strait. In 1642 the Governor-General of the VOC, Anthony van Dieman, sent out the cartographer Abel Janszoon Tasman who discovered Tasmania, an island lying south of mainland Australia, and New Zealand. Eschewing these finds as uncommercial, the VOC nevertheless kept this information to themselves.

The first English incursion into the Pacific under Frances Drake in the *Golden Hind*, had been purely political, in search of land not occupied or claimed by Spain. During his long circumnavigation from 1577 to 1581, Drake claimed California as New Albion, though with no means of holding it, Spain and Russia subsequently colonised it. Thomas Cavendish and Edward Davis followed, but English interest waned for a century, until William Dampier's privateering and official voyages.

In 1504 the French navigator Gonneville from Honfleur brought back a native from South America in his ship *Espoir*, and the French traded to Chile from 1695 until 1720, when the Spanish stopped them. Despite this setback, during this period the French produced some of the best charts and accounts of South America.

But it was the lure of the great southern continent that drew European interest inexorably towards the Pacific and made that vast ocean the crucible of exploration, turning mere circumnavigation into an ever tightening spiral web of hydrographic data acquisition. In 1721 Jacob Roggeveen set out, but his discoveries were confined to Easter Island and other islands in the East Indies, many of which were rediscoveries. French efforts to discover Gonneville's land, believed for a long time to have been Australia not part of South America, resulted in the expedition of Bouvet de Lozier, a captain in the French East India Company's service. On New Year's Day 1739, Bouvet sighted Cape Circumcision, thought to be the tip of Terra Australis. It was in fact an island, subsequently named after Bouvet and difficulties associated with relocation (due to the as yet unresolved longitude 'problem') confused subsequent navigators.

It was war with Spain that in 1740 encouraged the British to send a raiding squadron back into the Pacific under Commodore George Anson in HMS *Centurion* of 50 guns. Accompanied by some feeble-armed inferior ships, and crews which consisted largely of pensioners, Anson might reasonably have been expected to achieve little. In fact he lost 1051 of his 1955 men, mostly to scurvy, along with five of his six ships, but he sacked the Spanish colonial town of Paita in Peru, played havoc with Spanish shipping and captured the Spanish treasure ship *Nuestra Señora de Cobadonga*, securing loot to the tune of £400,000.

Although Anson's voyage achieved little in real terms beyond making him a personal fortune, it had a number of important consequences. It proved the power of a distant striking squadron and thus the potential of sea-power in an area hitherto considered a Spanish lake; it accelerated Anson's career and enabled him to carry our far-reaching reforms in the Royal Navy as First Lord of the Admiralty, and it renewed British interest in the Pacific. Finally and on social terms, by far the most important consequence though long in implementation, was that James Lind finalised his epochal treatise on scurvy in 1753, recommending lemons as an anti-scorbutic.

In addition to arousing general interest in Britain, Anson's account also inspired the men of the Royal Society of London, which in common with learned societies in other European cities was taking an interest in the natural sciences. These bodies were increasing in influence and, driving the intellectual life of Europe, producing encyclopaedic works and turning the philosophical mind away from spiritual speculations to more earthly certainties. They saw as their purpose the general promotion of knowledge for the benefit and betterment of the human race.

In Dijon, itself a centre of learning which had recently acclaimed the philosopher Jean-Jacques Rousseau, there was published in 1756 a thesis propounding the theory of the existence of a land-mass in the southern hemisphere to counter-balance those in the north. Charles de Brosses' *Histoire de la Navigation aux Terres Australes*, generated enormous debate and reasserted the existence of Gonneville's Land. De Brosses' theory was taken up by Alexander Dalrymple, hydrographer to the Honourable East India Company of London who had been steadily and privately amassing a folio of charts for the use of their ships. Dalrymple became friends with de Brosses and produced his own work; his (Dalrymple's) work also stimulated interest in the Royal Society in London. Pivotal in British interest was the young, highly gifted Joseph Banks. In a society rapidly opening its mind to the wonders of science, Banks was uniquely placed, for his wealth opened doors which his intelligence exploited. Banks' natural curiosity had led him to make a botanical expedition to Newfoundland in 1766, and from 1768 to 1771 he sailed as naturalist on Cook's circumnavigation in *Endeavour*.

Rich, personable and influential, Banks became a passionate advocate of exploration and scientific enquiry, dominating the Royal Society in London.

As soon as the Peace of Paris ended war with France in 1763, the British sent out Commodore Byron in June of the following year. Byron commanded the frigate *Dolphin* which had been experimentally sheathed in copper, along with the sloop *Tamar*. Byron had served in one of Anson's ships, HMS *Wager*, which had been one of those wrecked. Byron and his shipmates had consequently been subjected to the utmost hardship and privation before they eventually returned home. On his new voyage Byron arrived off the contentious Falklands shortly after Commodore Bougainville, who was on a similar expedition on behalf of the French. Thereafter Byron proceeded with a circumnavigation by way of the East Indies chiefly remembered for bad weather. Byron's voyage achieved little beyond unforgivably infecting his crew with scurvy, conferring upon its commander the soubriquet 'Foul-Weather Jack' and inspiring his grandson, Lord Byron, with material for his epic poem *Don Juan*.

Six months after her return, in August 1766, HMS *Dolphin* put to sea again under the command of Simon Wallis. Wallis was accompanied by Carteret in the elderly sloop *Swallow* and a storeship, the *Prince Frederick*. Carteret's ship was to be exchanged for a frigate, but this failed to materialise at the rendezvous and Carteret lost touch with Wallis in the Strait of Magellan. Wallis, however, succeeded in reaching Tahiti where, after a fight with the natives, peace was restored and for some time the Tahitians and British led a happy lotus-eating co-existence. For the islanders the interlude was to be a time-bomb of disease; for the British the beginning of scientific and commercial interest in the Pacific. When he returned in May 1768, Wallis had not lost a single man and his report was conveyed at once to Lieutenant James Cook, who was preparing to leave on an expedition sponsored jointly by the British Admiralty and the Royal Society.

As for Carteret, he continued to the westwards after being separated from Wallis and although losing men and suffering badly from the usual problems associated with life at sea, carried out several running surveys and added to previous knowledge, locating and naming the Admiralty Islands. On his way back

Carteret fell in with and was boarded by Bougainville himself who quizzed Carteret on his achievements but slyly did not reveal his own identity, having just completed his circumnavigation.

Bougainville's voyage, between November 1766 and March 1769, followed almost exactly the same route as the three English voyages that preceded it. Bougainville commanded the frigate *La Boudeuse*, with the sturdier *flûte Etoile* in support, commanded by Chesnard de la Giraudais. They too visited Tahiti after Wallis where they claimed they acquired syphilis, thereby starting the argument as to who first infected the easy-going islanders which has raged ever since. Bougainville's contribution to botany is probably better known than that to hydrography; his published works were scanty of scientific fact and provoked a reaction only from Diderot which reached scandalous proportions.

James Cook came of humble stock and had gone to sea in the merchant ships of Whitby. By dint of application he rose to the post of mate, the officer second-in-command to the master, in colliers operating on the east coast of England. It was an arduous trade and Cook became a complete master of his chosen profession. When war broke out with France in 1756, Cook volunteered for service in the Royal Navy as an able seaman (a position that matched his social standing). Appointed to HMS *Eagle*, he soon came to the notice of her then commander, Captain Sir Hugh Palliser. Palliser encouraged the gifted and intelligent young man in his studies of navigation, geography and astronomy and in October 1757 Cook's skills were employed aboard HMS *Pembroke*, which was bound up the St Lawrence River in the fleet under Admiral Saunders with General Wolfe's army embarked. Wolfe's landing and defeat of Montcalm (in whose forces Bougainville was serving) transferred Canada from the French to the British crown. For Cook, the event secured his reputation as an hydrographic surveyor, for he had carried out extensive charting of the St Lawrence prior to Wolfe's landing. When Palliser became governor of Newfoundland, Cook followed his patron to carry out a full survey of the island and the adjacent coast of Labrador. An account of an eclipse he had observed during this sojourn brought his work to the attention of the Royal Society.

The Royal Society and Admiralty were planning a joint expedition to observe the transit of Venus from the Pacific. When, in the manner of Halley and Dampier, Dalrymple, the expedition's chosen leader wished for a commission as captain in the Royal Navy, the Admiralty refused, and immediately Palliser recommended James Cook who, with the deserved promotion to lieutenant, might be fitted to command and to carry out the necessary observations. A large, opinionated and difficult man, Cook nevertheless possessed important attributes in his innate self-confidence, sense of justice, utter reliability, integrity and determination. Having been a common seaman, his care for his men was exemplary. He was also a willing horse which, with little recompense, the Establishment proceeded to flog, and he was only reluctantly promoted at the end of his career.

Cook's first voyage was to be in the *Endeavour*, of 366 tons, built as the collier *Earl of Pembroke*. She was a small, sturdy 'bark', an unpretentious ship which had been employed in both the coastal and the Scandinavian trade and in which Cook would have felt thoroughly at home. Just 97.7 feet (29 metres) on the lower deck, her beam was 29.1 feet (9 metres). Refitted for the expedition, her hull was doubled with oak against the worm, this oak being heavily studded with wide-headed iron nails. Her total complement of scientists, officers, marines and seamen was ninety-four when she sailed from Plymouth on 26 August 1768. Thirty-eight were to die and one was to desert before the ship returned to Dover on 12 May 1771. Chief among the scientists was the dilettante Joseph Banks who struck up an immediate friendship with Cook. It was an unlikely alliance, but a critical one for both men and although Banks did not accompany Cook on his subsequent voyages, Cook was to enjoy Banks' confidence to the end.

Cook doubled Cape Horn, crossed the Pacific by way of Tahiti where he carried out his mission of observing the transit of Venus, coasted New Zealand and the Great Barrier Reef of Australia and returned by way of the East Indies and Cape Town. The accuracy of his running surveys have to be seen to be believed.

Cook's second voyage was made with two chartered colliers, HM barques *Resolution* and *Adventure*. Cook commanded the former as Master and Commander, not the post-rank he desired, with Tobias Furneaux, who had sailed aboard *Dolphin* with

Wallis, commanding the latter. Among the midshipmen was George Vancouver, later to chart areas of the Pacific himself. The expedition left Plymouth in early July 1772 and returned to Portsmouth on 30 July 1775. Although Cook went back to Tahiti, it was to refit his ship, for the purpose of the second voyage was to discover the great southern continent; not Australia, but Antarctica. In January of 1773 Cook reached 67°15' South latitude, without sighting land and again, in January the following year he reached 70°11' South with the same negative results. His conclusion that no great continent existed was wrong, but his achievement is undiminished by this failure, for his further progress was impeded by ice. It was during this difficult and dangerous voyage that Harrison's fourth chronometer proved itself.

Cook's third expedition, again aboard the *Resolution*, with another converted collier, the *Discovery* commanded by Charles Clerke, a former lieutenant of Cook's, sailed on 12 July 1776. Vancouver was again a midshipman and Cook's sailing master was one William Bligh. The *Resolution* and *Discovery* proceeded to Cape Town and then by way of the Kerguelen Islands south of Australia to New Zealand and on to the Cook Islands and the Friendly Islands. Thereafter Cook was charged to proceed north and he visited the coast of the Pacific northwest of Canada, Alaska and passed through the Bering Strait into the Arctic Ocean. Vitus Bering, a Dane in the Russian service had, in 1728 and in 1741 established that the continents of North America and Asia were not joined. Cook was unable to discover the western entrance to the North West Passage that was to become an obsession with polar explorers. The two ships wearily turned south again, to winter at Hawaii. Cook had been unwell for some time and here he met his untimely death in 1779 in a skirmish with the natives on the beach. Courageously Clerke took the ships north again and then home, via Kamchatka, Macao, Batavia and the Cape of Good Hope.

Although the Frenchmen La Pérouse (1785–1788) and d'Entrecasteaux (1791–1794) followed Cook into the Pacific; the latter's expedition was a search for the former. French efforts at exploration had been marred by tragedy. De Surville in *Saint Jean Baptiste* discovered one island in the Solomons in 1769, but lost most of his men to scurvy; Marion du Fresne with the *Mascarin* and the *Marquis de Castries* gave his name to the Marion Islands in the south Indian Ocean, but was killed by Maoris in the Bay of Islands, New Zealand, in June 1772 and his crews were also much reduced by scurvy. Yves Joseph de Kerguelen de Trémarec led two expeditions south. The first with the *Fortune* and the *Gros-Ventre*, claimed to have discovered the great southern continent. In fact, like the Marions, he had found yet another island in the remote south Indian Ocean. Kerguelen's braggart nature cost him a prison sentence, for the large, expensive operation which was intended to claim Australia for France was a disaster. Fortunately for French fortunes, the British had suffered defeat in the world-wide war which had followed the rebellion of their American colonies. This circumstance and the humiliation felt by the French after Kerguelen's spectacular failure, led to the expedition by Pérouse who intended to emulate Cook. He sailed with *La Boussole* and *L'Astrolabe* in August 1785. These ships were two former merchantmen, the *Portefaix* and *Autruche* which were converted and reclassified as frigates. Jean-François Galaup the Comte de Pérouse (the commander) was a professional sea officer who had achieved fame in August 1782 by attacking two British posts in Hudson's Bay which had been considered inaccessible.

As with Cook's voyages, the auxiliary acquisition of any knowledge adding to the natural sciences was encouraged and experts sailed with the expedition to accomplish this. La Pérouse was also charged with testing the strength of Spanish rule on the Pacific coasts of the Americas. Passing into the Pacific, the ships reached the Alaskan coast where they lost three boats' crews, and made a brief stay at Monterey, before abandoning any further interest in the Spanish. Proceeding north and west, La Pérouse ventured to the coasts of Korea and Japan and reaching the coasts of Tartary, finally arrived at Petropavlovsk in September 1787. In this remote place he received orders to go south; rumours had reached Paris of a British settlement on the Australian coast and La Pérouse was to investigate it. Arriving for water at Samoa, his ships lost men to a native attack and deaths by scurvy increased. It was with relief rather than triumph that they reached Botany Bay on 26 January 1788 and ironically La Pérouse sent his report home by a British ship, announcing that once recruited he was leaving to achieve 'absolutely everything enjoined upon me by my instructions'. Leaving Botany Bay on 10 March 1788, *La Boussole* and *L'Astrolabe* were never seen again.

Despite the distractions of a mighty revolution, Contre-Amiral, the Chevalier d'Entrecasteaux, a French naval officer with experience of eastern waters was sent in search in September 1793. Two converted 500-ton merchant ships, *La Recherche* and *L'Espérance* were fitted out as 'frigates', but the effects of the Revolution in creating first trouble among the crews and later problems with the Dutch in the East Indies (with whom France was at war), were compounded by poor storing, scurvy, injury and sheer bad luck. Although some excellent surveying was carried out, particularly on the Tasmanian coast, D'Entrecastaux's expedition was a failure and the fate of La Pérouse remained unknown.

Meanwhile José Bustamente and Alexandro Malaspina, an Italian in the service of Spain, made a voyage of discovery in the ships *Descubierta* and *Atrevida*. Leaving Cadiz on 30 July 1789, the ships visited the northwest coast of North America and crossed the North Pacific, making observations on gravity ashore *en route*. Reaching Macao they recrossed the Pacific by way of Peru, to return to Spain in 1794. Malaspina was imprisoned for his liberal ideas and sank into obscurity, while his colleague Bustamente became an admiral whose treasure ships were deliberately attacked by a British frigate squadron in 1804 to precipitate war with a Spain that refused refuge to British shipping.

It was left to the British to complete the exploration of the Pacific, despite the renewed efforts of the French who, at the turn of the century and under the auspices of their new First Consul, Napoleon Bonaparte, made efforts to reassert their claims to unknown lands by the expedition of Nicolas Baudin. George Vancouver surveyed the Pacific North West, leaving Falmouth on 1 April 1791, and Matthew Flinders completed that of Australia, discovering, with his colleague George Bass, that Tasmania was an island. Flinders lost his ship, the sloop HMS *Investigator*, and was later captured by the French, languishing for several years as a prisoner on Mauritius. He died prematurely, back in England, on the eve of the publication of his account of the voyage which would take his name. Fame eluded this remarkable man who had learned his trade under William Bligh on Bligh's second voyage to take breadfruit to the West Indies. He is remembered in the name of the correcting bar of soft iron placed before a ship's magnetic compass to minimise deviation.

Flinder's famous meeting with Baudin in what became known as Encounter Bay bespoke a more civilised age than our own. It occurred on 8 April 1802, and both commanders believed their countries were still at war. In fact the Peace of Amiens had been signed a few days earlier (though it was not to last). The two ships ran out their guns but, a flag of truce being hoisted, Flinders went aboard Baudin's ship and asked to see Baudin's passport from the British Admiralty. Having sighted this, he offered his own passport from Paris, which Baudin declined to inspect and the meeting passed cordially in a discussion largely about the geography of the Bass Strait.

Baudin commanded the 350-ton corvette *Le Géographe* and in company with the storeship *Le Naturaliste* (Capitaine de Frégate Hamelin), had sailed from Le Havre on 19 October 1800 to explore and survey Australia. This he achieved in part, although his crews were decimated by scurvy.

As Flinders and Baudin were completing their Australian surveys the Russian Adam Ivan von Kruzenshtern aboard the *Nadezhda* was setting out from the Baltic port of Kronstadt with the *Neva* in company. Both Kruzenshtern and his second-in-command Lisiansky had, like many other Russian officers, served with the Royal Navy and it was in purchased British vessels that they made their voyages. These were diplomatic and commercial in their purpose and not purely exploratory, for Russia had trading posts both in Alaska and along the American coast which she did not abandon to the United States until the 1840s.

At the conclusion of the Napoleonic War there was a proliferation of scientific voyages, but the Pacific was no longer the frontier. It was the polar regions which were now attracting attention, but these remained unconquered until the twentieth century. Explorers there were a-plenty. Kotzebue in the tiny brig *Rurik* along with Golovnin, Lutke, Wrangel, and Bellingshausen, who took the *Vostok* deep into the Antarctic Ocean, represented Russia. France sent out Freycinet in *L'Uranie*, Duperrey in *La*

Coquille and Dumont d'Urville. D'Urville sailed in the same ship as Duperrey, though he renamed her *L'Astrolabe* and, in 1826, went in search of La Pérouse. In fact the wreck of the earlier *L'Astrolabe* had already been found and D'Urville confirmed this as having occurred on Vanikoro Island in the New Hebrides. The mystery was only partly resolved, as there was no trace of *La Boussole*, though the second ship was finally located in 1964, not far away from her sister.

British interest revived in the 1820s, when HM Frigate *Blossom* of 26 guns under Captain F. W. Beechey led the first of several scientific expeditions into the Pacific where her officers heard an account of the *Bounty* mutiny from the last surviving mutineer on Pitcairn, before proceeding to the Bering Strait to rendezvous with Sir John Franklin's expedition coming westwards through the North West Passage. Such expeditions were by now equipped with the tinned food introduced into the navy at the end of the Napoleonic Wars. What was not appreciated was that the tins were secured by lead soldering and Franklin's failure owed as much to lead-poisoning as to the hardships and privations he faced in the Arctic. In 1831, two years after Beechey's abortive attempt to complete Franklin's grand design, Captain Fitzroy's voyage in HMS *Beagle* sparked off the great scientific controversy of the century by inspiring Charles Darwin's 'Essay on the Origin of Species'. Darwin, the expedition's naturalist, had made many observations of living creatures which led him to theorise on the diversity of species and the manner in which so many had developed. His conclusions encouraged him to propound the theory of evolution some years later, which embroiled him in a protracted, furious and acrimonious debate in which science and religion fought for supremacy. Thus, the 10-gun *Beagle*, like the *Santa Maria*, has by her association with great events, assumed an importance out of all proportion to her size. She marks the importance of the ship generally in having contributed to the advances in mankind's knowledge and the hypotheses upon which such knowledge aspires to advance.

The nineteenth century saw the final exploration of the world's coasts. Dumont d'Urville in *L'Astrolabe* with La Zelee went south into the Antarctic ice in 1837, and the Englishmen Kellett and Belcher were busy surveying for Admiral Beaufort, then the British navy's hydrographer. The exploration of the world had turned to the more mundane, though no less personally exciting challenge of hydrographic surveying. Despite the overwhelming might of its navy, Great Britain was slow to realise the responsibility of an Admiralty in providing charts of sufficient accuracy for its ships to navigate by. It was 1795 before the Hydrographic Department was formed and even then it was necessary to employ a former HEIC officer, the same Mr Alexander Dalrymple whose demand for a commission had so outraged Their Lordships when they set him aside for the obscure Cook. Hydrographic surveyors had been modestly busy since Stuart times and those best known at the beginning of the nineteenth century were Graeme Spence, who had assisted Nelson out of Harwich in HMS *Medusa* in 1801, and Messrs Murdoch and Mackenzie. But Dalrymple did not prosecute an active policy of surveying, it being left to officers on station to initiate these. Many men, both naval officers and merchant masters alike, contributed surveys. Men like the East India commander Captain Huddart, who, along with James Horsburgh and Commander Broughton, carried out surveys of the Far East, but once Captain Thomas Hurd succeeded Dalrymple in 1808, things changed rapidly. Many of the old and warrant masters and mates who were specialist navigators, became staff captains and staff commanders, employed solely upon surveying duties. Moreover, in 1814 two designated survey ships appear in the navy list and this had doubled four years later with further expansion following. Names such as that of Hurd himself, Smyth, Kellett, Bullock, Vidal, Owen, Denham and Bayfield may still be found on twentieth-century charts. But even when, in 1823, the polar expert Rear-Admiral Sir William Parry became Hydrographer, the Secretary to the Navy regarded charts and sailing directions an unnecessary luxury. Parry was succeeded by the remarkable Sir Francis Beaufort, who served until he was eighty. Beaufort elevated the profile of hydrography and convinced the reactionary Admiralty Board of the necessity of charts and sailing directions, promoting navigation alongside gunnery as a desirable expertise in a navy with global commitments. The outcome of this labour made the British Admiralty chart one of the most respected achievements of cartography. But other nations made significant contributions to the nautical sciences, not least the Americans who, in the person of Lieutenant Matthew Fontaine Maury may be said to have undertaken the first study of the world oceanic weather. Such enterprise had had many amateur forbears, mariners like the Arctic whaling captain, William Scoresby who was as accomplished surveyor as well as a keen observer of 'atmosphereology'. Nor was this business without risk and danger. Many young hydrographic officers had blood-curdling brushes with death and even on the east coast of England, the business of surveying could prove dangerous, as the loss of HMS *Fairy* off Southwold during a ferocious gale on 13 and 14 November 1842 testified. What these men initiated has proved an endless, but thoroughly worthwhile task, for the requirements change with the development of shipping, increases in draught, physical changes both natural and man-made, and the exploitation of the environment by the endless restlessness of our species.

These changes were supported by other developments. One of the first bucket dredgers was built by the Cornish steam engineer Richard Trevithick in 1806 and while an early graving dock is known to have been at Portsmouth in 1495, the introduction of steam dredges and plant greatly assisted the general construction of both dry and wet docks elsewhere. Ships could now be overhauled and repaired properly, and also lie afloat all the time they were working cargo with less stress placed upon their hulls. London had had wet docks at Rotherhithe and Blackwall in the seventeenth century, but in the period between 1753 and 1830 some 370 acres of wet dock were available in England, largely due to the expansion of London and Liverpool.

Whilst the development of canals in Britain was for an inland transport system, the canals in France and The Netherlands were for coasters and even deep-water sailing ships, so that while the history of the merchant ship during the eighteenth century and first decade of the nineteenth is relatively slow-moving, the infrastructure serving it was in the grip of rapid expansion.

As the new era of peace dawned in 1815, with the British Royal Navy pre-eminent at sea and an aggressive new maritime nation flexing its muscles across the Atlantic, the pace of change slips into a higher gear. The first steam ships were making a tentative appearance. But with the first hiss of steam plant can be discerned a touch of impatience that things in the world were too slow: speed was now the great thing!

CHAPTER EIGHT

Sea Power I

Although rapid demobilisation of the Royal Navy occurred after 1815 and the British fleet was reduced to a mere 127 commissioned warships by 1820, the global responsibilities of Great Britain still required the maintenance of a relatively large navy. Twice, in 1816 and in 1827, British battle squadrons combined with other navies to put a fleet in the field. The first occasion was the bombardment of Algiers in 1816 by a heavy squadron under Admiral Lord Exmouth, formerly the frigate captain Edward Pellew. The object was to bring to book the Dey of Algiers whose vessels committed acts of piracy with impunity and who had enslaved many European seamen and the British consul. The Barbary corsairs had already been the victims of one punitive expedition under Captain Stephen Decatur of the United States Navy.

At Gibraltar, Exmouth was joined by a Dutch squadron under Vice-Admiral Baron van Capellen and prepared to attack the formidable defences of the city. The ensuing bombardment was terrible and lasted until well after nightfall when the attacking allied ships were virtually out of ammunition. Exmouth boldly prepared to renew his attack the next morning, but terms were acceded to, despite some severe damage to several ships. The 98-gun *Impregnable*, for instance, had over a hundred men killed and fifty wounded; after the action 233 heavy shot were found embedded in her hull.

The second action consisted of a small squadron of three line-of-battle ships, *Asia*, *Genoa* and *Albion* together with two frigates all under the command of Vice-Admiral Sir Henry Codrington, which combined with a Russian squadron under Heyden and a French squadron under De Rigny. At Navarino this Allied fleet attacked a Turco-Egyptian Fleet of sixty-five vessels under Ibrahim Pasha, with a view to forcing the Turks toconcede independence to the Greeks. The battle was characterised by the extreme ferocity of the bombardment by both sides.

Such punitive enterprises demonstrated what might be achieved with sea-power and generally such heavy measures were undertaken only with the consent or tacit approval of other powers. Even so, it was Great Britain who, by virtue of her naval supremacy, was both expected to carry out such acts out and, increasingly, felt it her duty as her imperial obligations increased.

Such flexing of naval muscle was a direct consequence of the lessons learned from the Napoleonic War during which Great Britain had resolutely opposed, at times, the whole of Europe ranged against her under the banner of Napoleonic France. With comparatively slender resources, she had achieved this by the judicious deployment of her navy.

In his last exile on St Helena, Napoleon remarked that wherever there was water to float a ship, there one might find a British man-of-war. This was no exaggeration. Nor were these foreign stations necessarily occupied by large ships; on the contrary, a small cruiser might be all that was needed to exert influence where necessary and to this end the Royal Navy maintained its large force of frigates and sloops (described in Chapter Six), as well as numerous smaller ships, schooners, cutters, gun-brigs, some of which were hired from private owners, such as the little cutter *Admiral Mitchell* which regularly patrolled the waters off Boulogne. These patrols, known then as 'cruises' were maintained at critical points where, for instance, merchant ships might make significant landfalls and where the French and later the Americans might be expected to prey off that trade with privateers or cruisers of their own, or where enemy activity might indicate an attempt by a squadron of frigates to break out on a raiding expedition.

Patrolling this was just one of the tasks for frigates, along with their support of the battle squadrons. Just as important, and very unpopular with their young commanders, was the crucial duty of convoy escort. Ships bound to certain destinations, such as the East or West Indies, because of their reliance upon seasonal winds, left at the same predictable times and were thus vulnerable to capture by French corsairs from, for example, St Malô when leaving or entering the Channel. While merchantmen might disperse when west of the 20th meridian, their husbanding thus far was imperative and the powerful sugar lobby in the House of Commons was vociferous if losses occurred among the West Indiamen. But ships sailing to Canada, the whaling grounds of Jan Mayen or the Davis Strait, or the vessels of the Hudson Bay Company required convoy just as much as the Indiamen. Equally vulnerable were the small vessels trading, like Cook's *Endeavour* in her former life as the *Earl of Pembroke*, with the Baltic, for not only did English coal go to Scandinavia but naval stores, timber, turpentine, flax and rosin came back. Thus the Baltic trade required escort, as did the coastal trade of the home coasts as well as that from the United States, until war with Washington began in 1812 with the spectacular defeat of a handful of British frigates.

The consequence of this blow to British pride and prestige was an increase in the size of British frigates, but more importantly it brought the increasing weight of blockading squadrons across the Atlantic in the wake of the first defeat of Napoleon in 1814. No longer necessary around the coasts of Europe, they soon began to exert a fatal stranglehold on the United States. It was by means of blockade that Great Britain held the key to naval mastery and it is ironic that it was only in the age of sail, when the price of technical superiority was relatively low and manpower readily available through oppressive coercion, that any country could afford, or was able, to maintain such a vast number of ships at sea. With the escalating costs of warships, particularly in today's technological age, no nation could now do this with such effectiveness.

The purpose of a blockade was to deny an enemy the use of the sea at all, by maintaining at least one squadron of observation off every major port, with a fleet in the offing capable of concentrating on any point on the enemy coasts where a major exit of men-of-war might be possible or which merchant ships might use. The most significant French arsenal was Brest, whence a fleet might escape, as it had done in 1779. With the prevailing wind behind it, such a force could swiftly dominate the English Channel and such local superiority might cover an invasion, or a descent upon any one of the several ports, both commercial and naval, that existed along England's south coast.

Other major French ports were watched; L'Orient and Rochefort on the west coast, for instance, and Toulon in the Mediterranean, while similar measures were taken against Spanish ports such as Cartagena, El Ferrol and Cadiz as and when required. It was also necessary to deny the enemy the benefits of a coastal trade and to prohibit movements along the enemy's shoreline. Thus, while frigates might be stationed off the Black Rocks watching shipping in Brest Road, the Channel Fleet would be cruising out in the Atlantic, to the west of Ushant, kept in touch by a line of frigates or smaller cruisers. Even in bad weather, when driven into Tor Bay, the Channel Fleet might be off Ushant very quickly, and while early commanders such as Howe and Hood were content with the distant blockade, Sir William Cornwallis, known as 'Billy Blue' to his men, perfected the close blockade. He rotated his ships on station and supplied his fleet at sea with wood, water, fresh vegetables and livestock by means of small hoys.

While the major part of the British fleet was disposed against Brest, large squadrons operated elsewhere and the coastal trade was interdicted by lesser vessels like the *Admiral Mitchell*. The anti-invasion flotilla, which was briefly under Nelson in 1801, watched the ports of Calais and Boulogne, but the Schelde, the Elbe and the approaches to the Baltic were also kept under view, many with small, shallow-draught gun-brigs, schooners and cutters. These often lonely and exposed posts were sometimes under captains acting as commodores or senior officers, but were more commonly commanded by masters-and-commanders and lieutenants-in-command, men whose prospects were poor but whose skill enabled their little ships to keep the sea in all weathers. It was this blockade-duty that caused the majority of losses of British warships to be largely sloops and gun-brigs, caught on the lee shores of France and her allies and subjects.

To exert influence elsewhere, as well as protect local trade carried in British merchantmen, the Royal Navy maintained its foreign stations and dockyards. At Halifax in Nova Scotia, in Bermuda, Antigua, Port Royal and Jamaica, dockyard facilities were maintained, as they were in Gibraltar and Malta (from 1800), Bombay and Madras. As circumstances altered, a presence was also maintained at Curacao (1807), Martinique (1794–1802), Cape Town (1795–1801 and from 1806), Minorca (1799–1801) and Lisbon (1796–1799 and 1808–1814). Even Napoleon's birthplace of Ajaccio on the island of Corsica was briefly a British naval base between 1794 and 1796.

In the spring of 1795 the Royal Navy of Great Britain had five fleets on foreign service at sea on active duty. The East India squadron consisted of five ships of the line, five frigates and two smaller cruisers. Two fleets were in the West Indies, that at the Leeward Islands was commanded by the area commander-in-chief with a subordinate admiral and comprised eight ships of the line, ten frigates and ten smaller cruisers. The second squadron under a second subordinate admiral based at Jamaica, consisted of three ships of the line, nine frigates and seven sloops or smaller cruisers.

Further north, at Halifax in Nova Scotia, a junior admiral commanded a squadron of three ships of the line, six frigates and two sloops and a subsidiary Newfoundland squadron, under a senior captain or commodore, consisted of two sloops. Across the Atlantic, the Mediterranean fleet was under a commander-in-chief with four subordinate flag-officers who commanded a total of sixteen ships of the line, eleven frigates and four or five sloops and lesser cruisers.

In addition to these ships, half a dozen sloops were deployed on special services, usually patrolling cruises, while three ships of the line, twenty-six frigates and twenty-two lesser sloops and cruisers were occupied solely in the protection of trade and these were augmented abroad by the frigates and cruisers attached to the foreign stations.

But this was not all; in Home Waters the prime fleet – the Channel Fleet – sometimes referred to as the 'Western Squadron' lay off Ushant under Admiral Howe as commander-in-chief and six subordinate flag-officers. It consisted of twenty-six ships of the line, sixteen frigates and three smaller sloops and despatch vessels.

More men-of-war were disposed along the coast, protecting the inshore trade, interdicting smugglers and looking out for enemy cruisers and privateers. At Plymouth two flag-officers commanded seven ships of the line, a frigate and five smaller cruisers. A line-of-battle ship, seven frigates and three sloops were based at Cork on the south coast of Ireland, while a commander-in-chief in a ship of the line, two subordinate admirals in frigates with a further dozen frigates and six sloops formed the anti-invasion flotilla based in The Downs. The Nore, the Thames and the Medway supported a further flag-officer, twelve of the line, thirteen frigates, and thirty-one smaller men-of-war, while the main reserve under the commander-in-chief at Portsmouth consisted of fourteen line-of-battle ships under four subordinate admirals, with fourteen frigates and fifteen lesser cruisers, all either ready for despatch to sea or absent on patrol. There were also eight small cruisers protecting the Channel Islands and Sir Sidney Smith commanded three frigates and twenty-six smaller vessels raiding and patrolling the northern coast of France. Finally, in Spring 1795, two admirals with six ships of the line, two frigates and three sloops were on passage to reinforce either Howe's Western Squadron, or the West Indies fleet.

At the beginning of the Peninsular War which broke out in 1808 and lasted until Napoleon's first abdication in 1814, the picture had changed significantly and is worth the labour of further iteration, for although the number of ships and squadrons had increased, the command structure had simplified.

By the summer of 1808 the East Indies squadron had a commander-in-chief and a subordinate flag-officer (it was to suffer from this double command) and consisted of six of the line, seventeen frigates and nine lesser men-of-war. At the Cape of Good Hope, an admiral commanded four of the line, two frigates and eight small sloops, while across the Atlantic off Brazil another admiral had at his disposal six of the line, three frigates and four smaller cruisers. The Leeward Islands station was commanded by an admiral with five of the line, ten frigates and no less than forty-eight sloops and small cruisers, while his colleague at Jamaica commanded one line-of-battle ship, fifteen frigates and twenty-seven smaller men-of-war. The North American squadron of two ships of the line, nine frigates and twenty smaller cruisers, was based at Halifax under an admiral, whose neighbouring but junior colleague at Newfoundland to the north, commanded four frigates and half a dozen sloops.

To support the main British military campaign in the Iberian peninsula a commander-in-chief with a subordinate admiral commanded a fleet of eleven ships of the line, five frigates and four sloops off the Portuguese coast, protecting the supply lines to Lisbon. Even more influential at this time was the Mediterranean. Britain's second most important fleet was commanded by a commander-in-chief (Lord Collingwood) who, with four subordinate admirals, twenty-nine ships of the line, twenty-six frigates and twenty-nine smaller cruisers maintained British influence there, and gave the sea which broke upon France's southern shore the appearance of a British lake.

By this time, with Russia an ally of the French, an additional fleet was on station in the Baltic under a commander-in-chief (the Guernseyman Sir James Saumarez) who, with two subordinate admirals, enforced the blockade with thirteen line-of-battle ships, four supporting frigates and nine sloops. A further two ships of the line, eight frigates and four cruisers were on independent trade protection.

These constituted the foreign deployments, to which must be added those men-of-war retained in home waters. From Leith on the Firth of Forth, an admiral in a ship of the line with two frigates and a dozen sloops, covered the east coast trade. Seven small cruisers were based on a similar mission on the open roadstead at Great Yarmouth, controlled by semaphore from the Admiralty, as were nine more at Sheerness. Cruising in the North Sea under an admiral were three ships of the line, two frigates and eleven sloops. In The Downs another admiral with five of the line, two frigates and some thirty sloops covered the eastern Channel. An admiral was based ashore in Guernsey, directing three frigates and thirteen smaller cruisers in the protection of the Channel Islands. Another flag-officer was ashore at Cork, with eight frigates and seven sloops, a port-admiral commanded at Plymouth with a dozen small cruisers to protect the Channel trade, another port-admiral was at Portsmouth with two frigates and fourteen small cruisers. Throughout, the most important British fleet remained the Channel squadron which, in the summer of 1808 was commanded by a commander-in-chief with five subordinate admirals. It consisted of eighteen ships of the line, twenty frigates and nineteen smaller cruisers.

It will be seen from these dispositions that the number of frigates and smaller warships had increased, reflecting the greater vulnerability of British trade and the necessity of protecting it. The shifting alliances of the Continental Powers still confronted Britain with the possibility of a combination of fleets and this explains the smaller, but more widely dispersed squadrons of ships of the line, particularly the fleet under Saumarez in the Baltic.

The Russian Tsar, Alexander I, had fallen under the Napoleonic spell at a supposedly highly confidential meeting between the two men on a raft in the middle of the River Niemen at Tilsit in 1807. Among the secret clauses agreed was the seizure of the Danish fleet to be combined with that of Russia and France. The British got wind of this and sent an expedition to destroy the Danish fleet in the dockyard of Copenhagen. They also seized the Danish island of Anholt which commanded the Skagerrak and held it for the rest of the war. By such decisive blows and the main-tenance of blockading squadrons, the possibility of serious combinations were neutralised.

Thus in 1808, the whole Royal Navy comprised over 600 ships in commission. Yet there were still 53 ships fitted out for harbour duty, with a further 167 laid up 'in ordinary', that is 'ready for sea' service at short notice. A further 111 were under construction, including 14 of the line. Some 99,000 seamen and 32,000 marines manned this impressive naval armament which cost the exchequer just under 20 million sterling.

It might be supposed that with all this naval power, even with the vacillating loyalties of the Tsar of Russia, the Emperor of Austria or the King of Prussia, the British Admiralty had the enemy in check. Not so; in the days of wind-driven ships nothing could be relied upon, except eternal vigilance. This was best appreciated by the American naval historian, Captain Alfred Mahan who recognised the contribution to history made by, in a famous and oft quoted sentence, 'those storm-battered ships upon which the *Grande Armée* never looked but which stood between it and the mastery of the world'.

The squadrons of storm-battered ships blockading the Atlantic coasts of France, usually had the west wind at their backs. Although casting them upon a lee shore, their presence mewed up the French and made escape from Brest, L'Orient and Rochefort difficult. But the prevailing gales might be so violent as to compel the British fleet to seek shelter in Tor Bay. By the time the wind moderated and before the main force could resume station, there was the danger that the French could slip out, brushing aside the handful of small cruisers which were always left on the doorstep, to escape into the wide Atlantic. Some British admirals closed the blockade by stationing an inshore squadron of 74-gun Third Rates where they could hamper an escaping French vessel and inflict damage, while falling back on the main force and despatching news of the enemy's attempt to break out.

Despite such measures, French ships did break through the blockade; not in large numbers and usually not of much force, but light easterly winds combined with fog and a selection of inshore passages, particularly from Brest, enabled frigates to slip away, to reach the South Atlantic and the Indian Ocean where they could pursue the *guerre de course* on their own terms.

The French, with a long history of commerce raiding and a tradition of *panache* and *élan* attaching to this mode of warfare, developed the frigate for precisely this form of attacking their traditional enemy, the English, or more accurately in this case, the British. Long range, a turn of speed and a comparatively large crew were all factors incorporated in the concept. French 'national', that is naval, frigates were active throughout the period, to be joined later by their famous American counterparts, but so too were their privateers, many of which were much smaller vessels, such as luggers or *chasse marées*. Generally these corsairs operated from small commercial ports which, while under the general surveillance of the Royal Navy's Channel patrols, were not subject to the close blockade of the major naval arsenals and were thus less confined.

But these efforts, for all their spirit and dash, were in the long run unable to make sufficient inroads on British trade. Although Napoleon's 'Continental System' officially closed all European and Russian ports to British goods, it was largely ineffective. Sweden always ignored it, Russia periodically abandoned it, as did Portugal and Spain after 1808, and Napoleon was forced to depose his own brother Louis from the Dutch throne for breaching the rules. Europe, especially a Europe dominated by French fashion, was hungry for luxury goods as well as the necessary staples 'civilised society' was beginning to consider indispensable, and which only the mercantile British could supply. As a consequence British trade ironically doubled between the outbreak of the French Revolutionary War in 1793 and the fall of Napoleon in 1815, and customs duties tripled, notwithstanding the illegal fraternisation due to the so-called 'free-trade'. Smuggling was carried out by nationals of both sides in relative amity and while the import of duty-free luxuries to Britain was actively opposed by the revenue officers, the export of goods and manufactures from Britain was as actively condoned and encouraged.

When, as part of the seizure of Danish assets, a British squadron took the then Danish island of Helgoland in 1807, this insignificant post at the mouth of the Elbe became the site of numerous warehouses owned by British merchants intent on evading Napoleon's proscriptions on trade, hence the Emperor's famous remark about the English being a nation of shop-keepers!

The responsibilities of the British Admiralty and its associated offices did not end with the maintenance of the squadrons outlined above. In order to support the 'conjoint operations' conducted with varying degrees of success in several theatres, and especially the complex logistics organisation that supported the British Army in the Iberian peninsula between 1808 and 1814, the Transport Board was responsible for mustering considerable shipping. The most remarkable achievement of the Transport Board, under the command of James Bowen whom we last met in Chapter Seven asking Lord Howe for a lieutenant's commission on 1 June 1794, was the embarkation of Sir John Moore's expeditionary force from La Coruña in January 1809. At this time the Transport Board was responsible for providing 18,000 tons of horse transport, with ships specially fitted out for taking cavalry remounts to Spain, 77,400 tons of vessels capable of acting as troopships as well as victualling vessels to serve both the army, (some 4000 tons) and the blockading squadrons (16,500 tons). With the standard size of a 'transport', the generic naval term for a chartered merchantman, at about 300 tons, some idea of the magnitude of the task may be grasped. Over 300 transports were occupied ferrying troops and supplies to Portugal and Spain, plus another 120 operating to and from Gibraltar, with yet others supporting the West Indies, Halifax, Brazil, South Africa, the Baltic and the 'listening post' at Helgoland which, in addition to being used for trade, was a staging post for spies.

By means of this flyspeck island, one of several maintained by Britain off the enemy's coast, one of the boldest examples of arrant sea-power was accomplished. After Napoleon had deposed King Ferdinand of Spain and installed his elder brother Joseph in his stead, Spanish forces were subsumed into the *Grande Armée*. A force under the Marquis de la Romana was sent to garrison southern Denmark where, when the Spanish revolted against King Joseph's rule, it found itself marooned. The British sent an agent through Helgoland to contact Romana, and despatched a squadron under Rear-Admiral Sir Richard Goodwin Keats to wait off the coast. The agent, a Catholic priest named Robertson, disguised as a cigar and chocolate vendor, arranged a rendezvous and Keats withdrew most of Romana's men who were transported home to Spain to fight the national enemy.

Refinements to the line-of-battle ships which constituted the British fleet have been outlined earlier, but these were minor, and the only warship type to alter significantly during the long struggle with France and her allies between 1793 and 1815 was the frigate. The British navy never managed to have enough of them and their shortcomings were cruelly exposed when in action with the large new frigates sent out by the United States government in 1812.

The rationale behind the design of the American frigates was bold and simple. They were built expressly to 'possess in an eminent degree the advantage of sailing, that separately they would be superior to any European frigate of the usual dimensions . . . that they could never be obliged to go into action but on their own terms'. They carried thirty long 24-pounders on their gundeck with a dozen 32-pounder carronades on their upper deck and their hulls below the main gundeck level had the scantlings of a British Third Rate. Despite this their numbers were too few to achieve much, and their psychological impact was out of all proportion to the real damage they did to British sea-power. Had they not engaged the British cruisers at all, and thus dealt such a blow to the Royal Navy's self-esteem, thereby inviting retribution, they might have achieved more by acting solely as long-range commerce raiders. In the event they stimulated concern in augmenting the power of British frigates.

Not all the expedients the British were driven to in satisfying the demand for more and larger frigates were successful. Frigates built of the readily available pine and fir were notorious for the splinters caused when pine was hit by round shot, and, like all soft-wood hulls, were subject to waterlogging rot. The Parsee yards of Bombay produced some durable cruisers, one of which, HMS *Trincomalee* built in 1816, survives to this day. In general the trend for frigates to become longer on the gundeck enabled batteries of heavier cannon to be carried. Larger hulls supported a proportionately larger sail plan, and the longer waterline length produced small increases in speed, but nothing dramatic.

Nevertheless, even as small steam-powered vessels were making a tentative appearance at sea, there were alterations in the hull form of warships which, in retrospect, seem to have been wasteful, especially in terms of timber. The quest for ever larger ships, particularly of line-of-battle ships, was exacerbated by the growing shortage of timber. Both long lengths of hardwood and the 'compass timber' required for naturally curved frames, posed a critical problem for the British Admiralty. This was largely solved through the efforts of Sir Robert Seppings.

In 1811 Seppings was subordinate to the Surveyor to the Navy, Sir William Rule, but supervised the experimental construction of the new 74-gun Third Rate *Tremendous*. He fitted additional frames running diagonally between the usual ribs and deck beams. The whole structure of the hull was thus made more rigid, it worked less and therefore admitted less water, while the inside of the hull was kept drier and consequently lasted longer. Seppings succeeded Rule in 1813 and his new system became standard thereafter. Seppings' method no longer limited the size of a wooden hull and in due course proved strong enough to accept the installation of steam engines and the shaft of a propeller. Early Seppings ships were heavy and gained a reputation for poor sailing qualities, but as size increased, up to gundeck lengths of 250 feet (76 metres) by the 1850s, the larger hulls compensated for the increase of weight.

Seppings was the Royal Navy's last Master Shipwright to be Surveyor of the Navy. After a general overhaul of naval administration in which the old Navy Board was abolished, the post was taken up by a naval officer, William Symonds, who was an amateur ship designer. Concerned with lack of speed, Symonds refined the entrance of the hull and a steep rise of floor, giving a deeper 'vee' section to a man-of-war. Although this enabled a large line-of-battle ship to make around 13 knots, Symonds' ships gave a pronounced leeward lurch, were lively and proved poor gun-platforms. The introduction of iron hulls and steam propulsion swept the problem aside, a fact which also eclipsed Symonds' other achievement, the round bow and stern which not only increased the strength of these areas and rendered them less vulnerable to raking fire, but enabled cannon to be permanently mounted to improve both bow and stern-chase arcs of fire.

This was an extension of Seppings' curious 'lighthouse stern', designed to improve the field of fire of chase guns across the stern and to deter raking. One of the first ships to be so fitted, HMS *Unicorn* of 1824, now preserved at Dundee, makes an interesting contrast with *Trincomalee*. Both frigates were nominally sister-ships of the same, numerous *Leda* class designed in 1794, based on the French frigate *Hebe*, captured in 1782. At the time of the introduction of the 'lighthouse stern', the invasion of the captain's quarters by additional guns was not popular with commanding officers, particularly as they had just persuaded designers to rehabilitate the open stern walks abolished a generation earlier!

Unicorn also bears witness to the expedient resorted to in finding a way round the shortage of naturally bent wood. Iron knees and braces, the first hint of the composite hull to be used briefly in the construction of tea clippers and small warships later in the century, were used throughout her hull and have proved astonishingly durable.

Most men-of-war retained the conventional ship-rigged sail plan with topgallants above topsails. Royals, run up from the deck, were increasingly popular in frigates and sloops. Fore and main masts set studding sails, but it was the adoption of staysails between the masts from about the mid eighteenth century, augmenting the fore and aft sails set between bowsprit and foremast, that began to sharpen the interest of naval officers in sailing performance. In his *Treatise on Practical Seamanship* of 1777, William Hutchinson compares the virtues of lying-to in heavy weather under shortened down square sails, with using only reduced fore and aft sails.

Reorganisation of the rating system was also undertaken after the peace. In 1816 First Rates still bore 100 or more guns, but Second Rates now included 80 or more gun ships, while the Third Rate commenced at 70 guns. The Fourth Rate weighed in at 50 guns, the fifth at 36, the sixth at 24. Innovations in gunnery were largely developments of the slide-mounted carronades and guns up to 32-pounders could be mounted on slide carriages which traversed over a wide arc. As can be seen by any visitor to

HMS *Warrior* in Portsmouth, such a traverse occupied a vast deal of deck space and while it might make more scientific the laying and pointing of an individual gun, the loss of mass, that 'weight of metal' inherent in a single, concussive broadside, might have proved a drawback had a major fleet action ever had to be fought by ships so armed. In the event it was not necessary; like the sailing warship, the smooth-bore gun which had changed little since its inception, was to become obsolete well before the end of the nineteenth century.

One important element of the sea-power wielded by Great Britain at this time, both in terms of men-of-war and merchantmen, lay not in the great ships of the line, nor in their dashing consorts, the frigates. For many of those ships, which Napoleon complained the British had everywhere it was possible to float a hull, were unrated cruisers, and much of her wealth was sustained not by the majestic Indiamen, but humbler 'bottoms' whose moments of glory rested upon the few, which were taken up from their trades and sent on voyages of exploration.

As the design of contending men-of-war converged, producing a broadly similar type as the most successful for each type of warship, and as the larger ocean-going merchantmen, although developing with recognisably national characteristics, were nevertheless identifiable for their role by a commonality of appearance, quite the reverse occurred to the smaller seagoing and coastal ship, whether she be cruiser or coaster.

In the pre-railway days of poor roads and a canal system that could not cope with the expansion of trade, notwithstanding Napoleon's theoretical 'closure' of the continent of Europe to British trade, the carriage of cargoes by sea was very important. The multitude of small brigs, barks and cats which hauled cargoes coastwise during the last decade of the eighteenth century to the final defeat of France in 1815, can no longer be enumerated. Impressive though their numbers must have been, their largely mundane, often unexciting existences, have been rendered down by historians into tables of economic data. Transport, by its very transitory nature, and perhaps by its very commonplace appearance in the daily life of the times, is an easy thing to forget. It is always Derby winners, not workhorses, which are remembered.

Coastal trade bore commodities like the 'sea cole', which warmed the gentry in London, south to the capital from its point of production in the north of England. Traders also took imported goods to smaller ports from the great entrepôt of London. Among cargoes exported to Europe both to Britain's allies and in defiance of the Continental System, were the finished goods for which Britain was already acquiring a formidable reputation as the manufacturing processes gained momentum after the Industrial Revolution. It is said that Napoleon's *Grande Armée* marched to Moscow on boots made in Northampton; true or not, a vigorous clandestine trade was carried out through Helgoland and adjacent Hamburg. Not least, among a huge list of commodities coming into Britain from abroad and which included sugar, spices and slaves, were the Scandinavian 'naval stores' necessary to maintain the British fleet. These consisted of Scandinavian mast-timber, but also what was known as 'Dantzig' oak, pitch, tar, rosin, turpentine, tallow, hemp and sail cloth, much of which came from Russia. As we have seen earlier in the chapter, protection of this vast range of goods and the shipping bearing it, received the protection of convoy.

In 1809, when Napoleon was at the height of his power, the British Royal Navy had 709 vessels in commission and fit for sea service. Two dozen were troop, store ships and auxiliaries, and there were 113 of the line, then rated from 60- to 120-gun ships (of which latter there were two). Of the 684 cruisers, the most numerous class were the seventy-six 12-gun gun-brigs, followed by the larger and more seaworthy sixty-nine 18-gun brig-sloops, fifty 18-gun ship-sloops, forty-seven 16-gun brig-sloops, and thirty-three 10-gun brig-sloops. The largest class of frigate proper, of which there were forty-four, were the 38-gun frigates bearing a main armament of 18-pounder guns. When due consideration is given to other facts, such as that there were also sixty-three cutters, carrying from 4 to 14 guns, the importance of small cruisers begins to emerge.

The increased requirement for small cruisers and the difficulties beginning to be experienced in acquiring sufficient supplies of timber, prompted the Surveyor's office to reconsider the method of building small warships which had hitherto been a scaled down version of frigates. The *Cruizer* and *Cherokee* classes of brig-sloop, besides being the most numerous, introduced the flush-decked hull (though some had light raised upper poops and 'topgallant' forecastles). They also adopted the raked keel found in cutters with the deeper 'vee' hull which Symonds later introduced to ships of the line with the problems and resulting unpopularity of which we have already remarked.

The Royal Navy did not find experimentation entirely inimical. About 1773 a master's mate named John Schank had observed the encased, drop keel being used in American colonial boats which lowered through a slot in the keel proper. At Boston the following year he had a boat built incorporating this idea which improved windward performance and was useful in shallow water. It was not new but its significance, as a 'local' development suiting local conditions, was typical of some ideas which had to be, as it were, 'rediscovered' for formal incorporation into Western naval architecture. By 1791, Schank was a post-captain and his submission to the Admiralty resulted in the cutter *Trial* being fitted with three drop keels. Such was her success that she was used on inshore patrols along the Channel coast of northern France. Four years later, in 1795, the 16-gun ship-rigged sloop *Cynthia* was built on the Thames at Rotherhithe and fitted with three of Schank's keels, while in 1799, Schank built the brig *Lady Nelson* with sliding keels and she was sent in support of Matthew Flinders on his surveying voyage of Australia in 1802. Schank's drop keels were incorporated in Samuel Bentham's two 'sloops', *Dart* and *Arrow* of 1795. Bentham, the brother of the political philosopher was to become Inspector General of naval works in March 1796.

Of a highly innovative turn of mind, his two highly unconventional experimental vessels are of considerable interest. Although ship-rigged, almost everything else about *Dart* and *Arrow* was unusual and their classification as sloops was a mere convenience. Round of bilge, with what we should today call a cruiser stern and a bow of hollow entry, their main decks were flat, with no sheer and they had a short, raised quarterdeck and forecastle. Their beam increased above the waterline which was intended to make them stiffer and resist heel, and because of this their framework curved less than was customary. Their armament was twenty-four 32-pounder carronades on the main deck with two more later added on the quarterdeck and two on the poop. All these were of a lightweight, 1.25-ton design by Sadler, mounted on recoilless slides. The two ships were found to be fast, but slow in stays, so some additional timber was added to their keels.

Arrow's fate illuminates something of the history of smaller cruisers. Employed as an escort in February 1805, she had in company the bomb vessel *Acheron* and both of these ships were protecting a convoy of thirty-five merchantmen off Cape Caxine, North Africa. The convoy was bound from Malta to London when two sails were sighted and *Acheron* signalled they were enemy frigates. Richard Budd Vincent, commanding Arrow, cast off the merchant brig he was towing, ordered the 'warlike-looking transport' *Duchess of Rutland* to lead the convoy, then placed his ship alongside *Acheron* between the French National frigates *Hortense* (Capitaine-de-Frégate La Marre-le-Mellerie) and *Incorruptible* (Capitaine-de-Frégate Billiet). The former was of 40, the latter 39-guns and in the light, fluky winds, it was dark before the ships got into action. Just before daylight, *Hortense* shot away some of the *Acheron*'s upper spars, but was raked by *Arrow*, and the ships continued to manoeuvre as the convoy drew slowly away. By about half past seven in the morning, *Incorruptible* drew abeam of Arrow and exchanged broadsides, moving on to the easier *Acheron* while her consort, *Hortense*, came up to engage *Arrow*. In the ensuing *melée*, *Arrow* raked both enemy ships and was herself raked, but the weaker British ships were now pounded by the French. After suffering heavy losses and much damaged, the two British ships struck their colours. They were so disabled that *Arrow* sank almost at once and *Acheron* was considered useless by her captors and set on fire. Attacking the convoy afterwards, the French frigates took only the *Duchess of Rutland* and two other merchant ships. Such self-sacrifice was expected of escort commanders in protection of trade and their surrender would have been accepted as honourable by the court martial.

Bentham's hull form was used in some later schooners and he incorporated watertight bulkheads to replace the plethora of heavy timber frames in some hulls. Another advanced hull design was produced by a Captain Gower of the East India Company. Gower's 'Despatch Vessel' *Transit* of 1809 had a slim hull (130 feet by 22.5 feet), with hollow lines, a sharp deadrise, or 'vee' form, and outward sloping sides similar to Bentham's concept. *Transit* had four masts. The foremost bore yards, the other three had a fore and aft rig spread by horizontal gaffs, a rig which required fewer hands to operate. Warship designers had no such economic imperative as they needed large crews to work the guns. Effectively *Transit* was a barquentine and her line drawing shows a hull with elements of the fast sailing merchantman of a generation later in the century. When unusual tasks occurred, ships were still taken up from trade.

The *Acheron*, lost with the experimental sloop *Arrow*, was one of a number of merchant vessels purchased into naval service. All Cook's ships were so acquired as was the notorious *Bounty*, and it was the exceptionally strong build of many small merchant ships that so well fitted them for long, dangerous voyages. This strength recommended them for purchase and conversions to bomb vessels, but in 1812, the Admiralty built the *Vesuvius* and *Hecla* classes, three of which were destined to perish in the Arctic – the *Fury* in 1825, the *Erebus* and *Terror* in 1848. Several of these sturdy little ships were converted for exploration or surveying at the end of the Napoleonic War. *Erebus* and *Terror* were ingeniously fitted out for Sir John Franklin's doomed quest for the North West Passage. Reduced from ship to barque rig to conserve crew size, they had 25 horsepower steam engines fitted. These had been bought from the London and Greenwich Railway as 15-ton locomotives from which the front wheels were removed before lowering them into the hold, onto the cross-timbers of the former main mortar bed. A 32-feet shaft drove a screw which, being highly vulnerable in ice, could be lifted into a well and the gap filled with chocks to avoid it becoming clogged with floes.

Erebus and *Terror* were also fitted with a desalinating plant which heated food while distilling water. This fresh water was stored in iron tanks and the ships had a heating system to improve the lot of those on board. Despite the capacity required to contain all this additional plant in a hull only 105 feet in length and of 29 in depth, *Erebus* and *Terror* held stores for three years, including 1.75 tons of tobacco and almost 2000 gallons of liquor, as well as the scientific apparatus necessary for the study of magnetism, geology, astronomy, zoology and botany. They also carried preserved stores in the fatal lead-soldered tins which had come into service use at the end of the Napoleonic War. Such outfitting, seen in context with the other surveying vessels commissioned in this period, bespeak the commitment of the British to exploration and hydrography. The fate of Franklin, a *cause célèbre* of its day, tragic as it was, acted as a spur to a dogged people. Franklin's widow personally sponsored four Arctic expeditions in search of her missing husband after the official searches had been abandoned and several intrepid Victorian yachtsmen made their own voyages into the Arctic Ocean, beginning a tradition of cruising in small boats which extends to our own day.

The fine-lined hulls of Bentham and Gower, before their time though they were, were not original and it is significant that neither man was a dyed-in-the-wool naval officer. Experimental enthusiasts like Schank or Symonds (who started designing as a lieutenant) were rare in the ranks of the Georgian navy. Ideas migrate and move with such speed that it is almost in vain that reviewers of history seek to pin down the person responsible, or isolate something as 'the first' of its kind. Something seen may influence subconsciously as well as through calculation, and it is now accepted that concepts may flourish within the spirit of an age and flower simultaneously in different parts of the world.

Nevertheless the fast hull that was to transform the merchant ship in the nineteenth century, seems to have emanated, if not exactly originated, from North America. Slaving and privateering were potent impulses in the search for speed and the ready supply of forest timber combined with an active, opportunist culture, encouraged individual development.

The hollow lined hull evolved gradually, and is usually associated with the schooner rig which is essentially an American rig whose origins are complex, difficult to define and as much part of the history of boats as of ships. Two-masted sailing vessels had been in existence long before the reputed chance remark at the launch of a New England two-master in 1713 coined the name 'schooner'. The Dutch had developed the form with leg-of-mutton sails in the sixteenth century and two- and three-masted fore and aft rigged vessels hoisted sprit and lug sails in Europe long before anyone thought of calling them schooners. Whereas in general American schooners dispensed with yards after about 1825, British and French schooners retained them to the end; moreover the schooner rig became a popular yacht rig in America, while in Europe, with a prevailing wind system that seemed to perennially require windward work, it was less favoured, the cutter being the more efficient windward performer until the masthead sloop dished her more elegant predecessor. The working schooner was to reach her peak in the Grand Banks fisherman of the early twentieth century, and it was to be from her New England home port of Marblehead in Massachussets that some of the first fishing schooners had come.

The schooner rig was already popular among slavers and the general West Indies trade of the eighteenth century with the American colonies. Speed preserved perishable cargoes, so the rig was ideal for the rapidly expanding fishing being carried out from the shores of New England in the early eighteenth century. There were over one hundred 50-tonners fishing from Marblehead in 1721 and by mid century this had almost doubled. Able to bear a small defensive battery of cannon, which many carried even as fishing vessels for defence against French cruisers and corsairs during the Seven Years War, it was their speed that attracted attention and was reported by British naval officers. The first schooner in the Royal Navy is believed to have been a 130-ton, Virginia-built vessel named *Barbadoes*. She was bought at Antigua in 1757, but details about her are hazy. More certain is the purchase of six Marblehead schooners to protect the New England fisheries. Eventually fifteen of them were taken into the Royal Navy, one by Commodore Palliser in 1764, six by Lord Colvill in the same year and a further eight in the period up to the outbreak of the American War. One of Colvill's purchases was the unfortunate *Gaspée* which was put into the colonial revenue service. Her burning by American 'Whigs' was but one step on the colonists' road to revolt. Two copies of the original batch, the *Earl of Egmont* and *Sir Edward Hawke*, are believed to have been laid down at New York about 1767, but their fate is not clearly known.

It was not only the Royal Navy that admired the speed of these schooners. During the Seven Years War the French acquired a few 'Marbleheaders' for their own use and sent them among their own kind as privateers. Seen afloat, such schooners appeared unremarkable, but the secret of their performance lay in their under-water lines. With a significant, though not extreme rise of floor, the lines at bow and stern were concave, allowing the hull to move easily through the water when driven by an ample sail plan. They bore square topsails on both masts as well as their large gaff sails and jibs. Individual developers of the schooner rig were not interested in conforming to any system of classification and the combinations of square yards, and the ward-robes of light weather sails carried by enterprising commanders, make rationalisation impossible. Requiring fewer men than a square-rigged brig or ship-sloop, the British Admiralty built several classes including the 'Fish' and 'Bird' types, although they tended to favour the native English cutter rig for the smallest class of cruiser.

It need detain us no more than to make a passing mention of the French equivalent, the splendid *chasse marée* lugger which, multi-masted and fore and aft rigged, avoided straying into the schooner camp. Whether used as a naval vessel, smuggler or privateer, the lugger was a large (often very large) boat, rather than a ship, much like its arch-rival the English man-of-war cutter. Both bore extravagant sail plans and were often replete with men and small cannon, and both sought to out-do each other in the bloody skirmishes which characterised warfare in the English Channel during the late eighteenth century. But neither ultimately contributed much to the development of the ship. With the schooner proper, however, it was quite otherwise.

Areas in North America other than New England had produced significant schooners by the end of the eighteenth century. The pilot schooners of Virginia were never more than boats, but the larger vessels produced on Chesapeake Bay were of a different mettle and were precursors of the apogee of the sailing ship.

One such was the American *Nonpareil*, built in 1801. She was seized by the British at the capture of Montevideo, condemned by a prize court as a blockade runner and taken into the Royal Navy in 1808. Her length was 89.5 feet, with a beam of 23 feet. Just as the Grand Banks schooners were known as Marbleheaders, *Nonpareil* and her sisters were generically known as Baltimore 'clippers', a name which was to alter in meaning as radically as the ships so described.

CHAPTER NINE

Science, Steam and Screw Propulsion

The century following the defeat of Napoleon witnessed the flowering of the steam age at sea, as well as a revolution in sea warfare. The technology which had begun to remove much of his toil from the agricultural labourer was also to dispossess the seaman of some of his traditional skills as power finally ousted sail. But this process took place gradually, allowing steam and sail to co-exist until the frenetic acceleration of war finally overwhelmed the sailing ship as a viable carrier of the world's goods.

It was the quest for fast predictable schedules and for timed delivery to the point of distribution or sale that ensured the demise of the sailing ship. The quest for speed was not new. Revenue cutters had long pursued smuggling luggers, frigates had 'chaced' enemy blockade runners, and fast passenger services, such as that of the Leith 'smacks' which ran from London to Edinburgh, had driven men to develop speed under sail. But the unavoidable vagaries of the wind itself always forced a concession to the unpredictable, and what appealed to the imagination of the entrepreneur, was the potential of steam to defy nature.

Tentatively, and with mounting success, the steamship took over the delivery of manufactured goods to the burgeoning markets of the world, bringing back to the growing manufacturing industrial bases of Europe and America the raw materials which provided the means of production as well as the luxuries demanded by the new wealthy. Steamships also started to carry troops, mails and passengers, forging the links of the empire, leaving to sailing ships those high bulk, low value trades where either the wind served or speed did not matter.

The belief that there was competition between steam and sail is a myth; the truth is that the transition was not a clean break of the future from the past. Steam was initially incapable of taking over from sail, and as the marine steam engine improved, it left room for sail not only to thrive, but to reach its zenith in the tea, wool and passenger clippers of the nineteenth century, and decline, still useful and still being improved well into the twentieth.

The development of mechanically-driven ships suffered from serious, periodic set-backs. The low power of early engines and the weaknesses of boiler design proved to be hurdles that could not not be speedily overcome; the need for vast stocks of coal on board, reduced the space available for revenue-earning cargo, while contrariwise, the solution of the British in stockpiling fuel at world-wide coaling stations tended to inhibit experimental innovation. There is an historic irony in the coincidence occurring in 1866 when, at the height of their development, the tea clippers *Ariel* and *Taeping* entered the English Channel neck and neck to make a spectacular end to their race from China. In the same year, the steamship *Agamemnon*, first of three vessels owned by an obscure but innovative engineer from Liverpool named Holt, steamed the other way. Three years later Ferdinand de Lesseps' canal cut the isthmus of Suez and thereby reduced the route between Europe and the Far East by 3000 miles.

Alfred Holt's high-pressure boiler and compound double expansion engine, installed in the *Agamemnon* and her sister-ships *Ajax* and *Achilles*, produced steamships that were truly viable alternatives to sailing vessels on ocean trade routes. From this point, shipowners could exploit the economies of scale they had spent half a century searching for. If there is any real comparison to be made in this early period of change, it is not between steam and sail, it is between the pragmatically conceived merchant ship and the mighty influential man-of-war, the cost of which was not normally considered. Both began with the steam-powered paddle wheel. This proved a dead end, useful only in limited applications, though it was to dominate the nascent steamship. The drawbacks inherent in paddle design called first for an alternative to be harnessed to the simple engines of the day. Then, with the acceptance of the screw propeller, the problem of engine efficiency and fuel had to be addressed. Crew expenses rose with the employment of engineers, greasers, trimmers and firemen (or stokers as they were called in the navy) in addition to the traditional true 'seamen' necessary to handle the sails to which these primitive engines were really only auxiliaries.

The Royal Navy had no shareholders to answer to, nor did it have manpower problems and, as we shall see, it engined its fleet of wooden, broadside firing line-of-battle ships so that, prior to the Crimean War, Prince Albert, the Prince Consort, could write enthusiastically of the whole Channel Fleet steaming into the wind at 11 knots with sails furled. But even the British navy proceeded with caution; the first steamers appeared on rivers, lakes and canals, where coal stocks were accessible, and breakdown was not a disaster.

Paddle steamers began to appear in the early years of the nineteenth century on the Clyde in Scotland, the Thames in England, the Hudson in the United States, the Elbe and Rhine in Germany and the Neva in Russia. They bore passengers upon the lakes of Europe and even the Brahmaputra in India. Most had engines of British design and manufacture.

The potential of the paddle had long been known. It was no more than an extension of the treadwheel, and cranes driven by such mechanisms were familiar in dockyards. The Romans and the Chinese had independently conceived slave-powered paddles, but human potential was clearly limited and it was the possibility of harnessing steam to drive a paddle that had first attracted the attention of a French physician, Denis Papin, whose atmospheric engine was later developed by Newcomen, Savery and Watt into a reciprocating engine with steam being admitted to both sides of the cylinder by way of a slide valve, giving thrust to both strokes.

It was another Frenchman, the Marquis de Jouffroy d'Abbans, who persisted in experimenting, and on 15 July 1783 his steamer the *Pyroscaphe* steamed against the flow of the River Saône for a full quarter of an hour. Similar early paddle-boats tried their luck on the Delaware, Potomac and Passaic in the United States and on Dalswinton Loch in Scotland. They achieved modest speeds of 3 to 5 miles per hour and one carried a 'cargo' of 2 tons. But it was not until 1801 that the first working paddle steamer was built under the patronage of Lord Dundas. She was fitted with engines by William Symington who, together with Patrick Miller, had already built several steam boats. The *Charlotte Dundas* had a wooden hull 50 feet in length driven by a single paddle wheel recessed in the stern. Symington's single horizontal cylinder of 22 inches in diameter bore had a piston stroke of 48 inches. The power it generated was rated as the equivalent of ten horses. In March 1802, the *Charlotte Dundas* towed two barges, each laden with 70 tons, along 19.5 miles of the Forth and Clyde Canal. A strong wind headed the little ship and she chugged away for six hours to achieve this modest passage. Sadly, anxiety about the effect of her wash upon the canal banks resulted in her being laid up to rot, her engine builder a disappointed man.

The following year, a restless and inventive American named Robert Fulton who had witnessed the *Charlotte Dundas* under weigh, carried out a successful steam boat trial on the Seine. Despite the short-lived career of the *Charlotte Dundas*, it was from this time that steamers played an increasing part in inland and sheltered navigation. Having been frustrated in Europe (his design for a submarine had been turned down by both Napoleon and the British Admiralty) Fulton transferred his enterprise back home. He formed a partnership with one Robert Livingstone, who had farsightedly acquired the exclusive right of steam navigation on the Hudson and eventually their twenty-one steamers thrashed up and down past the New Jersey Palisades. An attempt to break the partners's strangle-hold on this growing trade was made by John Stevens, but his steamer, the *Phoenix*, was driven off the Hudson and in 1809 coasted down to the Delaware, thereby making the first offshore, short-sea passage by a steam vessel.

Appropriately, it was 1815, the year when Napoleon was finally routed and sent to his final exile on the remote island of St Helena, when a steamship made what may justifiably be claimed as the first true seagoing voyage under steam power. Soon to be a world centre of marine engineering, it was the banks of the Scottish River Clyde from which the *Duke of Argyle* was launched in 1814. Shortly after her completion, she was sold to London owners who renamed her *Thames* and ordered her south. She set out by way of Dublin, along the wild Pembroke-shire coast, St Ives, Plymouth and Portsmouth, steaming 758 miles at a creditable average of 6.2 knots. On her arrival in the London River, she was put into service between the capital and Margate.

Thereafter steamers proliferated in coastal trades and numerous smart packet services were inaugurated. By the accession of George IV, there were regular sailings across the Irish Sea and the English Channel, and British influence in Sweden led to the establishment of a Stockholm to Türku service across the Baltic. In 1818 the aptly named *Ferdinando Primo* became the first steamship to enter service in the Mediterranean, powered by a British engine.

Despite this progress in Europe, more than one hundred steamers were operating in the United States, twice as many as could be boasted of in the entire British Empire! The growing population of the United States of America was moving inexorably westwards. The great rivers, the seemingly inexhaustible source of firewood, the energy and ambition of the American people, their inventiveness, resource and new-found wealth, acted as great incentives to the impetus of change. Where Fulton, Livingstone and Stevens led, others swiftly followed.

Steamers went into service on the Mississippi-Missouri (where the novelist Mark Twain was first a pilot); they appeared on Long Island Sound, on the Potomac and Lake Champlain; they ran up the coast to New Brunswick in Canada, restless products of a restless age. Nothing, it seemed could stop them, despite the poor design of their boilers and the frequency of devastating explosions. Between 1816 and 1848 there were 233 horrific accidents, but the risk was considered acceptable, for these waters were ideal for paddlers and the demand for cheap transport was high. Such vessels, particularly the famous Mississippi stern-wheeler, dominated United States inland navigation for a century, to become enshrined in the legend of the American West.

From a seaman's viewpoint and after some early problems of control, the paddle steamer proved easy to manoeuvre through the medium of the mechanical telegraph by which engine commands were transmitted to the engine room by the operation of chain-linked levers and indicators. True, the increasingly sophisticated design with its box and sponson set outside the ship's parallel body was liable to damage when coming alongside, but compared with a vessel under sail and at the mercy of the wind, most crucial when manoeuvring in port or on a coast, the paddle steamer was a joy. Although many American paddlers, like the *Charlotte Dundas*, retained the stern wheel to facilitate berthing head on to riverside landings, the conventional twin-wheeled form won early advocates, despite its vulnerability. But the paddle had another disadvantage which soon revealed itself as these steamers ventured out into the open sea.

Without the pressure of wind in her sails, a steamer rolled easily and a rolling ship buried one paddle wheel while exposing the other. Then, if steadying sails were set, the resultant heel still drove one paddle deeper than the other, making the steering of a straight course difficult without a constant angle of counter helm adding drag to the progress of the ship. Moreover, the massive consumption of coal rapidly diminished a vessel's draft and affected the designed depth at which a paddle was at its optimum performance.

There were other more esoteric considerations. Despite the mechanical devices of eccentric trimming rods which feathered the blades, or 'floats' of the paddle, it was important for the hull form to present a flat water surface for the paddle to bite into. As a ship moves through the sea, the bulk of its hull throws a pair of bow waves out from its 'entrance', the curve of the hull from the bow to the parallel body. Behind the secondary wave a flat waterline prevails for a while before the drag of the stern waves build up under the run of the after part of the hull. In order to achieve this theoretical plane surface, fine-lined, slender hulls were necessary, with low block co-efficients, and this further militated against cargo capacity and thus against the ability of a paddle steamer to earn her keep other than by carrying mails and passengers.

Nevertheless, these early steamers were rapidly increasing in size. The first to be registered at Lloyds was the 448-ton *James Watt* of 1821, built by John Wood at Port Glasgow was the largest steamship of its day. Only four years later the 'leviathan' *United Kingdom* measured 1000 tons. Such vessels were also increasing in range and soon making oceanic passages from their British builders to their new owners' areas of operation. Among them were the *Conde de Palmella*, which steamed and sailed from Liverpool to Lisbon in 1820; the *Rising Star* which reached Valparaiso in 1821 and the *Enterprize* which in early December 1825, dropped anchor in Balasore Road, Calcutta, after a 113-day passage, two thirds of which was under power. Sent out under the command of a former naval officer, Captain James Johnson, in an attempt to win a prize of a *lahk* of rupees (about £10,000), she failed to achieve the passage within the limit of seventy days. Indeed her passage was not even an improvement on the average Indiaman's passage of ninety days under sail, but she did succeed in doubling the Cape of Good Hope and proving the feasibility of the voyage.

The *Enterprize* measured some 500 tons and was 141 feet in length. She was built at Deptford by Gordon and Co., with engines by Maudslay, Son and Field, of Lambeth. Her paddles could be ingeniously hoisted inboard when under her three-masted, lug-sail rig. She carried 380 tons of coal which she burned at about 11 tons per day. Most significantly, she was fitted with a corrosion-resitant copper boiler. She served in the Burma War then afterwards as a tug before being sold to Bombay owners who put her into service with another steamer in an attempt to develop the overland route to Bombay via Suez. In 1834 she took the Bishop of Calcutta to the extremities of his diocese at Singapore, but four years later she was condemned for breaking, though her engines were removed into a second ship of the same name. By then steam-powered paddle steamers, tugs, tenders and even dredgers were common on the mighty Hooghly River.

The Royal Navy for its part, sent the steam survey tender *Lightning* on a round voyage to Algiers in 1824, and another to the Russian naval arsenal of Kronstadt in 1826. At the same time, HMS *African* steamed to Sierra Leone and then the Adriatic. But none of these voyages were commercial ventures, carrying cargo; they might almost be described as dilettante expeditions.

It was not that commercial enterprise was lacking. Although James Johnson had been unable to secure financial backing from the General Steam Navigation Company for the *Enterprize*, in 1826 the company made a trial voyage to Lisbon and the next year another to St Petersburg. Both were commercial failures with their costs exceeding their profits. Nor was the vaunted first crossing of the Atlantic by a steamer quite what the hype had promised. Although the American steam vessel *Savannah* made her eastbound passage in the summer of 1819 in twenty-nine days under Captain Moses Rogers, the same man who had taken the *Phoenix* from New York to the Delaware ten years earlier, it was mainly under sail and her bunkers were empty when she arrived in the Mersey.

Then, in 1833, the Canadian-built *Royal William* crossed the Atlantic in nineteen days en route to new owners. This was accomplished mostly under power, and the possibility of regular voyages attracted increasing attention. In 1838 a competition was held between the *Sirius* and the *Great Western*. The latter was a product of the inventive genius of Isambard Kingdom Brunel, who had conceived her as a trans-Atlantic extension of the Great Western Railway, hence her name. She left Bristol after the *Sirius* had steamed out of the Cove of Cork, but completed the passage in fifteen days and five hours, *three days and five hours* less than the *Sirius*, though her rival received line honours at New York. The significance of this event lay in both vessels being under continuous power, and it may be said that they initiated the era of passenger, mail and cargo services across the Western Ocean, founding a new maritime tradition, that of the ocean liner.

Among the 'lines' established at this time was the Peninsular Steam Navigation Company, which secured an early government mail contract in 1837, ousting the naval-run Post Office packets running to Spain, Portugal and Gibraltar. Serving the Iberian peninsula with seven paddle steamers, the company quartered the red and gold of the Spanish royal house of Aragon and Castile, with the blue and white of the Portuguese Braganzas to produce a 'house-flag' better known today as that of P&O. Prior to being granted the mail contract, the company had been struggling financially, but the government subsidy ensured its success. Later acquisition of the Indian mails monopoly which carried a huge subsidy, was to render the Peninsular and Oriental Steam Navigation Company impervious to many commercial vicissitudes, a fact complained of by other ship-owners such as the redoubtable Alfred Holt.

Mails between Britain and North America were first carried by the paddle steamer *Britannia* and her three sister-ships of the British and North American Royal Mail Steam Packet Company, forerunner of the Cunard Steam Ship Company. In 1840 *Brittania* opened a monthly mail service which was to earn her successors the title of R.M.S., or Royal Mail Ship. While these ships ran to Halifax and Boston, the *Great Western* plied her route to New York, though competition was also springing up from American companies such as the Collins Line.

In a statement made to the Institute of Civil Engineers in 1841, Samuel Seaward said:

'notwithstanding the numerous improvements which have been made in the form and dimensions of steam vessels, and the perfection to which the machinery has been brought, still the weight of the latter, together with the space required for the fuel, has rendered it hitherto impractical to extend the duration of the steam voyage beyond the period of twenty days, without the necessity of taking in a fresh supply of coal.'

The situation was to remain thus until Holt's breakthrough a quarter-century later (see Chapter Eleven), despite the intervention of the Royal Navy to force the pace of innovation.

The Lords Commissioners of the British Admiralty recognised early the advantages of steam power for a multitude of uses. Propelling the line-of-battle ship was not one of them; instead they envisaged steam as a provider of auxiliary services. In 1822 a steamer named the *Comet* served as a naval tug and survey tender. Four years later, the author Captain Frederick Marryat recommended the use of the Honourable East India Company's paddle steamer *Diana* for service on the Arakan coast during the Burma War. A small, Bengali-built tender used for ferrying passengers from the anchored Indiamen upstream to Calcutta, the *Diana* rated only 32 horsepower but could tow the boats of men-of-war up the River Irrawaddy. Here she was joined by the *Enterprize* and these little ships thus became the first steam vessels to participate in hostilities.

As we have already remarked, fast paddle steamers were also run by the navy on behalf of the Post Office to carry mails, both across the Channel and down to the Iberian peninsula. By 1845 the number of steamships in naval service had risen to 113, but they were all small fry, for Their Lordships remained steadfastly uncommitted to empowering the line of battle. The reason for this reticence was the simple fact that seaborne artillery was still muzzle loading and broadside mounted. Boilers, engines, paddles, boxes and sponsons occupied the position of a third of the armament of a ship of the line. For Their Lordships, such a sacrifice in firepower was unacceptable. The argument that paddles conferred the tactical advantages of manoeuvrability and steaming to windward, were promptly countered by their own vulnerability to enemy shot and, since opposing ships still had to be within cannon-shot of each other, these were not seen as significant. What changed Their Lordships' minds was the screw propeller.

Some early experiments in screw propulsion had already been carried out, but traditionalists so loathed and feared piercing a hull below the waterline, that these had petered out. Moreover, naval experts believed that motive power provided at the stern would make it impossible for a vessel to come up into the wind. However, in 1840, the appropriately named *Archimedes* successfully trialled a screw, though she failed to prove herself faster than the Post Office paddle-packet *Widgeon* and thus failed to impress. Then, in 1843 Brunel built a successor to the *Great Western*, the *Great Britain*, which was specifically designed to cross the Atlantic under screw propulsion. She was fitted with a six-bladed propeller of 15.5 feet diameter which, driven by four 85-inch cylinders developing 1500 horsepower, turned at 53 revolutions per minute, driving her 3618 tons displacement at a creditable 9 knots. Despite this, Brunel furnished her with an efficient six-masted jackass-barque rig which could set 15,000 square feet of canvas.

It was no accident that inspired Brunel to adopt the screw propeller for his iron steamer *Great Britain*. The properties of a helix had been known since ancient times, and screw propellers had already been tried at sea several times without real success. Then, in 1835 a farmer named Frances Pettit Smith built a small model boat and propelled it with clockwork and a screw propeller on the village pond at Mill Hill, northwest of London. Having patented the device in 1836, he proved it on a larger launch with a remarkable coastwise voyage from the Thames to Folkestone. Smith had now secured financial backing from a banker named John Wright and the well respected engineering partnership of the brothers Rennie. These men founded the Screw Propeller Company and sought the patronage of the influential Second Secretary to the British Admiralty, Sir John Barrow. Barrow was interested in Arctic exploration, and was an early advocate of steam engines. Following some suggestions from him, the steamer *Archimedes* was laid down at Limehouse on the Thames. Built under the auspices of the Screw Propeller Company at a cost of £100,500, *Archimedes* measured 200 tons and was fitted with Smith's screw, a horizontally mounted continuous helix of one revolution, or 'single thread.'

At the same time a British-domiciled Swedish army engineer named John Ericsson patented a helical device. This was even more ingenious, consisting of two contra-rotating bladed screws running on concentric shafts, each blade forming a sixth-part of a full 'thread'. Securing American support, Ericsson's first two vessels were named in honour of American nationals, the *Frances B. Ogden* after their consul in Liverpool, the second after a post-captain in the United States' Navy, *Robert F. Stockton*. The former achieved a remarkable 8 knots and the latter, with her direct-drive engine, towed four 100-ton coal barges up the Thames at 5 knots. Smith was present at this trial and, having found that the loss of part of his helix had actually improved performance, suggested to Ericsson that he drop one of his propellers. The result bore a remarkable resemblance to the modern screw. Sadly, this exemplary co-operation was not to last, Ericsson was squeezed out and Smith's influential establishment backers secured the interest of senior naval officers including Sir Robert Otway and the wonderfully eccentric Earl of Dundonald, the former frigate-commander Lord Cochrane. Both men remarked on the superiority of the *Archimedes* over paddlers. The Admiralty's ultimate response was the *Rattler*, a steam screw-driven sloop which was to usurp that place in history which, in many ways, belongs to the little *Archimedes*.

The *Archimedes* did her best to demonstrate her talents in a voyage around Britain, but a boiler explosion and other difficulties resulted in her rarely exceeding 8 knots, an unimpressive comparison with contemporary paddle steamers, especially the Post Office packet *Widgeon*. She was thereafter put up for sale, but the Admiralty declined to buy her and for the time being the Royal Navy failed to appreciate the screw's potential. Ironically, *Archimedes's* last duty in home waters was in April 1843 when she towed the *Rattler* from her builders at

Sheerness to receive her engines in the East India Dock. She ended her days ignominiously hauling coal from New South Wales to Chile, passing into obscurity like Smith himself, while The Ship Propeller Company and Wright's bank went out of business.

To Smith's disgust, Brunel had undertaken supervisory duties on behalf of the Admiralty in the installation of *Rattler*'s engines. He had, moreover, made some crucial observations and brought this knowledge to the design of the *Great Britain*, as we have already noted. Not least of these was the realisation that the waterflow to the propeller and thence to the rudder was vital.

Brunel's *Great Britain* marked the ultimate in steam vessel design then possible. She had an iron hull, built from plates brought down the Severn to Bristol from the ironworks in Coalbrookdale, and she had screw propulsion. But her engines and boilers still lacked the efficiency that would confound the engineer Samuel Seaward's stated limitations of voyage length to three weeks, and while she remained the pre-eminent carrier on the North Atlantic, further expansion of steam services awaited an engineer capable of building on Brunel's achievement.

The provision of a screw, although it obviated the problems of reducing draft and allowed a full-lined hull to carry extra bunkers, still did not give the commercial operator sufficient space for a viable quantity of cargo. Meanwhile, the continuing risks of boiler explosions made insuring underwriters nervous, and the rather insignificant propeller did not seem, to those with only a primitive understanding of hydrostatic physics, so convincing a choice as the demonstrably threshing paddle-wheel, which retained many admirers. This dilemma irked Their Lordships at the Admiralty.

To resolve the superiority of one over the other, two naval steam vessels of almost identical tonnage and equal power were ordered to carry out trials. On a perfectly calm day in April 1845, they were coupled up stern to stern and their steam-valves opened up. The screw propelled sloop HMS *Rattler* successfully dragged HMS *Alecto* astern at a speed of 2.8 knots as the latter's paddles flailed ineffectually in the opposite direction. Thus, with the backing of the Royal Navy, *Rattler* displaced *Archimedes* as the first real exponent of successful screw propulsion!

This proof was convincing, but the adoption of the screw now perversely threw up a new set of problems. The gland in the stern through which the driving shaft passed, had to be resistant to the pressure of water trying to force its way into the hull. This was achieved by packing. But a far greater problem lay in the basic incompatibility of the screw and the wooden hull. A wooden hull is made up of many parts; it flexes and works in a seaway, or when taking the ground, as many merchantmen did to load and discharge cargo. Moreover, since a steam vessel could now ply to windward, a wooden hull was subject to pitching and, in the worst conditions, pounding forces, for which sail provided no precedent and the traditional 'apple-bow' actually made worse. John Wood, the builder of the *James Watt*, is credited with being the first to incorporate the hollow lines of hull entrance that helped overcome this, but added to these factors, the early steam engines, particularly when powering paddles, threw vibrating stresses through the hull which became worse as hull size increased. The screw, with its long shaft was inimical to a flexing wooden hull; whip in a steel shaft was a very real problem, only exacerbating the leaking of a stern gland and most of the after-part of a hull.

The only answer to this was a more rigid hull constructed of iron and the success of the *Great Britain* proved this. Nevertheless, it was not until 1852 that the government rescinded its stipulation that mail steamers had to be of wooden construction, allowing iron hulls and screw propulsion to become the norm.

The Royal Navy did not rush to build iron hulls. Its power remained vested in massive 'wooden-walls' which retained the muzzle-loading cannon and possessed the virtue of extreme longevity. The size of all rates of warship increased dramatically, notwithstanding a shortage of timber caused by the Napoleonic War, particularly the compass oak required for the manufacture of the frames, or futtocks, with which a line-of-battle ship was generously furnished. The First Rate *Victory*, rebuilt in 1803, though launched fifty years earlier, measured 186 feet on the gundeck; the *Victoria* launched in 1859 possessed a gundeck of 250 feet. Similarly the frigate *Euryalus*, which signalled the emergence of the Combined Fleet before Trafalgar and had been built two years earlier in 1803, had a gundeck of 145 feet against the *Undaunted* of 1860, which equalled the *Victoria* in length.

In order to maintain their fleet and to increase the size of gundecks, the British built their last wooden ships of the line using the system devised by Sir Robert Seppings who, in 1811, had incorporated diagonal frames over the deck beams and futtocks (see Chapter Eight). This stiffened the hulls, enabling shorter lengths of timber to be used and facilitated the fitting of steam engines with far fewer problems than were experienced in the smaller or mercantile wooden hulls.

Despite the fact that several British ships of the line which served in the Crimean War had been commissioned in the Napoleonic War and had steam engines fitted, the Admiralty built the *Vanguard* class of eleven two-deckers as late as 1835, several of which never had engines at all. There was insufficient money or time to convert all existing two- and three-deckers to steam, so priority was given to the best hulls. This conversion programme started in the 1840s and was only terminated after the Crimean War.

Steam frigates had entered service in 1842 when HMS *Penelope*, built in 1829, was cut in two and lengthened from 152 feet to 215. The new section contained her engines, boilers and paddles. Significantly her armament reduced from 46 guns to 16. Nineteen frigates including one of iron were built in the next decade. None mounted more than 21 guns and most bore no more than 6. However the *Amphion* was converted to a screw when building and the screw frigate, as we have observed, soon became a very large ship. In 1859 and 1860 the frigates *Mersey* and *Orlando* were built measuring 300 feet on the lower deck, and were the largest unarmoured ships built for the Royal Navy. The strain on their hulls was excessive and the last wooden frigate, the *Newcastle*, lasted only six years, being decommissioned in 1880.

In order to reduce drag when under sail, the screws fitted to these ships could be disconnected from the shaft by means of a simple clutch and hauled up into a recess under the quarterdeck, a technique it will be remembered from the last chapter, first developed for the Arctic-bound bomb vessels *Erebus* and *Terror* of Franklin's expedition.

*

We shall examine the colonial sailing ship and the iron hull in the next chapter, but the Australian gold rush and the Crimean War created such a demand for shipping that there were, in fact, cargoes for all. Indeed the Crimean War called up almost every available steam ship for charter to the British and French governments as troop transports.

There had been a marked rise in American competition too, a circumstance terminated by the American Civil war and the slump which followed the end of the Crimean War with Russia. These market forces had done little for the rights of the sailor. His lot was an unfortunate one in the vacuum left by the repealed Navigation Acts. In 1854 the British government passed the seminal Merchant Shipping Act which regulated the examination of masters and mates, manning, scales of pay and conditions, and sought to correct many abuses. It also empowered the Board of Trade to 'undertake the general superintendence of matters relating to the British Mercantile Marine', clearing a plethora of arcane and outdated legislation and establishing the foundations for the future. This did not secure either rights or justice for seamen, but it brought some control of mercantile shipping into the hands of the state.

The passage of this act also raised the plight of seamen in the public consciousness largely, it has to be said, because of passenger losses. In 1859 the *Royal Charter*, homeward bound from Australia, was lost off North Wales at the cost of 500 lives, not to mention gold from the Ballarat fields, and between 1867 and 1882, no fewer than 5987 passengers were drowned at sea. Overloading was considered the significant cause and a Newcastle ship-owner named James Hall first mooted the idea of restricting the depth to which a ship could be loaded by suggesting marking the hull at the maximum possible draught. The idea found a sponsor in a reforming member of parliament named Samuel Plimsoll. The line took his name after legislation initiated by him was passed by parliament. Plimsoll's legislation was but a part of a series of acts covering such subjects as anchors and cables, Australian passengers, and casualty investigations. These paved the way for a second great act of consolidation, the Merchant Shipping Act of 1894, of which more in Chapter Eleven.

The regulating examinations of masters and mates for certificates of competency, colloquially known as 'tickets' by their recipients, was long overdue. For many years the Royal Navy had relied upon recruiting its professional navigating branch from the merchant service with the warrant rank of sailing master. However a gradually increasing insistence on professionalism among junior commissioned officers, rendered them largely redundant, though they laboured on honourably in the hydrographic surveying branch. These men had obtained their professional certification from Trinity House, which was run by former masters in the mercantile marine and who were empowered under the terms of their royal charter to carry out this duty. Some merchant shipping companies also submitted their officers to a similar examination at Trinity House, but a proper qualification of competence was now to become standard.

Techniques of navigation differed little from earlier times, though some refinements in the resolution of sights had occurred. Lead, log and lookout had, as we have seen, been joined by longitude as the fundamental data required by a ship's navigator, but the paddle steamer was to leave one enduring legacy, the ship's bridge. This enhanced both the conning of a steam vessel and the accuracy of fixes, since the navigator was close to a ship's tipping centre. Traditionally a ship was conned from aft, where the officer of the watch could see the disposition of the yards and sails, and command the deck when manoeuvring. The imposition of the paddle boxes ruined this aspect, but a greatly improved view of the deck could be had from a wooden bridge established across the tops of the paddle-boxes. Compass platform and steering position followed, as did the structure of the wheelhouse to accommodate them and the engine controllers, or telegraphs.

However, the mass of metal below decks in the engine and boiler rooms, introduced errors in compass headings. This feature was not entirely new to ships and had already been addressed to a limited extent by men such as Matthew Flinders, but complex compensating arrangements were necessary and compass work began to form an important part of the syllabuses for the new examinations of officers, although a full under-standing only became imperative with the coming of the iron hull.

*

Steam power was also beneficial in the matter of lighthouse construction and Trinity House, having been empowered by an Act of 1836 to acquire all the private lighthouses of England and Wales and thus align 'South Britain' with the northern part of the United Kingdom, built special screw steam tenders, the *Hercules* and the *Arrow* to undertake the rapid erection of granite towers on the isolated and notorious reefs of the Eddystone and Wolf Rocks. The corporation was already employing steam vessels as buoy tenders, having built its first, the *Vestal*, in 1835 with the Commissioners for Northern Lighthouses following soon afterwards.

Thus it was that the steam engine had made its impact upon the maritime world and, although it had yet to replace the sailing ship as a carrier of the world's goods, by the mid-1860s it was set fair to relieve the wooden auxiliary warship and had already captured many of the shorter passenger and packet routes.

Despite these successes and its obvious potential, the 'steam kettle' was unable to prevent the sailing ship from enjoying a constant improvement and reaching its culmination in the tea and wool clipper, producing the most beautiful utilitarian artefact ever formed by the hand of man.

CHAPTER TEN

The Apogee of Sail

The expansion of trade and demand for shipping which produced the final successes of the sailing ship are generally attributed to the repeal of the protective British Navigation Acts. This assumption is an over simplification. In fact repeal did not take place until 1849, prior to which the acts had been steadily eroded, largely by the British government's policy of removing preferential duties. From about 1824 this was actively pursued with those countries who would reciprocate. When America and Britain had gone to war in 1812, one of the points at issue was the American demand for 'free trade', so by 1830 American ships could carry their own produce directly to any British possession and carry exports from any British territory to any foreign country; they were even able to trade directly from Great Britain to India, part of the East India Company's monopoly having been abolished as early as 1813. Moreover the new republics of South America recently liberated from Spanish and Portuguese rule, rivalled the West Indies in the quality and price of their produce, and smuggling was widespread enough to make serious inroads into the revenue the Navigation Acts were supposed to generate. Together with a few exceptions, these factors combined to reduce by half the amount of British trade still governed by the acts.

The long depression that followed the Napoleonic War resulted in a world-wide slump which suppressed rapid change, and although countries such as The Netherlands suffered the most, British merchant shipping declined by twelve per cent. Then, as Huskisson's reciprocity policy bit, trade began a steady and eventually spectacular expansion. By 1861, British merchant tonnage had increased by fifty per cent of its 1849 level. More significantly, the number of ships loading and discharging at British ports also rose spectacularly. But many of these were American, for the United States's merchant fleet had almost doubled in the same period that Britain's had grown by half, while in Europe the newly independent state of Norway had become a serious rival. One reason for this change in circumstances was the cost of new construction. The British could not build wooden ships as cheaply as the Americans, the Scandinavians or the Germans. Even the Dutch, who were able to borrow money at cheaper rates, could produce merchant ships more economically than Britain. Apart from East Indiamen, only two wooden sailing ships of over 1500 tons were ever built in the United Kingdom. This serious decline was partially halted by the switch to iron construction later in the century. By these means Britain was able to reassert a commercial ascendancy equal to her naval supremacy, though both were somewhat tenuously held advantages.

Within these stern economic influences other factors played their part. The mechanisation of agriculture and the movement of the huge numbers of the British population to industrial towns with the resulting problems of overcrowding, cholera and insufficient work, encouraged emigration to America, Canada and Australia. The consequent establishment of a crack packet service across the Atlantic created a demand for faster passenger ships, accelerated by the horrors of the Irish famine of 1845–51. The expansion of mail services also helped to stimulate interest in speed.

However, following the removal of the Indian monopoly, there was also a sharp decrease in the passage times of the lumbering East Indiamen. Whereas comfort had hitherto been a guiding principle of their conduct, and they had shortened sail at night to ensure the secure slumbers of their passengers, the effect of competition was to sweep away these leisurely procedures. In 1816 a fleet of thirteen round-bowed Indiamen took only 109 days to reach the London River from Canton, whereas such a passage had formerly taken from four to six months!

But it was the gold rushes to California in 1849, Australia in 1852 and New Zealand in 1861 that gave a tremendous boost to the quest for speed as the numbers of would-be prospectors rocketed. Even by the mid nineteenth century the steam engine could not yet satisfy this demand for swift, long distance shipping services. The failure of the steamship at this important juncture was only partly a technical one. Because of the high running costs, passage in a steamship was expensive. Most emigrants were impoverished to the point of desperation and travelled third class, unable to afford anything better.

Thus, there were a number of diverse trades, traditions and economic pressures all impinging upon the world's two most competitive merchant marines, that of Great Britain, and that of the United States of America. Consequently the opening of the China coast, the boom of 'Forty-nine' and the subsequent finds at Ballarat and Otago gave the sailing ship a stay of execution. This period, when wind-powered ships remained the only means by which fast passages might be achieved, became the apogee of sail.

The tradition that the Americans were responsible for the introduction of the fine-lined hull derived from the breed of ships generically known as Baltimore clippers, is only partly true. The tasks of privateering and blockade-running had placed the demand for speed above that of capacity. A similar rejigging of priorities was eventually to dominate two trades in the middle years of the nineteenth century: the carriage of opium and tea. Both involved highly valuable commodities whose prices, and therefore the shipowners' profits, depended upon safe delivery. In the first, speed was essential to avoid interdiction; in the second a volatile, seasonal market meant that early shipments fetched the highest prices.

Although, as we have remarked, the Indiamen made efforts to improve passage times, the regime under which they operated belonged to the old century. They were swiftly sold, relegated to the status of hulks or opium receiving ships, or broken up. The Thameside shipbuilding yards of Blackwall turned their skills to constructing speedier emigrant ships, popularly known as 'Blackwall-frigates', or 'Blackwallers', a cognomen that lingered along with many of the ships well into the 1870s. These were not revolutionary vessels, although the tendency to adopt the hollower hull form was soon accepted. The first of these, the *Seringapatam* was laid down in 1837 and completed two years later by R. & H. Green. A wooden ship-rigged vessel of 818 tons burthen, she measured 152.5 feet (46.5 metres) in length, and 34.5 feet (10.5 metres) in the beam.

Blackwallers were built for the emigrant trade and enjoyed widespread reputations, their tribulations and triumphs featuring in the newspapers. The popularity of a master or a ship guaranteed her earning power and the public began to take an interest in passage times. However, though profits might be made from those who sought a change of fate by emigration, they were relatively small compared with the rich pickings available in another trade, the dividends from which would have exceeded the dreams of the most avid 'digger' who shipped out to Ballarat after the discovery of gold in 1852.

The fierce competition in the India trade, taken as the first sign that the post-Napoleonic slump would not endure, was followed in about 1830, by a commercial opportunity the unscrupulous found impossible to resist. The immorality of the opium trade to China is unquestionable; it was carried out in direct opposition to the wishes of the Chinese government and its enforcement by steam warships is of little credit to Great Britain. The old imbalance of trade to the Far East which derived from a lack of oriental markets for British exports, and the lingering importance of the 'country trade' to fund outward passages, is one reason why Britain went to such unreasonable and unjustifiable lengths to protect the opium trade. Opium preyed on the weakness and indigence of hundreds of thousands of addicts, fed on the corruption of the mandarins and enriched the British, American and Parsee houses who shipped it. Nevertheless the traffic produced the first spectacularly fast merchant sailing ships and opened trade with the Middle Kingdom which in turn led eventually to the expansion of the tea trade through the Treaty Ports conceded by the Chinese government after the Opium War of 1839–42.

The actual outbreak of hostilities was caused by the seizure of opium by the Chinese mandarins and their subsequent attempt to prosecute the traffickers. The British counter-claim that Chinese courts had no jurisdiction over British nationals caused an open rupture with the Celestial Empire. A naval bombardment of Canton and the occupation of Hong Kong added that island to the colonial garland; from 1842 the Middle Kingdom was opened to the rapacity of western trade. This was the ultimate consequence of the Ming Emperor's fateful decision four centuries earlier, based upon the unpromising findings of Zheng He's expeditions, that maritime exploration had nothing to offer.

Opium had been the solace of the Chinese coolie for a thousand years, but the demand was always greater than the supply and when the Indian government began exporting it, a market was to hand. The ships required to carry this highly valuable cash crop had to beat their way across the Bay of Bengal and up the South China Sea against the prevailing northeast monsoon. On the south coast of China the opium was transferred into receiving ships, which were often former Indiamen. These were armed and manned to hold their treasure until it was dispersed by smaller clippers along the coast to the Chinese opium smugglers who would as soon have seized the clippers and murdered their crews, as deal with them. During transactions at which neither side trusted the other and the temptation to double-cross must have been well-nigh irresistible, the illicit cargo was paid for in Mexican silver dollars, ingots or antique ware, much of which was then melted down.

Chinese pirates in junks lay in wait for the opium smugglers, whether outward bound with their chests of opium, or homeward with their ill-gotten specie. The clippers were therefore fiercely armed, and fitted with 40-feet sweeps which could propel them in a calm at 4 knots when each was manned by half-a-dozen men. Crews were mixed, but their officers were young blades, men of good families, ex-naval officers and those who, a generation earlier, would have sought employment with John Company or the Royal Navy.

In addition to the contrary winds of the monsoon, the calms that might beset the opium smugglers along the coast, the pirates and the dangers of the uncharted inlets in which they made their rendezvous, there was the added danger of a typhoon. Such conditions made strenuous demands upon the masters and officers. Gunnery, cutlass and small-arms drill were as important as smart sail and ship-handling as a means of survival in what was, for all its amorality, a highly dangerous activity. Nor were the hydrographical accomplishments of the characters who served in these opium runners inconsiderable and as a nursery for seamen these opium runners rivalled the slavers of the previous century. It was therefore no surprise that the traffic attracted men now cheated of the opportunities they believed the Napoleonic War had offered their fathers and elder brothers. Such was the 'gentrification' of this trade that officers are reputed to have retired rich to the United Kingdom to inherit their clergymen father's livings, or take up seats in parliament. Moreover, early traders who profited from the coolies' misery, became highly respected institutions in the orient.

An opium cargo consisted of about three hundred chests, and therefore it could be carried in a small vessel. Schooners and 'clipper-brigs' proliferated, particularly those trading for American interests. Best known of the British opium clippers was the Earl of Yarborough's former yacht *Falcon*, of 351 tons. She had been built in 1824 at Fishbourne on the Isle of Wight, modelled upon a 20-gun corvette. Yarborough was the commodore of the Royal Yacht Club, later the Squadron, whose members fitted out splendid yachts at their own expense, which might be used as naval auxiliaries in time of war. Yarborough paid his crew extra to conform to naval regulations and they had to sign acceptance of the necessity of flogging for the preservation of discipline. The earl had 11 guns mounted in the *Falcon* and is said to have commanded her as an adjunct to Codrington's fleet at Navarino. More significantly, Yarborough attended the evolutions of the experimental naval squadron that engaged in what amounted to races, rather than scientific attempts, to produce better hull and sail plans for the Royal Navy.

Across the Channel the French were similarly engaged, developing a large class of fast brig heavily influenced by American pilot boat hulls, of which the *Cygne* may serve as an example to compare with *Falcon*. Both were notionally 20-gun vessels, though the *Cygne* bore the full complement of 24-pounder carronades and both were 110 feet (33.5 metres) in length with similar beams of 26.3 feet (8 metres). Both vessels were built in 1824, the *Cygne* at L'Orient, but *Falcon* seems to have been the faster and was said to have been difficult to overtake. In 1835 Yarborough had a serious fall at sea which combined with an attack of influenza to persuade him to sell *Falcon* to London speculators. These were the Baring Brothers who wrote to Russell and Company in Hong Kong that she was ideal for opium running, believing she would 'sail faster than any ship in that trade'.

Falcon did not carry opium immediately, bringing two cargoes of tea to London and disappointing Barings who tried to sell her for twice what they had paid. In 1839 *Falcon* was dry-docked in Liverpool and is supposed to have been fitted with steam engines in the hope she would be chartered for use in the Burmese War. This seems an apocryphal story such as might accrue to so notorious a ship and there is no mention of engines after she was bought by Jardine, Matheson and Company for £6000 and finally put on the opium run.

Though superficially a conventional round-bowed corvette above the waterline, the secret of *Falcon*'s speed was attributable to the fact that she was 'sharp as a wedge in her entrance below'. *Falcon* possessed a long, flat bottom which turned into a fine run aft and these qualities, matters of some subtlety, enabled her to stand up to her canvas in a blow, bear her guns well and yet enabled her to make way in light weather. Able to hoist either short or long topgallant masts depending upon the weather and season, she carried a powerful sail plan and her masts 'seldom went more than a few inches beyond the rigging that supported them'. Said to have been particularly blessed in the person of her sailmaker, her deep sails when she was close-hauled were 'held like boards by sheet, tack, brace and bowline ... leaving no rift 'twixt spar and canvas ...'.

Falcon proved her mettle in the opium trade, as did her crew. In three days at sea, they rerigged the lower masts one by one, sending the top-hamper down from each in turn. This sort of practical seamanship set the standard for the China trade, and engendered both expertise and *esprit de corps*, qualities that were to carry over into the tea clippers that were to follow.

Falcon's astonishing ability, particularly her performance full-and-bye, which seems to have been exceptional for her times, owed everything to her sail plan. This presages the deep sails of the early clippers. It was the long vertical sides of the square sails which, suitably tautened by trimming, enabled her to work to windward. But she is believed to have been the only ship-rigged opium clipper.

More typical of the generality of these vessels was the 305-ton *Sylph*, built at Calcutta in 1831. The *Sylph* was schooner-rigged and had such a reputation for speed that the naval authorities wanted to charter her for the Opium War in 1841. This the Banajee family refused; instead the *Sylph*'s owners kept her running opium during hostilities with a full European crew. During the war and in company with another Parsee owned clipper, the *Cowasjee Family* and Jardine, Matheson's *Lady Hayes*, the appropriately named Captain Vice of the *Sylph*, found himself surrounded by a large fleet of Chinese war junks. The three opium runners fought a fierce action, shattering the Chinese squadron.

Once the British had forced the opium issue, the Americans moved in. The small schooner *Anglona* was sent out for Russell and Company, who began to represent American interests in the Orient. The *Zephyr* was typical of the American clippers which followed, being built in East Boston by Samuel Hall on the lines of a pilot schooner. Constructed of oak and elm, she was heavily sparred and even more heavily armed. With a broadside of four brass 18-pounders a side, she carried a traversing brass 18-pounder *en barbette* on the forecastle and a massive traversing 68-pounder gun amidships between her masts. Her master, Captain T. M. Johnson, claimed that 'on the wind I do believe there is not anything that can beat her'.

The passages that all these ships made are impressive. *Sylph* ran from the Sandheads, off Calcutta, to Macao in sixteen days, the *Antelope* and *Coquette* were twelve days from Calcutta to Singapore and the former, an American brig, was among the few square-rigged vessels capable of beating through the Taiwan Strait against the strength of the northeast monsoon. A veteran of battles with both pirates and the legitimate war junks trying to interdict the illegal trade, *Antelope*'s master, a Captain Watkins, ran down two government junks and sailed into Macao Roads with a Chinese victim suspended from each yardarm, an unpleasant tale whose consequences linger yet.

By the middle of the nineteenth century, sail was yielding to steam, although schooners were still in use. In 1845 Jardine, Matheson and Company chartered the schooner *Torrington*. She had been built by Alexander Hall and Sons of Aberdeen and her hull was characterised by what was to become famous as the 'Aberdeen bow'.

The inception of this new feature was due to economics rather than a desire for speed. During the late eighteenth century tonnage dues had been levied from merchantmen based on a formula deriving from a ship's dimensions and intended to approximate the weight of cargo she could carry. During the slow convoys of the Napoleonic Wars, owners had been at pains to increase capacity without alterations of registered tonnage. Because tonnage measurements were not taken abaft the heel of the sternpost, raked sterns became common to avoid the otherwise ruinous levies which would have been imposed on extended hulls. In 1836 the tonnage regulations were overhauled; it was intended to use internal measurements at three standard 'stations' within the hull. These were at the bow, where the stem met the keel, amidships and at the juncture of keel and sternpost. While mid-sections had to remain full, by reducing the bow and stern sections, a ship's registered tonnage could be minimised. The deck length could then be increased by raking the extremes, particularly the stem. Thus the lines of British hulls began to taper at bow and stern, with long overhangs and this was found to increase speed, endorsing the performance of the hollow Yankee hulls which owed their inception to other factors.

In 1839 the Aberdeen yard of Alexander Hall and Sons built a new schooner for the Leith to London packet service. The *Scottish Maid* capitalised on the new concept and was followed by the opium clipper *Torrington* built for Jardine, Matheson. Hall's next orders were for a more legitimate Chinese cargo – tea.

In 1834 the East India Company's last shipping monopoly was lifted and the entire trade of China was opened up. Although local restrictions and levies imposed by the corrupt mandarins were to frustrate them, British and American merchants were not slow to react. However, the Baring Brothers of London had to relinquish a speculative investment in silk for lack of a ship fast enough to deliver a cargo on time and they must have regretted their sale of the *Falcon*. But the demand for tea was far greater than that for silk, and it was upon this traffic that commercial interest swiftly focused.

Initially the tea trade had been conducted in a time-honoured and leisurely manner. The cargo was loaded in October and the ships carried the favourable northeast monsoon down the South China Sea, through the Sunda Strait and southwest across the Indian Ocean towards the Cape of Good Hope. But towards 1850, following the harvest, tea began to arrive at the loading ports earlier, creating a demand in London which attracted higher prices for the first cargoes of the season. This incentive, added to the necessity for the ships to combat the last of the southwest monsoon down through the South China Sea, a comparatively shallow stretch of water littered with coral reefs, islets and pirates, formed the conditions for which a faster sailing ship had to be produced.

Hall built two ships for the new trade, the *Bon Accord* of 1846 and the *North Star* of 1847. Both had the now celebrated 'Aberdeen bow', but neither was noted for speed. Indeed the fine entry produced a hull with little reserve buoyancy forward, and Hall's ships acquired an early reputation among seamen for being wet, of plunging their fore parts and sweeping men from their bowsprits.

Nevertheless the manner of building ships was taking a different turn. Advocates of engineering and hydrodynamics were elbowing aside the master shipwright as a vessel's chief midwife. Along with the changes to the tonnage rules, followed by a further revision in 1854 these factors swept away old concepts. James and William Hall succeeded their father in 1830 as manager and designer respectively and William is thought to have used tank-testing, or at least some form of it, such as tethering models in running streams.

Hall was not the only builder in Aberdeen; Walter Hood and Alexander Duthie were also producing ships for the China tea trade, and 1848 saw all three yards launch tea ships. Duthie's *Countess of Seafield* and Hood's *John Bunyan* rolled down the ways and took to the water with Hall's *Reindeer*. The last had an interesting feature in that her greatest beam was aft, a swelling outwards of her quarters which gave her reserve buoyancy in a following sea and countered the tendency of such ships to submit to pooping. The new ship also had an outward flare in her bulwarks, the reverse of tumblehome, which resisted heel when she was under a press of canvas. *Reindeer* was 141.5 feet in length (43 metres), had a beam of 22.7 feet (6.9 metres) and a tonnage of 328 under the new rules. In 1850 she was the only one of the three Aberdeen ships to beat against the southwest monsoon and managed a very creditable passage time of 107 days back to Britain, though later passages were disappointing. By 1852 she was off the China run, trading to South America and was finally lost on the coast of New South Wales in 1856.

Although Hall improved upon *Reindeer* in *Stornoway* of 1850 and *Chrysolite* of 1852, the China trade was now experiencing fierce competition from American ships.

With its growing perception of the United States as a world leader, Congress had backed the establishment of the Pacific Mail Steamship Company in order to improve communications with the American west coast via the Strait of Magellan. When gold was discovered in California in 1847 however, the company was on the verge of bankruptcy and it was the fast American sailing ship which filled the breach and bore thousands of eager speculators to the goldfields.

American construction turned at once to speed, developing their native style from the Baltimore clipper hull. The ship *Rainbow* was of similar length and beam to the Blackwaller *Seringapatam*, but of very different form. Designed by John W. Griffiths, she was eventually launched in 1845 from the New York Yard of Smith and Dimon after a long delay during which her backers threatened to pull out. The plain head traditional among American ships gave her bow an austere, but elegant profile when it was combined with her fine lines. With a high transom stern she seems to have been the first ship which might with justice be called a 'clipper' and conformed to our modern notion of the type. Griffiths' masterpiece was delayed in the building and then dismasted on her first voyage, fulfilling the gloomy prognostications of her critics. While *Rainbow* had been under construction another ship, the *Howqua*, was being built in the neighbouring yard of A.A.Low. The *Howqua* was largely the brainchild of Captain Nathaniel Palmer.

Palmer had gone to sea at the age of fourteen in a blockade-runner during the War of 1812. In 1820, at the age of twenty-one, Palmer commanded the sealer *Hero* and sighted the Antarctic peninsula that bears his name. His experiences in slow ships led him to persuade William Low to build the *Howqua* on hollow lines. Not quite a full clipper, the *Howqua* nevertheless justified Palmer's ideas and sailed on 31 May 1844, reaching Canton in ninety-five days. The success of *Howqua* persuaded the hesitant investors in *Rainbow* to resume her building, and despite her dismasting and the opposition of the monsoon on her maiden voyage, Captain Land reached Hong Kong after 102 days. On her second voyage, *Rainbow* made Hong Kong in ninety-nine days and returned her cargo of tea to New York in eighty-four days.

Both Griffiths and the partnership of Palmer and Low were shortly to be outdone by the Nova Scotian Donald McKay, whose *Flying Cloud* was a truly outstanding ship. *Flying Cloud* was built at Boston in 1851 for the Californian emigrant trade. Longer than *Rainbow* at 229 feet (69.8 metres), she was only nine feet wider, with a beam of 40.8 feet (12.4 metres), and registered 1782 tons. Her passages were exceptional and she twice sailed from New York to San Francisco westwards round the Horn in eighty-nine days. It was not just her speed that confirmed McKay's genius, but the care with which he attended to the details of her design, allowing *Flying Cloud* to operate with a crew of about twenty men, two thirds of the crew then carried on British ships of similar tonnage.

Having taken eager prospectors out to the gold fields, there was little to bring back except gold dust and it became the practice for *Flying Cloud* and her competitors to cross the Pacific in ballast to China and load tea for either Boston or New York, increasing the pressure on the market price and squeezing the British. Then, in 1850, the American clipper *Oriental*, commanded by Nathaniel Palmer's brother Edward, arrived in Hong Kong direct from New York in an unbeaten eighty-one days. She was immediately chartered to load tea at £6 per 40 cubic feet notional ton. The cargo was for London and her departure left British ships empty in Hong Kong. They were finding it difficult to fill their holds at £3.5 per ton of 50 cubic feet, such were the fickle nature of freight rates. Sailing against the southwest monsoon, the *Oriental* arrived in London after a fast passage of ninety-nine days. In drydock she attracted immediate interest, not least that of the Aberdonians. She also burst upon the British consciousness as a media-hyped threat to Britannia's supposed pre-eminence. Thereafter, for a brief period of under twenty years, the so-called 'tea races' became something of an obsession with the British, who took increasing notice of their mercantile marine.

The ships produced in this Indian Summer of sail were, without doubt, wonderful creations combining beauty and utility to an extraordinary degree. Emigrant ship or tea clipper, they created an enduring legend. As the poet John Masefield, who served briefly in sail, wrote: 'They mark our passage as a race of men. Earth will not see such ships again.' Masefield gave voice to a nostalgia which has attached to them ever since, yet they were built for money making and were hard-driven by hard-bitten men.

In a period of naval stagnation, it was their masters who became household names, men whose self-reliance and resourcefulness were legendary and whose reputations were frequently colourful if not formidable. Poorly paid, many merchant seamen deserted when the lure of the gold-fields proved too great an attraction. In 1852 numerous sailing ships were laid up in Melbourne for lack of crews and one master desperately advertised for seamen at the unheard of wage of £30 per month. Arriving at the same city, in the *Marco Polo*, Captain 'Bully' Forbes 'who lost men, spars and his temper on every voyage' had his entire crew thrown into gaol for safekeeping until the *Marco Polo* sailed again.

These ships frequently suffered dismastings such as overtook *Rainbow*, and although they were manned by able seamen whose expertise has perhaps never been surpassed. Masters of equal ability were much rarer; it took great nerve to drive a fine-tuned clipper, to hang onto sail in a blow to maximise speed, yet to judge the moment when canvas must be taken in before it was too late. The bottle helped some and hindered others, as did religion; one master jumped over the side, assailed it is believed by a fit of conscience at abusing a passenger. It was a remote and lonely life. Masters were expected to keep the deck and many catnapped in canvas deck chairs for days while they drove their ships to the utmost. Navigation in the confined waters of the South China Sea caused great personal anxiety, for reefs abounded, charts could not yet be trusted absolutely and haze frequently frustrated the taking of sights. Many fine ships piled up on the Macclesfield Bank, Pratas Reef or the Ladrones Islands. There were, of course, some outstanding commanders among them: Andrew Shewan of the *Norman Court*, Robert Kemball of the *Thermopylae*, Anthony Enright of the *Chrysolite* and *Lightning*, and Captain John Keay of the *Ariel*, whose ship's struggle with her rival *Taeping*, commanded by Captain McKinnon, described later in this chapter, epitomised the spirit and competition of these clippers and their masters.

*

Initially it was incontestably the Americans who led the field. The British press agonized over the 'humiliation' inflicted by the *Oriental* in 1850, although the Hall-built *John Bunyan* had taken only 101 days between Shanghai and The Downs. In 1852 the very fine-lined American *Witch of the Wave* had taken ninety-two days to reach London from Canton, the monsoon having been in her favour. Her arrival in April sparked off wild speculation as to the relative merits of British and American clippers and the American Navigation Club of Boston put up stakes of £10,000.

The five clippers which sailed in July 1852 from either Canton or Whampoa on the Pearl River, had to beat south against the southwest monsoon. The British *Chrysolite* took 105 days to reach Liverpool, the same destination as that of the American *Racehorse* which took 125. Of the three bound to London, the American *Surprise* took 107 days, beating the British ships *Stornoway* and *Sea Queen* by a few days. However, a faster passage of 106 days was made over the same run in August by the American *Challenge*. Meanwhile, leaving Shanghai in July and covering a greater distance against the wind, the British *Challenger*, built on the Thames by R. & H.Green as a response to the Yankee *Challenge*, was home to London in 112 days, with the American *Nightingale* taking 133. Poor Captain Fiske of the *Nightingale* was so disgusted that he resigned on arrival!

In 1853 *Nightingale* and *Challenger* both left Shanghai on 8 August and the British ship beat the American to the Downs with a passage of 110 days, two less than her rival. Of course conditions played a part in these passage times, and a clipper was usually held to be either a witch in light airs, or a racer in a blow, rarely giving outstanding performance in each extreme. Much also rested with the care and skill of the master and his officers, and matters such as the precise trim of the hull were debated and experimented with. Fast ships could give poor passages, particularly the wooden American hulls, despite having been built like knives. Donald McKay's *Sovereign of the Seas* which could log 19 knots and had covered over 420 miles in a day's run was one of the ships which left Shanghai for London in 1855. She disappointed her new German owners by taking 170 days to reach London, having lost eleven of her crew to cholera.

In the same year, four of the five American ships carrying tea from Foochow to London made long passages and the interest of American owners in carrying tea to London began to dwindle.

In 1856, during the favourable northeast monsoon, the British ship *Kate Carnie* took only ninety-two days to reach the Downs from Shanghai against the American *Kingfisher*'s ninety-six; then in 1857 the British clipper *Fiery Cross* took only ninety-nine days from Foochow to London, leaving during the southwest monsoon, the first time a British clipper had made a decisively faster passage than an American. Despite this the American ships's reputation for speed sustained the belief among shippers that they were faster, and the shorter passage times to Boston or New York helped maintain this flawed expectation. The seventy-four days achieved by the *Sea Witch* from Canton to New York set a standard which did not seem unreasonable to expect of a ship bound for London, and it was thought American ships could perform equally well on both passages. There was, however, a significant difference, pointed out in the researches into the oceans' winds conducted by Lieutenant Matthew Maury of the United States Navy. Maury noticed that although the increased distance to Britain was only about five hundred miles, the global wind pattern in the North Atlantic favoured the reach towards North America, rather than the long beat through the northeast trade winds which had to be undergone before Channel-bound ships picked up the westerlies.

In 1858 only two American ships loaded for London, although there was a brief upsurge in 1859 with a dozen cleared for Britain despite a very poor freight rate of £2 to £3 per ton. But the *Challenger*, under James Killick, soundly beat the *Bald Eagle* and the outbreak of the American Civil War two years later finally snuffed out American competition.

From the eclipse of the Americans, there now rose a challenge to the formidable ascendancy of the Aberdeen- and London-built clippers. The Clydeside yard of Robert Steele and Company of Greenock soon established a reputation for composite building. Steele had produced a number of fine wooden ships including the *Serica*, before turning to composite construction with the *Taeping* of 1863. Built of teak and greenheart bolted to iron frames by phosphorated metal bolts, *Taeping* measured 184 feet in length (55.9 metres) with a beam of 31 feet (9.4 metres). Notwithstanding her iron bowsprit and lower masts, she was dismasted in a typhoon homeward bound on her maiden voyage. Rerigged, she took eighty-eight days to reach the Downs, proving herself among the 'cracks' and earning a reputation of doing well in light winds.

In 1865 Steele launched the *Ariel*; ten feet longer than *Taeping* and four feet beamier, she proved a very fast ship. Her eighty days to Hong Kong was 'scarce believed' in London, wrote her master, Captain Keay, given that it was against the monsoon. Her great race with the *Taeping* in 1866 was notable chiefly because after a passage of 13,000 miles, both ships came up the English Channel side-by-side, an extraordinary circumstance and a most wonderful sight.

At Foochow *Ariel* had loaded 550 tons of tea at £5 per ton and her bills of lading bore the customary endorsement that an extra ten shillings (£0.50) would be paid on every ton if she was the first sailing vessel in dock. Engaging an inefficient tug, Keay towed out of the Pagoda anchorage, down the Min River and through the gorge, but failed to get over the bar and had to anchor. Here he had the mortification of watching the *Fiery Cross* towed past. Having crossed the bar the following day, 27 May, Keay made sail in company with the *Serica* and the *Taeping*; a fifth ship, the *Taitsing* sailed on the 28th. All the contending ships reeled off the miles with runs well in excess of 300 miles for a day's work and on the morning of 5 September, *Ariel* and *Taeping* passed the Lizard in sight of each other, logging 14 knots with *Serica* not far behind them. At about eight o'clock the following morning, *Ariel* arrived off Deal ten minutes ahead of *Taeping*, with *Serica* appearing in The Downs four hours later. Keay's choice of tugs was again flawed and *Taeping* was towed into dock at just after a quarter to nine, half an hour ahead of *Ariel*. *Serica* got in half an hour before midnight, just before she was locked out, and *Fiery Cross* arrived four days later on the 10th.

Ironically, the arrival of three clippers simultaneously, depressed the price of the crop, and the premium, divided equally between *Ariel* and *Taeping*, was afterwards abolished. Nevertheless *Ariel* secured a better freight rate the following year and although leaving late, Keay passed every other ship ahead of him except *Taeping* and *Fiery Cross*.

In 1868 Keay handed *Ariel* over to Captain Courtenay, formerly her first mate, a tradition which was supposed to maximise the potential inherent in the next most experienced officer familiar with the ship who had, it was assumed, imbibed the skills of his predecessor. But the days of the tea trade were numbered in the wake of the opening of the Suez Canal. In 1870 *Ariel* was dismasted off Yokohama and in January 1871 she left London for Sydney, to be posted missing and never heard of again. She is thought to have been pooped, a fate very fine-lined ships were vulnerable to. With a long, slender run, they possessed little reserve buoyancy aft beyond the outswelling of their counters; if that was insufficient to raise them to meet a heavy following sea, the wave broke over them, carrying all before it and finding its inexorable way below to flood and overwhelm the ship.

It was characteristic of these late composite clippers that, although ship-rigged, they sported all manner of light weather sails, the rigging and handling of which called forth great skill and precision from their officers and men. Light square sails ascended to heaven, with skysails and moonsails topping the conventional royals. Ringtails extended the spanker aft, 'Jimmy Greens' were suspended beneath the bowsprit and water sails hung beneath the lower studding sail booms. On gaffs abaft the fore and main masts, spencers or trysails were spread and individual 'flying-kites' were experimented with by masters and mates hell-bent on performance. Never before or since has the success of a trade rested so completely on the skill of a master and crew. Under a press of such canvas the appearance of these clippers must have been breathtaking.

The best known of them today are the *Thermopylae* of 1868 and the *Cutty Sark* of 1869. Both were built too late for the trade for which they were designed, but both did well in the Australian wool trade into which many tea ships were transferred in the 1870s. The mechanical press which compacted the wool into bales enabled it to be squeezed to such an extent that it could be carried half way round the world and still be cheaper in Britain and Europe than German and Spanish products. Annual competition to bring the season's 'clip' back to London caused a degree of interest in the 'wool races' and while these never quite seized the public imagination like the tea races, the trade was to prove a refuge for many former tea clippers.

While *Cutty Sark* has her partisans, there are those who claim the palm for her great rival *Thermopylae*. Composite built in 1868 by Walter Hood of Aberdeen, she was of almost identical dimensions to the *Cutty Sark*, being six inches shorter, though her registered tonnage was greater at 947. Her lower main and fore masts, together with their course yards, were of iron and in the 1870s she had double-topgallants fitted. *Thermopylae* seems to have possessed something of the combined virtues of being able to ghost in light airs as well as stand up to a blow, though she was better at the former while her rival excelled at the latter.

Until Richard Woodget commanded the *Cutty Sark* in the wool trade, she suffered from never having a master quite of the calibre of Captain Robert Kemball of the *Thermopylae*. Prior to Woodget taking command, the only time the ships were in a straight race, disaster overtook the *Cutty Sark* off the Cape of Good Hope. Although *Thermopylae* had passed the Sunda Strait ahead, *Cutty Sark* had gained a lead of four hundred miles by the time the two ships had worked their way down off the Cape of Good Hope. Here *Cutty Sark* suffered her misfortune, losing her rudder in bad weather. The subsequent fitting of a jury rudder at sea was a feat of outstandingly brilliant seamanship and courage, for the portable forge overset itself as the ship wallowed in the trough of the sea. Once back under command, *Cutty Sark* was obliged to proceed under easy sail; nevertheless she arrived only a week after *Thermopylae*.

Thermopylae was built for George Thompson's Aberdeen White Star Line and on her maiden voyage took only sixty-three days from London to Melbourne, clipping two days off the record set by the *James Baines* in 1855. Sailing up to China, she loaded tea and was ninety-one days from the Min River to London. Despite several successful voyages she failed to load tea in 1879 and 1880, and although shipping a cargo home in 108 days in 1881, was transferred to the Australian wool trade. Thompson sold her in 1890 and, like the *Cutty Sark*, she passed eventually to Portuguese ownership becoming the training ship *Pedro Nunes*. In 1907 she was towed out of the River Tagus and sunk by gunfire.

Cutty Sark's ancestry is as curious as her construction which bankrupted her inexperienced builders, Scott and Linton of Dumbarton. After that she had to be completed by Denny Brothers. Her bow is said to have been modelled by her designer,

Hercules Linton, on *The Tweed*, the favourite ship of her owner John Willis. In April 1863, in the aftermath of the Indian Mutiny, the East India Company's naval force, the Bombay Marine was disbanded. Two of its paddle steamers were on passage to Britain to have screws fitted and were put up for sale on arrival in the Thames. The Scots shipowner John Willis bought them both, the *Assaye* to sell on at a large profit, the *Punjaub* to be rechristened *The Tweed*. More importantly, Willis removed *The Tweed*'s engines and, as a full-rigged ship, she was to make her name as a crack sailer under the command of Captain W. Stuart.

Having laid the Persian Gulf telegraph cable, the ship brought the Seaforth Highlanders home from India in seventy-eight days and proved her worth as a sailing ship. *The Tweed* enjoyed a successful career, though she had her fair share of bad luck. In 1882, when running her easting down in the southern Indian Ocean she lost much of her upper main and foremasts. Notwithstanding this handicap she made 2000 miles in a week and arrived in Sydney under jury-rig only ninety-three days out. Finally, in July 1888, bound from China to New York, she was dismasted off Algoa Bay, South Africa. She was towed into Port Elizabeth by the steamship *Venice*, but was not considered worth repairing and her teak timbers were taken to roof a local church.

The *Punjaub* had been designed by Oliver Lang and was built of teak in Bombay by the Parsee Cursetjee Rustomjee. In conceiving her hull, Lang is said to have been inspired in his turn by the wreck of an old French frigate, an improbable tale since his new ship was 285 feet overall with a net tonnage of 1745. Captain Stuart certainly knew how to drive her and found the means of trimming her to advantage, for years later, the apprentices of *The Tweed* discovered her old ten 68-pounder carronades as ballast in her after hold.

Willis had *The Tweed*'s lines taken off and in addition to the *Cutty Sark*, he used her hull form for the *Hallowe'en* and the unlucky *Blackadder*. Though she inspired clippers, *The Tweed* herself was considered to be a Blackwaller. John Willis her Scots owner, though hailing from the banks of the River Tweed, ran her out of London in what was broadly considered a passenger trade.

Her last connection with the *Cutty Sark* was that the clipper's first master, George Moodie, had been *The Tweed*'s mate. Able but not exceptional, he was inferior to Woodget and *Cutty Sark* did not truly prove herself until under the latter's command in the wool trade where she ran her easting down in the Roaring Forties in fine style. Despite Woodget's driving, Willis sold the *Cutty Sark* to the Portuguese shipowners Ferreira, who named her after their family. The sale probably saved her from destruction in the First World War, though she was dismasted off the Cape of Good Hope in 1916 and rerigged as a barquentine. In 1922 she changed owners under the same flag, becoming *Mario do Amparo*, but she was rescued by a British master mariner, Captain Dowman, who moored her at Falmouth, restoring her to her full-rigged splendour. Later she became a training ship for merchant naval officer-cadets at Greenhithe and she now lies preserved in dry dock at Greenwich, a fitting tribute to a great epoch.

The *Cutty Sark*'s gross registered tonnage was only 963, yet some of the largest sailing ships of their day were, like her, composite built. The two largest being the *Andromeda* of 1864 which was built on the Mersey by Jones, Quiggin & Co with a registered tonnage of 1876, and Devitt and Moore's famous passenger ship *Sobraon*.

The composite hull consisted of wooden planking laid over a light, iron frame. To some advocates it was seen to offer solutions not only to the timber shortage, but to the problem of an iron ship's magnetism affecting her compasses. In addition, composite construction was said to be stronger than iron, not much heavier, and cheaper. Compared with all-wood construction it was cheaper, lighter, more easily repaired, stronger and more durable. To others it was not so much composite as compromise, for the two materials were incompatible, producing localised weaknesses. In fact the lifespan of the composite sailing ship was short, though several of the most outstanding sailing ships were built by this method and the *Sobraon* was so well known in her day as to be worthy of further examination.

Built by Alexander Hall and Sons in 1866 for the firm of Devitt and Moore, ship-rigged and capable of carrying over two hundred passengers in two classes, the *Sobraon* was one of the most popular late 'Blackwallers' on the Australian run. Amazing sea-cures were attributed to her and much of her success was due to the one man who commanded her for almost the whole of her working life, Captain J. A. Elmslie. The *Sobraon* was manned by a crew of sixty-nine, which included four mates, eight apprentices, sixteen stewards, two stewardesses, an engineer plus the usual petty officers and ratings: a carpenter, sailmaker, boatswain, two boatswain's mates, twenty-six able seamen, four ordinary seamen and two boys.

Elmslie, one of the first merchant officers to hold a commission in the Royal Naval Reserve, always departed from London in late September, leaving Australia homeward bound in early February and returning via Cape Town and St Helena. Here he landed provisions while his passengers wandered up to view Napoleon's last home at Longwood. To cater for their comfort and provide fresh meat and milk, *Sobraon* carried livestock to the tune of three bullocks, ninety sheep, fifty pigs and three milking cows, to say nothing of several hundred poultry. But conditions were not always such that these provisions could be enjoyed. Outward bound in the southern Indian Ocean in 1889 the *Sobraon*'s passengers were battened down for three days while the ship was battered by the worst weather she was ever compelled to endure. Having lost the foresail, essential to such a vessel in storm-force conditions to keep her head before the wind, Elmslie ordered his crew to set another. It took thirty prime seamen four gruelling hours to bend the new fore course and as they did so the fore upper topsail blew out above their heads. Even under the new reefed course and the fore and main topsails, *Sobraon*'s log ran out at 14 knots. Later that night a sea pooped her, washing away one of the boats and smashing its davits, stoving in a length of the port bulwark and the main skylight, washing some of the unfortunate passengers off their feet and gutting the galley and donkey engine house on the main deck. After a useful life *Sobraon* was retired in 1891 to end her days as a training ship moored in Sydney Harbour.

By 1861, British owners had emerged from the shadow of their American rivals. London-based Richard and Henry Green, Duncan Dunbar and the appropriately named Money Wigram, invested in the new Australian trade. Ten years earlier, it had been Richard Green who, at a City dinner, had publicly announced his intention of building a ship that would beat the

Americans at their own game and in due course his ship was launched as the *Challenger* whose exploits have already been touched upon. In Liverpool, meanwhile, Pilkington and Wilson (later founders of the White Star Line which built the ill-fated *Titanic* and not to be confused with Thompson's Aberdeen line of the same name), James Beagley and James Baines headed a group who bought wholesale a fleet of American Atlantic packets. These ships were put straight onto the Australian run and, at the same time, their owners ordered new tonnage from yards in New Brunswick and Boston. James Baines contracted with McKay for the *Lightning, Champion of the Seas, Donald McKay* and *James Baines*. In the last ship, delivered in 1854, McKay produced what is considered to be his masterpiece. So confident was Baines in his new Black Ball Line, that he signed a contract with the postmaster-general to deliver the Australian mails within sixty-eight days or suffer a daily penalty of £100.

But McKay's ships failed to enjoy the long life of most wooden ships, a factor which had hitherto automatically slowed ship development, for they were built of North American softwoods which soon became waterlogged. Moreover, American shipbuilding was depressed by demands for higher wages after the Civil War.

It was to iron construction that, as has already been mentioned, the British merchant fleet now turned, incidentally discovering the drawbacks concomitant with any new enterprise: iron hulls 'sweated', producing condensation and bilge water. The effluvia produced were highly contaminating to valuable cargoes of tea and coffee, which were highly susceptible to taint. In addition, the rivetting process set up a permanent magnetic field in an iron hull, the implications of which were only slowly grasped. A ship's deviation was now added to the earth's variation to compound Dampier's dilemma all over again. Wild compass errors caused a number of serious marine disasters and the British Admiralty set up a Compass Committee to examine the matter. Before the age of the iron ship, Matthew Flinders had carried out a lot of work on the subject of compass error and had introduced a soft iron bar born vertically on a binnacle to reduce it. To Flinders' bar the committee of Sir George Airy and Sir William Thomson, later Lord Kelvin (who also invented a deep-sea sounding machine) now added two soft-iron spheres. The two savants determined the effect of deviation was not constant and varied according to a ship's cargo and her heading, a fact which required constant vigilance. It could be partly mitigated by the twin spheres, borne on either side of a ship's standard and steering compasses, and these are irreverently known to seamen as 'Kelvin's balls'.

Despite these technical set backs, the advantages of iron to increase hull size were not long in being realised. Emigrant ships, overshadowed by the racier clippers, nevertheless claim their own place in the development of the ship if not of humankind, for they were responsible for the diaspora which followed the twin imperatives of the Irish famine and the Industrial Revolution. American ships alone shifted 90,000 people from the east to the west coast of the United States in the gold fevered year of 1849. The British trade was larger and lasted longer.

Iron ships were much employed in the emigrant trade to Australia. Outstanding among them was the *Patriarch*, built by Walter Hood for Thompson at almost the same time as *Thermopylae*. George Thompson's shipping empire had been founded in 1825 when he was only twenty-one years of age and it was to have a significant impact on long-haul steamships as we shall observe in the next chapter. In 1842, Thompson acquired an interest in Walter Hood and Company and the forty-ninth ship to be built for him in Hood's yard was the iron ship *Patriarch* of 1870, which grossed 1405 tons, was 221 feet (67 metres) in length and 38 feet (11.5 metres) in the beam. On her maiden voyage under Captain Pile she anchored at Port Jackson seventy-four days out from London, returning home in sixty-nine days, establishing a reputation for fast passages which she upheld. After a useful life, during which she had given the *Cutty Sark* under Woodget a close run on the same occasion that the clipper overtook the steamer *Ballarat*, she was sold by the unsentimental Thompson and ended her days carrying timber and sugar around the world. Having cost a substantial £24,000, her devaluation to a sale price of £3150 brought tears to the eyes of her last master, Captain Breach, as he handed her over to her new Norwegian owners in 1898, for the improvement in steamships, pioneered by Thompson himself, had so reduced the value of sailing ships. *Patriarch* was wrecked off Cuba in February 1912.

Noted for being a dry ship, *Patriarch* was popular with passengers and had a poop 90 feet (27.3 metres) long beneath which forty saloon passengers were accommodated. Luxury was not confined to the steam liners with which it has come to be associated. Ships like *Patriarch* vied with each other as owners competed for the army officers and colonial officials who made up the first-class passenger lists.

The London firm of Devitt and Moore built the 1447-ton *Rodney* especially for this end of the market as late as 1874. Launched from the Sunderland yard of Pile and Company which was well known for building wooden 'Blackwallers', though the yard was on the River Wear, not the Thames. The *Rodney* was 235.5 feet (71.5 metres) in length with a beam of 30.3 feet (11.6 metres). Sixty first-class passengers were accommodated in twin-berthed cabins opening from her long saloon. Each cabin contained a lavatory and chests of drawers, while her bathrooms provided cold or hot baths and smokers were no longer banished to the deck, but could enjoy a Havana cigar or a Burma cheroot in her new smoking room.

The *Rodney*'s saloon was lit by large skylights whose stained glass depicted tempting views of Antipodean ports while more practically her galley could feed five hundred a day. She was also equipped with a distilling plant which produced 500 gallons of fresh water, essential not merely to cosset the saloon passengers, but to cater for the less favoured mortals between decks. A fast ship, in 1882 she reached Melbourne under Captain Loutitt in sixty-nine days and five years later under Captain Barrett equalled the *Patriarch*'s record of sixty-seven days to Sydney.

In 1889–90 *Rodney* made her fastest homeward passage of seventy-seven days, leaving Sydney three days ahead of *Cutty Sark* on 31 October bound round Cape Horn. Both ships were in sight of one another off the Horn a month later and Barrett thought the *Rodney* was in the lead when they lost sight of the famous clipper. On 22 December both ships were becalmed together just north of the equator, then *Cutty Sark* picked up the trades and drew ahead. Nevertheless the *Rodney* passed the Lizard only hours astern of the famous clipper. Despite her speed and the luxury of her accommodation, *Rodney* was sold to the French who renamed her *Gypsy* in 1897. Loaded with Chilean nitrate she became a total loss on the Cornish coast on 7 December 1901.

*

Just as the name 'Blackwaller' lingered on, far detached by now from London's river if not from London owners, so too did the term 'clipper'. Ships built by Liverpool owners for the jute trade from Calcutta called their ships 'jute clippers' and many made notable passages. But the days of the ship-rigged vessel were drawing to a close. Fewer skysail yards were seen aloft, topgallants were doubled and the long lower masts that gave the early ships such deep courses, had vanished. As iron gave way to steel, so sail gave way to steam, conceding first the crack tea and passenger routes.

In America the adoption of iron for shipbuilding was slow, despite the impetus of the Civil War. In addition to the availability of cheap, soft timber, the government of the United States clapped a tax on iron, effectively stifling construction and leaving the field clear for British and European yards. The Germans built their first iron vessel, the brig *Hoffnung*, on the Rhine in 1844 and their first steel hull, the barquentine *Hedwig* forty years later. Although the Dutch were not slow to follow, they favoured composite construction for a while.

As the number of ship-rigged merchantmen flying the red ensign of Great Britain began to dwindle, so did the supremacy of the British mercantile marine. Men such as the yachtsman and circumnavigator Lord Brassey and the directors of Devitt and Moore became concerned and in 1890 these men manned the beautiful but ageing iron ships *Hesperus* (commanded by Barrett) and *Harbinger* with officer cadets. The two ships were later succeeded by the ship-rigged *Illawarra* of 1881 and the *Macquarie* of 1875, which were replaced in turn by the four-masted barques *Port Jackson* and *Medway*. Eventually, however, as the Royal Navy abandoned sail-training after the over-whelming of the training brig *Eurydice* by a Channel squall, the British merchant marine followed suit. Devitt and Moore established a training school at Pangbourne on the upper reaches of the River Thames. It was not the tidal waters of Blackwall; officers destined for steamships no longer had to know how to hand and reef sail. Though sail was to continue to exist in tandem with steam and significant improvements and developments were to keep it viable, it had passed its heyday.

Ahead lay only a glorious twilight.

CHAPTER ELEVEN

The Power-driven Vessel

In 1844 Brunel's pioneer iron screw liner *Great Britain* ran aground on the Irish coast. She was floated off eleven months later and after repairs re-entered service. The incident was dramatic proof of the superiority of the iron ship.

Similarly, the screw propeller confounded its worst doubters; in the event its effect of thrusting water onto the rudder, proved quite contrary to the predictions of the Admiralty's Jeremiahs. After the *Great Britain*, the screw became common and rapidly superseded the paddle-wheel. Brunel was not to abandon the paddle, for while steamship development made no startling advances, Brunel now exploited the proven strength of an iron hull to design the *Leviathan*, presaging the great Atlantic liners of the future.

Better known by her final name of *Great Eastern*, this enormous ship was 680 feet (207 metres) in length, with a beam of 83 feet and a gross tonnage of 18,915. Her displacement was in the region of 30,000 tons. Built by John Scott Russell on the Thames in 1858, it was to be 1901 before a larger ship was constructed. Her immense size was to enable her to carry sufficient fuel to steam from the Thames to Ceylon (Sri Lanka) via the Cape of Good Hope without taking bunkers, and thus make ends meet by economies of scale. She was intended to do 15 knots, but it was found not possible to engineer a shaft capable of transmitting this power to the propeller. Brunel overcame this by fitting both propeller and paddles. The 24-feet diameter screw was directly connected to a four-cylinder horizontal engine generating 4890 indicated horsepower; the paddles were driven by a four-cylinder oscillating engine of 3410 indicated horsepower. Under her screw the *Great Eastern* made 9 knots; under paddles, 7 knots. The combination just failed to give her the 15 knots Brunel had calculated. She carried six masts and a crew of 400 officers and men.

Brunel's fertile brain had incorporated other innovations which long afterwards became standard. He divided the *Great*

Eastern transversely by watertight bulkheads and carried her double-bottom plating up to the waterline to form a double skin. Her main deck was likewise doubled. She was as plain as she was monstrous, for Brunel forsook the elegant overhanging and embellished figureheaded bow which steamers had inherited direct from the sailing ship. Such an elaboration would have been difficult to construct, so she was built with a simple vertical stem. Having taken the unusual step of building the *Great Britain* in a dock, the same in which she lies today in Bristol, Brunel now constructed his huge new vessel *along* the bank of the Thames, rather than at a right-angle to it.

Not surprisingly, the *Great Eastern*'s career was chequered. She stuck fast during her sideways launching, which was held to have been a bad omen. She bankrupted Russell her builder, and afterwards her owners, the Eastern Steamship Navigation Company, despite her huge bunkers and capacity for 6000 tons of cargo. She was fitted with accommodation for 800 first-, 2000 second-, and 1200-third class passengers, but as a passenger ship she was a failure, for she rolled with an uncomfortable motion and few ports could accept her vast bulk.

She did, however, lay the first trans-Atlantic telegraph cable in 1865, an achievement which surely justified her existence. When finally broken up in 1888, the body of a riveter was found in her double bottom, accounting for her misfortunes in the perception of the superstitious.

The significance of *Great Eastern*'s direct-drive screw propulsion was largely attributable to the Swede John Ericsson, whom we have already met in Chapter Nine. The horizontally opposed configuration of the cylinders had arisen from the naval necessity of keeping a low-profile engine below a warship's waterline and the main deck, which could not be extensively pierced without weakening a wooden hull. This type of engine suffered from wear and was difficult to work on; moreover subsequent versions failed to reduce coal consumption. It was the Clydeside engineers of Thompson and Company who rotated the engine and produced a vertical configuration which became the norm for the standard marine steam engine.

The adoption of direct-drive was one reason for the general failure to improve coal consumption. As engines became increasingly able to supply the optimum revolutions necessary to a screw, which were clearly higher than for paddles, they required more steam and hence more coal. The design of boilers and the production and economic use of steam therefore became an object for investigation.

The boilers of Brunel's *Great Britain* worked at 5 pounds per square inch. By the 1860s boiler pressures were around 20 to 25 pounds per square inch, as were the *Great Eastern*'s, but the associated heat losses and steam leaks made them grossly inefficient. Furthermore the steam thus produced, having expanded in a cylinder, was vented and wasted. As it did this, while it thrust the piston, it lost heat to the cylinder itself so that the next injection of steam was itself cooled. The space taken up by bunkers was already excessive and an increase in consumption was unthinkable. Not only did the coal itself take up space, but the provision of engineers and firemen, their accommodation, pay and stores, were no less considerations inhibiting long-haul steam voyages.

Ironically, a solution to the problems lay at hand and had done for some time. The idea of using steam first in a high pressure cylinder and then in a second, lower pressure cylinder had been exploited in several early steamers, notably the *James Watt* of 1829. This 'compounding' was the product of the genius of Jonathan Hornblower and Arthur Woolf who had patented a compound engine in 1791 and such marine engines were common in ships by the 1850s, supplied by boilers working at about 25 pounds per square inch. Though this marked an improvement, it was a small one and did not successfully address the major problem of consumption. The best that might be achieved with this level of pressure was exemplified by the *Carnatic* of 1863, one of a class of long-haul steamers built for The Peninsular and Oriental Steam Navigation Company. The engines were designed by John Elder under a patent of 1853, and built by Humphrys and Tennant. By the application of super-heat, a remarkable halving of coal consumption was achieved. A second distant water shipping company, the Pacific Steam Navigation Company, had achieved some success with their paddle steamers *Inca* and *Valparaiso* of 1856. However, these companies were compelled to freight out to coaling stations large quantities of good quality 'navigation coal', an expensive business, even when carried in sailing ships.

Thus it was that, in addition to improvements in glands and packing, attention began to be focused on boiler design itself. The newer universities with faculties for the study of engineering had already founded the science of thermodynamics. But safety considerations enforced by the Board of Trade and the classification societies, meant boilers with higher working pressures could not be fitted to ships. This frustrating situation was overturned by one man who did more than merely 'solve' the problem of steam propulsion; he brought to the design of merchant ships what we should today call a 'holistic' approach. This man was Alfred Holt.

Holt came from humble, industrious Lancastrian stock. His family had migrated to Liverpool, bringing with them a strong Unitarian tradition. Alfred's father prospered with interests in cotton and finance, and bound his son apprentice to Edward Woods, chief engineer to the Liverpool and Manchester Railway. A singularly able fellow, Alfred added to his knowledge of engineering an inherited acumen and entrepreneurial skill. He soon established himself as a consulting engineer before finally going into ship-owning in a modest way with his brother Philip. When forced out of the West India trade by strong competition, the brothers sold their little fleet, retaining one vessel, the *Cleator*, for experimental purposes. This was not merely a bold move, it proved inspired.

In Liverpool shipping circles it was axiomatic that 'steamers may occupy the Mediterranean, may tentatively go to Brazil ... but China at least is safe for sailing ships'. This was much as Samuel Seaward had claimed in his limitation of a steam voyage to twenty-one days. To the Holt brothers, such a shibboleth seemed ripe for destruction. Alfred Holt knew the key lay in proving the safety and practicability of a boiler with a higher working pressure than those permitted under the Board of Trade rules. Encouraged by his friend and employee Captain Isaac Middleton, Holt modified the *Cleator*, and in December 1864 fitted her with new boilers of his own manufacture. He based the design on the braced, or stayed, boilers found in locomotives with which he was familiar. These boilers raised steam at 60 pounds per square inch.

Harnessed to these, Holt fitted his own design of a tandem compound engine with the high pressure cylinder mounted above the lower, powering a single crank. The valve gear was driven by an extended spindle emerging from the top of the high pressure cylinder, but although this made the engine tall, the arrangement permitted a greater angular deflection of the short connecting rod and allowed the main framework of the engine to be low and light. More significantly, the engine took up little longitudinal space.

This combination not only increased the speed of the *Cleator*, it reduced her coal consumption by a staggering forty per cent when Middleton took her on a proving voyage to France, Russia and South America. Meanwhile Alfred and Philip had contracted with Scotts of Greenock to build three identical steamships at a cost of £156,000. On 11 January 1865, the Holt brothers registered the Ocean Steam Ship Company, and on 19 April the following year Middleton sailed for China in the *Agamemnon*, of 2347 gross registered tons. *Ajax* and *Achilles* were to follow, for the Holts considered their venture a great odyssey and all their subsequent vessels sailing under their distinctive light blue and black-topped funnel were named after Homeric Greeks and Trojans. *Agamemnon* and her sisters were workman-like vessels; they were barque rigged, with plain, straight stems and although steaming at 10 knots, burned no more than 20.3 tons of coal a day. 'This result as far as I know,' Holt wrote, 'is not approached by any vessel afloat.' Nor was their ability to steam the 8500 miles between the Mersey and Mauritius without coaling, and still find room for 3500 tons of cargo!

Holt's ideas were not confined to engineering; he also took an interest in hull form. What became known as the 'Holt Standard' was a merchant hull built on the ratio of eight beam-widths to length. Holt attributed the loss of two Bibby Line ships, the *Calpe* and the *Catalonian* to their excessive length and narrow beam. He also built immensely strong ships.

Until 1962, Alfred Holt and Company's vessels were constructed to a standard above that required by the classi-fication societies' ✠100A1, a fitting tribute to the legacy of a man who not only enabled the steamship to come of age, but possessed the wit to run a profitable shipping company. In 1868 *Diomed* and *Nestor* joined the fleet and thereafter the company expanded steadily, carrying its own insurance. As mentioned in Chapter Nine, the coincident opening of the Suez canal in 1869, reduced the distance from China to Europe by 3000 miles and this advantage fell fortuitously into Holt's lap. His ships were soon nicknamed 'the China boats'. In 1891, to counter the threat of Dutch competition, Holt founded the Nederlandsche Stoomvart Maatschappij Oceaan N.V. in Amsterdam, and in 1902 bought out the competition of the China Mutual Steam Navigation Company.

The numerous derricks fitted to Holt's ships made them self reliant for cargo-handling and this feature combined with their speed and capacious holds, recommended them for government service during the First World War. Seventy-nine were engaged and sixteen were sunk by the enemy, a further twenty-nine being damaged. To make good these losses, the Indra Line, which possessed refrigerated ships, was acquired in 1915 and the Knight Line in 1917. These purchases coincided with the opening of the world's second great canal, through the isthmus of Panama, and what now became colloquially known as the 'Blue Funnel Line' had routes encircling the globe.

Finally in 1935 the Holt fleet was enlarged by the purchase of the Glen and Shire Lines, of which we shall hear more in Chapter Seventeen. The Glen Line had long been fierce rivals in the China trade. In 1874 the *Glenartney*, with a cargo of tea, made the passage from Woosung to London in forty-four days via the Suez canal. Until the Holt line's demise in the 1970s, the Glen and Shire Line ships retained their distinctive red and black funnels. They also held onto a curious blue pennant of a white Maltese cross on a blue ground which was flown above their rectangular house flag of a red and white bordered Union flag. This was originally known as a 'steamer's cornet' and was adopted by early auxiliary steamships to distinguish them from sailing vessels, since different rules of conduct governed them at sea, and collisions had resulted from being unable to assess whether or not a vessel was power driven when funnels were hidden behind canvas.

One of the company's steamers, the *Glenfruin*, opened the Tilbury Dock in 1886 and provides a good example of the final development of the steam reciprocating engine. Built in 1880 and of 2985 gross registered tons, the *Glenfruin* was fitted with compound inverted engines and two, double-ended boilers producing steam at 80 pounds per square inch. At 60 revolutions per minute, the ship was capable of 13.5 knots, although the coal consumption was 95 tons per day. Then in 1891 she was refitted with single-ended boilers of 160 pounds per square inch which drove new, triple expansion engines and reduced her coal consumption to 56 tons a day.

The first steamer to be fitted with triple expansion engines was the *Propontis*, built in 1874 by John Elder and Company for the Liverpool shipping house of W. H. Dixon. Although the new engines produced the desired fuel economies, she was dogged by trouble in her water-tube boilers which were unable to sustain the high pressure steam of 150 pounds per square inch required by triple expansion. These had been fitted at the insistence of Dixons who were seeking low fuel consumption, but had to be replaced two years later.

The purpose of compounding was, as we have seen, largely to minimise temperature loss and reduce the production of condensation on the cylinder walls. This had been partially achieved with such double expansion engines as Holt had built, but John Elder realised that multiple expansion was possible, and took out patents for triple and quadruple expansion machinery. The principle required a number of cylinders of increasingly large bore to be set sequentially, and it relied upon steam at very high initial pressure. Once again it was boiler design that frustrated progress. Hitherto wrought iron had been used in boiler-making but the Siemens process for producing steel provided a strong new material which could be rolled, reducing the staying necessary in flat-plated iron boilers, and the outcome was the 'Scotch boiler.' It was a pair of these, working at 90 pounds per square inch, which were put into the *Propontis* in 1876.

Despite the best endeavours of marine engineers, it was shipowners who made the decisions and few had the technical background of a Holt. The case of the *Propontis* demonstrates owners were not infallible. Consequently, however, it was a commercial assessment made in the boardroom of George Thompson's Aberdeen White Star Line that finally brought the steam reciprocating age to the brink of its final phase of development. Thompson decided to inaugurate a forty-day service to Australia by steamship, though the vessel would be rigged, as was customary, as a barque.

History of the Ship

The vessel proposed for this service, the *Aberdeen*, was to be a steam-driven vessel employing triple expansion machinery. Accordingly a three-crank engine was fitted. Its high pressure cylinder had a bore of 30 inches, the intermediate a bore of 45 inches and the low pressure cylinder a bore of 70 inches. The stroke was 54 inches and the plant could generate 2600 indicated horsepower. In order to minimise condensation the intermediate and low pressure cylinders were fitted with water jackets operating at 50 and 15 pounds per square inch respectively. Trials indicated that for a service speed of 13 knots, coal consumption would be around 40 tons a day. In order to contain the then high working pressure of 125 pounds per square inch, the *Aberdeen*'s two steel Scotch boilers were braced to withstand a test pressure of 250 pounds per square inch. This made them to a higher specification than Lloyds required but, with such boilers vulnerable to poor firing resulting from uneven temperatures and local super-heating, the additional incorporation of Samson Fox's corrugated furnaces circumvented any problems. Indeed their furnaces were capable of adjustment, to take account of the calorific value of the fuel in use, for the ship bunkered with coal from the Welsh valleys for the outward passage, and from the mines of New South Wales for the homeward voyage. The *Aberdeen* of 1881 proved a highly successful ship and earned her engine designer, Dr A.C.Kirk (who had designed the power plant for the *Propontis*), and her builders Robert Napier and Sons, a well deserved reputation. Kirk also developed the evaporator which was first used at sea in Napier's *Damascus*. By 1883 the Napiers were building larger engines at higher pressures for the *Oaxaca* and *Tamaulipas*.

Other builders soon caught on and permutations of the basic engine began to appear, designed largely to avoid the payment of royalties to patent-owners. William Denny of Dumbarton who had taken over the building of the *Cutty Sark*, built two 9000-ton steamers for Shaw, Savill and Albion in 1894. Although retaining the now anachronistic clipper bow and a barely necessary four-masted jackass rig, the *Tainui* and *Arawa* were in the van of progress. At Denny's suggestion, these ships were fitted with a four-cylinder, two-crank type of triple expansion engine. The high and intermediate pressure cylinders were mounted above two low pressure units, sharing the third stage of low pressure expansion between two pistons. This ingenious arrangement produced the all-important short power plant.

As the size of the *Arawa* and *Tainui* compared with that of Holt's ships of twenty years earlier shows, the tonnage of ships was rising dramatically as Brunel had known it would. And while the greater the waterline length of a vessel, the faster the hull could theoretically be driven, it needed machinery capable of achieving this potential. Super-heating steam was one answer, forced draught was another and this latter replaced the natural updraught in the boilers caused by a tall funnel.

The problem of producing more power without taking up more than the absolute minimum of space seemed but a repetition of earlier challenges. In reality the materials and techniques available to exploit long-held ideas were only now to hand, and the triple expansion engine afforded a starting point from which even small improvements accrued tangible benefits. Early forced draught systems relied upon pressurised boiler rooms with consequent difficulties in moving coal from bunkers to boiler-room and was abandoned for the time being.

The Inman liners *City of New York* of 1888 and *City of Paris* of 1889 had their closed systems removed in 1891 and replaced with the Howden system, which became standard. This used an open boiler-room fitted with fans which supplied a heated airstream to the Scotch boilers. The ducting was fitted with a form of non-return valves to prevent blow backs when the furnace doors were opened for firing or raking.

However no advance is without its attendant drawback and the steel which enabled the construction of higher pressure boilers, now proved more susceptible to corrosion than iron. This was little understood and became the subject of investigation by a British Admiralty committee, while the Board of Trade took increasing interest in it. Not only the feed water, but oil and grease picked up during the expansion process and carried into a boiler, caused problems, the grease breaking down and forming acids. Scale also built up, causing local over-heating and impairing efficiency. Various expedients were adopted such as chemical treatment and the fitting of filters and de-aerators which heated the feed water.

Such improvements were dramatic and, as we have seen with the Inman Line, occasioned the re-engining of perfectly service-able, but mechanically obsolete ships. The Union Line, facing fierce competition from the rival Castle Line as both companies responded to the demands of the South African gold-rush of 1886, re-engined the Athenian only five years after her com-missioning and the *Tartar* within seven.

In 1879 electricity was first introduced to light the passengers' dining saloon and the engine room in the Inman Line's largest steamer, the *City of Berlin*. Built in 1875 she too was re-engined in 1887, with triple expansion machinery built by the Laird Brothers of Birkenhead and briefly held the Blue Riband for the fastest Atlantic crossing.

All these improvements compounded; even in the long-haul, low freight runs, steam became increasingly attractive, steadily but inexorably eroding the advantages still enjoyed by the sailing ship. Cargo-steamers were launched in growing numbers, dispensing with the fancy fol-de-rols of clipper bow, spencer-gaffs and yards, in favour of a plain stem and derricks. The raised forecastle and poop, hand-me-downs from sailing vessels and useful for the accommodation of the seamen and officers respectively, was now augmented by the addition of the centre castle. It was common to house the master and mates close to the bridge, which had become no mere catwalk, but a substantial athwartships structure; the engineers lived in side cabins along the centre castle alleyways, and the firemen, greasers and trimmers bunked down aft, in the poop, which thereby rapidly lost its aristocratic status in merchant ships!

Just as the Blackwallers and other sailing ships retained the black and white chequer of 'painted ports', some steamship owners developed their own hallmarks in addition to thematic names, individual funnels, house flags and colour schemes. Until the 1960s William Thompson's Ben Line retained 'staining and graining' on its deck houses in imitation of the wooden housing of Scottish fishing boats; of equal longevity were Alfred Holt's huge blue funnels whose colour was said to derive from a tin of paint the young Alfred discovered on a second-hand vessel he bought for his West India venture. Perhaps the most extreme was the attachment of the Danish East Asiatic Company, who retained until the late 1950s a configuration of four tall masts in admiration of the sailing ship and up which the thin funnel exhausts led. Such devices set shipping companies apart, spiced rivalries and earned loyalty. They were a form of advertisement to potential shippers, and seamen prized their ability to distinguish ships by a knowledge of these recondite facts.

The search for reliable schedules and predictable speeds had been solved by the last decade of the nineteenth century. Progress at times had been painfully slow, but the fact that all this had been accomplished in seventy-five years is remarkable. It took time to design and build a ship, time too, to evaluate her performance, particularly if she was lost and that cause had to be established by a formally convened court of enquiry.

In 1894 the British Government consolidated the plethora of administration now regulating the mercantile marine. The new Merchant Shipping Act of 1894 stood as the legislation governing the red ensign fleet until the last phase of its existence, seeing it through two world wars. The act was not universally appreciated, for its minimum subsistence scales of pay and provisions were all that was required of a shipowner to remain within the law, and it was often abused by unscrupulous, scrimping owners who ran their 'pound and pint' ships according to its meagre provisions.

Losses of steamships still occurred, speed and fog being a dangerous combination particularly when a vessel's master was reckless, headstrong, or under pressure to maintain his owner's mail schedule. But the advantages of the steamship were well understood by the general public, many of whom had made voyages inconceivable to their parents. These may have been the one-way ventures of impoverished emigrants, or the leisurely toings-and-froings of the servants of the Raj, but they had in common an understanding of the ship as a most remarkable achievement of the human race, bringing ordinary experience face to face with the mighty forces of nature.

Bigger and faster ships were constantly demanded. In 1857 it was decided to refit the *Great Britain* for the Australian service. A propeller which could be disengaged from the shaft, hoisted and housed in her counter when the ship proceeded under sail, was considered adequate. Thirty years later ships on this service had twin screws and set what sails they had merely to steady their rolling for the benefit of their passengers.

In 1888 the Inman Line put into service on their North Atlantic run their new Clyde-built steamer the *City of New York*. Five-hundred-and-twenty-seven feet long she bore two engines which drove twin screws, the first to be used on a trans-Atlantic ship, giving a speed of 21 knots. The *City of New York*, at 10,650 tons, was the first ship to exceed the gross tonnage of the *Great Eastern*. She and her sister-ship, the *City of Paris*, were built by Thomson's of Glasgow. They had long elegant hulls, with clipper bows and counter sterns and were also rigged as barquentines, but these aesthetic anachronisms belied a very advanced design. Not only did the ships have twin screws, but they possessed considerable internal subdivision, with fifteen transverse bulkheads extending well above the waterline. They were fast ships too, the *City of Paris* making record-breaking runs in both east and west crossings on her maiden voyage, and with two power plants they proved the true reliability of the steam engine to the relief of shipowners and insurers. Following their success, passenger ships could dispense with masts and yards, clear their decks of the residual hang-overs from sail, and construct the long central superstructure with which we have become familiar. The subject of a curious buy-in, the two ships were acquired by American interests and allowed to fly the stars and bars by special act of Congress. Renamed *New York* and *Paris*, they were requisitioned during the Spanish-American War, fitted as armed merchant cruisers and again renamed, becoming *Harvard* and *Yale* respectively. As the USS *Yale*, the *City of Paris* was in action off Cuba, but was largely unscathed. Returning to regular passenger service she was not so lucky, running aground in fog on the Manacles Reef, Cornwall, when on passage west from Southampton. Salvaged and rebuilt in Belfast, the *Paris* underwent yet another name-change, to *Philadelphia*, and lost one funnel and a mast. Her remaining funnels were extended, alterations which ruined her lovely profile. When America entered the Great War in 1917, *Philadelphia* became the US troopship *Harrisburg* and conveyed some 30,000 soldiers to France, returning the survivors after the armistice. In the post-war slump this much-named ship was purchased by the New York-Naples Steamship Company. Bound for Constantinople she got no further than Naples when her owners went bankrupt. She was put under arrest, her already disaffected crew were further humiliated by imprisonment and the ship herself drifted ashore, a derelict. Sold for scrap, she was finally broken up at Genoa after a career of extraordinary vicissitudes.

In 1899, eleven years after the building of the *City of Paris*, the White Star Line's second *Oceanic*, laid down at Harland and Wolff's in Belfast, was also fitted with twin screws and steamed at 20 knots. Entering service in 1901, grossing 17,040 tons and 704 feet overall (209 metres), she was the first ship to exceed the *Great Eastern*'s length. Her displacement was 28,500 tons and she was described as 'the greatest and most elaborately fitted vessel ever constructed'. She too had a sad end, being requisitioned by the British Admiralty on the outbreak of war. She was put under naval command, her regular master serving in a subordinate capacity and she was lost on the Shetlands in bad weather on 8 September 1914.

An advantage of twin screws was not only an increase in thrust, but an ability to manoeuvre a long, thin hull and adding a safety factor in having a second power unit available. The former advantage also commended twin screw configuration to smaller ships which carried out a lot of evolutions. One great benefit of the triple and also its rarer and more expensive development, the quadruple expansion engine, was that it possessed almost equal thrust in reverse. This was not the case with the steam turbine which required a special independent turbine to go astern and complicated gearing to reduce its revolutions to a speed low enough for effective screw propulsion. Nor could the direct-drive diesel run at low speeds. Thus it was that in vessels that needed to manoeuvre a lot, or which needed to run at slow speed for long periods, the triple expansion engine survived. Tugs and cable ships used such steam plant until the 1960s and Trinity House laid up the lighthouse and buoy tender *Ready* as late as 1977. Later, both of these requirements were solved either by the installation of the diesel-electric power plant, or the constant-running diesel engine fitted with a variable pitch, controllable propeller.

Companies vied with each other to produce increasingly lavish first-class accommodation to attract prestigious passengers. Consequently, the quality of general passenger care improved steadily. The first *Oceanic* of 1871 had broken new ground by having a passenger deck, with cabins extending to the ship's side, rather than accomodation either below decks or in deck houses. This heightened freeboard allowed the fitting of rails rather than bulwarks, enabling water to run more freely off the deck. Sails had been dispensed with completely by the turn of the century for passenger ships. In 1904 the Cunard Line laid down the *Mauretania* and *Lusitania*. The company had suffered severe competition from the French Line's *La Lorraine* and *La Savoie*, the White Star Line's *Teutonic* and *Majestic* and the Inman Line's steamers. There was also a fine fleet of German ships in service, the *Kaiser Wilhelm der Grosse*, the *Deutschland* and *Kronprinz Wilhelm* among them. In 1906 the 19,000 tons *Kronprinzessin Cecilie* was intended to be a record-breaker with a speed of 23.5 knots, once her reciprocating engines had bedded in. In the event her only claim to fame was to be the last North Atlantic liner to be driven by 'up-and-down' machinery, for she was to be outclassed by both the *Mauretania* and *Lusitania*.

The *Mauretania* seized the coveted Blue Riband from the *Kaiser Wilhelm II*. This prestigious award was given to the vessel making the fastest trans-Atlantic crossing. It was to be retained by the Cunard liner for twenty-two years until it was captured by the Nord-Deutscher Lloyd's *Bremen*. The *Mauretania* was 790 feet in length, 88 feet beam, drew 36.2 feet and measured 37,938 tons gross. She possessed seven decks, crossed by fifteen bulkheads which gave her 175 watertight compartments. Most significantly she was powered by steam turbines generating 70,000 horsepower, and propelled by four screws. This formidable array gave her a speed of 27.4 knots which whisked her 560 first-class passengers in the lap of luxury from Southampton to New York. She also carried 475 second-class and 1300 third-class passengers, plus mails, baggage and cargo. A veritable floating town, her permanent population was a crew of 812 officers and men.

A fair proportion of this establishment was employed in the business of firing her, for her voracious appetite for steam meant a heavy consumption of coal. While labour was cheap and uncomplaining, manning such great ships was not a problem, but shipowners are not philanthropists and the associated costs were a significant factor in their continuing pursuit of mechanical efficiency.

The Power-driven Vessel

Although the *Lusitania* was a sister-ship, her tragic loss on 7 May 1915 when she was torpedoed off southern Ireland by *U-20*, prevented her gaining the unsurpassed reputation of the *Mauretania*.

The liners of the North Atlantic Ocean captured the public imagination. Because of the deep water terminals at either end of the run, the trade could support the world's largest ships and it became a matter of national pride and company prestige as to which ship held the Blue Riband. The symbolism inherent in linking the Old World with the New was not lost on a burgeoning media who made much of the ships' speeds and the celebrities on their passenger lists. The masters of such ships were men of considerable status who, if they failed to make the fortunes of their East India predecessors, nevertheless became household names.

The trans-Atlantic run was not, of course, the only sea-route, and for the British it was not the most important; that lay in the opposite direction, east, through the Suez Canal to India. But there were many others, mostly linking the colonies, dependencies and dominions of the Empire, while some, like those to South America, were of economic rather than imperial importance. All had one thing in common: they were dominated by passenger ships and passenger-cargo ships flying the red ensign.

The British Mercantile Marine, that generic name for a disparate collection of ships owned by a thousand shipping houses, was not solely composed of such grande-dames of the sea. By the end of the first decade of the twentieth century, in almost every port in the world on any given day, a British 'tramp' steamer could be seen. Such ships literally 'tramped' the world in search of the world's commodities, willing to transport raw materials like iron ore to either the manufactures of Great Britain or Europe, or haul them half way around the world to any destination for which a viable freight-rate could be secured. They carried foodstuffs such as grain, fertilisers and exported goods from Britain too, railway lines, pig iron and finest Welsh 'navigation coal' often for the bunkers of their grander sisters, to be dumped at the coal depots of Gibraltar, Port Said, Perim and Singapore.

The tramp ship was the power-driven equivalent of the sailing ship, built with capacious holds and usually a single 'tween deck, designed primarily as the carrier of an homogenous cargo, whether it be in bags or bulk. She was driven by a triple expansion steam engine fired by a Scotch boiler and grossed anything from 4500 to 6000 tons, plodding the oceans of the world at 7 to 10 knots burning 40 tons of coal a day.

At the outbreak of the First World War there were about 2200 such tramp ships and they rapidly fell prey to the German U-boats who had no trouble in catching them on the surface. A few were converted into decoy, or Q-ships, to tempt submarines, thereafter revealing concealed guns and counter-attacking the sea-wolves. Some, like the *Baralong*, acquired a reputation as dubious as that of their enemy. Generally, however, these ships lived their lives and earned their keep in unglamorous roles. It was the loss of hundreds of them with their vital cargoes, largely of grain, to the U-boats' torpedoes, that brought Great Britain to the brink of defeat in 1917. Only the belated introduction of the convoy system saved this desperate situation. Even so, it had to be forced through against the doubts of senior naval officers and ship's masters. At the height of this crisis the then Chancellor of the Exchequer, Bonar Law, made a tactless speech in the House of Commons, boasting of profits he had made from compensation paid him for losses of ships in which he had an interest.

Tramp ships were not usually owned by large companies, but by small concerns with one, two, or perhaps a dozen ships. It was these vessels that acquired the unenviable reputation of 'pound and a pint' ships, run on the absolute minimum scales laid down by the Board of Trade, ships whose voyages lasted the full two years of their articles and whose crews were paid off with a few pounds and a kit-bag of possessions, to ship out a few days later when they had blown the cash. This nomadic and polyglot population found itself possessed of a reputation as discredited as that of their ships. They represented the lowest ranks of imperial society and were popularly considered 'the pickings of the prisons officered by the sweepings of the public schools'. Such generalisations, as inaccurate as they were unjust, nevertheless pigeon-holed the status of merchant seafarers in the minds of many, and were deeply resented by those so labelled.

Lady Astor, the first woman member of parliament, endeared herself to merchant seamen by suggesting they should wear a yellow armband to identify themselves as potential carriers of venereal disease, yet it was these men who saved the United Kingdom from starvation, and suffered a mortality rate in the Second World War higher in percentage terms than any armed service.

As we shall see, even this sacrifice went largely unappreciated.

It was neither the tramp ship nor the luxury liner that formed the great proportion of the British merchant fleet, but the cargo liner in all her manifestations which carried the world's goods. Built with greater sub-division and up to three 'tween decks, these ships also generally carried a number of passengers, usually in a single class. They were often constructed with a specific trade in mind and sometimes complex permutations of on-board facilities were provided where appropriate. Frozen meat plants had been established at Sydney and Melbourne in Australia in 1861, but early experiments by French owners to ship frozen meat from the Argentine to France in 1868 had failed and only a proportion arrived in good condition at Rouen aboard the *Frigorifique* in 1877. Nevertheless it was the experiments and developments of Ferdinand Carre and Charles Tellier which enabled the *Paraguay* to deliver 5500 frozen carcases loaded in Buenos Aires, to Le Havre the following year.

In 1880 the *Paraguay*, fitted with Carre's ammonia compressor, arrived in London with 40 tons of prime frozen beef and mutton. Here she was inspected by an Australian shipper, Andrew McIlwraith, who afterwards chartered the *Strathleven*, owned by the Glasgow house of Burrell. This ship had been fitted with a 'cold-air machine' built by Bell, Coleman and Co. They had first installed one in the Anchor Line's *Circassia*, and the second went into Burrell's ship. At the same time the Albion Line's sailing ship the *Dunedin* had also been fitted with refrigerating plant and brought the first consignment of frozen New Zealand mutton to the United Kingdom. Other owners were not slow to follow this trend and in 1884 Turnbull, Martin and Co ordered the *Elderslie*, the first custom-built refrigerated ship.

In the Antipodean trades the proportion of insulated, freezer space was large, almost the whole of a ship being given over to it.

These vessels carried dairy products and fruit as well as meat. Some trades needed less freezer capacity and would perhaps devote one or two holds to it, while others specialised in all-chilled cargoes, carrying fruit at relatively high speeds. Such ships operated from the ports of the West Indies with bananas, or the Iberian peninsula with oranges. To achieve these speeds, the steam turbine, the development of which is described in the next chapter, was increasingly used. The New Zealand Shipping Company's *Otaki* built by William Denny in 1908 was capable of stowing 286,000 cubic feet of refrigerated cargo and 273,000 cubic feet of bales. In order for her to make 14 knots, two triple expansion steam engines flanked a central Parsons turbine driven by the exhaust steam from the two engines. By the outbreak of the First World War, over 200 refrigerated ships were in service and they too were targeted by German submarines.

Other cargo liners were constructed with tanks for the carriage of liquid cargoes. Thus 'parcels' of palm or coconut oil, latex, linseed or the fabulously valuable Tung oil, were borne in ships otherwise full of chests of tea, bales of rubber and hemp, hides and pelts, or bags of gum copal; indeed they might, and often did, carry anything. Other specialist space was devoted to secure lockers in which spirits and currency could be carried outwards, and valuable commodities such as silk, ingots of antimony or tin homeward. Such items as personal effects and mail naturally travelled in both directions. The carriage of valuable freight earned their bearers good rates, and the degree of care that companies afforded their ships and cargoes, earned their popular reputations.

Complacency, ever the precursor of disaster, struck the shipping world in April 1912 when the 'unsinkable' liner *Titanic*, owned by the White Star Line, struck an iceberg and sank on her maiden voyage. Although subdivided by athwartships watertight bulkheads so that she could supposedly contain and survive extensive flooding, the iceberg opened a long gash in her side. She sustained massive damage which no ship could survive but by a curious process of history, the tragedy has made the *Titanic* famous, rather than infamous. The circumstances and drama of that calm night captured the imagination of the public in an enduring and fascinating way.

The extensive loss of life, chiefly once again, of fare-paying passengers, provoked a reaction, initiating an examination of safety at sea, particularly in passenger ships. Although Captain Smith had ordered the then equivalent of an SOS or Mayday radio distress signal, it had done *Titanic*'s people little good, for although she exceeded the legal requirement, she remained deficient in lifeboats for the evacuation of all her passengers. The first International Convention for the Safety of Life at Sea, held in London, tackled this matter. It concluded with recommendations on watertight subdivision, the number of lifeboats to be provided and the method of launching them. Although the standard radial davit was to remain in service for many years, companies such as Welin of Sweden and Schat of the Netherlands began developing more efficient methods of getting boats loaded with survivors away from a ship which might well be taking a hostile list. The complex hand-hauled method of the radial davit was slowly replaced by the luffing quadrant davit, much used in wartime when boats were kept swung outboard, and later by the modern Schat and Welin Maclachlan 'gravity' type davits.

Other matters were also addressed by the Convention, such as improved and mandatory radio communications, and provisions for fire-fighting. Many of these recommendations were retro-fitted to existing tonnage, such as the *Titanic*'s sister-ship, the *Olympic*, the last vestige of which, the panelling from her first-class smoking room, may still be seen in the ballroom of the White Hart Hotel at Alnwick in Northumberland.

Shipbuilding boomed even while the Convention deliberated. In 1913, no fewer than 1750 merchant ships were built, some 3.3 million gross registered tons, a gross ton being a measurement of capacity of 100 cubic feet. Fifty-eight per cent of this new building was in British yards, but enormous losses to German submarines created a shortfall in merchant shipping which reached crisis proportions, for it was further exacerbated by other factors. Promised a short war, British builders turned to the production of warships and no new merchant tonnage was constructed. Moreover, there was no credible salvage industry available to save damaged merchant ships which were, of necessity, often sunk by friendly fire and thus repair of crippled merchantmen was virtually unknown. Unfortunately, it was the

Germans who had come to dominate the salvage market and so the British Admiralty took matters into their own hands, building large tugs capable of towing in disabled vessels and thus saving hull and cargo.

This situation required a crash building-programme to be instituted in 1917 as the United States entered the war. Emergency shipbuilding was vigorously started in Britain and the United States, with the concept of the 'standard ship' being born, simplifying existing designs, construction methods and, most significantly, custom-building new yards which were designed for mass production.

This innovation was not possible on the banks of British rivers where shipbuilding yards were small, confined almost to the tide-lines, with the little houses of the workers crowding in tiers of terraces close-by. In such circumstances a yard could accommodate less than ten building slips. It is often a wonder how such yards produced the leviathans they did, until one recalls the digging of deep trenches in the opposite river banks, as happened on the Clyde for the launching of the *Queens* (*Queen Mary* and *Queen Elizabeth*), Brunel's sideways launching method having been largely forgotten. In the United States, however, there was plenty of real estate, and yards such as Hog Island at Philadelphia were laid out with fifty such building ways. As a consequence, the Americans were able to build on a scale never before dreamed of. To this happy expedient, thousands of tons of German shipping interned in American ports were released to the Allies, a factor not apparently appreciated by the German High Command.

Nor were the Americans and British alone in this accelerated shipbuilding. Their oriental allies, the Japanese, also embarked on an ambitious programme of standard ship construction, founding an industry that was to supplant the others and marking the end of Japan's reliance upon western technology.

As for the standard ship, in her several varieties she was to save the situation, not just in the First World War, but later, in the Second.

The passing of sail was a significant enough fact to seafarers, but it also marked an important transition for humanity ashore, for in discarding the natural motive power of the wind, the human race began to embrace an independent means of power, first in the form of the steam engine, later the internal combustion engine. These forms of energy required fuel and while coal was to continue as a prime source for a long time, oil became increasingly important because of its higher thermal energy. In the prospering West, oil was to dominate merchant shipping as much as it was to dominate politics, diplomacy and daily life.

While the tramp ship might carry dry homogeneous cargoes such as grain and wheat or sugar in bulk, and the specialised cargo liner might fill her so-called 'deep-tanks' with relatively small parcels of 200 or 300 tons of palm oil, the demand for oil eventually produced a new ship type: the tanker. The earliest carriage of oils had been in Viking barrels, or Roman amphorae. In Burma similar earthenware jars had been used to transport oil on the Irrawaddy, and in 1210 Marco Polo remarked upon the shortage of barrels compelling oil to be shipped in the holds of ships sailing from Baku, on the Caspian Sea.

Demand for oil began to increase after the Napoleonic War as it became popular for streets in the better parts of cities to be lit, and for oil to fuel domestic lighting. Hitherto only obscure places such as Whitby, with its imports of whale oil coming in from its own fleet of whalers could afford such enviable luxury, but the Argand burner which improved the glow of a lamp by surrounding the flame with a tube, and which had already transformed the quality of lighthouses, was also finding its way into household use. Gradually the common fuels of fish, whale and vegetable oils were demonstrably bettered by shale rock oil. In 1859 the Pennsylvania Rock Oil Company successfully drilled the world's first well at Titusville, western Pennsylvania. This yielded up to 10 barrels a day, but within two years another was producing 3000 barrels and shipments were already being made across the Atlantic.

Oil had been regularly carried in two 4-gallon cases held together in a wooden frame in all classes of ships, when it was known as 'case-oil', and this idea was extended to the installation of large iron tanks in the holds of existing ships. These were of around 30 tons in the lower holds and about 12 tons in the 'tween decks. In 1862 two iron sailing ships, the *Atlantic* and *Great Western*, were built at Newcastle upon Tyne for the carriage of oil in bulk. Their holds were made into four cargo tanks, expansion being accommodated via hollow masts and on 17 February that year the first full cargo of oil, 2888 barrels aboard the American ship *Nineveh* arrived in London. Soon other European cities were also receiving large consignments.

Ten years later three steam tankers were laid down at Palmer's on the Tyne for Belgian owners. The first of these, the *Vaterland*, was fitted with proper tanks and a double skin with a central trunking to allow for expansion of the cargo. Unfortunately the owners also wanted passenger cabins to be fitted alongside this trunking. As a consequence the United States authorities refused to allow passengers to be embarked in such accommodation and in turn the Belgians refused permission for the construction of a tank farm at Antwerp.

Perhaps appropriately enough, the first successful steam tanker entered service where the first bulk oil carriers had been seen in 1210 by Marco Polo, at Baku. Here in 1873 Robert Nobel conceived the notion of investing in the oil business. In partnership with his brothers Ludvig and Alfred (inventor of dynamite and the peace-prize), they eventually bought and rebuilt a well and refinery. By 1876 they tried to persuade Russian shipowners with vessels navigating the inland waterways of Russia to improve their ships, but to no effect. Nothing daunted, the brothers ordered Motala Verkstad in Sweden, to build a small steam tanker, the *Zoroaster*, in which initially eight tanks were installed. After a year these were removed and her holds were filled directly, increasing her capacity by 160 tons to 400. Other ships followed and by 1884 no fewer than fifty steam tankers were working on the Caspian Sea while barges, some of wood, some of iron, served the network of waterways that extended distribution of petroleum products as far as Poland and Finland. One of these latter, the *Martha Poseidnetza* was 504 feet (154 metres) long and carried 9000 tons of oil.

Nor was this rapid and prophetic increase in capacity the only portentous development to be seen on the Caspian. In 1903 the Nobel brothers took delivery of a river barge named the *Vandal*; she was built at Nizhni Novgorod's Sormovo Works. With a length of 241 feet and a cargo deadweight of 650 tons, her chief claim to fame lies in the fact that she was fitted with diesel-electric propulsion. Rudolph Diesel had demonstrated his oil engine at the Munich Exhibition of 1898 and three 120 horsepower diesels, each coupled to generators, powered the three electric propulsion motors which drove her three shafts.

Other owners were equally bold. In the 1870s the Norwegian Hansen company converted its colliers to carry oil, and a decade later Alfred Suart converted existing tonnage, then ordered the first British tanker from William Gray at West Hartlepool. This ship, the *Bakuin*, had a pump-room where tank levels were recorded, and from which extended spindles allowed central control of all master valves.

A few sailing ships were, as we have seen, purpose-built tankers, but others were successfully converted to power. One such was the *Speedonia* which had been built as the *Urania* for German owners. The four-masted barque was bought by the Anglo-Saxon Oil Company in response to an acute shortage of tankers in the closing stages of the First World War and renamed *Scala Shell*. Her masts were taken out and twin triple expansion engines fitted, giving her a speed of 9 knots. Her deadweight was 5000 tons and like most tankers she carried her engines aft, a form of design that proved an elegantly aesthetic product of practicality. With her long bow and figurehead, she kept the evidence of her origin until she was broken up in 1931.

Broken up the same year, the *Dolphin Shell* had begun life at Port Glasgow in 1897 as the steel, stump-topgallant rigged barque *Haytor*. She was purchased by Anglo-Saxon in 1918 at the height of the tanker shortage and converted into a twin screw tanker capable of carrying cased benzine and crude oil in bulk. She retained her rig and was given a bridge above her 'midships deckhouse. Two Bolinder diesels were fitted and her stern strengthened to take her stern tubes. The *Dolphin Shell* was employed in the Indian Ocean and South China Sea, largely under a Captain Baxter, who commanded her for twenty years. The risk of explosion inherent in oil cargo meant that traditional forms of oil lighting were forbidden by the classification societies such as Lloyds who insisted upon electric lighting being fitted in all tankers. She was also fitted with wireless.

The dangers of fire and explosion were very real. It had been concern for this risk that had encouraged the 'engine-aft' configuration as much as a desire to place the tanks contiguously. Explosions did occur, accumulations of gas in empty tanks being the greatest danger, and ships undergoing repair were particularly vulnerable. A disastrous explosion occurred in 1891 when the *Tancarville* blew up in dry dock at Newport, Monmouthshire. In the same year the *Lux* was on passage from Batum to Antwerp, passing through the Greek archipelago when her cargo of kerosene caught fire and the ship became a total loss.

Several of the Nobels' barges had been built by Armstrong Mitchell of Wallsend-on-Tyne. Here, one of the directors and the chief naval architect was a Colonel Henry Swan. For some time Swan had been mulling over the specifications being demanded by various owners and he came up with a design which incorporated the best features. This permitted the carriage of cargo right out to the shell plating; cofferdams were fitted at either end of the cargo tanks; all valves were operable from the upper deck; a cargo main ran through the bottom of all tanks and pipework vented vapour to the atmosphere from the expansion trunking. Moreover, the ship would be capable of loading salt-water ballast for a return voyage.

Swan persuaded his fellow directors to build a ship to his design as a speculation and work was in hand when the Bremen agent for the American Standard Oil Company saw her. Herr Heinrich Riedmann had become involved in the carriage of oil in 1884 when he had had the sailing ship *Andromeda* fitted with seventy-two steel tanks in her holds, 'tween and orlop decks, with an expansion tank on each level. This ship remained in the oil trade until she was run down in February 1919. He was immediately impressed with Swan's tanker, bought her and named her *Gluckauf*, meaning 'good luck.' He also ordered several more ships of the same class. Although structurally successful and the true progenitor of all subsequent tanker tonnage, the *Gluckauf* caused problems in America when longshoremen, tinplate and barrel manufacturers realised that their services were not required to handle her cargo. Sadly the ship was lost in a gale after grounding on Fire Island, New York, in 1893.

Riedmann's other ships were purchased by the company for which he had been agent, the American Standard Oil Company which in 1888 also formed a British subsidiary, the Anglo-American Oil Company.

At about the same time Marcus Samuel, scion of a Jewish family whose business was the importing of shells for decorative purposes, held discussions with a shipowner and broker named Fred Lane, concerning a joint venture selling Russian oil in the Far East. Lane and Samuel visited Baku and the Black Sea port of Batum whence oil was delivered by rail. If a tanker fleet could transport oil via the Suez Canal the joint venture might be brilliantly successful, but up to that time all tankers attempting to transit the canal had been rejected by the authorities as too high a risk. Samuel therefore requested specifications for a tanker which would be acceptable to the Suez Canal Company and armed with this information, ordered three ships from William Gray of West Hartlepool on the Tees Estuary. His ships, *Murex*, *Conch* and *Clam*, each of 5010 tons deadweight, were the first Shell tankers.

Lane and Samuel had used their contacts to prepare facilities at Batavia (modern Djakarta), Singapore, Bangkok, Saigon, Hong Kong, Shanghai and Kobe so that the venture achieved early success. *Murex* became the first tanker to pass through the Suez Canal on 24 August 1892 and her appearance took the rival Standard Oil Company by surprise, initiating Shell's invasion of the hitherto uncontested Far East trade.

In 1907 Shell Transport and Trading merged with Royal Dutch Petroleum to give a combined fleet of thirty-four tankers. The British arm of this early multinational corporation was known thereafter as the Anglo-Saxon Petroleum Company Ltd. At the same time the Anglo-American (Standard Oil) fleet comprised four case-oil steamers and sixteen sailing tankers. Another company, founded by Lord Cowdray in 1912 to transport Mexican oil and hence naming its ships after Latin American saints, was the Eagle Oil Transport Company. Cowdray's ships made a conceptual leap by their size, for Eagle Oil's first ten tankers were of 16,000 tons deadweight, with a further nine of 9000 tons. The larger class immediately demonstrated the economy of scale by carrying their oil more cheaply than their sisters. The consequence of this was an immediate post-war order for twenty ships of 18,000 deadweight tons into which steam turbines were fitted in place of quadruple expansion engines.

Tanker designs were to steadily push ever upwards with the American *William Rockefeller* of 1921 grossing 14,054 and able to lift 22,600 tons deadweight, though the majority remained between the 10 and 15,000 ton range between the wars. Only after the Second World War did the supertanker proper appear and before such mammoth hulls were possible, a number of constructional difficulties had to be overcome.

The dominating problem was that of longitudinal strength. The all-aft design that enabled the tanks, their pipework, venting and controlling valves to be together, put intolerable strains on conventional hulls when the tankers were light, lightening or loading. The buckling of the bottom of a hull was not unknown and the increasing demand for larger ships only exacerbated this problem, so shifting the engines amidships was tried. This necessitated an increase in the number of cofferdams, those empty void spaces isolating the cargo tanks, and taking the shaft tunnel through the bottom of the after tanks. The rivetted construction of steel ships was not rigid and the result was that as a hull worked, gas filled the tunnels. Thus a new type of hull construction was sought and the answer was provided largely by a former Lloyd's surveyor, Joseph Isherwood. What became known as the 'Isherwood System' effectively turned steel ship design around, and instead of relying upon a multitude of frames rising from a single keel, ran frames lengthwise, in the form of several longitudinal girders, crossed by deep transverse floors. The first tanker using Isherwood's method was the *Paul Paix*, built in 1908 and by 1914, another 276 ships had been built in the same way.

Other building techniques came into use between the wars. The configuration of early tankers, where the 'tween deck found in conventional ships was longitudinally subdivided by two bulkheads, allowed a central expansion trunk to serve the tanks situated in the old hold space, and provided side wing, or 'summer' tanks, which were not filled when a tanker was engaged on a winter voyage and required additional freeboard. Such arrangements coped with the effects of free surface, which we shall examine in Chapter Nineteen, and also allowed bulk cargoes of an almost liquid character such as grain, or coal slurry, to be carried without endangering a ship. Such homogenous cargoes spawned the bulk carrier which was to rival the tanker in gargantuan competition, indeed eventually producing a ship capable of responding to the variations of the market, the OBO, or oil/bulk/ore carrier.

Ore carriers had been built in the 1880s, often in Britain for Scandinavian owners. Such ships as the sail-assisted *Gellivara* of 1888, built by Swan and Hunter on the River Tyne, employed strengthened hulls, with central trunking and wing tanks to counter the exceptional strain the hull was subject to. Iron ore, being immensely heavy, requires a larger hull to carry it than the volume occupied by the mass of ore. Moreover, ore lying at the bottom of a hull makes the ship uncomfortably 'stiff', with a violent, short roll period stressful to hull and humans alike. While the *Gellivara* carried her cargo over deep double bottoms and probably used her sails as much to steady her as for anything else, the *Vollrath Tham* built by the neighbouring firm of Hawthorn Leslie had her cargo hold raised well above the double bottom tanks to lift her centre of gravity. This ship could not only dispense with sails, but was self-discharging with electric cranes and carried over twice as much ore as the *Gellivara* though she was only some fifty feet longer. A year later the largest single-decked vessel of her day, the *Sir Ernest Cassel*, rolled down the ways of Hawthorn Leslie, capable of carrying 10,800 deadweight tons of iron ore. Like the new oil tankers, she had her engines aft and her bridge amidships.

The first ship to carry combination bulk cargoes, the *G. Harrison Smith*, was built in the United States by Bethlehem Steel for Canadian owners in 1921. Fitted in similar style to the Hawthorn Leslie ships, the ore was carried in central hoppers set in the middle of the hull and around which was a void space. Divided by bulkheads this void space could be filled with oil and thus the *G. Harrison Smith* carried Mexican oil southwards and brought back ore from South America.

Despite the economic advantages to be derived from such ships, the concept was slow to catch on and it was over thirty years before such a ship was briefly the world's largest. The *Sinclair Petrolore* of 56,100 deadweight tons was built at Kure, Japan in 1956 for the American owner Ludwig. Her complicated equipment permitted self handling of an ore or grain cargo, while she could also carry oil.

In the interim, those ubiquitous carriers, tramp ships, continued in their traditional role. To handle bulk cargoes some were produced using patent 'turret' and 'trunk' systems of construction designed and built by Doxford or Ropner to good effect. A large number were ordered by Cayzer, Irvine and Company, given the names of Scottish clans to become the first ships of the Clan Line. Stimulated by the visit of the *Charles H. Wetmore*, an American whaleback ship to Liverpool, naval architects such as Doxford's designer Arthur Havers, conceived ships with a narrow central raised trunk or turret of about half the beam, flanked by side decks. This arrangement had several derivatives, but its basic advantage was to self-trim a homogenous cargo and inhibit its natural tendency to shift, find its natural 'angle of repose' when a ship rolled, and at best induce a ship to take up a drunken 'loll' or at worst to capsize her. The turret ship also had deep double-bottoms to raise the centre of gravity of the cargo. Furthermore because her net tonnage was low in relation to its deadweight, the turret and trunk ship was attractive to those owners trading through the Suez Canal, where until 1911 dues were based on the former.

The subdivision of a tanker's hull subsequently made the carrying of several types of petroleum products possible and the increasing demand for such fuels meant that not only were large, ocean-going vessels required, but so were coastal tankers, distributing smaller quantities of petrol and diesel fuel from the refineries where the crude oil from Mexico, Baku or the Persian Gulf was cracked into its derivatives.

Ironically, early tankers relied upon coal to fire their boilers and it took some time for oil to be adopted as a boiler fuel. Its potential as the primary power source produced a number of experiments the most successful of which was Rudolph Diesel's 'rational heat engine', patented in 1893. It was not long before firms such as MAN of Augsburg in Germany, Sulzer of Winterthur in Switzerland, or Burmeister and Wain of Copenhagen in Denmark were granted licenses to build industrial diesels. Sulzer installed a diesel engine to a lake steamer in 1904 and, as we have seen, the Nobel brothers fitted them to their barges operating from Baku. The first sea-going diesel by Werkspoor of Amsterdam was installed in the small Shell tanker *Vulcanus* built for the Dutch East Indies coastal trade and in 1912 the Danish East Asiatic Company fitted twin Burmeister and Wain diesel engines in the *Sealandia*. This 5000-ton cargo liner made a special call at London when outward bound on her maiden voyage and was visited by British shipowners and the Admiralty, including the young First Lord, Mr Winston Churchill. The *Sealandia*'s voyage was a commercial success, proving the claims of her engine builders, that the diesel engine took up much less room than a steam reciprocating engine or a steam turbine, each of which required not only boilers and bunkers, but tanks for fresh water. Moreover, the plant weighed less and required only a handful of greasers to tend it, not an army of firemen who had by now, acquired a fearsome reputation as the most fractious members of a merchant ship's crew.

With such a mood for innovation abroad, some curious hybrid engines appeared, designed to improve still further the fuel economies perceived as achievable by shipowners who, as ship size increased, were interested in the exponential nature of economies in scale. An example was the Scott-Still engines fitted to two of Alfred Holt's Blue Funnel liners. The *Dolius* of 1924 was powered by a pair of combined steam and diesel power units in which oil was burned on the down stroke and steam, produced in the cylinder jackets and held in a reservoir, was applied to the underside of the piston on the up-stroke. The *Eurybates* of 1928 utilised separate two-cylinder, non-compound, double-acting engines coupled to the forward ends of her twin diesels. A better means of effecting greater power output was achieved by Dr Alfred Buchi who in 1920 used the dynamic and thermal energy otherwise lost in exhaust gases, by passing these through a turbine driving a centrifugal fan which in turn forced air into the engine at the start of the cycle, thus 'turbo-charging' the whole process. By these means the diesel engine proved itself suitable for most types of merchant ship propulsion, except where very high speed was required.

Since the first, tentative appearance of the steam engine, the progress made in merchant shipping had been steady, based upon the pragmatism born of sturdy commercial requirements. This was to continue, for change in shipping is always slow, but in due course the economical and reliable 'rational heat engine' would come to provide the heartbeat of the modern power-driven merchantman. The story of the warship, however, is not quite so straightforward.

CHAPTER TWELVE

Armour, Turrets and Torpedoes

At the Battle of Trafalgar in 1805, HMS *Victory* was already fifty years old and although she had undergone several refits, had not significantly changed from her original form. One hundred years later, the commissioning of HMS *Dreadnought* changed the concept of naval warfare overnight and initiated a naval arms race which, in itself, can be seen as a contributory cause of the First World War.

During the intervening century the pace of naval change had gained momentum. Rapid development and counter-development became a feature of international warship design from about 1850, and steam power finally succeeded sail. New weapons such as the torpedo, the breech-loading rifled gun and the submarine were now to be added to the naval inventory.

The dominating power throughout the period was Great Britain; unassailable at sea for the first half-century, she came under increasing pressure from other countries in the second. Britain's strength lay not only in her mastery of the sea at the end of the Napoleonic War, but also in her huge industrial power which, when provoked by a foreign threat, shifted into a higher gear to confound her rivals. Thus, when the French navy of Napoleon III's Second Empire began to cause unease in high places, Great Britain's answer was to produce more and better ships. This was possible because Britain's output of coal, steel and munitions was greatly superior to that of France.

As with merchant shipping, Britain also built men-of-war for other countries, such as the new South American republics in whose liberation from Spanish rule Britain's naval officers had played no small part. Another customer was Japan, whose British-built warships destroyed Rhozhdestvensky's Russian fleet at Tsu-Shima in 1906. It was only after this victory that Japan began to break away from a reliance upon British industry and inventiveness, although she was not seen as a threat to Britain's interests until after the First World War.

France remained the traditional focus for British xenophobia until the rapprochement known as the *Entente Cordiale*. France had, in any case, a love affair with her army, not her navy, and the latter service had not flourished under a poor naval administration around the turn of the nineteenth century. Nevertheless France, in possible alliance with the unstable Russia of the Tsars, itself a by no means contemptible naval power, impelled the British to establish a naval policy based on maintaining parity with the fleets of any two world powers. This became enshrined in the Naval Defence Act of 1889, and it was not abandoned with the *Entente Cordiale*, for another focus for British misgivings had arisen.

It was Germany who proved to be the real menace, despite the ties of blood and kinship which united the two ruling houses of Saxe-Coburg Gotha and Hohenzollern. Germany, as the result of the recent unification of loosely knit Germanic states, had risen rapidly to a world power with avowed intentions of achieving major status under the young Kaiser Wilhelm II's policy of *Weltmacht*.

This was possible because the industrial power and dynamism of the German Empire increased after its victory over France in 1870. The German population rose rapidly during the last decade of the nineteenth and first decade of the twentieth centuries and while this created social problems for which imperial ambitions were a useful diversion, this upsurge occurred at a time when there was no similar increase in either France or Britain.

The world has found to its cost since 1945 what it might have learned from the unifications of Italy and Germany in the last century – that newly created states fervently embrace an aggressive nationalism. It was the especial genius of the Germans to organise their economy in such a way that their output of coal and steel, the sinews of a great armaments industry, soared. In 1890, Britain's steel output was 3.6 million tons, about one million more than Germany's. Yet only six years later both countries produced about the same quantity. By the fateful year of 1914, although Britain made 6.5 million tons, Germany was producing 14 million.

Nor was this increase in industrial capacity, without which naval expansion was impossible, to affect Germany alone. As mentioned above, Japan was to benefit from it and so was

America. Japan, recently emerged from the shadows to achieve the humiliation of Russia in the Far East, awoke to the possibilities of joining the imperial powers, while the United States were to be drawn out of isolation by the events of the First World War.

Long before these processes were maturing, the ambitious had sought to topple Britain from her naval pedestal. Small nations, even factions, encouraged the exploitation of small warships. It was, for instance a Fenian, funded by American Irish, who built one of the earliest submarines, just as it was the American rebels who had tried to sink Lord Howe's flagship, HMS *Eagle* in New York harbour in 1775 during the War of Independence, all of which will be discussed later in the chapter. Such aspirations brought into the world the torpedo and the mine, both forms of destruction which demanded a new means of delivery.

Capital ships remained the yardstick by which naval power was measured and displayed, and from 1906, the moment when HMS *Dreadnought* rendered every other capital ship on the face of the earth obsolete, it was German warships that proved a formidable rival to the British. Ironically, the dynastic ties which it had been assumed bound the British and Germans so closely, gave to German merchant shipping the tacit protection of the Royal Navy. Thus it was that from the moment the young Kaiser, supported by his naval chief Admiral Alfred von Tirpitz, began openly to challenge the naval supremacy of Great Britain, the Kaiser's empire already possessed a merchant fleet second only to that of his grandmother's.

In response to the situations and events outlined above, the changes in later nineteenth-century warship design reflected a shift in the balance of world power, an accelerating rate of scientifically driven innovation, and an alteration in the strategic and tactical maxims governing naval consciousness. Not all proved justified and some, such as the abandonment of the convoy system, were very nearly disastrous.

By the end of the century, the turmoil thus created had removed all the old certainties. For several years prior to the appearance of HMS *Dreadnought*, obsolescence had already been accepted as being built into a warship. Although the period was littered with bush-wars, colonial expeditions and the occasional short and bitter conflict between the so-called civilised nations, the *Pax Britannica* ensured that no major war occurred in which the ideas and methodology of naval orthodoxy, whatever its current status might be, could be put to the test.

Instead, just as the design of army uniforms frivolously reflected the style of the latest victorious power, navies reacted at far greater expense to the current advantage displayed by some relatively minor action. This nervousness created exactly the right conditions for arms races, and explains why the period threw up so many false starts and apparently crackpot concepts. Inventive minds with an eye to the main chance proliferated, and though those characters occupying the offices of the Lords Commissioners of the Admiralty in London might often have seemed insuperable obstacles, there was a certain subtle genius in which the British played this deadly game.

It was difficult enough; British public opinion, expressed in the penny-press or parliament, could and did prompt almost hysterical responses to foreign developments or inventions with often wild claims that without immediate adoption of such developments, Britain would instantly surrender her maritime supremacy. The Admiralty tried to manage this clamorous demand, although they were not always successful. One such outburst culminated when Captain Coles, who had been critical of the design of HMS *Monarch*, an early example of a battleship with turret-mounted guns, was permitted to design a ship to his own specification. The result, HMS *Captain*, capsized in a gale off Cape Finisterre in September 1870 taking Captain Burgoyne and most of his ship's company to their graves along with Coles himself.

Another such example was the response inspired by public opinion to the commissioning of two Russian cruisers, the *Rurik* and *Rossia*. Her Majesty's Ships *Powerful* and *Terrible* were huge 'cruisers', far longer than contemporary battleships, though without the armour or the armament to make them useful for anything much more than blue-water flag-waving. They were, moreover, hideously expensive and consequently off the active list by the outbreak of war in 1914. Had they been seen as precursors of that handsome, but unsuccessful warship, the battlecruiser, their fate might at least have served as a caution to the introduction of that class, but alas, this was not to be the case.

Such erratic events were mirrored by other countries, a situation summed up by Admiral Tirpitz himself. 'When I became State Secretary,' he wrote, 'the German navy was a collection of experiments in shipbuilding surpassed in exoticism by the Russian navy of Nicholas II.' The British could ignore the problem, Tirpitz argued, 'There, money is of no importance; if they build a class of ship wrongly, they just throw the whole lot away and build another...'.

The only time this was literally true was in 1906, with the coming of HMS *Dreadnought*.

As has been mentioned in Chapter Nine, steam was initially adopted for small or auxiliary men-of-war, despatch vessels, surveying tenders and tugs. Despite a slow start, the fitting of steam plant into wooden line-of-battle ships had become general by the Crimean War. Nevertheless, sail continued to be carried on heavy warships not entirely out of hidebound conservatism, but because of the fear of breakdown and of the economies it offered on long distance passages and cruising on foreign stations. It is often forgotten when the era under consideration is reviewed, that Britain had overcome the might of Napoleon by maintaining battle squadrons at sea, on blockade duty, and to do so under power would not merely have been extremely difficult logistically, but excessively expensive. The attempt to address these problems resulted in the policy of distant blockade as practised by the British Grand Fleet between 1914 and 1918 when the ports of the German Bight were 'watched' from Rosyth and Scapa Flow. This was manifestly flawed since the essence of blockade is to prevent the enemy emerging at all. The policy of distant blockade allowed the enemy to escape and was to expose the British to the unsatisfactory outcome of the Battle of Jutland.

Although by the mid nineteenth century it was realised that the modern battle would be fought under power, sail was retained for the line of battle until about 1880 when its final demise occurred due to the effect of windage on speed, as the latter became increasingly important as a factor in warship performance. By this time, iron and later steel hulls were in general use, steam plant and boiler design had improved significantly and the Royal Navy maintained coaling stations at strategic points. Nevertheless, small sloops and gunboats, those ships whose duty it was to show the flag world-wide, carry out colonial policing or exploration and surveying, continued to carry auxiliary sails. One constant remained, however, and was to remain until the Second World War and the advent of the aircraft carrier: naval might was measured by the battleship.

During the French Revolutionary and Napoleonic Wars, increases in armament had begun to blur the old distinctions of the rating system. First, carronades were introduced, although excluded from the 'official' number of guns a warship might carry; then additional guns upon the upper decks on forecastle and poop made a further nonsense of the old classifications. Frigate sizes increased steadily, with the Swedes and Americans fitting continuous upper 'spar-decks' to large super-frigates from 1790 onwards. The weight of guns grew likewise, so that the firepower of a large frigate, apart from trouncing nominally equal, but markedly inferior ships, rivalled that of a line-of-battle ship.

Sir Robert Seppings' diagonal construction, referred to in Chapter Eight enabled a wooden hull to be elongated considerably, and as speed is a function of waterline length, this was another augmentation in favour of such increases in scale. The cumulative consequence of these changes meant the new breed of heavy frigate eclipsed that old stalwart of the line, the '74'.

Such a metamorphosis struck deeper, for it took with it the name 'frigate'. 'Cruiser', the hitherto generic title for any warship excluded from the line of battle and not attached to a squadron, became more specific, while the fashionable French import 'corvette', served to denominate a smaller man-of-war. Both corvette and frigate were to be resuscitated in the 1940s as countermeasures to the submarine.

Contemporaneously with these developments, large guns were often carried by small warships on traversing, centreline carriages. Schooners, whether employed as men-of-war, privateers or slavers, adopted this means of delivering a heavy punch when required. Carronades had for some time been mounted on partially traversing slides, and the mortars of bomb vessels were fully trainable by the Battle of Copenhagen in 1801. Thus heavier guns with a centre, traversable mounting became accepted as a possible substitute for the massed broadside of the old wooden wall. Along with this increase in 'weight of metal', projectiles also underwent the transformation from the dead weight of an iron ball, to the exploding shell developed from the bomb vessel's 'carcass', though with an impact-fuze, not a burning one. This new form of projectile was at first spherical and fired from a rifled barrel, the twist of which, engaging in the shell's driving band, imparted a spin to the shell in trajectory and hence improved directional stability and aiming. Finally, in the 1860s, the opening breech was introduced to the largest naval artillery.

During the nineteenth century, progress in naval ordnance, like the quest for speed, armour and other preoccupations, seemed at times to become disproportionate. Lack of real combat experience meant that steady serviceable designs, with the slow improvements in detail which characterise evolution, were almost entirely lacking. When ideas were tested, usually the result of disaster rather than battle, it was always at the expense of the lives of seamen.

The Victorian mariner enjoyed a fashionable love affair with the Victorian public and the pre-eminence of the Royal Navy with its high profile, extended this perception. Sailor suits, nautically inspired brand names and naval images dominated the expanding worlds of advertising and fashion. As for the naval sailor himself, he still led a fairly miserable, over-crowded existence. Although tinned rations and relatively pure water were now used throughout the fleet, the stratified hierarchy of the peacetime Royal Navy became ever more rigid. Life on the lower deck could be oppressive, and while a world of rum, bum and baccy is a gross over-simplification of the naval sailor's lot, there were notorious ships such as HMS *Essex* whose reputation for sodomitical practice was so well known that when she was in the Medway, the women of Chatham reversed their aprons over their bottoms.

For an officer to make a reputation he either had to be lucky enough to distinguish himself in a colonial action, become known for his expertise in some field, or do his best to ameliorate the condition of his men. In an era of eccentric senior officers, that most useful breed of peacetime naval officer, the hydrographic surveyor, went about his business without much acknowledgement. For the officers of the battlefleet, family connections, dynastic alliances and a private income, were indispensable requirements for advancement. Talent was not a prerequisite, and while the memory of Nelson reached its apotheosis during the Victorian period, the independence of the great hero's spirit was quietly murdered.

With the Crimean War, the hitherto calm pace of change began to quicken. The first influence on this was the not entirely accurate view that 'wooden walls' were vulnerable to penetration by explosive shells; the second was the use of iron both as a material for hull construction, with its attendant advantages to steam power, and for armouring a warship against assault.

The exploding shell was first fired offensively from long guns in the Battle of Yucatan in 1843, during the secession of Texas from the Mexican republic. Ironically one of the defeated Mexican ships, the auxiliary paddle steamer *Guadaloupe*, was fitted with two heavy pivot guns but was mauled by a pair of Texan brigs. She had been built by John Laird at Birkenhead as a speculation in anticipation of becoming the first British iron frigate. Instead she was rejected and sold to Mexico.

Then, in 1849, Danish warships suffered from the shellfire of Prussian field guns, but it was not until Osman Pasha's Turkish line was utterly smashed at Sinope four years later, that the devastating effect of shellfire upon wooden ships became generally feared. Although fired from smooth-bore, muzzle-loading guns, the projectiles from Admiral Nakhimov's Russian squadron decimated their enemy with terrible loss of life.

In the 1840s, Britain had already begun a programme of large iron frigate construction in private yards, but a reaction against iron hulls, largely due to theoretical objection rather than the practical experience of the *Guadeloupe*, resulted in these being downgraded to troop transports. One of these, the *Birkenhead*, built by Laird, was fatally altered by the piercing of some of her watertight bulkheads. When trooping to India in 1852, she struck a reef off the South African coast and foundered with heavy loss of life.

The controversy over iron raged for some time. Secret trials as to the efficacy of iron to withstand shot were inconclusive; political considerations and the prejudices of that mediocre naval constructor, Sir William Symonds (who we met in Chapter Eight), weighed more heavily than practicalities. For reasons other than those propounded at the time, the decision was correct, for early wrought iron was not suitable for warship construction, becoming brittle at low sea-temperatures, and lacking resistance to the direct impact of shot or shell.

The French Navy had similar second thoughts, their chief constructor, the brilliant Dupuy de Lôme, having visited Laird and examined the *Guadeloupe*. They too began to build iron corvettes, but retreated from this initiative at the same time as their *trans-Manche* rivals. The French, however, were crucially aware of the potential of shellfire as an offensive weapon, since they had adapted it for naval use following the theories of Colonel Henri Paixhans who suggested that instead of shells being fired on a high, arcing trajectory from mortars, they might be employed to greater effect by firing them horizontally. Heavy guns using such shells demonstrated their ability by destroying the redundant French wooden wall *Pacificateur*. Hitherto the sinking of a wooden man-of-war by gunfire was extremely rare; they were usually reduced to an immobile shambles with sufficient dead or wounded to constitute reason enough for an honourable surrender. However, heavier guns, even without the benefit of exploding shells, began to change this. At the Battle of Navarino in 1827, the flagship of a combined French, Russian and British fleet, Admiral Codrington's *Asia*, completely destroyed her Turkish opponent, and several more of Ibrahim Pasha's squadron were sunk in the action. The opportunities offered by the possibility of actually destroying a ship, something taken for granted in modern war, seemed ideal for those interested in ending British supremacy. In addition to Paixhans, the Americans had also experimented as early as 1814 with horizontal shellfire. It was clear, even to the advocates of this novel form of ballistics that an antidote also had to be found in the form of effective armour. There had been trials of oak-backed iron plating and this was used in the Royal Navy's heavy frigates. Another idea was to incline iron plates to deflect shells, and the Americans adopted this when they planned the construction of a highly sophisticated 1500-ton screw-powered steam warship armed with breech-loading, rapid fire guns. Despite an outpouring of funds, little came of the matter and building was halted in 1856, fourteen years after the signing of the contract for her construction.

It was the inability of conventional warships to bombard the Russian forts in the Crimea as well as the effect of Russian shellfire at Sinope that changed matters once and for all, making the provision of armour an imperative. Ironically the Russians were opposed by a fleet that allied the naval rivals, France and Britain, and the temporary co-operation between these two nations resulted in heavily armoured floating batteries. Basically bluff wooden hulls, they were protected by 4-inch thick plates. The French batteries, *Dévastation*, *Lavé* and *Tonnant* were part of a force which attacked the fortress of Kinburn in October 1855. Their contribution was unimpressive, but the patronage of Napoleon III who took a great interest in artillery, guaranteed their employment. In the words of the British naval Commander-in-Chief, Admiral Lyons, 'you may take it for granted that floating batteries have become elements in naval warfare ...'

The final result was not quite as Lyons' condescension had foreseen. Inadequate though the *Dévastation* and her sisters might have been, they prompted Dupuy de Lôme to design a full sized, seagoing warship. This vessel was a heavy wooden 90-gun ship of the line, razéed to a 60-gun frigate whose hull was reinforced with iron knees and an iron deck. She was given a reduced, fore and aft rig, but was steam powered and screw propelled. Most significantly, her strengthened oak hull was covered in iron plates 4.5 inches thick. Commissioned in 1859 as the *Gloire*, this 'ironclad' man-of-war began the first real naval arms race and was the single greatest influence on warship design in the nineteenth century, not because of what she was, but because of what followed.

In fact *Gloire* was not herself a success, for she failed to take innovation far enough and any subsequent developments were frustrated by France's inability to produce enough high quality iron. Having said that, De Lôme did build an all-iron follow-up, the *Couronne*. Notwithstanding the fact that her hull proved durable, lasting until the 1930s, the *Couronne* was little more than an iron version of *Gloire*, unprotected by internal sub-division. Nevertheless, De Lôme's concept of the ironclad as the logical successor to the ship of the line and prime naval unit was correct. De Lôme, hampered by the lack of iron, was compelled to launch his ironclad programme with one ship a year. The British were not so restricted. When it came, the response was fast and formidable.

Although the British were launching a wooden line-of-battle ship as late as 1858, they were not slow to react to *Gloire*; the *entente* of the Crimean War was at an end. Late in the war, the Admiralty insisted on some of the floating batteries having iron hulls as well as armour. The news of the *Gloire* and a projected fleet of up to sixteen ironclad sisters alarmed no less a person than Queen Victoria, who ordered a Parliamentary Committee of Enquiry to look into the matter. Expert witnesses testified that although it was not necessary for Britain to innovate merely for the sake of it, since such a practice was liable to make her own fleet obsolescent, it was a different matter when a foreign power set a precedent. This was something of a simplification, since Britain had pioneered most maritime innovation and a navy could not ignore the improvements made in commercial shipping without automatically emasculating itself. Nevertheless, on the basis that the expense of major changes should not be accepted until a foreign power took the initiative, conservatism had prevailed. Thus, the appearance of the French ironclads changed the tempo irrevocably.

Paradoxically, the armaments manufacturer William Armstrong had produced a breech-loading rifled gun which, it was happily claimed, would make armour obsolete. In fact gun-power and armour were to march in tandem for some time, until the former finally overcame the latter. In 1860, however, matters were seen rather differently. Napoleon III, nephew of the once infamous Disturber of the Peace, was generally mistrusted by the British and it became imperative to counter his dangerous new ships. Progress of the French building had been monitored with some alarm; the weak, minority Tory government was short of money and this fuelled the debate as to how the French ships would affect the Royal Navy. The question had not been helped by the piercing of experimental plating by a Whitworth rifled gun, although the gun had simultaneously exploded! Further trials of wood-backed armour versus all-iron had been carried out using floating batteries as targets. The wood-reinforced *Meteor* had stood up to fire better than the iron *Erebus*. To some extent this vindicated Dupuy De Lôme's decision to build *Gloire* as he did, but in fact it was the weakness of the bolt-heads which proved the problem, although the oak dispersed the initial shock of impact. De Lôme used heavy screws to secure his armour, the British were to use rubber washers.

What finally tipped the balance in favour of a full-blown reaction was the realisation of the British as to the exact nature of the French ships. *Gloire* was continually referred to as 'a frigate' and the debate about armour seemed to be about the range at which it would be expected to accept punishment. The British Admiralty Board wanted a ship which, in accordance with De Lôme's idea of superseding the wooden wall, made a quantum leap forward and was manifestly and convincingly superior to the French ironclad.

The result of these deliberations was to be an iron-hulled improvement on the heavy *Mersey* class built to a design of Surveyor of the Navy Baldwin Walker, one of the Committee of Enquiry's chief experts. The *Mersey* was the longest wooden warship ever built and was heavily armed for long-range gunnery, conceived as an antidote to a new type of large American commerce raider. The new ship was to carry out the same battle-plan, but with the advantage of her central hull 'being encased with Wrought Iron Plates'. This iron cladding was to extend from the sheerline to five feet below the waterline and, so as not to over-burden her, would stretch for 200 of her 380-feet hull. Her extremities were to be subdivided and her bow capable of ramming. To achieve this, however, a heavy iron knee was built into her bow and contributed to her trimming by the head. Combined with this defect, her great length made her difficult to manoeuvre and she was a poor station-keeper. Nevertheless a feature of her specification which was to be later forgotten, was an insistence that her midships gunport should be at a freeboard of 9 feet. She was also to be as fast as the *Gloire* with a speed of 13.5 knots and capable of cruising under sail, so a banjo frame and retractable screw, along with lowering, telescopic funnels were all to be fitted.

In the event, despite the perceptions which had formed the specification, the new ship became not the first of a new generation of battleship, as De Lôme had postulated, but a great iron frigate, or cruiser. She was nevertheless, an immensely powerful ship and was commissioned as HMS *Warrior* in October 1861 under Captain A. L. P. Cochrane, third son of the Tenth Earl of Dundonald, one of the Royal Navy's former most daring and brilliant frigate captains. Despite being a poor station-keeper, *Warrior* proved herself a fine sailer, easily achieving her designed speed of 13 knots under sail, and slightly better under power. She was 420 feet (128 metres) long overall, 58 feet (18 metres) in the beam, on a draft of 26 feet (8 metres) and she displaced 9137 tons. She was powered by a twin cylinder horizontally opposed Penn trunk engine. Although intended to mount conventional smooth-bore guns, *Warrior* came into service with two 100-pounder Armstrong rifled, breech-loading guns as bow chasers, with a third on her poop; also on the upper deck were four 40-pounder Armstrongs on trucks, while below on her main gundeck a further eight 100-pounder rifled breech-loaders supported her main armament of twenty-six conventional smooth-bore 68-pounders on truck carriages. All except six of these lower-deck guns were inside the armoured citadel. Shortly afterwards, *Warrior* was joined by her sister-ship *Black Prince* and these two warships were assigned to the Channel Fleet where they were described as 'black snakes among rabbits'.

Every ironclad warship which followed these two powerful men-of-war introduced minor improvements. Moreover, although their deliberations took some time, the British Admiralty had reclassified its fleet so that every major warship over 1000 tons displacement and fit to lie in the line of battle, with the exception of two freak sloops and some coastal defence vessels, was either a battleship or a cruiser. By 1870 the Royal Navy possessed twenty-five of them with another five under construction; by an astonishing *coup de main*, Britain, far from relinquishing her sea-power, had augmented it and once again led the world.

What followed in terms of major warship development now concentrated on the best way to accommodate heavy guns. One idea was the armoured turret, germinated virtually simul-taneously by the Swede John Ericsson, whom we met earlier in Chapter Nine over the matter of screw propulsion, and who was still working for the Americans, and a British naval officer, the aforementioned, ill-starred Captain Coles. This rotating device was a logical development of the centreline swivel mounting. Another idea was a central, armoured citadel; yet a third was the

French concept of a barbette, an armoured tower, which protected the ammunition hoists and upon which the guns rotated. To avoid top-weight, the turret necessitated a potentially dangerous low freeboard, but enabled very heavy guns with a good field of fire to be mounted. Furthermore, by locating two twin-gunned turrets in echelon, a 360 degree field of fire could be obtained. The citadel, on the other hand, allowed a high freeboard but restricted the field of fire and the calibre and weight of metal of the guns. It also allowed only half the guns to come into action on either beam, since it was essentially a broadside system. Finally, the barbette system allowed medium to heavy calibre guns to be sited at a good freeboard, but with their crew exposed.

The Royal Navy favoured the turret and the central battery and incorporated the ram bow. An outstanding armoured central battery vessel built according to these principles was HMS *Bellerophon*. She was the first heavy British ship designed to ram and had a short, beamy hull which, with a balanced rudder, made her exceptionally manoeuvrable. In concert with several other such ships, she was later fitted with torpedo launching apparatus.

These concepts had driven American designs on both sides during the Civil War of the 1860s. The *Merrimack* was captured by the Confederates and converted to an armoured battery ship which was renamed *Virginia*; she was formidably armoured, but mounted inadequate guns. To counter this vessel the Union authorities commissioned Ericsson to design an ironclad. Ericsson's *Monitor* was of very low freeboard with a single rotating turret mounting twin 11-inch Dahlgren guns. In danger of foundering en route, *Monitor* nevertheless engaged the *Virginia* in Hampton Roads in a four hour long and inconclusive duel on 9 March 1862. *Monitor* was later lost in a gale off Cape Hatteras but her enduring legacy was to bestow her name on all heavily armed shoal-draught, shore-bombarding craft.

There was a sequel to the Royal Navy's experiment with Captain Coles's ill-fated turret ship, HMS *Captain*, built to his own design, whose loss was attributed by the Chief Constructor, Edward Reed, to a lack of freeboard and the top-hamper of her full rig. Reed produced a better version of the type in HMS *Devastation* of 1871, which carried two turrets, each of which mounted twin, muzzle-loading 12-inch guns. The weight of armour and coal capacity required in such a vessel rendered a sailing rig superfluous. HMS *Devastation* was an ugly ship, but was based upon sound principles, and the British Admiralty was content with this modest progress, continuing to await the developments of foreign navies in order to react by trumping the potential enemy's ace. Since naval orthodoxy increasingly favoured heavier and heavier guns and British manufacturers were building these for foreign powers, it was ironic that an upheaval was to be caused by Armstrongs themselves.

The nascent nationalism of Italy caused her people to decide upon building a small but highly effective force of battleships. The first two, *Dandolo* and *Duilio*, were designed by Benedetto Brin who was offered Armstrong's 15-inch, 50-ton guns, which he accepted for *Dandolo*. However, Armstrong's latest 17.7-inch, 100-ton gun was bought for *Duilio*, Brin's ships were fitted with two turrets each mounting their muzzle-loading monsters. The turrets were situated amidships in echelon, surrounded by a citadel of 21.5 inch Creusot steel armour, with 17-inch steel protecting the turrets themselves. Their speed of 15 knots now caused a new debate and the theory was born of allowing a capital ship the speed to dictate the range at which she engaged: this was to have consequences later. Despite the power of the Italian ships' guns, their rate of fire was slow. Nevertheless, the Royal Navy adopted the 16-inch, 80-ton gun for the *Inflexible* of 1876. Although fitted initially with an inadequate brig rig for training, this soon disappeared. HMS *Inflexible* suffered from the same defects as the Italian ships, but she incorporated several novel ideas which included electric power, torpedo launchers and anti-roll tanks. Her engines were three cylinder compound units capable of delivering 14.75 knots on trials.

Battleship design now concentrated on balancing the triple equation of gun-power, armour and speed. Guns performed better when the shell leaving the barrel did so with the maximum possible speed. The greater the speed, the flatter the trajectory, giving greater gun-control and increased range. In order to achieve this, rifling made a contribution, but a combination of slower burning explosive charges and longer barrels was also found to be necessary. The short muzzle loaders relied upon the barrel length permitting the muzzle to be dropped within a 'glacis' in order for the mechanical rammers to reload; long barrels prohibited this, for larger guns made breech-loading unavoidable. Early use of breech-loading guns had proved unsuccessful, and the seal of early patent Armstrong guns had not proved gas-tight, a problem which had dogged artillerists since the fifteenth century. This was overcome by 1880, largely by superior engineering, and longer barrels were produced by abandoning the old method of boring, and employing a technique of building up a barrel either by shrinking successively larger tubes onto each other, or winding wire around a central hollow forging.

In order to increase muzzle velocity, a slower propellant was required that applied thrust to a shell travelling along a rifled barrel for a greater duration than that provided by fast-burning black powder. This was achieved by adopting slower burning powders and later nitro-cellulose propellants such as cordite. Moreover, longer shells were more destructive, but the chemicals used in both shells and charges were dangerously liable to spontaneous combustion if temperature was not tightly controlled. When the USS *Maine* exploded in Havana Harbour in 1898 it was probably due to this cause, although the American government accused the colonial Spanish of sabotage and used the 'incident' to declare war.

For some time French designers, having favoured the barbette, were also able to produce ships with a high freeboard and this produced better sea-keeping qualities in the classes of battleships initiated by the *Amiral Duperré* of 1879. French ships were built with exaggerated tumble-home, an inward curving of the topsides which allowed side mounting of guns on sponsons. The Italians too, had already adopted the barbette system and in 1887, HMS *Collingwood* became the prototype of the *Admiral* class of barbette battleships, marking the transition from ironclad to what later became known as the 'pre-dreadnought'.

With the barbette, the *Admiral* class carried some very heavy guns. HMS *Benbow* mounted two huge 16.25-inch calibre guns, each weighing 110 tons. The problem with breech-loading barbette guns was that in order to load them they had to be trained onto the centreline and their breeches lowered to align with the ramming gear situated in the rear of the barbette. In a sense, however, these ships had wrapped up the concept of the central battery by carrying a secondary armament in wing turrets intended to ward off the attacks of torpedo craft, of which more later in this chapter, and indeed carrying torpedo tubes as well.

The *Admiral* class suffered from lack of freeboard due to a tonnage limitation and were very wet ships. Its chief effect was to allow sea-water to sweep boats, ventilators and deck fittings away in even moderate weather. However, it was rectified in the *Royal Sovereign* class of seven battleships all built between 1891 and 1892 free of political constraints. The *Royal Sovereigns* achieved this with increased freeboard, helped by their all-steel construction and wide beam. Steel armour proved lighter and more effective than iron, and it was possible to taper the armour at its extremities to save weight. At 380 feet on deck, the same length as the *Warrior*, the *Royal Sovereigns* were beamier, at 75 feet and drew 28 feet with a displacement of 14,150 tons. Though still driven by steam reciprocating engines, the fastest of the class achieved speeds of 18 knots, had a main armament of 13.5-inch guns, well supported by a secondary battery of 6-inch guns with lighter armament for warding off torpedo boat attacks.

In all, forty battleships based on William White's design were built for Britain and similar ships for foreign navies; some of these formed Tojo's victorious fleet at Tsu Shima. The *Royal Sovereign* herself was built in record time, two years and eight months, and this in a Royal dockyard, a result of White's reorganisation of the dockyards in 1889–90.

These ships still suffered from the drawbacks inherent in the barbette mounting, but this was partially rectified in subsequent smaller groups until the *Majestic* class, which broke new ground by being armoured with improved steel. Even though the thickness of armour was reduced from 18 to 9 inches, protection was as good. The weight thus saved, could be taken up elsewhere, and the guns were covered by an armoured gunhouse, soon again colloquially known as a 'turret'. Thus a standardised main armament of 12-inch guns came into being. The new mounting revolved on top of the barbette, enabling loading to take place while the gun remained aligned with its target. This meant subsequent salvoes could be corrected, rather than redirected at every shot.

These and other late classes of pre-dreadnoughts were designed by Sir William White. His tenure of office coincided with the Naval Defence Act which set the 'two-power parity' standard for the Royal Navy. Seen in this context, the rapid

The diminuitive first Holland boat, HM *Submarine No. 1*, lies alongside her depot ship, HMS *Hazard*, a converted torpedo boat gunboat. Five such 'Hollands' were built.

The adoption of steel, taking up 40 per cent of gross tonnage as opposed to 50 in the case of iron, also allowed ships of greater size to be constructed. Russell and Co. of Port Glasgow built this 3609 net registered tonnage 'four-poster' for Anglo-American Oil. The *Brilliant* was used in the case-oil trade and she was one of the largest four-masted barques ever built.

The five-masted barque *France*, one of the 'bounty-ships' subsidised by the French government. Built of steel in Glasgow by Hendersons in 1890 for A. D. Bordes, she was smaller than other five-masters at 3784 tons. Not to be confused with the larger *France II*.

HMS *Dreadnought* dressed overall at a Fleet Review heading a line of pre-Dreadnought battleships.

The German armoured ship (*panzerschiff*) *Admiral Graf Spee* was diesel engined, capable of long-range operations and intended for commerce raiding. Extensively welded to save weight, the class nevertheless exceeded the limitations of the Versailles Treaty. Although her gunnery control suffered from vibration, she inflicted damage with her 11-inch guns when cornered by three British cruisers off the Rio de la Plata in December 1939.

In the pre-1939 arms race, Germany discarded all treaty restrictions and built the *Scharnhorst* (shown here) and the *Gneisenau*, which at a declared tonnage of 26,000, actually displaced 35,000 tons. Variously classified as battlecruisers or fast battleships, they were, if accepted as the former, the only successful examples of the type. Fast and well-armoured, *Scharnhorst* was finally destroyed by the *Duke of York* off the North Cape on 26 December 1943.

Great Britain took the limitations of the Washington Treaty seriously. The *King George V* class battleships were heavily armoured and firepower was sacrificed to this end. The compromise solution of a quadruple turret for eight of the 14-inch guns carried was only partially successful and the forecastle was very cramped and wet. Shown here in 1948, HMS *Duke of York* sank *Scharnhorst* with gunfire in the Battle of North Cape.

This profile of the Japanese aircraft carrier *Shokaku* gives some idea of the large size of such ships. A veteran of several actions, she was sunk in 1944.

The German merchant U-boat *Deutschland* was used for running cargoes from the United States, but on America's entry into the war, she was armed as *U-155* with two 15-centimetre (5.9-inch) calibre guns.

With her 68,000 shp steam turbines driving her quadruple screws at 24 knots, *Lusitania* regained the Blue Riband for Great Britain in September 1907 on her second voyage. On 7 May 1915 she was torpedoed off the Old Head of Kinsale, Ireland by a German U-boat. The deaths of American nationals among her passengers drew the United States into the First World War.

In both world wars, much faith was pinned on camouflage painting breaking up a ship's profile and either making it difficult to see in the first place, or thereafter awkward to lay a gun accurately using optical sights. Here the beautiful Cunard liner *Mauretania*'s silhouette has been broken up by chequers forward and a sunburst scheme aft.

The elegant French trans-Atlantic liner *Normandie* at Le Havre. The after funnel was a dummy and contained the ship's animal kennels. The ship was powered by turbo-electricity and this generated 160,000 shaft horsepower, making it the largest such installation of its day.

The passenger terminals of New York in the heyday of the trans-Atlantic liner. Both Cunard's *Queen Elizabeth* and the United States Line's *United States* dominate the scene.

Flying over the Cunard Line's RMS *Queen Elizabeth* (83,673 gross registered tons), a Boeing Stratocruiser heralds the end of the ship's usefulness as a passenger carrier. In 1957, 1,036,000 people crossed the North Atlantic by sea; a year later the number going by air had increased to exceed this.

The most famous standard merchant ship of them all, the 10,000-ton deadweight Liberty ship. Between December 1941 and October 1945, 2710 of them were built, each taking about sixty days. In 1943, at the height of the battle of the Atlantic when victory depended on the Allies building more ships than the Axis could sink, three Liberty ships were commissioning every day. After the war, Liberties formed the bulk of the world's tramp fleet until the 1960s. This is *Samarkand*, built at Bethlehem-Fairfield at Sparrow's Point, Maryland, where the first Liberty ship and 384 successors were constructed. On commissioning, *Samarkand* served under Alfred Holt's management and then subsequently under various flags until her scrapping in 1978.

building programmes and swift adoption of change is a perfect example of the British Admiralty's policy of reaction, to which, through all the vicissitudes of the period, it had steadfastly held. As for Sir William, his outstanding career was marred by the late introductions to the new Royal Yacht he had built for the old Queen. When docked for fitting out, the courtiers and the Queen herself suggested so many modifications that on being floated out, the *Victoria and Albert*, fell on her side. White retired in 1902, his real work done, but on the eve of momentous changes.

White's ships were keenly observed and followed by foreign builders, especially in the United States and Germany, where the industrial giant Krupp was producing guns and armour to rival anything produced by Armstrongs and Vickers. Matters were shortly to come to a head more dramatic than the *Gloire* versus *Warrior* crisis of 1860 and in order to understand the magnitude of change which had occurred in half a century, it must be remembered that steam-engined, screw-propelled wooden ships of the line had still formed the core of the fleet in 1855. By 1905, the modern battleship was a fully steam-powered, twin-screwed armoured ship of 14,000 to 15,000 tons, with a central citadel surrounding the boilers and engines. Fore and aft she carried a main armament of 12-inch, rifled breech-loading guns in twin armoured turrets. Amidship, her secondary armament was a dozen 6-inch guns. In the *King Edward VII* class these were supplemented by 9.2-inch secondary, and 6-inch tertiary batteries. She would also boast submerged torpedo tubes, though how and when she would fire these was something of a poseur, for this was the potent slingshot she feared most from the enemy.

Just as the mighty battleship was the standard by which a navy's might was measured, so its annihilation preoccupied the inventive minds of those bent on its destruction. Two methods of accomplishing this had been developed: the torpedo and the mine. The latter was a passive weapon, moored opportunistically in shallow water and could be triggered by contact with a passing vessel.

The moored mine could be laid by fast ships under the cover of darkness, and the minelayer later became a significant warship type, with many smaller warships being capable of this deadly task. Early attempts to sink a warship by stealth had tried to adopt the mine by a forlorn hope in a small, inconspicuous boat or a submersible. David Bushnell's *Turtle* of 1775, crewed by the daring American sergeant, Ezra Lee, was one such attempt. The concealment offered by an underwater approach was attractive to those determined to humiliate Great Britain and it is significant that no-one aboard the *Eagle* had the least idea that the attempt had taken place. Poor Lee abandoned his attempt when overcome by carbon-dioxide narcosis

Earlier experiments are alleged to have included a clinker-built cylindrical boat which was rowed underwater with King James I as a passenger. This unlikely story is followed by a shadowy project of the Russian Yefim Nikonov who, in 1720, produced a secret vessel for attacking ships.

A second inventive American whom we have already encountered in Chapter Nine, was Robert Fulton, who built a submarine craft of copper and demonstrated it to Napoleon on the Seine in 1801. Fulton's *Nautilus* bore a sail which collapsed as the vessel reached its operational area, whereupon, like Lee before him, the unfortunate submariner was obliged to hand crank the *Nautilus*'s screw. Fulton's boat trimmed down by means of a ballast tank in its bottom. Alas, the Emperor of the French was meditating a truce with Britain, and Fulton's submarine met the same response as his proposals for steam power. Not one for being over-burdened with moral doubts, Fulton crossed the Channel and demonstrated his machine by exploding a charge under the brig *Dorothea* anchored in the Downs, within sight of Walmer Castle, to which the British Prime Minister William Pitt frequently retreated. The First Sea Lord, Earl St Vincent, poured scorn on Pitt's subsequent enthusiasm by declaring that Pitt was 'the greatest fool ... to encourage a mode of warfare which those that command the sea did not want, and which, if successful, would deprive them of it'. These words were to prove prophetic, but for the time being, early pioneers of submarine warfare were to be deprived of the crucial element: success.

The idea was next resurrected in 1850 by a Bavarian named Wilhelm Bauer during the Prussian-Danish war. Bauer's iron submersible, the *Brandtaucher*, submerged, but could not withstand the pressure, with the result that the hull collapsed and sank to the bottom of Kiel Harbour. Bauer courageously ordered his crew to wait until the ingress of water increased the pressure of the trapped air, whereupon the hatches burst outwards and Bauer and his men shot to the surface. Bauer went on to work for the Russians, whose experimental ventures in many ship types were, as Tirpitz was to observe, 'exotic'.

But the idea of a submarine failed to sink with Bauer's diving boat. While it had at least been proved feasible to get a hull to submerge, even to escape from it when disaster struck, the means of propelling such a hull seemed an insuperable problem. An effective weapon to justify further development was also needed. During the American Civil War, the impoverished Confederates built several steam-powered 'Davids' to attack the 'Goliaths' of the Union navy. One such was armed with a 'torpedo', which in the parlance of the time meant any underwater explosive charge. The David's 'spar torpedo' was poked violently against the target's hull, exploded and in theory sank the enemy vessel. An attack was made by this method on the *New Ironsides* in Charleston Harbour in October 1863, but the conspicuous funnel of the submersible was observed in its approach and the explosion of the torpedo achieved only minor damage. The steam plant was dispensed with in the *H. L. Hunley* which attacked the Union steam sloop *Housatonic* in February the following year. This attack was a Phyrric victory, for although the *Housatonic* was sunk, so was the *H. L. Hunley*. The Confederates also employed 'torpedos' in the form of the primitive moored mine with some success.

Meanwhile a significant and largely ignored contribution had been made by a Spaniard named Montjuriol. In 1862 he built a double hull, using the space between the two for ballast to sink his boat. Montjuriol provided chemically produced oxygen to his steam plant which functioned underwater. The submarine was brought to the surface by driving out the ballast with compressed air. Unaware of this major advance, the following year the French admiral Simeon Bourgois and an engineer named Brun, used compressed air to drive their boat, the *Plongeur*. However, she proved longitudinally unstable.

The successes achieved in the American Civil War, however, had focused attention on the possibilities offered by this kind of warfare and were to result in a collaboration of a rather more sinister kind. The Reverend George Garrett was an Anglican clergyman who, when touring in Europe, observed torpedo attacks made by Russian craft on Turkish ships on the Danube. To be successful, Garrett charitably concluded, they had to be made unobserved underwater. Raising £10,000 capital from his father and some business associates, Garrett built the 14-foot *Resurgam*. With a hand-cranked screw, the vessel's buoyancy was reduced using a piston which admitted the sea to alter the volume of the hull. This curious prototype functioned sufficiently to encourage Garrett and his backers to follow it in 1879 with the steam-powered *Resurgam II* of 30 tons. For this craft a rather more sophisticated power-unit was installed. Water was heated to a high pressure and, upon diving, the smoke escape and fire door was shut and the residual heat continued to provide steam at a working pressure, enabling the boat to travel about 12 miles at 3 knots. To trim the boat down, Garrett fitted amidships hydroplanes, but this method seems never to have succeeded in submerging the boat fully, though Garrett appears to have claimed success when operating in Liverpool Bay.

By February 1880, Garrett was in contact with Torsten Nordenfelt, a successful Swedish armaments manufacturer who was interested in submarines. Attempting to tow *Resurgam II* to a rendezvous with Nordenfelt in Portsmouth, the submersible foundered off North Wales, but this set-back did not prevent the two going into partnership. They built several boats without impressing observers, although they seemed able enough to persuade governments. Submerged times were disappointing and submerged depths no more than a few feet, largely because the method of trimming down was mechanical rather than hydro-dynamic. However, in 1886 the Greeks bought one of their boats and although it never went to sea after reaching the Piraeus, such was the state of naval nervousness that the Turks promptly ordered two! None of these were a success, but they brought Garrett a commission as commander in the Ottoman Navy, an unusual honour for an Anglican clergyman.

Nordenfelt and Garret's *Nordenfelt IV* was built at Barrow-in-Furness for Russia, but she failed to reach the Tsar's naval base at Kronstadt in 1888 and also proved a costly failure. The Russians had had a longstanding interest in experimental submarines. A General Schilder built an iron submersible in 1834 and during the Crimean War, boats were built for service on the

Baltic and the Black Seas by Nikolai Spiridonov and General Gern. A compressed air plant was put into Ivan Aleksandrovski's 115-feet submarine of 1866, but the outstanding Russian contribution to submarine design was made by S. K. Drzewiecki who conceived five different types and developed or refined ancillary equipment for the Russian and foreign navies, which extended the Polish-Russian's career into the present century.

Running in tandem with the evolution of the submarine, is that of the torpedo. By 1866 Robert Whitehead had introduced a practical design to the world's navies. Initially seen as a battleship-killer and mounted in fast 'torpedo boats', it was not immediately adopted for submarines. However, when the Nordenfelt-Garrett partnership built their 1886 boat for Greece, they fitted it with torpedo tubes, enabling torpedoes to be launched underwater for the first time. This kit then became standard and was fitted in all submarines built for the Turks and Russians. These ideas were only taken up slowly and progress continued erratically. Nordenfelt's boats never submerged properly and their latent-heat steam units were hopeless for proper underwater use. In 1888, when the Spanish naval officer Lieutenant Peral designed and built a submersible boat with an electric motor, ballast tanks and a torpedo tube, the Spanish naval authorities took no notice.

In the end it was a Fenian Irishman named John P. Holland, a lay-brother of the Irish Christian Brothers, who achieved the first real prototype submarine. Having emigrated to the United States and left the order because of ill-health, he became fascinated by the anti-British potential of the submarine boat. He built a working model and demonstrated it to fanatically enthusiastic members of the Boston Fenian Society: money thereafter flowed in. As a result Holland built a small boat in 1878, which sank on trials, but was afterwards salvaged, made to float properly and failed again when its petrol engine refused to start. Undaunted, Holland piped steam in from an escorting launch and soon got under way and later submerged.

There followed a series of similar boats which threatened to ruin Holland, until already strained relations between Britain and France worsened, and Congress put up $200,000 for a submarine. Holland's design defeated his only serious rival, Simon Lake. Despite the government's backing, the

Plunger, of 1895, was never finished and finally abandoned. Then Holland's luck changed. His sixth boat was launched on St Patrick's Day, 1897 and purchased by the United States Navy in April 1900, when Lieutenant Harry Caldwell was appointed to the USS *Holland*, becoming the first American submarine commander. Five more *Holland* class boats were ordered; they used a 50 horsepower petrol engine on the surface, which gave them 7 knots, and an electric motor for running underwater at 6. The main ballast was carried amidships, and they had trimming tanks fore and aft. The disappointed Lake went on to design complex submarines, conceiving the type to be for full submarine warfare, with a detachable diving bell to enable divers to cut telegraph cables and wheels to run along the seabed.

Meanwhile in France Dupuy de Lôme had died, but not before designing a submarine which was completed by his colleague Gustave Zédé. The *Gymnote* was 59 feet long (19 metres) and was remarkable for using almost 600 electric cells to power her 55 horsepower motor. However, her debut in September 1888 was marred by the same problems that had dogged the performace of *Plongeur*. Despite these failures, the giant-killing potential of the submarine was recognised by the French Admiralty. After Zédé's death, Maxime Laubeuf became the principal French designer and it was he who fulfilled the French specification for a boat capable of running submerged for 10 miles and with an overall range of 100 miles. Laubeuf's concept was a torpedo boat capable of submerging to deliver her attack. A steam reciprocating engine was used on the surface and while it took some time to shut this down to dive, *Narval* and the sisters which followed, could recharge their own batteries. With these boats, the French were therefore the first to have viable submarine squadrons in service, and seventy-six boats were completed by 1914.

In London the British had observed the French with customary suspicion. A contemporary of the *Narval*, the battery-powered *Gustave Zédé*, had carried out a mock attack on a battleship in December 1898. In itself it was not alarming, because the exercise had been somewhat unrealistic, but reports on the more potent *Narval* altered matters irretrievably. Once again, the British Admiralty bestirred itself.

In 1900 the American Electric Boat Company had acquired John Holland's rights and a Mr Isaac Rice, travelling on behalf of the company, was introduced to the British Admiralty by Lord Rothschild. Despite opposition from the Controller of the Navy, Admiral Sir Arthur Wilson, who declared that submariners should be hanged, a contract was swiftly concluded between Rice's company and Vickers Sons and Maxim at Barrow-in-Furness. Although no provision had been made in the naval budget for the acquisition of submarines, the awkward matter was by-passed by the explanation that they were required to train surface ships in anti-submarine warfare. Construction was to be supervised by two torpedo specialists in conditions of great secrecy. In fact it took place in a yacht-building shed, where ostensibly, the assembly of a new pontoon was being carried out. *Holland I* slid unobtrusively into the water on 2 October 1901, with sea-trials following in the new year. She was commanded by Lieutenant F. Arnold-Foster, the junior superintending officer.

Early difficulties had first to be overcome, but five of these 'Hollands', petrol and electric powered, were soon followed by the thirteen A-class boats built between 1903 and 1905. These early British submarines bore their ballast tanks inside the 64-feet (21-metres) pressure hull, a configuration known as 'spindle form'. They could fire an 18-inch torpedo through a forward tube and proved capable of 25 miles underwater at 7 knots. They were guided by a rudder and after hydroplanes; with no conning tower, surface navigation ran the danger of swamping, but their dive time was significantly superior to the French *Narval* and her successors. One of the innovations which owed nothing to Holland and was introduced by Captain Bacon, the senior superintending officer, was a periscope, a device already used by the French. By the time HMS *Dreadnought* was commissioned in 1906, larger B-class boats were entering service and improved designs were to follow.

At about the same time the Russians acquired a submarine squadron. These were based on designs by Lake and were unfit for active service. Like the British, the Japanese had also bought Holland boats, but none were ready before the end of the war with Russia in 1905. This was also the year that the Imperial German Navy took delivery of its first submarines.

It was to be the torpedo that made of the submarine so potent a weapon, not only as a threat to battleships, but more significantly, to merchantmen. Initially, the torpedo was not developed for submarines. As we have seen, the word 'torpedo', coined originally by that dangerously inventive American Robert Fulton, was an imprecise term. Whatever form it took, the purpose of a torpedo was to blow a hole in a ship's side of sufficient size to sink her. Several varieties were tried in the American War of Independence, the second Anglo-American War of 1812–14, the Crimean War and the American Civil War, but it was not until an Austrian soldier named Giovanni Luppis conceived the idea of a self-propelling 'locomotive torpedo', that the genesis of the modern weapon occurred. Luppis began work with an ex-patriate British engineer named Robert Whitehead who had workshops at Fiume (now Rijeka). Whitehead rejected Luppis's clockwork motor and substituted compressed air. Directional control was not a great problem with early, short-range torpedoes, but keeping the 'infernal machine' running at a constant depth, such that it would not break surface and be seen, nor under run its selected target, was a different matter.

Whitehead developed an ingenious hydrostatic control and the Austro-Hungarian Navy soon took up the new weapon. The British Admiralty followed in 1870, building their own 'Whiteheads' under license at Woolwich Arsenal. The Germans too followed, calling the weapon a 'Schwarzkopff'. There were some odd parallel developments such as the American fly-wheel powered Howell torpedo of 1889 and the British Brennan wire-guided weapon of 1880, but it was the compressed-air powered Whitehead system that was to provide the main-spring for torpedo evolution. By the end of the 1890s the 18-inch diameter nose was loaded with gun-cotton and the compressed-air engine was given extra range and speed by burning fuel in the compressed air.

How this radical new weapon was to be used was a question the British investigated systematically, forming a committee in 1873 which recommended four methods: on board existing warships; delivery to the point of attack by a warship's boats; building small fast craft; and lastly, building fast, larger seagoing ships. The first recommendation we have already remarked upon and torpedo tubes were fitted to most classes of larger warships.

It was this method by which the first Whitehead was launched at the Peruvian armoured rebel ship *Huascar*, from the British steam frigate HMS *Shah*. The *Huascar* outran the torpedo and stories about the torpedo's launching being off the wardroom table rather mocked the parable.

However, development of a dedicated torpedo delivery system was to be an amalgam of the remaining three options. A 'torpedo ram', HMS *Polyphemus* of 1882, was a low-profile experimental vessel which was similar to an American ship, the *Spuyten Duyvil* of 1864. With a good turn of speed (17 knots) for her day, *Polyphemus* carried out a spectacular penetration of Berehaven in Western Ireland in the exercises of 1885, smashing through the defensive boom extended across the anchorage. More significant was the *Zieten*, built on the Thames for Germany in 1875 and capable of 16 knots. She was followed by similar small ships for most European navies, but while these might be seen as diminutive light cruisers, they were too slow to take much advantage of the weapon's giant-killing possibilities. The US Navy's *Katahdin* was a very late example of the ram.

Eventually the British resolved the situation by building two types of craft capable of delivering the torpedo as an offensive weapon. They were the torpedo boat, a light, swift, hit-and-run attack craft, and the torpedo boat destroyer. The Royal Navy's first torpedo boat was HMS *Lightning*, an 80-foot, 18-knot craft, built by Thornycroft in 1876 and finally fitted with a bow tube rather than side drop-collar launching. A few years later the length of such boats had doubled, speed had risen to 25 knots, and the number of tubes had also doubled.

Young officers viewed the new boats with enthusiasm, seeing in them opportunities to distinguish themselves, but their masters at the Admiralty were more concerned with the dramatic rise in the numbers of these boats in the French and Russian navies. At the time the combination of the two powers was greatly feared, along with the potential of these craft to destroy British naval superiority by sinking her battlefleet at its moorings. A whole range of defences appeared: battleships, to the misery of their crews, had to hoist out booms and rig heavy, anti-torpedo nets; and greater internal sub-divisions were added to the already overweight hulls of capital ships while harbour breakwaters were built to protect fleet anchorages. Most effective, however, was the rapid firing 'quick firer' gun, which could pierce the light hulls of the attackers and against which the early torpedo boats adopted the turtlebacked bow made of strengthened boiler-plating.

Hotchkiss, Nordenfelt, Gardner and Gatling were the eponymous geniuses producing these weapons and, with the fitting of recoil cylinders in the early 1880s, the foundation of the rapid firing 3-pounders and 6-pounders soon grew into the 12-pounders, 4.7-inch and 6-inch calibres. What now took place was an escalating arms race in miniature. Successively larger classes were set to catch their smaller predecessors and in 1886, an extensive class of fast armed ships were ordered as 'torpedo catchers' or torpedo gunboats. Later these fragile vessels, which proved too slow, were superseded by 'torpedo boat destroyers' (TBDs). The TBDs proved the nemesis of the torpedo boat, over its offensive function as well.

With detailed design left to individual builders, speed became the obsession of the day. For this the Scotch boiler rapidly proved inadequate and locomotive boilers were tried. As these were found unsuitable for the larger boats, something bigger was called for that would produce steam as fast. The solution was found in the water-tube boiler. This worked by passing water through the furnace rather than the reverse. There were a number of problems associated with the early water-tube boilers and manufacturers vied with each other until, in 1893, the whole controversy was laid to rest by Admiral Sir John Fisher, by now Controller of the Navy and therefore the head of procurement. Laird, Thornycroft and Yarrow each built a pair of destroyers to their own designs, but also to naval specification. These 26-knot, steel vessels were fast, well-armed and carried torpedoes. They were thus able to keep the sea with the fleet, destroy enemy torpedo boats *and* deliver their own torpedoes into the heart of the enemy battlefleet. Later, in order to improve sea-keeping qualities, the forward turtlebacks were replaced with raised forecastles in the 'River' class of 1903–5, an idea the Germans, with a large torpedo boat fleet, had already incorporated in their flotilla leaders.

Such small, waspish vessels were uncomfortable but popular; their discomfort began almost immediately to erode the stiff formality which threatened a kind of social rictus to the late Victorian Navy. Destroyers, known colloquially – but only to those who served in them – as 'the boats', were popular because they were a comparatively junior officer's command and therefore offered opportunities not previously available in great numbers. In many ways the effect such small warships had on the social fabric of the Royal Navy was to be as significant as the new tactics they inspired. As one would expect with such ships enshrining the aspirations and views of young men, speed and in particular the speed achievable by the notional enemy, dominated the continuing development of the destroyer. At the Diamond Jubilee Fleet Review held at Spithead in 1897, the reviewing squadron was led by the Trinity House yacht *Irene* astern of which followed the Royal Yacht *Victoria and Albert*, the Admiralty Yacht *Enchantress*, the Peninsular and Oriental Steam Navigation Company's liner *Carthage*, Cunard's *Campania*, the *Danube* and *Wildfire*. After Queen Victoria, flying her royal standard and the flag of Lord High Admiral, this squadron bore the dignitaries of the British Empire and its guests: Indian maharajahs, Malayan princes, foreign royalty and nobility, the *corps diplomatique*, ministers of the Crown and the great Dominions of Canada and Australia, colonial officials, peers from the House of Lords, members of parliament from the Commons. Even the Kaiser was there, dressed as an honorary admiral of his grandmother's fleet. This solemn procession proceeded between thirty miles of moored warships, each of which was immaculate in new paint with her ship's company lining the rail. The space between the columns was empty but for the steady formation of the reviewing squadron.

Suddenly, a small, low, grey vessel dashed out from between the lines of immobile men-of-war. A large flag streamed out from a vestigial mast and a solitary figure posed negligently on the deck. Her Majesty's torpedo-boat destroyers of the newest and fastest class went in hot pursuit, but proved unable to catch the insolent vessel and her conspicuous commander. The small but flamboyant *Turbinia* sped away from her pursuers at the sensational speed of 34.5 knots!

With this piece of inspired daring, Charles Parsons convinced the hitherto sceptical Admiralty that his steam-driven turbine was a vastly superior power-unit to the conventional triple expansion reciprocating engines in the destroyers. He achieved 2000 horsepower and drove his privately funded venture at this incredible speed by fitting three screws in tandem to each of three shafts. The Admiralty got the message. HMS *Viper* of 1900 was the prototype turbine destroyer in the Royal Navy and although she was wrecked the following year, she proved the feasibility of the system, which was to be introduced for many classes of fast ship, both naval and civilian. As for the destroyer, the Royal Navy was to have 225 of them by 1914 of which the latest L-class were ships of 270 feet in length, displacing 1100 tons. They were armed with two twin rotating torpedo-tube mountings for the new 21-inch weapons, and three 4-inch guns. Their Parsons turbines generated 24,500 horsepower, giving a top speed of 29 knots and they were to achieve a glamour not seen since the days of the sailing frigate.

Although some of these little ships were to see service on foreign stations, their development was closely allied to that of the battlefleet. To fulfil its world-wide obligations, the Royal Navy had, as we have remarked, also derived the long-range cruiser from the frigate. This type of warship had a variable role, but its inception as a medium-sized warship, evolving its own classes, occurred at the point at which the addition of armour distinguished the battleship from the old ship of the line. The cruiser was to raid the enemy's commerce, protect imperial trade, police the colonies and show the flag where British influence was required or British interests were in jeopardy.

For foreign navies the options were less onerous – protection of their own trade but, more important, damaging that of an enemy. To this end there was really only one potential enemy whose trade was so extensive as to be vulnerable, notwithstanding the great size of her navy: Great Britain. The US Navy began building large cruisers in anticipation of a war with Britain after the end of their Civil War. The trend alarmed the British Admiralty which sought to protect its own merchant ships by building large, long-range ships itself. Many of these were 'protected' by a belt of armour, a requirement justified by the failures of HMS *Shah* and her consort HMS *Amethyst*, to defeat the Peruvian rebel vessel *Huascar*.

Once again, developments elsewhere upped-the-anti in British design and the 'armoured' cruiser appeared, different from her 'protected' sister in having side armour. It was to be expected of those masters of *le guerre de course*, that the anglophobic French should promote the type and the *Dupuy de Lôme* of 1895 had the traditional French tumblehome enabling two 7.6-inch guns and six 6.4-inch guns to be mounted in her. She was also the first warship to have triple screws.

Ironically the British Armstrong company built a class of cruiser which was exported in substantial numbers, sufficient to call for orders for the Royal Navy while the reaction to the commissioning of the Russian *Rurik* and *Rossia* has already been alluded to. All the major navies built or bought cruisers. Like torpedo boats they were potential anti-British weapons, useful for destroying imperial trade, but also useful for at least creating the illusion in less well-informed quarters, that the appearance of a national cruiser suggested naval parity with Britain.

The Germans were also building modern light cruisers. Designed to scout and screen their new High Seas Fleet, to destroy the destroyers and to launch in their turn the torpedoes which it was believed would send Britain's Home Fleet to the bottom, the tough *Gazelle* class demonstrate some of the insanity inherent in arms races. At the other end of the scale were the huge battlecruisers, of which more later, but the 'cruiser' as a generic type was to include a number of sizes of warship. There were several types of these smaller sloops and gunboats, from seagoing craft to riverine gun-platforms such as served on the Nile and the Yangtze-Kiang, but they were minor tools of empire and scarcely significant in the history of the ship.

One further innovation claims our attention before the debut of HMS *Dreadnought*. In 1898 Guglielmo Marconi had transmitted a wireless message from the North Foreland lighthouse in Kent to the East Goodwin lightvessel, a few miles away offshore. The following year the same lightvessel broadcast the first radio distress message, having been run down by a steamship. The Admiralty were immediately interested and by 1906 were carrying out radio trials in HMS *Montagu* in the approaches to the Bristol Channel. Beset by fog and hopelessly out in her reckoning, the battleship ran aground on Lundy Island. She became a total loss, though her guns were salvaged. Notwithstanding this mishap, British interest in naval wireless telegraphy increased, but the technology lagged behind the advances made in high explosives, gunnery, armour and speed. Despite the harnessing of electrical energy and impulses, and despite the inception of an epoch-making new class of battleship, the Battle of Jutland was to be no repeat of Trafalgar.

Flag-officers feared that lack of control would lead to a free-for-all and were emphatic that command and control must never slip from the grasp of the senior admiral afloat. To this end they were soothed by the cosy assumption of the signals experts that what worked majestically in the Mediterranean or during summer exercises in the North Atlantic, would suffice under battle conditions in the North Sea.

Funnel smoke, mist and the ship's wind inherent in steaming at speed in line ahead, complicated flag signals, while the lack of effective encryptable short-range, ship-to-ship radio communication combined with aversion to a new technology and preoccupations of secrecy further inhibited the outcome. Moreover, the one radio which might have rendered a signal service, in a plane operating from HMS *Engadine*, broke down.

At Jutland, the very concept of rigid control, essential to the way the British Royal Navy had been trained to fight, was the first casualty. Contact was lost: Scheer turned away and the opportunity for which the officers of Tirpitz's High Seas Fleet had long been drinking toasts, vanished. When it came, *Der Tag* (The Day), saw the British fleet badly bloodied with two battlecruisers lost and a third severely damaged. Six thousand Britons were dead, but Admirals Jellicoe and Beatty remained in possession of the field while Hipper and Scheer scuttled home. In the end, despite the disappointments, the achievement of Jutland was not so contemptible. For mewing up the expensive investment of the High Seas Fleet's great ships until their men mutinied was annihilation by another name. The trouble was that the High Seas Fleet was not the only German naval weapon; the other was more deadly. For the alternative released upon the world the strategy of unrestricted submarine warfare and submarines found easy pickings in the last of the windjammers.

CHAPTER THIRTEEN

Twilight for the Gods

It was profit and not romance that kept sailing ships at sea. Sailing ships took with them to the end, their deserved reputation for being hard work with few rewards; for being poor feeders with wretched conditions. Seamen are not bedazzled by their ships, though they may acknowledge a loyalty to them which has more to do with shared experience and mutual reliance than any false amatory emotion.

After the steamship defeated the clipper on the fast tea routes, the clippers found more meteorologically congenial routes where the winds were almost always predictable in the Australian wool and grain trades. The ageing crack ships ended their days either in this arduous employment (a full circumnavigation by way of both capes), or in the jute or sugar trades. Many, particularly after the First World War, were bought up by the Alaska Packers Company of San Francisco, renamed *Star of ...*' and made an annual voyage up the west coast of North America. Outward, they carried men and stores, to return at the end of the summer laden with packed salmon, having been anchored in those beautiful northern waters as depot ships. But even this work diminished. Slowly these ships, culled from many famous lines with many bearing even more famous names, were sold for scrap, laid up mast-less or moored outside United States' territorial waters as gambling and drinking dens. A pair went to Hollywood for filming and by the outbreak of the Second World War only one, the *Kaiulani*, was fit for sea, the last windjammer to fly the Stars and Stripes. Many other sailing vessels, especially the smaller clippers, such as the *Cutty Sark* were reduced to barques, barquentines, or stripped of their lofty spars to become coal hulks.

Sad though the ending of these ships was, it was inevitable; their sail plans were extensive, their cargo capacity relatively small. As a consequence they required large crews and were heavy on gear and these factors reduced their profitability. So, while steam advanced, there took place a parallel and final development of the sailing ship which had its last stronghold in the long-haul, blue-water trades where low freight, bulk cargoes could still turn in a profit in the face of competition from tramp steamers.

The full-rigged ship of the late nineteenth century had by 1865 already adopted the division of the topsail into an upper and lower sail; in about five years from this time, the single topgallant was phased out and divided, to be replaced by double sails which were easier to handle. In due course the ship-rig itself gave way to the larger four-masted barque. The extreme clipper design which had excelled in carrying the small high-value cargoes of tea from China was superseded by the medium-lined clipper of the 1870s. As composite construction was replaced by iron, the size of ships and the height of their rigs increased. A spate of dismastings occurred, which persuaded builders to curtail mast height and add a fourth mast. Such ships as Craig's *County of Peebles*, and *County of Caithness* were the first of a dozen four-masted iron ships built between 1875 and 1887 by Barclay, Curle and Company, while the Fernie Brothers replaced their lost *Eulomene* with a second ship of the same name in 1891 and chose the four-masted ship-rig for her. A steel ship, she too went missing in the North Sea in 1905. Gillison and Chadwick, whose ships' names were always prefixed *Drum*, had the Clydeside shipbuilders John Scott Russell & Co build the four-masted iron ships *Drumburton* in 1881 and the *Drumcliff* in 1887. But the four-masted ship needed as large a crew as an extreme clipper, and the extra expense in gear eroded profits at a critical time for sailing shipowners. Just as the extreme clipper had sacrificed her after yards and become a barque, the four-masted ship, handsome though she was, rapidly gave way to the four-masted barque.

There were, of course, idiosyncrasies in the basic concept. What became known as 'the English rig' consisted of single, deep topgallants and royals with a gaff-rigged spanker on the fourth, or jigger mast; while 'the Scottish rig' favoured double top-gallants, royals and a leg-of-mutton spanker. The Germans, on the other hand, developed a distinctive, easily reduced, double spanker, with twin gaffs. Despite these variations, it was the four-masted barque which was to be the last, archetypal deep-water merchant sailing vessel.

*

Steel contributed greatly to the increase in size of these last sailing ships. For a decade after the widespread adoption of Henry Bessemer's blast furnace for its production, steel enjoyed a brief vogue. At first it was used for deck fittings, masts and yards. Then it was seen to offer promise as a competitive and effective material for the manufacture of all types of hull. Unfortunately the quality of the material proved inconsistent, and it was not until 1878, when the Siemens-Martin process had eliminated this, that steel hull construction became the norm.

Steel was lighter, cheaper and stronger than iron; it also permitted the introduction of the cellular double bottom, greatly strengthening the rigidity of a hull and giving it protection against grounding. This also conferred the not inconsiderable benefit of providing space for water-ballast.

In 1882 Harland and Wolff of Belfast launched their first steel-hulled full-rigged ship, the *Garfield* for Thomas Ismay. The same year Alexander Stephen and Sons of Glasgow, built the small but fast barque *Helenslea* for their own management. Other British yards like Russell on the Clyde, particularly well known for a conventional and almost standard barque known as a 'Clyde four-poster,' excelled at steel shipbuilding. But so did Dutch, German and French yards, and it is to the latter that acknowledgement for the final innovation must be given.

In contrast, however, the vast soft-wood forests of North America yielded an inexhaustible source of building material and American yards built a few large 'shipentines', the name by which the four-masted barque became known in the United States. In 1889, Arthur Sewall and Company, of Bath, Maine, built three large shipentines, the *Susquehanna* of 2591 tons, the *Shenandoah* of 3154 tons, and the *Roanoke* of 3347 tons, all of which set skysails over royals and single topgallants. With the exception of the *Great Republic* of 1853 (4555 tons), the *Roanoke* was the largest wooden vessel ever built.

These large American barques suffered from the inherent disadvantage of wooden construction. When carrying heavy cargoes such as iron ore, the weight of the cargo acted in the opposite direction to the upward pull of the rigging and consequently a wooden hull worked and strained so that the daily ordeal of pumping, traditionally a hated and laborious task, only became worse. In a man-of-war with a huge complement this provided work for otherwise potentially idle hands; in a hard-pressed merchantman it was a heartbreaking task for which shanties were an inadequate compensation. The iron, and later the steel ship did away with this, much to the relief of sailors, though the chipping hammer, employed to remove scale on a steel hull, provided a substitute activity of monotonous and noisy tedium.

Some American shipowners purchased British-built four-masted barques, but Arthur Sewall also became the principal American builder working in steel and built the barque *Dirigo*, in 1894, using plates and frames fabricated in Glasgow and shipped across the Atlantic by steamship. 'Dirigo' means 'I lead', the motto of the state of Maine, and while Sewall might boast, it was the British designer J. F. Waddington from Liverpool who supervised construction. Even so, it was Sewall who, in 1899, built the *Kaiulani*, already noted as the last Cape Horner to fly the American flag.

As the size of these barques increased, so subtle changes were introduced. For instance the distance from the fore mast to the stem lengthened, and so the bowsprit and jibboom with its long elegant, but vulnerable overhang, became redundant and was replaced by a shorter, more practical spike bowsprit. Masts too, could be fabricated from steel and so the lower and topmasts were made in one section, a method much favoured by German and French builders. It was found in some British ships like the *Lawhill*, and is common today in sail-training ships, being used not only in the small British brig *Royalist* and the barque *Lord Nelson*, but in the large modern, Polish-built, Russian full-rigged training ship *Mir. Jigger* masts were usually, though not exclusively, made in one section.

Increasing economic pressures forced the 'cutting down' of tall rigs so that they were more easily managed by smaller crews. This was achieved by removing the skysail and royal yards. As it was first introduced in 1887, the year of Queen Victoria's golden jubilee, the innovation was called the 'Jubilee' rig. It was also known as 'the stump-topgallant', or 'bald-headed' rig. The Clyde-built *Routenburn* of 1881 was a standard four-poster of 2000 tons. Sold by Shankland to foreign owners she became the

Swedish *Beatrice* and was reduced to a bald-header, a circumstance which was claimed not to alter either her speed or her sailing qualities. Once it showed itself a practical proposition, both economically and technically, barques were built with the rig, though these were mostly unlovely, wall-sided workhorses.

Thereafter the bald-headed rig became the hallmark of the late commercial sailing vessel. The *Lawhill*, built in 1892 by Thompsons of Dundee, was a steel four-masted barque of just under 3000 tons. Lacking royals, her yards were wide and though not elegant, spread as much canvas as if she had set the upper yards. Pole-masted to the topgallant hounds, these were doubled *abaft* the topmasts, an American idea first used in the *Great Republic* and which enabled the upper yards to be more effectively trussed and the topgallants easily handled.

Never a flyer, the *Lawhill* once took 176 days on a passage between Hong Kong and New York, but she was commanded by some able masters such as J. C. B Jarvis and Reuben De Cloux. Their seamanship and commercial acumen, combined with the soundness of her practical design, made her very easy on men and gear, and she was a highly viable ship, able to survive economic depression and still turn in a profit. Not surprisingly, she ended her life registered in Mariehamn under Gustav Erikson's flag, of whom more later.

In parenthesis her sister-ship, the *Juteopolis*, achieved a certain notoriety as the last deep-water ship to fly the red ensign. Although registered in Montreal, she ended her days as the *Garthpool*, owned by Sir William Garthwaite. On a hazy day in 1929 she ran aground off the Cape Verde islands and became a total loss. Her demise was almost symbolic and, perhaps prophetic for red ensign ships in the succeeding century. British merchant sailing ships had become over-capitalised and expensive, not so much due to the costs of men and gear, but by the inexorable and ineluctable rising tide of bureaucracy that was a consequence of the First World War. Expertise too, was on the wane; ambitious seamen could not afford to be romantics. They went into steam and diesel.

There were other innovations alongside the bald-headed rig. Simple, labour-saving technology such as the provision of donkey boilers to produce steam power for deck machinery in the form of capstans, windlasses and pumps became increasingly common.

Generators to produce electric light and the provision of double-bottom tanks for water ballast have already been mentioned in Chapter Eleven, but both were incorporated in the bald-headed four-masted barque *Bermuda*. The *Invercauld* was rigged with sails along the foot of which holes allowed the 'dead wind' to escape, which was said to improve the driving power of a sail and eased the job of furling. Latterly, even stockless anchors were fitted, entirely dispensing with the labour of fishing and catting anchors, or of breaking or bending cable. The most outstanding of these devices was the brace winch, developed by Captain Jarvis. Consisting of conical drums upon which the hauling part of the lower braces were wound, they enabled the yards to be swung with a handful of men. As crew size diminished, so the demand for such equipment increased, while its provision enabled the shipowner to argue for less qualified and able-bodied men, and an increase in the number of 'apprentices'.

Not that any of these devices ruled out much use and abuse of heavy manual labour. Bracing yards with Captain Jarvis's winch was no easy matter, and the gearing on capstans and halliard winches had to be so low that the tasks took a long time. Although technology could produce steel masts and yards, chain sheets and wire braces; and while this gear could stand the worst weather and spread sails which were short in the leach and spread on long yards, the material was unsympathetic. Cold-burns to the skin were not uncommon, injury aloft could be fatal and it was vested interest and profit as much as the great winds of the open ocean that drove these ships.

Perhaps the gear was too strong; there was no way rigging could be cut away when a ship was laid down on her beam ends in a storm, such as happened to the *Moshulu*. Her lee lower yards were in the water, her cargo shifted and she must have been dangerously close to achieving negative stability. Nevertheless, steel spars, chain sheets, wire braces and stout double-zero grade canvas enabled men like Captain Hilgendorf of the *Potosi*, to carry their topgallants through the worst weather. Such a thing would have been unthinkable in a China clipper.

The *Potosi* was one of the last great sailing ships, built specifically for the trade in nitrates between Chile and Germany and her master was known as 'the Devil of Hamburg' for his uncanny knack of divining the wind. Robert Hilgendorf merely studied the data collected by the Hamburg hydrographic office and put the information to good use. He was one of an outstanding generation of German windjammer masters, most of whom worked for the Hamburg owners Reederei F. Laeisz.

All Laeisz's ship's names began with 'P', and this fleet of fine vessels was known as the 'Flying P Line'. They were mostly four-masted barques, though Hilgendorf's *Potosi* boasted five masts and the company produced a five-masted ship, the *Preussen*, which met a sad fate off Dover, being run down by a cross-Channel steamer whose officers misjudged the great ship's speed.

The big sailing vessel of the early twentieth century could, by virtue of her gear, be driven far harder than her predecessors and handled by a much smaller crew. Most of these great barques could and did sustain good speeds, comparable with the fine-lined clippers of the previous generation. Far less complex in their gear, they were far simpler to handle. Gone were the lofty masts of timber, the studding sails and the deep top-gallants, the long, vulnerable jibbooms and the multiplicity of odd, light-weather sails – the 'Jimmy Greens', ringtails, watersails and so forth. The four-masted barque could be officered and manned by relatively young men, whose fitness and enthusiasm contributed in no small measure to their success.

Because of their inherent strength, these vessels could take full advantage of the global wind system and consequently spent most of their time running before the wind, exposed to the danger of pooping. A large, wall-sided four-masted barque was difficult to steer and customarily yawed twenty degrees either side of her course. A pooping meant more than the mere flooding of the officers' quarters; it might mean the destruction of the wheel and binnacle, the washing overboard of men, the smashing of boats on the skids. This occurred to the *Beecroft* off Cape Leeuwin in 1910. The same year the *Glenshee* was buried so deep that the watch on deck only survived by taking to the rigging. The men at the wheel were fortunately lashed, but the violence of the sea took her boats, part of her bulwarks and the poop rail. In March 1905 the four-masted ship *County of Linlithgow* lost her wheel and much of her deck cargo of timber from this cause.

Another danger was that of broaching, of falling broadside into the trough of a heavy sea. With the pressure of a gale in the top hamper pinning a broached vessel down, she ran the added danger of her cargo shifting, usually a fatal circumstance. This fate was narrowly avoided by the *Moshulu*, but the four-masted barque *Torresdale* was not so lucky. She lay on her beam ends at the mercy of the sea for two days in 1903. A similar fate overtook the *Inverclyde* in January 1915. Crossing the Great Australian Bight, the vessel shortened sail as the sky darkened and the barometer fell. The wind veered and backed fitfully, varying in force between a strong breeze to severe storm force 11. During the early hours of the 21st the wind increased to hurricane strength and several sails blew out of the gaskets, shredding away to leeward. In the effort to save canvas, one man was 'beaten off the main topsail yard and landed on the deck'. The ship was eventually hove-to under bare poles, but listed badly and continued to heel so far that the main hatch was dipping under the water, as were the lee yard arms of the lower spars. Water began to pour below. Gaining access to the holds, the crew were now turned-to to jettison or shift the *Inverclyde*'s cargo of wheat and, by a prodigious effort which lasted until the 24th, succeeded in righting the ship and regaining command of her.

Another more avoidable and pernicious risk to which both ships and men were exposed, was poor ballasting. The growing competition from steam which forced the design of the late sailing ship to sacrifice speed for capacity tended in general to diminish inherent stability. In essence there was less bottom weight in the unladen hull and the strong, heavy, resistant rig increased weight aloft. Without a hold full of cargo an unballasted ship, even lying at anchor, was liable to capsize.

Payment for ballast was a disbursement made by a master and it was accepted practice for a master to augment his meagre salary by ordering and paying for an amount of ballast which was delivered short. The master and supplying agent would pocket the value of the shortfall. Inadequate and poor quality ballast such as slimy wet shingle which was liable to shift, caused problems to several ships and it was not unknown for discharged vessels to fall on their beam ends when at anchor or alongside a dock wall. Not until the cellular double-bottom tank was incorporated into the design of a steel hull and, much to the relief of penurious shipowners and the irritation of masters, salt-water ballast could be pumped into a big sailing ship, could she be kept safely upright.

Laeisz, and the major French company of A. D. Bordes, employed their ships in the Chilean nitrate trade, taking coal and timber outward and loading a homeward cargo of saltpetre for fertiliser and explosives. Such operations represented not merely considerable investment in men and ships, but in the infrastructure of the nitrate ports, particularly at the open roadstead of Iquique. Both companies had their own tugs and lighters, so that their ships were not subject to the vagaries of delay, nor their masters compelled to bribe the local officials. Nor was it only for towing lighters out to her that the late merchant sailing ship relied upon steam tugs . She herself often needed hauling in and out of port. Often, if for instance a foul wind prevailed in the English Channel, a big barque would tow well down to the westward before dismissing her tug, not casting off until she had sea-room to beat her way quickly and effectively offshore. It was this use of steam power to minimise the disadvantages of sail which helped preserve the sailing ship for so long.

Whereas the British maintained a distance between their merchant and naval seafarers, based upon social differences as much as differences in expertise, only introducing a naval reserve with reluctance, the more egalitarian French displayed a pragmatic, Gallic approach to their merchant seamen, seeing in them a pool of ability, useful both in times of war and as a potential instrument for national prosperity. The fleet of sailing ships run by Antoine-Dominique Bordes et Fils, though managed with as much skill as that of Ferdinand Laeisz, also profited from this national belief in the maintenance of a strong, skilled seafaring community. French merchant ships did not admit the polyglot crews that manned merchantmen sailing under the red ensign; their complements had to be made up of French nationals and were therefore simultaneously naval reservists. In exchange, a seaman attaining the age of fifty with half that time spent at sea, was guaranteed a small pension.

More importantly, in 1881 the French government subsidised ship construction and underwrote voyages, paying a franc for every gross ton that travelled 1000 miles. This meant that a French vessel could make a passage in ballast to pick up another cargo without suffering loss, and thereby increased the versatility of French shipping. At a time when owners sailing under other ensigns were cutting back and paring costs in order to retain slender profits, the French were able to continue to develop and improve their ships.

Perhaps, therefore, the final flowering in the design of the deep-water merchant sailing ship may be found in the *France II*, the second vessel of that name to be built for the Bordes flag at Bordeaux in 1911, and intended for the ore trade from New Caledonia to France. Although not by any means the last large sailing vessel, she nevertheless incorporated the most up-to-date ideas and was clearly intended to represent the then state-of-the-art, whereas all those that followed her retained traditional features. Built under the French tonnage bounty system by Forges et Chantiers de la Gironde, she was the largest sailing ship ever built, a five-masted barque grossing 5806 tons, with a long forecastle, centre-castle and poop, reducing her well decks to short intervals in her sheer, which was steep at her extremities. All her running gear was belayed on the upper decks and these were linked by short catwalks over the well decks. In total her standing and running gear consisted of 38 miles of manila hemp and 42 miles of flexible steel wire. Her length was 419 feet, with a beam of almost 56 feet and a depth of 25 feet.

Designed to carry a few first-class passengers in the midships house, this also accommodated the donkey boiler, supplying steam to the numerous winches and capstans with which *France II* was endowed. Although stump-topgallant rigged, all the braces and halliards led down to winches. Moreover her decks were well fitted out with steam cargo winches and capstans to aid the business of mooring and, more important to her seamen, the laborious task of shifting sail.

Intended to be independent of tugs, *France II* was fitted with twin eight-cylinder single acting two-stroke auxiliary engines of 295 nominal horsepower. She also sported a steering engine, a generator for electric lighting, pumps and a radio. Her engines, however, were not a success and she was compelled to use tugs, causing considerable anxiety on one occasion by breaking loose from those tugs engaged to tow her from the Tyne to the Lizard.

France II carried stockless anchors which stowed completely in hawse pipes and dispensed with the work of fishing and catting, bending and unbending cable. Her steel hull was also built with cellular double bottoms, a fore-peak tank and two deep tanks which together could hold some 2685 tons of ballast. Her four, foremost masts were constructed with the lower and topmasts in a single pole, the topgallants being secured with long doublings, while her after-jigger, or spanker mast, was a single section of rolled steel; her spike bowsprit secured directly onto the forecastle, following the steep line of her sheer. She was controlled from her poop, on the forward end of which was a house containing the steering engine. Above the wheel, standard compass and extending bridge wings gave her master and officers a commanding view of both her decks and the horizon. Should the steering fail, the traditional after wheel could be resorted to by way of an emergency system, and this was more powerfully geared than was usual. The crew accommodation was more like a contemporary steam vessel and while not lavish, was certainly comfortable.

France II was an interesting combination of new ideas and the traditional lessons of hundreds of years of empiric development, and she deserved a better fate. Unfortunately her career was short-lived and she seems not to have achieved the 17 knots expected of her until her engines were removed and the drag of propellers eliminated. Nevertheless she was capable of a creditable 14 knots and, in the autumn of 1921, she earned the distinction of lifting the largest wool cargo carried in sail, 11,000 bales with 6000 casks of tallow. It was on this ninety-day passage from Wellington, New Zealand, to London that she achieved a remarkable 420 miles for a day's run.

Early the following year she loaded a cargo of cement, steel rails and trucks consigned to the ore mines of New Caledonia. Having discharged this and ballasted in Tchio, her Breton master, Captain Leport, was taking her along the coast to load 8000 tons of nickel ore at Pouembout when, on 12 July 1922, the current set her onto a coral reef some 60 miles from Noumea where a ground swell pounded her badly. Although her distress signal was responded to by the *Canadian Transporter*, the steamship's arrival was too late. *France II* was already bilged and Leport had ordered his crew to abandon her. Despite engaging salvage interests in Australia, such was the world-wide slump in shipping at the time that only her sails, cabin fittings and wireless were ever recovered. The rest of this fine barque was left to rust.

One can speculate as to whether, with engines still fitted, although she might not have made that fabulous run of 420 miles, she would have avoided this sad fate. Light winds and unpredictable currents have bedeviled the sailing ship since time immemorial, but the contemporary prejudice against auxiliaries, partly due to the innate conservatism of the deep-sea sailorman and partly due to the embryonic state of marine diesel engineering, may have indirectly contributed to the total loss of the *France II*.

Unfortunately the history of the auxiliary engine in these later-day sailing vessels has been confused by sad and often mysterious circumstances. Whilst the French bounty-system compensated an owner for the space lost to an engine room, it is clear that advancing technology had persuaded other nationalities to consider fitting auxiliary diesels. In 1907 Danish shipowners, like their Belgian and German contemporaries, ordered from Burmeister and Wain of Copenhagen a four-masted barque as a training vessel for officer cadets. Sail-training was then universally held to be a prerequisite for any merchant sea-officer, irrespective of his subsequent career. As a consequence, a number of large barques such as the *L'Avenir*, *Herzogin Cecilie* and *Viking* were built. These ships were intended to carry a full, commercial cargo, but were distinguished by their long quarterdecks, intended to provide the extra accommodation, class rooms, and so forth, but which incidentally immeasurably improved the comfort and weatherliness of these great vessels. Just like her Belgian and German equivalents, *Viking* was to end up under the Erikson flag, being sold to the Finnish house in 1929.

At the time of the outbreak of the First World War, Danish interests had ordered a second, larger training vessel from Ramage and Ferguson of Leith, Scotland. The vessel was requisitioned by the British Admiralty as an oil fuel tender and never completed so, at the conclusion of hostilities, the East Asiatic Company re-ordered, initiating the construction of the largest sailing vessel ever built in Britain.

Four-hundred-and-thirty feet overall, the five-masted barque *København*, measured 3965 tons gross, with a capacity of 5200 tons deadweight. Incorporating features originally developed for power-driven vessels, the *København* was sub-divided by watertight bulkheads, fitted with water ballast tanks with a capacity of 1245 tons; she had cellular double-bottom tanks in her after holds in which she carried 204 tons of oil fuel. She was also fitted with 3-ton cargo derricks served by diesel winches and the windlass could be operated traditionally by the cadets *en masse* or if required, by power. Her decks were served by warping capstans, halliard and brace winches, the latter operable by one man. Accommodation comprised cabins for her master, officers, instructors and doctor with their saloon, pantry, bathrooms, dispensary and hospital under the poop; a cadets' deck house was situated between the jigger and mizen masts, and a centrecastle contained the sail room, crew cabins, galley and services.

As befitted a prestigious training ship she carried a tall sail plan, with royals above double topgallants. Her four square-rigged masts rose 197 feet above the keel, and her lower yards were 90 feet from yard-arm to yard-arm and weighed 4.5 tons each. She was also beautifully finished with a teak figurehead of the warrior priest Absalom, said to be the founder of the Danish capital. But it is in her engine that her chief interest lies, for she was fitted with a single screw driven by a four-cylinder diesel Burmeister and Wain 4125-litre engine, developing 500 break horsepower at 180 revolutions per minute. Bilge pumps were run off this, and while one Bolinder generator provided electric power for lighting and heating, another provided power to the ballast pump. The engine was irreversible, so the twin-bladed propeller was an early example of variable pitch, controlled by a Zeise clutch which, in addition to reversing thrust for stern power, also varied forward pitch in order to provide thrust commensurate with the speed under sail. This power-assistance could be used to great advantage, particularly when working to windward in confined waters. Moreover, the propeller blades could be stopped vertically, in the arch of the stern-frame to minimise drag.

One benefit the engine conferred on this fine barque was an ability to transit the two great canals of Panama and Suez, reducing voyage time and the wear and tear of flogging round both capes. Although not a flyer, she made good passages, taking only sixty-seven days in 1926 to sail from the Lizard to Adelaide after departing from Copenhagen. Her best day's run was 305 miles and she averaged 11 knots for twenty-one days running her easting down in the south Indian Ocean.

On 14 December 1928 the *København* sailed from Buenos Aires under the command of Captain Andersen who had formerly served as her chief officer. She had on board fifteen officers and ratings, and forty-five cadets; all were Danish, as no-one but Danish nationals were permitted to sail aboard her. She was never heard of again.

Posted overdue, extensive searches failed to yield even a clue as to the reason for her disappearance. Finally posted missing at Lloyd's on 1 January 1930, her tragic disappearance remains a mystery to this day. Gloomy pundits inevitably pointed to the propeller. *France II* had shed one and, long afterwards, the *Pamir* was to do the same. It was thought that possibly the shaft had drawn, but all was speculation. Perhaps the case of the *Pamir* does give some indication, along with the testimony of a few remaining Cape Horn seamen, and it had nothing to do with engines or propellers. Perhaps, like the *Pamir*, the *København* foundered in extreme, hurricane force winds and in fact her gear was too strong. It is possible the great ship was overwhelmed by the immense forces of nature somewhere in the vast Southern Ocean, her crew unable to release her over-burdened hull from the driving force of her heavy rig. A similar fate overtook *L'Avenir* just before the Second World War. Renamed *Admiral Karpfänger*, and acquired as a training ship for the Hamburg-America Line, she went missing on her first voyage under her new name.

Perhaps at the end of the long struggle to harness the wind and turn its power to their own use, men had produced in the last windjammers a machine so technologically effective that it left no margin for escape from the very worst the sea was capable of.

The large barque was not the only sailing rig to compete with steam to the bitter end on the blue-water routes. In an effort to cut costs, a number of large barquentines were laid down, the two most notable being British built, but for the Hamburg owners A. C. De Freitas and Co., namely the four-masters, *Beethoven* and *Mozart*. These were not exceptionally large vessels, though designed for the Cape Horn trade and comparable in size with the standard four-masted barque of the day. Their chief virtue was a smaller crew and whilst a big four-masted barque could be run by a shrewd, parsimonious owner with crews as small as two dozen, a barquentine of similar tonnage could be manned by three-quarters of that number.

Mozart, of 1987 gross registered tons, was built by the Grangemouth and Greenock Dockyard company on the Clyde in 1904 for the nitrate trade. She had a complement of sixteen, plus twelve cadets, but her later owner Hugo Lundqvist, Erikson's rival at Mariehamn, reckoned on a total crew of fourteen. Cheap to run, she was a trial to her crew who endured agonies of sail handing to avoid her great gaff sails chafing to bits in light weather.

It is possible, had matters been allowed to develop unhindered by war, that the big barquentine might have offered the sailing ship a longer lease on viable life than the four-masted barque, for she combined the advantages of square sails with gaff rig and could out-perform even a large schooner on a long passage. But she suffered in general from the flaw of having too few masts for her length. Thus the gaff sails became huge and difficult to handle, their topsails likewise, needing donkey engines to haul their throat and peak halliards taut. Their advocates among seamen were not vociferous enough to convince conservative doubters that barquentines had a future. In any case, the First World War was about to disturb the whole pattern of global trade.

In the last two decades of the nineteenth century, the economics of ship-owning were such that they continued to favour the sailing ship in the low-freight, bulk trades. Bunker coal was expensive and while crew wages remained relatively low, stokers were an additional burden on the wage-bill of a steamer. In the narrow margin between profit and loss there remained room not only for the sailing ship, but for new tonnage.

As the century drew to its end, the Spanish–American and Boer Wars caused an upsurge in freight rates for steamships, and in 1897 an increase in insurance premiums for sailing vessels made inroads into the slender profit enjoyed by the sailing shipowner. By the end of the first decade of the twentieth century this was eroded to such an extent that sailing vessels were being put on the market, only to resell at a quarter of their building cost. Matters were paralysed upon the outbreak of war in 1914. Trade protection was no longer achieved by the time-honoured method of convoy, but by British cruisers patrolling the trade routes, ready in theory to intercept and destroy enemy surface raiders, alerted by the alarm calls of merchantmen under attack.

It was not a success. Submarine warfare, though it began by obeying the Geneva convention, soon became unrestricted. Merchant ships, both sail and power, were sunk in huge numbers. Hulls were in increasing demand to carry the raw materials which accelerated war-economies craved. Freight rates began to rise rapidly, threefold by 1917, being paid in advance, to the ill-concealed delight of shipowners. Moreover, the indemnities paid by the British government to owners losing ships, were generous, as witness Bonar Law's tactless parliamentary speech (see page 172). While a seaman's pay stopped the day his ship was sunk, his owner could look forward to a real profit without the least inconvenience. Fortunes were made as old, laid-up sailing ships were recommissioned to make up for lost tonnage and ships became worth twelve to fourteen times their pre-war value. New sailing vessels were built and the schooner in particular gained a new lease of life.

Perhaps the grandest if ugliest exemplar of the type was the huge seven-masted schooner *Thomas W. Lawson* of 5218 tons. She was built in 1902 by the Fore River Shipbuilding Company at Quincy, Massachusetts for the Coastwise Transportation Company of Boston. Unlike most native-built American vessels, the *Thomas W. Lawson* was constructed of steel and while she had steam power on deck, which was maintained all the time, she carried no auxiliary engine and was considered something of a wall-sided monster. Despite her labour-saving rig, she proved very difficult to handle, both on deck and in manoeuvring. Notwithstanding this she was a commercial success.

Almost all of these last wooden sailing ships were built in the United States. None were laid down in Britain, which concentrated on steam tonnage for the very practical reason that, at the eleventh hour, the convoy system was reintroduced as the only effective means of protecting trade. Sailing ships could not be sailed in convoys tight enough to escape the depredations of submarines; U-boat gunfire was the effective end of the independently proceeding British merchant sailing ship.

After the war there was a brief boom, followed by a slump that resulted in the Great Depression. All shipping was affected. Ageing tonnage went rapidly to the wall, both steam and sail. Only the best run, most economical shipping companies survived without subsidies. Among these were a mere handful of sailing ship-owners. Although sail was to continue to hold its own for some time in world-wide coastal trades, there were only two deep-water sailing fleets of any significance in existence after the First World War.

It was left to the great Hamburg shipping house of Ferdinand Laeisz to build the very last commercial post-war four-masted barques, although, as we have seen, the Danish East Asiatic Company took delivery of the ill-fated auxiliary five-masted barque *København* from Ramage and Ferguson of Glasgow in 1921. Laeisz had ordered the *Priwall*, 3105 gross, from Blohm and Voss at Hamburg in 1916, but it was 1920 before she sailed on her maiden voyage and she had proved very expensive to complete. The *Padua* of 1926 was of similar tonnage and built by J.C. Tecklenborg of Geestemunde. Both German four-masted barques remained doggedly trading until 1939, achieving fast passages: sixty-six days from the Elbe to the Spencer Gulf, for instance. These ships continued to carry cargoes of Australian grain until reverting to the Chilean nitrate trade in response to the acceleration of German industry in the 1930s. As late as 1938, *Priwall*, under Captain Hauth, made the record doubling of Cape Horn to the *westward*, against the prevailing wind, taking five days fifteen hours to storm from latitude 50°S in the Atlantic, to latitude 50°S in the Pacific.

Priwall was at Valparaiso on the outbreak of the Second World War and was later presented to the Chileans who turned her into the auxiliary *Lautaro*. Carrying a cargo of nitrates, she later caught fire and burned out. Her sister survives still, for the *Padua* became a war prize of the Soviet Union and was renamed after the great Russian navigator Ivan Kruzenstern. The *Kruzenstern* has become familiar in sail-training races and now flies the flag of Russian Confederation. Once again, her future, like that of other former Soviet sailing vessels, seems uncertain.

The other great post-1918 sailing fleet was that of Captain Gustaf Erikson, of Mariehamn in the Finnish Åland Islands. Erikson bought up old ships such as the *Lawhill*, and even former 'Flying-P' liners, retaining some of the best of the great four-masted barques until the upheaval of the Second World War. He relied upon a source of cheap, enthusiastic labour both from the Åland Islands and the romantic youth of the world at large, many of whom sailed as 'apprentices' for the thrill of the experience. A shrewd operator and no romantic himself, Erikson could operate only so long as old ships were to be found at rock-bottom, post-slump prices, and the grain cargoes of Australia could be shipped at rates too low for steam or motor vessels. His ships were not over-capitalised, since they could not depreciate, nor did he insure them, allowing them to carry their own loss.

Essentially it was war that knocked the last nail in the coffin of the traditional merchant sailing vessel, accelerating industry and economics, beyond the point at which in any trade, the bulk-carrying, long-range sailing ship was in any sense viable. But it would be foolish to think these ships had any kind of monopoly on a right to exist. They have acquired a romantic aura quite at variance with the harshness of the conditions they worked in, or the conditions they generated for their crews. Erikson's ships were short-handed and hard work. Several, like the beautiful former German *Herzogin Cecilie*, the ex-Belgian *L'Avenir*, or the ex-Danish *Viking*, had been built originally for large complements of cadets and lacked even the rudimentary labour-saving devices designed by Captain Jarvis. Erikson and his fleet survived the Second World War – just. He died in 1947 and his remaining ships, *Viking* and the former Laeisz 'Flying-P' liners, *Pommern*, *Passat* and *Pamir*, soon ceased trading. *Viking* was the only one to make a post-war voyage under the Erikson flag, later being preserved at Gothenburg. Sold on and with U-boat engines fitted as auxiliaries, *Pamir* and *Passat* made their last commercial voyages in 1949 with bagged wheat from South Australia to Ipswich. Both were unprofitable.

After being sold for scrapping, these two fine four-masted barques were rescued and eventually returned to the German flag to be used as training ships. The loss of the *Pamir* in 1956, when she foundered in heavy Atlantic weather, brought this to a halt. In the traumatic reaction to her loss, the *Passat* was laid up as a museum ship at Travemunde, near Lubeck on the Baltic.

The British had long before abandoned any attempt to train its future naval officers in sail. A Royal Naval training ship, the *Eurydice*, had been lost in severe weather in the English Channel in 1878, followed by the *Atlanta* in 1880. Their Lordships finally gave up the idea in the Edwardian period. British merchant apprentices, however, were bound to qualify in sail if they wanted a full master's certificate, but the introduction of the 'steam-ticket' and the effects of the First World War upon the number of sailing vessels on the British Register eroded this need. Inevitably a ticket in sail became a prestigious but arcane qualification.

Before the harsh realities that burst upon the world in the aftermath of the events of 1914 to 1918, some British owners had fostered sail-training. Most notable was the firm of Devitt and Moore whose fine vessels, *Port Jackson* and *Medway* have been referred to at the end of Chapter Ten. The former was torpedoed in April 1917 and the latter was, along with other sailing ships such as the *Haytor*, converted to a tanker and renamed the *Myr Shell*. She was finally broken up in Japan in 1933.

A few sailing vessels were in fact purpose-built tankers. The *Quevilly*, of 3480 tons, was built at Rouen on the Seine under the French bounty-system in 1897. She was a fine five-masted barque, carrying royals above double topgallants. She was designed not for case-oil, but for petroleum products in bulk and for the first fourteen years of her life operated solely under sail, though a diesel generator provided her with the electric lighting required by the classification societies for tankers. Shortly before the First World War she was fitted with twin screw auxiliary power, but the outbreak of hostilities restricted her to service as a depot bunkering tanker. In 1923 she was sold to Norwegian buyers, who renamed her the *Deodata*, removed her masts and fully converted her. She survived until 1939, when she was mined in the opening months of the Second World War.

It seemed, certainly with the loss of the *Pamir* in 1956, that with the exception of the international fleet of pure sail-training ships, the commercial, pelagic sailing ship's day was over. But the utility and beauty of sail will not quite go away. New sources of wealth and consequently new sources of 'cargo', have combined with a new consciousness of ecological values, the finite resource of fossil fuels and technology itself, to revive interest in commercial sail. Today luxurious, hi-tech sailing vessels operate in a niche of the cruising market, in contrast with attempts to fit auxiliary sail to powered vessels to conserve fuel, which have not been successful.

At Mariehamn, the *Pommern* remains as she did when she came in from the sea in 1939 and was interned for the duration of the war. Today she is a museum and memorial to these great ships and no less to the breed of men who sailed them. In a sense she epitomises them all, for she was British built in 1903 as the *Mneme*, a typical 'Clyde four-poster' of 2376 tons for B. Wencke Sohne. Later she was bought by Laeisz and renamed, then after the First World War she was Greek-owned. In 1922 she was acquired by Erikson and inherited by his children on his death. They in turn presented her to Mariehamn. Truly international in her inheritance and her personal history, *Pommern* and a handful of her sisters remain in good hands. Elsewhere, a few ships remain in various states of preservation. Others lie in odd coves and upon remote reefs in desolate corners of the world, decomposing slowly, remnants of a hard, uncompromising way of life which was never romantic, but was not without its glory.

CHAPTER FOURTEEN
Fear God and Dreadnought

The British Government staved off the potentially disastrous rivalry between Great Britain and France after the Fashoda incident in 1898, but was unable to prevent the effects of the rise of nationalism in a Germany ruled by Kaiser Wilhelm II. Wilhelm was not only the king's nephew, he was an honorary admiral in the Royal Navy and his main contribution to that Service seems to have resulted from a complaint that no two officers ever saluted him the same way. It is a measure of the dynastic deference of the day that Their Lordships immediately standardised the naval salute.

It seemed unthinkable that Wilhelm would pursue a provocative policy, or confront a country whose language he spoke fluently and for which he protested the greatest admiration. The Kaiser was a keen yachtsman who raced annually at Cowes, but his admiration for all things British was tainted by the corrosion of envy. This envy was harnessed by several of his imperial satraps, especially Alfred von Tirpitz. The Secretary of State for Naval Affairs encouraged his megalomaniac monarch to expand the German Navy by sanctioning a series of Navy Laws passed by the Reichstag and authorising the formation of a considerable fleet. Tirpitz conceived the High Seas Fleet to challenge the British Royal Navy, not on a global scale, but at least for domination of the North Sea. Had Uncle Edward lived longer he might have prevented the horrors of the First World War, but the King's death in 1911 left the stage clear for the posturing and ungovernable Wilhelm. European governments had so enmeshed themselves in a web of treaties that an Austrian declaration of war on Serbia following the assassination of an archduke in the Serbian city of Sarajevo, drew the nations of Europe into four years of appalling warfare.

Although the issue was finally decided on land, there were significant developments at sea and these were the fruits of the arms race led by Tirpitz and his British counterpart, Admiral

'Jackie' Fisher, a charismatic and energetic admiral with a well-established reputation as a specialist. Fisher foresaw the importance of maintaining superiority at almost any cost, using to the full Britains's huge industrial resources remarked upon by an envious Tirpitz.

A 1903 paper by an Italian naval designer, General Vittorio Cuniberti, entitled *An Ideal Battleship for the British Navy*, proposed a heavily armoured ship of some 17,000 tons, mounting triple 12-inch guns and capable of 24 knots. This would, he said, give the Royal Navy a significant lead over any potential rival. Although the decision to adopt an all big-gun design had already been made by the Admiralty, the publication of Cuniberti's paper in Fred T Jane's *All the World's Fighting Ships* gave the debate a public airing.

The first response had already been made. The 12-inch and 9.2-inch armaments of the *King Edward VII* class, for instance, increased firepower, but were not effective at much over 6000 yards because the shell-splashes could not be distinguished. Indeed, the routine 'practice shoots' which the battleships undertook, rarely exceeded 4000 yards and this proved a highly fertile breeding ground for complacency. One of Fisher's protégés, Captain Percy Scott, began a much needed if slow revolution in gunnery by introducing continuous aiming and salvo firing, with high quality optical rangefinding and spotting to update and correct misses. The result, though far from perfect, began to increase the ranges at which heavy calibre guns might hit their targets.

Curiously, it was in this matter of gunnery control, that the *Dreadnought* and all her big-gun successors were at best a compromise. As the range of gunnery increased, the fall of shot became harder to correct. The first step was to centralise gunnery control to a high point in the ship, the so-called Director system. Smoke from *Dreadnought*'s funnels was to obscure the view of the spotting teams and required urgent modification, but this was not the only problem, for a moving gun-platform firing at a moving target must necessarily fire off the direct line of bearing in order for the projectile and target to meet at the fatal moment. As ranges and speeds increased, the requirement for this refinement likewise increased exponentially.

It was a civilian, Arthur Pollen, who offered a solution to the Royal Navy. Interested in prediction as it applied to gunnery,

Pollen deduced that the solution lay in determining the rate at which the variables changed and he employed differential calculus via an analog computer to resolve the problem. While being subject to the accuracy of the optically acquired input data, Pollen's apparatus was a dramatic improvement on the plane trigonometrical offsets unique to each salvo which was then common practice.

Unfortunately, although Fisher embraced Pollen's idea to the extent that he was persuaded that a ship so equipped could dispense with a substantial amount of armour, the intervention of a gunnery specialist, Captain Dreyer, compromised the Fleet's gun accuracy by recommending his own cheaper, trigonometrically-based system. As a consequence, although the Pollen apparatus was fitted experimentally to a few ships, the Grand Fleet's fire at Jutland was poor, and out-classed by that of the Germans, largely because of the superiority of Zeiss stereoscopic rangefinders. It was only after the First World War that Pollen's method was adopted and only after it incorporated range data input from radar in the Second that it finally came of age.

Extending the range rendered the smaller calibre weapons superfluous and also allowed the battlefleet, in theory at least, to annihilate enemy torpedo-craft before they could deliver that great giant-killer, the torpedo. Moreover, the removal of secondary guns made room for more heavy weapons, fuel and armour.

In the United States, which was another growing naval power, similar developments were progressing under the leadership of Captain William Sims. While Fisher discussed the concept with W. H. Gard, the Chief of Naval Construction at Malta, Commander Poundstone of the United States Navy had gained the ear of President Theodore Roosevelt to win approval for a study commencing in 1903 into the feasibility of an 'all big-gun' battleship for the United States Navy. As a consequence the construction of the USS *Michigan* and the USS *South Carolina* were authorised in March 1905. These were built with eight 12-inch guns in two turrets forward and two aft, the higher 'superfiring' over the lower. These ships also bore twenty-two 3-inch guns for countering torpedo attacks by small craft if these succeeded in penetrating the battleships' outer screen.

The significant drawback in these American ships was the time they took to build, some five years. To a British Admiralty under the direction of the new First Sea Lord Admiral Fisher, such a protracted building-time was unacceptable.

Fisher became Second Sea Lord in 1902 and a year later he was Commander-in-Chief at Portsmouth. By this time Gard had moved from Malta to Portsmouth and when in 1904 Fisher became First Sea Lord, the idea over which the two men had been deliberating for some time began to take form. Gard came to the Admiralty as Assistant Chief of Naval Construction and was tasked with the preparation of plans for the super-battleship the two men had nicknamed HMS *Untakeable*. From 3 January 1905 Fisher chaired a Committee of Designs to consider the configuration of what was later to become HMS *Dreadnought*.

Events were accelerated by intelligence from the Far East. British naval officers were embarked as observers in Admiral Togo's British-built Japanese fleet when it engaged the Russian Baltic fleet in the Strait of Tsu-Shima. Togo crossed ahead of Rozhdestvensky's line and fire was opened at 20,000 yards, with the first hits registering at 13,000.

The Russian Far East Fleet had been destroyed the previous autumn in a surprise attack by the Japanese before any declaration of war. The Tsar therefore ordered the Baltic Fleet to steam 18,000 miles from Kronstadt, round the Cape of Good Hope, to avenge their fellow Russians. Denied any support, Rozhdestvensky's shambling voyage achieved one distinction: his warships were the first battle-fleet to refuel at sea, loading coal out of a supporting flotilla of seventy chartered German merchantmen.

On the morning of 27 May 1905, as Togo's six battleships 'crossed the T' of the Russian column, they engaged with all their heavy guns. The Russian fleet was systematically annihilated. Reported on by the British observers, this seemed to confirm all the theories inherent in the employment of the big-gun, and HMS '*Untakeable*' began to take form. HMS *Dreadnought* was to displace almost 18,000 tons and to mount ten 12-inch guns in twin turrets, with twenty-seven 3-inch (12-pounder) guns for her anti-torpedo defence. The main armament was to be disposed in three centreline turrets, one forward and two aft, with two turrets amidships on either beam. This allowed an 8-gun broadside, but also permitted 6 guns to fire forward or aft.

Although this 'all big-gun' concept was thought to be the main advance inherent in the design of *Dreadnought*, it was a greater gamble for Fisher and his committee to adopt the Parson's steam turbines for the new battleship's propulsion. For such a large vessel, this was truly revolutionary and these turbines combined to deliver some 23,000 horsepower to four shafts and gave the ship the incredible speed of 21 knots; incredible because *Dreadnought* had armour 11 inches thick amidships, tapering to 4 inches at the ship's extremities.

But the superlatives were not to end there. Eschewing the great private yards on the Tyne and Clyde, the Admiralty opted for building the new ship in the Royal Dockyard at Portsmouth (which had previously shown it could beat the private yards). *Dreadnought*'s keel was laid on 2 October 1905, less than nine months after her design was decided by Fisher's committee; four months later, on 10 February 1906, King Edward launched the great 527-feet (160 metres) hull. Furious activity followed and HMS *Dreadnought* was ready for basin trials on 3 October 1906. Her final loaded displacement was just under 22,000 tons.

This remarkable ship had been built in fourteen months, a prodigious feat in itself, and one not lost on observers in Berlin. Such was the impact of the *Dreadnought* that her name became generic, both for her successors and retrospectively for her predecessors, for she reduced every other capital ship in the world to 'pre-dreadnoughts'.

Imitation being the sincerest form of flattery, it was not long before other navies followed suit. Tirpitz ordered two 'dreadnoughts', the *Nassau* and the *Westfalen*, to be armed with a dozen 11-inch guns. The two followed from the United States in 1910, but with a speed of only 18.5 knots. Two years later, however, the *Texas* and the *New York*, mounting ten 14-inch guns also mounted a secondary armament of twenty-one 5-inch guns. At 27,400 tons displacement and a speed of 21 knots, these two ships were early exemplars of the final consensus view of 'typical' battleship philosophy. The French, on the other hand, building the *Danton* in 1909, retained mixed calibres, four 12-inch guns with side turrets mounting twelve 9.4-inch weapons. However, they fell into step with the British and Americans in

1912 with the *Courbet*. The Russians, humiliated by the victory of Japan, built four dreadnoughts of 23,360 tons. The class ship, the *Gangut* commissioned in 1911 with her 12-inch guns mounted in four triple turrets, a configuration followed by the Italians with their *Dante Alighieri*. Both of these classes achieved 23 knots.

While Argentina ordered dreadnoughts from the United States, British yards built them for Brazil and Chile, and they proved to be more powerful ships than even the Royal Navy possessed. One of the Chilean ships was requisitioned as HMS *Canada* during hostilities, and did not arrive in Chile as the *Almirante Latorre* until 1920; another was later completed as the aircraft carrier, HMS *Eagle*. Britain also built dreadnoughts for Turkey, but one of these also ended up under the white ensign as HMS *Erin*, while the *Rio de Janeiro*, being built in Britain originally for Brazil, was purchased by Turkey, and was then commandeered by Britain and commissioned as HMS *Agincourt*. In the event the only big-gun ship to serve the ailing Ottoman Turks was the *Yavuz Sultan Selim*, a German battle cruiser SMS *Goeben,* purchased in 1914, and whose passage through the supposedly British-dominated Mediterranean caused something of a scandal in the corridors of the Admiralty in London. The *Tegetthoff* and her four sisters were built between 1912 and 1915 by the Austo-Hungarian navy in response to the Italian *Dante Alighieri* and *Cavour*. Their gun turrets were of an advanced design, and built in the Skoda works. These 21,600-ton battleships carried the prodigious armament of twelve 12-inch guns, three to a turret, with two superfiring turrets forward, and two aft. They also mounted secondary batteries of a dozen 5.9-inch guns.

With the 'big-gun' concept now accepted, the debate now centred around the vexed equation of armour versus speed. Fisher's specious belief that accurate, long-range gunfire could place a warship beyond the reach of retribution, produced a type of ship which was not only supremely eye-catching, but also fatally flawed.

Conforming to the well-known principle that what one learns from history is that no-one learns from history, the hard-won experience of the Napoleonic War in respect of the defence of trade was forgotten. Convoy, it was believed, was an outmoded idea, belonging to the age of sail and not consonant with twentieth-century naval war. Part of the role of cruisers was to patrol the well-established routes of imperial trade and engage enemy raiders when they struck at merchant shipping. Meanwhile these versatile ships with their long endurance, would strike in their turn at the enemy's seaborne commerce.

But the restlessness of naval thinkers, having extrapolated the cruiser from the sailing frigate, had developed the cruiser into several derivatives. The light cruiser, sometimes called a 'scout', lightly armoured and fast, could either operate as a lookout or a picket ahead of a battlefleet, or as flagship to a flotilla of destroyers, for such small warships were best deployed in large numbers. A cruiser might also act independently. The armoured cruiser, developed from the Victorian first-class cruiser, bore heavier guns, similar to the medium-calibre weapons recently discarded from the battleships' inventory. These ships theoretically operated and fought in squadrons, usually in support of the battlefleet. They carried both belt and deck armour and were in effect second-class capital ships and are exemplified by the American *Tennessee* class of 1903–5 which displaced 14,500 tons, bore four 10-inch, sixteen 6-inch and twenty-two 3-inch guns. They could, moreover, steam at 23 knots.

As Fisher's Committee on Designs was finalising the *Dreadnought*, the Japanese were flouting naval orthodoxy with the *Tsukuba* class of 14,000-ton fast armoured cruisers, said to be capable of 23 knots and mounting four 12-inch guns, a dozen 4.7-inch and two lighter weapons. Considering these new ships and the clear tactical advantage of speed in Togo's fleet at Tsu-Shima, Fisher's committee concluded the Royal Navy also needed a high-speed super-cruiser and ordered a class of three 'dreadnought armoured cruisers'. HM Ships *Invincible, Inflexible* and *Indomitable* displaced almost as much as *Dreadnought*, some 20,000 tons laden, but at 567 feet (173 metres), were longer, and had 7-inch armour. However, their four screws were driven by turbines generating 41,000 horsepower which powered them at over 25 knots. Since the ships carried an armament of eight 12-inch guns in four twin turrets, two of which were *en echelon* amidships, they packed almost as great a punch as *Dreadnought* herself. Commissioned in 1907, they were soon followed by even bigger ships, an improved *Invincible* class comprising two ships, HMSs *Indefatigable* and *New Zealand*, and then 'the splendid cats' of the *Lion* class. HMS *Lion* commissioned in 1912 displacing 29,700 tons loaded and carrying a main armament of eight 13.5-inch, supported by sixteen 4-inch secondary guns. At 700 feet (213 metres) she was longer than the largest battleship and, with 70,000 horsepower turbines, could steam at 27 knots. In order to achieve this she sacrificed weight by having relatively light armour, only 9 inches thick amidships. She was the largest, fastest and, at £2,086,458, the most expensive warship in the world. Her crew comprised 997 men, many of them stokers who, in order to maintain the speeds demanded of her in action had to shovel 950 tons of coal a day! In fact when at full speed almost a hundred men shifted coal from 'one steel chamber to another without ever seeing the light of day or the furnace fires'.

Lion's sisters *Queen Mary* and *Princess Royal* followed, with the modified *Tiger* making a fourth. HMS *Tiger* displaced 35,000 tons with 108,000 horsepower turbines and was to fight at Jutland using Pollen's gunnery control system with which she had been experimentally fitted. Almost simultaneous with the production of these 'splendid cats', British yards were building four 32,000-ton *Kongo* class for the Japanese. These ships not only mounted eight 14-inch and sixteen 6-inch guns, but were capable of 27.5 knots!

Such huge ships were classed as 'battlecruisers' in 1912, an ambiguous designation which was to cause confusion as to their true role. Having swallowed so much money and carrying heavy guns at high speed, it was inconceivable that they should be spared to patrol trade routes, so a role was invented for them: they would operate ahead of a battle-fleet, engaging and drawing an enemy fleet down upon the heavy guns of the main battle-squadrons.

Despite the flaws inherent in this concept, it was not to be expected that the British would go unchallenged, Berlin ordered first the 25-knot *Von Der Tann* with eight 11-inch guns, and then the *Moltke* class which were the first European warships to adopt the superfiring turrets already fitted to the USSs *South Carolina* and *Michigan*. It was the appearance of the *Moltkes* which prompted 'the splendid cats'. These, and an improvement, the *Seydlitz*, were in service by 1913 by which time the *Derfflinger* was on the stocks. Only slightly smaller than *Lion*, this battle-cruiser and her sisters, had slightly thicker armour with better protection afforded to vital parts. Indeed German capital-ship design was to prove generally superior to that of Great Britain in both world wars on two important counts: internal, watertight subdivision and the sophistication of the disposition of armour. Concessions had to be made to achieve this, largely by small sacrifices in speed, but these were to pay dividends in allowing major German warships to endure greater punishment than their counterparts. The reason for these advantages was simple: the Germans were acutely sensitive to the fact that they were starting from an inferior position. They could not hope to equal the might of the British fleet, at least not until they had inflicted a defeat upon it, and therefore, even at a great cost, had to enable their High Seas Fleet to maximise the chance it would get on *Der Tag*, The Day.

They seemed about to achieve this at the outbreak of war when Von Spee's armoured cruiser squadron inflicted a humiliating defeat on a squadron of elderly British cruisers off Coronel on the coast of Chile. But then the British Admiralty under Fisher and the First Lord of the Admiralty, Winston Churchill, sent the *Invincible* and *Inflexible* south under Vice-Admiral Sturdee to reinforce the cruisers in the South Atlantic. After a long chase, Von Spee was destroyed off the Falkland Islands on 8 December 1914.

But in the indecisive engagements in the North Sea culminating at Jutland on 31 May and 1 June 1916, the weakness of the battlecruiser was revealed in shocking and dramatic form. Superior gunnery on the part of the German van under Hipper not only inflicted near-disastrous damage on Vice-Admiral Beatty's flagship, *Lion*, but blew apart the battlecruisers *Indefatigable* and *Queen Mary*. In both ships armour-piercing shells penetrated magazines which detonated with devastating effect. Although some serious hits were landed on the retreating German ships, their ability to absorb punishment proved impressive. Well might Beatty, a master of the *sang-froid*, comment that something seemed 'to be the matter with our bloody ships today'.

Churchill accurately extracted the kernel of the lesson learned on that fateful day. 'I do not believe in the wisdom of the battlecruiser,' he wrote. 'To put the value of a first-class battleship into a vessel which cannot stand the pounding of a heavy action is false policy.' How right he was, and he also wrote, 'If it is worthwhile to spend more than the price of your best battleship upon a fast, heavily gunned vessel, it is better … to give it the heaviest armour as well. You then have a ship which can do everything. [The battlecruiser] should be superseded by the fast battleship, i.e. fast strongest ship, in spite of her cost.'

In spite of her cost… . Therein lay the rub. A more perceptive analysis of the whole programme of the age had been made in a speech by Sir Edward Grey in Manchester in February 1914. Grey had told his audience that he thought:

> 'This dreadnought era is one to be deplored and very wasteful … we are a business country and … as thinking men, we have the foreboding that, in the long run, exceptional expenditure on armaments, carried to an excessive degree, must lead to catastrophe, and may even sink the ship of European prosperity and civilisation.'

Grey's prescient speech is remarkable, not merely as prophecy, for that is to attribute to it a supernatural quality, but as an example of clear, logical thinking, unfettered by the hysteria of his time. It is, in short, an example of an intelligent man using history as a means of extrapolating the probabilities of the future. Grey was of course ignored, yet in the event he was right. Moreover, the history of the battlecruiser is not only evidence of Grey's foresight, but of the emotional and patriotic seductions inherent in the acquisition of armaments, of manifesting a desire for power exceeding the ability of a national economy to pay for it. It was to prove as true for the British Royal Navy around the middle of the century as it was for Soviet Russia at its end.

There were serious problems in communications which cost the British a decisive victory at Jutland, and the battle was at best a Phyrric success, for the Royal Navy was left in possession of the field but at a cost far greater in men and ships than had been suffered by their opponents. The High Seas Fleet deferred *Der Tag* until another day – which, to the anger of the officers of both fleets, was never to dawn. Both battlefleets were to suffer the corrosive effects of inactivity and frustration, the Germans to end in defeat, mutiny, surrender and scuttling; the British to be denied the chance to bring the High Seas Fleet to battle a second time.

One of the problems at Jutland was the failure of the main British battle squadrons to stay in contact with Hipper and his Commander-in-Chief, Scheer, long enough to inflict decisive damage. There was an irony in this because the Battle Cruiser Fleet included in its ranks what was to prove one of the most successful classes of capital ship, the *Queen Elizabeth* class battleships. These mighty battleships served the Royal Navy through two wars and though rebuilt and modified, proved the soundness of their original design.

Experiments having proved the penetrative superiority of the 15-inch shell, eight of these guns were adopted as the main armament for the *Queen Elizabeths*, situated in two twin superfiring turrets forward and two aft. The hulls were armoured with 13-inch plate, tapering to 6-inches at the extremities of the 646-feet hull. Ten- and 11-inch armour was carried on the barbettes and turrets respectively, but despite this, they were capable of 24 knots, powered by turbines of 75,000 horsepower. Designed by Sir Philip Watts, the Director of Naval Construction who had also worked with Fisher and Gard on *Dreadnought*, the class were fitted with oil-fired boilers, to the relief of all concerned. In the United States, the battleships *Oklahoma* and *Nevada* had been ordered in 1911 and had commissioned in 1914 with similar boilers. Hitherto the main British objection to dispensing with coal was due to a reluctance to rejecting what was a huge national resource. Accordingly a Royal Commission on Oil Supply was set up and chaired by Fisher, who had been recalled from retirement prior to his reappointment as First Sea Lord. As a result, £2.2 million pounds were allocated by the government to acquire controlling interests in the Anglo-Persian Oil Company, the forerunner of British Petroleum. The consequence of this was to secure oil for the Royal Navy, and thus provide fuel for new tonnage.

The generic name 'dreadnought' for a while superseded even that of battleship, and while there were 'dreadnoughts' and 'pre-dreadnoughts', the five ships of the Queen Elizabeth class, *Queen Elizabeth*, *Warspite*, *Valiant*, *Barham* and *Malaya* and their 13.5-inch gunner predecessors were considered 'super-dreadnoughts'. The 'QEs' long and useful lives also proved their design was not only capable of being updated, but due to their high speed, really bore out some of the ideas supposedly provided for by the battlecruiser.

But the battlecruiser possessed a glamour that did not easily die, and defied death by logic even in the aftermath of Jutland. Fisher's fertile and dynamic brain was, like that of Churchill his political master, capable of eccentric ideas. During the First World War, the First Sea Lord conceived the idea of attacking Germany's northern Baltic coast with very heavy guns. For this he required large, shoal-draught hulls and the order for *Courageous*, *Glorious* and *Furious* specified a speed of 31.5 knots, thus debarring from the field the recently built heavy bombardment craft, the monitors. Classed as large light cruisers to evade an undertaking to the Cabinet to build no more battle cruisers, they had very long hulls (786 feet) and only 3-inch armour. The first two carried two twin 15-inch turrets, the third, an enormous single 18-inch gun which was never exceeded in size and only equalled by the Japanese Yamato class of the Second World War. None of the trio were finished before Fisher resigned and in the event their chief interest lies in their ultimate fate. Only the 18-inch after gun was ever fitted to *Furious*, and before completion her forward turret was replaced with a flight deck. Meanwhile her sisters, *Courageous* and *Glorious*, were to become full-decked aircraft carriers. Their history will be taken up in the next chapter.

Of the wartime battle cruisers, only *Renown* was to survive, having served with some distinction, though never exposed to the fury of the enemies that disposed of her sister *Repulse* or her charismatic and glamorous successor, *Hood*. *Repulse* and *Renown* bore out the accuracy of Sir Edward Grey's prediction, costing the British taxpayer hundreds of thousands in their continual updatings, such that they were called *Repair* and *Refit* by their ratings. *Repulse*, along with the new battleship HMS *Prince of Wales*, was lost to Japanese aircraft in 1941.

HMS *Hood* had been laid down after Jutland as one of a class of four. Wartime shortages resulted in the cancellation of her three sister-ships, but *Hood* was given armour nearly equal to the *Queen Elizabeth* to make her a 'fast battleship'. She was commissioned in 1920, the largest warship in the world and to many considered by far the most beautiful, 'then and ever'. Displacing 41,200 tons, 860 feet (262 metres) long, with a beam of 104 feet (38 metres) on a draught of 28.5 feet (8.7 metres), *Hood* mounted eight 15-inch guns with a secondary armament of twelve 5.5-inch guns. She was capable of 31 knots, driven by turbines generating 144,000 horsepower. It is interesting to review her armour: her hull was divided by bulkheads 4 inches to 5 inches thick and her main belt was 12 inches thick amidships, tapering to 5 inches at her extremities. Her barbettes were variously protected by 12 to 5 inches of armour plate, her turrets with 15 to 5 inch plate. Her gun director was cased in 6-inch armour and her conning tower 11-inch, all of which was betrayed by the thinness of her deck, a mere 3 inches at its *maximum* thickness. By the mid 1930s her protection against aircraft attack and long-range gunfire, that is to say her deck armour, was recognised to be inadequate and it was planned to refit her in the manner of *Repulse* and *Renown*, but war intervened and she was sent in chase of the *Bismarck* when the German battleship broke out into the Atlantic to menace British seaborne trade. On 24 May 1941, a plunging shot from a salvo from *Bismarck* is believed to have detonated her after magazine. Only three of her company survived, one more than from the *Indefatigable* at Jutland a generation earlier. The evidence from eye-witnesses and survivors is so sketchy that it is impossible to say with certainty what exactly caused her loss.

That the battlecruiser concept finally produced a class of successful warships by default, will be reviewed later, but this was due to the fact that there was no confusion of role with potential, no muddled thinking or arrogant assumptions. Again and again the weakly armoured capital ship failed to live up to its promise because it was almost never employed in the task for which it had been conceived, and because it became a dinosaur, too big, too cumbersome and conspicuous to carry out a task performed by ordinary cruisers and even converted merchantmen.

Following the horrors of the 'war to end all wars', it was concluded by the victorious powers that naval strength should be limited. The rising cost of fleet maintenance, echoing Sir Edward Grey's concern, brought all the interested parties to a consensus and this was enshrined in the terms of the Washington Treaty of

1922. Britain, the United States, France, Italy and Japan agreed to put a moratorium on building for ten years and to limit the maximum calibre of gun to 16 inches, the tonnage of battleships to 35,000 tons displacement, with a life of 20 years. Refits were only to take into account improvements to counter submarines and aircraft.

Overall tonnage limitations were agreed: Britain was permitted 580,450 tons, the United States 500,320 tons, Japan 301,320 tons, France 221,170 tons and Italy 182,000 tons in what was popularly known as the '5-5-3 ratio'. To ameliorate bitter disagreements, each country was allowed to convert two capital ships to aircraft carriers, not exceeding 33,000 tons each. In the United States capital shipbuilding was stopped, and the *Lexington* and *Saratoga* took advantage of this option, as did the French battleship *Béarn*. Japan was deeply resentful of her relegation to a subordinate status to the United States. She agreed to the scrapping of two unfinished battleships, the *Tosa* and *Kaga*, and nominated the battlecruisers *Amagi* and *Akagi* to be completed as carriers, but the *Amagi* was badly damaged in the earthquake of 1923 and, having disposed of the *Tosa* as a target, the *Kaga* was resuscitated and completed as a carrier instead.

The Washington Treaty contained a provision for a review to be held in London in 1930, just before the expiry of the capital shipbuilding moratorium. The world-wide recession had already started when the national representatives convened and an arms race was out of the question. But the Pax Britannica was an outmoded concept and policing the world's oceans was no longer held to be a prerogative of the British. This view was strongly advocated in the United States while a rising tide of nationalism, fuelled by the war reparations clamped onto Germany by the Treaty of Versailles, and in Japan and Italy as a result of changes in the political life of those countries, cried out for manifestations of national grandeur. In all this Great Britain was both exemplar and cause; exemplar because of her imperial status, and cause because of the perceived immensity of her military power. In the late nineteenth century every European power and, to some extent, the United States, had rushed to acquire an empire in emulation; now these states wanted the trappings that went with the assumption of the purple. Despite, or perhaps because of the economic depression, the representatives coming to the conference table in London in 1930 had other objectives than the diplomats who had convened in Washington eight years earlier, exhausted and haunted by the horrors of war.

Although the depression affected naval budgets generally and an extension of the moratorium for a further five years was proposed. In 1929 Germany had completed a major warship named the *Deutschland*. Under the Versailles Treaty, the defeated country had been limited to a 10,000 tons maximum per ship with a gun calibre not exceeding 11 inches. Typically, the Germans made the best of a bad job. The *Deutschland* was to be followed by more of what the Germans came to call euphemistically, *panzerschiffen* (armoured ships), but which the English press was to call 'pocket battleships'.

France refused to ratify the agreement, aware of German plans for more *panzerschiffen*. Italy, already in the grip of fascism and wary of France, also refused. Japan, although willing to abide by the five-year extension, announced her intention of breaking with the spirit of the treaty at the expiry of that period. Thus a second London Conference in 1936 surveyed a changed world; European rivalry had spawned a second, more terrible arms race than that which preceded the First World War.

Britain conformed to the Washington Treaty and subjected its great navy to the axe. Hundreds of career officers were super-annuated and many of their ships were broken up, including all the older capital ships and a host of destroyers. In the two decades following, only Britain stuck to the terms of the treaty, producing the curious nine 16-inch gunned *Nelson* and *Rodney* of 1927 which at 33,950 tons (38,000 fully loaded), just fell in line with the terms of the treaty. Heavy, 14-inch armour reduced their speed to 23 knots, and the disposition of the three turrets forward of the main superstructure broke with tradition. But less obviously, they incorporated all the First World War lessons, particularly magazine protection.

The updatings permitted under the Washington Treaty on existing tonnage resulted in re-engining and the fitting of anti-torpedo 'bulges', all of which were carried out by the Royal Navy on the *Queen Elizabeth* and her sisters, together with a group of smaller battleships, the 'Royal Sovereign' class. Similar modifications were made to American capital ships, while the

Japanese paid scant attention to provisions of the treaty and carried out improvements beyond its terms. Lengthening the 1913 vintage battlecruisers of the *Kongo* class increased their speed to 30 knots and altered their classification to battleships. Similar major reconstruction was carried out by the Italians, effectively producing a different, more powerful ship, though they still bore the name of the old.

The big-gun also survived in an odd class of ship first built by the Union Navy for coastal and river work. Of lineal descendant from the bomb vessel, the monitor of the twentieth century was properly a weapon of offence. The history of British monitors is a complex story of taking over ships being built for Brazil and Norway, or of fitting guns taken out of obsolete pre-dreadnoughts while later and larger vessels used American guns and spare 15-inch turrets ordered for a Greek battlecruiser being built in Germany! In fact the *Furious*'s two 18-inch monsters were mounted in fixed monitors in two of the *Lord Clive* class. These pointed to starboard and were used in conjunction with the conventional 12-inch turret forward to bombard German positions on the Belgian Coast at the end of the First World War. Basically these odd ships possessed low, beamy hulls with a conspicuous gunnery control tripod. Armour varied from 4 to 6 inches thick. British monitors were idiosyncratically named after soldiers and, in the case of two built in 1915, after *French* soldiers from the Napoleonic era! The *Marshal Soult* and *Marshal Ney* were fitted with diesel engines, although these only managed a speed of 6.5 knots. They also bore their single 15-inch twin turrets on a tall barbette. This feature was followed in the *Erebus* and *Terror* of 1916, both of which saw service in the Second World War, during which only two monitors were built, the *Abercrombie* and *Roberts*, the latter proving to be the last British ship to carry 15-inch guns and which did not finally disappear from naval service until 1965. Such ships were, however, historical asides, derivative by-blows of the greater struggle for naval dominance. It was the renascent German *Kriegsmarine* and the Imperial Japanese Navy which possessed the power to astonish.

By 1917, German U-boats had reduced the ability of the British to wage war to such an extent that Their Lordships advised the

Cabinet that they considered defeat an inevitable consequence of unrestricted submarine warfare. Despite this chilling fact, even in 1939 surface raiders vied with U-boats for their potential ability to destroy the seaborne commerce upon which Great Britain depended. This misperception of admirals may in part be attributed to a justifiable fear of the historical depredations of commerce raiders as practiced by both the French and the Germans, and in part to a failure to grasp what they did not understand through ignorance. But much may be attributed to the influence of the *panzerschiffen* themselves for they were in fact what the battlecruiser should have been: fast enough to overtake most merchant ships and outrun most small warships, strong enough take punishment if caught by enemy cruisers and able to return fire with interest, as *Graf Spee* was to do when assailed by three British cruisers off the River Plate in December 1939. Their diesel engines gave them an immense range and with supply ships refuelling and revictualling them at remote rendezvous, endurance became simply a factor of crew morale.

The *Deutschland* (later renamed *Lützow* by the Nazi government for fear of the moral effect of her loss if she retained her original title) was followed by the *Admiral Scheer* of 1931 and the *Admiral Graf Spee* of 1932. In response the French built the battlecruisers *Dunkerque* and *Strasbourg*, completed in 1937 and 1938. These were armed with eight 13-inch guns, displaced 26,500 tons and achieved 30 knots. The Italians also responded with the battleships *Vittorio Veneto* and *Littorio*, nominally displacing 35,000 tons but exceeding the treaty limits at over 40,000. They carried nine 15-inch guns in three triple turrets as did a third, larger ship, the Roma, completed in 1942.

The spiral was now moving out of control: the *Littorios* provoked the French to lay down the battleships *Richelieu* and *Jean Bart*. Only the first was finished to serve in the Second World War and at 38,000 tons broke the terms of the treaty. She carried eight 15-inch guns in two quadruple turrets, both mounted forward to give protection to her vitals. Germany, now under the Nazi government of Adolf Hitler was moving inexorably towards war. In 1935, as the French laid down the *Dunkerque* and *Strasbourg*, the Germans cast aside the mask and began construction of the battlecruisers *Scharnhorst* and *Gneisenau*, ships of such power that they are also classified by some authorities as battleships, for their nine 11-inch guns were adopted in order to allow them additional armoured protection, while their design provided for a later replacement by 15-inch guns. At 34,800 tons displacement they were capable of 31 knots and their subdivision enabled them to absorb terrible punishment.

When war loomed once again and Grand-Admiral Raeder realised Hitler was likely to precipitate events before the German fleet was large enough to challenge the Royal Navy, he remarked that if his capital ships 'ever had to grapple with the British fleet, they would just about be able to show that they could die with dignity'. Acting out such tragic, Wagnerian hyperbole, was to be the fate of the *Scharnhorst* when, in the gloom of an Arctic night, she was to be overwhelmed by the Home Fleet under Admiral Sir Bruce Fraser and Rear-Admiral Burnett on 26 December 1943.

Long before Germany renounced any formal conformity with naval agreements in 1939, Raeder had ordered two more capital ships. These, the 41,700-ton *Bismarck* and a slightly modified 42,900-ton *Tirpitz*, laid down in 1936, were unequivocally battleships, armed with eight 15-inch, twelve 5.9-inch and anti-aircraft armament of 4.1-inch guns. Though splendid ships, the *Bismarck* was sunk by the Royal Navy in May 1941 after a long and bloody chase during which she sank the *Hood*. Thus she preceded *Scharnhorst* in acting out Raeder's prediction, whereas her sister the *Tirpitz* only fired her guns offensively at defenceless mine installations on the island of Spitsbergen and spent most of her life 'a chained dog' in the fiords of occupied Norway. Finally, hit by RAF heavy bombs after being damaged by midget subs, she ignominiously capsized.

By the time of Japan's withdrawal from the international naval treaties she had already embarked on a programme of expansion in eastern Asia. Under the guise of founding a 'co-prosperity sphere', the Japanese army invaded China and annexed Manchuria, in effect starting what was to become the Second World War. In 1934 plans had been drafted for four immense capital ships. Aware of the military necessity of destroying the United States' Pacific fleet the Japanese naval command had embarked on a similar process as their allies, the Germans. By building superior ships, it was falsely assumed that they could thus compensate for numerical inferiority. Thus were born the 'unsinkable' *Yamato* class. In the event only two were built, a third being converted to a carrier, and a fourth cancelled. Nevertheless, they were formidable ships.

The *Yamato*, completed at Kure in 1942, displaced 69,990 tons when fully laden and, at 863 feet (263 metres) was less than a metre longer than HMS *Hood* and only eight metres shorter than the American *Iowa*. However, she was much heavier and, at 27 knots, slower, due to her heavy armour which consisted of a belt 16 inches thick, with decks of 9 inches and her turrets were protected by an incredible 25.6 inches of steel. Her armament too was tremendous, for she mounted the heaviest broadside ever, nine 18.1-inch calibre weapons in three triple turrets. Nor did the *Yamato* appear deficient in secondary or anti-aircraft weaponry, for she carried a dozen 6.1-inch, batteries of 5-inch high-angle and numerous lesser guns down to light machine guns. Seven aircraft completed her inventory.

Yamato was followed in 1943 by her sister-ship, the *Musashi*. This ship was sunk by American aircraft in the Battle of Leyte Gulf (23–26 October 1944) when a triple pronged attack was mounted on Admiral Halsey's Third Fleet and Vice-Admiral Kinkaid's Seventh Fleet covering the American beach-head in the eastern Philippines. The Japanese attack, brilliant in conception, underestimated the American capability at using the twin dominant forces of modern naval war. Admiral Kurita's squadron was attacked first by submarines which sank two cruisers, including his flagship *Atago*. Thereafter his force was continually harried by aircraft from Halsey's carriers. The *Musashi* was assailed by about forty direct bomb hits and eighteen torpedo strikes before she capsized. Though the action was not decided until a few days later, Leyte Gulf was one of the decisive battles of modern times, for it was a battle of annihilation, proving the big-gun was no match for aircraft.

Interdiction of the capture of Okinawa was the purpose of the *Yamato*'s last sortie in April of 1945. Vice-Admiral Ito had been ordered to 'fight to [the] finish'. His squadron also included the cruiser *Yahagi* and eight destroyers, a wholly inadequate force for its purpose. American carrier-borne aircraft found Ito's squadron 250 miles away and 380 torpedo and dive bombers were launched against him. Four damaged destroyers escaped total destruction. As for the *Yamato*, she was hit by at least a dozen bombs and seven torpedoes, and took Ito and 2400 men to the bottom of the East China Sea. This was the last great naval action of the war and confirmed what the Japanese themselves had demonstrated with such devastation four years earlier, that carrier-borne aircraft were the crucial key to the exercise of twentieth-century sea-power.

Like the British *Rodney* and *Nelson* of 1927, 16-inch guns were also adopted for the United States Navy's treaty-permitted *North Carolina* class which were in fact not completed until 1941. Serious attempts were made to conform to the 35,000-ton limitation, but they finally displaced 37,500 tons. Armed with nine 16-inch guns with twenty 5-inch secondary weapons, they made 27.6 knots due to light armour. Their successors, the four *South Dakota* class were commissioned in 1942, by which time the United States was involved in the Second World War. Radical redesign of their propulsion machinery enabling greater armoured protection over a shorter length, made these ships as fast on the same tonnage. In November 1942 the USS *South Dakota* received hits of 14-inch and 8-inch calibre from the Japanese battleship Kirishima without them penetrating her armour.

The speed of the *South Dakotas*, however, was felt to be too slow and an enduring super-class, the four *Iowas* followed. Of 57,540 tons loaded displacement, USS *Iowa* commissioned in 1943 mounting nine 16-inch and twenty 5-inch guns. She was 887 feet (270.4 metres) in length, 108 feet (33 metres) in the beam on a draught of 36 feet (11 metres). Her armour was 12.1 inches thick amidships, tapering to 12 and 6 inches at her extremities. Turbines generated 212,000 horsepower and sped her along her way at 32.5 knots. Joined by USSs *New Jersey*, *Missouri* and *Wisconsin*, two remain in reserve today, having served in the Second World War, the Korean, Vietnamese and Gulf Wars, and, fitted with Tomahawk cruise missiles, in the Persian Gulf against Iraq. Although a larger, *Montana* class was planned, a steel shortage in 1943 led to their cancellation.

Scrupulous in her intention to abide by the Washington Treaty as much as to reduce the cost of increasingly expensive weapons, Great Britain had laid down five battleships of the *King George V* class which were completed between 1940 and 1942. The primary battery of 14-inch guns was fitted in three turrets, a quadruple fore and aft, with a twin superfiring over the forward quadruple. Built to conform with the treaty, their loaded displacement was 36,750 tons and they were 745 feet (227 metres) in length. Their steam turbines generated 125,000 horsepower and they were capable of 28 knots. Their secondary armament was sixteen 5.25-inch guns in twin turrets supported by pompoms and other light weapons which were updated as the experience of war required modifications to be made. The *Prince of Wales*, having been badly blooded by the *Bismarck*, was lost to Japanese aircraft in company with HMS *Repulse*, but it was HMS *Duke of York* which successfully led the fight against *Scharnhorst*. The Home Fleet flagship, HMS *King George V* was in action against the *Bismarck* and served with distinction as flagship of the British Pacific Fleet.

Heavily armoured with belts 15 inches thick, similar plating on the main turrets, 6 inches on the secondary armament and 6 inches on deck, the designed speed of the *KG-V* was higher than that actually achieved. The class also lacked sheer and were wet because of a Staff Requirement to allow forward guns to fire ahead at zero elevation, but they were generally regarded as successful ships. Although larger 30-knot successors, the *Lions*, were laid down in 1939, labour problems and material shortages led to their cancellation. However, a pre-war project design was revived, using the twin 15-inch turrets removed when Fisher's 'light battlecruisers' *Courageous* and *Glorious* were altered to aircraft carriers. A modified *Lion*, HMS *Vanguard*, 'a new battleship with her great-aunt's teeth', was commissioned too late to take part in the Second World War. *Vanguard* incorporated most of the lessons learned in two wars and proved a remarkably fine sea-keeper with her 130,000 horsepower turbines enabling her to achieve 29 knots even in poor weather. But they were lessons learned too late for the Royal Navy; indeed she might with some justification have been named HMS *Rearguard*. She was not merely an anachronism, she was a liability. Sir Edward Grey's foresight was proving too true and Britain had finally spent her imperial treasure. The end of a war in which, whatever her faults, she had stood alone for a year as the champion of freedom, found her bankrupt. And there were others eager to take up her old, discredited role of global policeman.

CHAPTER FIFTEEN

The Skies Above:
The Seas Below

The restoration of peace in 1918 is a more significant event in the history of the warship than that of the merchantman. The expected clash of mighty battlefleets had somehow misfired and had, as far as it went, proved something of a disappointment for the British. Because of this, the effect on the German High Seas Fleet is often overlooked.

The demoralisation which later wrecked the German Navy may be dated from the Battle of Jutland in 1916. Mutiny, surrender and the scuppering of Tirpitz's *Hochseeflotte* followed, and with it the humiliation of the terms of the Treaty of Versailles, inflation, poverty and the consequential rise of Nazism.

Notwithstanding the extraordinary luck of Scheer in avoiding a defeat at Jutland (31 May 1916), the Germans had to admit that only the U-boat could give them victory. Even though the gamble of achieving that victory by destroyong Allied seaborne trade before the Americans could bring their might to bear in Europe failed, the U-boats came close in 1917.

Realising the importance of airpower, the Royal Navy since 1911 had been investigating ways to use aircraft for spotting and reconnaissance. By 1917, the concept of the aircraft carrier had become well enough established to see large numbers of aircraft operating from ships, and in 1918 HMS *Hermes*, a specialist aircraft carrier, was laid down

In fact several other naval shibboleths required re-evaluation. Although the powers sought to limit the size of navies with the Washington Treaty and its successors, the inter-war years produced a number of developments which, despite being under funded, only half thought through and sometimes marginalised by old-fashioned preferences, nevertheless ratcheted up to full production and potential after the onset of the Second World War.

For their part the Germans also made considerable advances in warship design, while the Italians, Japanese and American navies were no longer in the shadow of the British. Perhaps the lasting legacy of Jutland was not the limitations of its achievement, but its toppling of the once incomparable British navy from its pedestal. In the event, the big-gun was exposed as less than the perfect weapon it was supposed. Received wisdom asserts that the three great influences upon modern naval war are the submarine, the aircraft and electronics. Oddly, the latter *inter alia*, did bring the big-gun into a brief, ironic and sunset prominence.

The idea of using aircraft at sea was initially in support of the battlefleet, that hypothetical concentration of dreadnoughts which would seek out and destroy the battlefleet of an enemy. Lack of accurate intelligence of enemy movements, along with the flawed concept of distant blockade, had cheated Admirals Jellicoe and Beatty at Jutland, and they had been worse served than Nelson before Trafalgar. Had Jellicoe and Beatty had aeroplanes, the sequence of events might have gone better for them, although it is interesting to note that the seaplane carrier *Engadine* had been operating in a forward position during the opening phases of the action, although a technical fault prevented her seaplane from sending a sighting report.

Just as the Holland submarine had come from America, so did the heavier than air flying machine. The Wright brothers offered the British Admiralty all their patents in 1907, but the Royal Navy politely declined the purchase. By this time Graf von Zeppelin was building lighter-than-air dirigibles and the Blériot monoplane was assuming pre-eminence in the burgeoning world of heavier-than-air aviation after its eponymous aviator had flown the English Channel in July 1909. It was clear that a dirigible could not operate from a ship although they had excellent endurance and could to a degree reconnoitre and give air cover. However, in early 1909 the first naval airship, as long as a contemporary armoured cruiser, broke its back in a cross wind and the Admiralty dismissed the idea for a while. Raids by German 'Zeppelins' revived interest and numerous non-rigid 'blimps' were built. Rigid dirigibles *R33* and *R34* were ordered and the latter made a return trip across the Atlantic in 1919. Naval airships fell victim to post-war economics, although gas-filled barrage balloons were hoisted above merchant ships in convoy between 1939 and 1945 to ensnare enemy aircraft in an array of wires.

The United States Navy, however, did perfect the dirigible, and flew them as long-range anti-submarine patrol craft up to the 1960s, but they were never seriously used in concert with large groups of warships at sea. Besides their ponderous progress, dirigibles were large and vulnerable targets. But it was clear from an early stage the heavier-than-air machine had the versatile potential which promised the kind of death-machine the military intellect took such an interest in. As Blériot had crossed the Strait of Dover he flew over the French destroyer *Escopette*, racing him at the destroyer's full speed of 26 knots. While her crew waved, the *Daily Graphic* commented, 'a machine which can fly from Calais to Dover is ... an instrument of warfare of which soldiers and statesmen must take account.' The newspaper might have added 'sailors'.

Then, in 1911, one of those periodic innovative civilian interventions in naval affairs occurred. A Mr Francis McClean offered to teach some naval officers the rudiments of flying using his own private aircraft based at Eastchurch on the Isle of Sheppey in the Thames Estuary. No fewer than 200 young officers volunteered for this service and in the 1914 Spithead Review a flight of sixteen seaplanes flew over the Royal Yacht *Victoria and Albert*. By the end of the war that began four days later, the Royal Naval Air Service boasted a strength of 55,000 men. The year McClean made his offer of training, a seaplane built by A. V. Roe took off from water, focusing early Admiralty attention on the seaplane as the ideal form of aeroplane for naval work.

Across the Atlantic, the Americans were already experimenting with carriers. A short platform was rigged over the bows of the USS *Birmingham* and in Norfolk Harbor, Virginia, on a November afternoon in 1910 a civilian pilot, Eugene Ely, just managed to get his Curtiss Model D airborne, although it dragged its underbelly in the water. Nevertheless, the idea warranted further investigation, especially the possibility of landing, and a long flight deck was laid down over the after turret of the USS *Pennsylvania*, rising slightly at its forward end. On the morning of 18 January 1911, Ely brought his aeroplane in at about 35 knots and landed safely. He had been dragging grapnels and the ship had rigged athwartships lines, lifted a little above the wooden deck by draping them over railway sleepers and tensioning them with sandbags. Having landed successfully, Ely then took off again. The following year, in addition to coming up with the idea of arrester hooks and wires, the United States Navy also tried to launch an aircraft from a catapult.

In 1912, however, the Royal Navy achieved similar success. A Lieutenant Samson flying a Short S27 'hydroaeroplane' flew off a ramp on the foredeck of the anchored battleship HMS *Africa*. The same year he repeated his feat from HMS *Hibernia* which was steaming at 10 knots. The experiments were not followed up as Europe was engulfed in war and the seaplane carrier provided the Royal Navy with its first air-strike force. Taking up a number of cross-Channel ferries from their usual profession, the Admiralty fitted them with a hangar and crane aft. On Christmas Day 1914, seven seaplanes, launched from *Engadine*, *Riviera* and *Empress*, attempted to bomb the Zeppelin sheds at Cuxhaven, at the mouth of the Elbe. Fog prevented accurate bombing, but the return of the aeroplanes over the Schillig Road caused a flurry among the ships of the High Seas Fleet anchored there, providing the Admiralty with an accurate intelligence report of their whereabouts.

Ultimately, however, the difficulties in launching these small aeroplanes in the usually choppy conditions of the North Sea combined with the even more uncertain business of recovering them, persuaded the Admiralty that such a method was fraught with difficulties. There was also the consideration that such was the pace of technical advance, it was necessary to think ahead and the clear superiority of an aircraft disencumbered of its floats, persuaded the planners to revise their ideas. The Cunard liner *Campania* had been converted to a carrier by the fitting of a 200-foot flight deck, originally intended for flying off seaplanes from trolleys. Unfortunately the ship was sunk in collision in 1918, but she had provided the key for future progress. It was hoped that superior-performing wheeled aircraft could be used from existing units of the fleet, rather than undertaking the expensive development of a whole new class of warship. Accordingly, following some further experiments with cruisers, a flight was made from a platform mounted on B-turret of the battlecruiser *Repulse*. Thereafter all the battlecruisers were equipped to fit a platform over the superfiring B-turret which could be trained into the wind and from which the wind speed was sufficient to enable a small fighter to take off. Many capital ships were similarly fitted with this, as well as light cruisers. However, this method of launching an aircraft meant a one-way ticket, since recovery at sea was not only difficult, but would have left the stationary parent ship prey to a torpedo from a prowling submarine. The cost of these primitive aircraft was low and once they had achieved the aim of sighting an enemy, this consideration, beyond concern for the pilot, did not weigh very heavily. Even when the provision of catapult-launched amphibious spotting aircraft became standard for cruisers and capital ships between the wars, the aircraft were often abandoned.

These were, however, experimental teasers which avoided the logically costly conclusion of providing a proper sea-worthy operating platform. The real impetus to carrier development was the appearance of the Short 184 in 1915, a biplane which could launch a torpedo. The potential of such an airborne weapon, flown off a ship in an advanced station either alongside the battlefleet or operating almost as a capital ship, was immediately obvious; matters now proceeded apace. The light battlecruiser *Furious* was fitted with an experimental flight deck forward of her bridge. Upon this, Squadron-Commander Dunning, skilfully avoiding the turbulence created by the ship's superstructure, made a successful landing in a Sopwith Pup. Repeating the feat later, however, Dunning's machine burst a tyre, fell over the side and he drowned.

It was then decided to construct a second area for landing abaft the funnel, but although in July 1918 seven Sopwith Camels successfully flew off *Furious* to raid the Zeppelins at Tondern, most of the pilots flew onwards to neutral Denmark, rather than attempt to land back on *Furious*. Those two who did return, opted to ditch alongside rather than risk their necks fighting their light aeroplanes through the turbulence created in the lee of the battlecruiser's funnel and superstructure. It was obvious that the solution to taking off and landing required an unimpeded flight deck, long enough for the incoming aircraft to slow to a stop as the ship steamed into the wind. To achieve this, an Italian liner, the *Conte Rosso*, then being built in Britain, was requisitioned as HMS *Argus* and completed with a continuous upper flight deck and a hangar underneath. Only a small, retractable chart-house broke the horizontal purity of her otherwise flat profile. HMS *Argus* survived to the end of the Second World War, although her birth was at the very end of the First, when she proved the potential of the dedicated 'aircraft carrier'.

Meanwhile *Furious* herself was taken in hand and her after 18-inch gun was removed, destined, as we have remarked, for service aboard a monitor. She was again rebuilt and recommissioned in 1925 as a flush-decked carrier, capable of supporting thirty-five aircraft. With her speed of 31 knots she was further confirmation of the value of such a ship and her half-sisters *Courageous* and *Glorious* (22,000 tons) were also docked for similar work, emerging in their new roles in 1930 as fast and capable carriers. Sadly, both were destined for tragic ends in the early part of the Second World War. The first was operating in the Channel on anti-submarine patrol when her quarry struck first and she was sunk by a U-boat. *Glorious*, her decks cluttered with aircraft after the evacuation of Norway, and her captain anxious to carry out two courts-martial, had no aircraft aloft when she fell under the guns of the *Scharnhorst* and *Gneisenau* in June 1940. She was sunk by shellfire while her attending destroyers sacrificed themselves with customary gallantry. These two losses were to have an ironic and merciful effect on the thinking of the German *Seekriegsleitung,* or supreme naval staff, effectively halting German carrier-development.

The British gained a further carrier from the conversion of the sister to the battleship *Canada,* which had been under construction originally for the Chileans. Purchased in 1917, this hull was partially converted by 1918 and then fully converted to become HMS *Eagle* (22,600 tons). She too was destined to be sunk during operations to relieve beleaguered Malta in 1942. The first 'custom-built' aircraft carrier laid down for the Royal Navy was the *Hermes.* She was a smaller ship than her predecessors, displacing a mere 10,850 tons, with a speed of 25 knots. Her complement of aircraft was limited to twenty and this was later reduced to fifteen. Sadly, she too was lost in the Second World War, falling victim to Japanese carrier-based bombers in the Indian Ocean.

The advent of the aircraft carrier was to sour relations between those former allies, the British and Americans. Aware that in seaborne aircraft they were involved in a 'stern chase' the Americans took an intense interest in British developments. Unfortunately, the British had relegated naval aviation to a curious hybrid status because the government succumbed to the seductive argument, 'the air is invisible'. In 1918 the Royal Naval Air Service was amalgamated with the RFC to form the RAF. Thereafter, aircraft on British naval carriers were supplied by the Royal Air Force, together with air and ground crews, with an RAF officer embarked as a senior air officer. In the days of simple biplanes with short take off and landing characteristics, this did not unduly matter, but after a protracted and unedifying competition for limited funds the late revival in 1936 of what became the Fleet Air Arm was too late to equip British carriers with first-class aircraft by the outbreak of war in 1939. The fleet therefore had to fall back on the primitive Swordfish, its unsuccessful derivative, the Albacore, the Skua, the Roc, the inadequate Fairey Barracuda and inadequately strengthened conversions of land-based fighters such as the Hurricane and Spitfire which were adapted to naval use as the Sea Hurricane and the Seafire. These were of insufficient strength to withstand the rigours of carrier operations. Starved of a really effective carrier-borne fighter which could intercept incoming bombers, the Royal Navy considered it must protect its carriers against such attacks, and enclosed their hangars accordingly.

Meanwhile the United States Navy forged its own path. By 1930 the Americans had only two carriers, albeit large ones, which like so many of their generation, were built on the hulls of suspended battlecruisers. They entered service as the *Saratoga* and the *Lexington*. It was, however, the development of dedicated and highly successful fighters, fighter bombers and torpedo bombers which rapidly gave the Americans a consider-able advantage over the British. In due course aircraft such as the Grumman Avenger and Hellcat, made their much needed appearance on the flight decks of His Majesty's aircraft carriers, where they were enthusiastically embraced by their young pilots. Such fighters and fighter bombers were designed for heavy landings, with immense integral strength and in all respects suited to naval air-war. Up until this time the British navy's Fleet Air Arm had suffered the inevitable consequences of political in-fighting and had gone to war with largely ineffective and out-dated aircraft operating from their carriers. That such obsolescent aircraft as the Fairey Swordfish, fitted with radar and an 18-inch torpedo or depth charges, became a highly effective U-boat killer, is almost entirely due to the incredible endurance of their aircrews. As for the carriers from which these courageous young men operated, their story is less murky and, at the end, proved them to possess some virtues unappreciated by the Americans until young men of a similar stamp but a different nationality, drove their lethally loaded fighters into their unarmoured flight decks in acts of self-immolation.

The limitations of the Washington and London Treaties were designed to curtail the development of the prime weapon of the age, the 'big-gun' battleship, and the carrier was barely affected, a circumstance which resulted in the size of carriers exceeding the real needs of aviation at the time. This was, of course, partly a consequence of four of the world's navies having redundant capital ship hulls. Although profiting to a degree from this, in fact Britain was the loser because she had cancelled large ship construction in 1914 and, as we have remarked, already had several converted carriers in service. Both the Americans and the Japanese incorporated 8-inch guns, the largest calibre permitted under the terms of the treaties, and, although these proved useless in practice, both naval staffs realised that the Pacific theatre needed large carriers.

These two countries therefore again reviewed the possibility of other expedients, such as the conversion of merchantmen. The Japanese built three fast auxiliary warships capable of rapid conversion to carriers and also subsidised liner construction to provide hulls for quick adaptation following requisition. There were few suitable hulls in the American Merchant Marine, but in 1936 a Maritime Commission was formed to revive the post-slump merchant fleet. Born out of their First World War experience of standard shipbuilding, the Americans sponsored a liner convertible to an auxiliary or carrier in time of national emergency. This, the *P-4P*, was designed with its engine uptakes offset, to allow quick fitting of a flight deck, but was not ready for the outbreak of war. The end result was that simpler conversions were actually made in defiance of pre-war theory.

The Royal Navy had a more complex dilemma. The protection of the world-wide Empire trade routes required cruisers, and the new large carriers were earmarked for service with the main fleet. A compromise was sought with trade-protection carriers, a concept which could not be developed in 1939 because of a lack of aircraft. The six fleet-carriers under construction were designed to operate with the heavy units as part of the battlefleet. When the treaties expired and capital ship construction was revived, scarce funds were made available, but the six carriers had not been delivered by the outbreak of the Second World War. Indeed, it was soon realised that a greater priority had to be given to cruisers, corvettes, destroyers and frigates.

In 1935 the British Admiralty had laid down a large new purpose-built aircraft carrier, HMS *Ark Royal*. Eight hundred feet long, displacing 22,000 tons with turbines generating 102,000 horsepower to give a speed of 30 knots, the new ship was fitted with sixteen 4.5-inch guns and six multiple pom-poms for air defence. Protected by a belt of 4.5 inch armour and with decks of 3-inch steel, she was commissioned in 1937. Frequently 'sunk' by German propaganda, she scored a propaganda coup of her own by being influential in name only, persuading the unfortunate *Kapitan-zur-See* Hans Langsdorff to scuttle the *Graf Spee* off Montevideo rather than come out and be sunk by the guns and aircraft of the British navy. *Ark Royal*'s Swordfish biplanes carried out a raid on the *Bismarck* sufficient to damage that great ship's steering gear, delay her, and deliver her to the guns of the *King George V* and the *Rodney*. But in November 1941 HMS *Ark Royal* was sunk, torpedoed off Gibraltar by a German U-boat.

By this time more carriers had joined the fleet, HMSs *Illustrious*, *Indomitable*, *Formidable* and *Victorious* all entered service between 1939 and 1942. Classed as fleet carriers and capable of 31–32 knots they possessed similar dimensions to *Ark Royal*, but had armoured flight decks. The raid on the Italian fleet at Taranto in November 1940 was made by aircraft from *Illustrious*, and aircraft from *Victorious* also hit *Bismarck*. As an historical footnote, *Indomitable* was to have joined the *Prince of Wales* and *Repulse* as a reinforcement to the Far East Fleet, but ran aground off Jamaica and the two capital ships thus had no air cover when Japanese aircraft located and destroyed them. The larger *Indefatigable* and *Implacable* had quadruple screws and Barracudas from the former struck at the *Tirpitz* in her Norwegian lair; afterwards *Indefatigable* and the other armoured carriers served as part of the British Pacific Fleet alongside the United States Navy, where their flight decks proved more effective against the Japanese *kamikaze* attacks than those of the USN.

One virtue of the carrier was the relative rapidity with which it could be constructed, despite its size. Pre-war warship construction in the United States had concentrated on battleships because they took so long to build. Nevertheless the *Ark Royal*'s larger American contemporary, the USS *Yorktown*, could handle almost a hundred aircraft, twenty-eight more than the *Ark*'s nominal seventy-two. The *Essex* class which eventually numbered twenty-four ships, was ordered just before Pearl Harbor, largely due to the foresight of President Roosevelt, and were followed by the larger and more sophisticated *Midway* class – giant 60,000-ton ships, which did not enter service until the very end of the war.

As the war progressed, building priority on both sides of the Atlantic was shifted away from battleships and large carriers, to concentrate not only on convoy escorts, submarines and destroyers, but on merchant ships and small carriers. Although the big carriers were to play a vital part in several major naval actions in the Pacific War, the important matter of convoy protection demanded air-cover, locally and continuously if possible, above and around the flocks of laden merchantmen that kept the armies of the Allies in the field.

Several 'answers' addressed this problem. Single fighters could be catapulted from merchant ships (Catapult Armed Merchantmen, or CAM-ships), but this launched a pilot on a one-way mission and the card could only be played once. A second expedient was to build a mercantile hull which could carry cargo, and superimpose a flight deck with a handful of fighters operating from it. These 'merchant aircraft carriers', or MAC ships, were only a partial answer. The best solution was the escort carrier (CVE), a small, rather ugly 'flat-top', a converted merchant ship's hull fitted with a flight deck. Ugly hybrids they might have seemed, but they were fully fledged carriers and served with distinction in the North Atlantic and especially on Arctic convoys when the merchant ships were exposed to air attack from occupied Norway throughout their passage to Russia.

These ships did not long outlive the Second World War; in fact several were reconverted to merchant ships. A more enduring type was the light fleet carrier. The loss of the *Prince of Wales* and *Repulse* had alerted the Admiralty to the vulnerability of capital ships to air attack, and the carrier losses sustained with the sinking of *Courageous, Ark Royal, Glorious* and *Hermes* meant that alternative plans had to be drawn up. Strained to the limits of their capacity, British shipyards produced 16 of these replacement carriers, of about 14,000 tons displacement. They were capable of nearly 25 knots and operating nearly forty aircraft, but only four entered service before the end of the war. The hulls had been built to Lloyd's classification standards, allowing construction by non-specialist shipyards. Five, *Ocean, Glory, Triumph, Sydney* and *Theseus,* were called to action during 1950–53 for various periods of service during the Korean War. Two others were completed as aircraft maintenance ships and as a test-bed for the new steam-catapult which was to allow jet aircraft to operate from carriers. Several were scrapped or transferred to the Commonwealth navies of Canada, Australia and India, while others were sold to the French and the Dutch, afterwards finding their way into the Brazilian and Argentinian navies. (HMS *Venerable*, for instance, became first the Dutch *Karel Doorman* and then the Argentine *Veinticino de Mayo*.) The last of the class, HMS *Leviathan*, was towed from her builders on the River Tyne to Portsmouth in 1946, to lie idle until 1968 when she was scrapped, a distant whisper of Sir Edward Grey's warning blowing about her windswept and deserted flight deck.

The later delivery of four larger 'intermediate' fleet carriers allowed design modifications to take advantage of post-war development, particularly in strengthened flight decks for the operation of jets. By the mid fifties, the Royal Navy was operating the Sea Hawk and Venom with the Blackburn Buccaneer following in 1962. The Buccaneer was an outstandingly successful subsonic low level attack aircraft with a highly robust airframe which outlived the ships capable of launching it. While the former aeroplanes operated from three of these ships, HMSs

Albion, *Bulwark* and *Centaur*, all of which had slightly angled flight decks, the larger Buccaneer was too heavy, and therefore *Albion* and *Bulwark* were converted to commando carriers. They thus assumed a new role, deploying a rapid-response force of Royal Marine commandos, air-lifted by helicopters. The fourth ship of the class, HMS *Hermes*, was not delivered until the late fifties and was strengthened and reconstructed several times during her life. Commissioned with a fully angled flight deck her later modifications enabled her to carry large Sea King helicopters and a Royal Marine commando and, with a ski-jump forward she could fly-off the revolutionary Sea Harrier. In this guise she served as Rear-Admiral Woodward's flagship off the Falklands in 1982, while her half-sister ship, the *Veinticino de Mayo*, whose presence at sea might have made an enormous difference to the outcome of the campaign, remained in port.

Of the heavier fleet carriers ordered in the war, only *Eagle* and a new *Ark Royal* were ever completed, in 1951 and 1955 respectively. Sister-ships of 36,800 tons displacement, they had flight decks just over 800 feet in length. Both underwent extensive refits and finished their lives with fully angled flight decks, side lifts, sophisticated landing guide arrangements and steam catapults. The fully angled flight deck enabled flying operations to take place continuously, essential when a carrier was in action. This configuration provided a fail-safe flight path for any returning aircraft which missed the arrester wires, as well as a park for refuelling and re-arming aircraft landing from combat air patrols, while the steam catapult, serviced by a lift, enabled more aircraft to be launched from forward.

In 1950, the war-built British aircraft carrier *Victorious* was completely reconstructed in Portsmouth, after first being almost reduced to her double bottoms. She was equipped with the most modern features so that when she re-entered service in 1958, she was virtually a new ship. The carrier force of *Victorious*, *Ark Royal* and *Eagle* could operate with airborne early warning radar carried in the Fairey Gannet which acted as an advanced picket for the carrier, but all had been scrapped when the conflict with Argentina over the Falklands arose in 1982. Only months earlier the *Ark Royal* had been broken up and so *Hermes* was thrust into the breach, alongside a new type of small carrier which could operate only half the number of aircraft *Hermes* hosted.

This ship was HMS *Invincible*, which had been conceived as one of three Through Deck Cruisers. These were victims of both a battle of political semantics and cancelled plans. Intended as support for a large strike-carrier (*CVA-01*), the government of the day, convinced by spurious RAF arguments, cancelled *CVA-01* on the grounds of excessive cost, compelling the newly unified Ministry of Defence to re-evaluate the role of naval aviation. The concept of a 'garage' for anti-submarine helicopters was replaced by Through Deck Cruisers, a euphemism intended to conceal from the politicians any pretence to aircraft carrier status. The three ships planned were to be the core of anti-submarine groups, with sonar-equipped Sea Kings capable of dropping homing torpedoes. The number of helicopters was then reduced from the projected fifteen in favour of accommodating an additional five Sea Harrier Short Take-Off/ Vertical Landing (STOVL) aircraft to provide a limited strike capability and to deal with Soviet reconnaissance aircraft. Three were eventually built, but the first, HMS *Invincible*, was about to be sold to Australia when the Argentines invaded the Falklands in April 1982. In the event *Invincible* sailed in support of *Hermes*, and HMS *Illustrious* was hurried to completion in June 1982. The ships are fitted with ski-jumps, to increase the fuel or weapons pay load of the Sea Harrier with its guns and air-to-air missiles. With the lesson of carrier airpower re-learned in the South Atlantic, these three 20,000-tonne carriers are today the mainstay of the Royal Navy in the post-Cold War age.

Although these ships lack the full range of capabilities of the 100,000-ton nuclear carriers (CVNs) of the US Navy, their Sea Harriers provide local air superiority, deterring attack on the fleet and providing more than adequate offensive capability against land and sea targets. Their weapons now include medium range AMRAAM air-to-air missiles and Sea Eagle anti-ship missiles.

The close co-operation between the British and United States Navies at the end of the First World War evaporated and opened into a rift during the 1920s, but not before allowing the American navy to profit from the Royal Navy's battle-experience. American naval staff war games encouraged the belief that it was essential to use the greatest possible numbers of aircraft with a battlefleet. Thus, American tactics preached the dictum of getting there 'firstest, fastest with the mostest': air strikes were to be delivered *en masse*.

A converted naval collier, the USS *Langley*, was put under the command of a Captain Reeves who rejected the practice of striking aircraft below into the hold, not only because the ship had no hangar deck, but also because he considered this too slow. Instead, he shunted landed aircraft forward, put up an athwartships barrier and handled his incoming aeroplanes on the after two-thirds of the deck. The chief advantage thus gained was that larger aircraft could be operated than could be accommodated in the hangar or stowage area below the flight deck. Although flight-deck accidents were frequent, Reeves stuck doggedly to his principles. Chaos was averted by imposing a rigid disciplinary system and subjecting pilots to the instructions of landing signals officers who corrected glide paths and ordered the cutting of engines. Three significant ideas arose from Reeves' foresight: arrester wires, a high rate of aircraft handling and very robust air-frames. It explains the lead the Americans established over the unfortunate British, for the United States Navy controlled design and development of its naval air arm from the beginning. This combination of dash and inherent strength obviated considerations of airflow over the flight decks, a subject that obsessed the British with their much lighter aircraft and the experience of HMS *Furious*, around whose 'island' wind eddies caused havoc for early naval aviators. The US aircraft industry was also on a sounder footing, unlike the British, who produced endless prototypes.

Early Royal Navy carriers had double hangars, with aircraft flying off the lower forward deck directly from the hangar. Even after this configuration had been abandoned in *Hermes*, the internal hangar concept prevented the British from accommodating large air groups. Not until Lend-Lease provided newer American types did the British carriers have robust high-performance aircraft.

The Americans pursued another route with the *Lexington* and *Saratoga*, which were launched in 1925 and displaced 43,000 tons fully loaded. 888 feet overall (271 metres), they were fitted with 7-inch armoured belts, though their decks were much weaker. But they were fast, with turbo-electric motors nominally running at around 180,000 horsepower, but capable of being boosted to 210,000, giving the huge carriers a speed of 34 knots, a legacy of their original role as battlecruisers. Odd in profile, their four uptakes were combined into a huge, ugly funnel, separated from the fore-bridge which, in carrier-parlance was 'the island'. Manned by 1788 officers and ratings, over a third of whom were air personnel, these two ships could carry a minimum of sixty aircraft. To deter surface attack by cruisers or destroyers, eight 8-inch guns were mounted in conventional turrets (a configuration never entertained by the Royal Navy, which more correctly recognised the risk of carriers engaging in a gun-battle), while a dozen 5-inch high-angle guns were carried for air defence. Huge and expensive, even by American standards, they were not exceeded in size until after 1943 when the three *Yorktown* class (25,000 tons) were followed by the 35,000-ton *Essex* class. Subsequent carriers did not copy the 8-inch armament, but what the *Saratoga* and *Lexington* did leave as priceless legacies to their successors was the concept of the open hangar deck and the large air group.

The flight decks of these two early American carriers were raised superstructures, below which a lower deck, that could be enclosed in bad weather by shutters, enabled aircraft to run up their engines, prior to being lifted to the flight deck for launching. Repairs and servicing were carried out in the hangar proper, which lay another deck down, within the hull. This left them vulnerable to a determined enemy.

When conventional attacks failed, the Japanese turned to the *kamikaze* ('divine-wind') attack which was used against both British and American carriers operating in the Pacific. Carriers of the former were back in service quicker than those of the latter due partly to their armoured flight decks which limited the damage, and partly to superior fire precautions. American yards were frequently used to repair and refit British ships during the war and when HMS *Illustrious* was docked at the Norfolk navy yard in 1941, her armoured flight deck had attracted much interest. Thus, in the design which followed the *Essex*, United States Navy designers, eager to maintain the rapid rate of turnaround of aircraft, embraced the armoured deck, but rejected the enclosed hangar, placing batteries of 5-inch AA guns below the flight deck on either side. What began as armoured versions of *Essex*, doubled in tonnage to become the *Midway*, of 60,000 tons loaded displacement, capable of 33 knots and with a flight deck of 968 feet (295 metres). Such a massive ship possessed the ability to handle no less than 137 aircraft.

As a curious footnote to this story, whilst the Royal Navy's armoured flight decks proved superior against *kamikaze* attacks, the advantages of the open hangar system recommended it in turn to British planners who were alarmed at the pilot losses from flight deck accidents. It was thus adopted for the *Malta* class, a carrier design which was cancelled at the end of the war.

As a contemporary of Britain's rebuilt *Victorious*, the Americans built the *Forrestal* in 1955. She was to be the first of a five-ship class, and had a flight deck 1039 feet long, which was built above a hull, with a beam of 130 feet. The ship incorporated an angled deck off to port, with a side-lift, and an extension on the starboard side supporting the island with three more side-lifts. This gave the carrier an extreme beam of 252 feet. Anti-aircraft armament was provided by 5-inch guns in side-sponsons, plus surface-to-air missiles. Steam-catapults launched the squadrons of jet fighters and fighter bombers, up to a hundred of which could be carried, and these were manned and serviced by a complement of 3412 officers and ratings. Propelled by turbines of 280,000 horsepower, the *Forrestal* was capable of up to 34 knots. Such a ship combined all the lessons of the Second World War and many of those acquired in the early years of the Cold War, a technical revolution which we shall examine in Chapter Eighteen.

The Allied carrier task forces deployed in the north western Pacific against Japan proved the weight of sea-power that could be applied by such a force. This concept confirmed the ultimate expression of the battlefleet, displacing the flawed logic of the all big-gun fleet which had been but an extension of the traditional line of battle. The vast distances of the Pacific required sea-borne supplies and the development of the fleet train in which numerous Allied merchantmen of all flags so nobly served, was essential to its maintenance. But the sharp end of this endeavour was the carrier strike-force which took war to the very coasts of the enemy, and launched air raids of supreme devastation.

Japan was beaten to her proud knees by two culminating forces: neglect over the importing of absolutely vital raw materials by protected convoy, and the overwhelming effect of seaborne airpower. Yet it was Japan herself who had unleashed this terrible form of war upon the world, and Japan's misfortune in doing so, that her surprise attack on Pearl Harbor on 7 December 1941 had failed to destroy the American carriers which were absent from the Hawaiian naval base on that fateful day.

As an ally of the United States and Great Britain in the First World War, Japan's relationship with Great Britain had hitherto been close. The Imperial Japanese Navy had a carrier, the *Hosho*, under construction in 1920 when a British naval air mission visited the country. Exchanges between the two nations resulted in the Japanese closely conforming with British carrier-practice, in particular adopting the closed hangar. They too converted two battlecruisers, the *Kaga* and *Akagi*, using the lower flying-off deck like HMSs *Furious*, *Courageous* and *Glorious*. Japan's early break with the limitations imposed by the Washington Treaty allowed her to increase her carrier fleet, but it also severed the ties of co-operation, and thus Japanese carriers never carried British-type catapults.

During the war the carrier *Taiho* exploded from a build-up of avgas fumes in her enclosed hangar deck after a torpedo-hit, but Japan's devastating carrier losses in the Battle of Midway (4–6 June 1942) effectively destroyed her strike capability. The Japanese fleet never recovered, lacking the capacity, the industrial base or the resources to replace these ships in sufficient numbers, although it did build its largest carrier, the *Shinano*, as late as 1944. Over 800 feet long and displacing 72,000 tons loaded, she was heavily armoured and capable of 27 knots. Bearing forty-seven aircraft and defended against incoming attack by sixteen 5-inch guns, the *Shinano* had been laid down as a battleship of the *Yamato* class, a late conversion in this saga of adaptation. The Japanese losses at Midway in the southwest Pacific decided Imperial naval thinking in favour of a last carrier. Shortly after she completed sea trials, the *Shinano* proved to be the largest warship ever sunk by a submarine, being torpedoed by the USS *Archerfish* on 29 November 1944 while en route to the Inland Sea to be completed.

Although, as has been noted, several lesser navies were to acquire redundant British-built aircraft carriers post-war, only the

French had a carrier in service at the outbreak of the Second World War. The *Béarn* followed British practice, but was slow and carried too few aircraft. She was built from an incomplete and suspended battleship and launched in 1920. As a unit of the navy of the Nazi-collaborating Vichy French regime, she escaped destruction by the Royal Navy. Instead she was interned in the West Indies, being handed over to the free French in June 1943 and was thus among French warships which repossessed Vietnam in October 1945. Two new 28,000-ton carriers were abandoned in June 1940.

Italy began a carrier programme very late by converting a liner, the *Aquila*, but this was incomplete at the capitulation of the Fascists in 1943. For her part, Germany laid down the carriers *Graf Zeppelin* and *Peter Strasser* as part of the 1936 naval-building programme, but very little work was done on the latter, and the former proceeded intermittently. She was launched at Kiel on 8 December 1938, but then work ceased, a spurious vulnerability being attributed to carriers after the losses of the British carriers *Courageous* and *Glorious*. After the Japanese sank HMSs *Prince of Wales* and *Repulse* by land-based aircraft, the German building programme resumed. The chaotic state of German naval thinking, early Luftwaffe problems in providing suitable aircraft, and the overwhelming demand for U-boats, was to halt the *Graf Zeppelin* yet again. Other German plans had included the conversion of passenger liners, but nothing ever came of them and the incomplete *Graf Zeppelin*, which had been moved to Stettin, was eventually scuttled on 25 April 1945 to prevent her from falling into the hands of the Soviet Second Assault Army. She finally sank in 1947.

Had Adolf Hitler not rushed so precipitantly into war, Grand-Admiral Raeder's ambitious 'Z-plan' might well have provided Germany with a highly capable strike force, which would have avenged the fate of Tirpitz's High Seas Fleet long before the run-down British Royal Navy of the 1930s had resuscitated itself into the efficient force it was to become by 1943. Ironically, this was the very year Hitler had originally told Raeder he should be ready for war with the British Royal Navy.

Within the confused legacy of Jutland were the questions of enemy whereabouts, from which deductions of enemy intentions were possible, and the whereabouts of friendly forces, without which overwhelming concentrations of force were difficult to achieve. The reconnoitring potential of patrolling aircraft was quickly appreciated. It was, moreover, vastly cheaper, simpler, quicker and thus more effective than extended squadrons of light, scouting cruisers. It also became obvious that if a ship was vulnerable to attack from the air, then such an attack might be staved off at a distance by defensive air combat, rather than leaving it until the enemy got in close, in the rather pious hope that he could be shot down. Moreover, such aeroplanes could also provide air defence for a squadron of ships.

The three purposes of carrier-based aircraft were therefore established as reconnaissance, attack (or striking), and defence. As the British found out, these huge ships were vulnerable to submarine attack, and the idea of using them to hunt for U-boats was dropped initially, although it became clear later in the Second World War that the idea was a sound one, providing the method of execution was efficient.

Reconnaissance, which was also the first line of defence in depth, was carried out by combat air-patrols of small groups of fighters flying over given areas surrounding the squadron or convoy. Later such aircraft carried radar sets to transmit data back to the mother-ship's plotting room. By this method surfaced submarines could be attacked before they had time to dive. The effectiveness of radar which came into service early in the Second World War, revolutionised early interception. A few fighters flying an air patrol could be vectored onto incoming bombers, while the early warning thus provided, robbed an attacking force of its element of surprise.

Concern about the effects of Japanese *kamikaze* attacks on American carriers was a great incentive to the pursuit of electronic countermeasures such as radar warning receivers. Destroyers were fitted with long-range radar and were stationed well out on the flanks of a task force as pickets. Nor need this role be sacrificial, for the fleet carrier provided local air-cover.

None of these criteria, once established and understood, has altered radically. The heavy, jet strike fighters such as those in service with the United States, Royal and French Navies, replicate the tactics of the piston driven machines of the Second World War, albeit to a highly sophisticated degree. Only the

British Sea Harrier has proved revolutionary, with its short take-off and vertical landing capability (STOVL). This aircraft is now combat-proven and has resulted in an American derivative, the AV-8B Harrier II. An aircraft carrier is a mere target without its aircraft, for these provide its eyes and its teeth. This ability of the carrier to deliver punitive strikes from the boundaries of the enemy's territory ensures that the carrier is at the heart of the modern battle group.

Control of the skies above a battlefleet was not only essential for its survival as an entity, it was equally necessary to enable it to operate offensively. But beneath the surface of the ocean lurks another environment, one which naval officers had been examining the potential of since David Bushnell launched his *Turtle* against HMS *Eagle* in New York in the American Revolution. In the period leading up to 1914, the submarine played no great part in the strategic planning of admirals. Regarded with distaste by surface warriors, its chief virtue seemed to lie in its ability to act as occasional giant-killer. A few possibly remarkable exploits were expected of it, but the idea of the great, annihilating gun-battle remained the entrenched view of the naval strategists, and to achieve this, the ultimate weapon to keep to hand was the battlefleet.

On the other hand, there was the disturbing thought that an enemy might attempt a coup against one's own capital ships, and submarines seemed the most likely way of doing this. The Imperial German Navy had taken delivery of its first submarines in 1906, the year HMS *Dreadnought* commissioned into the Royal Navy, and means were desultorily considered to combat it. More important and dangerous were enemy capital ships, and for the British it was their vulnerable trade they fretted over. Even at the beginning of the Second World War, the British Admiralty could not ignore the surface raider as a threat to Britain's overseas lifeline. In the light of the experience of the First World War this seems incredible, but in a sense inevitable. Informed naval opinion concluded that Jutland had been botched, that an opportunity had been lost and a few scapegoats were identified. The real reasons were not properly appreciated until later and were connected with the fact that the range of heavy guns exceeded the range that admirals, using visual reports, could evaluate and exploit the tactical situation. Naval doctrine, although far from as confident as it had been, still lay under the thrall of the big-gun. This was compounded by euphoria.

The outcome of the war lulled the British into a false sense of security. They had after all won, or at least been on the winning side. They were world leaders in naval aviation and they had found an answer to the submarine menace, the challenge of which had almost defeated them. The question of submerged submarine location had been addressed by the formation of an Anglo-French 'Allied Submarine Detection Investigation Committee' (ASDIC).

Since sound travels well under water, hydrophones had been used for listening for submarines, and by U-boats to listen for merchant ships. The hydrophone was a passive receiver, so the quarry had to come within its range and German submarines routinely rigged for silent running. Operating against unescorted ships, they also routinely avoided detection and sank British merchantmen – a lot of them.

What was required was an active means of probing the ocean, and this was provided by a 'beam' of sound, directionally controllable by a transceiver which not only sent out the pulse of sound, but received its echo if this was returned by an object. It was fitted to a few trial ships by early 1919, with results described as 'promising'. British destroyers first began to be fitted with the operational ASDIC from 1923 and ten years later all newly built destroyers were equipped with it. The Admiralty Staff declared, 'the submarine should never again be able to present us with the problem we were faced with in 1917.' In March 1939 the 'damned un-English weapon' had been licked; after a demonstration off Portland, Winston Churchill wrote a memorandum to the then British Prime Minister, stating: 'The submarine has been mastered.'

The devastating effect of the German submarine aces of the Kaiser's Imperial German Navy was apparently history.

Largely due to the opposition of Tirpitz, the German Navy was the last major naval power to commission submarines, *Unterseeboot No 1* (*U-1*) was built at Kiel in 1906 to a modified French design prepared for the Russians. Eschewing the then unreliable diesel engine and the highly dangerous petrol engine,

U-1 was fitted with a Körting paraffin engine which laid a trail of sparks by night and yellow exhaust fumes by day. Nevertheless, this late formation of a submarine arm allowed the Germans to profit from the mistakes of others and provided them with a state-of-the-art fleet when war broke out.

Early British submarines were largely rendered obsolete by the 'D' class of 1909 which were fitted with diesel engines capable of 16 knots on the surface and electric motors giving 9 submerged. The main ballast was carried in saddle-tanks and the class were also the first to be fitted with wireless and a gun on deck. Their three 18-inch torpedo tubes, one aft and two forward, improved the lines at the bow and stern. The 'D' class, built by Vickers at Barrow-in-Furness, incorporated what was to become the classic configuration of the submarine type and they were regarded as capable of offensive operations off an enemy coast. Succeeding these, the 'E' class (667 tons surfaced, 796 tons submerged and with a length of 181 feet) were slightly larger and capable of laying mines. They formed the backbone of the Royal Navy's submarine force between 1914 and 1918, and were equal to the best in any navy.

To ensure development was not impeded by Vickers' virtual monopoly, British officers visited the FIAT San Giorgio yard at La Spezia, to examine Italian developments. Consequent upon this visit, orders for experimental submarine, *S-1-3*, were placed with Scotts of Greenock to build a Laurenti design under licence. A similar trip to Toulon resulted in contracts being awarded to Armstrong Whitworth on the Tyne to build *W-1* to *W-4* to a Laubeuf design. None of these boats performed well in the North Sea and all were sold to Italy during the First World War, but there followed a series of experimental boats in which size and the demand for speed increased. The quest for the latter sent the Admiralty back to Laurenti who, disliking diesel, fitted a steam engine. The result, HM Submarine *Swordfish*, was a failure and was converted to a surface patrol boat.

Because of its ability to provide high speed, steam was still favoured by the French despite its disadvantages. It took a long time to close down a steam submarine for diving and once dived the residual boiler heat spread throughout the submerged boat. On the outbreak of war, the French, though they had about forty submarines operationally suitable, had lost the initiative to the

British. In America the United States Navy had embarked on a parallel programme to the British and by 1914 the small, 392/521-ton 'K' class had a surface range of 4500 miles and was thus capable of distant operations.

So although the British had seventy-five submarines in commission and a further twenty-five building, only sixteen belonged to the 'D' and 'E' classes, whereas the Germans possessed twenty-nine in service and nineteen on order. The Royal Navy was therefore quantitatively inferior to the enemy and to rectify this the Admiralty ordered boats from America and Canada, although the former compromised American neutrality and were embargoed until the United States entered the war in 1917. These, known to the British as the 'H' class, crossed the Atlantic, with a little occasional help from their escorts and lasted in some foreign navies until 1944.

The Admiralty also reacted to stories that the Germans possessed a 20-knot submarine and this revived a Staff Requirement of an 'underwater destroyer', a fast, fleet submarine. The consequences of this unfounded rumour were disastrous as the British sought to outdo this chimera. The *Swordfish* was not yet fully evaluated, so few misgivings were voiced about steam in a submarine and the British 'K' class was ordered. Large, at 339 feet overall, with a surface displacement of 1980 tons (2566 submerged), they achieved the high surface speed required of them, some 24 knots and were impressively armed with ten torpedo tubes, a 4-inch and a 3-inch gun. They required some detailed modifications and went into service in 1917 looking like patrol boats on the surface, with two funnels that folded down when they dived. They proved fatally vulnerable as they dived due to the large air intakes that required shutting by machinery. Ordered to dive in a Scottish sea loch, *K-13* sank when her intakes were left open in error. Though the most serious, this was but one of several accidents that overtook the class. Perhaps more significant, was the incident in the Firth of Forth which took place in January 1918 when a flotilla of K-boats was operating at speed ahead of the battlecruiser fleet in the very role for which they had been conceived. Two of the submarines were involved in a collision and in the ensuing chaos, the battlecruisers rolled over them, sinking two in what became known as the 'Battle of the Isle of May'.

Operationally it was the 'D' and 'E' class which proved themselves. Some of these operated in the Baltic, working with the Russian fleet, others attacked the Turks in the Sea of Marmora. The extremely hazardous nature of submarine operations gained their commanding officers several decorations. Among these was a certain Max Horton, a submarine commander whose exploits put a price on his head and earned the Baltic the rueful German nickname of 'Horton's Sea'. With what interest Horton was to return the compliment remains to be seen, but it was not the staff officers in either Berlin or London who defined the role the submarine was to play in war, but the young Max Hortons on both sides, and especially those of the Imperial German navy.

In August 1914 the Imperial German Navy had in fact only six diesel-engined submarines, *U-19* to *U-24*, in full operational trim. But these were capable of a surface speeds of 16.8 knots. The high command immediately ordered seventeen more and took over five boats then building for the Austro-Hungarian Navy. The capture of Belgium persuaded the Germans to develop small coastal submarines, some of which were designed, like the Russian *Krab*, to lay mines. But it was well offshore where the Kaiser's young officers were to prove their mettle, operating U-boats which were typically of some 1200 tons surface displacement. Capable of the high surface speed of 17.5 knots they were faster than the average merchantman and at 7 knots submerged, the equal of many of their quarry.

In the early days of the war U-boats ambushed their victims by surfacing and ordering them to stop, in compliance with the Hague Convention. Providing the arrested merchantman did not transmit an emergency wireless signal, the crew were given time to evacuate and take to the boats before their ship was sunk, usually by gunfire to avoid the expense of a torpedo. This courtly state of affairs did not last long. British masters had an understandable dislike for losing their ships so passively and transmitted alarm signals, only to be fired upon for refusing to relinquish their charges, and often before all the crew had abandoned ship. Others delayed and prevaricated, hoping a patrolling British warship would arrive on the scene, for most of these incidents occurred in the waters of the Channel, the North Sea or the Western Approaches. The odds were heavily stacked in favour of the Germans, so British ships were then fitted with guns, defensively mounted on the stern to comply with international law. The Germans chose to interpret this as depriving merchantmen of their non-combatant status and a propaganda war of accusations and recriminations flew back and forth between London and Berlin. But British merchant ship losses continued to mount alarmingly. The countermeasure of the decoy, or Q-ship was introduced. This was an elaborate hoax. Merchant ships were fitted with hidden guns which appeared when 'lifeboats' sprang apart, or bulwarks dropped, to open a devastating fire on the submarine. The enemy had to be lured close by dramatic play-acting. Part of the Q-ship's crew went through the motions of taking to the boats, even dressing up for the purpose, carrying ships' cats and parrots in cages. Theatrical though this ploy seems, its real effect was not significant.

Feeling in merchant ships ran high. On the one hand a merchant seaman was not supposed to take offensive action. When he did the most dire consequences could befall him, as happened to Captain Fryatt of the Great Eastern Railway Company. The company's ships maintained an irregular service between Harwich and the Hook of Holland in the neutral Netherlands and were frequently chased by U-boats, but their speed usually helped them avoid capture. The company's steam packet *Brussels*, under Fryatt's command, had outrun her pursuers five times during 1915 and on one of these occasions, on 28 March, Captain Fryatt had attempted to ram his tormentor, *U-33*, which lay between his ship and his destination. The incident received wide publicity and Captain Fryatt and his officers were commended by their owners and the Admiralty. Then, on 22 June 1916, the *Brussels* was surrounded by torpedo boats, captured and escorted into Zeebrugge. Although his crew were interned, Captain Fryatt was shot for his temerity. The German justification lay in the fact that Fryatt's action was unlawful as he 'was not a member of a combatant force' and this legal judgement lent a nicety of status to the plight of the beleaguered merchant seaman for, on the other hand, his pay stopped the day his ship was sunk and he had the consolation of knowing that his struggle for life in a boat was an unpaid excursion.

The ambivalence of this situation was salved by the adoption of the exiguous collection of ships being, so to speak, 'ennobled' by order of King George V as 'the Merchant Navy'. However this honour was not conferred until *four years* after the war. And while officers of most companies including the Great Eastern Railway's marine officers, wore a 'livery', an official uniform was prescribed by the British Board of Trade. But what the merchant seafarer could not comprehend, was why the convoy system was not reintroduced.

The year 1917 was crucial to both sides, and was the turning point in the war. In Russia the Tsarist government collapsed and by secret prior agreement with Germany, Lenin was able to take Bolshevik Russia out of the war. German troops were moved to the Western Front where the fighting was as bloody as it was fruitless. In Britain grain reserves were reduced to a mere six weeks' supply and the Admiralty advised the Cabinet that defeat was imminent. Against considerable opposition the Prime Minister, David Lloyd George, was persuaded by his Cabinet Secretary to order an immediate resumption of the ancient practice of convoy, thus ending the high remuneration earned by shipowners who lost their ships. But convoy in the First World War was remarkably successful, considering the primitive state of submarine detection. Escorting destroyers might rush back and forth about a convoy and deter all but the most determined attack, but their hydrophones were unable to distinguish between friend and any lurking foe. Their only real method of counter-attack was either the somewhat self-destructive tactic of ramming, for which they needed to catch the enemy on the surface, or the dropping of depth-charges, explosive devices which could be triggered at a pre-determined depth by hydrostatic detonators. Since there was no accurate method of predicting the position of a target, it was all rather vague, literally hit-or-miss.

Annihilation was the object of the unrestricted submarine warfare ordered in 1917 by an increasingly desperate Kaiser, and annihilation was what was practiced by his young submarine commanders. These cultivated the enduring image of the lone wolf. Commanding *U-35* in the Mediterranean, *Korvettenkapitän* Arnauld de la Perrière sank fifty-four ships on a single twenty-four-day cruise in 1916. This was a total of 90,150 tons, a record unequalled in either war, and de la Perrière's gross total is said to have been some 400,000 tons.

Another 'ace' was *Kapitänleutnant* Walther Forstmann who, in *U-39* is credited with 380,000 tons. Serving with Forstmann and later in command of his own boat was Karl Dönitz, later Commander-in-Chief of the navy of Nazi Germany. There was a darker side to the reputations of some of these young men; U-38's commanding officer Max Valentiner was alleged to regard killing as 'a pastime', and *Korvettenkapitän* Wilhelm Werner of *U-55* was said to have behaved in 1917 'with particular savagery'. On 8 April 1917, the turret steamer *Torrington*, of 5597 gross tons, was torpedoed without warning. Her crew were picked up and the master was taken prisoner. The remainder of the crew were lined up on the submarine's casing after which the U-boat dived. Such stories fuelled the British perception of German frightfulness, but were equally an indictment of the Admiralty's failure to do its job properly. Lloyd George told a journalist privately the 'Admiralty had been awful and the present submarine menace was the result ... [and] the apathy and incompetence of the naval authorities were terrible'. The Germans took a more active line.

In the year of *U-35*'s success the German navy commissioned 108 submarines and these each carried as many as sixteen torpedoes, could motor at 17 knots on the surface and 8 to 9 underneath. The following year therefore augured well for the Imperial navy. The Germans had sunk a prodigious amount of allied shipping, not least by its surface raiders of which the former British barque *Pass of Balmaha* had become SMS *Seeadler* under the courtly command of Graf (Count) Felix von Luckner. But chivalry was not a conspicuous feature of submarine warfare, and it was to bring a powerful ally to the assistance of the hard pressed Western Powers.

It was the depredations of German U-boats that eventually persuaded the United States to enter the war in 1917. Without warning, on 7 May 1915, the Cunard liner *Lusitania* had been torpedoed off the Old Head of Kinsale, Ireland, with the loss of 1198 lives. Among these were a number of Americans. Up to this moment American public opinion had been anti-British, a traditional reaction to what was seen as the equally traditional high-handedness of the British at sea, interdicting trade with their enemy. The loss of the *Lusitania* began to swing American opinion right around. When more Americans were killed in the torpedoing of the cross-Channel packet *Sussex* on 24 March 1916, matters approached crisis point. The switch in American public opinion was a blow to the Germans, especially when it erupted into open hostility. The Germans had in fact been importing vital nickel, rubber, tin and copper from the United States, running the British blockade with some success. Some of these cargoes had been run in specially-built mercantile submarines, of which the most enterprising was the *Deutschland*, capable of stowing 900 deadweight tons. When the Americans came into the war, the *Deutschland* was taken in hand, refitted and commissioned as an armed U-boat, *U-155*. Along with her sisters *Bremen* and *Oldenburg*, the three became cruiser-submarines with two 5.9-inch guns each.

But it was too late, the outcome was decided elsewhere and the Kaiser's government sued for peace. Nevertheless, for the British it had been a close run thing. In total 2479 British merchant ships of 7,759,090 tons, at a cost of 14,287 lives had been destroyed by the enemy. Only four had been lost to aircraft, and 117 to raiders, cruisers and torpedo boats. A substantial number had been mined, some 259 grossing 673,417 tons, but by far the most had been lost to U-boats, a staggering 6,635,059 tons, 2099 vessels, many of whose crews escaped death, but whose total loss was 12,723 souls.

In the aftermath of this appalling total, British representatives at the Washington and London treaties wanted the submarine banned, but the 1922 conference considered only limited gun-calibre to 8-inch. The best that could be done in London in 1930 was a limitation on tonnage to 2000 and an overall maximum per signatory. Needless to say compliance was partial.

The British built large-gunned cruiser-submarines known as the 'M' class. One of these, M-2, was later fitted with a catapult-launched seaplane, crane and hangar, but two were lost and the fourth never completed. The French built the *Surcouf*, which was also fitted with a seaplane for reconnaissance and twin 8-inch guns. Her 361-feet long hull was laid down in 1927 and she took seven years to complete, displacing 3250 tons surfaced and 4304 submerged. She was sunk in collision in 1942.

Britain, France and America also built mine-laying sub-marines and one of the French *Saphir* class, built between 1930 and 1937, the *Rubis*, laid 683 mines in twenty-eight patrols between 1940 and 1944. Japan poached the best ideas from all the Western submarines, conceiving the submarine to be a fleet attack craft. The Japanese never, however, really took the war on trade seriously. It was, moreover, the Japanese whom the British considered to be the next enemy as the Emperor's soldiers rampaged through Southeast Asia, establishing the euphemistically named Imperial Co-prosperity Sphere. As a consequence the Admiralty began building larger submarines of the 'O', 'P' and 'R' classes. These submarines were fitted with asdic (renamed sonar in 1948) and suffered from persistent leaks of fuel from their exterior tanks. Many of these classes were lost in the Second World War, but the 'T', 'S' and 'U' classes of better quality were advances. Despite the sinking of the *Thetis* in 1939 while on trials from her builders, Cammell, Laird of Birkenhead, the 'T' class, of which fifty-three were built between 1937 and 1945, were very successful. Even *Thetis*, though sunk with all hands, was raised and served as HMS *Thunderbolt* until her loss in action in 1943. Displacing 1090 tons surfaced and 1575 submerged, the 'T' class were 275 feet long, carried a 4-inch gun and ten 21-inch torpedo tubes. Their diesel engines were rated at 2500 horsepower and gave 15.5 knots on the surface; her 1450 horsepower electric motors, some 9 knots below.

British submarines achieved notable successes in the Mediterranean, not least of which were several voyages to run essential stores through to besieged Malta and to return with the survivors from merchant ships lost on passage to the fortress island. Royal Navy boats also served in the Far East and carried out patrols on the coasts of occupied Europe. American submarines were highly effective against Japanese shipping, restricting the supplies of raw materials from its co-prosperity 'partners' to the Imperial heartland. They were not, however, the main arm of the Allied navies, as was the case with the Nazi *Kriegsmarine*.

Although banned from owning submarines by the Versailles Treaty, Germany had begun secretly creating a new submarine design-capability in the Netherlands. In March 1935 Hitler finally repudiated the terms of the Treaty of Versailles, and in June of that year, due to an increase in Soviet submarines, Hitler negotiated an agreement with Britain which allowed him to build submarines to forty-five per cent of British tonnage, with parity under certain conditions. The first German boats were commissioned in a very short time thereafter; by June 1937 the first of the Type VII U-boats which were to form the backbone of the German submarine arm was ready. The class was largely the result of the thinking of Dönitz, whose combat experience under Forstmann and in command of his own boat, had persuaded him that torpedoes not guns should be the submarine's main weapon, and that a successful U-boat was of such a size that it could dive and escape pursuit quickly, was manoeuvrable at periscope depth and possessed the greatest possible range.

Early classes were limited in their range, but adjustments in their successors ensured improvements increasing diving time, range and hitting power. By January 1939 the Type VIIB had become the Type VIIC. Of the 691 Type VIIs produced, 650 were of this highly successful type. Two-hundred-and-twenty feet long, they displaced 750 tons on the surface and 850 submerged. Capable of 17 knots, twice the speed of the average convoy, their cruising range at 10 knots was 8700 miles. A skilled crew could dive a Type VIIC in 20 seconds and she could submerge to 650 feet, some 200 metres. Compared with a 1918 U-boat, diving time was a third and the maximum safe depth had increased almost five-fold. Under water maximum speed was 8 knots. Variants followed, doubling the displacements in the Type VIIF which was actually 0.5 knots faster, and had a range of 14,700 miles at 10 knots.

A parallel design was the Type IX, with a range of 10,500 miles, this was increased by later modifications to a staggering 31,500 miles. Later Type XXI boats were fitted with snorkels, air intake tubes which enabled them to run at periscope depth using their diesels. Their whole purpose was high underwater speed and they achieved 17.25 knots, over one knot greater than their surface speed. Ingenious attempts to obtain an underwater propulsion unit which gave improved performance on the electric motor, resulted in the fitting of the Walther turbine which used the steam generated by burning fuel with hydrogen and a catalyst. The cost of the hydrogen peroxide was exorbitant and this disincentive plus the late entry of the Type XXI into service, produced few operational boats and negligible impact.

*

With 115 boats, the Italians had the largest submarine fleet when Mussolini joined his German ally to form the Axis in June 1940. Four of them, the class ship of which was the *Ammiraglio Cagni*, were specifically designed for attacking merchant ships. They carried fourteen 18-inch torpedoes, and had proved operationally successful supporting General Franco's Fascists in the Spanish Civil War by sinking merchant vessels supporting the Republican government. During the existence of the Axis, Italian submarines scored some notable successes working alongside their German allies.

After the Bolshevik Revolution the navy of Soviet Russia had contracted to become a coastal defence force. Ironically the Russians had begun increasing their submarine force with secret German help during the rapprochement of Rapallo-Politik. This co-operation had produced the Soviet 'S' class, based on the Type VII. When the two doctrines motivating their respective governments inevitably drew apart, it was this expansion which enabled Hitler to turn to the weak British government and negotiate a 'legitimate' increase in the numbers of German submarines. During the Second World War, the proximity of German capital ships in the fiords of occupied Norway, the hostility of Finland and the invasion of Russia by Germany, awakened the Soviet *Stavka* to the dangers of relying upon defensive measures. When, moreover, the *Admiral Scheer* moved into the Kara Sea to shell shore installations and the Royal Navy began to arrive in Russian waters alongside Allied merchantmen loaded with supplies for the Red Army, a change of heart occurred. Little progress was to be made initially, for the great land-battles of the Eastern Front preoccupied Russian energies. Nevertheless the Russians developed a smaller and more numerous coastal *Shch*-type of submarine which was deployed against Axis shipping movements along the polar coast of occupied Norway. The know-how acquired in submarine operations by Russian naval officers during the Second World War, led the Soviet Navy to expand its submarine fleet during the post-war years with what results we shall examine later in Chapter Eighteen.

Despite the successes of German submarines in the First World War and the number of classes of warships which carried torpedoes, the design of these highly expensive weapons was found to be faulty by German submarine commanders. Many of these young men were frustrated by the inexplicable failure of their weapons to detonate. It was some time before the German officers convinced Dönitz that there was anything at all wrong with their weapons.

The British had similar troubles which in one case, that of the cruiser HMS *Trinidad* operating in the Barents Sea, resulted in a torpedo reversing course and exploding in the side of the ship which had fired it. Torpedo design rapidly improved once the deficiencies were acknowledged. The Germans produced an acoustic weapon which homed on propeller noise and was particularly dangerous to fast-moving escorts. One method of deceiving what the Allies called the German Naval Acoustic Torpedo (GNAT) was to tow a 'foxer', a device which caused turbulence in the wake of an escort and decoyed the 'Gnat' to explode in the vessel's wake. But torpedoes of one kind or another proved efficient enough to achieve losses in merchant-men as near fatal to the Allies in 1942–43 as they had been in 1917.

Submarines were vulnerable to airpower until they could submerge to great depths for a long time. To do this they needed a new propulsion system. After the Second World War the British, in emulation of the German Walther boats, built two high-test hydrogen peroxide (HTP) powered boats, HM Submarines *Excalibur* and *Explorer* which were capable of 27 knots underwater, but they were a design blind-alley. Nuclear power offered so much more that the HTP experiments were abandoned.

Effective though the submarine had become, its development thus remained deficient in the matter of its propulsion. Two separate methods, diesel and electricity, one relying upon the other and not yielding the underwater speed theorists claimed was possible for a submerged hull was clearly unsatisfactory. The solution of course, lay in nuclear power which was to convert the submersible into a line submarine, a fully fledged underwater capital ship so deadly that she is capable of destroying civilisation itself, a formidable rival to the nuclear powered aircraft carrier.

CHAPTER SIXTEEN

Port Out, Starboard Home

The liner, affirmed Kipling, was a lady 'by the paint upon 'er face, An' if she meets an accident they count it sore disgrace ...'. By contrast, the man-o'-war was ''er 'usband', imagery that was entirely consonant with imperial pretensions. The British, with 39.3 per cent of the world's tonnage in 1914, possessed the largest mercantile marine in the world. In 1921 shipping registered in Britain remained the same, but as a proportion of the global total it had fallen slightly to 32.8 per cent. Although no-one would have remarked it at the time, this was the beginning of a long decline, made worse by the slump that occurred in 1920 after the brief post-war boom.

In this year a Merchant Marine Act was passed in the United States 'to provide for the promotion and maintenance of the American Merchant Marine'. This was for defence purposes, born out of the experience of war and because of the enormous number of emergency standard merchant ships which had been built on government account in American yards. Advantageously-backed American shipping companies therefore took up trade routes previously handled by British companies, and many of the latter fell victim to what they saw as sharp practice by the Americans. One such was the Union Steamship Company of New Zealand, a British owned subsidiary of P&O, which was unable to take advantage of the lucrative passenger trade between the West Coast and Hawaii because it was considered by the Americans to be a 'coastwise' trade. By 1936 American shipping had almost doubled, while a rising proportion of world trade was borne in Scandinavian and Japanese ships. The Japanese, moving into high, industrial gear, subsidised their merchant fleet, introducing a 'scrap-and-build' policy in 1932, and doubled *their* tonnage between 1920 and 1939. Of the Scandinavians, Norway's fleet had become the world's fourth largest by the outbreak of the Second World War, a fact that was to prove highly significant in due course, because the fleet came over to the British side and thereby augmented Allied tonnage.

Up to 1914, the Germans had possessed the world's single largest shipping company in Albert Ballin's Hamburg–America Line. The company, known as Hapag, owned 175 ships totalling 1.3 million tons and its phenomenally rich owner, although a patriot, entertained a deep and profound conviction that ships, free trade and peace were what the world needed. A son of the traditionally free-trading city of Hamburg, Ballin made his name in direct competition with Hapag's rival, the Bremen-based firm of the North German Lloyd. As director of Hapag's passenger ships at the age of twenty-nine, Ballin introduced better service and more ships on the North Atlantic run. At the age of forty-two Ballin had become managing director and shortly before the outbreak of the First World War his company ordered the liners *Imperator* (1912), *Vaterland* (1913), and *Bismarck* (1914). The *Imperator* was laid down as the *Europa*, but the interest of the Kaiser was aroused in this prestigious new liner and on 23 May 1912, six weeks after the loss of the *Titanic*, Wilhelm II launched the huge 919 feet hull from the slipway of the Vulcan Shipyard into the Elbe. Consequently she was christened in his honour. This ship, then the largest in the world, grossed 52,000 tons and carried 4594 passengers, catered for by a crew of 1180, at a speed of 23 knots. Her bunkers contained 8500 tons of coal and her glass-domed first-class saloon could seat 700 people. A significant and conspicuous feature of her design was a large searchlight fitted to her foremast for spotting icebergs, a reaction to the loss of the *Titanic*.

Statistics such as the fact that the *Imperator*'s rudder weighed 90 tons, became part of national folklore, learned by enthusiastic schoolboys who marvelled at the superlative qualities of these ships. By the same token, rumours that all was not well with a ship could seriously compromise passage bookings and hence affect a ship's viability. Although she had bankrupted her builders, ruining her owners was something not to be countenanced when reports claimed the *Imperator* rolled abominably. Her funnels were therefore truncated, a huge bronze eagle was removed from her bow, upper deck panelling was replaced by lighter materials and tons of cement were poured into her bottom.

The outbreak of war in 1914 saw the *Imperator* laid up for the duration, only to be taken over as a troopship by the

Americans who afterwards laid her up again in New York in 1919. It was open season on German assets and she was claimed by Britain as a replacement for the lost *Lusitania* and joined the Cunard fleet as *Berengaria*. Formally purchased in 1921, she became the company's flagship. She was taken in hand and converted to oil-fired boilers, her new bunker capacity being 6500 tons to provide the 700 tons of oil necessary every day for the Southampton to New York service. To further improve stability, marble was removed from her first-class accommodation and more cement went into her bilges. In conformity with the 1921 American immigration quota regulations, her passenger capacity was modified to 972 in first class, 630 in second class and 515 in the euphemistically styled 'tourist' class. Along with *Aquitania* and *Mauretania*, the *Berengaria* formed one of the so-called 'big three' which maintained Cunard's weekly trans-Atlantic service in competition with the White Star's *Majestic*, *Homeric* and *Olympic*.

In 1934 the Cunard and White Star Lines merged, and the trans-Atlantic passenger trade slumped because of growing restrictions on immigration in the United States; there was consequent overcapacity in ships. *Berengaria* had acquired the nickname of 'Bargain-area', and although in September 1935 she made a record turnround in Southampton of thirteen hours fifteen minutes, during which 1000 passengers and baggage were serviced, 4000 bags of mail tallied, one million gallons of fresh water and 7000 tons of fuel were pumped aboard, the ship had passed her prime. It was intended to keep her in service until replaced by the new *Queen Mary*, but in 1938 a serious fire on board in New York caused the United States Coastguard to withdraw her passenger certification. She returned rather forlornly to Britain devoid of passengers, was taken to Jarrow and cut down to the waterline. Here she languished, reduced to her cement-laden double bottom until 1946.

Ballin's second liner, *Vaterland*, had also been laid down at the Blohm and Voss yard in Hamburg under another name. Ballin persisted in wanting to call a new ship *Europa*, for he deplored the growing rivalry between Britain and Germany and built his three great ships as a commitment to peace. He was to be bitterly disappointed, for not only was his new ship given a jingoistic name, but in the aftermath of the terrible war his patron unleashed,

Vaterland passed to the United States. She was initially interned in New York in 1914, where she hosted fund-raising gala evenings for the strong German communities there. Then when the United States entered the war in 1917 she was seized and recommissioned for trooping under the name *Leviathan*. Acquired by the United States Line and rebuilt after the war, she returned to passenger service in 1923 where she became one of the most popular trans-Atlantic ships right up until her sale in 1929, coincident with the Great Depression. With the subsequent loss of revenue she was soon laid up and, in 1938, scrapped.

The third of Ballin's great trio, the *Bismarck*, was launched by the Prussian statesman's grand-daughter. When the bottle failed to break on the ship's bow, the Kaiser stepped fatefully in and finished the business. It might have been a metaphor for the dreams of all idealists. Building was suspended when war broke out two months later and *Bismarck* was incomplete when she passed to the British as a reparation for the loss of *Britannic*. She finally entered service as White Star's *Majestic*, her completion being resentfully carried out by German workers under the supervision of the British Allied Command. Steel was in short supply; delays, a fire and dockyard shenanigans (her master's cabin was fitted out as a closet) culminated in *Majestic*'s completion with the name 'Bismarck' on a hull painted in Hamburg-America colours. She finally steamed away to carry out her trials in the Irish Sea, only gradually attaining a reputation for splendour after this inauspicious start. In Cowes Week 1922, King George V and Queen Mary paid her a visit, but at the onset of the Depression, *Majestic* offered American visitors cruises 'offshore', thinly disguised temptation to a supposedly 'dry' American public enduring the years of prohibition.

The financial difficulties of the White Star Line led to the ship's neglect and she was disposed of when the company merged with Cunard. She was purchased by the British Admiralty as a naval training ship, rebuilt and commissioned in 1937 as HMS *Caledonia*, to be moored at Rosyth in the Forth. At the outbreak of war she was taken in hand for conversion to a troopship, but caught fire and became a constructive total loss. At one time this ship had, at 56,551 gross tons, been the largest in the world. Even by the time she was scrapped, she was still the fourth largest.

Bound up with the history of ships, are those characters who inspire, pay for, design and build them. Ballin had based his genius upon the principle laid down a century earlier by the Duke of Wellington, that of, 'an infinite capacity to take pains'. Born a few yards from the waters of the River Elbe he had been a true a son of the great Hanseatic city which had based its prosperity upon trade. It was his tragedy to be caught up in the rise of Prussian militarism and to lose his fleet as a consequence. In the wreckage of his country and his ambitions, Albert Ballin took his own life.

There is yet a post-script to this remarkable man's life. After the war Hapag possessed only a handful of coasters, but it ordered from Blohm and Voss a small class of medium-sized liners, one of which was named *Albert Ballin*. The four ships grossed about 21,000 tons with speeds of 15 to 16 knots and carried about 1500 passengers across the Atlantic. The ships were popular with Germans emigrating and with German-Americans paying return visits home, so in 1930 new boilers were put in to increase the *Albert Ballin*'s speed to 19.5 knots. Four years later she was cut in two and a fifty-foot section lengthened her to 677 feet. Accompanying adjustments raised her speed to 21.5 knots, but an unfortunate accident in the shipyard while she was being moved, resulted in her sinking the tug *Merkur* and seven of the tug's crew were drowned.

Then in 1935 the Nazi government ordered her name changed; Albert Ballin had committed the sin of being born Jewish. And so the ship that had been named in his honour was rechristened *Hansa*. Used as a static training ship by the German navy between 1939 and 1945, she left Gdynia in March of that cataclysmic year, laden with refugees fleeing from the wrath of the Red Army. While on passage, she struck a mine and sank slowly in shallow water, allowing her terrified passengers time to take to the boats. Four years later she was salvaged by the Russians who first repaired her in Antwerp and then rebuilt her in Warnemünde, not far from the position of her mining. Work was slow and it was the autumn of 1955 before she recommissioned as the *Sovietsky Soyu*, the largest ship in the growing Soviet merchant fleet. In 1971 she was overhauled in the Taikoo dockyard in Hong Kong, and was in service on Soviet government service in the Far East until 1982 when she was finally scrapped.

*

In contrast with their competitors, the British rarely gave subsidies, but Ballin's prestigious liners had provoked one such uncharacteristic act earlier in the century. Perturbed at the possibility of German usurpation of Britannia's trident, Cunard was granted an annual subsidy of £150,000 and built the ill-fated *Lusitania* and her successful sister *Mauretania* in 1904. In the aftermath of the First World War repeat of such a thing was unthinkable, particularly as the assets of Imperial Germany were open to plunder. Nevertheless, as we have remarked, boom soon turned to bust, and with the slump came the first hint of British decline.

There followed a series of shipping mergers which affected not only the large liner companies but many small, one or two-ship firms disappeared completely. In 1914 some 120 such outfits maintained registered offices in Cardiff. By 1939 there were about twenty left. After 1918 British shipping passed increasingly into the hands of an autocracy of great families: Bibbys, Inchcapes, Brocklebanks, Ellermans, Holts, Runcimans, Denholms, Vesteys and so forth.

Nevertheless these dynasties owned enough ships to create the illusion that little had changed. The remaining companies were run under a hundred house flags which, although ultimately owing financial allegiance to these select, patrician shipowners, all had their own traditions, whether it be their colour schemes, their names, the distinctive and distinguishable design of their ships, or their company 'liveries'. Some called their masters 'commanders', following the tradition of the old East India Company; some called their apprentices 'midshipmen'; some painted their passenger ships white and their cargo ships black and buff; one (Brocklebank's), on account of being the oldest British merchant shipping house, flew their private house flag at the foremasthead, instead of the more traditional main. Seamen could recognise a Blue Funnel cargo liner long before she was hull-up, and could tell individual ships while they were a vague blue-grey silhouette on the horizon. Such liner companies still maintained large fleets, containing competition by running 'conference' rates, controlling charges and excluding cheaper operators. Each company therefore dominated a particular service or route and became famous for it. Best known was the

Peninsular and Oriental Steam Navigation Company (P&O) service east of Suez, which served India, and effectively became an arm of the Raj.

P&O, like Cunard, was unusual in being a recipient of a government subsidy to underwrite communications with the jewel in the British crown imperial. In 1923 P&O owned 460 ships totalling over 2.5 million gross registered tons. The company was one of the 'Big Five' British shipping houses, of which the others were Cunard, Ellerman, Royal Mail and Furness Withy.

Comfort might never quite have reached the opulence of the trans-Atlantic liners, but the white-hulled, yellow-funnelled *Carthages*, *Cathays*, *Himalayas* and *Straths*, for such names were often used successively, plied the shipping routes with clockwork regularity. They took out the mails, the army recruits, and the young officers to their regiments; they brought back the mails, the invalids and those going on furlough. They took out the hopefully expectant young women in search of husbands (unkindly known as 'the fishing fleet') and they brought back the retired and the recalled. They provided employment for thousands of men and not a few women. Masters, officers, engineers, radio-officers, pursers, cadets, seamen, stewards, stokers, firemen, laundrymen, cooks and bakers crewed this huge fleet. They were of mixed races: British, Goanese, Indian, Sudanese, men possessing a variety of skills and trades, but there was also the 'infrastructure', an even more varied population replicated in every great port and imitated in not a few smaller places.

Itinerant barbers, sew-sew women, bumboat vendors, fortune tellers, magicians and thieves made a precarious and uncertain living from the ships' crews and passengers. But the pilots, their cutters' crews, port health officers, harbour masters, their launch crews, tug crews, port surveyors and cargo surveyors serviced the movements of shipping, while tally-clerks, stevedores, lightermen, coolies, wharfies, longshoremen, watchmen and hatch and tank-cleaners attended the mails, baggage, and cargoes. Gangs of untouchables and coolies plied chipping hammers when a chief officer required a little supplementary maintenance. Hired painters and other tradesmen could paint an entire hull, or chip, red-lead, undercoat and paint two masts while they trembled under the loads swinging shorewards on the very derrick whips suspended from them.

This huge infrastructure was, like the ships it served, graded into its finely differentiated classes, from the grandest and most idle, to the meanest and most overworked and had yet to take account of dry-docking and repair facilities. While the master and officers of a Peninsular and Oriental Steam Navigation Company liner dined like viceroys, they were beaten hands down in the vice-regal stakes by the pilots of the Hooghly River Pilotage Service which, from its immaculate pilot-brigs cruising on the Sand Heads, to the moment their small boats took them to the club in Calcutta after they had moored or berthed an inward bound ship, was lathered in subservience. Each pilot boarded from the brig's cutter with a servant who would provide a change of immaculate whites, for fear the pilot's own ducks had been soiled in ascending the pilot-ladder. He was attentively cosseted during the passage for his vital knowledge of the channels which lay between the treacherous, shifting banks and bars of the great river.

It was no wonder that when passengers booked their cabin in these ships they stipulated 'port-outward, starboard-home', to obtain accommodation on the cool side of the ship as it steamed down the Red Sea and across the Arabian Sea in the days before air conditioning. Nor was it any wonder the acronym thus produced by the booking-clerk's abbreviation has come to mean privileged and swanky.

Peninsular and Oriental were but one empire within an Empire when, in the post First World War period these rich shipping houses went on a binge of mergers, consolidations and rationalisations. Many of these mergers were at inflated prices, leaving the new controlling companies in a weak position to deal with a slump. Lord Kylsant's Royal Mail Group owned eight different shipping companies, all running cargo and passenger liner services pre-1914. In 1919, using some of his £20 million wartime profit, Kylsant added a further three companies plus seventy-seven standard ships built under the government's wartime emergency programme; these were dispersed about his fleets.

The liner trades began a fierce price war at the onset of the slump in 1920 and Kylsant, believing he had a duty to preserve jobs, continued to borrow and invest in new shipping, particularly diesel motor ships. Among his purchases at this time were the White Star Line from the Americans, the remainder of Shaw, Savill and Albion, and the Australian Commonwealth Line, so that eventually he owned fifteen per cent of the British merchant marine. Unfortunately, outstanding government loans came with these companies. Kylsant had over-geared his empire and made share transfers of which he alone knew the complexities; he was acutely vulnerable to foreclosure if trade did not pick up, and trade did not pick up, it dried up.

Then in 1928, along with the news that one of his ships, Lamport and Holt's *Vestris*, had foundered, came a demand for the repayment of all government loans. In 1930 the Royal Mail Group collapsed and the unfortunate Kylsant spent a year in prison for issuing a false prospectus. What could be rescued and reorganised was carried out by Richard Durning Holt, of Ocean, and Sir Frederick Lewis of Furness Withy, but the long-term consequences were that investment in shipping almost ceased and British shipowners did not borrow. The British Merchant Navy that had served as the 'Fourth Arm of Defence' between 1914 and 1918 was acquired in a considerable proportion, by foreign owners. Ultimately of more significance, the overall age and general inefficiency of the ships now increased.

Kylsant's collapse was followed by Britain's abandonment of the gold standard and devaluation of the pound sterling. Import duties imposed after the war were further extended so that only private companies like Holt's Blue Funnel Line (which by 1939 had supplanted Royal Mail as the fifth of the 'Big Five' shipping companies), and T. and J. Harrison, also of Liverpool, continued to profit. Not only was the *Garthpool* lost in the Cape Verde Islands, but the barquentine *Waterwitch*, the last square-rigged ship to ply on the home coast and thus enable pilots to maintain square-rig experience, ceased trading in 1936.

Any gain obtained from devaluation was marginalised because of the excessive numbers of British ships and when trade began to improve, the effects were again lessened because of the numbers of laid-up ships available. To compound the problem, foreign governments, eager for invisible earnings from shipping, began subsidising their own merchantmen at the first signs of an upturn. In 1932, first Italy underwrote her ships, then in 1933

Germany and the Netherlands followed suit, with France joining in 1934. It was 1935 before the British woke up to the damage being done to their economy. A rather pathetic £2 million was granted to assist the dwindling numbers of tramp owners to load cargoes at less than the standard rates, a pale imitation of the French 'bounty-system'.

A series of internationally agreed measures to fix certain trade-rates began to stabilise the situation from 1935 and, following the Japanese example, a 'scrap-and-build' scheme was set up for tramp ships. Ninety-seven old ships were broken up and replaced by fifty new ships totalling less than half the tonnage of the old. The scheme backfired because many of the decrepit ninety-seven were deliberately purchased abroad from foreign owners.

This cynical act was followed by an upswing in trade due to the Spanish Civil War and the Italian invasion of Ethiopia, then called Abyssinia. To a large extent cargo liners operating either within the British Empire or within spheres of British influence (such as the Argentinian frozen beef trades), managed to survive. But the North Atlantic liners were as exposed as the tramps and the immigration policy of the United States government which, as we have noted above, subjected them to severe restriction in fare-paying passengers during the 1930s. The British government declined to underwrite the loss, probably quite correctly, for there was chronic overcapacity. The British government did, however, agree to underwrite that portion of the insurance which was not taken up on the market for Ship No. 534 then building at John Brown's Clydebank yard. This government subsidy was, however, conditional upon the merger between the Cunard and White Star lines.

In 1934, this great ship rolled down the ways, with the sparks flying from the hundreds of tons of scrap chains she dragged with her, driving stern-first across the narrow river into the cut specially excavated from the opposite bank. She was launched by the consort of King George V, and named after her, *Queen Mary*. Laid down in 1930, construction of Ship No. 534 had been halted at the onset of the Depression in December 1931 and nothing was done until the granting of the government loan enabled work to resume in April 1934. Only rain therefore marred the launching on 24 September. As with all the great ships of the era, statistics about her abounded, perhaps the most telling of which was that the *Queen Mary*'s gross tonnage equalled that of the entire Cunard fleet of 1876.

In the hiatus of her building the French Line had produced what was arguably the ultimate trans-Atlantic liner, the *Normandie*. This magnificent ship's pedigree was impeccable, following in the wake of the *France* of 1912, the *Paris* of 1921, the *Ile de France* of 1926 and the *Champlain* of 1932, from each of which she drew inspiration, quality or function. Laid down in January 1931 at the St Nazaire yard of Chantiers d'Atlantique, with a subsidy from the French government of $60 million, she was intended to be the most luxurious, largest and fastest North Atlantic liner in the world. She was intended also to bear the honour and prestige of France, but destined to mirror the tragedy about to overwhelm her natal land.

The *Normandie* was influential in the world of fashion and setting an impeccable style, but her building was dogged with controversy as the world sank into the Depression. Many French citizens protested she was an extravagance and objected to taxpayers' money guaranteeing the risk of her construction. The 1029 feet (313 metres) hull was launched by Madame Lebrun, wife of the French president, on 29 October 1932. As the hull displaced the waters of the Loire a wave swept more than a hundred people into the river, an omen that presaged ill and was followed by her being laid up unfinished, like her great competitor in England. By May 1935 the *Normandie* was finally finished. On her maiden voyage she made 29.98 knots, immediately capturing the Blue Riband from the Italian liner *Rex*. This aroused tremendous public interest and not a little national chagrin elsewhere. The *Normandie* was widely admired for her clean lines, the absence of ventilators and her long, overhanging bow, traces of which can be seen both in the *France* of 1961 and the *Queen Elizabeth 2* of 1969.

Her outward elegance was one thing, her sumptuous interior was quite another. The *Normandie*'s first-class dining saloon was decorated with Lalique glass and bronze fittings. It extended three decks from floor to ceiling, one can scarcely say deck to deckhead, and seated 1000 diners. She housed an indoor pool 25 metres long, a 'Winter Garden' with spray fountains and caged birds. Aubusson fabric upholstered the furniture in the glass-panelled lounge and a theatre staged live performances. Each first-class cabin suite was decorated individually and two especially luxurious 'apartments' were remotely located on the sun deck. There were, moreover, quarters provided for the domestic servants for those who could afford such luxury and could not exist without.

As her great rival the *Queen Mary* was to roll, so *Normandie* vibrated, and it was not long before new propellers had to be fitted. Also added was a new after deckhouse, which increased *Normandie*'s gross tonnage from 79,280 tons, to 82,799 tons, in response to news that the new Cunard giant now nearing completion on Clydebank would gross at least 80,000 tons. Such was the paranoia of the age!

The *Queen Mary*, finally weighed in at 80,774 gross registered tons, arriving in Southampton on 27 March 1936. She left for her trials a month later, passing the *Berengaria* on her way. She entered service and sailed on her maiden voyage on 27 May. The new ship made no record-breaking passage and the French considered the *Normandie*'s record to be unassailable. Then, after three months, the British ship made a serious assault on the coveted Blue Riband and in August 1936 the Queen Mary stormed across the North Atlantic, averaging 30.14 knots, thereby seizing the Riband from the *Normandie*. In the following March, the French liner struck back with a run of 30.9 knots, regaining the honour and improving her position with a speed of 31.2 knots in August. Her pre-eminence now seemed assured until August 1938 when the *Queen Mary* finally wrestled it from her with a speed of 31.69 knots, driven by her 160,000 horse-power steam turbines and their quadruple screws.

The great '*Queen*' was 1018 feet long overall, with a beam of 118 feet on a draught of 39.6 feet. With a complement of 1001 crew, she carried 1939 passengers. An austerely elegant and powerful ship with her three raked funnels, she had the more tangible distinction of being the only large liner of her time to make a profit. Sadly her trans-Atlantic career was terminated by the outbreak of World War Two, by which time she had been joined by a slightly larger half-sister ship, the 83,673-ton *Queen Elizabeth*. The two *Queens* were to have run a weekly, two-ship service, but the new ship was to carry no fare-paying passengers for a long time.

The *Queen Elizabeth*'s building had not been subject to delay initially. Her design was less conservative than the *Queen Mary* and had incorporated many of the ideas the French had built into the more modernistic *Normandie*. She was launched by the queen consort of King George VI, Queen Elizabeth (now the Queen-Mother) on 27 September 1938, but as the war loomed, fitting out dropped in priority, as production switched to warships. There was wild talk of selling her, but on 6 February 1940, more or less complete but with her interior fitted out only with essential services, she was ordered out of Britain, though the *Luftwaffe* sent aircraft to bomb the Southampton dock where it had been deliberately rumoured she would complete her out-fitting.

The *Queen Elizabeth* grossed 83,673 tons and was, like her half-sister, built by John Brown and Co, Clydebank in Scotland. She was 1031 feet in length (314 metres), with a beam of 118 feet (36 metres) on a draught of 39.5 feet (12 metres). Her speed of 28.5 knots was generated by four screws driven by geared steam turbines generating 200,000 shaft horsepower. This immense ship bore a crew of over 1000 for the benefit of 823 first-class, 662 cabin and 798 third-class passengers.

After a brief period stationed together in New York, the *Queen Mary* sailed to Sydney, Australia, where she was converted for trooping, operating in Admiralty grey paint across the Indian Ocean to Africa, returning with the wounded, refugees and prisoners of war. Having been completed at least nominally as a passenger ship in the then neutral United States, the *Queen Elizabeth* followed, first to Singapore and then on to the Indian Ocean as a troopship.

The enemy knew of the *Queen Mary*'s presence in Suez Bay in early October 1941 and sent two Heinkel HeIII bombers of KG20 to strike at her and her 'cargo' of soldiers. Fortunately the *Queen Mary* had left the area earlier that afternoon and in the bright moonlight the German bombers struck at the anchored freighter *Thistlegorm*, which having a full military cargo, blew up.

In 1942 the *Queen Mary* returned to the grey Western Ocean and began running between the Clyde and New York, never quite repeating her track and carrying some 15,000 American and Canadian servicemen at such a speed that she outran both escorts and enemy submarines. Indeed the power of her momentum was to contribute to a tragedy on 2 October 1942 when the *Queen Mary*, making a rendezvous with the cruiser *Curaçoa* in the northern approaches to the Irish Sea, cut the cruiser in two when the *Curaçoa* misjudged the great liner's speed and tried to cross her bow. The *Queen Mary* sliced through the warship with scarcely a tremor and 338 men died in her wake. There were only twenty-six survivors.

Despite this, the contribution made by the *Queens* in their swift and efficient trooping was prodigious; Churchill considered, with some hyperbole, that they shortened the war by a year. In July 1943, the *Queen Mary* bore no fewer than 16,683 souls across the Atlantic – the greatest number of people ever embarked in a single ship.

By 1947, both *Queen Elizabeth* and *Queen Mary* were functioning in their Cunard colours and designed role. Denny-Brown stabilisers were fitted to ease their tendency to roll, and improve passenger comfort. Their beautiful rival was not so lucky. Like the *Queens*, the *Normandie* had also been laid up in New York when war broke out in Europe, her crew of 1320 reduced to a skeletal 115. Speculation about her future havered between her becoming a troopship or an aircraft carrier. Her position became even more precarious after the fall of France in the spring of 1940. Then in December 1941, the Japanese attack on Pearl harbour brought the United States into the Second World War on the side of the Allies. *Normandie* was immediately requisitioned by the American government, to become the United States Navy's transport *AP-53*. Her costly innards were dismantled and she was sent to Boston for dry-docking before returning to New York for completion as a troop transport.

Now renamed the USS *Lafayette*, rather tastefully in view of the Marquis' contribution to American independence, she was overrun by workmen. One of those wielding an oxy-acteylene cutting torch ignited a pile of kapok-stuffed life jackets. Fire rapidly swept through the ship, and in the attempts to save her, so much water was pumped into her that she became unstable and capsized. The salvage operation that followed necessitated the reduction of much of her upper works and it seemed that the great hull might yet serve as an aircraft carrier when it was righted in 1943. The naval bureaucracy postponed the decision and the hulk lay in Brooklyn for two years until, overtaken by events, peace put an end to American interest in her. An attempt by her designer to rebuild a more modest ship out of her remains, was dismissed and in October 1946 she was towed ignominiously to Port Newark, New Jersey and what the oxy-acetylene torch had begun, it finished.

Her end might have been seen as symbolic of all her type. It is easy today to regard her over-blown extravagance as a manifestation of something improper; certainly the critics at the time of her building considered her to be pandering to the millionaire market. During the hungry decade of the 1930s, this was understandably questionable, but the arrival of peace revived, at least temporarily, expectations of a return to what people had come to think of as 'normal'.

Just as the two Cunard '*Queens*' resumed the role for which they had been built, the passenger liner, relieved of its wartime transport grey, resumed its old routes all over the globe. For the victorious Americans, the prestige of the United States could not ride on the broken, burnt hull of a French wonder-ship: they had to have their own ocean greyhound.

The American Merchant Marine consisted of great shipping lines equivalent to their British counterparts. Bull, Moore-McCormack, Pope and Talbot, Matson, Lykes and Isbrantsen were names as influential in their way as the Brocklebanks, Harrisons and Holts. And while one of the major American trans-Pacific shipping lines named its ships after American presidents, the major trans-Atlantic American service was run by the United States Lines, an unequivocal claim to pre-eminence among American owners!

Operating both cargo and passenger services, the company's post-war forty cargo liners, all prefixed *American* ... were of the standard C-2 type. But the United States Lines are best known for passenger ships of which the record-breaking *United States* must serve as the finest example. She was the creation of attorney-turned-naval architect, William Gibbs, the man who had rebuilt the *Leviathan* and designed many other ships. Gibbs was a man of extraordinary energy and determination. A champion of high-pressure boilers he studied every influence likely to affect his master-project: the reasons why the *Titanic* sank, why the *Morro Castle* burned, the effects of torpedo attack, and how his dream ship might be financed. But the times were not auspicious; great liners were not making money, America was suffering economic problems at the hands of the maritime trade unions and Congress was no longer interested in merchant shipping. Gibbs wanted three-quarters of the cost of his ship to be subsidised and while he might raise half direct from the government, he twisted a little more out of the naval budget by pleading the 'national defense' aspect of the project. She would be an exceptionally fast ship, highly suitable for trooping, and she would have two engine rooms to provide against possible torpedo attack. So successful was this ploy that he convinced the American public the new ship was not really intended to be a luxury liner.

Gibbs stretched the tonnage measurement rules to the extent of their elastic limit to provide a prestigious gross tonnage for the *United States*. Completed in 1952 by the Newport News Shipbuilding and Dry dock Company in Virginia, she was 990 feet overall (302 metres). Gibbs managed to have her registered as being 53,329 tons, though strict interpretation of the American rules seems to indicate she was no more than 38,216. On trials the *United States* proved to be everything Gibbs envisaged. In fact capable of 38.23 knots, this prodigious top-speed was kept as a state secret, as were her five-bladed outer screws (she had four, of which the inner two were four-bladed). On her maiden voyage she seized the Blue Riband from the *Queen Mary* with a speed of 34.48 knots, considerably less than her maximum.

Notwithstanding this triumph, nor that she carried over 2000 passengers in air-conditioned luxury, nor that most of her superstructure was made of light-weight aluminium, she was already an anachronism. Rising fuel costs, labour troubles and tug strikes on both sides of the Atlantic beset all these great ships in their twilight years. Economically suspect, the passenger liner had become redundant, replaced by the airliner. Britain continued to build them, with the *Southern Cross* (1955), the *Oriana* (1960) and *Canberra* (1961) for the Far East and Australian services; so did the Swedes with the *Gripsholm* of 1957 and the Dutch, with the *Rotterdam* of 1958, but their days as 'liners', sailing on schedules between passenger terminals, were over. Nevertheless they fought a gallant rearguard action.

Shaw, Savill and Albion's *Southern Cross*, for instance, was built by Harland and Wolff in Belfast as a single-class passenger ship devoid of any cargo in order for her to avoid delay on her four annual round-the-world voyages. She was of 20,214 tons gross, measured 604 feet (184 metres) in length, with a beam of 77 feet (23.5 metres) and a draught of 26 feet (8 metres). Her steam turbines and twin screws drove her 1160 passengers across blue-water at 20 knots. Her engines-aft design gave unparalleled space for her accommodation and she had the luxuries expected of such a ship: a swimming pool and lido, a cinema and lounge, a taverna, dining saloon, reading and writing rooms and a long sports deck. To reduce the effects of the ship's motion, she was fitted with Denny-Brown stabilisers and to provide a pleasant environment for her human freight, she had full air conditioning; indeed it would be hard to imagine anything that could have been added to improve passenger comfort.

By contrast, Alfred Holt's *Centaur* of 1962 carried only 200 passengers. Always pragmatic, the Blue Funnel Line made an attempt to fill a niche market by marrying a demand for passenger accommodation with the carriage of live sheep or cattle from Australia to Malaysia for which the aptly named *Centaur* was especially fitted. But it was not enough. The Second World War had advanced technical knowledge on almost every front and the range and power of aircraft was no exception. The long-haul airliner had already stolen its vocabulary, its crew uniforms and ranks from nautical culture; it was now to supplant the passenger ship as the means of global transport, relegating the great *Queens* to ignominious ends, the *Mary* to a 'hotel and amenity complex' at Long Beach, California, and the *Elizabeth* to a floating university, which caught fire and finally sank in Hong Kong harbour. Other passenger ships went a-cruising, tapping an increasingly lucrative trade which today has ships such as P&O's new *Oriana* of 1995, built specifically for this luxury market.

This swift decline of a specific ship type was not confined to the passenger liner, nor was air travel to be the only influence impinging upon post-war shipping. The crisis caused by the oil-producing Arab states which occurred in 1973–4 combined with other, minor revolutions, to destroy the cargo liner too. Her capability of carrying passengers diminished rapidly through the 1960s, and many liners lost their passenger accommodation, briefly improving the lot of their crews. Then, a decade later, the cargo liner with its break-bulk cargo and its long periods in port was swept away by the container carrier, or 'box-boat', and the roll on/ roll off, or 'roro' ship. Only the all-refrigerated ship, or 'reefer' continues to co-exist with her bigger, uglier sisters and still manages to retain some of the grace and beauty of an age that had not considered aesthetics an improper feature of ship design.

Whatever exterior changes this revolution ushered in, there was one feature that maintained the comforting linear progression upon which history is supposed to proceed: the diesel engine. The diesel engine had proved itself suitable for ship propulsion of most types, except where high speed was an absolute requirement. As speed became less and less important, the engine gained an ascendancy which, even in 1929, could produce speeds of 21 knots.

The *Asama Maru* built by the Mitsubishi Shipbuilding Company in their Nagasaki shipyard was one of a pair of liners built for the Nippon Yusen Kaisha's trans-Pacific, Yokohama to San Francisco service. The two 'NYK' or Japanese Mail Line ships were, at 16,975 gross tons, the largest liners then to have been built in Japan. The *Asama Maru* was fitted with four Sulzer diesels which were geared to quadruple screws. These made their running costs significantly lower than their competitors, such as the American President or Canadian-Pacific liners. Very well equipped with gyrocompass, radio direction finder and two motorised lifeboats among the twenty-two in the davits, her public rooms boasted an international variety of styles and she carried over 7600 tons of cargo with a refrigerated capacity of 300 tons. Her passenger accommodation held 239 in first class, 96 in second and 504 in third, many of the latter being Japanese immigrants bound for the United States.

In September 1937 the *Asama Maru* was dry-docked in the Taikoo dockyard in Hong Kong when a typhoon warning was received and the ship was moved to a 'safe' anchorage. Sadly this move proved otherwise. The onslaught of the typhoon was to part her cables and she drove hard ashore. A considerable effort was required to get the stranded ship off, so high had she gone, and she had to be lightened by 3500 tons. To achieve this it was necessary to lift out two of her Sulzer engines. Six months later she was refloated, taken to Japan for repair and was back in service by September 1938. By 1941 the *Asama Maru* was a Japanese naval transport and in 1944 she was sunk by the US Submarine *Atule* in the South China Sea.

This Japanese liner was but one of several large medium-speed diesel-powered liners in service before the Second World War. Gradually the diesel became increasingly used in ships of all classes, proving a versatile, reliable and economical power-unit. It had its drawbacks, though. It was not always suitable for ships involved in frequent manoeuvring or which required changes in screw revolutions until the variable pitch propeller came into use. Heavy manoeuvring requirements could be achieved by using diesel-electric propulsion and this expensive power-unit was fitted into smaller ships such as passenger ferries.

The diesel engine and welding combined to produce both an economic power-unit and hull construction method. As with sail to steam and steam to diesel, the transition period was prolonged. Oddly, although welding only gained general acceptance through the massive shipbuilding programmes of the Second World War, it had already been around for some time. In 1919 the Liverpool company T. and J. Brocklebank ordered a small 420 ton gross registered ship from Lairds of Birkenhead. She was named *Fullagar* and built on a revolutionary new principle that abandoned the use of rivets. Instead a mild steel rod was wrapped in an asbestos flux which was designed to exclude air during the fusing process. The rod was placed close to abutting plates and frames which required joining and an electric current was passed down the rod. This created an arc across the gap, melting the rod and fusing it to the adjacent steel of the plates or frames to be linked, joining the whole into a continuous unit.

Although problems were encountered in the consistency of welding, the system employed in the *Fullagar* was successful. As a coaster she was hard-worked and she soon grounded in the River Mersey when fully loaded with coal. When she arrived at Belfast and discharged, her bottom was found to have been set in a foot over a length of 70 feet, but a subsequent dry-docking in Birkenhead revealed nothing worse that a buckled bottom and a dent in her master's pride. Despite this she was written off as a constructive total loss. The ship had been fitted with an experimental diesel to the design of H. F. Fullagar, but this was not considered to have been successful and may have contributed to the decision to dispose of her. The ship was taken to Scotland and converted to steam. Here too her hull was straightened and strengthened and she was sold on, enduring a series of name and ownership changes over the succeeding years. By 1937 the *Fullagar* traded under the name *Cedros*, and had been reconverted to diesel power. By then she was owned by O. L. Rodriguez of Ensenada, Baja California. On 31 August she was in collision with the *Hidalgo* and sank, an obscure but remarkable merchant ship which took to the bottom of the Sea of Cortez a hull which had endured hard usage but at a survey in 1931 had shown no sign of failure or rusting in her welding.

The benefits of welding were enormous. Far less steel was required and thus weight and fuel were saved; the method was much simpler from the steel fabrication point of view, less labour intensive and, because no particular physical strength was required, could be undertaken by women, a fact to be thrown into sharp relief after 1941. While there were to be serious failures in welded ships, they were due to poor quality work exposed in rigorous sea conditions, not a failure in the method itself.

As we saw in a previous chapter, steam survived in some ships, either in its reciprocating form, in the steam turbine, or in its more sophisticated derivative, steam turbo-electric propulsion.

Conventional steam turbines had driven the gloriously fine-lined *United States* to enable her to seize the coveted Blue Riband with more than 3 knots in reserve. Steam turbines were also to drive warships at even faster speeds until superseded by the gas turbine. Nuclear-powered steam turbines were fitted to the United States of America's experimental cargo liner *Savannah*, but in commercial terms she proved a failure. Great Britain held on longer than most nations to the steam propulsion she had pioneered. Cunard's prestigious *Queen Elizabeth 2* was fitted with steam turbines when launched by Queen Elizabeth II from John Brown, Clydebank in 1969, but they became troublesome even on her trials in November 1968, and Cunard refused to accept her. Her maiden voyage was postponed and she became a constant problem, losing huge sums of money for her owners who, in 1971, were bought out by Trafalgar House Investments.

She also suffered successive publicity disasters. In 1972 Royal Air Force bomb disposal experts parachuted into the Atlantic alongside her to be lifted aboard in response to a terrorist bomb threat which turned out to be a hoax. She was the centre of an 'incident' in the long antipathy between Israel and the Arabs when on an Israeli charter, and she was immobilised by boiler trouble off Bermuda on All Fools' Day, 1974. On this occasion her passengers were rather humiliatingly taken off by a Norwegian cruise ship. The following year she ran aground off Nassau, and in July 1976 a fire broke out in the engine room. None of these highly publicised events attracted passengers and costs of refits, fuel and personnel rose inexorably. Although requisitioned for trooping service in the recapture of the Falkland Islands in 1982, she was kept well away from the front line, unlike P&O's *Canberra*, and rumours circulated as to her reliability. Even her spurious claim to be 'the flagship of the British Merchant Fleet' had a sonorously hollow ring as the British register dwindled into decline.

Eventually she was taken in hand and her troublesome turbines were removed, being replaced by MAN diesels in 1987, not in Britain, but in Germany. It was a sign of the times: even P&O's *Oriana* of 1995, was built entirely in Germany. This new ship's naming ceremony carried out at Southampton by Queen Elizabeth II in the Summer of 1995 might be seen as marking the death of British merchant shipbuilding, if not quite the demise of ships under the British red ensign.

Notwithstanding this sad history, the fitting of diesels seems to have given the '*QE2*' a new lease of life and although depletion of fossil fuels may in due course revive the nuclear power plants such as *Savannah*'s or those in some Russian icebreakers, it is Rudolf Diesel's 'rational heat engine' that has come to provide the heartbeat of the modern power-driven merchantman. Such a ship is, however, a very far cry from the elegant liners of the early and middle part of the century, for at its close there is only a dwindling place for ladies: only hard worked and functional androgynes thrive.

The *Queen Elizabeth 2* was fitted with both satellite and the radio-navigation system known as Omega, but these methods were, at the time of her launching and along with the older established Decca, only just succeeding traditional methods of position-finding among merchant seamen. Ocean navigation had undergone no radical changes since the introduction of steam power, but being less capricious than the wind, steam enabled the practice to become less of what King Charles II had called 'an arte and mysterie', and more of a science.

Basic navigation consisted of dead reckoning, calculating direction and distance from a known point, called the 'departure position'. Up to distances of 600 miles this was solved by traverse tables and for greater distances, slightly more complicated, but fundamentally simple calculations were done. But dead reckoning was mere estimation and took varying degrees of account of the vagaries of wind, tide, oceanic current and so forth. It was essential that latitude and longitude were regularly determined as often as possible during a passage.

Latitude had been determinable from ancient times, using either the Pole Star or the altitude of the sun when it 'culminated', that is reached the highest point of its daily rise at local noon, when it was on the meridian of an observer. Such measurements, made by various instruments such as the astrolabe and quadrant, were finally best achieved by the sextant. Longitude could not readily be determined until Harrison produced his accurate chronometer, thereafter the subsequent contributions made by the American master, Captain Thomas Sumner and the French naval officer, Marc St Hilaire enabled mariners to monitor their ship's position with confidence. The solution of the 'PZX triangle' became the basis upon which all astro-navigation now relied and this solution was arrived at by means of a physical observation combined with calculations.

This triangle is conceived to lie upon a theoretical celestial spheroid which is viewed by an observer on the earth from the inside, at its centre. This repudiation of Galilean astronomy is necessary to resolve the problem on the basis of relative, observed phenomena. The observer has a point in the heavens vertically above his head which corresponds in angular values to his latitude and longitude on earth, and which is known as his or her zenith; this is point Z. When he or she takes the altitude of a star, which may of course be the sun, the star selected marks point X on the celestial triangle; while point P is the elevated pole, that is the nearer pole in the same hemisphere as the observer; this is a fixed point. The angle subtended between PZ (an arc on the observer's meridian) and PX (an arc of the meridian or hour angle of the star), when related to the Greenwich Meridian, gives the longitude of the zenith and hence of the observer immediately below. Meanwhile the angle PZ (the co-latitude), when subtracted from a right angle, gives the latitude. The value of ZX (the zenith distance) is calculable from sextant observations and the angle between arc PZ and arc PX at the elevated pole, P, may be found from a second calculation using the time at Greenwich combined with the 'ephemeris', data obtained from a nautical almanac. If at twilight 'sights' of five or six stars were taken as nearly simultaneously as possible, an accurate fix could be obtained by the solution of a formula to resolve the unknown values of the PZX triangle. An alternative method was to take a 'running fix', using two observations separated by a few hours of a single heavenly body like the sun, with a carefully measured course and distance between each.

Such course and distance was determined by compass and log. The former relied less and less upon the magnetic compass, because the gyrocompass was increasingly used in merchant ships from about 1920 onwards. The chip log had long been replaced by the impeller type developed by Thomas Walker in 1861 and which had several variants thereafter. This towed astern, imparting its spin to a series of 'clocks' which recorded distance and which was secured to a ship's rail. Liable to be fouled by weed, nobbled by sharks or carried away in bad weather, Walker's log could only be streamed on a long passage and not when manoeuvring. Such data was required by naval officers, and in 1917 Captain Chernikeef of the Russian Navy developed a log which dropped an impeller through a watertight gland and sluice valve in a ship's bottom plating. In rotating, the impeller made electrical contacts which registered on the bridge as speed and distance.

Substitution of a pressure-measuring device, named after Henri Pitot who in 1730 discovered the principle that pressure increased with speed, produced the pitometer log and both types were fitted to warships during the Second World War. Their introduction to merchant ships was not common until some time afterwards, but they measured speed through the water, not speed over the ground and solution for this far more significant problem had to await the impact of the great technological revolution that was now imminent.

CHAPTER SEVENTEEN

Sea Power II

On the very day that war broke out in Europe, 3 September 1939, the British Donaldson liner *Athenia* was torpedoed by *U-30*. Although the U-boat's commander, Lemp, thought she was an armed merchant cruiser, the sinking of this passenger liner caused the British to assume unrestricted submarine warfare had broken out. There were other uncomfortable similarities to events in 1916 and 1917: twenty-eight Americans lost their lives.

By the summer of 1940, Britain stood alone against a Europe dominated by Germany, maintaining a precarious existence by holding onto command of her own airspace and her ocean supply lines. This she managed by dint of self-sacrifice until the full might of America was drawn into the conflict after the Japanese attack on Pearl Harbor in December 1941. As we have seen, the defeat of Japan was due to carrier-borne aircraft and the only successful submarine campaign against trade, whereas the defeat of Germany was due to two factors: Russian pressure from the east, which eventually turned the tide of German fortunes; and the amphibious invasion of occupied France in the west with chiefly American, British and Canadian forces. This invasion, the greatest combined operation in military history, was executed from the south coast of Britain.

The maintenance of Britain as the outwork of the Allied front-line in the west was due to the transfer of supplies, munitions, troops and all the *materiel* of war across the grey and tempestuous North Atlantic. Early in the war, the United States had agreed to supply Britain with 'guns and butter' under the terms of the Lend-Lease concordat reached by President Roosevelt and Prime Minister Churchill. Russia also benefitted from Anglo-American aid, either via the Arctic supply route, the Persian Gulf or across the Pacific. Prior to Pearl Harbor, America had also assisted with 'protection' of her own neutral shipping in the Atlantic and lost a destroyer, the *Reuben James*, to a U-boat torpedo on 31 October 1941.

*

371

Victory for the Allies hinged entirely upon command of the sea, and the shipping of supplies either across the Atlantic to Britain by convoy, or across the Pacific to the Allied battlefleet by the Fleet Train. The fiercer of the great battles of supply in these two oceanic theatres was that which took place in the Atlantic. Although Admiral Dönitz had not in fact ordered unrestricted submarine warfare in September 1939, it was soon to be introduced and the battle of the Atlantic was to become the longest battle of the Second World War. It was also the most crucial, for quite simply, its loss meant defeat for the Allies.

The Germans developed the tactic of the 'wolf pack,' spreading out lines of patrolling U-boats to watch for the telltale smoke of a convoy, then concentrating a group to converge and strike at the steadily plodding merchantmen. To achieve this, U-boat headquarters used encoded radio messages, and could supply their wolf packs with fuel from submarine oilers known as 'milch cows'. The high surface speed of the Type VIIC U-boat meant it could trail and report a convoy until headquarters had vectored sufficient support ahead of the convoy to strike. Attacks were usually made at night, to cause the maximum confusion, and hinder the counter attacks of the escorts.

At the beginning of the war, Britain, which adopted the convoy system immediately, remained short of adequate escorts. As a consequence the U-boats had easy pickings. Later, as counter-techniques, expertise and numbers built up against them, U-boat commanders followed the example of Otto Kretschmer, and worked their way inside the columns of the convoy itself and made night surface attacks, unaffected by the probing asdic. The outcome of this battle depended on a series of advantages gradually accruing to the Allies: sufficient effective escorts, increasing air-cover to locate surfaced submarines, and a sufficiency of merchant ships capable of transporting the sinews of war across the North Atlantic.

Basically the matter revolved around a simple question: could the Allies build more merchant ships than the Axis could sink? For a long time the matter hung in the balance, but in the end the answer was in the affirmative, and the affirmative largely took the form of the standard ship. The concept of the standard ship had grown out of the desperate need for shipping in the First

World War. By the armistice of 1918, some 420 standard vessels were completed to the orders of the British government and these all bore names prefixed by the word War. Acute though the situation was in the First World War, it was greater by the Second. The idea of standardised construction was revived and the most famous of the standard ships produced was the 10,000 ton deadweight cargo-type known as the Liberty ship.

During the Depression the British shipyard of Thompson's at Sunderland on the River Wear had planned to take advantage of an upturn in shipbuilding by modernizing their facilities. In 1935 they built the coal-burning 10,000-tonner *Embassage* for Newcastle owners. This rather unprepossessing ship was not merely the prototype for a class of identical sisters, but was in fact the forerunner of hundreds of ugly-duckling half-sisters. Faced with crippling losses to German U-boats, the British Ministry of War Transport (MOWT) took up the design and ordered the '*Empire*' *Liberty*. Forms of the basic type were ordered on both sides of the Atlantic, but more particularly in America where the most innovative builder was the American engineer Henry Kaiser. Kaiser had specialised in mass-production and prefabrication techniques in dam and bridge building, and he was assisted by Cyril Thompson of the Sunderland yard, who had crossed the Atlantic to help extend production in Canada.

Kaiser developed prefabricated construction sites across the States, transporting components for assembly in the huge new shipyards whose multiple slipways lined the hitherto virgin banks of numerous American rivers. The US Maritime Commission financed eight new shipyards on the Atlantic coast consisting of 62 slipways; four on the Gulf of Mexico with 35, and six on the Pacific coast with 62 building ways. This required a prodigious investment of $300 million. The first of Kaiser's Liberty ships was launched on 7 September 1941 at the Bethlehem Fairfield Yard, Baltimore, Maryland; she commissioned three weeks later as the *Patrick Henry*, after an orator of the American movement for independence who had made a passionate speech in which he cried 'give me liberty, or give me death!'

American Liberty ships were all named after prominent citizens of the great republic; some two hundred of them manned by the British were prefixed *Sam* ... . They were all distinguished by being oil fired with midships accommodation and although their names were popularly assumed to be a reference to Uncle Sam, it was entirely due to the bureaucratic terminology of the British MOWT which denominated them as 'superstructure aft of midships' types and the acronym was incorporated into the name.

By contrast Canadian-built standards had 'split' accommodation and asymmetrical sampson posts serving the hatch between bridge and funnel deck, a misalignment designed to confuse attacking U-boat commanders. Many of these were named after *Parks* and were Canadian crewed. The British-manned Canadian-built ships were named after *Forts* while all standard ships built in Britain were named '*Empire ...*', a form of name which also included captured ships and ships taken into government service from trade.

It had taken about 225 to 230 days to build the early Liberty ships at a cost of $1.78 million each and took about one million work hours, but the average time of construction rapidly dropped to around forty-two days, although the more usual time was sixty. However, spectacular results affected this average, the fastest being the *Robert G. Peary* which was launched from No. 2 slipway of the Permanente Metals Corporation of Richmond, California on 12 November 1942, some four days fifteen hours and thirty minutes after the keel was laid. The ship was fitted out and ready for sea three days later, demonstrating the advantages to be derived from prefabrication, and while President Roosevelt might have considered them 'dreadful looking objects', their armament of an after 4-inch low-angle surface defence gun, and an anti-aircraft defence system comprising a 12-pounder, 40 mm Bofors and 20 mm Oerlikon guns together with PAC rockets, made them a welcome sight to their crews. They could moreover, steam at a respectable 11 knots, a great improvement on the normal 8 knots of the standard slow convoy.

The alliance between mass production and pre-fabrication ensured the building rate exceeded the rate of attrition and so, by 1943, the crucial year in the battle of the Atlantic, *three Liberty ships were completing every day*. One of the innovations espoused by Kaiser was the then relatively new technique of welding (described in Chapter Sixteen), and although some serious problems were encountered with this method of ship construction, particularly in heavy or cold weather, these were overcome and many Liberties lived long and useful lives after 1945, some undergoing a variety of conversions, including being lengthened to increase their deadweight or being converted to passenger ships. By and large however, they formed the back-bone of the world's post-war tramping fleet, still providing about forty per cent thereof as late as 1960. Such was their dominance, the phrase 'Liberty-size cargo' meant a standard bulk shipment of 10,000 tons, and passed into the argot of the chartering markets.

Several other standard types were built; the T2 tanker proved a vessel as important as the Liberties and the faster derivatives of the *Patrick Henry*, the *Victory* class in which the reciprocating engines had been replaced by turbines, were capable of 15 knots. The standard C-type which followed was even faster. Many *Victories* ran in first-class cargo-liner services in the years after 1945 before suitable replacements were built, and the United States government not only laid up considerable numbers of Liberty and Victory ships in mothballs, it fostered a replacement building programme of standard ships. Hulls of the C-type were to serve not only as the first experimental container ship (the Matson Navigation Company's *Hawaiian Merchant*, a C3-S-A2), but lived long enough to be converted into fully fledged 'box-boats.'

The requirement on both sides of the Atlantic during the war was not merely for merchant ships. The British were desperate for convoy escorts with a substantial and effective anti-submarine capability. They were to produce a remarkable little ship which, although far from perfect for her role – she was slower than a surfaced U-boat – nevertheless bore the brunt of the Battle of the Atlantic while faster and more sophisticated successors were designed, built and brought into service. These were the *'Flower'* class corvettes, a numerous and stalwart batch of ships whose origins lay in the inhospitable waters of the Antarctic Ocean where the oil-fired steam whale catchers remorselessly pursued their prey.

In the 1930s, the British Admiralty sought a ship design capable of being built quickly and in large numbers by modest yards familiar with small merchant ship construction. The

Smith's Dock Company of Middlesbrough on the River Tees submitted a concept based on their whale catcher, *Southern Pride*, which was simple, reasonably fast for a small hull and possessed proven sea-keeping qualities. Originally intended for coastal patrol and escort work, the '*Flower*'s were soon at home in the grey wastes of the North Atlantic, along with their largely 'hostilities-only' crews. These amateur sailors were stiffened by a handful of key regulars and commanded either by reserve officers from the merchant service (RNR) or later in the war, by volunteer officers (RNVR), many of whom were promoted from the lower deck.

They exactly fitted Jackie Fisher's perceptive remark made a generation earlier that a convoy escort needed to be 'something that would last six months and could be driven by the man in the street'. Although fitted with a 4-inch gun forward and a pathetically small 2-pounder anti-aircraft gun amidships, it was the racks of depth charges and their side launchers along the after deck which posed the real threat to the U-boats once they had been located by the asdic, or sonar. Later Oerlikons were added to beef-up the AA capability as were the forward-firing hedgehog mortars to hurdle the problems of losing their underwater quarry as they made their final approach.

The standard anti-submarine attack was made by running down the bearing of a submerged submarine located and held in the asdic beam by its operator. But as the corvette approached the point above the U-boat from which it would deliver its attack, the asdic beam could not be depressed far enough and lost its clarity in the noises produced by the attacking corvette. The hiatus between losing contact, passing over the quarry and lobbing the depth charges over the stern, often allowed a cool and experienced U-boat commander to escape. By allowing an attack to be made ahead, while the intended victim was still in the beam of the asdic, the Hedgehog offered a better chance of a hit. It delivered a smaller amount of high-explosive fused to detonate on contact, though, and this was improved upon late in the war by the Squid, a forward-firing mortar which delivered a pattern of depth charges set in accordance with data from Asdic.

Kretschmer's tactic of surface attacks at night robbed convoy escorts of the use of their asdics, so from May 1941, the corvettes were equipped with the Type 271 surface radar, its scanner concealed in a weather proof 'lantern'. This unit was primitive, but it proved effective, and demand outstripped supply. The 271 radar was one of the first 'modular' systems. The 'lantern' and the operator's 'office' were installed as a single unit.

The *'Flower'* class corvettes were powered by simple triple expansion steam reciprocating engines fed by Scotch boilers. They had a good endurance of 4000 miles at 10 knots, but were quick to accelerate to their top speed of 16 knots and quicker to turn, possessing a large rudder, something that made them able submarine hunters in the right hands.

Their main disadvantage was their short, round-bilged hulls, which rolled horribly and pitched badly in the heavy seas of the Atlantic. Later modifications such as extending the fore-castle in HMS *Verbena* and her successors, made them drier and more comfortable, but their 200-feet hull was really too short for ocean work. Curiously, their main opponent, the Type VIIC U-boat was also too small for her task, and her crew's living conditions were even worse than those endured aboard a corvette. In total 300 corvettes were ordered, some 148 of the class were built in British yards for the Royal Navy, plus a further 16 for the French, who also built four of their own before their defeat. In Canada a further 130 were completed with 25 going to the United States Navy, an example of 'Reverse Lend-Lease'. As the Royal Navy subsumed the 'free navies' of occupied nations, *'Flower'*s flew the ensign of almost every Allied nation. Escaped Schelde pilotage staff manned one, the Greeks four, the then Royal Yugoslavian Navy manned another, the Dutch one, while both the British white ensign and the French tricolour flew side by side in the corvette *La Malouine*. Like the Liberty ship, many of the *Flower* class enjoyed long lives, passing to the post-war naval services of Portugal, Eire, Israel, Dominica, India, Thailand, Chile, Italy, Argentina and Nationalist China, while others were converted to merchantmen. A further four became ocean weather ships (OWS) and some even became involved in pelagic whaling.

The Admiralty had sent the *Flower* class corvette into the Atlantic on the assumption that a convoy's escort would only be required westwards to about longitude 20°. They were very effective, but forced the U-boats to hunt in deeper waters. The fall of France and use of the French Biscay ports by the enemy, combined with the long range of the German U-boat, moved the battleground to the middle of the Atlantic. The requirement for a better version was obvious, but the improved *Castle* class was ordered from those yards incapable of building long hulls. Superior asdic sets were fitted to the *Castles* and the Hedgehog was replaced by the more effective Squid, mounted forward of the bridge, shunting the 4-inch gun to a wet and vulnerable position on the forecastle. A great improvement though they were, the *Castles* were inferior to the frigate classes then coming into use and production was cut back. Five were completed as convoy rescue ships and commissioned under the blue ensign with *Empire* names. Those which survived the war were reclassified as frigates, though they were not long in post-war service. Nevertheless, four were recommissioned from mothballs in the mid 1960s to serve as replacement ocean weather ships, displacing the last *Flowers* under the British flag. Two of these even underwent major refurbishment in the 1970s and ended their careers as OWSs *Admiral Beaufort* and *Admiral Fitzroy*.

Prior to the war, the Royal Navy had developed a number of small escort and patrol ships, born of the experience of the First World War. During this period the most significant were the thirty-six sloops which culminated in the *Black Swan* and *Egret* classes. These were substantially the same and proved fore-runners of the large frigate classes which superseded the hurriedly built corvettes. Expensive and relatively sophisticated ships, the sloops were most effective when withdrawn from escort work and deployed as independent 'support groups', the most famous of which was that commanded by Captain 'Johnnie' Walker. In HMS *Starling*, Walker headed a team of superb professionals who quickly found the answer to the Gnat acoustic torpedo. This device homed in on the noisy propellers of fast moving escorts, just one example of the ebb and flow of advantage and disadvantage that swung between the Allied and Axis forces throughout the long war. While destroyers assigned to escort work towed crude baffles called foxers in their wake to divert and explode the noise-seeking Gnat as it dashed in to the attack, Walker made his kills by dropping the speed of his 19-knot sloops to a 'creeping pace' and hunted in a pack. Two of his ships held the located U-boat in the beams of their asdics and vectored the rest of the group onto the pinned-down target to destroy the enemy submarine by persistent depth charging.

The success of the sloops generally persuaded the Admiralty to produce a cheaper derivative, reviving an old name long usurped by the now much grander cruiser, that of the frigate. There were three classes, the *Rivers*, *Lochs* and *Bays*. The *Rivers* began to enter service in 1942 with over eighty serving in the Royal Canadian Navy, a few in the United States Navy and sixty-five in the Royal Navy. A further twenty-one similar frigates were built for the Royal Navy in the United States in 1943, originally as the American *Asheville* class, but which hoisted the white ensign under the names of imperial colonies. The *Rivers* had a 300-foot hull, the accepted minimum for oceanic work, and most were powered by two sets of corvette machinery to give a top speed of 20 knots, though a handful were fitted with geared turbines. Like the corvettes before them, the design was kept as simple as possible. Prefabrication was not entertained because of the difficulties and delays inherent in setting up such a system. Instead the traditional skills of the small merchant yard were again pressed into service. Armament was similar to the *Castles* and later *Flowers*, but the improvements in speed and endurance were considerable. Canadian and Australian versions were built with minor differences in armament, but the class generally presented a handsome, workman-like appearance.

The thirty-one *Loch* class frigates built between 1943 and 1945 carried a light anti-aircraft armament along with the 4-inch forward. The *Lochs* sting lay in their two Squid mortars which had effectively displaced the gun and were a foretaste of post-war anti-submarine frigate development. Although most of the class were powered by the conventional triple expansion engines, two of them, HMSs *Loch Arkaig* and *Loch Tralaig* were driven by turbines and like their half-sisters could do a creditable 20 knots. Prefabricated welded construction was used in these ships, giving them an ugly straight line sheer.

The two dozen *Bay* class were essentially an anti-aircraft version of the *Loch* class mounting two twin 4-inch guns, with reinforced Bofors and Oerlikon batteries. They were built late in the war with an eye on the continuation of the war in the Far East after the defeat of Germany. In the event, four of them were completed not as frigates, but as HM Surveying ships

Cook, Dalrymple, Dampier and *Owen*, truly swords beaten into ploughshares.

British desperation for escorts in 1939 was not solved by the building of the *Flower* class corvettes, though they provided the backbone of the Royal Navy's response to the demands of war. The British possessed a considerable number of fine fleet destroyers, particularly the new *Tribal* class, but many of these were retained in home waters or on foreign stations in support of capital ships, nor did fleet destroyers make adequate long-range convoy escorts.

To provide these, the British, still fearful of enemy raiders, commissioned a number of fast liners as Armed Merchant Cruisers under the white ensign and armed them with 6-inch guns. Some, like the Bibby Line's *Worcestershire*, had been built with specially strengthened positions to accept gun-mountings. They took with them to war some of the glamour naturally associated with liners and soon made a name for themselves when the *Rawalpindi,* under Captain E. C. Kennedy, on a northern patrol off Iceland, was sunk by the *Scharnhorst* on 23 November 1939 after a gallant but hopeless defence. Similarly a year later, on 5 November 1940, the *Jervis Bay,* under the command of Captain Fogarty Fegen, covered her scattering convoy by engaging the *Admiral Scheer* at suicidal odds. The *Scheer,* having despatched the *Jervis Bay,* also shelled some of the fleeing merchantmen, but most of the convoy escaped. Other liners were taken up as Ocean Boarding Vessels whose task it was to intercept and board neutral shipping in an attempt to stop vital war materials reaching Germany. One such, the former Blue Funnel cargo liner *Maron,* was fitted for this task with two 6-inch guns. In common with those hurriedly mounted on the sterns of most British merchantmen, they were antique: one was dated 1903, the other 1897. Despite the deep-seated fear of surface raiders, a fear which, incidentally, had the obsolete 'R' class battleships sailing with some trans-Atlantic convoys, it was the U-boat offensive that posed by far the greater threat.

The negotiations between Prime Minister Churchill and President Roosevelt transformed the United States into 'the arsenal of democracy' and Lend-Lease held the promise of help out to a beleaguered Britain. As part of the deal, fifty elderly destroyers built by the United States Navy at the end of the First World War, were loaned to Britain. They were not really up to Atlantic service, but were commissioned into the Royal Navy as the *Town* class. Some, like HNorMS *St Albans*, served under ensigns other than the British and one, HMS *Campbeltown*, was used on the St Nazaire raid where the explosives in her bow detonated when she was rammed into the gates of the dock in which the liner *Normandie* had been built.

In addition to fleet destroyers, the British built the *Hunt* class escort destroyers. Lacking the length and high speed of fleet destroyers, they were faster than the frigates, with a top speed of 26 knots. They had a formidable anti-aircraft battery and were much employed on the east coast of England and on Arctic convoys to north Russia. Powered by turbines and water-tube boilers, eighty-six of them were built in four groups, of which more later.

Numerous though these classes were, the demands of convoy work were remorseless. Further to the fifty *Towns*, numerous other American escorts were lent to the Royal Navy. Thirty-two diesel frigates of the 20-knot *Evarts* class, along with forty-six of the almost identical but turbo-electric and therefore faster 24-knot ships of the *Buckley* class were commissioned under the white ensign. These were grouped together as the *Captain* class and named after outstanding historical British naval captains.

The United States Coastguard also provided reinforcements in the form of ten of their 'cutters' – relatively small, 16-knot, flush-decked ships to which must be added the Royal Navy's own fleet minesweepers, 126 of the *Halcyon* and *Algerine* classes. These were more often used as convoy escorts, for they were slightly larger and faster than the *Flowers* and had good asdic capabilities. Many of these served on the remote station at Polyarnoe, near Murmansk in support of Arctic convoys, clearing the approaches to the Kola Inlet and providing both local and through escorts.

Many other ships served on convoy duty, particularly in the early part of the war. Anti-submarine trawlers gave yeoman service, as did other fishing vessels pressed into the depressing and nerve-wracking duty of minesweeping, an essential ancillary activity to convoy work on the east coast of England. It should not be forgotten that these short routes were deadly, subject not so much to submarine attack but to aerial and ship-laid mines, E-boats and air-attack. It was along these swept channels that many of the ocean merchantmen, who had transited the Atlantic, had to wend their way to their final destinations, or along which they made their way to the next rendezvous.

While deficiency in anti-submarine escorts could be made by the adaptation of distant water trawlers, the provision of anti-aircraft support, particularly for coastal convoys, was solved by another ingenious expedient, that of Auxiliary AA ships. Seven ships were taken up from trade for this purpose. They were not merely modified, but virtually rebuilt, the most thorough conversion being that of the fast Irish Sea packet *Ulster Queen* of 3791 tons gross, whose merchant origin could scarcely be guessed at on completion. Another Irish Sea ferry, the Isle of Man packet *Tynwald*, was the only steamship to be converted for an anti-aircraft role. Capable of 21 knots, thanks to her Parsons turbines, she and a sister-ship had already made a name for themselves by first ferrying the British Expeditionary Force to France in 1939 and then evacuating the men from the beaches of Dunkirk the following year. Two of MacAndrew's fruit carriers, the *Pozarica* and *Palomares*, both of 1890 gross registered tons, which had been built in 1937, and were capable of 15 knots also became AA auxiliaries. Usually employed in the carriage of oranges from the Iberian peninsula to the United Kingdom, they distinguished themselves, along with *Ulster Queen* and *Alynbank*, (5151 gross registered tons) in support of Arctic convoys to North Russia. The last named of these was one of three of Andrew Weir's Bank Line tramps which was converted to this role. While several of these gallant ships were lost on active service, *Alynbank* was deliberately scuttled as part of the great artificial harbour created at Arromanches on D-Day in June 1944. All of these ships were fitted with a basic anti-aircraft armament of twin 4-inch high-angle guns, backed up by a variety of 2-pounders, 20 mm Oerlikons and machine guns. In the case of *Foylebank* (5582 gross registered tons) a Fairey Fulmar fighter on a catapult was added, while *Ulster Queen* had an asdic and depth charges. All of the anti-aircraft auxiliaries had gunnery control radar and served usefully until the end of 1942 when they began to be replaced. *Foylebank* was sunk by Stukas off Portland in the English

Channel on 4 July 1940, an event from which a mortally wounded young gunner earned the first Victoria Cross of the war to be awarded to a rating.

In total, the British Royal Navy employed some two thousand escorts of all classes during the Second World War. At the commencement of hostilities, much use was made of extemporised, stopgap measures, but as time passed it was not just the quality of the hulls or that of their crews that improved. By 1943 the standard asdic/sonar and radar sets had become far more effective than early models. While range in both systems could be reasonably accurately measured, accurate bearing was a function of the overall mechanical efficiency of the design and this got much better. The deployment of good radar and asdic/sonar sets was one decisive factor in the war with the U-boats. But so too was the intelligence derived from the decrypts of the German Enigma signals sent from Dönitz's headquarters, and passed from Bletchley Park to the heart of British convoy defence and counterattack in the submarine tracking room at the Admiralty in London and the unobtrusive bunker beneath Derby House in Liverpool. From there, first Admiral Sir Percy Noble and later the former submariner Max Horton, commanded and co-ordinated the struggle for mastery of the Atlantic.

In winning this, air-power also played a major role and once long-range aircraft such as the British Sunderland, American Catalina flying boats, or the extended range VLR Liberator were able to fly anti-submarine patrols over wide areas of the ocean, the ability of the Allies to strike back at the German submarines was greatly enhanced. Brilliant, resourceful and courageous though the U-boat offensive was, it invited a war of attrition and received annihilation in full measure. The great battle, which lasted from the day war was declared in Europe until the German surrender, resulted in the sinking of many hundreds of ships. Along with the ships went thousands of seamen of all nationalities. In the poignant words of the German song, 'there are no roses on a sailor's grave'.

During the great days of her empire, Great Britain had maintained her prestige by 'showing the flag', by maintaining single ships or small squadrons of warships on foreign stations, often intervening in peacekeeping operations, assisting the civil power, or helping when a natural disaster struck. The warships most commonly used for this role were cruisers whose power, speed and armament were sufficient to impress. Cruisers were versatile ships with large crews and astonishing endurance and, as visible evidence of sea-power, were employed by all the major nations.

During the First World War the British Admiralty had originally assumed that cruisers patrolling the imperial trade routes would be sufficient deterrent to prevent the sinking of British merchantmen. As we have seen this assumption soon proved tragically optimistic. During the Second World War, the role of the cruiser underwent a subtle and successful change, and she found herself conforming more closely to the role that had been that of the old sailing frigate whose name she had usurped. Operating in small squadrons, engaging enemy raiders, or as the eyes of the fleet operating in advance of the main body, her task was to bring an enemy under the guns of supporting capital ships. British cruisers were remarkably successful, though losses were considerable. However, the AA armament of modern cruisers gave powerful protection to convoys as well as warship-formations.

Cruisers were subject to the limitations of the naval treaties of the 1920s and their design was thus heavily constrained, at least in theory. American studies argued in favour of fast cruisers with 8-inch guns to sustain United States' strategic requirements in the Pacific. The Americans therefore built their first 'Treaty' cruisers with a belt of armour and ten 8-inch guns in three triple mountings. In contrast, the Japanese fitted five twin turrets into their Atago class. In their quest for speed the Italians utilised a thin armoured belt but with light hull scantlings, while French cruisers abandoned armour completely. The British '*County*' class followed the Italian principle, with large, but strongly built hulls, heavily subdivided to absorb punishment and though deficient in fire power with only eight 8-inch guns, their high freeboard, high endurance, speed and sea-keeping qualities made them comfortable, weatherly ships, capable of about 32 knots at top speed. Thirteen were built, including two for the Australian navy. Two, *Dorsetshire* and *Cornwall*, were lost to Japanese aircraft in the Indian Ocean in April 1942, the latter having been hit earlier in the war on the raid on Dakar when she was struck by a heavy shell believed to have been from the French battleship *Richelieu*. *Norfolk* sustained two 11-inch hits from the *Scharnhorst* off the North Cape in December 1943 and the *Devonshire* sank the German raider *Atlantis*. Two slightly smaller and cheaper derivatives of the 'Counties', HMSs *York* and *Exeter*, were both lost during the war, but not before the latter had been part of a cruiser squadron which engaged the German *panzerschiff Graf Spee* off the River Plate in December 1939.

Exeter's consorts in this action were two *Leander* class light cruisers, *Ajax* and *Achilles*, built in the 1930s with eight, twin-mounted 6-inch guns. This departure from the 8-inch heavy cruiser brought in a greater diversity among British cruisers in the last decade of peace, reflecting the British Admiralty's concern over the probable developments in a future and increasingly likely war. Displacing around 7000 tons the first five of the class had lower freeboard and a long quarterdeck than the 'Counties', but carried eight 6-inch guns in four twin turrets. They were 554.5 feet overall, with a beam of 55.25 feet on a draught of 16 feet. Their anti-aircraft armament was a battery of four 4-inch high-angle guns which was later increased to eight. They also had eight 21-inch torpedo tubes, a seaplane and catapult, and were lightly armoured, with a belt of 4-inch steel tapering to 2 inches at bow and stern, with lighter armour on the deck, the conning tower and gun turrets. Steam turbines generated 72,000 horsepower and 32.5 knots at full speed.

Three improved *Leanders* were built in 1934 in which the main difference was to make flooding of the boiler rooms more difficult. The trio was transferred to the Royal Australian Navy just before the outbreak of war. In November 1941, HMAS *Sydney* brought-to a supposedly Dutch merchantman. The *Sydney* was too close and when the merchantman cast aside the mask of deception and revealed herself as the German raider *Kormoran*, it was with devastating shellfire. In the ensuing duel, the *Kormoran* was so disabled that she was scuttled, while the *Sydney* broke off the action in flames and was later lost with all hands. HMAS *Perth* was also sunk during a disastrous cruiser action in the Java Sea on 27 February 1942 when a Japanese squadron under Rear-Admiral Tagaki engaged a mixed Dutch-American-British Imperial force under the Dutch Rear-Admiral, Karel Doorman.

Smaller than the '*Counties*' were the four ships of the *Arethusa* class which, with only six 6-inch guns, gave good service, but were considered under-armed and too weak. A large improved class, the *Didos*, were consequently built between 1937 and 1939, using as a main armament not the 6-inch gun, but the same 5.25 high-angle weapon in twin turrets as the secondary armament of the *King George V* class battleships. The *Dido* and her sisters gained a distinguished reputation, although of the eleven constructed before the outbreak of war, three were torpedoed in the Mediterranean – *Bonaventure* by the Italian submarine *Ambra* in March 1941, *Naiad* in March 1942 by *U-565* and *Hermione* by *U-205* in July 1942. HMS *Charybdis* was torpedoed in October 1943 by German E-boats in the English Channel, having been leading a small force of destroyers in fog (one of the destroyers was also lost).

Three of the class, *Cleopatra*, *Euryalus* and *Dido*, together with an older cruiser, HMS *Carlisle* of 1917 and a force of destroyers under Admiral Vian defeated a mixed force of Italian warships under Admiral Iachino in the Gulf of Sirte on 22 March 1942. Iachino's fleet consisted of cruisers, destroyers and the battleship *Littorio*. It was anti-aircraft defence at which the class excelled, however, although two ships could not be fitted with their correct armament due to a shortage of weapons. These cruisers, HMS *Scylla* and HMS *Charybdis* had an outfit of 4.5-inch guns, and the *Scylla*, nicknamed the 'Toothless Tiger', provided formidable anti-aircraft barrages in defence of convoys to North Russia.

Possessing overseas territories, the United States of America had viewed the aggrandizement of Japan in the 1930s with alarm and had anticipated their own most likely future naval deployments would be in the Pacific. As observed earlier, the need for cruisers had been apparent to the Navy Department in pursuit of a policy of augmenting the United States fleet for extended service in that ocean, but cruiser design during the early 1930s began by falling short of expectation. The Americans had not been successful with the 10,000-ton *Pensacola*, because her triple and twin turrets were too congested. Initially the ship and her sister, *Salt Lake City*, lacked director control, but this was remedied before completion. Unfortunately they rolled badly, frustrating accurate gunfire and proved unpleasant to serve in. The United States Navy quickly rectified the limitations of the first two ships and produced the six-ship *Northampton* class, followed by two more derivatives, the *Portlands*. But it was in the *New Orleans* class that the Americans produced a fine, weatherly cruiser. Retaining the three triple 8-inch mountings, the new ships, built between 1933 and 1936 bore heavier armour, up to 5 inches around the hull with decks of half that thickness. Despite extensive use of welding and other expedients to save weight, such as constricting the space for the turbines and boilers, the class was over the weight limit stipulated by the naval treaties.

The *New Orleans* and her six sisters of 1933–1936, were a huge improvement on the *Pensacola* and hers. In 1936, the longer, lighter *Brooklyn*, together with eight sister-ships, although only developing ideas already in use, did so in such a way as to produce an exceptional type of cruiser from which the United States were to derive their highly successful wartime cruiser classes. Fifteen 6-inch guns were selected for the *Brooklyn*'s main armament, mounted in five triple turrets, three of them forward with the centre of the trio, the 'B' turret, superfiring over the others. These were supported by a secondary battery of eight 5-inch guns and fifty-two anti-aircraft weapons. The hull, over 608 feet in length (185.4 metres), incorporated extensive welding and longitudinal framing. The *Brooklyn*'s beam was 61.75 feet (18.8 metres) and with a draught of 22 feet (6.6 metres) she displaced 9767 tons. Her rather ugly transom stern accommodated up to six aircraft in a hangar and these could be launched from one of two catapults on the quarterdeck. A belt of 5-inch armour was superimposed over the hull plating and the decks bore light reinforcement, while the gun turrets were heavily protected. The *Brooklyns* were powered by steam turbines generating 100,000 shaft horsepower driving quadruple screws. Improvements in American expertise were much in evidence in these ships which, although unremarkable in their speed of 32.5 knots, possessed superior electrical installations and machinery, thus saving weight and improving their power-to-weight ratio.

Contemporaneous with these developments, the Japanese experimented with a small design, the *Yubari*. She was given armour, but this was built into the hull, and her displacement exceeded her designed weight. This failure was inherited by the subsequent larger ships of the *Furutaka* and *Aoba* classes, both of which had their 8-inch guns in triple turrets. In order to confer good sea-keeping qualities on the hulls, a high freeboard forward, dipped down at the stern to give a low centre of gravity and produced a wavy sheerline which became characteristic of Japanese warships. But they possessed a characteristic of a far more damning nature: centreline bulkheads designed to limit damage in the engine and boiler rooms. Alas, they had the contrary effect, inducing a capsizing moment when compartments were breached, and eight out of the dozen Japanese cruisers hit amidships during the war, turned turtle. Designed for a top speed of 34.5 knots, they also suffered from a lack of lateral stability and were given blisters to overcome this, a modification reducing their high speed to a more standard 33 knots. The same problems attended the four *Myoko* class cruisers, though their speed of 35.5 knots was impressive. These were followed by a similar class, the *Takaos*. The demands of the Japanese Naval Staff took precedence over the unfortunate naval architects ordered to accommodate all the ideas, for stability problems dominated Japanese warship design and culminated in the capsizing of the torpedo boat *Tomozuru*, which sank in bad weather in 1934. This refusal to compromise also resulted in serious departures from Treaty limits.

Undergoing construction at this time was the *Mogami*, a cruiser intended to carry fifteen 6-inch guns at a speed of 37 knots on a displacement of a mere 8500 tons. On completion the *Mogami* displaced 11,200 tons and made 36 knots, but she and her sisters sustained storm-damage in 1935 and were modified, increasing the displacement. This was again augmented in 1937 when Japan denounced the naval treaties and replaced the 6-inch turrets with 8-inch guns. The *Mogami* was to lead a charmed life, escaping destruction at the Battle of Midway, although she suffered tremendous punishment in the Surigao Strait action of October 1944. On fire and with the *Yamashiro* capsizing close by, the *Mogami* fouled the heavy cruiser *Nachi* but limped out of the fight.

When first commissioned, both the *Mogami* and the *Brooklyn* provoked reaction from Whitehall, and the British responded with the 9100-ton *Southampton* class. These new cruisers were armed with a dozen 6-inch guns in four triple turrets, protected by 4.5-inch armour, and achieved a speed of 32 knots. The first batch led by HMS *Southampton*, were built between 1936 and 1937 and consisted of eight ships. They were followed by *Edinburgh* and *Belfast* which were slightly larger and more heavily armoured to resist 8-inch shellfire. When war broke out, a subsequent class using the same thickness of armour as the *Southampton* class on a slightly smaller hull, known as the '*Colony*' class, were under construction. Three of the later ships never received X-turret to make room for an increased anti-aircraft battery. A last group of almost identical ships, the *Superb*, *Swiftsure* and *Minotaur* (afterwards the Canadian *Ontario*) were the last cruisers to commission during the war.

The 'Towns' and 'Colonies' had an eventful war. HMS *Southampton* was lost to enemy air attack in January 1941 when escorting a convoy to *Malta*, and *Gloucester* and *Fiji* shared the same fate off Crete. Manchester was also supporting Malta during Operation Pedestal when she was hit by Italian torpedo boats on 13 August 1942. *Sheffield* and *Jamaica* under Rear-Admiral Burnett, engaged the German *panzerschiff Lützow* and the heavy cruiser *Hipper* in the Barents Sea action of 31 December 1942. A year later *Glasgow* engaged German destroyers, while *Liverpool* was torpedoed twice, but survived. HMS *Trinidad*, after an epic effort to save her following a previous bombing, was sunk in Arctic waters by one of her own torpedoes during an action with German destroyers. Also lost in the Arctic was *Edinburgh*. As for *Belfast*, having survived a broken back from a mine she took part in the sinking of the *Scharnhorst*, the D-Day landings and today remains afloat as a museum in London. Others lasted well, particularly those built pre-war, several going into service with Commonwealth and foreign navies.

The light, fast 33-knot cruisers built by the French as the *Duguay-Trouin* class, consisted of two ships mounting eight 6-inch guns. They were followed by the *Duquesnes*, 8-inch cruisers able to do 33.75 knots, but the obsession to save weight caused their light hulls to be over stressed and they suffered from leaky seams.

The Italian Navy paid to their shipbuilders a bounty of one million lire for every knot above the designed speed, for the cruisers of the *Trento* class. This inducement produced ships able to make 36 knots on trials without armament, but they were 300 tons above the treaty limits, and speed dropped to 31 knots when the guns and extras were added. Both the Italians and the French paid more attention to armour in subsequent classes of cruiser, although the Italians later reverted to high speed in the *Bolzano*, which achieved 36 knots.

The Germans, who had produced the quintessential commerce raider in the diesel driven *panzerschiff*, also built cruisers of note once Hitler had repudiated the restrictions of the Treaty of Versailles. Five 10,000-ton cruisers, the *Admiral Hipper*, *Blücher*, *Prinz Eugen* and *Seydlitz* and *Lützow* carried 5-inch side armour, a main armament of eight, 8-inch guns in four twin turrets, supported by a dozen 4.1-inch anti-aircraft weapons and a further dozen 37 mm AA guns. They also carried twelve 21-inch torpedo tubes and four aircraft. But despite a thirty per cent overshoot of the Treaty limit these heavy cruisers failed to live up to their promise. The majority remained inert, in the words of an officer, 'like chained dogs'. The *Blücher* was sunk by shore-mounted torpedoes in Oslo Fiord during the German invasion of Norway on 9 April 1940, the *Seydlitz* was scuttled in 1945 at Königsberg and the incomplete *Lützow* was sold to the Russians in 1940. The *Admiral Hipper*, which was dry-docked as a result of British bombing, was also sunk by her own crew before falling into British hands, but perhaps most odd of all was the fate of the handsome *Prinz Eugen*, named after the Duke of Marlborough's ally in the War of the Spanish Succession. She was part of the squadron of ships moored in Bikini atoll for the atomic bomb trials held there in 1946, and her destruction was filmed for posterity at that awesome moment.

Some of the later American *Brooklyn* class incorporated major innovations. One, the USS *Wichita*, was armed with nine 8-inch guns and these, unlike the *Pensacola*'s, were mounted in individual cradles reducing the spread of salvoes and increasing the rate of fire. Two more of the class, the USSs *St Louis* and *Helena* were fitted with superior twin 5-inch mountings fitted as secondary armament, and these were adopted for a smaller class of cruiser, the *Atlantas*, intended to work with destroyers and given a heavy 5-inch armament.

These guns proved very effective against aircraft and were fitted to one old British cruiser, HMS *Delhi* of 1918, which underwent a wartime refit in the United States. Alarmed, particularly during the Italian annexation of Abysinnia (now Ethiopia), at the escalating efficiency of aircraft, the British Admiralty had embarked on a programme of re-arming some elderly cruisers with light, high-angle 4-inch guns, but they lacked an accurate control system. A general reappraisal of the anti-aircraft capability of cruisers occurred during the hasty arms race just prior to the outbreak of war, and this affected British ships far more than American. The provisions of the naval treaties were abrogated and some heavier armour was fitted. We have already mentioned in Chapter Fourteen the fate of the battlecruiser *Hood*, which did not get her new armour, but some British cruisers, built to conform to the treaties with light hulls, now became overloaded, strained and leaky. Nevertheless they none of them suffered the overweight and instability problems inherent in Japanese designs.

The outbreak of the war in Europe destroyed any final reservations about tonnage limitations in America. Ships laid down were hurriedly redesigned and among the cruiser classes affected were the *Clevelands*, which were modifications of the *Brooklyn*. Internal watertight sub-division was increased and one triple 6-inch mounting, 'C' turret, was omitted to make way for the twin 5-inch mounting just forward of the forebridge. Although they suffered from excessive topweight, twenty-nine *Clevelands* were built between 1941 and 1946, the most numerous of any class of cruiser. They were followed by a less extemporised design in which the calibre of the main armament reverted to 8-inch. The lead ship, the USS *Baltimore* displaced 14,472 tons light ship, increasing to 17,000 when fully loaded and armed for war. At 673 feet in length (205 metres), with a beam of 71 feet (23 metres) she could make 32 knots. Seventeen sister-ships were built between 1942 and 1945 and several were converted to missile armaments in the mid 1950s.

Immediately post-war the Americans commissioned the 17,255-ton *Des Moines*. With her sister ships *Salem* and *Newport News*, the class mounted a main battery of nine 8-inch guns, supported by a dozen 5-inch and two dozen 3-inch weapons. The first two were built by Bethlehem Steel, the last by the Newport

News Company. With turbines working up to 120,000 horse-power, these heavily armoured cruisers with their long, 716-feet hulls were capable of 33 knots. American gunnery developments had included automatic loading for the 6-inch weapon of the smaller, 14,000-ton *Worcester* class and the concept formed the basis for the 8-inch calibre weapons fitted to the *Des Moines* class. The old rivalry between the two calibres, based on the argument that the 8-inch was incapable of rapid fire and the 6-inch could not inflict lethal damage quickly enough, seemed finally settled in these ships. The *Des Moines'* guns could fire ten 335 pound 8-inch shells in a minute.

Whilst it was general United States' practice to name cruisers after American cities and battleships after states, two super-cruisers were completed in New York in 1944 with the then rather ambivalent names *Alaska* and *Guam*. They were just over 800 feet in length, with a beam of 91 feet and displaced 27,500 tons on a draught of 31.5 feet. Turbines powered them at 150,000 shaft horsepower and conferred a speed of 33 knots. Armoured with a 9-inch belt, their main armament was nine 12-inch guns, with twelve 5-inch secondary weapons and ninety anti-aircraft guns. The Americans conceived them as logical developments of the heavy cruiser, but in their expansion to the position of pre-eminent naval power they had arrived by another route at the battlecruiser.

Perhaps the ghost of 'Jackie' Fisher would have approved the idea, if not the flag under which these ships served, for one thing was irreversible. It was summed up by an exchange of signals reputed to have been made between a United States' warship and one of her British allies in the Pacific where a considerable British fleet operated alongside the United States Navy.

'How's the world's second largest navy?' asked the Yank.

'Fine thanks,' replied the Limey, 'how's the world's second best?'

Whatever were the qualitative merits of the Royal Navy at the end of the war, the resources of the British Empire were almost exhausted and it was Uncle Sam's star that was now in the ascendant. Nevertheless, the British had produced a prodigious war machine from limited resources. From their large merchant fleet they had extemporised warships, as we have seen, with varying degrees of success, but they had also developed new and successful forms of auxiliary vessels as the conditions and circumstances of the war had demanded. Among these were the *Glenearn* class cargo liners which were built just before the outbreak of war to the exacting standards of Alfred Holt and Company, who had acquired their old rivals a few years earlier. Not only were these ships strongly constructed, but they were fast, capable of a service speed of 17 to 18 knots, thanks to their twin screws and Danish Burmeister and Wain diesels. Furthermore, this speed could be increased if required. Fitted with one refrigerated hold, several tanks for the carriage of palm oil and latex, with heavy-lift derricks at Nos 2 and 5 holds, and a large complement of lighter 3- to 5-ton derricks at all hatches, they also possessed deep lower holds, and three 'tween decks. Additionally, a centrecastle deck embraced numbers three and four hatches making these ships capacious carriers. Several of the class were used as fleet supply ships and troop transports, but later in the war several were taken in hand to become large infantry landing ships, armed with three twin 4-inch mountings, Oerlikons and pom-poms to deter air-attack. Troops could be accommodated in their extensive tween decks (Holt's had specialised in the carriage of Muslim pilgrims for many years and some of their ships and most of their sea-staff were capable of handling large numbers of people) and these were landed from small landing craft, of which the *Glengyle*, for example, carried no fewer than twenty-seven, all of which were employed at Salerno and Normandy. *Glenartney* remained a supply ship, serving in the Pacific with the Fleet Train, that superb logistics force which kept the United States' fleets and the British Pacific fleet supplied with everything from aircraft to yeast. Best known of the 'Glens' was *Breconshire*, whose name was a vestige of the old Shire Line. Operating under the white ensign as a naval vessel, *Breconshire*'s contribution was vital to the supply of Malta and she was finally sunk on this service.

The Americans also converted standard ships into 'attack transports' used in the great sweeps across the Pacific archipelagoes, while on a descending scale of size, though perhaps an ascending scale of versatility, both the British and Americans developed a whole legion of landing craft for the assaults on the Pacific islands held by the Japanese as well as

German occupied 'Fortress Europe'. Landing craft were conceived for delivering all the varied hardware required at a beach-head, from tanks to foot soldiers. Others were also built to carry rockets or 4-inch and 4.7-inch guns, expendable 'ships' designed to get in close and soften-up enemy defences at short range with a furious saturation barrage.

The rather glamorous armed merchant cruisers mentioned earlier, were arguably the least successful of adapted Allied merchant ships. The Germans revived a different, though similar technique they had perfected in the Kaiser's War, that of converting nondescript cargo ships to commerce raiders. Nondescript in order that they could, with a little falsification – an added funnel, perhaps or dummy deckhouse to change their profile – deceive other unwary merchantmen to lure them under the concealed guns of the raider. The *Kormoran*, referred to earlier, was one such raider and sailed in December 1940. When she met her nemesis in the November following, she had sent eleven merchant ships to the bottom, totalling some 68,274 tons. The 14-knot raider *Stier* had begun life as the Atlas-Levante Line's *Cairo* and was fitted out with six 5.9-inch guns together with six lighter calibre guns. She also carried two Arado seaplanes and was fitted with torpedo tubes. On Sunday 27 September 1942 she was lying close to the supply ship *Tannenfels* revictualling and painting her hull when the American Liberty ship *Stephen Hopkins* hove in sight. Surprise was mutual, for rain squalls had hidden the ships from each other. The Liberty ship was sailing independently in ballast, from Cape Town to Pernambuco to load a cargo of bauxite for the manufacture of aluminium. At long range the *Stier*'s guns opened fire, as did those of the *Tannenfels*, but the target reduced as the master of *Stephen Hopkins*, Captain Paul Buck, turned her away. Buck returned fire with his 4-inch stern gun, manned by Ensign Willett of the naval Armed Guard. This gunfire was afterwards reported by the Germans to have been from 'six 4.7-inch' guns. Notwithstanding this, the German shells soon had the *Stephen Hopkins* on fire, her boilers hit and her port lifeboats destroyed. A shell blew up the after magazine and Willett was killed, as were successive members of his gun's crew. A cadet fired five rounds before the ammunition was expended, but by this time the ship was settling and Buck ordered her abandoned. Nineteen men got away in the remaining lifeboat under the sole surviving officer, Second Engineer George Cronk. Although four more men died during the passage, the boat made the coast of Brazil near the village of Barra do Itabopoana on 27 October. The American losses amounted to thirty-two of the original forty crew and nine of the fifteen-strong naval Armed Guard. Remarkably the *Stephen Hopkins* did not go unavenged, for Willett's gunfire had fatally combined with that of Second Mate Lyman who had charge of the 37 mm anti-aircraft machine guns. The *Stier* was so damaged that Captain Horst Gerlach was compelled to scuttle her and her survivors returned to Bordeaux aboard the *Tannenfels*. The action was afterwards commemorated by naming a Liberty ship after Captain Buck, and a destroyer escort after Ensign Willett.

The campaign of German surface raiders never became a real threat and was an expensive drain on German resources. As we have seen the *Graf Spee*, potent though she was, was neutralised early in the war and as Allied intelligence and control of shipping improved, raiders lost the initiative, dependent as they were upon the servicing of supply ships such as the *Tannenfels*. Best known of the latter was the *Altmark* which had supported the operations of the *Graf Spee* and aboard which Captain Langsdorff had sent his prisoners back to Germany. After the destruction of the 'pocket battleship', the *Altmark* made her lonely way back to Europe, holing up in a Norwegian fiord into which the then Captain Vian took the destroyer *Cossack*, in defiance of Norwegian neutrality, to rescue the merchant seamen.

HMS *Cossack* was but one destroyer in the Royal Navy's large force of these fast and potent small warships. As we have already observed, the role of the destroyer had undergone almost constant change since its inception as an anti-torpedo boat weapon in the 1890s. By the 1930s, ships like the *Cossack* were operating as fleet destroyers, supporting units of the main battlefleet and providing the anti-torpedo deterrent and the means to deliver the torpedo counterattack. But wars rarely fall out as planned, and few grand actions were to be fought by a British line of battle in the years to come. Additionally, by 1917 the destroyer had been compelled to become the principle anti-submarine weapon, and while she lobbed her depth charges with imprecise enthusiasm in that pre-sonar age, it was clear that her duties as escort to a vulnerable merchant fleet might put taxing demands on these ships.

Despite this, *Cossack* and her fifteen sisters of the *Tribal* class, were unashamedly fleet destroyers, weak in anti-aircraft armament but with a heavy main armament of eight 4.7-inch guns in twin mountings and four 21-inch torpedo tubes. At around 1900 tons displacement, they measured 377.5 feet overall (115 metres), 36.6 feet in the beam (11 metres) with a draught of 13 feet (4 metres). Geared steam turbines gave them a top speed of 36.5 knots and they were regarded as crack ships, which fought a hard war. HMS *Punjabi* was lost when she was struck by the *King George V* in poor visibility; her depth charges exploded as she sank, causing great loss of life, and serious damage to the battleship. The *Cossack*, *Maori*, *Sikh* and *Zulu* all engaged *Bismarck* in the classic manner and of the original sixteen, only four survived the war.

The 1937 *Tribal* class were the outcome of British destroyer design just prior to the outbreak of the war. Large numbers of destroyers had been built in the closing years of the First World War, but the enforced economies thereafter had resulted in most being scrapped and while more were built in the inter-war years, many of these proved inadequate to the subsequent demands put upon them. Fortunately, the British embarked on an ambitious destroyer-building programme in 1936 which continued the practice of naming classes after letters of the alphabet which the *Tribals* had interrupted. Begun again in 1926 with the 'A' class, the first wartime destroyers were the 'O' class which conformed very largely to the 'J', 'K' and 'N' classes laid down after Munich. The 'J's' were essentially more balanced versions of the *Tribals* with shorter hulls, six 4.7-inch guns, similar AA armament and ten torpedo tubes. The major innovation was the strong, longitudinally-framed hull, used thereafter through to the *Battle* class.

At the end of the war it had been realised the fleet destroyer must evolve into a more flexible fleet escort and many of the later 'war emergency' destroyers, from the 'O' class onwards, were converted to frigates. During the war these destroyers remained largely, though not exclusively employed in fleet operations. It was clear that convoy escorts were required urgently and the corvette and later frigate-building programme went some way to answer this demand as did the provision of the fifty 'four-stackers' lent by the United States. However, time was of the essence and various emergency options to provide quick escorts were examined. One expedient solution was the conversion of old First World War 'V' & 'W' class destroyers. These elderly ships were divided into two groups. One of these was the Long Range Escort (LRE), achieved by removing a boiler and fitting extra fuel tanks to increase endurance. Asdic and depth charges were added to make these ships submarine-hunters of some distinction, particularly during the crises in the Battle of the Atlantic. The second conversion programme was started in 1938 to improve anti-aircraft armament for the defence of coastal convoys. Since many of the destroyers taken in hand in this batch had names beginning with 'W', these were known as *Wairs* and it was the *Hunt* class, mentioned earlier, that afterwards augmented them.

The numerous *Hunt* class, successful though they proved, might have been more so, had not a curious mistake been made by the normally punctilious Director of Naval Construction's design office, which failed to notice a self-cancelling error in the calculations. This meant they could not accept the intended armament of three twin 4-inch high-angle guns and a set of triple torpedo tubes. As modified the first batch carried no torpedoes and only two twin gun-mountings. The second batch had a beamier hull, enabling the full gun armament to be carried and the third reverted to two twin guns and had twin torpedoes. Finally, when Thornycroft undertook the building of the fourth batch to their own design, but without staff limitations, they produced a very different ship, with a long forecastle, similar to later frigates, but which could carry the whole designed armament. The small size of the *Hunts* made them hard to modernise and they soon went out of service post-war.

Towards the end of the war the British built a new class of fleet destroyer, the numerous *Battle* class. These ships were much larger than their predecessors, adopting the American practice of enclosing the guns in gun-houses, which hitherto, because of gun shortages, had only been carried out in the sixteen 'L' and 'M' class. Paradoxically, the time taken to manufacture the complex 4.7-inch twin mountings resulted in four destroyers of the 'L' class, and some of the subsequent 'O' and 'P' classes, being fitted with the older 4-inch gun. In the event, these proved their worth in anti-aircraft defence, because the smaller gun could achieve a higher angle of elevation and was found particularly useful in such theatres as the Arctic. The *Battle* class mounted four dual-purpose 4.5-inch guns in two twin turrets forward. Some had a single 4-inch gun fitted abaft the funnel on the insistence of the First Sea Lord, Andrew Cunningham. Its purpose was to fire star-shell so that the forward turrets could load with high-explosive and the last batch had a 4.5-inch in that position. Their displacement varied slightly at around 2350 tons, and their hulls were 379 feet overall (115.5 metres), with a beam of 40.25 feet (12.3 metres), on a draught of 15 feet (4.5 metres). Geared turbines generated 50,000 horsepower and gave them a top speed of 36 knots. In addition to their 4.5-inch guns, they carried eight 21-inch torpedo tubes and a formidable array of anti-aircraft guns, several 40 mm Bofors guns being fitted aft instead of a large calibre gun. This reflected their role of carrier escort, for they were essentially designed to operate in the Pacific, stationing themselves on a carrier's quarter as 'plane-guard' to pick up ditched pilots and to cover the carrier from *kamikaze* attack. Most of the class were not completed until after the war and while some of these handsome ships went on to endure disfigurement in conversion to radar picket ships, most were scrapped. In the end only *Matapan* survived into the 1970s as an experimental sonar ship.

Also converted to radar pickets were the largely aborted *Weapon* class, only four of which were completed. Conceived originally as anti-aircraft destroyers, the end of the war terminated their construction as a numerous class. Three were fitted with the Squid, but *Scorpion* had the more effective 'Limbo' Mk 10. These ships were followed in 1949 by a group of super-destroyers which were almost small, light cruisers and were called the *Daring* class. At 400 feet long and displacing 2600 tons, they should have been capable ships, having absorbed the lessons of a long and arduous war, for they carried ten 21-inch torpedo tubes, the Squid anti-submarine mortar, half-a-dozen Bofors and six 4.5-inch dual purpose guns. These were housed in automatic, radar controlled enclosed twin-turrets, which were to become standard frigate weaponry. But four of the *Darings* experienced trouble with their experimental hydraulic and electrical systems.

After the end of the First World War, the United States moth-balled its superfluous destroyers, from which were drawn the famous fifty four-stackers leased to Britain. Because of this they were late in developing new destroyers, although this proved no disadvantage since their industry was capable of rapid expansion and they were able to build on the lessons learned in a series of classes built in the 1930s. They based new tonnage on the 5-inch dual-purpose gun introduced in the *Farragut* class and the later, heavier armed *Porter* class. High-pressure steam-power plants were fitted in the class named after the great American naval historian and Anglophile, Captain Mahan. The *Mahans* also had heavy torpedo armament, and this was further increased in the succeeding three classes. The 'war standard' design became the very numerous *Fletcher* class which incorporated all these benefits in a hull of 376 feet in length (115 metres), a beam of 40 feet (12 metres) on a draught of 13.75 feet (4.2 metres) and which displaced 2325 tons light and 2924 in full war load. One-hundred-and-seventy-five of these potent 38-knot flush-decked destroyers were built, a contrast to their predecessors. The *Fletchers* were followed by fifty-eight of the *Sumner* class which had three twin 5-inch mountings instead of the five singles of the *Fletchers*, but this additional weight forward made them poor sea-boats, liable to ship heavy seas and subjecting the hulls to excessive strains. This was partly compensated for by lengthening their successors, the *Gearings*, the last American destroyers built during the war. All these classes were designed as fleet destroyers, though they were not exclusively so employed; for escort work the United States Navy constructed 102 new destroyer escorts. These had a much lighter gun armament, some with 3-inch guns and others with two 5-inch guns, and were much slower at 24 knots, but they had a fine anti-submarine capability and were supported by several smaller and lighter classes of patrol and escort vessels.

The Germans also adopted the 5-inch gun as the principal weapon of their destroyers. The *Kriegsmarine* possessed classes of small destroyers which were called torpedo boats, a confusing nomenclature but with which the Allied form of Torpedo, or PT boat should not be confused. These had a 4.1-inch gun and six torpedo tubes and were excellent little ships, perfectly capable of carrying out most of the duties afterwards demanded of their successors.

After Hitler's repudiation of the Treaty of Versailles, the German navy began building a larger type of destroyer very similar to the American concept, also using a 5-inch gun and high-pressure steam plant. These were not a success, for their power-units proved highly unreliable, their stability suspect and although in theory they out-gunned their lighter British opponents, they found themselves outclassed in a seaway. This was bad enough, but later batches adopted an even heavier weapon, the 5.9-inch gun, and when a twin mounting weighing 97 tons was adopted, the problems were exacerbated. The calibre was roughly equivalent to that of a British light cruiser, but when a group of eleven of these destroyers and torpedo boats met two British cruisers, the elderly *Enterprise* and the modern *Glasgow*, they were shot to pieces.

The German ships had sortied to cover the arrival of the *Alsterufer*, a blockade runner at a French Biscay port. The *Alsterufer* was inward bound from the Far East with vital supplies, but a Czech-manned Liberator of RAF Coastal Command sank her, and on the following day, 28 December 1943, the cruisers fell in with the now redundant German escorting force which consisted of the eighth Destroyer Flotilla and fourth Torpedo Boat Flotilla. An attempt to engage the British with a pincer attack failed in heavy weather and in the subsequent fire-fight the destroyer *Z27* and the torpedo boats *T25* and *T26* were sunk.

Although the Second World War produced many other forms of merchantman and warship, the major naval campaigns in the great struggle, centred on the logistical battles without which the offensive actions that finally destroyed the fascist Axis, could never have taken place. But ships are nothing without the crews who man them and give them purpose and life. Of all the combatant forces engaged, the U-boat arm of the German *Kriegsmarine* suffered most; of all the Allies it was, in proportional terms, the merchant seamen of the British Empire and the United States that bore the greatest losses.

Throughout the history of the ship, it has been war that challenges the ingenuity of man, and produces the innovations which are denominated as progress. The added challenge of science, introducing steam power at the beginning of the nineteenth century, gave matters a greater impetus and guaranteed that thereafter war and science would join in an unholy alliance. After 1945, however, the shift of gear into an increasingly faster rate of progress was first to be stimulated by the Cold War, resulting from the ideological and irreconcilable differences of the capitalist West and the Communist world to the east, and by the rise of electronic technology which this extreme form of competition encouraged. When, in 1989, the Russian-dominated Communist world imploded, the exponential nature of the technological revolution was to continue.

It was to affect every walk of human life, and the world of the ship was to undergo a revolution comparable to the coming of steam, but at a pace far outstripping that slow development and with greater consequences for the world of the seaman.

CHAPTER EIGHTEEN

Technology, Turbines and Terror

By the beginning of the twentieth century sail had still not been entirely abandoned, even in the advanced countries of the western hemisphere. Sail continued to dominate the coasting trade, and wooden ketches and topsail schooners still ran themselves up on hard beaches and discharged overside into horse-drawn carts at low water. This was so old a practice that it is from the old English 'merekwearf' that the noun 'wharf' derives. Indeed Mockbeggar Wharf in Liverpool Bay and Redwharf Bay on the coast of Anglesey, still denominate sandy strands upon which loading and discharging once took place.

Those most economical and extraordinarily cost-effective sailing craft, the Thames sailing-barge, were regularly lifting cargoes of up to 200 tons deadweight and distributing them to the ports of the east and south coasts of England and the near-European continent. Scandinavian *galeases* hauled even larger cargoes around the Baltic, and Dutch *kofs* and *aaks* worked the extensive waterways of the Netherlands and her immediate neighbours. Heavily built ketch rigged trawlers hunted the fishing grounds of the North Sea from Lowestoft, while Dutch *tjalks* and *boiers*, Danish *kutters* and German *smacks* also worked the same areas. English smacks and bawleys fished the complex banks of the outer Thames Estuary and farther west Breton tunny ketches ventured into the Bay of Biscay, lines streamed from rods suspended from their heavy main masts. In the Channel, the lugger-rigged *chasse-marée* fished where once she had smuggled or slipped aristocrats escaping the guillotine over to England. Cruising to the westward of Lundy Island, on the lookout for an inward bound merchantman, those magnificent cutters built for the sea-pilots of the Bristol Channel, rode out the worst the Western Ocean could throw at them and were perhaps the finest example of the single-masted sailing ship.

In the Mediterranean Turkish *tchektirmes*, Greek *trekandinis* and *sacolevas*, Italian *navicellos*, Spanish *feluccas* and the *polaccas* and schooners flying several flags, continued the ancient trades of the Middle Sea, while the *dhow* still made her annual voyages between the Persian Gulf, Arabia and the east coast of Africa to Dar-es-Salaam and Zanzibar.

Across the Atlantic one of the most attractive fishing vessels ever built continued to work the line fishery of the Grand Banks, where schooners from Portugal, the first discoverers of the cod on these Atlantic shallows, met those from the New World. The American designs produced yacht-like craft which eventually crossed the boundary between a working ship and a vessel built to race, and made of the type a most elegant and beautiful craft, the last of which was constructed in the early 1920s. Tall masts, long booms, bowsprits, spoon-bows and overhanging counter sterns, gave the schooners of Massachusetts an appearance indistinguishable from custom-built yachts, although their decks were cluttered with the stacks of dories from which individual fishermen laid long-lines for the big cod that swarmed on the Grand Banks in due season.

But can these multifarious craft, echoed across the world in the junks of China or the *lancha chilota* of Chile, be classified as ships? And should they occupy a place in this history? Some were substantial in size, but essentially they remained coasting craft and one is tempted to dismiss them as mere boats. Yet they preserved the traditional skills of the seafarer, skills that had provided the means by which ships had been made to serve the ends of their masters throughout recorded time. A few continue to do so in the remoter corners of the Third World to this day, and they deserve a mention, albeit in passing. While these ancient abilities lingered in the shrinking fleets of deep-water barques, there was another type that attracted interest due to the national rivalry arising from polar exploration, the whaler.

The best-known whaling fleet operated from the New England ports of North America. The sperm whale 'fishery', characterised by Herman Melville in his magnificent novel *Moby Dick*, was carried out by barques working out of New Bedford and sailing to the distant waters of the South Pacific. Harpooning sperm whales in the time honoured manner from small, double-ended boats, they flensed the carcasses and tried-out the oil at sea, casking it and finally bringing it home when the ship was full, which might take three or four years!

In fact an older whale fishery existed and outlasted the Nantucket enterprise of the Starbucks and Ahabs. This was the European Arctic fishery for the Greenland right whale, seeking not merely oil, but the baleen, or 'whalebone' from which a multitude of artefacts, not least the stiffening in *fin-de-siècle* corsetry, were manufactured. Such small ports as Whitby, on the north coast of Yorkshire, and from which James Cook made his early voyages, grew rich on the trade. Whitby became the first town to have street-lighting from whale oil, though the town was later superseded in importance by Hull, and both were finally overshadowed by the Scottish port of Dundee on the River Tay.

It was the Dutch who had first gone north in pursuit of the right whale, so called because it floated after death and was therefore the 'right' whale to hunt. The Dutch pushed up into the Barents Sea to Spitsbergen and beyond, but by the nineteenth century, it was the British who dominated the fishery, braving the hazards of the Arctic. Many whaling commanders made considerable contributions to hydrography, of which the most outstanding must be William Scoresby, who was also one of the most successful whaling captains and, after a distinguished career which saw him elected to the Royal Society, became a parish divine.

By the end of the nineteenth century ships from the Scottish ports of Dundee and Peterhead were working up the Davis Strait and into Baffin Bay, catching seals as well as right whales. In 1903 over 317,000 seals yielded a value of almost £90,000, the oil selling in the United States at £28 per ton. As for whaling, this was equally profitable, baleen fetching £2500 per ton and the oil some £22.5 per ton. Oared whaleboats put off from their mother-ships to harpoon the right whale, exhaust it and finally lance its heart. In this, the right whale was far more docile than the sperm of the South Pacific, though what the northern whalers gained in the submission of their prey, they more than made up for in the hardship of their conditions.

The ships themselves were heavily built wooden barques fitted with auxiliary steam engines, facts that recommended them for polar exploration. The best known of them are the *Terra Nova* and the *Discovery*, both of which made voyages of exploration to the Antarctic and are thus associated with the names of Sir Ernest Shackleton and Captain Robert Falcon Scott. The *Terra Nova* was completely crushed in the southern ice, an event recorded on film, and the *Discovery* may be seen today in her home port of Dundee. Many other whalers were equally remarkable vessels. As late as 1903 the Dundee fleet acquired the *Vega*, built at Bremerhaven thirty years earlier. She had been commanded by Baron Nordensköld between 1878 and 1879, and had made a remarkable transit of the North East Passage, between Norway's North Cape and the Bering Sea across the top of the world. Unhappily that year the *Vega* was beset in the ice off Baffin Bay, becoming crushed so quickly that her crew barely had time to escape with their lives. Her forty-five-strong crew spent six days in the boats before getting ashore. Thereafter some of the crew made a further voyage of 300 miles in their boats before being picked up by the Danish steamer *Nov*, which later landed all hands at Aberdeen. Three other ships were also caught. The *Eclipse* and *Diana* sawed and blasted their way free after seventeen days, while the *Balaena* was beset for seventy days, before she broke through having lost her rudder.

Such ships had a hard tussle with the elements and their rewards reflected this. The *Eclipse* arrived back in Britain with a catch of four whales, thirty-three belugas, a single walrus and thirty-eight polar bears which yielded 49 tons of oil and 3.4 tons of baleen. This suggests a degree of balance between hunter and hunted, although as a sustainable harvest it was to fail by around 1908. In fact the year 1903 was to dramatically alter whaling, for two Norwegian companies had established themselves at stations in the Shetlands and began fishing with small, purpose-built steamers capable of 12 knots and armed with an exploding harpoon gun on their stem heads.

The first of these, the *Spes et Fides*, meaning 'hope and faith', had been ordered in 1862 by Svend Foyn of Tønsberg, a former sea-captain who soon built up a small fleet of the seagoing hunters. With the commercial demise of the right and bowhead whales, Foyn's objective was the fin whale which was not extensively hunted by the old method because the fin, or rorqual, was too quick for oared pursuit and tended to sink when dead. In 1873 Foyn was granted a patent, having overcome the technical problems in catching the rorqual while operating experimentally off the North Cape in the *Spes et Fides*. The industry soon boomed with the arrival of many competitors; 1910 saw the first British whaler built at Smith's Dock on the Tees, a circumstance important to the Royal Navy thirty years later (the first derivative *'Flower'* class corvette, HMS *Gladiolus*, being launched in 1939). Smith's Dock had also built Z-whalers for anti-submarine work in 1916.

Foyn's techniques were formidably successful and it was not long before the stocks of rorqual in Norwegian waters were following the right whale into oblivion. Quarry was sought farther away and by 1908 whaling companies were being established in South Africa. The concept of the shore station was largely abandoned, though they lingered in such remote locations as South Georgia and Deception Island. Instead, a large pelagic factory ship was sent in support of a fleet of catchers. The factory ship could accommodate a large workforce, process and store the reduced whale oil in tanks, and pack the meat. At first redundant liners or converted tankers were used as factories, and it was not until 1920 that the first purpose-built factory ship, the *Ronald*, was constructed, boasting pressure cookers and trying works. The same year aircraft were first used to spot whales off the Cape coast of South Africa.

Technology was now in gear: a steam bone-saw was invented a year later, and in 1922 the stern slipway was introduced, up which the carcasses could be hauled for processing. This was fitted into a number of converted ships, such as the former White Star liner *Athenic* of 1904, which became the Norwegian factory ship *Pelagos*. Two years later a centrifugal separator was developed to clarify the oil at sea where the technique of settling was inappropriate. In 1925 a stern slip was built into the *Lancing* and in 1929 aircraft served at sea from the *Kosmos*. Then, in 1930, the second British factory ship to be called *Sir James Clark Ross*, the first having been a converted cargo ship, was purpose-built with diesel engines to increase her endurance and range. Inventions followed fast and furiously, so that each 'expedition', as a company's annual undertaking was called, was a masterpiece of ingenuity and planning.

The catchers would hunt the whales; upon sighting the fine plume of spray from a blowhole, the skipper would leave the bridge by way of a catwalk which led directly to the bow platform where he would man the Bofors gun mounted there. On closing the whale, he fired a harpoon containing a charge. This exploded once the harpoon had penetrated the whale's body, extending the barbs and, it was hoped, killing the victim outright. Hauled alongside by means of the harpoon-line, the corpse was filled with compressed air and marked. Having completed their hunting the catchers would tow their collected prizes back to the factory ship where they were hauled up the stern slip by means of a great steel scissor-claw onto the deck. There the dead whale was flensed, butchered and processed to produce meat and oil. Hydrogenation, perfected in 1929, enabled the quality of the oil to be maintained so it could be used not only in such end products as soap, but in edible commodities such as margarine. Waste solids were no longer dumped but dried and stored for sale as *ersatz guano*.

After the Second World War the technology which had brought about the defeat of the U-boats, was now turned upon the cetaceans. Many now redundant corvettes, particularly ex-Canadian ships, were converted at Howaldtswerke in Hamburg or Kiel to become catchers or to be used to round up the marked whales and tow them to the factory ship. Amphibious Walrus aircraft, which had been the spotters for many a British cruiser, were stowed on the sterns of giant factory ships like the *Balaena*, to be craned overside when required to take off. Later, experiments were carried out from the *Olympic Challenger* using a helicopter.

But more significant were the properties of asdic, now universally known by the more appropriate American acronym 'sonar'. Although sonar was to transform all forms of fishing with dire consequences in due course, post-war whaling was to enjoy a boom; but it was to be short-lived, terminal and to become politically significant.

By the early 1960s the stocks of whales world-wide had become so reduced that the operations of most Norwegian and all the British companies involved were wound up. Whaling had always been a gamble, and diversification was the name of the game if survival was to be achieved. Dutch, American and German interests also pulled out, leaving the Japanese, for whom the taste for whale meat had become addictive, to continue decimating the remaining cetacean population for 'scientific purposes', and the Russians to continue fishing under their utterly corrupt 'managed economy'. Since the collapse of the Soviet system in the early 1990s, only the Japanese remain as a serious threat to the whale, while many small ships, including ancient former whalers, have now changed the colour of their coat and joined the conservation movement for whom the whale, as the earth's largest mammal and therefore a distant relative of man, has become an icon.

The human race feels less sympathy for the cold-blooded fish. At the beginning of the twentieth century, when we hunted under sail, there was some sort of equilibrium. Even when the small steam plant was fitted to drifters and trawlers, the ardour and hardships of the fisheries, the dangers and losses, particularly of iced-up and top-heavy trawlers cod-fishing in the polar seas, conferred upon the trade the spice and risk of danger.

Technology has put an end to this romantic notion. In fact technology has for a long time played an important part in fishing, where preservation of the catch is an overriding consideration in the economics of the industry. From early times, drying ashore, or salting down prior to shipping to market, were the only means of bringing home a catch from distant waters. Offshore fisheries often relied upon a fish-well, a hold open to the sea, in which the nets were emptied and the fish allowed to live until landed. Species such as prawns and shrimps were cooked on board and landed ready for sale.

About 1845 ice came into use, initially produced from fresh-water ponds and held underground until needed. Then, about 1870, it was shipped from Scandinavia to ports such as Hull, to be loaded into the holds of trawlers. Twenty years later Hull was producing its own ice, about 50 tons daily. The provision of ice allowed vessels to work the fishing grounds and transfer their ice-packed catches at sea to faster carriers which raced to the nearest railhead and then sent the fish onwards to Billingsgate market in London. This system allowed the big sailing trawlers to work farther and farther away, pushing up towards the Barents Sea in the wake of the whalers, where the eutrophic waters of the Arctic yielded a mighty harvest.

Steam, which rendered redundant wind-driven ships and allowed powerful trawlers to scrape the sea-bed bare, began operating about 1880. An enterprising tug owner named William Purdy, whose paddle tugs regularly hauled groups of sailing trawlers out to sea, came up with the idea of using the tug itself for fishing. In 1877 Purdy's *Messenger* left the River Tyne, bound for the grounds. Though successful in principle, the tug's paddles proved to be vulnerable and a nuisance, so the screw was quickly adopted and steam was embraced enthusiastically elsewhere, soon being fitted into existing wooden smacks and ketches. Donkey boilers provided steam for trawl winches and capstans about the same time, and in 1881, Earle's of Hull built the iron trawler *Zodiac* for owners across the River Humber in Grimsby. Steam-powered fishing vessels could venture further and within a quarter of a century had penetrated the White Sea.

Methodology differed little from that employed under sail; the tapering trawl was held open laterally by trawl doors which spread under the dynamics of the warps; the lower mouth of the net rolled along the bottom on heavy iron bobbins, while the upper edge, slightly in advance of the lower, was suspended by submerged, but buoyant floats. The fish were collected in the 'cod-end', and to recover the net the trawler turned across the wind and hauled it up to the steel-arched gallows. These were fitted on the starboard side, where the drag of the trawl countered the torque of the conventional, clockwise rotating propeller. The net was pulled inboard, and the narrow cod-end was lifted over the fishpounds by a tackle from the main mast, on which a steadying trysail might also be spread. The catch then cascaded into the pounds, where it was held prior to gutting and packing in ice in the hold. Once empty, the trawl was 'shot' again, over the lee beam, before the trawler resumed her course with the net towing astern.

The distant water trawler was soon established with a design somewhat different from the flush-decked sailing vessel she had replaced. Engines, casing and bridge and bunkers were aft, with the accommodation for her skipper, mates and engineers. Here too, was a mizen mast to spread a steadying sail. Forward the fish-hold and ice-room lay beneath the low waist, the deck of which was open, but for the massive trawl winch just forward of the wheelhouse and the wooden cleadings of the fish-pounds. Forward the deck reared sharply upwards, broken by a companionway to the dark and foetid 'fo'c's'le', the crew's accommodation, and the stores. This area, the forecastle proper, was formed into a turtleback or whaleback, so that this, combined with high forward sheer and tremendous flare to the bow, not only gave the 100- to 200-feet hull wonderful sea-keeping qualities, but protected the labouring crew as they toiled in icy winds to clean and stow the catch. This was the configuration that endured the transition from coal- to oil-fired boilers, and from steam to diesel. Such were the side-winding trawlers that worked the North, Norwegian, Barents and White Seas, distinguishable from the long liners by their heavy gallows.

The discharge of the catch into carriers at sea known as 'fleeting' was accomplished by small, two-man boarding boats, the capsizing of which was commonplace and often accompanied by drownings. Such conditions and working practices made the life of the fisherman extremely hard and they endured dreadful conditions for the often small consolation of bounty. But occasionally their skipper struck lucky and the popularity and reputation of a skipper depended upon his skill and expertise in first finding, and then netting, a good catch. Occasionally these men made huge sums of money, but the economy of fishing under the red ensign was almost always boom and bust.

The diesel engine fitted easily into small sailing craft and many of them enjoyed a long life. Indeed, like the Grand Banks schooner, Brixham owners were building their handsome, if heavy trawlers up until the 1920s. But the economy of the diesel recommended itself to distant water fishing and was exploited by the French, Portuguese and Spanish vessels sent to fish the Grand Banks. The French also pioneered the use of refrigeration using brine, but it was Britain, in the grip of post-war austerity and desperate for cheap alternative sources of food to feed her population, who produced the next major innovation.

Following experiments with a former *Algerine* class minesweeper renamed the *Fairfree* and which was fitted with refrigeration plant and stern slipway, Christian Salvesen's of Leith, built a new type of trawler which hauled its net up a stern-ramp. It was not entirely a crib from whaling, for catches were dragged over the stern in tuna clippers, and Syrian and American 'stern-draggers'. By about 1950 the German fish-filleting machine invented by Rudolf Baader and the multi-plate freezing equipment which processed fillets in large quantities had been developed by the American Clarence Birdseye in the ˙ˈ920s in association with the United States Bureau of Fisheries. A combination of these developments was to produce the factory ship mentioned earlier.

In 1954 John Lewis of Aberdeen launched the 2605 gross registered ton *Fairtry* for Christian Salvesen. She was 280 feet overall (85.3 metres) and with a crew of forty she was able to garner a large catch, process it on the grounds to preserve its freshness, and did so by shooting and hauling her trawl over the stern. Not only was this method safer, it could be done in heavier weather and was fully mechanised. *Fairtry* and her sisters, *Fairtry II* and *Fairtry III* all proved their ability to produce fillets from the rich cod of the Grand Banks before opening competition in the traditional British fishing areas. But too much capital was already invested in the traditional ships, and moreover trawler owners had their own tradition of putting profit before investment in the future. This intransigence was to signal the death knell of British fishing, though the throes were to be prolonged and agonizing.

During the 1930s the Japanese began an ambitious fishing industry, having learned much from the Cardiff-based British firm of Neale and West. Japanese owners had continued to follow developments in Europe and America and, along with the Russians and Germans, began to build their own stern trawling factory ships, beginning with the *Umitaka Maru* of 1956. The Russians used Lewis's plans to produce their two dozen *Pushkin* class ships and thereafter every Communist country of the Comecon group followed suit. Such ships not only fished on their own account, but grew larger and supported fleets of conventional trawlers, an extension of the 'fleeting' method and many innovative ideas were tried as a consequence. Voith–Schneider propulsion was fitted to a West German factory ship, the *Heinrich Meins* in 1957 and although it was afterwards removed on account of its complexity, the *Heinrich Meins* remained a whole-fish freezing ship, not reducing the fish to fillets. Another West German ship, the *Sagitta* of 1958, used a gas turbine plant.

Derivatives of the *Fairtry* were everywhere, built and operated by Japan, East and West Germany, Poland, Romania, Spain, France, Iceland and Belgium. It was not until 1961 that British owners ordered one, the *Lord Nelson,* a patriotic enough name, though the ship was built in West Germany. There followed the *Junella*, built for Marr's of Fleetwood, whereupon other operators followed suit, some building at home, some abroad in Poland or East Germany where new building was cheap.

To the inventory of gear the *Fairtry* experiments had also added the 'variable-depth' or 'pelagic trawl', which caught fish swimming in the mid-water layers of the sea. Trawlers equipped with this became so numerous and so efficient that in a comparatively short period their impact on fish stocks was catastrophic. The Comecon countries were indiscriminate in their catches, fishing as much for fertiliser as food, and efforts to conserve stocks were largely futile. Ironically, the replenishment of the piscean population by the enforced moratorium of the Second World War was thus squandered.

National fishing rights became increasingly jealously guarded. When the government of Iceland extended exclusive national fishing rights to 200 miles offshore, Britain tried to claim her traditional access to Icelandic waters. After some unpleasant and dangerous incidents in which the Icelandic Coastguard cut the trawl warps of British trawlers, the Royal Navy's sophisticated frigates confronted the Icelandic Coastguard's robust gunboats in what were called the two 'Cod Wars'.

British vessels were finally compelled to fish farther away and the loss of one, the *Gaul,* fostered rumours of her being spirited away by the Soviets for espionage, though a more plausible alternative was that she had foundered in heavy weather, possibly still fishing when she should have been hove-to. Some economic pressures are ineluctable. In the face of a spirited outcry led by fishermens' wives, the British government of the day commissioned a mother-ship to keep watch over the distant water fleet. The *Miranda* was sent north under the command of a retired naval officer and the auspices of Her Majesty's Coast Guard. Her presence was not wanted for long.

Elsewhere feelings ran high and incidents became common, even among member nations of the new European Union. Overcapacity compelled governments to pay owners to lay up

fishing vessels of all classes and many splendid trawlers ended
their useful lives in odd employments, such as research vessels,
seismic surveying ships, or guardships, watching over
engineering works in the English Channel, or as navigational
training ships for the Royal Navy itself.

The efficiency of these ships was only partly attributable to
improved size and method as, it also owed much to electronics,
as we shall discuss later, but although the problem of over-fishing
spread world-wide, trawling and long-lining were not the only
methods used. For many years mid-water fishing was done by
the passive technique known as drifting. A drifter streamed up to
2 miles of vertically hanging nets from floats known as 'buffs',
lay at the leeward end of this barrier and awaited her quarry, the
once immensely popular herring. This method was ended by the
pelagic, or mid-water trawl developed originally by the Dane
Robert Larsen. Larsen's net required a two-boat operation and
was used to catch the huge shoals of 'silver darlings' that
swarmed in season in the North Sea. The Germans reduced the
number of towing vessels to one, fitted with a stern slipway.
Combined with electronic fish-finding by echo-location, speed
and warp-length were varied to target a shoal and simply
engulf it.

Another highly successful two-boat method, universally
employed from a vast variety of craft world-wide, is the purse
seine net. This consists of a central bag with side walls; along the
foot of the net runs a purse line which when drawn, closes the
net. Purse seines can be enormous, around 300 feet in depth and
up to 3000 feet long, with some examples used in the Pacific
reaching depths of 900 feet. Purse-seining was originally
introduced in the 1880s by the Swedes as a means of catching
herring, but by 1904 the Californians were using it to catch tuna.
The purse seine is shot by a single boat which then steams round
in a half-circle to close the purse; other variants are the two-boat
Spanish 'pareja' or American 'menhaden' systems which operate
in a similar manner to entrap the fishes. The efficiency of the
Spanish method, in which the trawlers may work up to half a
mile apart and tow for ten hours before hauling, is stunning.
Catches of 180 tons are not unknown, and these are large enough
to deplete a whole ground, netting gravid fish, spawn, juveniles

and mature males. So great was the glut of fish lifted in a single haul that the sheer mass of the catch posed the next technical obstacle. Net winches helped, but the hydraulic-powered Puretic block, invented by Mario Puretic in 1953, enabled huge curtain purses to be deployed, the destructive power of which is awesome and indiscriminate. This is a far cry from the rod and line method, most elegantly exemplified by the lovely ketch-rigged Breton tunnyman.

Not only herring and tuna, but pilchard, sardine and mackerel can be caught by these methods, though the fishing craft employed are often boats rather than ships. Progress, insofar as fishing is concerned, has been akin to whaling and largely self-defeating. Greed has been the chief dynamic of change, perhaps best expressed by the adoption of the term 'klondyking', neatly summarising the most speculative form of fishing, that of the indigenous boats of a fishing ground catching, then selling on to foreign factory ships anchored in the fishermen's home waters. Factory ships from the former eastern bloc countries may still be seen in many remote western British bays, loading the catches of local boats, and it is almost impossible to police such a system. The point is fast approaching where neither pelagic nor demersal species will exist in sufficient quantities to justify the complex hunt for them, for they can no longer evade the huntsmen.

Once upon a time the location of fish relied upon a skipper's knowledge and experience. Secrets as to the exact whereabouts of lush grounds were guarded and radio-chat between trawlers working the grey waters of the polar seas would be spiced with untruths as these masters of dissembling bemoaned their uselessness at finding fish, while their crews hauled nets bursting with a gleaming catch over the rail or up the stern ramps. This was as much a part of the pitting of wills and skills as any other factor governing the industry. The explosion of electronic technology that swept the world after the Second World War was to render these traditional skills obsolete.

The echo-sounder and asdic relied upon timing the period in which it took a radiated sonic wave to reach and return from a contact, knowing the speed of sound in water. Although this is not an absolute constant, varying according to temperature, interpretation of sonic returns by a skilled operator increased the capability of what became universally known as sonar to be used effectively to search for fish. Given the directional control of a manipulable transponder/transceiver, bearing could be added to range and with a cathode ray tube display, this information could be represented visually. This removed much of the mystique which had formerly clung to the person of a grizzled fishing skipper, and transferred it to the expertise of a sonar operator. Technology, by its very precision, is the destroyer of that unquantifiable commodity, experience.

The transmission of sonic waves from an oscillator to determine short-range distance and direction under water was complemented and overtaken by the electronic emissions of high-frequency radiation in air. Originally designed as land-based early air warning for the detection of bombing raids on Britain, radar was to have a tremendous impact on the marine world, both as a weapon of detection, and thereafter gunnery and missile direction, but also as an anti-collision device and a navigational aid.

As early as 1901, Guglielmo Marconi had succeeded in transmitting a radio signal across the Atlantic. Wireless telegraphy using the Morse code had obvious applications both for naval and merchant shipping and during the Second World War very high frequencies were used for low range voice transmissions for the tactical control of, for instance, convoy escorts. By 1960 such VHF radio systems were common on merchant ships and used for port control, dispensing with flags and complex Morse messages, although these continued in use for long-range contacts.

Prior to the war, radio propagation was also used for navigation by establishing radio beacons which transmitted on advertised frequencies in the 250–420 kHz band. The first Bellini–Tosii aerial for radio-location was fitted to the Cunard Line's *Mauretania* in 1911, the year before her White Star rival *Titanic* transmitted her infamous distress message by wireless telegraphy (though it was not then SOS). Rough bearings could be obtained up to 200 miles away from the transmitting station, a great help particularly on the North Atlantic run where frequent prolonged overcast rendered the use of the sextant and chronometer impossible. However, this lack of real long range was addressed by the Consol system which could be used up to

1000 miles from a transmitter, although it was awkward to use and considered inferior to the long-range navigation system known as Loran developed in the United States in 1943. Loran shore stations generated low frequency signals available up to around 700 miles by day and around twice that distance at night due to the augmentation of sky-wave reflections. A ship's receiver measured the elapsed time between the origin and reception of a signal by displaying a time-base on a cathode ray tube and this was then laid on a charted hyperbolic lattice based on the time-base in microseconds. Several such hyperbolic position lines gave a fix, but the installation was expensive and tended to be more common in naval vessels.

A simpler hyperbolic system, though useable only in coastal waters was also developed in the Second World War. Intended for accurate bombing, the 'Gee' method used hyperbolae to plot the coincidence of phase-comparison of signals transmitted from a master and up to three slave stations. This system was abandoned by the Americans and was marketed by the Decca company with successive upgradings in sophistication. It remains, until the end of the century, the commonest and cheapest form of radio-navigation, eclipsing the radio-beacon system. The flooding of Western markets by receivers undermined the Decca company's monopoly and in the early 1990s, lighthouse authorities took over responsibility for maintaining the stations and providing the service.

So much for fixing a ship's position other than by observing cross bearings from land, or essentially doing the same offshore by the solution of a series of astronomical triangles by sextant and chronometer. But what of a ship's course, the direction she must head to reach her destination? For years this had been accomplished by the magnetic compass, subject as it was to the variation induced by the earth's inconstant magnetic field, and the deviations provided by the ship herself, an ever-changing value in respect of the course itself and because of alterations due to the movement of derricks or a magnetic cargo. A greater accuracy with far fewer errors, and hence corrections, was achieved by the use of the gyroscopic compass. This device relied upon the properties of the gyroscope, invented by the Frenchman, Jean Foucault who, in 1852, discovered that an iron wheel rotating at high speed within a system of gimbals which allowed its axis to assume any direction, would resist a considerable force before its axis would submit to change. If the axis was first aligned with a fixed star, such as Polaris, the gyroscope became a compass, maintaining alignment with the true meridian.

The first proper gyrocompass was developed in 1908 by a German engineer, Dr Anschutz. Three years later the American Elmer Sperry patented his version, with the British engineer S. G. Brown following suit in 1916. Slow though these expensive instruments were to be introduced to merchant ships, the properties of the gyroscope did not go ignored by scientists working on gunnery control. In addition to gunnery, a gyro-compass could also be used to control an electronic device linked to a ship's telemotor, the hydraulic transmissions of which moved her steering gear and hence the rudder. Shipowners quickly realised that just as, among other economic advantages, the diesel engine had disposed of that fractious fellow, the ship's fireman, the automatic steering gear made the helmsman equally redundant.

It was radar that enabled 'interfacing' to make its first impact on the maritime world. Radio detection, that is the obtaining of an electronic echo from an obstruction athwart the transmission, first began to be mooted as a theory as early as 1903 by a Herr Hulsmeyer of Germany. Marconi also saw its possibilities and the idea began to receive serious attention. Early sets were built and fitted in a number of ships, and the German *panzerschiff Admiral Graf Spee* had a gunnery set installed in 1936. The French liner *Normandie* was also equipped with a pioneer radar, but all results were disappointing, ranges being limited to a mere five miles. But then, in 1940, British scientists invented the magnetron which produced short wavelengths in ship-borne sets. By 1943, wavelengths of less than 2 centi-metres enabled U-boats, evading sonar detection by lying on the surface, to be picked up and displayed on the cathode ray tube 'screens'.

In the post-war period, simple surface radars became commonplace in ships of all classes, initially as anti-collision devices which were believed to have 'defeated' fog. Unfortunately a spate of 'radar-assisted' collisions resulted. These were caused by misunderstanding the data derived from the instrument which were concerned with relative motion. The most notorious of these was the terrible collision of the Swedish liner *Stockholm* and the Italian liner *Andrea Doria*, which occurred off New York in 1956.

By 1960 the gyro-stabilised true-motion radar displayed information on the 'plan-position indicator' which was a true plot of actual events in real-time, and twenty-five years later not only coloured daylight viewing was possible, but a standard merchant ship's radar could automatically plot up to twenty 'targets' and analyse their course, speed, closest point of approach and the time at which that would, or had occurred. With this level of sophistication available to merchant ships, the equipment fitted to warships was of a far greater order of accuracy and versatility. Interfacing gyroscopic directional control, radar or sonar detection and location (combining range, bearing and elevation or depression) with data processing by computer, enabled very accurate target information to be provided to gun, missile or torpedo control systems.

By the last decade of the twentieth century both the Americans and the Soviet Russians had launched artificial constellations of satellites which could not only receive and retransmit voice telephone messages and data across the globe, but could give positional information through the Global Positioning System up to the accuracy of plus or minus a few metres. This staggering level of locational detail introduced a whole new argument as to what the exact form the terrestrial spheroid, or geoid, actually took, and exactly where upon it, a place or person actually was. Nevertheless, whilst hydrographic experts and geomancers could split hairs to the thickness of infinity, a humble yachtsman could determine his position to something approaching a boat's length on a battery-powered device the size of a packet of cigars which cost him a week's wage! But a danger lurked amid this mind-numbing accuracy: the system could be degraded at the whim of the United States Department of Defense, for whom it was in itself a weapons component; it was not only radar that had changed warships.

After 1945 the old classifications of warships were swept away. While the terms destroyer, frigate, aircraft carrier and cruiser remained, these were increasingly qualified by abbreviations denoting role, while the escalating costs of quite modest ships meant that classes were often sub-divided into batches, some with a different armament. Bulk building was no longer possible, so small groups of almost experimental ships were built, each marginally improving on its predecessor as the acceleration of technology raced ahead in yet another arms race, fuelled by the Cold War.

While the aircraft carrier remains a potent and important capital ship, able to extend diplomacy by more forceful means, and was the backbone of the bushfire conflicts in the Falklands and the Persian Gulf, it has been the nuclear submarine which has had the greater if more subtle influence on the world's political calculations and the development of naval strategies.

It was clear in the aftermath of 1945 that German U-boats had almost succeeded in their sinister task. It was also acknowledged that in the Walther boats and the later 'electro' U-boat types, particularly the type XXI, the Germans were well in advance of the Allies. Both the British and the Americans experimented post-war on the backs of German developments. In 1948 the United States Navy launched the Greater Underwater Propulsive Power programme, which rejoiced in the acronym GUPPY. Both navies built submarines to exploit the possibilities of hydrogen peroxide which, it was assumed, would produce a closed-circuit system capable of high speed. Dr Helmut Walther's concept was dangerous, but seemed to offer the potential for improvement. The hull designed for his power plant was more successful and, abandoning the hydrogen peroxide unit, proved very fast when fitted with more powerful electric motors supported by additional batteries stowed in the larger and more streamlined hull.

It was these twin concepts that kick-started the GUPPY programme and the British experiments. As mentioned in Chapter Fifteen, the Royal Navy ordered HMSs *Explorer* and *Excalibur*, but these two boats were never one hundred per cent reliable, being known to their crews as 'Exploder' and 'Excruciator'. Their only achievement, beyond proving the folly of pursuing the Walther idea, was to serve as fast targets for training purposes. Nevertheless the German Type XXI 'electro-U-boats' which had appeared in the closing days of the war were capable of under-water speeds of around 16 knots, and the GUPPY programme initially concentrated on streamlining existing submarines and developing the fast battery submarine.

Some fifty boats were converted by the Americans and achieved speeds in excess of the Type XXIs, but although improved battery performance was achieved, it was at a price. In the event this, and the high cost of peroxide, which the British were still futilely trying to reduce, damned both concepts. It was clear that the only realistic way forward was to develop a plant that did not need oxygen at all. Thoughts reverted to steam, although this time the steam would be raised from water by the heat of a nuclear core and passed into a steam turbine from which it was to be re-circulated.

The United States Navy and the Westinghouse corporation were tasked to produce prototype reactors to power submarines. The project was overseen by Hyman G. Rickover, then a captain, later an admiral. Rickover's team selected the pressurised water reactor (PWR) as being small enough to fit into a submarine. The PWR had other advantages. Although water does become radioactive, the half-life of the hydrogen isotope is short enough to avoid major problems, so only the reactor area needed heavy lead shielding, and boiler and turbine were therefore accessible when under way. The water within the reactor was pressurised so that it did not actually boil within the reactor itself; moreover water served both to carry away heat and to provide the moderation for fusion control. The system was extremely stable provided the waterflow through the reactor was maintained. Thus a temperature rise slowed reaction and the temperature fell back, whereas a cooling produced more effective moderation, the reaction became more efficient and the temperature rose again. In fact the only drawbacks were the working temperatures and pressures available for the turbines, which compelled Rickover to revert to turbine technology abandoned in the 1930s.

No matter, Rickover and his team pressed on. The United States Navy began building a hull based upon the Type XXI, to accommodate the Westinghouse power plant. The result, the USS *Nautilus* was launched in January 1954 and twelve months later, on 17 January 1955, her commander, Bill Anderson, signalled 'underway on nuclear power'. Although her turbines fell short of delivering the designed 15,000 shaft horsepower, and thus failed to exceed the speed of the fastest Walther boats, they reached around 13,200, and *Nautilus* achieved underwater speeds of about 23 knots. But her great advantages lay in her complete submersibility and her endurance which, according to Anderson, was 'as long as the groceries lasted'. In August 1958, *Nautilus* made a passage from Honolulu to Portland, passing under the North Pole and in her first two-year commission she steamed 62,562 miles. Following refuelling with a new uranium core, she ran for 91,234 miles on her second, and 150,000 on her third core. Handling his 'boat', Anderson said, made him feel he 'owned the ocean'. Unfortunately he was not the only one who wished to do so.

The British nurtured ambitions to own a nuclear submarine fleet and having made a false start by making the mistake of selecting gas-cooling, as used in their early power stations, only to discover it was too large for a submarine, they then diverted resources to the production of electricity for civil use. Eventually they took delivery of a pressurised water reactor as fitted in the American *Skipjack* class attack submarines. The *Skipjack* was a larger production boat which followed the *Skate* class, the first slower production American nuclear powered submarines. The *Skipjacks* were tear-drop shaped and capable of 29 knots, their after hull form dictated by the single screw arrangement.

The acquisition of the nuclear plant from Washington was an arrangement largely attributable to Earl Mountbatten, then Chief of the Defence Staff. It was said to have been a quid-pro-quo for raft-mounting machinery, a device developed by the British to reduce noise and thus avoid detection, a fault inherent in the early US nuclear boats. By marrying the power-unit with its *Skipjack*-like stern section to a home-built steam propulsion plant, the Royal Navy obtained its first nuclear attack, or hunter-killer, fleet submarine. She was commissioned on 17 April 1963 as HMS *Dreadnought*.

The British are the only nation to benefit from American nuclear submarine technology, though abortive negotiations were opened with the Canadians and the Dutch. The French developed their own independent programme for building nuclear submarines, though they are fundamentally different. Their plant is smaller and noisier than that in the Anglo-American boats. But while the French and British were signatories to the North Atlantic Treaty Organisation, there was another pretender to the ownership of the ocean who was not.

*

The Soviet Russians gave the Americans a very nasty surprise.

Admiral Rickover had been meticulous in guiding his programme through its development phases, ever mindful of the welfare of his sailors; in the event, the emphasis upon the power-unit's safety distracted effort from the absolutes of speed and power. No such reservations were laid upon the Soviet Russians.

Under the impetus of Stalinism and with scant regard for the sanctity of human life, the Russians were able to make rapid advances. While Russian nuclear technology was cruder, the same could not be said for their hull design. The Project 627 hull was, like the *Skipjack*, tear-drop shaped, a blunt bulb tapering to a fine stern, but with twin reactors giving very high underwater speed of 30 knots which, with the ability to dive to 1000 feet, set new standards in operating norms. The sustainability of high, underwater speeds is a characteristic unique to nuclear boats and, for a long while even the Americans reckoned their vulnerable nuclear-powered aircraft carriers were immune to the submarine on account of *their* high speed. But Project 627, code-named *November* by NATO, could outrun many conventional surface warships and in 1968 a *November* class boat intercepted the mighty carrier USS *Enterprise* on passage to Vietnam. Thus, although not launching *K3*, the first of the class until 1958, the Russians immediately established themselves as highly viable competitors to the Americans and Leonid Ossipenko was soon one of an increasing number of captains in command of very fast Russian attack submarines.

Russian xenophobia had led to the Soviet Union building vast numbers of submarines, some of them conventionally powered. Obsession with the concept of submarine-launched missiles, the first of which had been fired from a Soviet boat in September 1955, led the then Russian leader Nikita Khrushchev to order a fast attack submarine intended to hunt and torpedo a Western submarine which might be so armed. In fact the first American submarine capable of firing ballistic missiles was USS *George Washington*, a modified *Skipjack* design which launched her first pair of Polaris missiles off Cape Canaveral on 20 July 1960.

The result of Krushchev's initiative was two-fold. On the one hand a class of boat code-named '*Alfa*' was developed. These attack submarines were intended to remain in port until targeted onto a threat when they would make a high speed dash to annihilate the enemy before the enemy annihilated Mother Russia. Small and with a light, strong, titanium hull, and a potent liquid-metal reactor, the six '*Alfas*' were capable of an incredible 43 knots, but US missile ranges increased so the '*Alfas*' would not be able to intercept in time and so these very expensive boats became obsolete. On the other hand, however, the Soviets possessed the ability to launch intermediate-range ballistic missiles from conventional, diesel-electric submarines by 1956, and three years later the Red Navy had also armed itself with an intercontinental weapon (ICBM). Nevertheless, the Soviet navy's role was conceived to be defence against Western attack and the destruction of carrier-led battle groups which might threaten Russian interests. Emphasis was therefore placed upon ship-to-ship missiles and nuclear boats, code-named the *Yankee* class, were built to deliver up to sixteen of these.

After several shifts in policy in the Kremlin, Russian capability to launch strategic ICBMs from submarines was re-established and escalated through several different stages in step with the American programme. The American reaction was to increase effort put into submarine-launched ICBMs. These ultimately went into production as the Polaris which, in its A-1 configuration, had a range of 1200 miles. To deliver these, President Kennedy ordered five modified *Skipjack*-type boats as ballistic missile-armed nuclear submarines (SSBNS). Between 1959 and 1961 these craft, each armed with sixteen nuclear missiles, were capable of concealing themselves anywhere in the depths of the ocean, the only criterion governing their position being the ability to reach targets in the territory of Soviet Russia or her allies.

One of the multitude of technical problems required to sustain the strategic advantage of such a weapon was that of navigation. Just as the power-unit finally selected for the perfect sub-marine capital ship had to be self-sustaining, so had its navigation system. While a submarine could surface to determine its position, neither the opportunity, nor the accuracy obtainable by this method recommended it to the strategists planning nuclear deterrence. The system finally developed and by which Anderson took the *Nautilus* beneath the pole, was SINS, meaning Ship's Inertial Navigation System. This was a complex self-contained machine capable of measuring movement and giving a constant indication of position without external reference. Inertial systems are stabilised in space and use the properties inherent in gyroscopes and accelerometers to detect movement in a horizontal plane on the two axes, east/west and north/south. A mechanical unit comprises a platform which supports the accelerometers, stabilised by three, single degree of freedom gyroscopes. This compensates for the earth's rotation, and the submarine's roll, pitch and yaw, all of which are minimised underwater at speed. Electronically controlled servo-motors interconnect these components and at equilibrium the axes of the platform lie parallel to the axes of the earth. The system also requires a true vertical and the angle subtended by the axis parallel to the earth's north/south axis and the true vertical equals the instrument's latitude, thus, from an initial condition at a known position, change in position over the earth's surface will disturb the accelerometers in either or both the north/south or east/west axes and planes. While the north/south reference provides difference in latitude, and the east/west reference shift in that plane, longitude is found by converting this shift to a difference of longitude with reference to the accurate knowledge of latitude. By integrating both references, distance, course and speed can be computed and displayed. Essentially the system measures displacement on the earth's surface in terms of shifts in northing and southing, and easting and westing. This provides the navigator with his current position, together with immediate data of progress. A SINS is a highly accurate reversal of the old traverse table, which sought to determine position by adding the progressive data. But the data obtained from a SINS is in real time and related to the terrestrial spheroid with a staggering accuracy. It is true that this data degraded over a long period of time with an accumulation of minuscule errors, but it can be corrected and updated by observations in a series of inertial crutches, and a hybrid system can resolve these discrepancies quite easily.

Such expense is only undertaken when driven by political and strategic imperatives and the American nuclear threat was soon countered by the Soviet Union. The world entered the age of aptly named MAD strategy, Mutually Assured Destruction, the consequences of which are too appalling to contemplate with anything other than the equanimity of the desensitised military mind. In its ability to annihilate the human race, the capital ship has come a long way from being an expression of monarchical power.

Polaris was seen as a 'second-strike' weapon, deterring a pre-emptive strike because it was itself immune from such an attack. It was conceived therefore as insurance against just such an event. In due course, submarine-launched ICBMs again increased their range with the Poseidon missile and this is now superseded by the Trident D5, a potent weapon with a range of 6000 miles. To launch the Trident a new generation of nuclear submarine was required and this was the *Ohio* class, first launched in 1979 and capable of launching twenty-four Tridents. *Ohio*'s huge hull, displacing 16,000 tonnes surfaced and 18,000 tonnes submerged, is 560 feet long (170 metres) with a beam/diameter of 42 feet (12.8 metres). In addition to her missiles, the *Ohio* carries 21-inch torpedoes for self-defence.

The British *Resolution* class of four nuclear-powered ballistic missile submarines were launched between 1966 and 1968 to carry Polaris A3 missiles. These have now been replaced by the Trident-armed *Vanguard* class, which are seventy feet shorter than the American *Ohios*, being armed with eight fewer Tridents. But the most awesome of all these craft are the 25,000-tonne Russian *Typhoon* class, so code-named by the West. They are unusual in carrying their twenty SS-N-20 ICBMs forward of the sail, a configuration making updating and rearming much simpler and cheaper than the conventional layout. It is known that six of these monstrous 'boats' were being completed as the Soviet system itself collapsed. Of similar length to the *Ohios*, their diameter is almost double, at 75 feet (12.8 metres), while their speed of 25 knots is not very different.

Advanced sonars obviate the use of periscopes, nuclear power does away with vast indraughts of air through snorkels, and carbon-dioxide scrubbers quickly restores air quality. While the groceries last such euphemistically named 'boats' have become true underwater, sub-marine ships, able to operate submerged away from their base for months at a time.

Nuclear power confers on warships the extreme flexibility once enjoyed by the sailing man-of-war, based solely upon the limitations of crew endurance. Admiral Rickover's dream was to produce an all-nuclear United States Navy and a formidable arsenal of aircraft carriers and cruisers using the plant have been added to the Department of Defense's quiver. Almost unlimited range, high speed and endurance gives a nuclear battle-group frightening strategical and tactical freedom. But there is always a price. There have been at least six known disasters affecting nuclear-powered submarines alone, and only the richest countries, or the less wealthy whose governments are prepared to put arms before the aspirations of their populations, can afford them.

The ingenuity of human beings can usually outflank the genius of a predecessor, and the cheaper gas turbine, with its short life and rapid replacement, has provided a cheaper method of propulsion, especially for craft designed to rob the nuclear submarine, whether of the attack, or the strategic type, of some of its terror.

During the brief Israeli–Egyptian war of 1967 the elderly Israeli destroyer *Eilat* was sunk by three missiles fired from fast patrol boats. Essentially these and their derivatives were the legitimate descendants of the early torpedo boats, although gas turbines had replaced steam engines and surface-to-surface missiles had replaced torpedoes. The fast boat was a cheap ship-killer, available to the small, locally deployed navies of many emerging nations. Both sides in the Second World War had developed the type in several guises, as torpedo launchers or gunboats, and the quest for rapid surprise attack led to them achieving very high speeds in the post-war world, not merely by adopting the gas turbine, but by exploiting advances in hydrofoil and multi-hull technology. Such craft, while they can pack a formidable punch in launching missiles of awesome power, cannot keep the sea, or operate in all-weather conditions and are therefore peripheral to the history of the ship.

As for the torpedo itself, it continues to occupy a secure place in the world's naval arsenals. It was a modified Mark 8 torpedo of Second World War design that was fired by HMS *Conqueror* to sink the Argentinian cruiser *General Belgrano* in 1982. The result of this controversial but pre-emptive strike was to ensure the aircraft carrier *Veinticinco de Mayo* remained mewed up in port and did not interfere with the operations of the British task force. *Conqueror* also carried the Mark 24 battery-powered, wire-guided torpedo which was suitable for anti-submarine work. Thus the nuclear hunter-killer, fleet submarines of the Royal Navy justified their potential, by racing at speed to lend their deterrent presence to cover the carrier task force sent south by the Thatcher government to retake the Falklands.

The potence of the hunter-killer, fleet or attack submarine was to be an ever present threat to the battle-group, and also to convoys of merchantmen or fast transports transferring reinforcements to a potential flashpoint. In 1967, HMS *Valiant*, a fleet submarine of the all-British designed *Warspite* class on which *Conqueror* and her sisters *Churchill* and *Courageous* were improvements, made a 12,000-mile submerged passage from Singapore to Britain, carrying out exercises on the way, and she took only twenty-eight days to accomplish this. The lesson of the Second World War, while so brilliantly exploited by the nations it had so recently threatened, also had to be countered, for it was not lost on the Soviet Union either, and anti-submarine warfare has preoccupied the naval mind constantly since 1945.

As has been related, many former British destroyers were converted post-war to anti-submarine frigates. Sonar technology improved rapidly, the British developing both search and attack sets which, combined with the ahead-firing Squid mortar, provided a marked improvement. But the fast, battery-driven submarines were capable of evading it and a new combined sonar with a 'four square' transducer was introduced. This detected a submarine's depth, range and bearing using a split sonic beam technique and was stabilised against roll, pitch and yaw. It tracked at 2000 yards and allowed the new automatic Limbo mortar to engage at 1000 yards. Trials in HMS *Scorpion* were successfully carried out in 1947–1949 and by the early 1950s a long-range scanning sonar had been developed to work in tandem with the attack equipment and locate a target at up to 18,000 yards distance. But the gear did not enter service until 1957, and was already being overtaken by submarine performance.

The Americans had moved along similar lines, although they still retained the elderly Hedgehog, but in a trainable mounting. A rocket-propelled depth charge called the 'Alfa' followed but proved unsatisfactory. Similar problems were encountered with homing torpedoes, which proved too slow to catch the faster submarines. However, as sonar ability improved, so did torpedo technology. Eventually, in 1956 the electrically propelled Mark 43 torpedo was deployed for anti-submarine work in American destroyers to replace the trainable Hedgehog. It was followed by the Mark 44, a larger 30-knot electric torpedo with a 75-pound warhead which allowed an attack to be made from a distance, since the torpedo was launched and ran into quiet water clear of the ship before assuming its search-pattern and final run.

In 1948 the British submarine force was assigned its primary role of anti-submarine warfare, foreshadowing the fully fledged hunter-killer nuclear boat. Search techniques were complicated by lack of space to incorporate the then large computers necessary to support the weapons system, and passive gear was fitted. When the British built HMS *Dreadnought*, they mounted an active/passive digital multi-beam sonar (DIMUS) array capable of detection at formidable ranges of up to 60 miles. But the weaponry to exploit any advantage lagged behind until about 1971, eight years after *Dreadnought*'s commissioning.

The Americans pursued a similar route, detecting snorkelling submarines at up to 20,000 yards and very low frequency passive sonar sets such as the BQR-4 had a range of 50 miles. A passively operating submarine could call in aircraft to effect a kill. Indeed, although high-speed electric submarines robbed the fixed wing patrolling aircraft of some of the potency it had enjoyed during the war, helicopters using dipping sonar arrays, such as the British 'King-pin', could act as effective submarine hunters. Initially, however, their size meant they had to operate from a carrier, and many smaller carriers found themselves relegated to the role of helicopter support. However, as time passed, new, lighter helicopters, with devices to secure them instantaneously to the deck of small warships of the frigate class, enabled such ships to become useful submarine hunters.

To some extent this answered the next problem confronting the anti-submarine warfare experts, for as the underwater speed of nuclear boats, unaffected by surface sea conditions and hydrodynamically superior in their hull forms to frigates and destroyers, rose above that of their pursuers, a weapon capable of reaching them from the slower platform had to be found.

The torpedo-carrying Westland Wasp helicopter operated from British frigates at ranges of up to 4 to 5 miles which, while being suitable for convoy defence, was not considered capable of annihilating a major threat to a battle-group. The Australian Ikara missile dropped a light torpedo over a sonar contact at ranges of up to 10 miles, but was not widely adopted by the British who wished to retain the more adaptable offensive capability of the helicopter, which could also be deployed against fast surface attack craft and could deliver not just an aerial torpedo, but nuclear depth bombs.

An alternative was the Mark 46 torpedo which could reach a speed of 45 knots at a range of 6 miles, or the ASROC, anti-submarine rocket, which was widely deployed in US and Allied warships from about 1960. Having located a target, the rocket-launched Mk46 torpedo is delivered above the submarine, detaches from the rocket and is parachuted to the sea where it goes into its search pattern and homes in on an area comparable to the lethal radius of the nuclear depth bomb.

In 1962 the *Thresher* class of United States' submarines, and four years later their quieter successors, the *Sturgeons*, had midships torpedo tubes, allowing their bulbous bows to be filled with a huge sonar transducer, the BQS-6, alongside a passive low-frequency array, the BQR-7. A passive classification set, the BQQ-3, was mounted at intervals along the hull and the data was processed by a digital fire-control system to guide a SUBROC nuclear missile to a detected target. This permitted a passive engagement that did not reveal the presence of the attacker which engaged with a remotely-set warhead at a distance of up to 40 miles. This, allied with the ASTOR, a wire-guided nuclear torpedo which had entered service in 1959, put an unacceptable emphasis on tactical nuclear weapons. This was not merely bowing to the anti-nuclear lobby; ASTOR was predicted by submarine crews to be lethal to the launching boat and it was phased out by 1977. Replacement took the form of a heavy, fast homing torpedo, the Mark 48. This 50-knot weapon was capable of achieving a range of 35,000 yards and entered service in 1971.

Thus the submarine not only hunted itself, but was hunted by small surface warships with their own helicopters, and by fixed and rotary-wing aircraft from carriers. Later, bottom sensors were laid in 'enemy' transit areas and wider ranging aircraft responded to signals obtained from these and then laid sonobuoys to fix a target. This enabled accurate tracking and dummy 'attacks' to be sustained against a future opponent.

Advantage swung back to the surface vessel as a submarine detector with the introduction of the towed sonar array. Developed originally for towing astern of a submarine, and capable of detecting another ship at a distance of an incredible 100 miles, such devices were adapted for use by some of the *Leander* class frigates of the Royal Navy. These frigates were an improved version of the Type 12, *Whitby* and *Rothesay* classes built in the 1950s and this large group supplied ships to the Commonwealth and foreign navies. The Australian, Dutch and Indian navies built their own *Leanders*, but Chile and New Zealand possessed British-built vessels, while the *Leanders* serving in the Royal Navy numbered twenty-six. Weapon suites and indeed hull dimensions have varied since the class ship *Leander* was laid down at Harland and Wolff's, Belfast, in April 1959, but broadly they may serve as examples of one of the best general purpose frigate-types used by the Western Allies and North Atlantic Treaty Organisation (NATO) navies between 1960 and 1990.

Displacing 2450 tons, with a draught of 18 feet (5.5 metres), they were 372 feet (114 metres) in length with a beam of 41 feet (12.5 metres) in the first sixteen ships, 43 feet (13 metres) in the last ten. They had, by naval standards, a modest crew of 260 men. Their main armament was mounted forward in the form of twin, semi-automatic 4.5-inch dual-purpose guns, supported by a pair of 40 mm Bofors, except those built after *Naiad* in 1964, which had a multiple Seacat anti-aircraft missile system. Additional anti-aircraft armament was provided by one or two Oerlikons, and anti-submarine Limbo Mk10 depth-charge mortars were fitted for close range anti-submarine work. In the 1970s the earliest ten British ships had the main guns removed and replaced by Ikara anti-submarine missiles, though this rearmament was not followed up, largely because it deprived the *Leanders* of their useful general purpose role and meant they needed air and surface defence cover. The Australian ships were known as the '*River*' class and carried a lighter weight Ikara on each quarter, retaining their forward gun and their versatile role.

However, a further ten of the class had their guns replaced by the French Exocet anti-ship missile which was bought in large numbers after trials in 1974. But these ships also lost their multiple capability, although they retained an anti-submarine weapon with two triple Mark 32 torpedo tubes and their helicopter. The final ten broader beamed ships, kept the gun. All the *Leanders* carried a Wasp or the larger Lynx helicopter for reconnaissance and offensive operations, largely against submarines. Capable of 30 knots and relatively quiet, with two double-reduction geared steam turbines generating 30,000 horsepower on twin shafts, the *Leanders* proved to be able sea-boats designed for the nightmare scenario of nuclear war, with pre-wetting facilities and an efficient early warning and weapon control electronics suite. The frequent updatings produced a mishmash outfit, for while their Australian mates managed to accommodate the missile systems and retain the gun forward, as did the *Leanders* built for Chile, the first British Exocet conversion, *Cleopatra*, appeared in 1975 with the Exocet box-launchers in place of the gun turret. Such a short-sighted policy has never been clearly explained. The first of the broad-beamed version, HMS *Andromeda*, was fitted with four Exocet launchers, improved sonar and the Seawolf anti-aircraft and anti-missile short range defence system together with new electronics.

As the *Leanders* were completing, the Ministry of Defence was engaged with the Polaris programme and additional frigates were built to a commercial design produced by Vosper-Thornycroft and Yarrow. These were the Type-21 frigates of the *Amazon* class, eight deceptively small-looking ships which had aluminium superstructures to save topweight; for an increasing problem facing naval architects is the weight and windage of radar aerials and arrays mounted high in a warship. Aluminium saved some 60 tons, but with appalling consequences when HMS *Ardent* was hit by a dozen rockets and HMS *Antelope* was bombed off the Falklands in May 1982. In thelatter case the bomb did not detonate, but exploded when being defused, and both ships burned furiously, with the added horror of toxic fumes from the burning insulation.

Armed with a single, 4.5-inch quick-firing automatic gun, Exocet and Seacat missiles, the *Amazons* also carried an anti-submarine helicopter and six anti-submarine torpedo tubes firing the Mark 46 weapon. The *Amazons*' chief interest as advances lay in their power plants. Following experiments in the 1955 steam-driven Type-14 frigate *Exmouth*, which in 1966 was re-engined with Olympus and gas-type turbines, the *Amazons* were fitted with two sets of twin Rolls-Royce gas turbines driving twin screws. The Tyne turbines of 8500 shaft horsepower were used for cruising, giving 18 knots and a range of 3500 miles. The larger Olympus units were available with 56,000 horsepower at short notice to boost power and give 30 knots, with a range at that speed of 1200 miles. Power was transmitted to the ships' twin shafts, the five-bladed propellers being variably pitch controlled. The saving of space and acceptable redundancy of such engines is of benefit, but it also removed bottom weight from a light hull which was susceptible to stresses and required strengthening. One major and significant advance they had on the *Leanders*, themselves an improvement on earlier ships, was that they required a crew of only 179 officers and ratings.

British naval planning was subject to fluctuating political influences as the cost of warships rose and the nation's role and wealth contracted. Projects centred around large carrier designs and the concept of battle-groups only produced aborted escort classes and the diversion of investment into nuclear submarines. Advanced radar equipment, under development with the Dutch for the battle-group idea was cancelled on grounds of expense. As a consequence a class of ships designed to be fitted with the Anglo–Dutch radar resulted in a single, very expensive destroyer, HMS *Bristol*. In the 1960s a class of eight guided-missile armed super-destroyers, the '*Counties*', were built. These were hand-some ships with a mixed and powerful armament; they used the then unusual steam turbine plant which was boosted by gas turbine for high speed at short notice. But they had large crews, their running costs were considered excessive and their Seaslug missile was only a qualified success. As an example, HMS *Glamorgan* underwent a hugely expensive refit between 1977 and 1980, survived an Exocet strike in the Falklands and was after-wards sold to Chile in the wake of several of her sisters.

The '*County*' class were superseded by the fourteen guided-missile destroyers of the Type-42 *Sheffield* class. At 3500 tonnes displacement, the first ten had a length of 412 feet overall, a beam of 47 feet on a draught of 19 feet. The later four, *Edinburgh*,

Gloucester, York and *Manchester* have 2 feet additional beam and 42 feet more length, hence their description as 'stretched'. All are gas turbine powered, deriving an 18 knot cruising speed from their Tynes, and 28 from the Olympus engines. Their main armament is the automatic 4.5 Mk 8 gun, with two 20 mm Oerlikons and a twin Sea Dart surface-to-air missile system. The Lynx helicopter is primarily for anti-submarine operations. State-of-the-art ships though these are, two of them, *Sheffield* and *Coventry*, were lost off the Falklands.

Their loss begs a few questions. Can a navy, especially a small, highly technical one, afford a few ships of such complexity and often disappointing armament? Or should simpler and more numerous hulls be the priority? Losses of ships in the Falklands were not inconsiderable and might have been much worse. What in a modern warship, is value for money to a nation with limited means?

Towards the end of the 1980s the Soviet Union were producing submarines as quiet as anything devised in the West. The *Victor III* and the *Akula* class utilised rafted propulsion and other silencing measures and this largely outflanked the passive sonar technology of the West. In 1991, however, the Soviet Union collapsed, bringing a pause at least to the long confrontation which had dominated naval thinking for almost half a century.

At the end of the Second World War theorists had postulated that airpower had robbed the warship of its potency and rendered it largely ineffective. It was true that Mutually Assured Destruction found the long-range bomber most suitable as its first strike delivery medium; it is true too, that the ICBM was later capable of achieving the same end via the borders of space itself, but military planners always seek the edge. Mutually Assured Destruction could be averted by deploying second strike weapons where they could not be detected, or where detection would be costly, and uncertain. Interest focused again on the capital ship which might hedge this maddest of politico-military bets.

At the core of the Cold War, unseen, yet infinitely sinister, lay the true submarine, the latest, most powerful capital warship devised by man, armed with horrendous weapons capable of laying waste vast tracts of the globe and ensuring the after effects might either contaminate or freeze the remainder. It was this hugely expensive ship that held the no man's land between the world's two opposing doctrines; this ship which, slipping through the still, dark waters of the Atlantic and the Pacific depths, somehow managed to help keep a fragile peace.

It remains to be seen what political and military imperatives will emerge to drive the naval thinking of the future.

CHAPTER NINETEEN

Boxes, Bulkers and Babel

Immediately after the Second World War it appeared that world shipping would pick up from where it had left off in 1939. The plethora of standard ships available filled some of the demands of general bulk trades, while major liner companies rebuilt their shattered fleets with ships that varied little in general principle from pre-war designs. Trade patterns too, seemed to have reverted to their previous state with the old colonial powers reasserting their authority and the United States moving into the power-vacuum created by the total defeat of Imperial Japan.

The British, already committed to policies of independence, particularly for the Indian sub-continent, nevertheless remained dominant in their traditional role as a major carrier. However, all was not as it seemed; the European countries were exhausted financially and morally by war, fearful of the greatly increased power and influence of Soviet Russia who had acquired her own post-war empire of buffer states in Eastern Europe. Woken to the importance of sea-power, the Russians not only began building a blue-water fleet of warships, they began a programme of building merchantmen, both in Russia itself and in her European satellites. Highly subsidised and with an eye to under-cutting the cosy freighting arrangements of the West, innovation marked the new Comecon merchant vessels which began to roll into the Baltic down the slipways of Gdynia, Stettin, Rostock and Leningrad. The Russians also exported ideology and the re-established colonial governments in Africa and Southeast Asia were soon in trouble as Marxist inspired rebellion became the mainspring of political activity. But the second half of the twentieth century has been characterised by a process of constant accelerating change and this dynamic has caused a revolution in the world of shipping as much as in the world at large.

Advances in electronics, increasing automation and the loss of traditional labouring work within the international free market; the decline of heavy manufacturing bases in certain Western countries and the rise of such industries on the Pacific rim; the steady increase in consumer demand and of all forms of commodity carriage by sea; these have all influenced the development of the ship. Political upheaval, such as the nationalisation of the Suez Canal in 1956 and its subsequent closure between 1967 and 1973, the threat of Comecon shipping, the oil crisis of 1974 and the formation of the European Union, have all had a profound effect, particularly upon the rather hidebound structure of the British merchant marine.

Although it enjoyed a brief, post-war flowering, after 1966 the once pre-eminent British 'Merchant Navy' went into a steep decline. By 1997 it has virtually disappeared.

The rise of air-passenger services has already been mentioned in Chapter Sixteen, but a more subtle influence arose from the intransigence of British dock-labour to automate after the war. Historically maltreated, it appeared to labour leaders that they too could enjoy a post-war golden age. Pilfering, particularly in the general cargo trades, was a serious problem and ironically the first containers were stowed in the 'tween-decks of cargo ships as additional secure stowage for valuable cargo. It was not long, however, before their great potential was developed and the docker was swept aside by the switch to automated terminals handling the world's general cargo transportation system in containers. Essentially, it was this rapid change in almost all forms of cargo handling that transformed shipping in the thirty years between 1965 and 1995.

The West's increasing dependence upon oil and the reaction of Western governments to instability in the Middle East prompted a search for new sources of this raw material. Oilfields in the North Sea and American Arctic were consequently opened up and the tanker *Manhattan* made her epochal voyage through the North West Passage which technology had rendered passable. In reverse, the depletion and burden of cost of north European coal and mineral deposits encouraged exploitation of sources in Brazil, Australia, America, West Africa and even Greenland. Industry has expanded in step with consumer expectations; raw materials are now required in precise quantities at regular intervals. Multinational companies have burgeoned, sweeping aside national boundaries, nowhere more so than on the high seas where a ship's ensign says little about the ownership of the vessel herself and may also be of a different nationality to the port of registry painted on the stern below.

Larger and larger ships have been built, manned by smaller and smaller crews. Expertise and experience are no longer so important; technology helps smooth a master's decision-making and the owner's office is only a satellite-linked telephone call away. Ships are no longer built for anything other than functionality and a crew is no longer necessarily expected to husband a ship for a long, productive life, but to deliver her from port to port, carrying out only what is essential to conform to the regulations of the flag state to which she nominally belongs. Although theoretically subject to international consensus in the matter of regulations under the auspices of the International Maritime Organisation (IMO), the flag of convenience (FOC) effectively provides the beneficial owner with a cheap option, and many take advantage of it. Flag of convenience operation permits cheaper manning and the avoidance of tax; in some cases standards of maintenance, equipment and competence are less than those under the more sophisticated and traditional registers. Of the four great ship-owning nations existing in 1991, Greece and Japan had more ships under foreign flags than under their national ensign, while the United States has national to FOC ships in a ratio of 4:3, and Norway 7:5.

As the old Swedish saying has it, 'only a poor country sends its sons to sea'. In the aftermath of the collapse of Soviet Russia, once one of the five largest ship-owning nations on earth, Russian ships and Russian seafarers are plying their trade at depressingly low rates of freight and pay. Nor are the Russians the only nationals providing cheap labour to the shipping world. The impact of the free market was immediate at sea; no protection existed for many traditional seafaring communities. Always opposed to interference in merchant shipping except in time of war – and then never to the advantage of the seaman – the British government, preoccupied as it was with Europe, simply abandoned its Merchant Navy to market forces. Described by the then Prime Minister, Mrs Thatcher, as a 'sunset industry', the sun rose elsewhere: British seafarers were simply too expensive in the face of foreign competition. Although still significant, a similar fate has to a degree overtaken the United States' merchant marine. Thus the two 'non-combatant' institutions which saved the world for the democracy and now made the shipping revolution possible, fell victim to its success. Great companies are no more; Alfred Holt's blue funnels no longer exist, nor do the long, lean hulls of the United States Line's fast cargo ships. Romance at sea was always an illusion, sadly, so too was tradition.

To some extent this decline has been artificially induced. United Nations' policy encouraged the formation of national merchant fleets in the countries of the Developing World and many future officers were trained in the fleets they were shortly to run off the high seas. The laudable intention of this was to reduce the disparity between rich and poor. Events were to overtake such philanthropy. While the United Nations inspired IMO conventions aimed at safety at sea, the elimination of pollution, the overloading of ships and basic standards in construction and conditions at sea, the vigour of the free market often sidestepped such initiatives to leave a legacy of unsafe ships, incompetent or underpaid crews, polluted seas and declining standards. Bureaucratic reaction to such unfortunate consequences only brings down a greater weight of regulation upon those disposed to abide by it. Such measures simply increase the likelihood of rendering uncompetitive the ships operating under responsible flag states; meanwhile the unscrupulous survive.

This has not always been the case, although the road to achieving the desired goal is often a long and stony one. Attempts to regulate theconduct of tankers following the loss of the 61,263-deadweight-ton *Torrey Canyon* off Cornwall in 1967, did not prevent the pollution of the Breton coast following the grounding of the *Amoco Cadiz* in 1978, or the disaster that befell the Alaskan coast in 1989 when the *Exxon Valdez* ran aground. But the subsequent insistence by the United States' administration that tankers calling at American ports should be double-skinned, though at first considered unacceptable by shipowners, has since become internationally acceptable by the 134-member nations making up the International Maritime Organisation. This point of view was given added force by the grounding of the *Sea Empress* in the approaches to the Welsh port of Milford Haven early in 1996.

The closure of the Suez Canal was linked with the soaring oil prices in 1973–4. Shipowners re-routed their ships round the Cape of Good Hope and the size of tanker, no longer constrained by the dimensions of the canal, rapidly began to increase up to 250,000 tons deadweight. Thereafter the profits from economies of scale, which took tonnage of the tanker and bulk ore carrier even higher, also prompted a similar increase in the size of cargo ships. A few large container vessels swiftly replaced a score or so of conventional-sized ships, even though these might have been fully converted to carry containers. Containerisation, though highly efficient compared with the operation of the old break-bulk system, nevertheless required massive capital investment. Large, fast ships and maximised speed of turnround in port clearly offered the best return on that capital, and while many container ships were built to pass the two great canals, even these have now followed tankers and exceed the maximum beam capable of transitting the isthmus of Panama. Highly priced fuel prompted the retro-fitting of improved power plants; the *Queen Elizabeth 2* was not the only ship to be converted from steam turbine to high performance, turbo-charged diesel engines.

Larger and fewer ships meant a reduction in new tonnage which, despite the steady increase in world trade, has resulted in a decline of shipbuilding, particularly in Britain where today there is virtually no substantial facility for the construction of merchant ships. Added to this must be the effect of the world slump following the end of the Cold War which, though relative, resulting in a steadying of demand rather than a decline, has nevertheless failed to generate a demand for new ships. Revolutionary though it might at present seem, the world's merchant shipping is already ageing.

The effects of these changes are still with us. The collapse of the Soviet empire has caused an East/West *detente* which is still under evaluation by the military. It is now debatable whether a country such as Britain, shorn of her imperial trappings and her merchant fleet, needs a Royal Navy for anything other than coastal defence. Without her merchant shipping to defend, why else should her taxpayers fund such a service?

Like most of the world's industrial production, the world's transportation industries are also increasingly international and the chief among these is shipping. Ninety per cent of the world's trade goes by sea and whether it be oil or its by-products, iron ore, coal, grain or the manufactured goods carried as general or containerised cargo, all have shown a steady increase in the last twenty years. It is these two decades then that have encompassed this extraordinary upheaval. Comparison with the change from sail to steam is specious, for although the earlier change had radical effects, as we have seen, it was gradual in its impact. Moreover this impact was far smaller than the effects of changes in world shipping since 1945.

The twentieth century has been increasingly dominated by oil. Originally seven companies, Esso (Exxon), Gulf, Texaco, Mobil and Chevron, all owned in the United States, and BP and Shell owned in Britain and the Netherlands respectively formed the 'oil majors' which controlled exploration, production and distribution, refining crude oil close to the oilfields and transporting the cracked products by sea. The experience of war and the general instability in the Middle East following the ousting of the British and the nationalisation of BP's Abadan refinery in 1951 ensured the processing plants were shifted closer to the major markets in North America, Europe and Japan. In step with other technologies, chemical engineering had developed so that there were finally no residual waste products from crude oil and still further substances could be made by blending derivatives from different grades. Since such grades came from the far corners of the globe, it was logical to manufacture this multiplicity of hydrocarbon products in the same place. Following the Middle East War of 1973, the oil producing countries gained control of their own raw materials and have begun to reverse this. Twenty years later, the *casus belli* of the Gulf War was oil, and the politics of oil remain as volatile as the fossil fuel itself.

The ships servicing this world-wide industry are varied. The crude oil carrier has grown in size since 1945, first to the supertanker of the 1960s, then to the Very Large Crude Carrier (VLCC), and finally to the Ultra Large Crude Carrier (ULCC) the tonnage of which may be in excess of 500,000 deadweight tonnes. Such great ships were developed to ply their trade from the oilfields of the Persian Gulf to the refineries of Europe, fuelling the post-war recoveries of the European and Japanese economies. Increases in size reduced unit costs and were further encouraged by the uncertainties surrounding the operation of the

Suez Canal, which were ultimately justified with its prolonged closure between 1967 and 1973. In fact the Japanese built, American owned *Universe Apollo* of 1959 and *Universe Daphne* of 1960 lifted a deadweight of around 115,000 tonnes and were designed to double the Cape of Good Hope. As technology put tools of increasing sophistication into our hands, it seemed it could deliver almost anything: after all, by 1969 men had landed on the moon. The economies of scale available to owners of ships shifting the world's most valuable commodity were not slow to pick up this point. Doubling the size of a hull increases the building cost by a factor of four, but it augments the earning power by eight times. Moreover the associated costs that bedeviled earlier attempts to benefit from advancing technology were no longer applicable. As the century advanced, steel production absorbed an increasing amount of recycled scrap and less raw ore, allowing cheap replacement, built-in obsolescence and minimal maintenance, so that expected ship-life reduced. A hull was only an asset and no longer an argosy. Combined with automation, this significantly reduced crew sizes even as tonnages rose. Similarly, communications systems and computers have affected savings in overheads and shore-staff.

The power required for a large ship does not rise in proportion to increase in size, but on a lesser scale. Thus a 60,000-tonne tanker of the 1960s, requiring a loaded service speed of 15 knots would require a plant capable of generating some 16,000 horsepower at a consumption of 53 tonnes of oil a day. A 260,000-tonne tanker of the 1980s, running at the same speed would need only 2.7 times the power, some 42,500 horsepower, at a daily consumption of 140 tonnes per day.

With such calculations dominating the economics of shipping, a golden age foreclosed on the seafarer, but opened for the shipowner.

As we have already remarked in Chapter Eleven, the Eagle Oil Company were shipping Mexican oil to Britain in 16,000-ton tankers before the First World War. The Second produced 620 'standard' T2 tankers of similar (16,400 deadweight tonnage) size. Like the Liberty ship's influence on bulk cargoes, the T2 became the unit size applicable to tanker loads. Both types were released to private ownerships and provided the world with the mainstay of its post-war capacity, both working and earning their keep well into the 1960s. Many such ships were taken under the Greek flag and entrepreneurial owners like Stavros Niarchos and Aristotle Onassis obtained long-term charters from the oil-majors, collateral with which to raise bank loans to build the first supertankers. By the time the T2s were rendered obsolete, Greek interests had built up the largest independent tanker fleets in the world. Later Hong Kong became the home of supertankers. The Island Navigation Corporation of C. Y. Tung, and the World Wide Shipping Corporation of Y. K. Pao, both registered in Hong Kong, were nevertheless financed by loans from Japanese banks. Such ships soon exceeded the 70,000 tonnes maximum capable of passing the Suez Canal. But by now the difference in distance between the Persian Gulf and Rotterdam via Suez and the Cape (6570 miles against 11,420 miles) was being offset by the benefits of size, for the rise in demand and the avoidance of canal fees had shifted the parameters. Shell realised this and by the end of the 1960s had a class of twenty crude carriers of 200,000 tonnes deadweight in service. These were the 'M' class, of which the Marpessa exploded in 1969.

As the owners of Brunel's *Great Eastern* had found, while the theoretical advantages of large ships were obvious in terms of return on capital investment, many ports were incapable of accepting such large ships and therefore new terminal facilities had to be built. In Europe the most significant of these was on the Maas at Rotterdam where, at the river's mouth, the huge new complex of Europoort was developed. Such a great port rendered obsolete many adjacent facilities.

However, human ingenuity being what it is, other solutions were found such as the single point mooring. This may be a buoy or large floating platform to which a ship not only moors, but from which she also loads. Such an installation sometimes takes the form of a permanently moored hull which is gradually filled and astern of which another vessel secures to load her own cargo by transfer. Such methods are used to export oil from certain North Sea fields and tankers specially fitted for bow-loading operate in this sector. Very large tankers requiring a lightening of their draught before entering a port unable to accommodate them in their loaded condition will anchor and discharge a part of their cargo to a smaller, 'lightening ship' close to their destination. Employment of lightening tankers saved several British ports from being subsumed by Europoort, but these operations provoked hysterical protest due to the risk of spillage. Weather affects both these expedients and faced with a problem of approaching their Danish refinery set in relatively shoal water, Gulf Oil built the 325,000-tonne ULCC *Universe Ireland* to deliver her cargo to storage tanks at Bantry Bay in Ireland. From Bantry the cargo was loaded into 100,000-tonne short-haul tankers and a similar installation was built in the Bahamas from where 60,000-tonners distribute the crude to American refineries.

Every progression in human history has its drawback and large tankers are no exception. The lack of water depth in the approaches to many ports imposes draught restrictions on them, and increasing size denies access to some parts of the ocean. Forced use of the Lombok Strait rather than the shallower Strait of Malacca between the Malay Peninsula and Sumatra, adds over 1000 miles to the Far East voyage of a VLCC. Another problem to emerge after the war was that of inexplicable and apparently spontaneous explosion, which overtook the *Marpessa*, among other ships. After a number of these tragedies, some resulting in the total loss of valuable ships, research finally concluded that the method of cleaning the tanks by high-pressure water jets produced static electricity which in turn, ignited residual gas. Various expedients were tried to combat this. Either the washing was done with crude oil from which the residues could in turn be recovered, or the tanks were filled with inert gases, reducing the oxygen content and thus the explosive potential of the gases in a tank.

The closure of the Suez Canal finally persuaded tanker owners to wholeheartedly back the large tanker and in the following years the VLCC was succeeded by the ULCC (Ultra Large Crude Carriers), a ship in excess of 300,000 tonnes deadweight. Such ships were relatively simple to construct and lent themselves to prefabricated construction. They were readily built by the newly resuscitated yards of Japan and the emerging shipbuilders of Korea. The latter located their yards on greenfield sites and rapidly assumed a dominance of the world market, backed as they increasingly became by banking interests which had historically considered investing in shipping a highly uncertain business. This situation soon led to overcapacity, exacerbated as it was by the tax demands of the traditional flag states under which the majority of these ships then still operated. Other factors were the panic that set in as a result of the forecasts of the imminently finite nature of fossil fuel reserves and the independent policy of the oil producers following the action of the American major Exxon (Esso) to cut the price offered for Middle East crude in August 1960. Saudi Arabia, Iran, Iraq, Kuwait and Venezuela formed OPEC (the Organisation of Oil Producing Countries) an exclusive, but influential body which eventually provoked the crisis of 1973–4 when oil reached a price of $5.19 a barrel, three times its face value three years earlier. This situation was made worse by the Egyptian attack on Israeli positions along the east bank of the Suez canal, in the Sinai desert. The Egyptian attack faltered and the OPEC countries called for an embargo of Israel. This failed, but the revelation of their power encouraged the OPEC countries to raise the price of oil still further, to $11.65 a barrel. For large tankers capable of hauling only one cargo over long distances, the wherewithal for their continued existence collapsed and a recession ensued. Various survival techniques were exploited of which the Rotterdam spot-market was one. Here oil cargoes were bought and sold by independent speculators: the oil majors had suffered a defeat and many large tankers were laid up world-wide having lost their economic advantages. 'Lots' of oil changed hands based upon the million-barrel tanker (at 7.5 barrels to the metric tonne), so that the 140,000-tonne tanker could handle two consignments of 500,000 barrels, the favoured amount. As such, great ships such as the *Seawise Giant* of 564,000 tonnes deadweight became redundant dinosaurs and it became clear such vessels had exceeded their own strength. Tanker owners traded at a loss, banks repossessed useless ships or let the owners trade on in the hope of better times. This seemed unlikely with a world surplus of 100,000,000 deadweight tonnes lying idle in 1975. Many new ships went from their building ports to lay up in the fiords of Norway or other deep-water anchorages, only to go straight to the breakers without ever loading a cargo; some few became bulk or combination carriers; other became static storage tanks. This was the fate in store for the abovementioned *Seawise Giant* which was acquired by the Iranian government during the war with Iran, although she was later bombed by the Iraqi air force. Only in Japan, where land storage is in short supply and expensive, did the government underwrite the use of ULCCs as holding tanks.

Part of the spiral of rising costs affected bunker prices which rose from $10 per ton in 1970 to $240 in 1979, so that those tankers in service steamed at a very slow speed to reduce fuel bills. At its inception, the supertanker had been fitted with steam turbines, but like the liner and the container ship, the improvement in the diesel ensured that the benefits in fuel savings justified the expense of retro-fitting.

But another consequence of the oil crisis and the dispossession of the oil-majors was to encourage prospecting in less hospitable environments and a whole new technology was spawned in Alaska and the North Sea, as well as in Mexico and Indonesia. Here the contiguous states were not OPEC members and, having suffered the effects of OPEC's power, were quite happy to undercut OPEC rates and assault the monopoly of the Middle East. Supplies lay closer to the markets and the ULCC finally died as other ships appeared, such as the offshore rig tender, thesupply and support vessel and the shuttle tanker.

When the Suez Canal was finally reopened in 1973 with international help, it was enlarged to take 170,000-tonne tankers, so that the world-wide 200,000-tonne ship has now become the norm. Today the market has picked up, but the remaining working tonnage is ageing and the size of its eventual replacement will prove interesting.

The crude oil carrier, or 'tar barge' as it is unkindly called by sailors, makes half of her voyages in ballast and effectively serves as the moving part of a pipeline between oilfield and refinery. Afterfractionating into its multiple products, oil becomes a number of varied substances, used in a multiplicity of ways. The distribution of these products became the task of the product tanker, a smaller vessel employed on shorter routes with design parameters dictated by the requirements of the individual trade. They carry cargoes of sophisticated specifications which are thus valuable commodities often requiring highly specialised treatment in their carriage. These requirements have produced a versatile ship with tank coatings and piping arrangements capable of handling parcels of oil derivatives of an inimical nature. Roughly divisible into two classes, the 'white' product carrier shifts cargoes such as petrol, kerosene (paraffin) and lubricating oils. The 'black' carrier handles fuel oils and many of these require heating before discharging, so steam heat is passed through pipe coils running through the tanks.

A further tanker type arising from the modern fractionating of crude oil and which may be regarded as a parallel to the product tanker, is the chemical tanker. It differs little from the former, but where it does so, the difference is notable. Modern chemicals are worse pollutants than plain oil derivatives which, unpleasant though they are, tend to be natural and to revert to natural substances in time. The generation of chemicals presents a number of challenges. Protection has to be afforded not only to the general environment, but also the ship's crew. Inert gas blanketing has to be applied to explosive substances. Others are highly corrosive, and ships have to be built with resistant tanks of expensive stainless steel. Other methods include the coating of the internal surfaces of a tank with zinc silicate, epoxy resins, various rubbers and so forth. Regulation and handling requirements are therefore stringent, the ships themselves being technically complex.

Consignments of chemicals rarely fill such a tanker, and there is therefore a demand for multiple parcels being borne in the same vessel. While most of the cargoes carried in these ships are petrochemicals, not all chemical or oil products are corrosive, poisonous or explosive. Some are quite edible, and ships capable of carrying these must be maintained in a scrupulously clean condition. For all these reasons cleanliness in such ships assumes a far higher priority than godliness. Palm oil, soya bean oil, animal oils such as tallow and grease fall into this category and form thirty-two per cent of the chemical trade, while molasses, although not used for human consumption and accounting for only nine per cent of the trade, often forms a useful return, or back-haul cargo, such are the global patterns of the trade. Such cargo-care stimulates higher freight rates and greater competence on the part of the ships' crews. This has caused many product and chemical tankers to remain with traditional flag states, to be manned by seafarers from well-trained national cultures.

Whereas the standard crude carrying tanker had, until recently, no double skin, a products or chemical tanker is filled with complicated sub-divisions. These chiefly require the cargo to be unaffected by stranding or collision, so the cargo tanks are not integral as in a crude carrier, but independent within the hull's structure and the larger vessels will house up to fifty such tanks. The provision of pumps is also much more generous than in a conventional crude oil carrier; to preserve the purity of the product, each tank has an individual pump and pipeline system.

Nowhere is this sophistication so important as in the liquefied gas carrier. The ratio of liquid to gas is about 1:600, so the carriage of gas has to be in liquid form and to achieve this either cooling or pressurisation or a combination of both is necessary. Since the relative densities of gas are low, typically around 0.5, capacity is defined by space in the form of cubic metres. Two types of liquefied gas are carried by sea: natural and petroleum gases.

Liquefied natural gas consists of eighty per cent methane which is carried at -162°C, since it is impossible to liquefy methane alone. Deposits of methane were found in Algeria and the world's first liquefied natural gas (LNG) carrier was the *Methane Pioneer* of 1960, a converted American standard ship into the holds of which tanks of 5125 cubic metres capacity were fitted. The British Gas Council had an interest in this ship and a special plant was built for receiving methane at Canvey Island in Essex. Two purpose-built ships, the *Methane Progress* and *Methane Princess* were afterwards built to develop the service. The latter, built by Vickers-Armstrong at Barrow in Furness, grossed 21,876 tonnes with a capacity of 27,400 cubic metres. She contained nine tanks in a hull 621 feet long (190 metres), 81 feet (25 metres) in the beam, 58 feet (18 metres) deep on a draught of 35 feet (10 metres). Her 13,750 horsepower steam turbine plant drove her at 17.5 knots by means of a single screw.

To sustain the low temperature of -162°C – roughly the boiling point of methane – special tanks are required and insulation between them and the ship's mild steel hull are essential. During a passage some of the cargo will boil off and rather than have it vent to atmosphere it is ducted to the boilers, a circumstance which has prolonged steam propulsion in this class of ship. Such cargoes, which are also loaded in Indonesia and Malaysia, Brunei, Australia and the Persian Gulf, are used for power generation on account of their cleanliness, and as a raw material for the chemical industry. Because of the complexities of its carriage, the LNG trade exists only where direct pipeline connection is impossible. Such a trade has to be underpinned by long-term contracts and is not therefore vulnerable to spot-trading opportunism. Even so, not all contracts have run their course and it is not uncommon for LNG carriers to take up cargoes of liquefied petroleum gas (LPG).

The LPG trade consists largely of butane and propane often carried together with other chemical gasses such as ammonia, either pressurised or cooled to about -55 °C. Both are derived by separation from natural gas, from crude oil when it is 'stabilised' for transport, or as a petroleum by-product. Quantities which boil off during a voyage are easily reliquefied and returned to the cargo tanks. Used for bottled gas and as a generating fuel or a chemical feedstock, they are nevertheless very dangerous. Explosions, known as 'bleves', cause terrible and immense damage, one occurring in Mexico being likened to a nuclear blast. As such, liquefied gas carriers are customarily conspicuously coloured and marked.

In addition to ammonia, other gases carried are the olefins ethylene, propylene, butadiene, and vinyl chloride monomer. Such parcels are contained in either fully pressurised spherical or cylindrical tanks, or semi or fully refrigerated tanks. The first of these classes are usually small ships which suffer from having their cargo spaces high up, making inefficient use of the hull capacity. The second class form the middle range, from around 2000 cubic metres to about 18,000. The third and largest class can carry up to 80,000 cubic metres and must have double barriers between tanks and shell plating, with inert gas interfilling the void spaces. Such vessels trade world-wide, many carrying the chemical feedstocks from the Middle East to the chemical plants of Europe, America and Japan. Ammonia is taken from the Caribbean to Europe, from the Ukraine to America and the Middle East to Japan and Korea.

Such sophisticated vessels are vulnerable to economic and political change. Those handling a single, dangerous cargo, such as phosphoric or sulphuric acid or caustic soda, are simpler to operate but helpless if demand for their specialised product falls off. Even so, many of these tankers run what amounts to a liner service, delivering their cargoes on a 'just-in-time' basis to their customers.

*

The promotion of consumerism that has evolved since the Industrial Revolution relegated shipping from the perilous adventure of the argosy to that of 'a bucket in the endless distribution chain that creeps across the world'. Such progress occupied the deep-water windjammer and the tramp ship, but increasing specialisation rapidly displaced the traditional tramp and the traditional cargo liner. The versatility of the Liberty ship and her wartime successors was continued with the SD-14 type, a post-war replacement developed on the River Wear, intended to provide carriage for the old bulk grain, ore and coal trades, but to which now had to be added increasing bulk cargoes of scrap steel, sugar, fertilisers, timber and wood-pulp. But tramp operation still suffered from the disadvantage of a one-way revenue-earning cargo as well as economic variables, as witness the cement traffic to Nigeria.

But on the whole the world economy has grown, demanding steady low cost supplies of raw materials to manufacturing centres, along with the world-wide distribution of finished products. The first phase of this bucket chain has resulted in the bulk carrier, an example of which was the *Sinclair Petrolore* of 1956 that has already been mentioned. These ships came into being to maintain this steady supply which operated regularly, under one charter or another. Bulk carriers vied with tankers to be the largest ships in the world because the same economies of scale applied, and the same return voyages had to be made in ballast for the next cargo. However, modern communications facilitate a closer control of supply and demand and operators and shippers are often able to make intermediate arrangements, so that another cargo can be carried on part of the return voyage, or in between voyage intervals, so that a ship capable of carrying a combination of bulk cargoes in a multiple trade itinerary was developed. This was the 'OBO', or oil/bulk/ore carrier, of which the *Sinclair Petrolore* was an early example.

The first of these ships were entering service in the 1950s and their hulls contained a central, elevated hold for ore, so that the vessel's centre of gravity was not too low and her motion not too stiff in a seaway. Since iron ore is an exceptionally heavy cargo, to lift a quantity of it requires a large hull much of which would be empty. By this subdivision of a central trunk, the surrounding deep double bottom and side spaces could be used as tanks, void when ore was carried, but which could be filled with oil, taking the ship down to her marks for a profitable voyage as a tanker.

The method, ingenious though it was, nevertheless wasted a huge amount of capacity and despite there being thoroughly good reasons for so doing, it irked the restless genius of men like the Norwegian shipowner Erling Naess. Naess appreciated that if the imbalances inherent in the dry bulk cargo trades could be further reduced, a ship would prove more profitable if she could further eliminate any days steamed in ballast. He wanted ships also capable of handling other bulk cargoes like bauxite, coal, phosphate rock and grain. He envisaged his ideal ship freighting coal and ore to Japan, then shipping back-loads of Indonesian oil to the source of the next out-bound load of coal and oil. After watching experiments by other owners which only partially reflected the magnitude of Naess's dream, the Norwegian headed a joint venture between British, Swedish and German interests. Consequently a Bremen yard delivered the *Naess Norseman* which, at 71,183 deadweight tons was regarded as the first true OBO. She drew almost 42 feet and was registered in Liberia in 1965.

The type took off: in ten years examples exceeded 200,000 tons deadweight, rivalling the tanker with her similar engines and accommodation aft profile. A typical OBO consists of up to eleven holds. These have large mechanised hatch covers to give access for bulk dry cargoes which are nevertheless gas and oil tight so that they can all serve as oil tanks. However some seven, alternately disposed longitudinally, can carry ore, thus distributing the weight in blocks rather than throughout the hull's length. Such a ship has deep double bottoms, carries ancillary equipment for cleaning her cargo spaces, and steam plant for heating oils. Although more expensive to build than either the tanker or the straight ore carrier, the OBO offers her owners the potential available from multiple cargo capability and the economies of large size.

In general OBOs require a degree of operational versatility and therefore need to be able to pass the Panama Canal. A typical standard Swedish-designed Panamax OBO has a limiting beam of 32.6 metres and lifts some 55,000 tonnes deadweight. This design, by the Uddevallavarvet yard, has a grain capacity of 65,795 cubic metres and an oil capacity of 63,000 cubic metres. However, the

OBO's susceptibility to economic variables makes her operation extremely complex, for she seeks to combine a regular bulk carrier service with a more opportunistic tramp service reacting to spot movements. This juggling of long-term contracts with short-term voyage charters has not proved easy in a period of surplus tonnage. The oil crisis of 1973–4 tempered enthusiasm for huge ships and in such a climate the OBO just fails as an ore carrier and just fails as a tanker, eliminating the attraction of her ability to switch commodities.

The industrial might of Japan which has to import all her raw materials, had small beginnings. In the 1950s Japanese shipyards recovered from the Second World War by lengthening Liberty ships to provide larger tonnage for bulk trades. They soon afterwards produced pure bulk carriers, picking up ideas from earlier American and Canadian experiments. In addition, complex international agreements were reached between the often state-owned oil and steel corporations of the West and the powerful Japanese trading companies who were experts in the matter of procuring raw materials; these resulted in joint ventures which were accelerated by the demands of the Korean War and the rapid gear shift of the Japanese economy. It was between 1953 and 1958 that the real post-war industrial boom began. This was characterised by a demand for steel, and hence iron ore and coking coal.

The single-purpose bulk carrier rapidly seized this trade from the tramp ship and while most are of Panamax size, many are larger. A 100,000-tonner can transit the newly enlarged Suez Canal and long-term charters can justify the building of single ships devoted to them. Such a charter was obtained by the Norwegian shipping company Bergesen dy AS who own a fleet exceeding 9 million tonnes in capacity. Securing a ten-year contract to feed the German steel industry with 4 million tonnes of Brazilian iron ore, Bergesens ordered two huge bulk carriers from the Ulsan yard of Hyundai Heavy Industries of South Korea. The first of these ships, the *Berge Stahl*, was built in 1986. She is 1125 feet (343 metres) long, 208 feet in the beam (63.5 metres) with a hull depth of 99 feet (30.2 metres) on a draught of 76 feet (23 metres), dimensions which give a gross tonnage of 175,720 tonnes. With seven holds her deadweight is some 364,767 tonnes or 199,324 cubic metres. The *Berge Stahl* is powered by an Italiani-Sulzer direct-drive diesel generating 16,900 horsepower which gives a service speed of 13 knots. She runs a joint service to Rotterdam with the slightly smaller *Bergeland* (320,000 tonnes deadweight) which was built at Ulsan in 1990, and these two huge ships form vital 'buckets' in that endless distribution chain which the seaman-novelist William McFee so aptly described.

Despite the development of such ships in the boom years of the 1950s there was still a requirement for the conventional tramp ship, hence the eagerness of the Japanese yards to 'jumboise' the Liberties, because the 10,000-ton load was no longer satisfying the demands of industry. Trade in commodities other than grain, oil and ore were growing and were required in places where the increasingly gargantuan ships could not go. But the domination of the tramp market by even the enlarged Liberty ship or her successors began to suffer from the age of the tonnage and this was reflected in rising insurance rates.

Three designs emerged to replace the old ships, the Canadian-designed and Japanese-built 'Freedom' class, the German 'Liberty-replacement' and the SD-14, designed and built by the Sunderland yard of Austin and Pickersgill and later built under license in Greece and Brazil. The SD-14 was first produced in 1968 with a deadweight of 15,250 tons on a draft of 28.5 feet and a service speed of 14 knots. Several subsequent marks have followed, the fourth having five holds, a five-cylinder diesel which drives the 15,000 tonnes of cargo at 15 knots on 25.5 tonnes of heavy oil daily. Capable of carrying grain, ore, coal, fertiliser and timber as well as general, break-bulk cargo, she is moreover self-sufficient, able to load and discharge herself with her own derricks. Over two hundred SD-14s have been built and many remain servicing spot trades. The German and Canadian/Japanese standard vessels had similar capabilities with a later Japanese improvement, the 'Fortune'-type, which has an increased deadweight of 20,000 tonnes. The versatility provided by the SD-14, Freedom and similar standard types of ship were reflections of the virtues of the general cargo liner whose trades were more regular. These became larger and more efficient cargo handlers with single 'tween decks, and wide or even twin hatches. Tonnage had risen to well over 20,000 tonnes deadweight and service speeds in excess of 20 knots. Such vessels had a self-

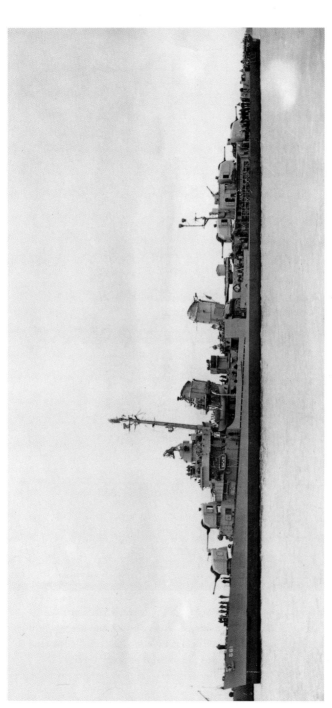

The United States Navy's most numerous destroyer class were the *Fletchers*, the name-ship of which was built in 1942 and the last, considerably modified, was the USS *Rooks* of 1944. Designed for the Pacific theatre, they were versatile, long-legged and able ships, their main armament being five of the efficient 5-inch (38 calibre) dual-purpose gun in single mountings.

The steam whale catcher was a far cry from the oared whale boats she replaced. With her tall mast providing a vantage point, and her powerful harpoon gun accessed directly from the bridge by way of a catwalk, the fatal march of technology quickly threatened the survival of many species of cetaceans. Thor Dahl's *Thorarinn* and her sisters were built in Norway by Akers Mek Versted in 1928–29.

W hile the whale catchers hunted, the factory ship processed the catch and provided all the base and back-up facilities for a fleet of catchers. This post-war mother-ship is the Norwegian *Norhval* of 13,830 GRT. Note the ramp in the stern, up which the air-inflated whale carcasses were dragged.

T he Soviet Union's *Sverdlov* class of large cruisers exemplified Stalin's over-ambitious naval programme. They also alarmed the navies of the West when the *Sverdlov* appeared at the Coronation Review of Queen Elizabeth II at Spithead in 1953.

The Soviet Union's Project 658 *Hotel* class (a NATO codename) were the world's first nuclear ballistic missile submarines. Three SS-N-4 missiles were carried in the fin, but could only be fired from the surface. The Hotel II was fitted with SS-N-5s which could be launched from a submerged position.

The shortcomings of land-based support hampered the British Pacific Fleet in 1944–45 and the loss of colonial bases focused attention on the maintenance of a fleet at sea by other means. The Royal Navy reacted swiftly by creating a more versatile Royal Fleet Auxiliary and in this 1967 scene, HMS *Victorious* is fuelled and stored simultaneously at sea. On her starboard side, the fleet oiler *Wave Baron*, of 12,000 tons and built in 1946, fills the carrier's bunkers; on the port side, the brand new combat support ship *Lyness* (16,800 tons) replenishes her ammunition and other stores. The distance lines to enable the three ships to maintain a parallel course are clearly visible forward.

The versatile and ubiquitous cargo liner is exemplified by Blue Funnel's *Anchises* lying at the loading buoys at Port Swettenham in 1966. Built in 1948, *Anchises* was one of seventy-eight ships then owned by Alfred Holt and Co. Eight to ten of such break-bulk carriers have been replaced by a single container ship.

The first major oil tanker disaster took place in March 1967. The *Torrey Canyon* (61,263 gross registered tons) struck the Sevenstones off Land's End, Cornwall, and awakened the world to the environmental damage caused by pollution.

The extremities to which ship development has specialised is shown by the floating advertising potential of a car carrier, in this case the former Datsun's *Kyushu Maru*. Fast, large and ugly, the chief feature of these ships, after their hideous box shape, is the ventilators that clear her decks of fumes when loading and discharging.

Nuclear power was fitted to the United States' merchantman *Savannah*. Named after the first steamship to traverse the Atlantic, she brought with her echoes of past problems and was not viable. Just as the early engineers and stokers had added a vast wage bill to the operation of steamers, the salaries of nuclear engineers were not consonant with the profitability of commercial shipping. This combined with rigorous safety conditions and a degree of opposition to nuclear power to render the experiment a failure – or perhaps ahead of its time. Seen here entering Southampton in July 1964, *Savannah* looks like a conventional cargo liner of her day, but minus funnels.

loading and discharging capability with heavy lift derricks and the capability of carrying part cargoes of containers. They were no longer called liners, but multi-purpose cargo carriers, although they still suffered from the long turnround time which had dogged the conventional cargo ship.

Although a number of general cargo vessels still run under the provisions of conferences, they are gradually being squeezed out of the marketplace by the container or ro-ro carrier. The configuration of the geared cargo ship persists in the 'reefer', the popular name for the refrigerated ship which retains some of the traditions of the old-fashioned cargo liner service with frozen and chilled spaces, 'tween deck capacity for general cargo and deck space for containers, but they still require a labour intensive servicing at their ports of loading and discharge. Both they and their supporting infrastructure are small in world percentage terms, that of frozen or refrigerated fresh meat, for instance, only grossing some 8 million tonnes world-wide, with about half as much again in the form of fish at the present time. Various methods of streamlining cargo handling have been adopted and unitization and palletisation have helped to improve efficiency. Since the 1960s the versatility of the reefer, allowing her to carry different cargoes at different temperatures, has improved profitability still further. Moreover, to seafarers the reefer is arguably the only type of deep-water merchantman to retain some of the aesthetic good looks once considered desirable in any vessel.

The demands of consumerism have also increased demand for more than the traditional supplies of exotic fruit. No longer do oranges and bananas alone constitute this trade; today our supermarkets are filled with mangoes, papaws, kiwi fruit and lychees, while exported apples travel to the new markets of the Far East. As a response to this upswing in demand, specialist companies like the Danish firm of Lauritzen have established subsidiaries in Singapore to cope with this manifestation of the ever increasing internationalisation of shipping as the boundaries of the global village shrink.

Just before the collapse of the Soviet Union in 1989, Russia and her satellites operated thirty-three per cent of the world's 1402 reefers, with 325 actually under the hammer and sickle. The flag of convenience registers accounted for about twenty-seven per cent. Panama possessed the second largest fleet (202 ships), with Japan a close third (201 ships). In the aftermath of the Communist fall, many of the former Soviet and Comecon reefers are plying under the Cypriot and other flags. However, much of the trade remains under the dominant control of the fruit-producing multinationals.

A further development is that of the refrigerated container which can be independent and contain its own plant, and these can be carried on regular container ships, allowing a door-to-door service to be provided. Combined with a computer information system, the transportation giant Sea-Land Service Incorporated of America, for instance, is able to provide a world-wide network able to move over 13,000 refrigerated containers which can be carried by rail, road or sea.

This exemplifies the advantages inherent in the container, but such an integrated system requires massive investment, not least in the matter of deep-water handling facilities with an adjacent road or rail infrastructure in support. The investment of Sea-Land mentioned above amounted in 1989 to over $150 million, so the complexities and scale of such enterprises is seen to incorporate not only the multinational giants, but national governments as well. And since the former do not seem to find pragmatic decision-making the ordeal that governments do, it is not surprising that the power of the former increases at the expense of the latter and that democracy may prove to be a fading dream in face of such aggressive and apparently irresistible expansion.

The limiting and expensive factors affecting liner operations up to about 1970 were the manual cargo-handling techniques used in a ship's holds and 'tween decks, techniques essentially unchanged since the preceding century. The cellular container system grew in part out of a simple idea aimed more at avoiding pilfering and speeding up handling than initiating a global integrated transport system. But the advantages of moving unitised cargo were appreciated as early as the 1950s when the General Steam Navigation Company of London used railway boxes for this purpose. In 1951 trailers from which the wheels had been removed were shipped as deck cargo from Florida to Puerto Rico. Then in January 1955 an American trucker named Malcolm McLean founded a company which in turn acquired the Waterman Steamship Corporation and its subsidiary, Pan

Atlantic. McLean transferred 33 feet long 8 feet square sectioned boxes from the road to the decks of Pan Atlantic tankers running between Houston and New York. The company soon converted their coastwise C-2 general cargo ships to take 236 boxes, using the road trailer chassis for the dockside handling with the ship's own gear for ship-to-shore transfer. McLean also saw the potential in wheeling the whole container aboard, but he rejected this on the grounds of wasted space, high trailer costs and the vulnerability of the load in a seaway.

The roll on/roll off idea was favoured elsewhere and a former British army officer, Frank Bustard, bought up some redundant landing craft and loaded them with lorries in emulation of the cross-Channel train ferries, thereby founding the Transport Ferry Service. Meanwhile McLean also converted some standard Second World War vessels in 1961, and began shipping containers to Puerto Rico, changing the name of Pan Atlantic to Sea-Land Service Incorporated. But by this time he was no longer alone. On 31 August 1958 Matson Line's C-3 type *Hawaiian Merchant* left San Francisco bound for Honolulu. She was one of six ships able to carry on deck seventy-five containers measuring 24 feet by 8.5 feet by 8 feet. In 1960, Matson converted another ship for 408 containers and the 'box-boat' was born.

By 1964 Sea-Land were considering deep-sea operations and along with Matson, further revolutionised shipping by switching to shore-based gantries, developed in concert with the American crane manufacturer Paceco. By virtue of their light steel construction, containers have a low tare weight. Their sectional dimensions, arising from US trucking regulations, have become standard (at 8 feet wide and 8.5 feet deep), with lengths varying at 10, 20, 30 and 40 feet. Much of the strength of the system has been from this standardisation and the low tare weight of 2.3 tonnes for a 20-feet unit, known as the base TEU, or 'twenty-feet equivalent unit', a phrase coined by Richard Gibney. Such a box can load about 21.7 tonnes of net payload. There are a variety of applications, with top-loading, open-top, ventilated, insulated and integrally refrigerated and bulk boxes. In addition flats and platforms allow non-gauge and non-containable items to be palletised, while the frame container with an internal tank permits the transport of a multitude of liquids. Handled by gantries at about thirty per hour, one man can locate a container within the guides that are fitted in the container ship. On deck locking is simple, and newer ships have guides to act as restraints. The development of ships to carry these boxes, from Sea-Land's early tanker conversions has been remarkable. Early Panamax ships carried their containers twelve deep, with ranks ten wide across the holds and thirteen across the deck. Later ships increased this to thirteen deep, with eleven across the holds and thirteen across the decks. Access fore and aft is via alleyways along the upper deck above which the last stacks of boxes lock. Their capacity is usually expressed in terms of the 20-feet standard TEU.

The traditional liner companies of the major maritime nations soon followed the American lead. The great German firm of Hapag–Lloyd and the Danish company Maersk were at the forefront of European container shipping. In order to raise the capital such a huge investment required, old British conference partners such as Ellerman, Port Line, Shaw Savill, Vestey's Blue Star, Holt's Ocean Transport and Trading, Furness Withy, P&O and British and Commonwealth rapidly formed consortia resulting in Overseas Containers Ltd (OCL) and Associated Container Transportation (Australia) Ltd. The first OCL ships came into service in 1969 named after bays; *Botany Bay* and *Moreton Bay* grossed 27,000 tonnes and had service speeds of 22 knots. The less romantically named *ACT 1* and *ACT 2* were slightly smaller, *ACT 1* being 713 feet (217 metres) in length, 95.3 feet (29 metres) in the beam, 52 feet (15 metres) deep on a draught of 35.5 (10.8 metres), gave a gross registered tonnage of 24,821. Such dimensions enabled the steam-turbined ship to carry 1414 TEUs at a speed of 22 knots.

A later generation of container ship is exemplified by the *Liverpool Bay* built by Howaldtswerke–Deutsche Werft of Kiel in 1971. The *Liverpool Bay* and her sisters were the result of reaction to Sea-Land's SL7s. These seven similar-sized ships burned 500 tonnes of fuel a day using four General Electric steam turbines driving two screws. The dividend was the astonishing speed of 33 knots. Competing British, German and Japanese companies worried about the incredible speed of the SL7s together with competition by the trans-Siberian railway on the all-important Europe–Far East route, formed a consortium known as Trio. They selected 27 knots as a more viable service speed, requiring as it did a more modest 300 tonnes of fuel daily. With a length of 950 feet (290 metres), a Panamax beam of 106 feet (32.34 metres), and a draught of 42.75 feet (13.03 metres), the *Bay* class grossed 58,889 tonnes and was driven at a service speed of 27.5 knots by four STAL-LAVAL steam turbines generating 81,132 shaft horsepower and geared through two shafts. At a later date, in common with many other ships and with significant reductions in fuel costs, they were re-engined with 50,880 brake horsepower diesels. Most significantly they were capable of handling up to 2661 TEUs. The oil crisis which now erupted, severely limited these speeds. The giant but expensive Sea-Land SL7s were not long in service and after only ten years they were purchased into the United States' strategic reserve fleet.

Attempts to increase capacity were made by Malcolm McLean who had left Sea-Land and taken over United States Lines, the flagship company of the American merchant marine. McLean produced a dozen so-called 'Econships' of 58,943 tonnes deadweight with a TEU capacity of 4480. In order to achieve this, the Econships dropped their service speed to only 18 knots, courtesy of an economical 28,000 brake horsepower engine and assisted by very fine-lined hulls. These were built by Daewoo at Koje in South Korea and were delivered in 1984–85, named after American states, such as *American California* and *American Alabama*. The Econships were intended to fit the then new concept of a round-the-world service, making up in numbers and capacity what they lacked in speed. In theory the idea should have been as successful as McLean's other venture the SL7s, but both extremes of the operational spectrum failed. The United States Lines went into liquidation and the Econships were acquired by Sea-Land following a sale and lease-back deal. They now operate in a trans-Atlantic consortium with TFL and Nedlloyd; their capacity has been reduced to 3200 TEUs and their speed marginally increased to 19 knots.

Succeeding container ships have settled on a service speed of around 23 knots and Panamax dimensions. This is the size favoured by the largest container ship operators, Maersk and Evergreen. Nevertheless the breakthrough made by the United States President Lines C-10 hull has ushered in a new generation of post-Panamax ships which are perhaps a culmination of the endeavours of Malcolm McLean. The C-10 *President Truman* is typical, with an extreme beam of 129.3 feet (32.26 metres) and, at 903 feet (275.22 metres) in length, has a beam to length ratio of almost 9:1 and thus the smallest block co-efficient since the SL7s. Built in 1988 by Howaldtswerke-Deutsche Werft at Kiel, the deadweight tonnage of the ship is 61,785 and the TEU capacity 4340. With a fine-lined hull, a single slow speed 56,960 brake horsepower Korean HI/Sulzer diesel will yield a service speed of 24.5 knots while burning 150 tonnes a day and carrying a full load of containers averaging 12 tonnes per unit. It is berthing and the danger of emergencies that call most upon a crew's energies, and while it is possible to run the C-10 on a very small crew, they are manned by nine officers and a dozen ratings.

Post-Panamax sizes are inching up. The Hyundai Merchant Marine Company has built a 5551 TEU carrier in its own yard capable of 25.6 knots and the economic growth of the Pacific rim is well served by such huge ships. The European–Far East service is somewhat constrained and the Rotterdam company of Nedlloyd, having carried out extensive research, took delivery of five ships each of 48,508 deadweight tonnes and 3568 TEUs. With a beam of 106 feet (32.26 metres), they remain operable via Panama.

While vestiges of the old mail and liner lines remain under the house flags of Nippon Yusen Kaisha (NYK), United States President Line and Hapag–Lloyd, internationalism is increasingly important in the container market. The Dart Containerline is an international consortium and flags of convenience proliferate. Developing countries have, however, succeeded in undercutting many operators with low running costs. The Taiwanese company Evergreen was, in 1988, the world's largest container ship operator with over fifty ships in service. Most significantly these ships run with crews of as few as seventeen men, and because of their speed and efficiency, are each able to do the work of up to thirty conventional cargo liners.

The container ship concept has spawned several derivatives. Most common is the much smaller 'feeder', often fitted with her own cargo handling gear and commonly operated by German and South East Asian owners. Such vessels distribute part cargoes of their larger cousins to smaller, shallower ports than the great entrepôts.

Greater versatility is found in the semi-container ship, which may additionally handle general or bulk cargoes, or roll on/roll off traffic. Such ships of medium size operate on short sea trades where economies of size are limited by distance or terminal facilities, part of the bucket chain which tends to fan out north and south of the equatorial traffic of the big box-boats. As well as producing the 5551 TEU giant, Hyundai's yards have also built other seminal ships such as the *Americana* of 1988, a 19,203 gross registered tonnage combined container-passenger ship which carries over a hundred passengers to cruise ship standard on her run between the east coast of the United States and Rio de Janeiro and Buenos Aires.

Specialised carriers exist in more numbers than hitherto. Since the search for efficiency hinges entirely upon the speed with which a ship is turned round, a special cargo may require a design tailored for it. A variant of the bulker is that for forest products, essentially timber and its related by-products. The forest product carrier (FPC) is usually able to handle her own cargo and operates at a faster speed than a conventional bulk carrier. She has larger hatches and large, smooth-sided holds, which makes her container-compatible and allows her owners to exploit charters in either the bulk or container trades, reducing the number of empty return voyages. This concept is also used by a class of ship known as the 'conbulker' which trades in the more conventional bulk trades.

Seen once as the container ship's great rival, the LASH vessel has fallen from favour, though some are still in service. The acronym stands for 'Lighter Aboard SHip', and was born out of the idea of not transhipping cargo when it was moved to a deep-water port by way of inland waterways, particularly if it was to be distributed at the end of the voyage by the same means. The extensive waterways of the United States are complemented by those of Europe and Russia, and the idea of leaving the cargo in its barge, or lighter, and attaching a pusher tug to move it to and from the deep-water port, obviated all the costs and delays associated with transhipment. Wharfage was not necessary, congestion could be avoided, idle time at anchor and the expense of dock labour all added to the simplicity of the concept.

The first LASH ship, the *Acadia Forest* of 1969 and 36,862 gross registered tonnes, lifted the lighters aboard by means of a gantry. She was built in Japan for New Orleans owners who shipped raw materials across the Atlantic for the manufacture of paper in Europe. The American ship-owning giant Lykes Lines employed a system of lifting two barges simultaneously, known as the Seabee method, but an alternative was to float the barges into the LASH ship's hull by pumping in ballast until she was partially submerged. Although still used by the Russians, the LASH idea has not caught on as extensively as theory suggests it should have done. The method is not as cheap as bulk carriage, nor as cheap as containerisation for higher value cargoes. This importance of margins emphasises the significance of the revolution that has transformed shipping since about 1960. It has been essentially a revolution in cargo carrying and handling, and it is the distinction between methodologies which defines the profitable survivor. Ships will never be cheap to operate and their profit margins will always be slender, so even what appear to be petty distinctions will make the difference between success and failure. Even the shipping revolution is littered with ideas which found favour with bankers but fell amongst the hurdles and pitfalls of the global marketplace.

There are no longer substantial numbers of ships which do lots of things; today the complexities of our modern world are such that ships can be designed when a specialised trade requires it. While the passenger liner has vanished, the name liner is quite inappropriately applied to those luxurious and fantastical vessels which ply in the cruise market, no longer exclusively in blue-waters, but taking the rich and adventurous to remote locations in that elusive quest for the exclusivity which money demands as the last dividend.

Among these may be counted the curious, hi-tec cruising sailing ship which sells a quite spurious promise of reviving a past age. This is more readily found among the sail-training yachts and ships, many of which are modern and crewed by eager young people, and which operate in tandem with preserved relics which are manned and maintained by enthusiasts. Sadly the tragedies that overtook the *Pamir*, lost in hurricane conditions in the North Atlantic in 1956, the *Marques* which foundered due to taking on water during a white squall in 1984, and the *Maria Assumpta*, which struck the Cornish coast and broke up in 1995, have over-shadowed this real revival of an ancient art.

Cargo-specialisation, however, reaches its peak in the car carrier. The idea of extending the roll on/roll off (roro) concept from the obvious short-sea ferry application to something more adventurous, not least of which is the trailer traffic from the United States to Puerto Rico which first inspired Malcolm McLean, is attractive for rapid loading and discharge and for quick distribution. It has other advantages in being suitable for non-unitizable cargoes such as special machinery, semi-bulk loads, palletised, baled or general parcels. While the majority of roros serve on the short-sea routes and are small or medium-sized ships, a large, deep-water class has emerged, operating on the same circumnavigation service as container ships.

They comprise multi-deck construction with internal ramps and loading/discharging access on one or both quarters. Apart from trucked cargoes, lorries, tractors and other wheeled plant can be carried. While early types also combine container stowage on deck, later versions have forsaken this hybridisation, and dispensed with the flexibility which proved in economic terms to be a false idol. In the main the large roro has had its day. High stevedoring costs and high building costs have contributed to this, but there is one important exception, and that is the specialist car carrier. These are simply huge, box-sided ships which not only carry motor cars, but advertise them on passage. Largely operated on behalf of Japanese manufacturers, it was the Swedish company of Wallenius which pioneered the type with the *Rigoletto* and *Traviata* of 1955. Today the company's *Aida* of 52,288 gross registered tonnes can carry 6200 cars. Nissan, Honda, Mitsubishi and Mazda transport their cars to the markets of the West in these ships, some of which are able to load trucks. Characterised by huge freeboard, slab-sides, side and quarter ramps and an upper deck which sprouts ventilators, only the bow and stern, tucked away under the knuckled limits of the car decks, proclaim them as ships. In addition to their main pro-pulsion, these vessels have bow and stern thrusters to aid their berthing, for they are susceptible to even light cross winds.

Good manoeuvring qualities are required of many modern ship types, especially the short-sea ferry, which is increasing all the time in size and sophistication. Most ferries combine the virtues of roll on/roll off capability with the vices of precinct shopping, bars, discotheques and hamburger outlets. They are eschewed by true sailors, but are what the public most com-prehends as the definition of 'modern shipping'. That the design concept is flawed and open to the threat of sudden capsize has been too frequently demonstrated by such disasters as the loss of the *Herald of Free Enterprise* off Zeebrugge in March 1987 and the *Estonia* in the Baltic a few years later. These were due to the entry of water on the flat expanse of the car deck which, owing to the effects of 'free surface,' sluiced to one side, inducing an irresistible capsizing moment.

All the foregoing specialist carriers have developed from the simple concept of selling space within a hull for the carriage of commodities. Even fishing vessels require a degree of capacity with which to bring their harvest to market. As a source of food and as a means of buoying up a laden hull, the sea has served the human race for generations, and seamen have learned their craft with a view to achieving these twin ends. In the last forty years of the twentieth century, however, another factor impinges upon the history of the ship: what lies below the sea-bed.

CHAPTER TWENTY

Whither, Oh Ship?

In December 1873, HMS *Challenger* sailed from Britain on a voyage of circumnavigation. This was no ordinary surveying trip, but a scientific expedition of oceanographic exploration. Among the tasks confronting Captain Nares and his people were an investigation of water circulation at all depths and a study of the seabed. The knowledge of abyssal plains, of deep chasms, seamounts and rocky ridges, of a rich carpet of ooze and the existence of holothurians at depths in excess of five miles, stimulated scientific interest enormously. Although it took a score of years before the last of the 'Challenger Reports' was published, even then the full import of many of the findings were not fully appreciated. The existence of manganese nodules were among the discoveries made by Nares and his men, yet it was many years before their significance as evidence of rich mineral deposits was realised.

To the world of the late twentieth century, with an increasing reliance on the internal combustion engine and an apparently voracious appetite for oil products, it was sub-sea deposits of oil that began to preoccupy oil companies as their future sources of supply. Shortly after the Second World War, the Americans began prospecting in the comparatively shallow and benign waters of the Gulf of Mexico.

Alden J. LaBorde, then president of the Ocean Drilling and Exploration Company (ODECO), had developed a primitive form of submersible drilling rig named *Mr Charlie*. In order to support it more effectively than the eclectic variety of craft then in use, 'Doc' LaBorde next turned his attention to designing the first rig supply ship. The *Ebb Tide* of 1955 was 119 feet (36 metres) in length, with a beam of 31 feet (9.4 metres) on a draught of 8.5 feet (2.58 metres), a revolutionary ugly-duckling which nevertheless established the configuration for a whole generation of subsequent, related vessels. Her wheelhouse, scavenged from an old tug, was placed on a short forecastle, leaving a long, exposed after deck for the carriage of drill pipes or whatever was required by the prospectors. *Ebb Tide* was followed by three sister-ships, all owned by Tidewater Marine Services Inc, a subsidiary of ODECO. *Ebb Tide* soon had her imitators: LaBorde had founded a new ship type. Soon afterwards the introduction of the jack-up rig and later the semi-submersible, required supply ships to develop new techniques for delivering plant and *Ebb Tide*'s configuration proved ideal. By dropping anchors ahead and working astern under the rig's cranes, supplies could be delivered in far from ideal conditions. By this time all the oil companies were involved and the steady demand for crude oil began to drive the new offshore hydrocarbon industry to the very limit, calling for a degree of technical expertise that had almost vanished from the sea.

The opening of the gas and oilfields of the North Sea begun in 1966 by the ODECO jack-up rig *Mr Capp*, rapidly imposed requirements on the design of these small ships to match an increasingly hostile working environment in ever deeper water. Responding rapidly to these demands, the adaptable simplicity of the *Ebb Tide* was capitalised upon to meet new challenges and the role of such tough little vessels expanded. Attendance of semi-submersible mobile exploration rigs required anchors to be laid out, so that the supply vessel also doubled as an anchor-handling tug and was fitted with a stern roller and winch, her engines capable of delivering greater bollard pull. This versatility has almost eclipsed the traditional deep-sea tug.

Today the modern supply vessel operating in the Norwegian Sea may be as large as 8000 tons deadweight and will be fitted with tanks, pumps and deck capacity to carry the full range of drilling mud, cement, fuel, water, pipes and the containerised cargoes necessary to support the complex logistic needs of the offshore installations she is tasked to serve. In the design and development of these vessels, the Norwegians have become world leaders.

The offshore industry has also generated a series of sub-specialist vessels: diving support ships, crane ships, semi-submersible indivisible load carriers, seismic survey vessels, production testing and well stimulation vessels, and the shuttle tankers mentioned in the preceding chapter. Disasters such as the loss of the prospecting rig *Sea Gem* in 1966 provoked reactive legislation which found employment for many trawlers as mandatory stand-by vessels, on hand to rescue victims of future misfortunes. These refitted ships were otherwise condemned to the scrapyard as the British distant water fishing fleet contracted in the face of government indifference, Icelandic hostility and rapidly dwindling fish stocks. They have largely been replaced by second generation fire-fighting-cum-rescue ships, whose profile was heightened by the catastrophe of the burning of the *Piper Alpha* production platform.

With the helicopter, these workman-like ships have opened up the further exploitation of sub-marine fossil reserves. Currently, exploratory operations are being carried out in the deep and exposed waters of the Fairaven and Schieaven oilfields to the west of the Shetland Islands for which the large new supply vessels have been developed. They and their kind are amongst the most sophisticated ships afloat, designed to operate in heavy weather and high latitudes with small, highly trained crews. In work of this kind reside the residual skills of the seafarer, very different from the remorseless drive of a tea clipper's master or the knots and splices of her able seamen; nevertheless the seafarers who earn their living in this arduous business, along with fishermen and a few others in specialised vessels, echo an ancient calling.

There are many other specialist ship-types; some have long histories, such as the lighthouse tender, the tug, the ice-breaker, the dredger and the cable ship; others are the products of our modern age. Waste and incinerator ships are the least environmentally popular, while livestock carriers are equally contentious, but there are also the heavy-lift vessels which have developed from the locomotive carrier with her special, heavy-lift derricks, to what is virtually an ocean-going floating dock. Vital though these varieties are to the specialised transportation they offer, they are offshoots to the general linear development of the ship, rather than belonging to its main stream. Perhaps in the future, however, no linear development will be discernible; ships will be unique to their purpose, diverse in their applications. The rig supply ship arose from the problem-solving expertise of one man, and Bergesen's two huge ore carriers which currently sail on a strict schedule from Brazil to Europoort to feed the smelting plant of the Ruhr are but one small, integrated cog in a complex global production process.

In addition to the revolution in cargo handling and the opening of the free market which has led both to an increase in the diversity of shipping, and a return to unscrupulous ownership, abuse and all the sad sociological spin-offs associated with a proliferation of flags of convenience, the last great influence on post 1960s shipping has been the impact of electronics. The manoeuvring of diving support and drilling ships owes as much to the computer as do the loading plans of a container ship or a tanker. The speed of information transfer is as fundamental a part of the cargo revolution as motorways, road trailers and box-boats themselves. Moreover, the ease with which the master of a ship in mid ocean can contact his owners, insurers, fuel suppliers or chandlers, has transformed ship-to-shore communications. Electronics have also had a dramatic effect upon navigation. No longer must a ship's navigating officer rely upon his skill at solving the PZX triangle; today an artificial constellation of geo-stationary satellites will give him instantaneous resolution of the problem of his or her position, along with course and distance made good, course and distance to the next way-point, the ship's speed over the ground and its elevation above the geoid.

As might be expected, this accuracy is taken a stage further in the offshore industry. Using dynamic positioning, a vessel can hold her station with absolute precision due to her computer controlled thrusters reacting to inputs from a combination of sources. Taut wires, transponders and the global positioning system refined by differential corrections provide the necessary data for this almost magical ability which disposes with the conventional and imprecise technique of anchoring.

The corollary to this modern wonder is that it is no longer necessary for a seafarer to acquire the skills only obtainable with the experience of long and arduous service. Revolutions always destroy even supremely useful traditions. The redundancy of hard come-by skills can be traumatic for those upon whom it impacts; historically it leaves a faint aura of lingering *tristesse*.

The sea was once a vast, mysterious enigma about whose margins a few people fished for food; later it became a means of transportation and of waging war. Today all these functions remain, but the sea is now seen primarily as the last of this world's frontiers beneath whose waters reside the mineral deposits without which the civilisations upon the adjacent continents cannot exist. And although this environment is no longer the sole preserve of the sailor, to carry out all these activities, even those reprobated by a minority's conscience, the ship in all her multifarious forms will continue to thrive.

In his reflective work 'The Mirror of the Sea', Conrad spoke of the fidelity of the ship as the servant of man. Of this there can be little doubt and on the edges of the abyssal plain, the ship continues this tradition. Yet it is easy to be seduced by the euphoria of triumph; to ignore the consequences of the human race's rapacity or the inanimate might of the oceans themselves. One of the world's oldest fisheries, that on the Grand Banks off Newfoundland, grounds that sustained generations of Portuguese, French, Canadian and American fishermen and produced the lovely Marblehead and Bluenose schooners, were closed down by the Canadian government in 1993. The vast shoals of cod, once so numerous that the sight could scarce be comprehended by the Europeans who first saw them, had vanished.

This is a single example; the global abuse of the ocean continues, so efficient have trawling methods become. In addition to usable catches, over 20 million tonnes of unwanted lifeforms are taken up and discarded annually in the world-wide process of fishing. The plight of the cetacean population is better known and it is not so much oil pollution that poses a problem to continuing life in the oceans, as chemical discharges, detritus and the profligate dumping of garbage of all kinds that now pollute the sea.

It was once convenient to blame ships for this; just another epidemic to hang like an albatross around the convenient necks of seamen. On a passage across the Atlantic in 1990 a master recorded that not one single day passed without a sighting of polystyrene from his bridge. The epidemic has become a pandemic.

Who cares?

The ship and seamen have unwittingly and often at great cost to themselves, been perpetrators of a great export of disease. Although it was from the West Indies that Columbus's men first imported syphilis so that within three years of their return a great epidemic raged through Europe, it was by way of ships that the world's populations have been infected with diseases originating largely from Europe. Either sailing packets or early steamships brought the potato blight from America to infect first Britain and then Ireland, with disastrous consequences for a population who so depended upon an annual crop. The original source of the blight became the refuge of the emigrants who sought to escape its devastation, an irony, given the effect of this shift in population on Anglo-American relations. This migration of disease and devastation continues. The sub-species of the gipsy moth indigenous to Russian Tartary has taken passage on modern forest product carriers and now devastates timber in the North West states of Canada and the United States. Moreover the infections and pollution carried in ballast water, shifting many hundreds of tons of say, almost raw sewage from the River Hooghly and discharging it into the ecosystem of the Great Lakes, can have a knock-on effect which is no less dreadful, though scarcely headline-seizing.

We may yet come to rue the day that we did not care enough. It is the price humanity must pay for the utilitarian advantages of the ship by which our modern world is bound together.

We have followed the ship throughout its remarkable history and fascinating though this is, history has no meaning of itself, unless it be to provide an insight that might help us to predict and perhaps plan for the future. Earlier in this work I suggested the great and epic day of the ship was over. Nevertheless, there is no doubt that the part the ship has to play in human history will be ongoing. The question is, what will we ask the ship to do?

Setting aside the highly unpredictable, diabolical and incontestably ingenious methods by which the warship will be asked to cope with any future conflicts humankind embroils itself in, it is the busy merchant ship that will be our workaday servant. Seafarers will continue to be employed at the lowest possible wages and, except on sophisticated vessels where a level of education is imperative, they will continue to be drawn from among the world's poor and exploitable, for it was ever thus.

Demand for fossil fuels will increase in the immediate future, even though in due course they must decline as resources fail.

Whither, Oh Ship?

Concern for the environment should combine with better control of standards at sea, helped by increased use of technology, though it is almost certain that crew sizes will continue to reduce, perhaps to the point at which ships are fully automated and require only supervisory monitoring. It is also possible that still greater fragmentation of cargo types may ensue, resulting in small shipments of valuables in high-speed catamarans, mirroring the increase in this sort of tonnage already operating on short-sea passenger services. Studies for the development of the 'fastship' are already under way, with analysis of North Atlantic weather providing sea-state data to enable the design of a new hull form capable of sustaining high speed in heavy weather. With equally high speed cargo handling to turn the fastship round and with optimum routeing thrown in, this might allow a scheduled service of hitherto unimaginable sophistication. Perhaps too, the submarine cargo carrier may be revived for special consignments. Some of these projects will come to nought; others will enjoy brief lives, submerged by the politico-economic shifts that still tend to defy prediction.

The wise observer does not attempt to make any such forecast, for fear of finding their words indigestible in the future. Whatever these changes might be, they will impinge upon the ship of the future as surely then as they have done in the past. International interdependence plays an ever increasing part in all our lives and we are constantly aware that we dwell in a global village. Multinationals may grow stronger than governments and the national frontiers which have obsessed our predecessors and already show signs of fading, may yet become complete anachronisms. This may be fatuous nonsense, or a pious hope, but while the free marketplace may be seen as a kind of latter-day tower of Babel, the only thing that can be predicted with certainty is uncertainty and the remorseless workings of the engine of change. As a restraint on over-weening optimism, a forecast based on recent experience must sound a warning. Cheap, badly run ships with exploited crews will continue whilst unscrupulous owners and shippers can make profits from them.

As I write, I can read of ships disappearing, mysteriously spirited away by modern piracy. Seafarers die in such incidents, and their dependants are left to fend for themselves. In addition, the world's fleet is ageing and the record of the losses of bulkers, for instance, is scandalous. It is generally accepted that these founderings are attributable to bad design, bad construction, neglect, age and abuse. The not so historic losses of the bulk-carrier *Derbyshire* and the LASH ship *München* remain unexplained. Should such events overtake crews of airliners, the world would rise in protest.

These circumstances, it seems to me, reflect the displacement of the ship from what it once was, to a subordinate position in mankind's perception.

In the Introduction to this book I mentioned the ship as having been among the most powerful of all the artefacts produced by mankind. Its development has been an expression of, as well as a means by which human beings have sought to dominate their environment; a means of surviving, of expanding and of conquering. The ship has answered humanity's restless quest, meeting the challenges often, though not always, with success and the fidelity ascribed by Conrad.

For those of us for whom the ship has served not just as a source of wonder, but the means by which we have earned our living and in whose long history we have played our tiny part, the best ships were those we served in, and they were best when we served in them. They were populated by the good and the bad; they themselves varied, but they bore us about our business as we guided them about theirs. We gave them names and they bound us to their story as we helped them write it.

The history of the ship is, and continues to be, one of the human race's greatest ventures.

Epilogue

In reviewing the history of the ship since this book was first published, it is interesting to note to what extent geopolitical events have affected the demands placed upon shipping. In purely technical terms the fastship has yet to make an appearance, as has the truly gigantic container carrier, although these steadily increase in size as port approaches and facilities strive to keep up. Competition in providing container terminals has become a feature of commercial shipping but it has had the consequence of driving ports further and further from major centres of population and out of the public eye. Where once almost everyone in, for example, London had seen a merchant ship handling cargo, only those actually engaged in the task are now familiar with the detail or the complexity of the task. This remoteness has been intensified by the terrorist attack on the World Trade Centre in New York on 11 September 2001, for merchant ships have become suspect as conduits of terror, potential carriers of men and bombs. A consequence of this is that their crews are still further alienated from the mainstream of life and, since shipowners continue to employ labour where it is cheapest, seafarers fall further down the scale of reward and of social acceptability. The excuse of 'security' now allows national agencies to wage a war of deprivation and exclusion against the hapless merchant seafarer in which a denial, or at least a severe restriction, of such a basic right as shore leave is an added burden.

Against this dismal social background, and against the greater threat of terrorist attack, whether imagined, exaggerated or real, the outbreak of war in Afghanistan and more especially Iraq has only served to focus the attention of Western marketers upon the issue of oil supply. It is, of course, too early to say what effect any future rise in oil prices will have on the economics of ship-owning, although the gradual phasing out of single-hulled tankers in response to the environmentally catastrophic grounding of the *Exxon Valdez* in Alaskan waters mentioned earlier is already impacting on the cost of new oil carriers. A series of ship losses affecting the perceived image of shipping generally has succeeded in focusing attention of the dangers that remain inherent in moving goods by sea, but usually with dire effects on those concerned. Despite his 'exemplary' conduct in getting all his crew off the tanker *Prestige* when his ship began breaking up in heavy weather off the Spanish coast in November 2002, Captain Apostoulos Mangouras was arrested by the Spanish authorities when he landed. Refused permission to bring his damaged ship into a safe haven – the traditional refuge if one was within reach – where the problem of her leaking cargo and its environmental impact might have been managed, Mangouras found himself and his profession institutionally criminalized. He was not the only master to be so treated, nor the first ship to be refused refuge. A similar fate befell the master of the *Erika*, which broke up in the Bay of Biscay in December 1999. Both disasters remain unresolved in their various legacies. The stories of these ships are only two in a series of similar incidents in which littoral states have closed their coasts as though to the plague.

The criminalisation of the ship master is an integral part of the history of the ship and an ironic part given the reliance we all have on 'the universal bucket chain' of William McFee's apt phrase. Whether or not the structural state of the ships concerned was up to the standard necessary to convey oil cargoes through the waters of the North Atlantic Ocean in winter is material to their fates, but was also a product of the market to which we all subscribe. The ferocity of competition that drives down prices, also drives down standards, while the dubious decision of littoral states to deny refuge for political reasons usually exacerbates the inevitable tide of pollution that eventually arrives upon their beaches. But equally importantly, the consequential fates visited upon men such as Mangouras are a serious and cruel injustice, not only breaking the obvious link of mutual interdependence between those afloat and those they serve ashore, but marking a more worrying lack of understanding on the part of the responsible authorities of that fundamental aspect of our increasingly complex world.

This shadowy and sinister side to shipping and its relation-ship with societies ashore is unknown to the great majority of people resident in those huge socio-economic groups. For them a perception of ships is more likely to revolve, as it has done for over a century, around the extremes: those large and luxurious vessels which are still denominated 'liners', though they run on no regular scheduled liner service as their predecessors once did. The modern cruise liner, such as the recently commissioned *Aurora* or the *Queen Mary* 2, offers a highly luxurious holiday to the wealthier sections of Western consumer society, concentrating on a high lifestyle on board and exotic ports on passage. Another manifestation of the desire of those fortunate enough to have escaped poverty to travel is the expedition ship which will take you into the icy wastes of the Antarctic, or along the cleaned-up coast of Alaska. Many former Soviet Russian research ships have been converted for this traffic which offers an extreme experience to those with robust interests.

A further interesting development is the rise of the Chinese national merchant fleet and the servicing of the world's most rapidly expanding economy. From a cheap manufacturing base, often acting as ancillary to its neighbour Japan, China has become what Great Britain was becoming two centuries earlier: 'the workshop of the world'. The extraordinary increase in the manufacture and distribution of Chinese-made goods is currently fuelling a boom in what are today technically now the 'liner-trades', that is the movement of goods in containers.

In recent years deployments in support of the so-called 'War on Terror' have occupied the major navies of the world. Few have accepted the more immediate duty of suppressing piracy. But if this continues to increase, it is probable that developing small pursuit and patrol craft will become a major feature of national navies, possibly acting in concert as seagoing UN forces as this form of asymmetrical economic warfare burgeons. Since there is no sign that the wealth differential is decreasing, this trend is likely to continue for the foreseeable future.

Such somewhat gloomy considerations may overshadow the oceans and those who go about their threatened lawful occasions upon the waters of the globe, but alongside this there remains our enormous dependence upon the ship in all her various mani-festations. She may exist largely out of sight, often misunderstood, and always in her cheapest form, but without her, as Kipling remarked so presciently a hundred years ago, we shall starve.

Select Bibliography

The following bibliography should not be considered exhaustive, although the listed titles are the main sources which I have used in the present work.

In general I have largely excluded those books from which a great deal of information can be derived, but which deal with associated subjects, such as naval warfare, maritime histories, trade histories, and so forth. The exceptions to this chiefly concern titles not readily available in the United Kingdom or the United States, but of which reference might prove useful to fellow enthusiasts.

I have made some use of information from learned journals such as those of the Royal Institute of Navigation and the Society for Nautical Research, and from magazines such as *History Today*, *Sea Breezes* and *Ships Monthly* but have not burdened the general reader with details. I have also gleaned much from the reading of accounts of voyages; again, I have omitted these as not being direct contributors to this book, though they are an inspiration to those who wish to set the ship herself, at various stages in her development, in her proper context and element.

Throughout, however, my chief source has been the appropriate volume of Conway's *History of the Ship* series, to which the present work was conceived as complementary. Each of the twelve volumes in the series presents a comprehensive bibliography to the period covered accompanied by an extensive bibliographic commentary. I should like to acknowledge my debt to all the contributors of this major work.

Archibald, E *The Fighting Ship in the Royal Navy*, revised edition, (London) 1984
Ballard, G *The Black Battlefleet* (Lymington) 1980
Bass, G F (Ed) *A History of Seafaring Based on Underwater Archaeology* (London) 1972
Beaglehole, J *The Exporation of the Pacific* (San Francisco) 1966
Bowness, E *The Four Masted Barque* (London) 1955
Branch, A E *Elements of Shipping* (London) 1964, 6th edition 1989
Braynard, F O & Miller W H *150 Famous Liners*, 3 vols (Wellingborough) 1987
Brosse, J *Great Voyages of Discovery* (Oxford) 1983
Brown, D K *Before the Ironclad: The Development of Ship Design, Propulsion and Armament in the Royal Navy 1815–1860* (London) 1990
Campbell, G *China Tea Clippers* (London) 1974
Cameron, I *Lodestone and Evening Star* (London) 1965
Casson, L *Ships and Seamanship in the Ancient World* (Princeton) 1971, new edition 1986
Chapelle, H *The American Fishing Schooners* (New York) 1973
  The History of the American Sailing Navy (New York) 1949, numerous reprints

Select Bibliography

The History of American Sailing Ships (New York) 1935, numerous reprints

The Search for Speed under Sail, 1700–1855 (New York) 1967, reprinted (London) 1983

Chapman, F H *Architectura Navalis Mercatoria* (Stockholm) 1768, reprinted (Rostock)1984

Conway Maritime Press, *History of the Ship* series, 12 vols (London):
The Earliest Ships 1996
The Age of the Galley 1995
Cogs, Caravels and Galleons 1994
The Line of Battle 1992
The Heyday of Sail 1993
Steam, Steel and Shellfire 1992
Sail's Last Century 1993
The Advent of Steam 1993
The Golden Age of Shipping 1994
The Eclipse of the Big Gun 1992
Navies in the Nuclear Age 1993
The Shipping Revolution 1992

Edgell, J *Sea Surveys* (London) 1965
Man is not Lost (London) 1968

Falconer, W *New Universal Dictionary of the Marine, 1815* facsimile reprint (London) 1974

Fox, F *Great Ships: The Battlefleet of Charles II* (London) 1980

Friedman, N *Battleship Design and Development 1905–1945* (London) 1978
Carrier Air Power (London) 1981
Modern Warship Design and Development (London) 1980
Submarine Design and Development (London and Annapolis) 1984

Gardiner, R *The First Frigates* (London) 1992
The Heavy Frigate (London) 1994
& Kolesnik, E (eds) *Conway's All the World's Fighting Ships 1860–1905* (London) 1979
& Gray, R (eds) *Conway's All the World's Fighting Ships 1906–1921* (London) 1985
& Chesneau, R (eds) *Conway's All the World's Fighting Ships 1922–1946* (London) 1980, reprinted 1987
& Chumbley, S (eds) *Conway's All the World's Fighting Ships 1947–1995* (London) 1995

Gleichauf, J *Unsung Sailors* (Annapolis) 1990

Goodwin, P *The Construction and Fitting of the Sailing Man of War 1650–1850* (London) 1987

Greenhill, B (Gen Ed) *The Ship* series 10 vols (London) 1980–81

Greenhill, B & Allington, P *The First Atlantic Liners* (London) 1997

Greenhill, B & Hackman, J *Herzogin Cecilie* (London) 1991
Greenhill, B & Morrison, J *The Archaeology of Boats and Ships: An Introduction* (London) 1995

Griffiths, D *Steam at Sea* (London) 1997

Harland, J *Catchers and Corvettes: The Steam Whalecatcher in Peace and War 1860–1969* (Rotherfield), 1992
Seamanship in the Age of Sail (London) 1985

HMSO *British Vessels Lost at Sea 1914–18 and 1939–45*, combined facsimile edition (Wellingborough) 1988

Hollander, N *The Last Sailors* (New York) 1984

History of the Ship

Hope, R A *New History of British Shipping* (London) 1990
Hornsby, D *Ocean Ships* (London), 3rd edition 1986
Howard, F *Sailing Ships of War 1400–1860* (London) 1979
Hutchinson, W *A Treatise on Practical Seamanship, 1777* facsimile
     edition (London) 1979
Hyde, F E *Blue Funnel* (Liverpool), 1956
Keble-Chatterton, *Fore and Aft* (London) 1912
Lambert, A *The Last Sailing Battlefleet* (London) 1991
Landstrom, B *The Ship* (London) 1961
Lavery, B *The Arming and Fitting of English Ships of War 1600–1815*
     (London) 1987, reprinted 1995
     Nelson's Navy (London) 1988
     The Ship of the Line, Vols 1 & 2 (London) 1983 & 1984
Lees, J *The Masting and Rigging of English Ships of War 1625–1860*
     (London) 1979, 2nd edition 1990
Lubbock, B *The Arctic Whalers* (Glasgow) 1937, reprinted 1978
     The Baltimore Clipper (Salem, Mass) 1930, reprinted (New York) 1969
     The Blackwall Frigates (Glasgow)1922
     The China Clippers (Glasgow)1929
     The Colonial Clippers (Glasgow)1921
     Last of the Windjammers, Vols 1 & 2 (Glasgow) 1927
     The Opium Clippers (Glasgow) 1933
     The Western Ocean Packets (Glasgow) 1929
Lyon, D *The Sailing Navy List* (London) 1993
MacGregor, D *British and American Clippers* (London) 1993
     Merchant Sailing Ships 1815–50 (London) 1984
     Merchant Sailing Ships 1850–75 (London) 1984
     The Tea Clippers (London) 1983
Moore, A *A Careless Word, a Needless Sinking*, American Merchant
     Marine Museum (King's Point, New York) 1984
Moore, J E *Warships of the Royal Navy* (London and Annapolis) 1979
Morrison, J S & Coates, J F *The Athenian Trireme* (Cambridge) 1986
     Greek and Roman Oared Warships, 399–31 BC (Oxford) 1994
Paasch, H *Vom Kiel Zum Flaggenknoff* (Hamburg) 1908
Paloczi-Horvath, G *From Monitor to Missile Boat* (London) 1996
Ritchie, G *The Admiralty Chart*, revised edition (Durham) 1995
Sawyer, L & Mitchell, W *The Liberty Ships*, Lloyds of London Press
     (London) 1985
     Standard Ships of World War I (Liverpool) 1968
     Empire Ships of World War II (Liverpool) 1965
Steel, D *Steel's Art of Rigging, 1818*, facsimile edition (Brighton) 1974
Steffy, J R *Wooden Shipbuilding and the Interpretation of Shipwrecks*
     (College Station, Texas) 1994
Terraine, J *Business in Great Waters* (London) 1989
Time-Life Books *The Seafarers* series 13 vols (Amsterdam) 1978
Tunstall, B *Naval Warfare in the Age of Sail* (London) 1990
Underhill, H *A Deep Water Sail* (Glasgow) 1963
Villiers, A *Falmouth for Orders* (Cambridge) 1976
     Way of a Ship (London) 1954
Wells, J *The Immortal Warrior* (Emsworth) 1987
Wells, P *Naval Customs and Traditions* (London) 1930
Williams, G *History of the Liverpool Privateers with an Account of the
     Liverpool Slave Trade* (London) 1897
Young, J *Britain's Sea War* (Wellingborough) 1989

Glossary of Terms and Abbreviations

Admiralty. The office responsible for the administration of the affairs of a navy, and in particular the Royal Navy. Originally it was headed by a Lord High Admiral, but later his duties were discharged by a Board of Commissioners known as the Board of Admiralty, comprising civilian politicians, senior sea officers and a secretariat.

aftercastle. A structure at the stern end of a ship, derived from the free-standing tower-like additions on northern European vessels of the Viking tradition and the raised platforms employed on Mediterranean 'round' ships (and, indeed, galleys). Over time the structure became more integrated with the hull topsides, developing into the half-deck, quarterdeck and poop arrangements of carracks and galleons. *See also* forecastle.

armourclad. Early term, synonymous with ironclad, for any vessel substantially protected with iron plates, principally on the vertical surfaces.

Armstrong. British engineering, ordnance and shipbuilding company founded by W G (later Lord) Armstrong (1810–1900) at Elswick on the Tyne. Armstrong's early achievements included advances in hydraulic machinery (the original product of the Elswick works), the first British breech-loading rifled ordnance, and eventually a shipbuilding yard whose designs included the famous Elswick cruisers.

Asdic. A British term for what is now called active sonar. The interpretation of the term is the subject of much argument. 'Asd' probably stands for anti-submarine detection: it is almost certain that the 'ic' does not, as is usually stated, refer to 'investigation committee'.

balener, baleinier, (and other various spellings). Etymologically connected with the English balinger, in medieval French and southern European usage, it was a light, shallow draught vessel suitable for privateering and used by naval forces for scouting. It may well have been rowed as well as sailed, and in fifteenth-century lists it is classed as larger than galiotes, barques and caravels but smaller than nefs. Later the term was applied to design continuity between these vessels and the previous employers of the name.

balinger. English late medieval craft possibly derived from the clinker-built double-ended craft descended from Viking boats known in the Middle Ages as galleys – ie capable of being rowed as well as sailed, as distinct from the sail-only cogs. In the fifteenth century they seem to have been the light scouting and raiding forces of the English navy. *See also* balener.

Baltimore clipper. An imprecise term applied to fine-lined American topsail schooners with an emphasis on extreme speed; not so much a specific type as a concept, their heyday was approximately 1870–1920.

barbette. Originally an open-topped armoured enclosure inside which was a gun mounting, usually on some kind of turntable, which fired over the top of the barbette wall. In the 1890s an armoured hood was added, the whole assembly coming to be called a turret.

bark or barque. As understood in the nineteenth century a barque was a vessel with three or more masts, square rigged on all but the fore-and-aft mizen, but earlier usage was more complex. The term was applied to a two-masted coastal trader of Italian provenance in the late Middle Ages, and the term was used in the North from the fifteenth century for a fast craft suitable for both naval and privateering employment. Mediterranean barques of the 1400s seem to have carried three lateen rigged masts, and the type was a predecessor of the caravel in Portuguese voyages of exploration.

barquentine. A nineteenth-century term applied to a vessel with a full square-rigged foremast but fore and aft rigged main and mizen. Not so much used for warships, except auxiliary steamers; later vessels had four or more masts.

battlecruiser. An armoured scout, carrying battleship sized guns, which sacrificed armour or number of guns to obtain higher speed. Designs, not built, after the First World War retained armour and gun power, obtaining speed by increasing size and hence cost.

battlefleet. The main fleet, centred on the battleship force, accompanied by battlecruisers, cruisers, destroyers and, latterly, aircraft carriers.

battleship. The most powerful unit of the fleet, suitable for fleet actions; descendants of the sailing 'line-of-battle ship'. Mid century technical developments confounded many of the old categories of warship types – some early ironclads were referred to as frigates because they had only one covered gundeck, for example, but eventually a clear division between the battleship and the cruiser was re-established.

bilander. A two-masted vessel with square-rigged foremast and square main topsail but a main sail set from a lateen; this latter was not triangular but had a vertically cut forward edge or luff. Not a regular naval rig and most common in North Sea and Baltic traders.

bireme. A galley with two tiers of oars; sometimes also used for vessels rowed alla sensile, that is, with each oar handled by one man with pairs of oars per bench.

Blue Riband. Until 1934, when Mr H K Hales presented a fine trophy (the Hales Trophy), the coveted Blue Riband was entirely a nominal title awarded to the passenger ship recording the fastest passage of the North Atlantic.

Bofors. Swedish gun manufacturer, famous for its 40 mm anti-aircraft weapon used through the Second World War and up to the present.

bomb vessel. A specialist bombardment craft designed to carry heavy mortars firing explosive shells. Earliest versions were ketch rigged and they were often, erroneously, called bomb ketches even when ship rigged from the 1760s onwards.

bonaventure mizen. A fourth mast, an auxiliary mizen, carried aft of the mizen proper, and like the latter carrying a lateen sail (and even a lateen topsail in some cases). Also called the counter mizen, it was generally confined to very large ships of the sixteenth century, and died out in the early decades of the 1600s.

bowsprit. Heavy spar (in effect, a lower mast) angled forward over the bow which provided the support for the foremast stays and allowed sail to be set far enough forward to have a significant effect on the balance of the rig.

boyer or boeier. Sprit-rigged Dutch coastal trader; by the mid sixteenth century the usual sail plan was a triangular jib, sprit main with two square sails and a mizen lateen. Boyers averaged about 100 tons.

Glossary of Terms and Abbreviations

breech-loading or breech-loader. Gun with a removable breech block through which the projectile and propellant was loaded. As long as a good flash-proof seal could be contrived, it had a number of theoretical advantages over the muzzle-loader it replaced: the gun need not be run in for reloading (important as guns became longer); it might be reloaded at a wider range of angles of elevation and training; it was easier to protect the crew inside a turret or casemate; it promised faster, and once elongated shells were introduced, more accurate gunfire. Early breech-loading guns were less reliable and more expensive than muzzle-loading while barrel length was not required with early fast burning propellant. In later usage, it distinguished guns which used ammunition, with the propellant charge in a fabric bag, from quick-firers.

brig. A two-masted square-rigged vessel but with a fore and aft gaff-and-boom main sail; very similar to a snow. Introduced to naval service from the 1770s but widely used in the merchant marine earlier.

brigantine. Originally more a hull form than a rig, presumably derived from brigantin, the term was associated with oared craft. By the nineteenth century it came to demote a two-masted rig, square on the foremast and fore and aft on the main; it was sometimes called a brig-schooner in some European countries.

bulk carrier. A cargo vessel designed for and employed in the carriage of single commodity cargoes in bulk, such as grain, ore, etc.

buss. From the fifteenth century a seagoing fishing vessel with bluff bows, a square stern and a relatively long hull; they were usually rigged with three masts, each with a single square sail, all except one of which were struck when fishing; the one remaining sail gave the vessel enough way to keep the nets taut.

buyscarveel. A development of the fishing buss at the end of the fifteenth century into a cargo carrier; seen as a step towards the evolution of the fluit.

C10 type. A series of five container ships built for the Pacific southwest service of American President Lines, and which exceed the limits for vessels using the Panama Canal. The lack of constraints applied to Panamax size vessels allowed greater freedom of design which produced what are widely regarded as the most efficient container ships in service.

capital ship. The largest and most powerful warship types; effectively synonymous with the battleship until the Second World War, latterly the term has been progressively applied to aircraft carriers and more recently nuclear submarines.

caravel. Relatively fine-lined Portuguese craft of the fifteenth and sixteenth centuries, originally a fishing craft or coastal trader, but most famously associated with the great voyages of exploration. They were originally lateen rigged on two or more masts, and were known for their weatherly qualities, but later variants adopted square canvas for better performance before the wind. *See also* caravela da armada and caravela redonda.

caravela da armada. A sixteenth-century development of the caravel, designed for more capacity and superior naval characteristics while retaining some of the better sailing qualities of the original type. They usually carried a forward-raked foremast with square sails and three other lateen-rigged masts.

caravela redonda. A caravel with square canvas on at least the foremast. There is an example as early as 1438–39 built by Portuguese shipwrights for Philip the Good of Burgundy and at this time the ships seem to have carried a square main and lateen mizen. Later three-masted versions became common, with square fore and main canvas and lateen mizen; most famous of the latter configuration was Columbus' rerigged *Nina*.

cargo liner. A vessel which operates a regular scheduled service on a fixed route between designated ports and carries many consignments of different commodities. It appeared significantly after the mid nineteenth century when steam propulsion, and the opening of the Suez Canal in 1869, made international scheduled services more possible.

carrack. The derivation of the word is uncertain: there were small Arab karaques in the thirteenth century, and the term may have been passed to the West via Muslim influence in Iberia, but the ship type seems to owe nothing to Arab craft. The carrack – called variously cocas, coggones or coche in the Mediterranean – was a developed as a compromise between the typical square rig of the northern European nations and the lateen rig of the Mediterranean. There are Venetian references to such vessels from 1302–1312, and a 'coche baonesche', or Biscayan cog, was built at Genoa before 1350; the main features were a square sail and centreline rudder. In English documents the words carrack or tarit occur from 1350, applied to vessels of this type and usually Genoese in origin. The carrack seems to have acquired more sail from quite early, a Catalan contract of 1353 specifying main and mizen, and the English captured a number of two-masters from the Genoese early in the fifteenth century. By the middle of the 1400s three-masted examples were known and the multi-decked forestage and aftercastle were becoming more marked. Carracks tended to be very large for their day, and with the application of the hull-mounted gunport, carracks became the capital ships of the sixteenth-century navies, until superseded in the latter half of the century by the galleon.

carronade. A design of a short lightweight ship's gun developed by the Carron Ironworks in Scotland in the 1770s.

carvel. A method of construction in which the strakes of planking butt at the edges, creating a flush hull surface – as opposed to clinker in which the strakes overlap and are clenched through this overlap. Carvel as a method of construction implies the initial setting up of a frame to which the strakes are fastened, which in turn means that some form of preconceived design is necessary in order for a properly faired shape to result. The term is closely associated with caravel and the technique was probably imported into northern Europe from the Mediterranean, where in late Antiquity frame-first carvel had replaced the earlier shell-first structure where mortise and tenon joints formed the connections between strakes.

centreline. Imaginary line drawn on deck from stem to stern.

chasse marée. French lug-rigged coastal craft.

Cinque Ports. An association of English Channel port towns that played a large part in the naval defence of medieval England. As its name suggests, there were originally five towns – Dover, Hastings, Romney, Hythe and Sandwich – but Rye and Winchelsea were added later. In return for commercial and legal privileges, the towns agreed to provide ships as required by the crown, so Cinque Port vessels formed the core of any naval armament up to the establishment of a permanent royal navy by Henry VII and VIII. The oldest surviving charter dates from 1278 but the exact date of its foundation is unknown; it still has a ceremonial function and the Lord Warden is currently Admiral the Lord Boyce, GCB.

clinker. Method of construction in which overlapping strakes are fastened

Glossary of Terms and Abbreviations

along the edges (usually with nails 'clenched' over roves, from which the term derives). It is a shell-first technique, without the benefit of a pre-erected frame, although strengthening timbers are sometimes added later.

clipper. Much abused term of no real technical precision, but generally denoting a fine-lined, fast sailing vessel. First applied to American small craft like the Baltimore clipper, the description was widely employed in the mid nineteenth century.

cog. The classic sailing ship of northern Europe in the high Middle Ages, the cog was developed on the Frisian coast from whence its usage spread down the North Sea coasts and into the Baltic before reaching the Mediterranean. Its capacious flat-bottomed form, with straight raked stem and sternposts, is believed to derive from the technology of expanded logboats, but by the thirteenth century the type had evolved into a seagoing vessel of several hundred tons in its largest form. It acquired a stern rudder on the centreline to replace the steering oars and was powered by a single square sail.

convoy. A fleet of merchant ships gathered together under naval escort; originally, however, the term applied to the escort rather than the escorted.

coppering. The process of sheathing the underwater hull of a ship with thin copper sheets (and later yellow metal alloy). This was originally intended to protect the hull from marine borers like *teredo navalis* but was found to have a very effective antifouling effect, the slow exfoliation of the metal preventing marine growths.

coracle (curragh). Small boat usually associated with the Celtic areas of Britain (Wales and Ireland predominantly), constructed of wickerwork and originally covered with hides but more recently pitch or tarred canvas has been used. The Welsh version is usually small and round (or a rounded rectangle) in shape, man-portable and designed to carry one or, at most, two people, usually for fishing on rivers and lakes. The Irish curach is larger, more boat-like, and very seaworthy.

corvette. French term for small unrated cruising vessels derived from the barque longue, equivalent to the British sloop. By the nineteenth century corvettes were sometimes regarded as intermediate vessels between frigates and sloops.

cruiser or cruising ship. Originally the term applied to any vessel on detached service but in the nineteenth century the meaning narrowed to ships not intended for duty in the battlefleet (see battleship), but designed specifically for scouting, commerce warfare, policing and showing the flag – previously the traditional roles of the frigate, corvette and sloop. Compared with battleships, cruisers were characterised by greater speed and endurance, but lighter armament and armour. Some were entirely unarmoured but by the end of the century, most were broadly divided into armoured cruisers (with vertical side-armour) and protected cruisers which largely relied on an armoured deck to protect the vitals.

davit. A beam of timber acting as a crane; originally applied to the fish davit that was used to hoist up the arms of the anchor, but from the late eighteenth century similar devices were used to sling boats from the quarters and stern of warships. The word has survived to the present in this latter boat-handling sense.

dead reckoning. The estimation of a ship's progress across the surface of the sea, arriving at the estimated present position by taking into account course steered and calculated distance run, after due allowance has been made for tides, currents and leeway, since the last known position.

depth charge. A cylinder containing about 300 pounds of high explosive which would explode at a pre-set depth.

destroyer escort (US Navy). Roughly equivalent to a British frigate.

destroyer. Shortened form of 'torpedo boat destroyer', a British designation introduced in the 1890s for a larger and more seaworthy opponent, initially to defend capital ships against torpedo boat attack but later usurping the role of the torpedo boat itself.

dhow. A generic term that covers the lateen-rigged sailing coasters native to the Red Sea, Persian Gulf and Indian Ocean (there are many sub-variants). Originally built by dowelled shell-first techniques, later examples have become frame-first, or partially so.

diesel-electric. Propulsion plant in which diesels drive electric generators which, in turn, drive electric motors connected to the propeller shaft.

displacement. The mass of the volume of water occupied by the ship when afloat.

dromon. Byzantine war galley, initially from the sixth century AD a fast single-level ship, but by the ninth century usually with two levels of oars and the standard ship of the battle line.

dugout. A dugout craft essentially constructed from a single piece of timber.

East Indiamen. Ships (not men) trading with the East Indies, which included not only the Indian subcontinent but modern Malaysia, Indonesia and Southeast Asia.

Empire type vessels. Term applied initially to British cargo vessels of about 10,000 deadweight tons in the Second World War, but later encompassing a wide range of vessels, from passenger liners to tugs. Given names prefixed with Empire.

Fifth Rate. In the British rating system originally a ship carrying no more than 24 guns (1651), but from the 1660s the Rate encompassed ships of up to 36 guns and for most of the eighteenth century it included those of 30–44 guns; after the Napoleonic Wars the re-rated 38-gun frigates (then officially 46 guns) were added.

fireship. A vessel either converted or purpose-built to be expended as a floating incendiary device; special fittings enabled the fireship to be ignited at the last moment, thus allowing the crew a chance of escaping by boat before collision with the target.

First Rate. Always the largest ships in the fleet, of 100 guns or more, but the lower end of the spectrum varied in British practice from 60 guns in 1651 to 80 guns in the 1660s and 100 guns after about 1700.

flag of convenience. A national flag flown by a ship registered in that country to gain financial or legal advantage.

flagship. The ship from which an admiral or senior officer commanded, so called because it flew the admiral's distinguishing flag.

Fleet Air Arm. The air arm of the Royal Navy. Formed in 1918 as part of the Royal Air Force replacing the seaborne component of the Royal Naval Air Service. Taken into the Royal Navy in 1938.

fleet in being. A strategic concept that argued for the preservation at all costs of a naval force as a bargaining counter, rather than risking it unnecessarily. The idea is often said to have been first crystallised by Lord Torrington after his defeat at Beachy Head in 1690.

Fleet Train. The auxiliary and support vessels, repair ships, depot ships as well as tankers, etc needed to operate a fleet away from the main base.

Glossary of Terms and Abbreviations

flotilla. An operational formation of small vessels, destroyers and smaller. In British practice, typically about sixteen ships in the First World War, eight in the Second and ever fewer in recent years, though numbers always varied.

fluit, fluyt, flute, etc. Characteristically Dutch merchantman, ship rigged and of large carrying capacity, extreme tumblehome and a narrow 'flute' stern. They were usually austere in decoration, with a plain stemhead, few if any guns, and a small crew relative to tonnage; there were, however, more conventional versions, with more powerful armament, for trading in dangerous waters. They were essentially a product of the late sixteenth century, but dominated the Dutch carrying trade in the seventeenth. Known as 'flyboats' to the English.

fore-and-aft sails. Those carried on gaffs, sprits or stays that at rest hung in the fore and aft axis of the ship; opposite of square sails which were set from transverse yards. A vessel whose principal mode of propulsion came from such sails was said to be fore-and-aft rigged, as opposed to square rigged.

forecastle. A structure at the bow of a ship, derived from the free-standing tower-like additions on northern European vessels of the Viking tradition and the raised platforms employed on Mediterranean 'round' ships (and, indeed, galleys). Over time the design became more integrated with the hull topsides, developing into the multi-decked defensible structures of carracks and galleons. *See also* aftercastle.

Fourth Rate. Smallest Rate to regularly justify a place in the line of battle, it comprised ships of 30–40 guns in 1651, 40–50 in the 1680s and 50–60 thereafter.

freeboard. The height of the top edge of the hull amidships, or the bottom edge of an opening in the ship's side, above the surface of the water when the ship is afloat.

frigate. As commonly understood, a fast and seaworthy cruising ship, too small for the line of battle, but large enough for independent action. However, it was originally applied to any nimble, lightly constructed vessel: for example, the frigates of the English Commonwealth were noted for these qualities – unlike the earlier great ships – even though they themselves eventually acquired enough guns to lie in the line of battle; by about 1700 the term was reserved for smaller craft.

gaff. A short spar to extend the head of a fore-and-aft sail; usually hoisted with the sail, for which purpose it was equipped with jaws that fitted around the mast. A larger permanent (standing) gaff was sometimes called a half-sprit.

galleasse. A sixteenth-century Venetian innovation, a hybrid that attempted to combine the versatility of oared propulsion with the greater seaworthiness and broadside armament of the new full-rigged ship. In effect they were a development of the great galley with a superimposed gundeck over the oars.

galleon. Seagoing full-rigged ship of the sixteenth century and later, characterised by a relatively high length-to-breadth ratio, a long beak under the bowsprit and a crescent profile rising somewhat higher at the stern than at the forecastle. Compared with carracks, the lines of the galleon were finer, the super-structures lower, and under sail both speed and handling were superior. Galleons were usually heavily armed, although they were not necessarily specialist warships. The term came to be closely associated with the Iberian powers, and in particular Spain, so that by the seventeenth century almost any large Spanish ship could be described as a galleon.

great ship. In general terms, more or less synonymous with the later 'capital ship', and used as such as early as the first decades of the fifteenth century. At the beginning of the seventeenth century it applied specifically to the large galleon-derived pure warships of the English navy. In the Stuart period there were a few even larger 'ships royal', and in the reorganisation of the 1650s the great ships were rerated as Second Rates.

Gross registered tonnage. A calculation of the total internal volume of a ship converted to weight by the formula 100 cubic feet equals 1 ton. Deducting non-earning spaces like machinery rooms, bunkers and accommodation gives net registered tonnage.

guerre de course. The strategy of war on the enemy's commerce, brought to a fine art by France but adopted by most other sea powers from time to time.

gun-brig. A British term for small but seagoing craft, derived from gunboats, but brig rigged. Commanded by a Lieutenant rather than the Master and Commander of a brig sloop.

gun-vessel. A short-lived British term intended to denote something larger and more seaworthy than a gunboat but not quite a sloop.

gunboat. Large boat equipped to carry a small number of guns (often one only); originally little more than ship's boats, they tended to become larger and more seaworthy in the late eighteenth and early nineteenth centuries.

gundeck. The main battery deck or decks, the number of which categorised a warship: even when quarterdeck, forecastle and possibly poop were heavily armed, it was the upper and lower gundecks that gave the two-decker its description.

the Hanse. A trading confederation originally based on north German towns but coming to dominate the trade of most of northern Europe and the Baltic. The Hanseatic League dates its foundation to Lübeck in 1159 and by the first half of the thirteenth century it included Hamburg, but eventually it was to unite the merchants of over thirty German towns into 'hansas' or chambers of commerce; it also set up outstations in important foreign entrepots like Bristol and London, Bergen in Norway, Visby in Sweden, and Novgorod in Russia. The Hanse aimed at commercial monopolies, and was particularly powerful in shipping and fishing, the characteristic ship-type being the cog, a very cost-effective carrier in its day. The League declined in importance from the late fifteenth century, as trade patterns changed, new methods of business organisation were introduced, and a more competitive spirit was fostered.

hedgehog. Spigot mortar used to fire patterns of small (65 lb) contact-fused anti-submarine projectiles ahead of the ship (used by Royal and US Navies).

Holt Standard. The combination of compound engine, screw propeller and an iron hull with a length:breadth ratio of about 8:1. Used by Alfred Holt for his cargo liners in the late 1860s and established as something of a norm for this class of vessel.

horsepower (hp). The early engineers described the power of their machinery in terms of the pulling power of horses, but seem to have chosen weak specimens to enhance the mechanical advantage of their engines. Eventually James Watt was instrumental in establishing a formula of 1hp = 550 foot pounds per second. Horsepower varies enormously according to how and particularly when it is measured; see indicated horsepower and nominal horsepower.

hulc or hulk. Rather mysterious ship type of North Sea origins whose working career paralleled, and eventually outlasted, that of the cog. What small iconographical evidence there is suggests a banana-shaped hull of very rounded form. A Dorestad coin of AD 800 may show one, and documents of the period indicate that the hulk was a very important carrier in trade between Britain and continental Europe. As a regular type-name the word declined in the fifteenth century, and eventually changed its meaning to indicate a dismasted vessel or one laid up and unfit for sea; if there is any connection between the two usages, scholars have been unable to make a convincing case for it.

Indicated horsepower (ihp). A measure of the pressure and volume of steam within a cylinder, gives the power available within the engine (1hp = 550 foot pounds per second). Once allowance has been made for power losses in friction, driving auxiliaries, etc, ihp may exceed real power output by as much as twenty-five per cent.

Ikara. An Australian designed anti-submarine missile.

ironclad. See armourclad.

jibboom. An extension of the bowsprit (in effect its topmast); from the end of the eighteenth century, a further extension, called the flying jibboom, was added.

jigger. Nineteenth-century term for a fourth mast; also applied in earlier times to temporary canvas carried on an ensign staff, for example.

katschip. A Dutch merchant ship; in effect a smaller and simpler version of the fluit, with pole masts, no topsails and a gaff mizen.

katt or cat. Merchant ship much used in the coal and whaling trades; characterised by bulbous round stern with narrow transom above, and plain stem.

keel. Lowermost structural member of a ship's hull; in a frame-built vessel effectively the backbone, the frames forming the ribs.

ketch. A two-masted rig characterised by a main and mizen (often said to be a ship rig without a fore mast); originally square rigged, but fore and aft versions became common later.

kites. Light good-weather occasional sails set at the extremities of the conventional sail plan; sometimes encompassing studding sails but more often confined to the unusual – skysails, moonsails, ringtails, etc. Sometimes called flying kites.

lanyard. Short piece of rope or line used to secure an item or act as a handle, such as the lanyard to a gunlock which allowed it to be triggered from a safe distance.

lateen. Sail or rig characterised by triangular canvas set from a long yard attached to the mast at an angle of about 45 degrees from the horizontal, the forward end being lower. It was a fore-and-rig rig dating from at least late Antiquity and was the usual form of sail for most types of medieval Mediterranean craft, including galleys. In the late Middle Ages it was also added to square-rigged vessels, usually as a small after sail to help balance the rig and aid going about, and retained this role with the development of the three-masted ship rig.

Liberty type. A series production standard type of general cargo vessel of about 7200 gross registered tons, of which 2710 were built in the USA during the Second World War.

light cruiser. Cruiser of any size with 6-inch gun main armament or smaller.

History of the Ship

light fleet carrier. Smaller aircraft carrier built to supplement larger aircraft carriers in main fleet operations; name officially used by Royal Navy for *Colossus*, *Majestic* and *Hermes* classes laid down 1942–45.

line fishing. A generic term which includes long line, hand line and trolling. Long line fishing involves laying stationary lines on the bottom, mid water or below the surface and hauling these at intervals. Hand line fishing involves hand-held lines operated at any depth, along a vertical plane. Trolling involves towing relatively short lines just below the surface.

line of battle. Tactical formation with ships more or less in a single line ahead, designed to exploit in battle the broadside firepower of the sailing ships of this era; the overwhelming domination of this tactic led the vessels to be known as line-of-battle ships, from which the modern term battleship is derived.

Lloyd's Register of Shipping. The oldest and largest of the ship classification societies. It has its origins with the Lloyd's of London insurance market, but during the 1830s became a separate organisation. The Register Book of Lloyd's Register of Shipping, published annually with monthly supplements, contains details of the majority of commercial vessels over 100 gross registered tons, and all vessels with a Lloyd's Register classification. Other classification societies include American Bureau of Shipping (USA), Bureau Veritas (France), Germanischer Lloyd (Germany), Nippon Kaiji Kyokai (Japan), Det Norske Veritas (Norway) and Registro Italiano Navale (Italy).

minesweeper. Vessel used to sweep mines either moored with a wired sweep or acoustic with a noise-maker (or any combination of these).

mizen. The aftermost mast of a ship or ketch, and the yards, sails and rigging pertaining to it.

monitor. Low freeboard coast defence turret ship, named after the progenitor of the type USS *Monitor* of 1862. The name was revived in the First World War for coastal bombardment vessels of shallow draught, but otherwise bore little resemblance to the earlier type.

Navigation Acts. A system of British restrictive legislation dating back to the seventeenth century (although there were even earlier precedents) which aimed at retaining British trade in British ships. Repealed in 1849 as part of Britain's new commitment to Free Trade.

Navy Board. The Principal Officers and Commissioners of the Navy, the body charged with the technical and financial administration of the Royal Navy under the direction of the Admiralty. The Navy Board was responsible for ship design and construction, and the dockyards, and oversaw the work of subsidiary organisations like the Victualling Board and the Sick and Hurt Board. Comprised of long-term professional members, both civilian and sea service, it was often at odds with the more politically appointed Admiralty and was abolished in 1832 to end the potentially damaging division of interest.

nef. Another ship-type designation that could mean little more than 'ship', but which had more precise meanings in certain situations. In early medieval England, for example, it was used for warships that were not cogs but belonged to the older Viking design tradition. In the Mediterranean, on the other hand, it was virtually synonymous with 'round ship', but in later usage it came to be reserved for the largest vessels: the famous Venetian Roccaforte of 1264 was so described; by 1354 both two- and three-decked nefs are documented; and by 1441 there is mention of a Genoese nef of 1500 tons.

Nominal horsepower (nhp). An early calculation of power based on the geometry of the engine. The formula was 7 × area of piston × equivalent piston speed, the sum being divided by 33,000. Piston speed for paddle steamers was taken to be 129.7 × (stroke) 1/3.35. Real power as expressed in ihp was usually greater than nhp and diverged more as engines improved, reaching ratios as high as 3–4 times nhp.

nominal rating. Round numbers of guns were often used to rate a ship, which might actually carry a few more; however, after the introduction of carronades (which were not counted as carriage guns), the nominal rating and the real gunpower diverged considerably, to the point where an 18-gun sloop might carry 28 guns. In 1817 the Royal Navy reformed the system, adopting nominal rates which were generally the same as actual numbers carried, although some ships of the line still had a few small poop carronades uncounted.

Noortsvaerder. Dutch term for a vessel in the Norway timber trade; they were usually fitted with special timber loading ports in the bow which were sealed before sailing.

Oerlikon. Swiss gun-maker. The most commonly used of their products was the 20 mm gun.

Oostervaerder. Dutch term for vessel trading with the 'East' (ie the Baltic); optimised for the shallow harbours of the region.

outrigger. A structure built out from the hull proper to improve the efficiency of the oar system. In the trireme it provided a position for the third, uppermost, set of tholes and was called the parexeiresia. In medieval and later single-level galleys it enabled the use of longer, more powerful, oars; and became known as the apostis or postizza.

packet or pacquet. Fast mail-carrying craft; usually government sponsored like British Post Office packets.

Panamax. The maximum size of vessel, by virtue of its breadth, which can transit the Panama Canal.

panzerschiff. Literally 'armoured ship'. The correct German name for what were popularly known as 'pocket battleships'.

parexeiresia. *See* outrigger.

pentecontor. A Greek galley propelled by fifty oars; versions with both one and two levels of oars have been postulated.

picket ship. Ships deployed at a distance from the targets being defended to provide radar early warning.

pinnace. In the sixteenth century, an English version of the Dutch pinnas but confined to smaller vessels; they were usually fast warships, used for scouting and dispatch duties – what a later age would call a frigate.

pinnas or pinas (plural pinnassen). A Dutch fine-lined, galleon-type vessel of the sixteenth and seventeenth centuries, usually employed as a warship.

Plimsoll Mark. A loading gauge painted on the outside of merchant ships' hulls; made compulsory for British ships by the Merchant Shipping Act of 1876, the work of Samuel Plimsoll, MP, a tireless champion of seamen's rights.

Polaris. The first American type of underwater, submarine-launched ballistic missile. There were three types: A-1 with a range of 1500 nm; and A-3 (also used by the British) with a range of 2500 nm. A-3 carried three multiple re-entry vehicles (MRVs) instead of a single warhead, and was further modified in Britain with an advanced MRV system, 'Chevaline'.

pom-pom. First applied to the 1 pdr of the Boer War, in a naval context it came to describe the Vickers 2 pdr automatic; the nick-name was supposedly derived from the sound of the gun in action.

post-captain. In the Royal Navy any officer in command of a ship – even a lowly Lieutenant in a gunboat – was accorded the honorific 'captain', but only a post-captain could command a ship of one of the six major Rates. His position differed from all lower ranks in that his future promotion was guaranteed by seniority, and if he lived long enough he must eventually become an admiral.

post-ship. A Royal Navy term dating from the late eighteenth century for a small Sixth Rate of 20–24 guns, too small to be properly regarded a frigate but large enough to be commanded by a post-captain; the next Rate down was the sloop which was the province of a Master and Commander.

privateer. A privately-funded warship licensed to attack enemy shipping; the privateer's sole purpose was warlike, but the otherwise similar Letter of Marque was issued to merchant ships which were thereby allowed to take prizes if the opportunity arose during the normal course of trading.

purse seining. A method of encircling fish using a large stationary net drawn together at the bottom by a purse line, while the top of the net is maintained at the surface by a large number of floats.

Punic. Relating to Carthage.

Q-ship. In the First World War the British used a number of merchant ships, including trawlers and sailing vessels, as traps for the German submarines attacking on the surface. If the submarine got into a suitable position, the flag would be replaced by the White Ensign and concealed guns opened fire. Initially, they scored some successes but as soon as German commanders were aware of their use, their value virtually disappeared.

quadruple expansion. The principle of four-stage utilisation of steam in an engine; a development of triple expansion.

quarterdeck. A deck covering the after end of the uppermost complete deck; the area from which the officers controlled the ship, so by extension the term came to refer collectively to the officers themselves (in contradistinction to the 'forecastle' in merchant ships or the 'lower deck' in the navy, which from their place of berthing referred to the seamen).

quinquereme. A Greek galley with five files of oarsmen per side; otherwise known as a penteres, or a 'five'.

razée. From French – a warship structurally cut down to a lower rate, usually by the equivalent of a single gundeck. Thus a two-decker might be made a frigate, and by the loss of its forecastle and quarterdeck a frigate could be made into a sloop. A useful modification for ships regarded late in their careers as too small for the current standard; retaining their more powerful main batteries, they then became formidable additions to their new rating.

reciprocating engine. One in which the power was developed by a back-and-forth motion (such as a piston working in a cylinder) rather than a rotary motion like a turbine. The term usually implied a steam reciprocating engine.

Red Ensign. The ensign originally used to denote the senior squadron of the English fleet. When the division of red, white, and blue squadrons was abolished in 1864, the Red Ensign, informally known as the red duster, became the ensign of the British merchant fleet and is today flown by all British merchant vessels.

reefer (refrigerated) vessels. Vessels in which the cargo carrying space is largely or wholly refrigerated.

schooner. Gaff-rigged vessel with two or more masts, originating around 1700; later examples had square topsails.

seaplane. An aircraft designed to land and take off from water using floats separate from the main fuselage. Often interchangeable with a wheeled undercarriage. Floats did not greatly reduce speed but they markedly reduced range and load carrying.

Second Rate. The Royal Navy's old great ships, of 50–60 guns, were so rated in 1651, but by the 1680s this category included ships of more than 80 but less than 100 guns; there were no significant alterations thereafter.

ship of the line. A major warship, usually with at least two full gundecks, arranged to fire on the broadside. The smallest ships so regarded carried at least 50 guns from the 1670s, 60 from the 1750s and 74 from about 1800, although ships as small as 30 guns had originally been admitted in the first decades of line-of-battle tactics.

ship rig. In the age of sail the ship, or full rig was defined as the principal driving sails on all three masts being square (in the nineteenth century a few four- and one five-masted full riggers were built, but the vast majority carried three masts; two square-rigged masts made the vessel a brig). The lower sail on the mizen usually comprised fore and aft canvas but as long as square sail was carried above it the rig was still rated as a ship.

Sixth Rate. The smallest ship in the Royal Navy commanded by an officer of full captain's rank; originally including ships of less than 16 guns (1651), by the eighteenth century it encompassed vessels of between 20 and 28 guns.

skysail or skyscraper. An occasional light weather sail set above the royals.

sloop. As understood in the nineteenth century a small cruiser, below a frigate but above a gunboat in size and status. Paddle sloops often carried out fleet duties, but the later screw sloops were mainly used for colonial policing duties. *See also* corvette and gun-vessel.

snow. Two-masted square-rigged vessel, with gaff-headed main course; in later eighteenth-century definitions, this gaff sail had to be hoisted on a rope horse or separate trysail mast (to distinguish the snow from the brig, which hoisted its gaff course directly on the main mast).

sonar. Sound navigation ranging echo-sounder device used for measuring distance from bottom of ship to seabed

sprit topmast. The small mast carried by seventeenth-century warships at the end of the bowsprit from which a small square sail called the sprit topsail was set; it survived in large ships until about 1720.

spritsail. A fore-and-aft sail extended by a spar called a sprit running from the foot of the mast to the top outer corner of the sail.

squadron. A division of a fleet; actual numbers varied. In English usage the fleet was divided into Red, White and Blue squadrons, each flying an ensign of those colours (the White Ensign did not become the exclusive naval flag until 1864).

square rig. Any sail plan in which the principal power was derived from canvas set from yards which crossed the centreline of the ship (the yards were 'square' – at right angles – to the centreline when the wind was directly aft).

square sails. Canvas set from yards that at rest were carried at right angles to the centreline of the ship; as opposed to fore and aft canvas set from stays or yards on the centreline, or nearly so.

Squid. British three-barrelled anti-submarine mortar firing ahead under

Asdic control.

steam turbine. A form of rotary engine in which power is generated by the action of steam on a series of revolving rings of closely set blades. The perfection of the marine turbine is attributable to Sir Charles Parsons, his first practical success being dated to 1892.

stern-wheeler. A paddle steamer with a paddle wheel at the stern; initially this was one single wheel but eventually the wheel was divided in the middle, giving two independently driven halves; this allowed the stern-wheeler some of the manoeuvrability of the side wheeler.

sternpost. The near-vertical extension of the keel aft on which the rudder was hung; the principal element in the construction of the stern.

superfiring. Arrangement of guns in which one mount is at a higher level, firing over the other. The lower mounting is exposed to considerable blast from the upper guns and special measures, such as blast screens, are needed to alleviate the effects.

supertanker. A term loosely applied to the largest tankers of the era, notably the 1950s and into the 1960s.

Surveyor of the Navy. In the Royal Navy the senior official of the Navy Board charged with the design, construction and repair of the ships; originally a single post, there were two joint Surveyors from the mid eighteenth century and three during the height of the Napoleonic Wars.

T2 type. A US-built standard type tanker (525 were built) from the Second World War. Propelled by turbo-electric machinery, of about 10,400 gross registered tons.

thalamios. An oarsman in the lowest file of a three-level ancient Greek galley, usually translated into English as 'thalamian', also descriptive of the equipment associated with such an oarsman. Thalamites was a Byzantine term for the same, and hence it is sometimes rendered in English as 'thalamite'.

Third Rate. In the Royal Navy originally a two-decker of 40–50 guns (1651), it later encompassed ships of 64–80 guns and included some 80-gun three-deckers. The most numerous battleship Rate.

three-decker. Ship with three whole gundecks plus upperworks; the largest type of sailing warship, although the Spanish *Santisima Trinidad* and some late First Rates had a continuous spar deck that might be regarded as a fourth gundeck.

Through Deck Cruiser. A large cruiser with a deck along its entire length; effectively a small aircraft carrier. The term was coined for the British *Invincible* class ships when they were first planned. 'Aircraft carriers' were politically unacceptable.

topcastle. Fighting top at the head of a mast; could be a lookout position in peacetime, but in war was used as a position from which to rain down missiles on the decks of enemy ships.

topgallant. The mast, yard, sail and rigging above the topmast.

topmast. The portion of a mast (and its rigging) above the top, usually separate from the lower section; its sail was called the topsail, which gave its name to the yard and running rigging.

torpedo boat destroyer. A British designation for an enlarged torpedo boat, originally designed to protect larger ships from torpedo attack, but eventually superseding its intended prey in offence as well as defence. With its designation shortened to 'destroyer', it became the prime fleet escort, with anti-submarine and eventually anti-aircraft duties added to its job description.

torpedo boat. Small, fast craft derived from steam launches designed to

Glossary of Terms and Abbreviations

carry out attacks on larger ships by means of a torpedo.

transom stern. Stern ending in a vertical, virtually flat, surface like a bulkhead. The flow past such a stern is equivalent to that past a longer ship giving a slight increase in speed. The broad stern associated with a transom makes easier the arrangement of such features as twin rudders, helicopter deck, mooring arrangements etc, and improves stability, particularly after damage in the after half of the ship.

triacontor. Ancient Greek galley rowed by thirty oarsmen.

triple expansion engine. Machinery in which the steam is subject to three stages of expansion, driving in sequence a cylinder at high pressure, then a larger one at intermediate pressure, and finally the largest at the low remaining pressure. Since the same amount of steam was made to do more work, it was far more economical than simple expansion engines and resulted in significantly increased range.

trireme. The Greek galley whose characteristic feature was three files of oarsmen per side, rowing at three levels.

trysail. A gaff-and-boom sail set from an auxiliary (trysail) mast or rope horse; the trysails that replaced staysails were called spencers in nineteenth-century navies. Trysail was also used of the reduced storm canvas employed by small craft in place of the regular main.

tumblehome. The curving-in of the ship's side above the waterline; this feature was abandoned in the nineteenth century, the resulting ships being described as wall-sided.

turret. Revolving armoured gunhouse. The principal early designs of the 1860s were the British Coles type, which traversed on a roller path below the weather deck; the US Ericsson turret, which was completely above deck and had to be jacked up to revolve on a spindle; and the American Eads turret, probably the most advanced of all with extensive use of steam power, but not widely favoured in the US Navy. In France Dupuy de Lôme introduced a turret that resembled the Coles type but was mounted over an armoured cylinder, anticipating the later barbette-turret, in which the open barbette style mounting was covered by an armoured gunhouse; in later usage turret usually meant this kind of mounting.

turtle-backed. A forecastle arrangement designed to throw off water at speed – a fore deck with exaggerated camber (curving down from the centreline to the deck edge) sloping down from the stemhead. A common feature of early torpedo boat destroyers.

two-decker. A ship with two complete gundecks plus upperworks; always the most common arrangement for line-of-battle ships. When frigates acquired a complete upper (spar) deck, they were described as double-banked rather than two-decked since they had no additional upperworks.

ULCC. Ultra Large Crude Carrier. A 'development' of the VLCC and first appearing in the 1970s. The term is applied to crude oil tankers of over 300,000 deadweight tons.

Versailles Treaty. The peace treaty at the end of the First World War between Germany and the Allies. Its clauses limited the number and size of German warships. The biggest permitted was 10,000 tons which led to the 'pocket battleship' design which were actually of about 11,500 tons.

Vickers. The British engineering, shipbuilding and aircraft manufacturing company of Vickers, Son and Maxim; shipbuilding mostly concentrated on large warships, was based at Barrow in Furness.

Victory type. A standard series-built general cargo vessel built in the

USA during the Second World War. A total of 531 were built, of which 414 were cargo vessels and 117 were a military transport variant. They were about 10,750 deadweight tons and had a speed of 16 knots.

VLCC. A Very Large Crude Carrier. A breed of crude oil tanker first appearing in the mid 1960s and applied to such vessels of about and over 200,000 deadweight tons.

water ballast. Water taken on board an empty ship, usually in double-bottom tanks, to compensate for the weight of the missing cargo and to ensure adequate stability.

water-tube boiler. One in which the boiler space was filled with tubes in order to increase the area of water exposed to heating. Initially the hot gases from the furnace passed through tubes in a body of water (the fire-tube pattern), but in the more efficient water-tube type, water passed through the tubes which were surrounded by the hot gases, allowing for more rapid and efficient steam generation.

West Indiaman. Any vessel trading with the West Indies, but usually confined to those built specially for the trade.

whale catcher. A small hunting vessel equipped with a harpoon gun operated in conjunction with a whale factory ship in the open sea.

whaleback. A curved deck placed above the main forecastle deck on certain classes of fishing vessels.

wolf pack. An operation unit of German submarines which, initially, would be deployed in an extended line to search for a convoy. When found and reported to U-boat command, the pack would be ordered to concentrate for a massed night attack on the surface.

zygios (plural zygioi). Oarsman in a three-level ancient Greek galley who sat on the thwarts (zyga), usually known in English as 'zygians'. As one time the upper level in two-level galleys, they became the middle level in triremes; in late-Greek (Byzantine) sources they are known as zygites.

Index

Index

Index

Index

Index

Index

Index

Index

Index

Index

Index

CUNARD

FAMOUS OCEAN LINERS IN THE WORLD

1922 Cunard introduced the first ever World Cruise. Now, in 2010, Queen Mary 2 will embark on a monumer